PRINCIPLES OF
ABNORMAL PSYCHOLOGY

Under the Editorship of
GARDNER MURPHY
COLUMBIA UNIVERSITY

～～～

PRINCIPLES OF ABNORMAL PSYCHOLOGY:

The Dynamics of Psychic Illness

A. H. MASLOW, Ph.D.

BROOKLYN COLLEGE

AND

BÉLA MITTELMANN, M.D.

NEW YORK POST-GRADUATE DISPENSARY SERVICE
OF NEUROLOGY AND PSYCHIATRY

HARPER & BROTHERS PUBLISHERS

NEW YORK AND LONDON

CONTENTS

v

FOREWORD

~~~~~~

This book attempts to present an integrated picture of what we know of the psychologically disturbed individual. In this attempt we have used contributions from a wide variety of sources—from clinical, experimental, hypnotic, comparative, psychoanalytic, and psychobiological observations. Our aim was to avoid polemics and to utilize and synthesize whatever good material was available. We have brought to this task two traditions that are certainly ready for fusion, namely, the experimental-academic and the clinical-medical.

We found that this synthesis could be accomplished best in terms of dynamic psychology. This word has several meanings for us. For one thing, it means greater stress on the motivational or conative aspects of psychic life, and, more particularly, on motivations of which the individual is not fully aware. Secondly, in the study of psychopathology it means an emphasis on the meanings and motivational roles of symptoms. Most important of all, perhaps, it means that every psychic state is, by definition, also a motivating state. For example, a state of fear always leads to further reactions, i.e., flight, submission, attack. We are interested not only in what special state the individual is in, but also what he does about it. Thus our emphasis is directed away from the purely static description, listing, and analysis of psychic states to the study of the dynamic interplay, interdependence, and motivational roles of these states. We emphasize the interrelation between the various responses of the individual, the broad patterns that are observable in his reactions—in other words, the integrated features manifested in his experiences and total behavior.

The concepts and terminology used have been derived from the study of abnormal psychological phenomena. Operationally, however, we have utilized and adopted observations and concepts from other fields of psychology. For example, conditioned responses mean to us not only a linear connection between stimulus and response, but a reaction pattern of the individual in response to situations, on the basis of previous experience, depending on his immediate state, and involving broad needs and goals such as complex physiological drives and needs for safety. Similarly, disturbances of conditioned reactions involve disturbances in the state of the individual and in the condition of his drives and needs.

We have been constantly influenced in our thinking by the methodology and concepts of Gestalt psychology; all data have to be considered and evaluated in terms of interrelated patterns which can be described as smaller and larger configurations and as varying relationships of the individual with the environment.

We have attempted to bring into this structure the psychological implications of modern anthropology and sociology. One of the authors has done psychological field work with a so-called "primitive" society. This ever-present contrast with our own culture has, we hope, helped us to be more sophisticated about the role of culture in the psychic life of the individual.

Pedagogically we have attempted to make this book not only intelligible but plausible to the average college student who is willing to read it carefully. We have used case material generously, a good deal of it from our own case files. A survey of the Table of Contents will show that this book differs considerably from other texts. It is our hope that this is an improvement.

We have tried to make the book less forbidding by having as few footnotes as possible, and by removing from the text as many bibliographical interruptions as we dared. We hope that the scientists, upon whose work we have built, will not feel this to be a lack of gratefulness; it is done for the student's sake. The bibliography is fairly full.

Our work received considerable stimulus from the conference

on the problems of interrelation between psychological and physiological disturbances called by Dr. Howard S. Liddell at Cornell University in Ithaca and sponsored by the Josiah Macy, Jr., Foundation. The participants were: Drs. F. Alexander, M. Altman, O. D. Anderson, C. Binger, F. Deutsch, H. F. Dunbar, S. Dworkin, J. Eisenbud, J. Finesinger, L. K. Frank, F. Fremont-Smith, H. Gantt, D. M. Levy, H. S. Liddell, B. Mittelmann, N. S. Moore, R. Parmenter, L. Saul, G. E. Sutherland, W. P. Van Wagenen, H. G. Wolff, and other members of Dr. Liddell's staff.

We have had the benefit of discussion with many leading representatives of the various points of view which have been influencing us. We wish to thank Drs. Ruth Benedict, Margaret Mead, Ralph Linton, Gregory Bateson, and the many other anthropologists with whom we have discussed the cultural aspects of our joint problems. Drs. Benedict and Mead were also good enough to read and criticize preliminary drafts of certain parts of the manuscript.

In addition to the writings of Freud and the many other authors quoted, we have utilized for this synthesis the recent psychoanalytic contributions, both verbally communicated and printed, of Drs. Erick Fromm, Karen Horney, Abram Kardiner, David M. Levy, and Sandor Rado, as well as the published contributions of Franz Alexander and other members of the Chicago Institute for Psychoanalysis.

We have also extensively drawn on the field of psychobiology as evolved in the writings of Adolf Meyer and the other authors quoted, particularly the books by Dr. Oskar Diethelm and Dr. Wendell Muncie. These contributions have become an integral part of psychiatric thinking.

One of the authors (B. M.) has collaborated with Dr. Harold G. Wolff at the Cornell University Medical College for several years in psychosomatic research, and has applied the results and formulations evolved in that investigation to the present synthesis.

We have been strongly influenced by the methods of Dr. Max Wertheimer and Dr. Kurt Lewin. Those who are familiar with their profound thinking will detect their influence in many pages of this book. The influence of Dr. Kurt Goldstein's important book, *The Organism,* is also to be noted.

One of the authors (A. H. M.) has benefited greatly by discussions with Dr. Alfred Adler, and has attempted to give proper emphasis to his contributions to psychopathology.

Dr. Clark Hull and his many collaborators are chiefly responsible for the understanding of the role that the Pavlovian conditioning theory may eventually play in abnormal psychology.

For reading various portions of the manuscript and for various helpful suggestions, we wish to thank Drs. Ruth Munroe, Frank Fremont-Smith, David M. Levy, Miss Jane Belo, and Drs. Walter Briehl, Eugene C. Milch, Jon Eisenson, and Gerald Lawlor.

We are especially grateful to Dr. Abram Kardiner, for his suggestions and formulations in the section on traumatic neuroses, and to Dr. David Rapaport and Dr. Ruth Munroe for their valuable aid with the section on projective methods of examination.

Finally, we wish to thank Dr. Gardner Murphy, the editor of this series, for his encouragement and his suggestions. Discussions with him have been most stimulating in achieving an adequate synthesis between "social" and "biological" considerations.

We are deeply grateful to Miss Ida Kramer and Miss Evelyn Green, our secretaries and assistants, for their many hours of untiring work and their many useful suggestions. We also wish to thank Miss Irma Grable for her typing and clerical assistance, Miss Frances Corn for her research and helpful suggestions, Miss Ruth Ritzman for typing, and Mr. John Honiggman for his help in preparing the index.

We wish to express our extreme gratitude to Miss Dorothy Thompson, of Harper & Brothers, for her indispensable help in determining the form of this book. We feel that her suggestions have made our thoughts much more lucid and understandable.

PART I

INTRODUCTORY CONCEPTS

CHAPTER I

INTRODUCTORY SURVEY: A TYPICAL CASE

~~~~~~

Before we go into the complexities and specific details of abnormal psychology, let us see if it is not possible to get some preliminary notion of the *whole* of the material. We are, after all, aiming in this book at a better understanding of human nature, of the total personality, in so far as this can be obtained through the study of psychopathology. The following case is typical enough so that we can draw from it some idea of the kind of phenomena with which we have to deal, of the difficulties we shall meet, and of the paths over which we shall travel toward better understanding. After this bird's-eye survey, the student may find it easier to enter the maze of problems and questions through which he must pass before arriving at his goal, a better understanding of himself and of the people about him.

A 28-year-old woman developed attacks of heart palpitation, difficulty in breathing, choking sensation, dizziness, and trembling of the hands. The attacks were accompanied by an acute fear of dying. At times, she felt that the walls were closing in on her, or that she was alone on a great height, or that she was a small thing in the mesh of gigantic circumstances. The patient was examined by a physician who found her physically healthy. The psychological examination revealed that the attacks started about two months previously, under the following conditions: She had been married three years. When she married, an unusual agreement was made at her husband's suggestion: if either of them should wish to dissolve the marriage, the other would make no objection. About

3

two months earlier, that is, just before the patient's attacks began, her husband announced that he was leaving to work permanently in South America. With this, he suggested that they dissolve the marriage. The patient was sad and was disturbed by this, but she raised no objections, according to their agreement. Not long after, she had her first attack of palpitation accompanied by the fear of dying.

During the past two months, the patient's work as supervisor in a library suffered. She frequently felt tired, or preoccupied and tense. On such occasions, she made mistakes in her work, found it difficult to concentrate and was easily exhausted. She became irritable, and had frequent disagreements with her colleagues. She did not sleep well. She lost her appetite. She was still living with her husband but derived no pleasure from sex relations.

Previous Difficulties.—About eight years before these attacks, the patient had had severe attacks of anxiety under the following circumstances: She went to the hospital for a minor operation which was not at all dangerous. In the hospital, however, she became terror-stricken, was afraid that she would die, and had palpitation and difficulty in breathing. During this period, she was much disturbed and frightened by the fact that she had to stay in bed for several days. Her discomfort continued after she left the hospital, but subsided in about a month.

The Patient's Condition Between Periods of Attack.—The patient was an efficient worker and had advanced in her position. She had some friendships of long duration. She enjoyed going to the theater, reading books, seeing friends, eating good food. A careful survey of her reactions and mode of living, however, showed that some difficulties were present practically all the time. She was often possessive and over-sensitive with her friends. She was tense in her work and she was apt to be upset by any mistake or criticism. She was occasionally moody and worrisome; she did not quite know why. At times she felt exhausted and had difficulty in carrying on her work. Her husband was the first man with whom she had been in love; she had never before been able to be close to men, even though she had longed for such closeness.

The circumstances of her attachment to him were also interesting. The people who introduced him to her told her that he was "flighty." He himself agreed with that statement. He pursued her ardently and praised her because of her appearance, her tastes, and her interests. He told her, even before proposing, that he wanted to have an affair with her. She, however, wanted to get married, but had not made up her mind whether she wanted to marry him. He later made the suggestion of their liberty to dissolve their possible marriage, and soon thereafter she fell in love with him. The marriage was a happy one, for they had many interests in common. He was jocular, gay, and complimentary. He was, however, often busy with his work in the evening; this troubled her at first. As far as she knew, he had always been faithful to her. She usually reached an orgasm, but with some difficulty.

Childhood History.—The patient was the older of two siblings. She had pneumonia when she was four years old; she herself did not remember this. Her father, a warm and affectionate person, died when she was six years old. She had been more attached to him than to her mother. Her mother, who was still alive, was emotionally unapproachable, never demonstrative, but worrisome and rather exacting in discipline. She (the mother) preferred the patient's sister. The mother was over-solicitous and rather strict about the patient's eating habits and excretory functions as a child. She was always strict in moral questions. The patient remembered being unhappy about her sister, and having quarrels with her. She was unhappy also when thinking about her father. As a child she was irritable, was afraid of the dark, and at one period was panicky if she was alone in the room, even for a short period. When she was seven years old she wet her bed for a period of time.

Treatment and Outcome of Her Condition.—The patient received mental hygiene treatment. She came twice a week for interviews. At these interviews, the information given above was obtained and discussed with her. After two visits, the patient's condition began to improve; she was permanently freed of her attacks of anxiety after six weeks of treatment. She separated from her husband and stood the separation well. The patient was seen by the therapist at six-month intervals for four years. It is significant that, after her acute symptoms and complaints subsided, she had the same difficulty in finding a man to whom she could be attached as she had had before she met her husband. Minor difficulties with her work and relationships with her friends likewise remained.

The type of treatment administered to her as a rule does not correct such character difficulties.

GENERAL DISCUSSION

This case has been chosen purposely. It is not a severe case. In no sense is the patient a "nut" or a freak. Depending on the definitions we choose, we may call her either "normal with severe maladjustment" or "mildly neurotic." She certainly is not "crazy" or "insane." She seeks the same things that every other person seeks—happiness, love, and self-respect. But she does this in a rather peculiar way. Furthermore, we from the outside can see clearly that her technique of seeking love and happiness is "bad," for it almost guarantees the opposite of what she is seeking.

Why does she behave in such a way? Why does she prevent herself from getting what she wants most? What peculiar logic forces her to feel and behave as she does? We shall make a few broad generalizations and then take up a few of the more technical aspects of this case.

First, let us say that in general the study of such patients will *always* show that the symptoms are the ways in which a certain kind of personality will react to the fact of frustration or conflict which is precipitated by an external situation and which threatens the loss of gratification or love or self-respect. These symptoms are meaningful and logical—even if the logic is private, personal, and peculiar—in the sense that most frequently they serve a purpose or fulfill a function. These processes guard the individual against further loss or hurt; or they serve to get revenge, to change the situation, to retrieve what was lost, to make some integration or compromise that gives partial satisfaction to all the conflicting elements in the situation, etc.

Methods of Analysis.—Since the character structure is so important in this picture, we first try to get some idea of what sort of person we are dealing with. There are two good ways of doing this, both necessary and both used simultaneously. First, we try to understand the etiology, the history, the genetic development of the personality. The question here is, "How did she get to be the way she is?" Usually the patient's childhood relationships to her parents are studied, for the chances are that the whole pattern of her personality, her attitude toward life, and the general trend of her style of adjustment to life were acquired in early life (not always but usually)

Second, we analyze the personality as we find it actually existing, in all its internal interrelationships and structures, and in all its relationships and reactions to the current problems set for the individual by the world she is living in. The first type of analysis we may call "genetic analysis"; the second type, "character analysis."

Now let us turn back to our patient. The outstanding fact on the genetic side is that she did not get enough love as a child (rejection). Her mother was not affectionate, and she preferred the sister (leading to sibling rivalry). Her father, who was affectionate, died when she was young. People who are starved of love when they are children usually grow up to be what we call "insecure personalities."

We know a good deal about such people and can describe their symptoms with fair accuracy. However, just putting a label on this patient and describing her symptoms does not help much. This is what is called *static*, descriptive psychology. If we want to understand her character to the point where we can help her, we must understand her *dynamically*. That is, we need to understand how she feels about her symptoms, how she reacts to and against them, what their function is, what they lead her to do. In a word, we wish to understand how these symptoms act as motives or drives to further processes.

Our patient's reaction to rejection and her consequent insecurity were a kind of defensiveness, a tendency to keep up her guard *always* so that she would not be hurt again as she had been in childhood. Mostly, this meant isolation from men, and a refusal to fall in love. She was afraid of love, because that meant letting her defenses drop and becoming vulnerable to hurt. When she sought for love as a youngster she was hurt; and she will tend to go through life with this habitual expectation. It is for this reason that it becomes difficult for her to let herself go, to fall really in love without any reservations. In a word, she is forced by her character, which is a creation of her past, to make reservations and restrictions all of which indicate fundamental mistrust and expectations of hurt. She does this to guard against further hurt; but while these guards defend her against hurt, they also make love impossible or difficult.

We do not wish to paint too black a picture. Many such people have been gradually weaned from this mistrustful attitude toward life by a psychologically good marriage in which they were loved over a long period of time. In such cases, as the defenses are slowly found to be unnecessary, they are dropped and may disappear completely; the individual may become trusting, affectionate, and loving. For our patient there was no such fortunate outcome because her husband left her. The person who is lifted slowly from the bottom of a deep well and is then suddenly dashed to the bottom again may be more hurt and more embittered than one who is not lifted at all. So with our patient, who had had a taste of how good life might be. Her symptoms were worse than any she had ever experienced before, and it did her little good to realize that they were made possible only by her own reservations and initial mistrust.

The Meaning of the Symptoms.—Such symptoms serve many purposes. In the first place, they represent in part a sheer defeat and discouragement reaction, sheer response to pain and suffering. But even this is complex, for this patient's suffering is in turn much intensified by her feeling of wounded self-esteem with its consequent sense of helplessness, and her feeling of greater insecurity resulting from this horrible rejection. Peculiarly enough, the symptoms are also an expression of the conflict which disturbed her initially, of simultaneously wanting love and being afraid of it. Of course she is hurt by losing her husband; but at the same time there is still a remnant of her original feeling that a husband is dangerous, so that deep down she even feels a little relieved at his loss and the removal of all the problems he represented.

The symptoms have still another meaning. It is as if they said, "See how helpless I am when you leave. I need you. Have pity and come back. I cannot do without you. I throw myself on your mercy. I am completely dependent on you."

Discussion of Some Technical Points

The foregoing paragraphs give a general picture, a bird's-eye view. Now, point by point, we shall go over the case history from the standpoint of each of the various chapters in the book, to show how all the subjects discussed in them are necessary in understanding any individual case.

What Is "Normal" ("Healthy") and What Is "Abnormal" ("Sick") in This Patient.—First we must understand our frame of reference, our main concepts, and our vocabulary. What constitutes normality? What constitutes abnormality? Obviously such questions must be answered at the very beginning, even if we are led into all sorts of unexpected bypaths, as in fact we shall be in these chapters.

In our patient, the symptoms of sickness or disturbance or abnormality were as follows:

1. Suffering and unhappiness.
2. Certain specific manifestations called symptoms, which are not present in healthy individuals, e.g., attacks of palpitation, overwhelming fear of death.
3. Impaired efficiency, e.g., difficulties in work.
4. Impaired ability to enjoy life, e.g., less pleasure in work, in food, in sexual activity.
5. Lack of adequate insight or conscious knowledge; e.g., the connection between her complaints and the precipitating situation was not understood by the patient.

6. Disturbance of the feelings of security and self-esteem.
7. Excessive defensiveness, chiefly in the form of isolation from men and from love, with great fear of being hurt and of being dependent.

All these symptoms are important. However, as usual, this patient came because of the second group, which were obvious and disturbing.

Now let us see what is normal or healthy in this woman. Until this last episode, she usually managed to get along satisfactorily enough without attracting undue attention. The psychologist, examining her some time previously, would probably have raised his eyebrows and been skeptical about her future psychic health. He would probably have said that she had a near-neurotic character structure, and he would have predicted that she would get along well enough as long as things went well with her, but that a shock would throw her over the line into frankly abnormal symptoms. All in all, since she carried on her work well, was not extremely unhappy, and had no overt abnormal symptoms, he would have called her normal enough to get by, even though he might have shaken his head about the future. Why his doubt about the future? Mostly because of her obvious over-defensiveness against falling in love with a man so as to avoid being hurt. Attempts to shut love out of one's life are not to be made lightly. People who do this usually come to grief in one way or another.

The Relation of Her Difficulties to Her Personality.—Careful examination of this patient's outlook on the world, on herself, on her work, and on her relationships with people shows that many features which are more easily observable during the acute period are also present during calm periods and persist after the acute symptoms subside. These reaction patterns are relatively permanent; such permanent attitudes toward the world, people, etc., may be called an aspect of her personality or character. Thus our patient had more or less permanent, even though mild, difficulties with her work, in her relationships with friends, in her attitude toward herself, and particularly in her relationships with men. The question may be asked, why are more acute manifestations of these difficulties observable during certain periods? The answer is, that they occur in response to particularly difficult or acute or threatening situations. Thus, the patient's severe difficulties began when she was threatened with separation from her husband. Similar symptoms had been observed once before, in the hospital episode, but they were not as severe.

The Personality as a Whole; Vital Needs and the Concept of Conflict.—The student must have felt by now that neurotic symptoms are not to be considered as foreign bodies within an individual's psyche but rather are closely interrelated with vital needs, with aims in life, and with attempts at solving life's problems. In other words, they have to do with the "total personality." It is also obvious from the above case that an individual's vital needs may be at cross purposes. This patient, for example, had a strong need for love, but was at the same time so afraid of it that she tried to put it out of her life. This clash of vital interests is called "conflict." The student should observe, however—and this is an extremely important point—that both of these conflicting desires really represented one and the same goal, namely, happiness, or, at any rate, comfort. There was never any question about the desirability of this goal; the only question was as to which was the best path to happiness or lack of pain. One of the most common misapprehensions of the beginning student of abnormal psychology is to think of the personality as if it were made up of several different parts which are absolutely incompatible and at war with each other. This is not so, except possibly for certain very sick people. All human beings want the same things. The trouble is that there are many possible paths to these ultimate goals. When we are presented with a choice of paths, we frequently choose foolishly because of poor attitudes toward the world, usually acquired in unfortunate experiences in childhood and usually carried about unconsciously. It is because of this unconsciousness that we behave foolishly. An unconscious desire is independent of logic and intelligence, and thus the first task of deeper psychotherapy is to make the unconscious conscious. Once it is conscious, our intelligence, our past experience, our sense of humor, our logic may be brought to bear upon solving the problem of how we may achieve what we want most, i.e., happiness, love, self-respect.

Limiting the Concept of Neurosis.—For other reasons also, the personality of the individual with neurotic symptoms should not be considered as completely different from the personality of a healthy person. All individuals with neurosis show strength, health, and normal functioning in many respects. Thus, in many situations they behave to all intents and purposes in a healthy fashion; it is only in certain other situations that they show severe disturbances. For example, the work of our patient was good as a whole. When she was not working under the stress of disappointment and frustration in other spheres of life, and when her work was not exposed to any criticism, she enjoyed it thoroughly and was almost perfectly efficient. When her friends showed adequate interest, were congenial, and flattered her enough, her relations to them were entirely satisfactory, at least externally.

Even here, if we examine behind the façade of the patient's functioning well in some situations, we see that there are impulses which represent certain measures she takes to function well by making the best of a bad situation. Thus she was very good in her library work and had written several scientific essays on the subject. But even in this best aspect of her work there was a factor that, by stretching the point, might be said to have a neurotic aspect. She relied on it too much; the satisfactory functioning of her personality was based almost exclusively on it; it might be said to be too important for her. Thus she had fantasies, not only that her publications would be very successful, but also that they were the most wonderful ones that had ever been printed. At times she pursued these grandiose daydreams with intense and elated emotions. We may say that they served the purpose of compensating her for her feelings of rejection and her lack of self-confidence in the rest of her life. Nevertheless, it was clear that in this aspect of her work she showed much less "neuroticism" than, for example, when her work was criticized. Then she grew highly emotional; if she was able to argue the point at all, she became illogical and incoherent, and either would not see the meaning of the criticisms or would distort them. She had to consider herself flawless and perfect in her work, and she elaborated various defenses to safeguard this picture of herself. This was the one way she had of consoling herself for other pleasures and satisfactions which she missed, and it was the main basis for building up her self-esteem, since she allowed no one to love her.

Psychosomatic Relationships.—Viewing the material from another angle, the student will see that no line has been drawn in this case history between the "mind" and the "body." This patient's symptoms were a fusion of psychic and somatic symptoms. For instance, in her anxiety attacks there were both somatic manifestations—heart palpitation, disturbed respiration, tenseness, and trembling of the muscles—and psychic manifestations —the thought of dying, feelings of panic, and various fears. In short, the whole person was involved. For a full understanding of such a case, we shall have to comprehend clearly the relationships between "psychological" and "bodily" manifestations in psychopathology.

Etiology.—It is not only desirable but necessary to understand the historical development that lay behind the patient's symptoms. It is true that a difficult problem, a terrifying situation, or a chronic frustration will precipitate a neurotic outbreak; but it is just as true that the reason why the individual cracks under the strain can be understood only if we understand the personality as it has been formed through his life. Thus we find ourselves, again and again, going back to the patient's earlier life for several reasons—so that we can understand the symptoms better ourselves, so that the patient may acquire insight into the meaning of his behavior, and so that we may know what specific therapeutic measures are necessary in addition to the general therapy which is used in practically all cases.

But there are two other aspects of the etiology of the personality. First, the individual is a biological organism, born into the world with certain strengths and weaknesses, with such and such a nervous system and glandular system. His biological equipment has an important bearing upon any understanding of his personality. We need not discuss the most obvious examples, such as innate feeble-mindedness, birth injuries to the brain, etc. The fact that, because of hereditary factors, he may be four inches shorter than the average man or have too large a nose—these are biological factors that will influence the personality. We must also remember that the human animal, like every other animal, is equipped with certain innate drives, such as hunger, sex, and thirst. Deprivation in these spheres may be tremendously important psychologically.

In one way the human animal is different from all other animals, for he is the only one that has a complicated culture, passed on from generation to generation, a culture that he begins to acquire from the moment of his birth. The particular kind of culture which he "interiorizes" will determine in large part the nature of his conflicts, lay out for him the ways in which he is permitted to satisfy his desires, allow certain defense processes and forbid others, etc. Our patient, living in a competitive, relatively insecure society, naturally tends to be competitive and relatively insecure. Our society has created certain gaps between the sexes; in general it is also characterized by an ambivalent attitude toward sex. It is natural, therefore, that in a large proportion of neurotic patients we should find conflict and ambivalence in sexual life. Thus in order to understand our patient, we must also understand her cultural background.

Psychotherapy.—It is only on the basis of all these types of knowledge which have been mentioned that a discussion of psychotherapy becomes possible and understandable. Psychotherapy is fundamentally different from all other forms of therapy and it cannot be grasped until adequate psychological knowledge is acquired. It is therefore impossible to say much about it at this point.

Résumé.—In handling any case, we must first understand the patient's relation to the norms of normality and abnormality. In the case cited above, we specified just why the patient was considered maladjusted or sick. We also saw in this case the intimate relations between psychic and bodily manifestations in motivation and emotion as well as in appearance of symptoms. It was shown briefly that the essential part of the picture was a subsurface phenomenon, almost entirely unconscious. The patient did not realize what her conflicts were; she was totally unaware of the unconscious defensive processes which she had automatically elaborated to handle the situation; she did not realize that her self-esteem and security were being attacked and that, in various ways, she was attempting to defend them. Some sources of her trouble were found in the immediate situation, and others in her character structure, which in turn was found to be a product of her life history. A certain type of therapy was used which relieved the severest symptoms. The particular disturbance from which she suffered is called "anxiety hysteria."

Thus we see that if we attempt to understand any case of maladjustment, we must bring to bear upon it all the resources of modern psychology. To put it in another way, in abnormal psychology everything relates to everything else.

SUGGESTED READINGS

Probably the best introduction to the study is a popularization by Bernard Hart, *The Psychology of Insanity* (332). We recommend also such popular treatments as Menninger's *The Human Mind*

(544), Hendrick's *Facts and Theories of Psychoanalysis* (341), Zweig (819), Allen (26), and other similar books. It would do no harm for the more serious student to check through the pertinent chapters in Murphy's *Historical Introduction to Modern Psychology* or Stone's historical article (730). Case readings are desirable if they are available. Some may be found in Menninger, some in Taylor's book of readings (740); of course, there are always a few in any textbook of abnormal psychology or psychiatry. An outstanding one is Muncie's *Psychobiology and Psychiatry* (581).

CHAPTER II

SOME FUNDAMENTAL CONCEPTS

The Field of Abnormal Psychology.—The field of abnormal psychology is the study of the maladjusted human being—the human being who has lost his subjective well-being, whose social relations are disturbed, who cannot use his capacities well, whose evaluation of reality is altered, or who has lost contact with the real world. We are interested here as much in the principles of general human nature that can be derived from the study of the maladjusted individual, as in the study of maladjustment for its own sake. Many important lessons about the normal human being can be learned from the study of the neurotic and the psychotic. The abnormal individual is not a different kind of human being; he is simply one who is attempting to solve the more serious problems of life but is doing so in an undesirable or inefficient fashion; he seeks for the same ultimate goals and the same pleasures as does the normal person, but he searches in the wrong directions, and he searches inefficiently.

The Concept of Adjustment.—We shall be interested more in functions and processes than in the sheer descriptive analysis of abnormality. In other words, we are concerned with adjustment and maladjustment to the world more than with making lists of weird symptoms and "interesting" quirks of human nature.

The essential characteristic of the concept "adjustment" is that it is a solution of problems. It is also important to remember that the human being recruits all his capacities and sum-

17

mons up all his abilities in the attempt to solve these problems as successfully as possible. The whole body—including the nervous system, the muscular system, the perceptual functions, the emotions—is used in the solution of these problems, and it is impossible to understand these capacities completely and validly except with respect to the problems confronting a person. In a word, we must deal with psychological capacities as tools of adjustment, rather than as automatic, self-governing machines, each functioning autonomously regardless of the needs of the organism. *Accordingly we shall define the adjustment of a person as the characteristic way in which he perceives, reacts to, and solves the main problems of life.* We shall see as we go along that, for various reasons, certain of these adjustments are considered poor or inefficient or abnormal. If we add to this definition a list of the various tools of adjustment and a statement of their efficiency, we shall find ourselves with a fair definition of personality as well.

The Main Problems of Life to Which Adjustment Is Made. —For the sake of simplicity we shall classify the main problems of life into three categories:

1. The problems set by external reality in its biological and physical aspects. As biological organisms we must get food to eat, we must have shelter, we must protect ourselves. In general, these problems are less important for us today than they were millions of years ago, because we live in groups that have more or less efficiently solved most of them for us. A culture is itself an adaptive device—indeed, the most efficient and amazing of adaptive devices that has ever been evolved.

2. The problems set primarily by the culture in which the person lives—its demands and prohibitions, its habits and taboos, and its internal conflicts and inconsistencies. These vary with the particular culture. In our culture such problems would be social-sexual adjustment, winning prestige and power, earning money, getting and keeping a position and advancing in it.

3. The problems set by relatively internal psychological demands; these in turn may be put under three heads:

a. The need for comfort, gratification, and equilibrium; the avoidance of pain and the satisfaction of drives.

b. The need for self-esteem, independence, achievement, adequacy, and strength.

c. The need for security, the love of our fellow men, community feeling, and warm emotional ties.

In solving these problems all possible adaptive tools are used, including intelligence, sensory and perceptual facilities, learning, remembering, forgetting, and thinking, as well as emotions and drives. As we study some of these modes of adjustment, we shall see that the psychological sickness or abnormality, the neurosis, and often even the psychosis may be solutions or attempted solutions of the main problems of life, sometimes the only possible ones. We shall realize that they may be defenses against even worse alternatives, e.g., catastrophic breakdown, suicide, murder. Furthermore, we shall realize that the necessities of adjustment may make us blind to things that are before our eyes, force us to forget things that happened only a short time ago, encourage us to construct and perceive sights and sounds that have no physical basis, make us hate people whom by all logic we should love, and even make us physically ill. We shall learn that what we say and feel and think is determined by our internal worlds as well as by the external real world, and in neurotics and psychotics perhaps even more by the former than by the latter. If we hold such a point of view, the hallucinations, delusions, phobias, and the worries and uncertainties of the maladjusted all immediately become "logical" attempts to achieve the same happiness and attain the same goals that other more "normal" people already have.

The Unity of Personality and Adjustment.—Let us come back again to the concept of adjustment. We must be careful to make clear that we are not studying particular mechanisms or processes or symptoms divorced from particular human beings.

If we speak of "projection" or "defense" in general, this does not imply that it is a part of a machine which can function by itself. It is not something that can be taken from human beings and studied in isolation as we might study the function of an automobile carburetor or battery. It is always a whole unitary human being who projects or rationalizes or defends himself, and these are responses to the problems that face him as a total human being in his adjustment to the world.

We can clarify this further by a discussion of Adler's concept of the "style of life" (12). It was his conviction that everything that a person does, everything that he feels and thinks is representative of him or characteristic of his whole personality. Most of his products, whether artistic or intellectual, will bear the stamp of his personality, of his way of living, of his world outlook. Thus a musician can easily detect the works of various composers. Anything by Mozart is Mozartian and is often identifiable with and characteristic of his personality.

If the student desires to convince himself on this point, he may do so by any one of a dozen little parlor games which have been used experimentally by Wertheimer. For instance, let him give brushes, paint, and paper to some of his friends and instruct them to paint in any way that they desire, whether geometrical designs, curves, blocks of color, or pictures. After a little practice, if he has good insight, he will frequently be able to say that this painting is the work of this person, that the work of that person, etc.

This sort of thing serves to illustrate the fact that people are somehow unitary, or total organisms. It will be well to keep this always in mind as we analyze this total unity in various ways, as "aspects," as "parts." We have to split up, to analyze, and to describe; but we do this only for convenience' sake, with the ultimate purpose of helping ourselves to understand the total unitary personality in all its uniqueness.

Mechanical Analogies.—The student must be cautioned along still other lines. Because psychology as yet does not have an adequate scientific vocabulary for its purposes, it often has to rely upon words that are used by analogy. Very frequently these are mechanical analogies. Therefore we shall have to speak of "forces," of "conflict," of "mechanisms," and the like. This is extremely unfortunate, for there is great danger of reifying these concepts, that is, thinking of them as real, palpable things that we can touch, feel, and see. A further danger is that of anthropomorphism, that is, talking about a particular mechanism or a part of the personality as if it had independent life of its own and could act autonomously. It is only an individual total human being, John Smith or Henry Brown, who struggles or inhibits or defends or represses.

The Role of Symptoms in the Study of Abnormal Psychology. —In this book we shall treat symptoms essentially as indicators of trouble, of maladjustment or of danger; and we shall always attempt to discuss the symptom not merely for its own sake, but for the meaning behind it, what it is a symptom *of*. In other words, we are interested not in disorders for their own sake, but rather in why we have them, what they mean, and what we can learn from them about human nature. The particular trouble behind symptoms can be determined not from a study of the symptoms in isolation, but only from an analysis of the particular individual involved.

Furthermore, we shall deal not with separate symptoms, but rather with groups of symptoms, with syndromes. A syndrome may be defined as a group of highly interrelated symptoms all presumably related to a single underlying cause or set of causes. This means that we shall classify our symptoms not in terms of "faculties," e.g., intelligence, perception, emotion, but in terms of their occurrence together and their putative relationships to more fundamental causation.

The Meaning of Psychodynamics.—Abnormal psychology must be dynamic psychology. Therefore, we shall be interested more in mainsprings of action and motivating forces, more in what the psyche *does* than in what the psyche *is*.

The differences between the dynamic and the static approaches to the problems of psychology may be illustrated by comparing a blue print of a machine and a description of what the machine does—how it functions, how one part affects another and in what sequence, what the machine does with the material that is given to it, what spots in the machine are likely to be weak, what kind of product it will turn out under various conditions, etc. A static psychology is essentially descriptive, whereas a dynamic psychology is essentially *functional*. We shall study the individual's total reactions to his problems, his ways of defending himself, of overcoming difficulties, of developing and changing and retrogressing. We shall be interested not only in the description of symptoms, but also in their meaning or purpose or function. And finally, a dynamic analysis of symptoms will treat them not as final products, but as initiators of action, as motives.

The Individual in His Culture.—It will help the student in his appreciation of abnormal psychology if he thinks of the human being as a biological animal immersed in a cultural field, and if he realizes that many of his conflicts and troubles are the result of his failure to integrate his biological demands with the cultural demands, taboos, conflicts, and frustrations imposed upon him by his society. Those anthropologists who have interested themselves in the psychological aspects of their work— e.g., Boas, Mead, Malinowski, Linton, Benedict, etc.—have shown that, with few exceptions, it is impossible to understand "abnormality" without reference to the cultural background of the individual and his specific social situation. We shall accordingly refer frequently to anthropological materials. We can consider primitive cultures as, after a fashion, ready-made "experiments" with different ways of solving the problem of man's relation to his culture and with various cultural ways of satisfying and holding in check man's biological demands.

There are other reasons for attention to primitive societies. They are useful as social experiments because they stand in the same relationship to our society as laboratory experiments to events in everyday life. For one thing, they are usually not as mobile or as changeable or as diverse as our society, and do not impose upon the individual the great strain of adjustment to rapidly changing standards, to great diversity of standards between generations, to rapid status change, etc. Furthermore, they are less complex and more homogeneous as compared with so-called "civilized" societies, and thus enable us to understand more fully the nature of our society by contrast.

The Biological Needs.—The biological needs of the individual that will concern us extensively are the need to avoid pain, to seek pleasure and drive fulfillment (gratification), and in general to maintain "equilibrium" or "comfort." There are other biological reactions which are not needs in the same sense as the sex drive is. We refer here chiefly to aggression. As we shall see, it is implicit in the psychological nature of man that in certain situations he will react with aggression. Whether or not it is a drive does not matter so much, for in any case the problem of controlling the aggression of its members is one of the most important problems facing any society. Generally it is fair to say that the two main biological problems which any culture has to solve are the problems of regulating sex and aggression.

The Interrelations Between Biology, Culture, and Psychology.—It is a general principle that biological forces have a tremendous determining effect upon the final features of personality, but that this effect is intermediated by and expressed through the particular culture in which the individual finds himself.

Let us use for an example the influence of organic inferiorities upon personality. There is no question whatsoever that being crippled, ugly, blind, deaf, or malformed has tremendous repercussions upon the individual. What is the exact nature of this process? In the past this effect has been thought to be a *direct* one. But we now know that it is rather an indirect effect which is intermediated by various cultural-psychological dynamic processes. It is not sufficient to say, "I have lost a leg, therefore I feel inferior." Now we would say, "I have lost a leg. In my society, people look down upon or pity or resent those who cannot make their own way economically, or those who are handicapped personally or socially. I recognize this loss of prestige and respect from others. Because of this I tend to lose respect for myself. Also, since I myself am a member of my society and share their beliefs, I feel toward myself as others do toward me." In other words, an organic inferiority leads to a feeling of inferiority only when this organic change is *defined by the society* as an "inferiority."

Another example may be found in certain forms of homosexuality. It is true that homosexuals frequently have bodily characteristics of the opposite sex; and to the untutored person it would seem that homosexuality is somehow a product of direct biological determination. But as soon as we examine the anthropological data presented by Benedict and Mead in various writings, we find that a man is not a homosexual just because he has a feminine body. He is a homosexual because he has a body which is defined by his neighbors as female, and also because these neighbors are firmly convinced that femininity of personality correlates with such a body. Mead points out that, in the first place, there are differences from culture to culture in definition of anatomical femaleness and maleness, as well as psychological maleness and femaleness. In the second place, in some societies these differences are considered to be of no importance, and in such societies there is little or no homosexuality.

In our society, having cross-eyes will affect the personality adversely; they will create feelings of inferiority and rejection. Can we say, however, that cross-eyes are universally an "organic inferiority" and always create feelings of inferiority? No, we cannot; for in various societies—for example, Arabia, Turkey—cross-eyes are an "organic superiority"; they are thought to be very attractive and they enhance "sex appeal." The ethnocentric Arabian psychologist is apt to come to the theoretical conclusion that cross-eyes, always and everywhere, heighten the self-esteem, just as the ethnocentric American psychologist may come to the opposite conclusion.

The effect of physiological forces, e.g., of hunger, of the sex drive, on the personality features is even more complex. We wish to state here generally that *it is the cultural definition of a biological fact that will create the importance or unimportance of this biological fact as a psychological determiner of personality.* Biological facts do not often act directly on the psyche; it is usually the cultural phrasing of these biological facts with which we have to deal.

SUGGESTED READINGS

The best single readings here are Mead's *Sex and Temperament in Three Primitive Societies* (539) and Benedict's *Patterns of Culture* (74). Pertinent chapters in Linton's *Study of Man* (497) will be found useful. A good example of the way in which the point of view presented in this chapter works out in an actual problem may be found in Dollard's *Caste and Class in a Southern Town* (187).

This general point of view from a more psychological angle is best expressed in the writings of Alfred Adler. His last book, *Social Interest* (12), is as good as any, but certain less expensive volumes may be more easily available to the student, e.g., *Understanding Human Nature* (7), *What Life Should Mean to You* (10), etc.

CHAPTER III

THE MEANING OF "ABNORMAL"

Various terms are commonly used in connection with the complaints and manifestations that are discussed in this book. Those most widely used are "abnormal," "pathological," "sick," "deviant." Furthermore, the terms have various meanings and implications. A discussion of these terms and their implications is necessary for two reasons. First, we can make clear what we are trying to say only if we clarify the terms in technical use, even if it is impossible to give hard and fast definitions. Second, the patient and the individuals in his environment may attach certain implications to these manifestations or to the words by which they are described, and the therapist may therefore have to deal with the harmful effects of these implications and attitudes. Such attitudes as the following are harmful to the patient and are incompatible with both the scientific and the clinical approach. (1) Some of the manifestations are shameful and the individual thus afflicted should therefore be condemned, punished, and ostracized. (2) A stigma is attached to these manifestations, for instance to "insanity," and any family in which it is present is disgraced. (3) Because some of the manifestations are condemned on religious grounds, the individual should be utterly disapproved of and made to feel guilty and sinful. (4) The individual is not living up to certain ideals and is therefore inferior and worthless. These connotations are most frequently attached to the word "abnormal" and, to a lesser degree, to "pathological," although not to the noun "pathology." A psychologist never gives any of these words such interpretations, and the student must not either. In the following, we shall discuss only concepts and implications which have some scientific validity.

Symptoms.—A symptom was defined earlier as a disturbance in some aspect of the individual's functioning which is often objectively observable and is usually connected with subjective suffering. The attack of anxiety described in the first chapter is a symptom, as are also hallucinations and delusions of persecution. If the symptoms are sufficiently acute, the individual is incapacitated.

Abnormality or psychic illness can be defined most simply in terms of symptoms. There need be no disagreement or theoretical argument about such a definition, once the symptoms are agreed upon by the members of the particular society.

Character Disturbance.—One of the greatest advances in the study of psychopathology was the recognition (Breuer and Freud, Adler, Janet) that symptoms have a "meaning," that is, that they are connected with the individual's needs, desires, fears, and life experiences. It was then recognized that less obvious phenomena than such overt symptoms as anxiety attacks or delusions required investigation in the individual who suffered them; for example, how he usually handled situations, e.g., stinginess, the need to produce flawless work, stubbornness, etc. In other words, the individual's "character traits" became a subject of investigation (Freud, Adler, Meyer). The terms "pathological," "sick," "abnormal" are often used to refer to these concepts. This amounts to an extension of their original meanings and thus brings even more confusion into their use.

It was found that the individual's symptoms and character traits are the results of various needs, fears, and life experiences. The person attempts to cope with his problems, with situations, in a certain manner. In many respects he apparently functions well, at least on casual observation; but closer investigation may show that he has to use various devices that the completely healthy person does not require. For example, the patient described in the first chapter worked well as a librarian, but she needed self-aggrandizing attitudes to overcome her feeling of inadequacy and helplessness in the situation. The terms "pathology," etc., have been used by some to refer to the "psychodynamics" of an activity, regardless of whether the activity was an obvious symptom, an obvious character disturbance, or an apparently normal performance which was, however, made possible by the use of such devices or "mechanisms" as are discussed in Chapter X.

As we said previously, the extension of the investigation from the symptom to character traits and dynamics represented a great advance in the field of psychopathology, but at the same time it raised a new and difficult problem. Everyone will agree that an attack of anxiety can be considered a sickness. But when "character traits" are concerned, the delimitation is much more difficult, and it becomes even more so when "dynamics" is concerned. To add to this complication, it was found that, at least to some extent, even those individuals who did not break down in normal situations of stress or in the face of obvious and severe threat had reaction patterns similar to the people who did break down; in other words, the desire to escape from a threatening situation is present even when the individual puts up a splendid battle and wins. Further, some of the healthy individual's daydreams and fleeting desires have certain features in common with the profound disturbances observed in sick people; thus harmless daydreams of achievement may look like the delusions of grandeur of the seriously "sick." Likewise, a disappointed but healthy person may find consolation in some other activity. This resembles the reactions of some seriously "sick" individuals who, after disappointments in relationships with friends, console themselves by eating excessively. If this consolation is denied them, they become emotionally depressed.

The recognition of similarities in some of the "dynamics"

of sick and healthy individuals is of great psychological importance. It implies, however, that in many respects the terms "pathology," etc., represent only quantitative differences. In other words, an individual may be more or less "sick"; no sharp line of demarcation can be drawn.

One can raise the question whether a senior who is facing the necessity of looking for a job after graduation when there are none, can be called "sick" if he becomes moody, loses his appetite, and cannot sleep. One can ask whether a girl who desires love and affection but finds no one whom she cares for, is "sick" if she is moody and does not sleep well. One can likewise ask whether unemployment leads to "sickness" because it makes the individual feel depressed and hopeless. All of these are situations in which the person is under stress, in a state of conflict; circumstances beyond his control prevent him from obtaining what he wants. Everyone will agree that people faced with such situations are under stress, but few will call them "sick."

Statistical Approach.—Most psychological traits are assumed to fall into a "normal" distribution, with most of the cases in the middle and few at the extremes. These extremes, which constitute only a small percentage of the total population, are arbitrarily lopped off and labeled "abnormal" or "pathological" or "deviant," and the far larger percentage clustering around the middle are arbitrarily called "normal" (247).

There is a descriptive value to this concept, if we recognize its limitations. Obviously, much of what lies at the extremes— delusions, anxiety attacks, etc.—will be definitely psychopathic. Genius, however, which is found at one extreme of the distribution, is a totally different matter. Furthermore, many of the traits which appear in a great number of individuals at a certain age can be considered minor "sicknesses." Thus, many children show an unreasonable type of fear between the ages of four and seven; such minor fears as a slight anxiety in reacting to harmless animals are particularly common in women.

Yet one would hardly call this a "healthy" reaction, even though it is present in more than half the population.

Cultural Norms.—The observations of anthropologists in primitive societies established the fact that modes of behavior and reaction patterns which are approved and followed by the majority of a group may be totally different from, and sometimes the opposite of, those followed by another group. In each group, however, those who do not follow the generally approved mode of behavior are usually considered "abnormal" or "pathological," or at least queer or different. The term customarily used by anthropologists to describe such individuals is "deviant" (73, 533).

These differences between various groups apply to a variety of phenomena. Thus, some societies expect the individual to show no strong ambition, to refrain from becoming emotionally or physically violent, and to cooperate with other members of the group. The individual is trained in this direction in various ways, either overtly or by implication and example, and the majority of the people follow this pattern (Zuñi). Other societies may put a premium on boasting, on ambition, on the accumulation of a certain form of wealth, on surpassing and vanquishing others, on certain states of violence, and on killing (Kwakiutl). Each of these two societies strongly disapproves of the other's modes of behavior. Similar differences and contrasts may be observed in various groups in regard to sexual behavior. Thus the Marquesan woman has several husbands, and the Mohammedan man sometimes has several wives; but a Mohammedan woman who tried to follow Marquesan custom in her own society would come to grief. Another striking fact is that certain special types of psychological phenomena, such as trances and certain kinds of visual and auditory hallucinations, may be highly prized and used for cultural purposes by one group, but be treated as "abnormality" and "sickness" by another.

These facts pose difficult problems which have not as yet been adequately solved, but the following general statements can be made.

1. The individual's reaction patterns have to be viewed in terms of his cultural background. This term refers to a complexity of factors, such as the general values held by the group, their actual behavior, the economic necessities of the social environment, the treatment given the individual from early childhood both by persons who are close to him and by strangers, etc.

2. The fact that a certain reaction pattern is accepted and valued by one group and rejected by another does not imply that the "dynamics" of this pattern are the same in both groups. Thus, dream states, hallucinations, and supernatural voices have different "dynamics" for a group that believes in supernatural communication with the individual than they do for a group that does not hold this belief. The reaction pattern of the group which values these phenomena may imply desire to develop in a certain direction, to better one's status, and to advance one's career successfully. For the group which rejects such phenomena, they represent an extremely unfortunate and catastrophic solution of conflicts, a state of helplessness—in a word, a state of psychic illness.

3. As Kardiner has shown (421), the reaction patterns and dynamics established in the individual members of a group are valuable in any attempt to construct the dynamics of behavior in another group. This must be done very carefully. We must first understand the dynamics of the reaction patterns and behavior approved of by the group. We must determine what stresses and strains its members have to face from the cradle to the grave, what inducements and rewards they are offered, which modes of meeting problems are encouraged and which are forbidden. In this way we can describe the dynamics, the stresses and strains for each society or group separately; we can describe their relative points of security and of gratification and happiness. In the light of these facts,

we can further understand the dynamics of those individuals who break down when confronted with unsolvable conflicts, with intolerable stress and anxiety.

The Concept of Anatomical and Chemical Disturbance.— The discussion of concepts thus far has implied that the individual's disturbed functions resulted from distressing experiences. However, many forms of mental disturbance are caused by a primary damage to the brain or to bodily chemistry and metabolism which influences the functioning of the brain. In such instances, of course, the term "sickness" is most apt.

SUGGESTED READINGS

From the cultural point of view, the best reference is Ruth Benedict's article, "Anthropology and the Abnormal" (73), which also forms the basis of the last chapter in her book, *Patterns of Culture* (74). Another excellent paper is Karen Horney's "What is a neurosis?" (368). Her two books (366, 367) also provide good reading in this connection. A discussion of the statistical approach is given in Foley's article (247). Wegrocki (768), Frank (250), Maslow (533), Hallowell (321), Horney (365), and Landes (451) are also useful. Perhaps it is well to hark back to the classical work in this field, Sumner's *Folkways* (736), which is still good reading. A popularized version is Ayres' *Holier Than Thou* (34).

CHAPTER IV

THE NORMAL PERSONALITY

Difficulties of Definition.—Many difficulties stand in the way of a definition of the normal personality. The most fundamental difficulty arises from the great contemporary influence of anthropology, with the consequent clear demonstration that abnormality is almost always *abnormality in a particular society*. That is, "abnormality" is relative to the cultural standards. The preceding discussions of this point should have made clear that the judgment of abnormality is usually a judgment of value and that values differ in different groups of people.

This brings us to our second main difficulty: it is practically impossible to separate clearly the descriptive (what is) from the normative (what should be). This difficulty is in many ways like the first one, but it is best described separately since it obtains within the confines of any single society (ours, for instance). We must face clearly the fact that to some extent the normal is always the desirable and the abnormal is almost always the undesirable. For this reason, any one person's description of the normal is apt to describe what he likes; his description of the abnormal is apt to include what he dislikes.

Another grave difficulty—one that is rarely realized in our society, except by very tolerant people—is that there are many kinds of normality, many kinds of adjustments. There is no single ideal of personality or normality in even the most primitive society, and certainly not in a complex society like ours. No particular form of good adjustment is set up as more desirable than any other form of good adjustment. In other

33

words, we must seek for the least common denominator for all the forms of good adjustment.

It is by now a truism that there is no clear dividing line between "normal" and "abnormal," that there are quantitative as well as qualitative degrees of each. We frequently say that abnormality consists of too much or too little of such and such a quality. What "too much" or "too little" connotes is constantly shifting in any society. Generally one criterion is the opinion of the group in which the individual lives. If the group regards his behavior as excessive, in bad taste, eccentric, beyond the necessities of the situation; or if, at the other extreme, he is so bound by the group that he has lost all "spontaneity," we say "too much" or "too little." Another criterion is that of sheer efficiency in dealing with the real world (Wertheimer).

This discussion also serves to indicate that every normal or healthy person has within him most of the seeds of abnormality or illness, and, conversely, that every abnormal individual may be considered an exaggerated normal person with all the possibilities of normality within him. Such an attitude has consequences. Except in the case of the clearly organic psychosis, we must not look for a "what," a "something," a "substance," or a "thing" in the abnormal person. To explain his abnormality we must conduct a historical and a cultural inquiry; we must ask not "What is there in this person that causes his abnormality?" but "How did this healthy person become sick, what was the process, how did the whole personality change in its development, what influences in his history sought out his weakest points and made him the exaggerated personality that he is, and what factors maintain his condition?"

Within a complex culture like ours, and particularly in the large cities, the culturally oriented psychologist is confronted with a difficulty that is hard to solve practically, but that must be reckoned with theoretically; this is the fact that there are many subcultures in our broad American culture, or subsocieties within the total society. A city like New York, for instance, has

Irish, Italian, German, and Swedish; Catholics, Protestants, Jews, Mohammedans; well-educated and poorly educated people. We frequently find in such a city a situation that can be described only somewhat paradoxically, namely, an individual may be well adjusted to his subculture but maladjusted to the total culture, or well adjusted to the total culture but maladjusted to his subculture. Thus a young woman may be completely maladjusted in her home, which is dominated by (let us say) immigrant parents, but at the same time get along fairly well with people in the outside world.

It seems hardly necessary to point out, in times like ours, that one's definition of the normal or abnormal personality will vary also with the political or economic or social attitude of the person who sets the standards. Much that has happened in the last few years has been confusing to the psychologist in his attempts to bring order and simplicity into his conceptual systems. For instance, what shall we say about the totalitarian states in Europe? The behavior that is being prescribed as average or desirable or ideal for the citizens of some of these states includes many characteristics that we in this country have called and still do call abnormal. An extreme cultural relativity would settle the question by saying that this or that is "normal" in a totalitarian frame of reference and "abnormal" in an American frame of reference. But the cultural relativist in America is now asking himself many questions that he never thought of before— Is it possible for a whole culture to be abnormal? Are there possibly absolute rather than relative standards of normality and abnormality? How far is he as a scientist to go in condemnation? Must he always say that a person or group is normal from his *point of view*? Or do we have universal criteria which enable us to say that such and such an action—cruelty, for example—is abnormal even if a whole nation participates in it? This question has been discussed in the preceding chapter, but its solution is left to the reader.

Some psychologists and sociologists—e.g., Dollard (189)—in

their discussions of the present problem have emphasized the fact that, in the last analysis, normality and abnormality are behavioristic concepts. To a large extent they are correct, for it is true that society labels a person normal or abnormal almost entirely on the basis of whether his *behavior* is normal or abnormal, acceptable or unacceptable, social or antisocial. From a sociological point of view it is obvious that society cares little about what goes on inside him as long as he behaves well.

However, for the psychologist this is an untenable point of view, because he is concerned not only with a person's effectiveness, inner as well as outer, but also with his happiness or unhappiness. The inner state will in any case determine external behavior in one way or another; if not immediately, then eventually. Two people may behave in the same way from a social point of view. One may meet social demands easily and naturally, with no feeling of thwarting or frustration; the other may meet them quite as effectively as far as outer appearances go, but still be storing up unforeseen breakdowns and eventual behavior disturbances because he has to *force* himself to do what society bids him to do. We cannot, as psychologists, neglect the inner state of well-being in dealing with normal or maladjusted or abnormal people. The case cited in Chapter I described an obviously sick person, but one who was at the same time fairly effective both socially and in her work.

An interesting point in this connection has been made by Linton (497) in connection with the concept of the "status personality." In brief, Linton shows clearly that personality is always relative to the status of the individual within the society. That is, people expect certain things of a man rather than a woman, of an older person rather than a younger, of a noble rather than a commoner, of a rich man rather than a poor one. A certain type of personality, a certain set of behaviors and attitudes are conceived by the group to go with the mere fact of status. Such is the malleability of human behavior that it is rare for a person who has a certain status in his society not to behave as he is expected to. Thus in our society, we expect different personalities, different attitudes, and different behaviors in a butler and in a banker. What is more, we are rarely disappointed in our expectations. (But this is complicated by the fact that an individual will *seek* a status compatible with his particular type of personality.)

There is another kind of relativity in normality, the relativity that emerges from our increasing knowledge of individual differences in personality. What is normal for one kind of individual may not be for another. Even in daily life we set up certain expectations as we get to know a person better and better. We recognize that there are inner necessities, that he is following a certain "path," that he has a "style of life"; and this means that we expect and predict certain things of him. If, for instance, a consistently selfish person suddenly grows kind, we are apt to say, as laymen, "There's something queer about it." The technical psychologist also is likely to look with some suspicion upon such behavior because it may be a superficial symptom of a deeply-lying conflict process. To put this in other words, certain people are expected to do certain kinds of things that, although normal for them, would be abnormal if done by other people.

Sick and deviant individuals are usually investigated more thoroughly and with different methods than normal individuals are. Much of what we assume about "normals" is based on the disturbed function observed in the sick or deviant individuals; that is, the opposite or a milder parallel is often assumed in the normal individual. These assumptions may be correct but their verification is difficult.

The above difficulties can be summed up as follows:

1. Normality is always relative to the particular culture or subculture in which the person lives.
2. Normality is also relative to status, age, sex, and type of personality.
3. It is difficult to separate the normative from the descrip-

tive; that is, it is difficult to describe the personality objectively, without reference to values, ideals, or individual political or social beliefs.

4. There are many kinds of normality.
5. There is no clear line between the normal and the abnormal.
6. Much of what we know about the normal is obtained by extrapolation from the abnormal, and so may be inaccurate.

Manifestations of Normality

We shall outline the manifestations of normality under twelve main heads. These characteristics, all of which are shown by the normal person, overlap a good deal. This is inevitable because the personality is a whole, an organic unit, and we do it theoretical violence when we split it into parts. Our justification is that we do this for convenience, that we must analyze in order to resynthesize on a more efficient basis.

1. *Adequate Security Feelings.*—Good rapport with society in general and with one's own group; a feeling of identification with it. One must have some feeling of being at home in the world and of being an accepted member of some social group, however restricted this group may be.

2. *Adequate and Firmly Based Self-esteem.*—Self-esteem is a form of self-evaluation. It is obvious that one's self-esteem may be too high or too low, even in our society where a fairly strong personality is the ideal. In such a society a conviction of permanent inferiority with its accompanying lack of self-confidence is such a handicap, particularly in men, that it may be quite incapacitating. On the other hand, too high self-evaluation in a society like ours, with its clear convictions of superiority and its tendency to dominate, may occasion resentment, jealousy, and even revolt in other members of the group.

3. *Adequately Free Expression of the Personality (Naturalness of Behavior, Spontaneity).*—This is characterized by:

a. The ability to drop the psychological defenses when necessary or desirable, to "relax" psychologically, to allow oneself to be psychologically "vulnerable," to drop one's mask or front.

b. The ability to express hostility or aggression freely when it is necessary or desirable.

c. The ability to smile and laugh freely and naturally.

d. Ideals of personality that are not too high or too alien to one's own capacities (self-acceptance, self-tolerance).

4. *Adequate Self-knowledge.*—We are often ignorant of important aspects of our own personality. Whenever we reject an impulse because it is unendurable or unacceptable to our social selves, it may sometimes be repressed; that is, we may have no conscious knowledge of its existence. The damage that such lack of self-knowledge can create will be clear when neurosis is discussed. An adequate self-knowledge includes:

a. Adequate knowledge of one's own major motives, desires, goals, ambitions, inhibitions, compensations, defenses, inferiority feelings, etc.

b. Objective and realistic appraisal of one's own assets and liabilities. The ability to appraise oneself honestly is based upon the ability to accept oneself as natural, and not to repudiate any important desire or thought. This, of course, does not mean that there must be *no* socially or personally unacceptable desires; they will always be present as long as one lives in a society. What is important is that these thoughts and desires be accepted as part of oneself, as common to human beings, as "natural." They must not be projected into the outside world, nor must one be afraid of them, for with such fears go repression and trouble.

5. *Adequate and Efficient Contact With and Use of Reality.*—Reality here means more than the physical world. It has at least three aspects with which the psychologist must be concerned: the physical world, the social world, and the internal world. One must be able to gauge all of these objectively and realistically, for as soon as he distorts or evades them he becomes

less efficient—less able to adjust to them and to adjust them to himself. Such use of reality involves:

a. An absence of excessive fantasy, daydreaming, escape, or flight.

b. A realistic and broad outlook on the world which is able to withstand all the ordinary shocks of life. A person who has not been too much sheltered from life but has had contact with a fair sample of the world, good and bad, is able to see and face the shocking and the terrible when necessary. A broad knowledge of the real world is an insurance against traumata or shocks. It is, of course, possible for a sheltered, over-protected personality to remain normal as long as his false and naïve idea of the world is not upset. In our society, however, such an idyllic state of affairs cannot last very long.

c. Good social equipment and social intelligence.

d. Adequate self-knowledge (see 4 above).

e. Adaptability, or the ability to change easily and gracefully if external circumstances or reality cannot be modified. A good phrase for this is "cooperation with the inevitable." This trait is also related to frustratability and frustration tolerance, the ability to withstand deprivations without suffering undue harm psychologically.

6. *Adequate Emotionality.*—This is characterized by:

a. Lack of emotional frigidity and of fear of emotions. This involves the ability to form strong and lasting emotional ties such as friendships or relationships of love and trust. The individual has the ability to fall in love and to be loved; he does not control his emotions excessively; his hostility can be given adequate expression. However, there must be a certain degree of emotional control.

b. Sympathy in a broad as well as narrow sense, that is, the ability to understand and share other people's emotions.

c. At least some degree of happiness and pleasure in life; the ability to enjoy oneself, to have fun, to laugh. Everyone is unhappy at times; but this unhappiness must have valid reasons which are justified by the group.

7. *Adequate Integration and Consistency of Personality.*—The personality is an organized whole; all its aspects overlap each other and have definite relationships with each other. In the maladjusted person this organization breaks up; instead of acting together, the various parts of the personality almost seem to be warring against each other. The personality may be unstable and shift about continually. Certain aspects of it may be entirely repudiated and repressed; this creates much indirect disturbance. The following are fundamental for a well-integrated personality:

a. No major conflicting or mutually incompatible trends within the personality.

b. No serious dissociation of personality, as in multiple personality.

c. Cultural folkways which are easily enough met so that they can be accepted without internal conflict.

d. Morals and conscience which are not too inflexible and rigorous from the group's point of view.

e. Fairly rounded development, versatility, several interests instead of just one, and no single ability or interest overemphasized.

f. Average continuity or consistency in time of the major personality trends.

g. Ability to concentrate, to keep a set, to fix attention.

8. *Adequate Life Goals, Purposes, Ambitions.*—This involves:

a. Achievable, realistic goals.

b. Reasonable persistence both of goals and of efforts to achieve them.

c. Goals which are not incompatible or inconsistent.

d. Goals which involve some good to society. They must not be too egocentric or selfish.

9. *Ability to Satisfy the Social Requirements of the Group; Adequate Inhibitions and Social Adaptability.*—The individual must be:

a. Not too unlike the other members of his group in ways that the group considers important.

b. Able to face the ordinary problems of life with a fair degree of confidence and success.

c. Adequately informed on the folkways of his group.

d. Willing and able to inhibit the drives and desires tabooed by his group.

e. Able to meet the fundamental personality demands of his society without too great difficulty; e.g., he must manifest activity, ambition, competitiveness, promptness, friendliness, democratic behavior, sense of responsibility, loyalty, patriotism, etc.

f. Interested in the games, sports, hobbies, interests, etc., favored by his group.

g. Willing to accept—at least to some extent—the group's set of folkways, or at least *some* set of folkways. He must feel that some things are good, others bad; some right, others wrong. In a word, he must not express universal cynicism.

10. *Adequate Emancipation from the Group or Culture.*— This involves:

a. At least some originality, individuality, and differentiation from other members of the group.

b. Some independence of group opinions; the ability to make up one's own mind on some matters.

c. The absence of an excessive need for flattery, reassurance, or group approval. The individual has within himself adequate reserves of self-respect and self-esteem.

d. Some degree of tolerance, cosmopolitanism, and appreciation of cultural differences.

e. Adequate spontaneity (see 3 above).

11. *Ability to Accept Love, Affection and Support.*—One aspect of normality is the ability to receive attention, love, affection, and even mothering, as well as the ability and desire to be dependent, filial, and even at times submissive. We might even say that one characteristic of a normal person is his ability to place himself temporarily in a dependent, subordinate, or even

submissive position without experiencing feelings of guilt or hostility toward the one upon whom he is dependent, or any loss of self-esteem or ego-security. Men who are over-ambitious or excessively independent unconsciously seek mothering from their wives or friends, rather than partnership; but at the same time they react intensely against this desire for mothering. The ability to accept love involves:

a. Some satisfaction of the need for dependency.

b. Some feeling of being loved by superiors or by those who are looked up to.

c. Some pliability and suggestibility, some susceptibility to the desires of others.

d. Ability to admit superiority or merit or ability in others; not too strong a will to power.

12. *Adequate Bodily Desires and the Ability to Gratify Them.* —This includes:

a. A healthy attitude toward bodily functions in terms of accepting them but not being preoccupied with them.

b. Ability to derive pleasure from the physical things in life such as eating, sleeping; having good fatigue recovery.

c. Ability to perform the excretory functions adequately without shame or conflict.

d. Sexual adequacy—healthy desire and the ability to gratify it without fear and guilt.

e. Ability to work.

f. Absence of an excessive need to indulge in any of these activities; and the ability to stand, at least temporarily, a fair amount of deprivation.

The Ideal Personality and Goals

As we said earlier, the ideal personality is not our primary concern. It is essentially a question of values and is therefore usually considered of intra-cultural rather than strictly scientific concern.[1] Most scientists think that statements about it are

[1] See, however, Köhler, *The Place of Values in a World of Facts* (441).

impossible unless these fundamental values are agreed upon in advance. What such values are we leave the reader to discover by searching within himself. If it is happiness that he seeks primarily, some statements about what is "good" and what is "bad" *for him* can be made, for a good many of the correlates of happiness are known. If it is the respect of the community, he can be given advice as to how he can best achieve his end. If it is the success of the state, then completely different advice is required. Perhaps wisdom is his foremost desideratum; again the advice must be changed. And so it goes.

This point is perhaps unduly emphasized; but this is necessary to bring out the fact that in most discussions of the ideal personality there may be a projection of the ideal of the particular individual who is carrying on the discussion. It is unquestionably worth while to bring one's own ideal to the forefront of consciousness. If for no other reason, this is good from a purely utilitarian point of view, for if one knows clearly what these fundamental values are, he then has it within his power to weigh them, to criticize them, and even to change them if he finds them lacking; at the same time he becomes a better member of society.

It is hoped that science in its onward march will eventually take over the whole problem of values for study. Even now there is some evidence that science is, willy-nilly, changing some of the values of western civilization and proving certain actions universally desirable, others universally undesirable. For example, in connection with the premise that life and health are desirable, the biological and medical sciences are changing not only our habits but also our value judgments—e.g., in relation to diet, cleanliness, sanitation, disease, etc. We see no reason to believe that this process will not eventually be extended so that most of our values, perhaps even all of them, will eventually come within the jurisdiction of science; but until this is true, any discussion of the ideal personality must be postponed.

SUGGESTED READINGS

The best textbooks now available on the normal personality are by Allport (27) and Stagner (721). Such general books as Burnham's *The Wholesome Personality* (122) and Morgan's *Keeping a Sound Mind* (573) are recommended.

CHAPTER V

PSYCHOSOMATICS: MOTIVATION, EMOTION, ETC.

〜〜〜〜〜〜〜〜〜〜〜〜〜〜〜〜〜〜〜〜〜〜〜〜〜〜

THE PROBLEM OF PSYCHIC-SOMATIC CORRELATION

Some of the data we obtain from sick individuals refer to observable, objective phenomena. Much, however, is of such a nature that we can know about it only if the individual chooses to tell us. Thus, in the case cited in Chapter I, an observer could see that, during an attack, the patient's facial expression was "anxious," she was breathing more deeply, her heart was beating faster; he could see her go to the window and open it. These are all observable phenomena. The following data, however, could be obtained only through her statements: During such attacks she was afraid that she might drop dead, that she might go insane; she had the feeling that she—an insignificant thing—was caught in a gigantic mesh of circumstances. In fact, her whole situation and the arrangement with her husband, while in a considerable measure referable to observable facts, represented her attitudes toward expectations of the future, and only she could tell about them.

An even more striking contrast between these types of data is furnished by such an example as the following:

The patient lies on the bed motionless, he does not react to pain, he does not answer questions, he does not attend to his wants; he remains in this condition for several weeks. His condition then changes and he becomes communicative. He says that, while lying on the bed motionless, he was not unconscious; in fact, when he made the attempt he knew everything that was going on around

46

him. This statement can be verified. He can actually relate minor incidents that occurred while he was lying in the unconscious state. He says that while he was lying in this state he was going through an intense and dramatic experience. He thought a gigantic battle was going on in the universe between good and evil; he, himself, was the battleground; the forces of good and evil were equally balanced. The slightest motion on his part could have decided the battle in one direction or another. He was not sure, however, what kind of effect his movements would have on the battle; therefore, he said, he lay without moving. Obviously, this rich and dramatic and significant experience of the patient could not have been surmised simply from looking at him.

On further examination of the problem of the two types of data, we find that the division between them is not sharp, that actually in a great many instances there is considerable correlation between them. The correlation is obvious in the two cases cited. The first patient had certain feelings and thoughts which regularly occurred with her bodily complaints. The second patient's fantasy and his lying motionless have an understandable connection.

There are numerous cases in which the two kinds of data show correlation in either psychologically healthy or sick people, e.g., when the individual is in a state of strong emotion, anger, or fear. In addition to the commonly experienced subjective feelings in such emotions, there are also changes in heart rate, salivary secretion, gastric secretion, blood pressure, circulation, etc.

Another example of correlation may be found in certain studies of electric phenomena in the brain. In these experiments electrodes are placed on the scalp and connected with an apparatus that records the electric current generated in the cortex of the brain. The tracing thus obtained shows so-called alpha waves, with a rhythm of about 10 per second. If the subject has his eyes closed, the alpha rhythm is very evident; but if he suddenly opens his eyes in the light, the alpha waves disappear.

Thus, there is a correlation between a subjective sensory experience and the observable record of the electrical activity of the brain.

Even more striking is the following experiment by Loomis, Harvey, and Hobart (502):

The subject was a patient who had been frequently brought under hypnotic suggestion for therapeutic purposes. When he was hypnotized, he still showed his normal waking (electro-encephalographic) record, with no indications of the changes characteristic of sleep. The eyelids of the subject were held open by adhesive tape and the room was moderately illuminated. After the subject had been brought to a suitable level of hypnosis, the hypnotist suggested to the subject that he was blind and could not see. The alpha waves appeared in the electrical record. The hypnotist suggested that the patient had regained his vision; the alpha waves promptly disappeared. Sight and blindness were suggested alternately sixteen times, and each time the EEG showed a corresponding change. The changes were essentially the same as if the subject had actually opened and closed his eyes.

Psychosomatic Concepts.—The ideal concepts would be those that refer to both introspective experiences and observable phenomena accurately correlated. Such concepts, however, are not always available, and for many important introspective data there are no observable correlates. Thus, in considering the concept of the feeling of helplessness, we should think not only of a subjective feeling, but also of changes in muscle tone, and, further, of actual situations in which the subjective and the observable phenomena appear. Many of the concepts to be discussed here will sound purely introspective; but they should be thought of in terms of widespread phenomena in the brain itself and in the periphery and interior of the body, and in terms of reactions to situations and various tasks which the individual has to face. As an illustration we may use some observations on experimental neurosis in animals by H. S. Liddell and his coworkers (494, 495, 29, 30).

A sheep was used as the experimental animal. Presenting it with a task which it had to solve but could not was the method of producing breakdown in its behavior ("neurosis").

The animal was trained to stand on a platform in harness. After a period of repeated struggle, it finally learned to stand quietly. The unconditioned stimulus was an electric shock to the foreleg of the animal. To this stimulus, or, in other words, whenever the electric shock was administered, the animal flexed his foreleg and then stood quietly again. The sound of a metronome beating at the rate of one beat a second was used as a conditioning stimulus in the following manner. The metronome started to beat and when, let us say, the fifth beat was reached, the shock was administered. If this was done a certain number of times, the animal behaved in the following way. He stood quietly both when the metronome was silent and when it started to beat. As the fifth beat was approaching, the animal started to flex his foreleg until the shock actually occurred. Then it stood quietly again. The animal could be conditioned in a similar manner if the electric shock came at the tenth, fifteenth, or even at the twenty-fifth second. It stood quietly up to shortly before the shock was delivered and stood quietly again after it was delivered. If, however, the interval was thirty seconds a profound disturbance occurred. The animal waited too long, then not long enough before the shock came. After such experiences, the animal's behavior changed. Henceforth, it was restless on the platform. Even when the metronome didn't beat it kept moving its foreleg. When the metronome did beat it flexed its foreleg with each beat. But still other changes were noted in the animal. Where it formerly went willingly to the laboratory on collar and chain, it now vigorously resisted going there and had to be placed by force on the table. But more than that, it became more restless even in the pen both during the day and during the night. Further, the animal tended to be withdrawn, to crouch in a corner, and to be more submissive in case of attack. And still further, the sheep's pulse became rapid and irregular as compared with that of the normal animal.

If such an animal is kept away from the laboratory for a year and a half its condition improves. If then the tests are resumed the sheep's "neurotic condition" will return. In one instance it persisted until the animal's death at the age of thirteen years and four months.

Such a "neurotic condition" did not occur if the sheep had to learn a simple maze where, if it could not solve a problem, it could turn its attention to other matters. If the same sheep learns to stand quietly and to restrain itself on the platform, it *has* to come to grips with the problem presented by the electric shock. If the problem (in the previous example, gauging the time interval) is too great and the sheep must face it, a breakdown occurs. To quote Liddell, "It is our belief that this restraint, first imposed from without, and then imposed by the animal upon itself, is the fundamental condition favoring the development of nervous strain with resulting neurosis."

The following points should be stressed in connection with the experiments on the sheep for the purpose of our discussion of human psychopathological reactions:

1. The "breakdown" of the sheep occurred in a *situation of stress*. The breakdown included changes in coping with and behaving in a wide variety of circumstances, and changes in the functioning of many organs of its body.

2. After the sheep in its helpless state developed a neurotic reaction and was exposed repeatedly to the traumatic situation, a permanent change occurred. It could not, even in the same situation, cope with tasks which it had been able to do previously. Its behavior altered in even different situations—for example, in the pen.

3. There were several significant aspects of the situation of stress: (a) the inability to master the problem presented by the situation; (b) the impossibility of escape from the problem; (c) "voluntary" or trained relinquishing of freedom; (d) conflict. Actually a multiplicity of conflicts is present: Thus the sheep "wants" to cope with the situation but has had the experience of being unable to do this successfully. It wants to escape but has an internal inhibition which makes it stay. It wants to run

away but is forced to stay; it wants to do the inevitable task but knows that it is helpless in the face of it.

4. The concepts which explain and describe best what happens to the sheep are stated in terms of forces and of being driven. The animal is forced to face an impossible task; it is driven to run away and simultaneously it is driven to remain. We now turn to some of these concepts.

The Concept of Dynamics.—As we have seen, both healthy and pathological behavior are best conceived of in terms of force, desire, goal, or drive. The individual wants something, or feels driven. Even if obstacles arise, he persists in pursuing the goal. He *has* to cope with the problems that confront him. He wants to solve them, or rather he feels forced to solve them.

The Concept of Capability and of Helplessness.—In the healthy reaction the individual usually feels that he is able ultimately to master the task confronting him. In the pathological reaction the individual feels that he has not adequate strength to dare even to want his goal. In other words, a healthy person pursuing a goal does so actively, dynamically, with his whole personality. In the case of a pathological reaction, the feeling of helplessness assumes great dynamic importance; it becomes an urgent, threatening force, and the individual feels forced to take all sorts of measures to meet the situation. For example, when the sheep on the platform fails repeatedly to cope adequately with the electric shock, it is driven constantly to do something about the expected shock. This is why the animal jerks its foreleg spasmodically although the metronome is not yet beating and the animal has not yet received a shock.

The Concept of Constellation; Genetic Considerations.—Now let us enlarge this concept of feeling helpless in a situation with which the individual has to cope. This is best accomplished if we consider an infant in his relationship with his wants, needs, and his environment.

The human being is, as a child, biologically dependent on adult individuals, because of the helpless state in which he is born and in which he remains for a period of time. The term "biological dependence" here means a need for actual help and support—that is, food, clothing, and shelter—from the adult.

In addition to his biological dependence, the newborn helpless individual is also subjected to cultural dependence; that is, the degree of his dependence on the adult is regulated and determined by the customs, goals, expectations, and actualities in his environment.

This biological and cultural dependence is later invariably accompanied by certain emotional characteristics and by emotional dependence. In his actual seeking of goals, in the sphere of ideals, and in his conflicts, the dependent individual, both consciously and unconsciously, is strongly influenced by the adult on whom he is dependent and whom he loves. He adopts the goals and ideals set for him by the adult; these goals become important and significant for him, and he values them. Furthermore, for the love and approval of the adult, or because of fear of him, he gives up other goals which he had previously pursued of his own accord. In this respect the child becomes compliant and accepts restrictions on his freedom somewhat as the sheep did when it finally was willing to go to the laboratory and cooperate with the experimenter.

Very early, probably during the first few weeks of life, the infant begins to differentiate between the external world and himself. Thus the concept of the "I" is formed. This "I" includes the image of his body and of his psychological processes. It includes many goals, both those he himself has chosen and those he has accepted from the adult on whom he is dependent. This image of the "I" is likewise treasured.

In these constellations and reactions, the child feels essentially safe, strong, and intact if the adult does not confront him with situations which are beyond his power to cope with. This corresponds to the stage at which the sheep could cope with the problem of the electric shock up to a certain point.

During this period of biological and cultural dependence some of the infant's most important needs are physiological, particularly his food, excretory and genital needs, as well as the need and desire for locomotion. In addition, in our society, he needs love and respect. All these needs are ordinarily fulfilled and regulated in his relationship with the adult. If in this relationship, however, taboos are introduced which are beyond his comprehension; if he is made to feel, in direct or indirect ways, that he is unloved or worthless; if he is always threatened with abandonment; if he is constantly disapproved of and punished; if he is always requested to renounce and is not given compensation, then a deep feeling of helplessness and worthlessness arises in him. This feeling is very strong because the child is actually dependent on the help and affection of the adult and because the adult is infinitely stronger.

There is a further development. The child becomes intensely resentful and hostile toward the adult who, he feels, refuses help, threatens, punishes, and frustrates. This resentment arises again and again, whenever the child is "unfairly handled"; and it has further consequences which are likewise very important. The helpless child may become intensely hostile to individuals on whom he is dependent, who are stronger than he, whom he needs to love, and who set his goals and ideals. This in turn leads to a strong fear of retribution, the fear of abandonment, the fear of injury, the fear of complete frustration in his bodily wants. Furthermore, the child feels helpless in the face of these threats. This conflict leads to a great devaluation of the self, and to a strong feeling of worthlessness and guilt. Thus a dynamic constellation comes into existence and becomes constantly active. The child pursues a goal; but he feels helpless and worthless, is resentful of those on whom he is dependent, and is afraid of being humiliated, abandoned, considered worthless, injured, or completely denied and frustrated. Because of the child's helpless and dependent state, his fear has a potentially catastrophic intensity. This condition—feeling helpless in a potentially hostile world—has been called "basic anxiety" (Horney).

The patient who was discussed in the first chapter was biologically and culturally dependent on her parents. As we said, her mother was emotionally distant, yet over-solicitous and over-bearing in her discipline and moral outlook. The patient, feeling herself dominated and rejected as well as humiliated, became resentful. Her resentment led to the feeling of abandonment, guilt, and worthlessness, and to the fear of injury. Thus, in its essential features, her later reactive constellation started in her childhood. Under these circumstances the experience of pneumonia was an additional serious threat. The loss of her father deprived her of the only source of affection that was in any way equivalent to her needs.

The Constellation Described in the Child Similar to That in the Adult.—The constellation described in the child has strong convincing value because his helplessness is obvious and unquestionable. In the adult, however, the situation is not quite so obvious; but it becomes clearer if we examine and observe him more carefully when he breaks down in the face of a difficulty. In such situations we have to go beyond the patient's statements, and we have to be aware of connections of which he is unaware. In other words, we have to see connections which to him are "unconscious," and we have to see evaluations, strivings, needs, and desires of which he knows nothing. If we do this, we find that in its broad outlines the constellation in the adult is very similar to that described in the child. The patient cited in the first chapter had as great an emotional need and in that sense felt as dependent on her husband as a biologically helpless and mistreated child does. She unconsciously considered him powerful and herself weak in comparison, just as the child does when he compares himself with his parent. She felt as profoundly rejected and unfairly treated and was as angry and hostile as a child. She was as much afraid of utter abandonment, of counterattack and injury, and of complete frustration as was the child we described. All this manifested itself in a compressed or telescope fashion in her attacks of anxiety.

How the general evaluation of the self and of the relationship with another individual becomes so deeply disturbed in later life will be discussed in other chapters.

Further Similarities Between Dynamics of Animal Neurosis and Human Breakdown.—In discussing the dynamics of neurosis in the sheep we stressed several points. There are similar ones in the dynamic constellation of a human breakdown.

1. The breakdown in the child or adult occurs in situations of stress, when he feels helpless in the face of problems with which he cannot cope.

2. There is intense conflict in such situations. For example, the helpless individual wants to escape from the situation but has to face it. He is hostile toward the "unfair" individual but is afraid of him. He wants to attack but he needs and wants help.

3. Once the breakdown is severe enough, it tends to continue even if the external situation of stress has temporarily abated.

4. The sheep's compliance in the situation is the result of training. When obedience was first asked of him, he struggled against it. Later he gave in of his own volition.

Dynamic Significance of Basic Anxiety and Its Derivatives.— We said earlier that, in the healthy reaction, the individual as a whole is bent on reaching his goal, whereas in the case of anxiety and helplessness the individual is also constantly driven to take some action about the distressing situation and the threatening danger. Let us now enlarge on this statement, particularly in the light of what we have learned about the "basic anxiety" found in the sick individual (see page 53). Only some general principles will be discussed here; details will be presented in later chapters.

The individual may try in various ways to relieve or remedy his fear and at the same time pursue some of his goals. Some of the means he adopts may appear only in special situations, others may be present as a constant drive, a seeking out of some situations and an avoidance of others—all for the purpose of allaying anxiety or reaching the goal, or both. If they are present almost constantly we can speak of them as character traits.

One of these measures may be the need to enter into a dependent relationship in which the other individual's strength is overvalued; he offers help and support to the small and helpless individual. This drive for love and attention may have a demanding quality. This desire for dependence was present unconsciously to a considerable degree in the patient described in the first chapter. It appeared in an observable form in her strong attachments to her friends and in her expectation and demand that they include her in all their plans.

Another measure which an individual may adopt is to do everything perfectly, to be flawless, to surpass everybody, to dominate and control. Here again the expectation is that this will guard him against the state of helplessness and worthlessness and will protect him against retribution. These trends also were strong and unconscious in the above-mentioned patient. They were observable in connection with her work; she felt constantly driven to do perfect work, was much disturbed by a mistake, had fantasies in which she had written the best pamphlet on library work, and was apt to be sharply critical and unreasonable when one of her subordinates made mistakes.

Another type of device which is observable in some individuals is the gratification of a bodily urge to relieve and protect against a catastrophic or distressing expectation. The function of eating, both in its self-preservatory and in its pleasure-seeking aspects, may be thus used. For example, a patient may eat whenever he is anxious, whenever he fears that he will be defeated. He may eat great amounts of sweets in an almost compulsive manner. He may eat as if he were protecting himself against starvation and as if the pleasure of eating guarded him against the catastrophic situation.

All these types of devices will be elaborated on in subsequent chapters. Here two dynamic topics which are of obvious and immediate psychosomatic significance will be discussed, namely, emotions and tension.

EMOTIONAL REACTIONS

The student will remember, from his study of elementary psychology, the demonstrations of the relationships between consciously felt emotions and bodily changes. In fear, for instance, the tonus of the body changes, the adrenal gland becomes more active, the gastro-intestinal tract and all its glands cease functioning, the heart beats faster, the breathing is rapid, the whole vasomotor system changes so that blood is withdrawn from certain areas and shifted to certain others, particularly the peripheral muscles, etc. (Cannon). A certain logic unites all these somatic responses with the individual's perceptions (of danger) and with his introspective, emotional content (fear). The individual with all his parts, with all his capacities, with all his past experiences in such a danger situation tends to react as a unit. He perceives a problem which his past experience tells him he cannot overcome but which may overcome him, and he prepares to do whichever has more survival value, i.e., to flee or to fight if cornered. In our jungle past dangerous problems were always very obvious—e.g., wild animals—and involved life or death. The problems of today have changed in nature a great deal. While they still sometimes involve danger to life and limb, they more often involve danger to our personalities—self-esteem, system of psychological defenses, etc. The problems may be much less dangerous and obvious than they used to be, but psychosomatically they are still the same (533).

To avoid confusion some discussion of vocabulary is necessary here. Today we distinguish "fear" from "anxiety." A simple differentiation is that fear is a reaction to something in the "real" world; anxiety is a reaction that seems unjustified or out of all proportion to the actual danger that is apparently involved. This description is further complicated by the fact that in anxiety, even though the emotional response itself may be conscious, the

situation that arouses it may be completely unconscious. For
instance, the patient described in the first chapter had attacks of
anxiety that were conscious. The causes of these attacks, however, were unconscious, i.e., the fear of being abandoned after
she had reached out emotionally toward her husband and had
thus made herself dependent and vulnerable.

But the concept of unconscious anxiety is even broader. This
unconscious anxiety is present constantly as an active dynamic
factor in many pathological reactions. It always contains an
anticipated helplessness, worthlessness, humiliation, or injury
(366). That is, it includes a state of anticipation of disaster or
catastrophe, as well as emotions of self-condemnation, guilt,
worthlessness, and so on. It is this anticipation of breakdown,
of the complete collapse of self-esteem, of the complete withdrawal of the respect and affection of others that we call the
fear of catastrophic breakdown. To repeat, anxiety may be
described from the changes in breathing, in blood pressure, etc.;
from various kinds of perceptions and from certain kinds of
feelings, such as helplessness or anticipated helplessness, vaguely
understood or wholly unconscious feelings of incipient danger to
the personality (catastrophic breakdown). But there is more
than just this description, for this whole state itself acts as a
motive, a drive, a cause for action. The entire organism girds
itself, starts to protect itself in various ways, does something
about the situation. In other words, it is a dynamic situation.[1]

[1] We can understand now why the problem of anxiety creates so much
trouble for psychologists. Some think of it as a kind of by-product, an
epiphenomenon that arises from the situation and floats above it like smoke
over a battlefield; but in itself it has no more influence on the situation
than does the smoke. It is, so to speak, caused by the battle, but has no
causal influence on it. These individuals think of anxiety as a purely
introspective phenomenon. But there are others who speak of anxiety in a
dynamic sense, as an influence that starts things going, as a cause; but if
one reads carefully, he can see that these people do not speak of anxiety,
as the first group does, merely as an introspective phenomenon; they think
of it in its total psychosomatic nature. That is, they include not only the
introspection but also the neural and physiological processes that give rise
to the anxiety. We have a choice as to how we shall use the word in this
book; we shall use it as a psychosomatic concept and not merely as a

The Fear of Catastrophic Breakdown (311, 366).—Perhaps at this point a concept that is ordinarily puzzling to the layman, but nuclear in its importance in psychopathology, can be made clearer. What are neurotics afraid of? It is not so much a "real" situation, an actual threat to the body, an actual danger of death. They are afraid of the situation because it happens to have a peculiar threatening or dangerous quality for *them as individuals*. This threat may not be at all apparent to other people in the same situation. Why then is it a threat? What does it threaten? It threatens the very structure of their personalities, their way of life, their philosophy of the world. In the neurotic character structure there is always a shaky, disturbed self-esteem, and shaky, disturbed feelings of security. These must be guarded, defended, buttressed, supported, strengthened, if the individual is not to fall into that black pit in which he feels absolutely worthless, rejected, overcome, and helpless. This is the ultimate psychological danger that can befall any human being. It can easily be understood, then, that anything that threatens the already shaky self-esteem, the already infirm feeling of security, or any of the supports or defenses for them, will be feared with the most intense fear (seen on the surface as anxiety). It is not the situation itself that is feared; it is the possible catastrophic breakdown (absolute worthlessness, absolute rejection) which the situation may bring that is feared. This catastrophic expectation is precisely the reason why "neurotic strivings" have such vital significance for the patient, such force, such persistence; this is why he persists in his peculiar behavior even at the cost of great deprivation and suffering. No deprivation is more to be feared than being deprived of self-esteem and security; no suffering can be more intense than the suffering inherent in catastrophic breakdown.

With this background of understanding, we can perceive the logic of bodily reactions in certain individuals in certain situa-

---

psychic concept, just as we shall also imply that any feeling, any psychic state is likewise a psychosomatic entity.

tions. For instance, all the somatic symptoms accompanying the emotion of wild elation may appear in an individual because of some trivial compliment or very minor victory. Such an apparently disproportionate somatic response can be understood if there is reference not only to the situation itself but also to the individual's self-esteem-security status. Probably the psychopathology of emotion can never be understood without reference to the negative factor of the fear of catastrophic breakdown, or to the positive factor of the removal of this fear or the actual support of the self-esteem and the feeling of security.

Anger, Hostility, Aggression.—The emotion of anger is also fairly well known in its psychosomatic relationships. Ordinarily anger and fear are treated as if they were contraries of each other. In psychopathology, however, we shall see that they are very closely related; and this close relationship may eventually be apparent in general psychology as well.

As far as the somatic reactions in anger are concerned, they are very simple; on the basis of present knowledge, they are the same as the somatic reactions in fear. We might ask at this point why this important fact has been overlooked by many, why fundamental similarities between fear and anger continue to be neglected. Again this is largely because of the use of the mind-body split. The introspective content of anger is, in the typical case, a feeling of wanting to attack; in fear it is usually the conscious feeling of wanting to flee. But let us analyze further. Anger of some kind is always present in every psychopathological individual; it is frequently overlooked because it is either unconscious or directed inward toward the self. The unconscious reaction of anger in its widest psychosomatic sense occurs in situations in which the individual feels disappointed in his vital expectations of help and affection, in which rejection is threatened or his self-esteem is attacked by threatened injury; it frequently is also aroused through sheer deprivation as well as frustration (See Chapter VII.) But these are the situations which we have already described as causing fear or anxiety.

This is not a paradox or contradiction. The simple fact of the matter is that where the individual's self-esteem or feeling of security is threatened, he will feel *both* afraid and angry. Introspectively or unconsciously both will be felt; sometimes one, sometimes the other will predominate. The somatic pattern involved is *one*, hence there is no contradiction on this point.

The essential difference, however, is in overt reaction. In fear and anxiety these reactions might be flight, defensiveness, giving in; in anger or hostility we tend to find aggression. But even here there is no black and white separation. Aggression may arise from fear as well as from anger, as in the cornered animal making a desperate last stand; the individual who has psychosomatic fear and is forced to flee or defend himself is also angry and aggressive.

Generally when one becomes angry with a more powerful or needed individual this will breed anxiety also because of the danger of manifesting such an impulse against a person who is so important. In psychoanalysis, when we go below the surface we frequently find that the key here is the fear of retribution, sometimes of actual physical retribution. An example would be a person who feels threatened and who fears or anticipates catastrophic breakdown. Let us say that he is threatened with abandonment by someone whom he considers powerful, on whom he feels utterly dependent, and whose approval he needs —his father, perhaps. Because of this threat and because of his fear, he will feel angry and hostile toward the one who threatens him with so much psychic pain. But several things may happen to this hostility. For instance, it is common to project it upon the feared object, i.e., to start feeling that his father is angry with him; this in turn increases his anxiety and fear of abandonment and retribution, which in turn increase his anger toward his father, and so on. But reactions of anger (hostility) and fear (anxiety) may also have strong effects on the patient's evaluation of his worth. Fear of the feeling of worthlessness because of condemnation by another individual gives rise to resentment against this individual, which increases the feeling of condemnation by this individual, which involves self-condemnation and guilt, which involves more anxiety, more hostility, etc.

In psychopathology, then, it is better to speak of a single entity, fear-anger or anxiety-hostility, and to speak of it in the widest psychosomatic sense. Fear-anger is a dynamic state of the total organism in which the body is prepared for either attack or flight or symbolic representations of either or both, and in which perceptions of the situation and the life history are all integrally bound together. It is not only a state of affairs (static) but also a tendency to do something (dynamic). The old philosophical difficulty of how a mental state can influence bodily reactions—or anything else for that matter—is seen to be a pseudo-problem so far as we are concerned; for fear-anger is not a mental but a psychosomatic state, that is, it is both a state and the total organism's reaction to that state.

Tension

Psychosomatic tension is present in all instances which involve problem-solving. The words "problem" and "solving" are used here in the broadest possible sense; for all situations which demand an answer of some kind from the individual are problems, and all such answers or attempted answers, whether good or bad, are "solutions."

The student is already familiar with Cannon's emergency theory of emotions. Cannon has shown that when a biological threat or danger faces the organism, the autonomic nervous system responds in a total fashion, so that in many ways the organism is changed. These changes all subserve the function of preparing it to fight or to flee more efficiently. We wish here to extend this theory almost to the point of universalizing it for all psychic activity, overt or covert, conscious or unconscious, cognitive or emotional.

From this point of view, *all* problems that confront the organism are to be considered "emergencies" in the same sense as Cannon's use of the term. Of course, these vary in severity, some being mild, others involving life or death. Cannon spoke only of the psychosomatic emotional response to an emergency. Our extension of the theory holds not only that the autonomic system responds in an emergency, but that the *whole person* responds with all his capacities, with all his adaptive tools, his intelligence, his perceptual abilities, his past experiences, his protective and defensive devices. This we may call a *general emergency theory of psychological adjustment*, in contrast to Cannon's special "emergency theory of emotional reactions."

Now, with regard to the specific problem of tension; we can understand why tension, both psychic and somatic, is a universal concomitant of problem-solving activities. Tension means readiness to act. If a muscle has to respond from scratch, so to speak, its response will be much slower, and therefore less efficient. It must have a certain preliminary tonicity, a constant tonic contraction from which the phasic contraction can emerge. Thus tonus means that the organism is facing a problem and is prepared to make a quick response (solution). Theoretically, its absence would mean that no problems confront the organism. Since, however, in waking life we are always in a state of tonus we must envisage the organism as *always* facing problems.[1]

Psychopathology of Tension.—In psychopathology the role of tension is, on the surface, very puzzling, for there is usually an extreme degree of over-tension, it is almost always present, and there is no overt reason for it because it is out of all proportion to the apparent problems facing the individual. The only way to bring order into this chaos is to go *behind* the overt picture, remembering that problems may be unconscious and

---

[1] The words "tension" and "relaxation" are used in various ways by the layman. By tension he usually means what we shall call "over-tension." By relaxation he usually means mild tension; however, this is a state of tonus which gives the organism just enough efficiency for problem-solving. Complete lack of tonus is not relaxation, but flaccidity. See the writings of Koffka and Lewin for discussions of the concept of psychic tension.

therefore not immediately perceivable. We can then find a logic of a kind in the situation.

The psychologically sick person always feels threatened and afraid; he is afraid of catastrophic breakdown, i.e., absolute feelings of worthlessness, helplessness, rejection, humiliation, isolation, and frustration. In other words, he is *at all times* faced with emergency problems which are so severe that he reminds one of a cornered animal fighting for its life. Threats come from every side and they are continuous. The situation is made worse for him by the fact that, in addition to his problems being severe and continuous, his answers to them are in the last analysis inadequate; deep down, he himself does not trust them. Not only must he fend off attacks from all sides, but he must do this with a pitifully blunt sword.

Thus he experiences introspectively a chronic and unbearable tenseness and strain; somatically he wears himself out as if he were trying to run a marathon at a 100-yard-dash pace.

It is at this point that there emerges the nuclear idea that must underlie any adequate psychosomatic medicine: a continually discharging autonomic nervous system must in the long run have many organic pathological effects. For instance, some form of gastro-intestinal disorder would be natural in a man whose digestion is frequently impaired, because he is always, so to speak, running for his life. Vasomotor disorders, e.g., high blood pressure, would be expected in a man who is always fighting enemies and whose body never rests. Disturbances in the functioning of excretory and genital organs would be expected in individuals who are thrown into a state of conflict by constantly recurring impulses from these organs which cannot be adequately satisfied (Kempf [429], Freeman [260]).

Experimental Study of Observable Vegetative Changes During Emotional Stress.—We said in the previous section that a sick individual may continually expect a catastrophic situation and thus be under severe chronic emotional stress. We mentioned earlier that the sheep, after its breakdown in the unsolvable situation, had a continuously rapid pulse. At other times it had an irregular pulse, particularly when placed in the traumatic situation.

Disturbances in the functioning of various organs which are not under the control of the will are frequent in patients. The patient described in the first chapter had a rapid pulse rate—120 per minute—when she had an anxiety attack; under usual circumstances when she was relaxed, her pulse rate was 72 per minute. Many such vegetative changes occurring under stress have been subjected to experimental investigation and to accurate measurement. As an example, changes in finger temperature accompanying emotional stress will be described here (Mittelmann and Wolff [565]).

The subject rested on a comfortable table in a constant-temperature room; the subject's hand rested on a pillow. Next to his fingers was placed a radiometer, an instrument which measures the temperature of the fingers by measuring their heat radiation. The essential principle upon which this instrument operates is that of the thermocouple, with which the student becomes familiar in the physics laboratory.

During control periods in which the subjects were in a relaxed condition, the finger temperature ran an even course at about 33°C. In order to induce affective states experimentally, a discussion was conducted dwelling on difficulties in the individual's life situation to which he reacted with signs of emotional distress. One subject was a high school girl in her late teens. She was an only child, whose parents had separated when she was one year old. Generally she lived with her mother, but had spent one bad summer with her father, who affected her emotionally. She was a very pretty girl, even beautiful according to some. Yet she was convinced that she was unattractive and that she had "pop-eyes." She was sensitive to disapproval and strongly desired praise and attention. She had many acquaintances but no close friends She was attached to her mother, whom she considered a "companion," but still she was often on bad terms with her because of criticisms and general disagreements. At such times, she would not speak to her mother for weeks, and felt bitter and helpless because she was dependent on her mother for support.

In one experiment, in which she was asked to repeat and retain a series of digits, her finger temperature dropped 4.8°C. in 12 minutes, then came back to normal afterwards. Her introspective report was that during the repetition of digits she was very eager to perform well, and was disturbed over mistakes because she considered the procedure to be a test of her intelligence.

The experimenter then engaged the subject in conversation about her mother with whom she was on bad terms at that time. Finger temperature dropped 13.2°C.! When the conversation was terminated, the finger temperature returned to normal. Her report was of anger, feelings of inadequacy and helplessness.

In another subject, who was having great difficulty with her husband, conversation about this situation produced, as in the first subject, the same tremendous drop in finger temperature, 13.2°C. She reported feelings of anger, rage, resentment, anxiety, and guilt.

This typical psychosomatic experiment demonstrates various other points that we have discussed. First of all, it shows the correlation between conscious happenings and bodily happenings. It shows, furthermore, that some of the reactions which we ordinarily regard as purely psychic are in reality psychosomatic, responses of the whole individual. The function involved here is an autonomic one, not under the control of the will; but strong reaction could be experimentally induced simply by conversation about sore points in the patient's life. Finally, such experiments help us to understand how private "introspective states," continued over a long period of time, may produce widespread pathological changes in the body.

DISTURBANCES RESULTING FROM GROSS ORGANIC DAMAGE TO THE BRAIN TISSUE

Up to this point we have discussed reactions and motivations, methods of coping with difficult situations when there was no gross organic damage either to the brain or to the organs of the body—in other words, conditions in which the difficulty was primarily psychological. In many cases, however, there is an organic damage either to the brain or to some organ in the body; and, correlated with that, there are disturbances in one or another psychological function. As an example of this, some clinical observations on human beings and some experimental observations on animals will be discussed.

The Effect of the Removal of Both Frontal Lobes.—Each half of the cerebrum is divided into several lobes, one of which is called the frontal lobe. This lobe is itself divided into various parts; the hindmost part, the so-called central gyrus, contains the centers of muscular activity. If this part is removed, the patient becomes paralyzed; but if parts in front of it are removed, there is no paralysis. If the pre-motor part of one side of the frontal lobe is removed, there are as a rule no noticeable disturbances in any of the psychological functions. Sometimes if the pre-motor area is removed from the dominant hemisphere, e.g., from the left brain in right-handed people, disturbances in some psychological functions do occur. They always appear if this area is removed from both sides.

The possible symptoms and the principles involved are illustrated in the following observations of a man whose frontal lobes (the pre-motor areas) were removed bilaterally (Brickner [98]).

The patient was a 40-year-old man, a successful broker on the New York Stock Exchange. He developed a tumor of the brain. During the operation large portions of his frontal lobes were removed on both sides.

The patient was not able to go back to his previous work. He talked a lot about going back, in a boastful manner, but never made any effort to do so.

In general the outstanding features in his behavior and speech were boastfulness and the tendency to self-aggrandizement. The patient's self-aggrandizing and boastful manner showed itself also in his considering himself the best conductor and the best dancer. It showed in his statement that he could lick anybody, that nobody in the world could fool him. It further showed itself in reminiscences and stories about his boyhood in all of which he either beat up somebody or fooled somebody. In all his stories about sexual exploits he showed the same trend. Together with that he was inclined to be facetious and euphoric (being in an elated mood). His memory for recent events was faulty. He sometimes forgot, for example, that he had gone to the movies the day before. He was incapable of logically following through a topic in thinking or in conversation if this topic was in any way complicated. Thus, at one moment he would say he did not believe in capital punishment for people who committed a crime when they did not know what they were doing; he would then say he did not believe in capital punishment for kidnapers, then he would say that kidnapers did know what they were doing. He would say he did not believe in torturing people under any circumstances as a punishment, but then he would say that torture was too mild a punishment for kidnapers. He was easily distractible.

On other occasions he behaved in a childish, angry, and abusive manner. He would refuse to get undressed in the evening and to wash his face in the morning. He would walk into a room where people were playing cards and would say, "You're all a lousy bunch of players. Do you want to start something?" An example follows of his manner of conversation illustrating his self-aggrandizement, his boastfulness, his inconsistency in thinking, and his distractibility:

"Dr. Brickner: One thing your illness lost you is the knowledge that you're not perfect.
"The Patient: It's a damn good thing to lose.
"B. Do you really believe in your heart that you are perfect?
"Pt. Yes. Of course we all have faults. I have faults like everyone else.
"B. Name some of your faults.
"Pt. I don't think I have any.
"B. You just said you had.
"Pt. Well, they wouldn't *predominate* on the Exchange.
"B. I mean personal faults.
"Pt. Yes, I have personal faults. I never give a man an opportunity to do what he wants to do on the Exchange, if I know it.

"B. Is that a fault?

"Pt. That's being a good broker.

"B. Can you name a personal fault? Do you really believe you're perfect?

"Pt. You bet I do—pretty near perfect—they don't come much more perfect than I am."

Often when the patient conversed, his attention would suddenly be attracted by something around him.

Patient talking about himself:

"Pt. You must have a certain mentality that catches on to the knack of executing an order. (To his wife, *referring to the colored stripes on the sleeves of her dress*) The yellow is for Princeton, the green for Irish, and the blue for navy.

"B. What's the white for?

"Pt. White is for the doctor—purity."[1]

Experimental Investigation on Frontal Lobectomized Animals. —The frontal lobectomized chimpanzee is distinguished from the normal animal by his restlessness and distractibility and "by a rather fatuous equanimity of spirit which one encounters in a good-natured drunkard, but never in a normal chimpanzee" (Fulton [299]). The intellectual performance suffers. Intellectual function and also memory are tested with the stick-and-platform test and the delayed reaction test.

In the more complex form of the stick-and-platform test, the animal has to use shorter sticks to gather in longer sticks beyond its reach, finally reaching the banana with the longest stick. In another complicated test, sticks of varying lengths are placed on two platforms. In order to get the banana, the monkey has to carry the sticks from one platform to the other. The normal chimpanzee is able to do this task successfully; but if the premotor areas in both sides are removed, the animal cannot do this (Jacobsen [385-391]).

The delayed reaction test is as follows: There are two cups in

---

[1] R. M. Brickner, *The Intellectual Functions of the Frontal Lobes*, The Macmillan Company, New York, 1936, pp. 45, 48.

the cage, separated from the monkey by the bars and a glass door. Food is placed under one of the cups. After a certain length of time, the monkey is permitted to reach for the food. In order to choose correctly, he has to remember under which cup the food was placed. The normal chimpanzee can do this task correctly after intervals of as long as five minutes. After bilateral frontal lobectomy, the chimpanzee is unable to do it after an interval of five seconds.

This test can be made more complicated by lowering an opaque screen after the food is put under one of the cups. The chimpanzee of course cannot see the cups until the screen is raised. At times, even normal animals become emotionally disturbed and fail in this form of the test. Thus an adolescent female, affectionate, cooperative, and eager to work in the problem situations, became greatly upset whenever she made an error in the delayed reaction test. In these circumstances she flew into a temper tantrum during which she rolled on the floor, beat the grate, defecated and urinated, and showed signs of diffuse sympathetic discharge. She finally refused to go into the problem cage. After the removal of both frontal areas, a profound change occurred in this animal. She ran eagerly into the experimental cage, did not get excited when the opaque screen was lowered, and never showed any emotional disturbance no matter how many times she made a mistake. "It was as if the animal had joined the happiness cult of the elder Micheaux and had placed its burdens on the Lord. Objectively the animal failed in the test even with only the glass door in operation" (Jacobsen).

Thus we see the similarities—intellectual and memory defects, distractibility, and euphoria—in human beings and in chimpanzees following the removal of the pre-motor area of the frontal lobes bilaterally.

Personality Aspects and Psychodynamics in Frontal Lobectomy.—The following data throw further light on the behavior, reactions, and emotional life of patients whose frontal lobes have been bilaterally removed. The situation is not as simple as it might seem. We cannot say simply that if certain parts of the frontal lobes are removed, certain symptoms will then appear. In general, the following occurs: (1) The patient's ability to perform certain tasks is impaired and his drives are altered; (2) some of his functions and emotional needs remain unchanged; and (3) he reacts to his deficiencies in terms of his altered drives.

It is obvious that in this whole process the patient's earlier personality is of paramount importance. The patient reported by Brickner had been a shy and quiet child, submissive to his dominant father and dependent on his mother. He married, but the aggressor in the courtship was his wife. After his marriage he wished to remain in his parents' home. Before his illness, he often showed a spark of facetiousness and frequently told humorous and sometimes boastful stories. In general, he was a mild and submissive individual who repressed all hostility and compensated for his feelings of inadequacy by a whimsical, humorous, and somewhat boastful manner. The one function that was good was his occupational activity. The results of the frontal lobectomy were: (1) impairment of the previously good intellectual function (memory and logic); (2) a decrease in self-criticism and self-restraint and, as a result of this, an increase in spurious self-evaluation, in the expression of previously repressed hostility, and in childish, dependent attitudes. The functions that he retained from previous periods were some ideals of achievement, a desire for the respect and praise of others, and some self-criticism.

It was a painful experience for this patient to realize that his intellectual functions had become impaired and that he was unable to live up to the ideals which he still cherished. He reacted to these disappointments and this realization in terms of the already altered goals and reaction patterns, namely, with a further increase of self-evaluation and dependence and with hostility. This is why he becomes boastful, almost grandiose, combative, and abusive. He makes no attempt to work. He grows more dependent on his mother, who bathes him and often dresses him. He never engages in normal sexual relations with his wife, but only in auto-erotic practices.

We wish to emphasize again that direct damage to the brain is not followed by a simple defect; the symptoms are determined by the direct effect of the damage and the reaction of the patient's total personality to this damage.

Personality Problems in Primary Disturbances of Metabolism and in Changed Appearance of the Body

Another type of psychological problem arises in some conditions in which there is a primary disturbance in some function of the body. This will be illustrated by a condition called adiposo-genital dystrophy (Fröhlich Syndrome), which is due to a glandular disturbance, particularly underfunctioning of the pituitary gland. The metabolism is usually low, and there is "general poverty of drive." The boys are stout and have small, underdeveloped genitals. Thus, the appearance of the body is altered. Such boys frequently lack ordinary skills and often behave passively. They are apt to play with girls and smaller children; at times, they are irritable, angry, and abusive. However, it is not as simple to explain their emotional difficulties as one might think. It could first be assumed that such boys are suffering from a glandular disturbance which *directly* influences their nervous system and with that their whole behavior (472); but on detailed examination the behavior is found to be determined by several factors (Mittelmann [562]) which will be discussed in connection with a case.

The patient was a stout boy with small genitals. His basal metabolism was –20. His mother was over-protective, strict, and dominant. He tried to play with other boys of his own age (about five), but was unable to compete with them effectively in sports. After a period of distress, he gave up further attempts and instead played with his sister, with other girls and with smaller boys. He was peaceful and never fought with other children. When he was ten years old his classmates, some of them nearing puberty, became increasingly rough and teased him about his stoutness and about his playing with girls. About the same time, while in the shower room, some other boys remarked about the smallness of his genitals. He felt bitter and inferior about this. His behavior soon underwent a considerable change. He became disobedient and abusive toward his mother; he beat his sister; fought with the boys if they called him "sissy" and started to play games with his classmates, picking quarrels with them frequently.

The treatment of the patient at the age of 13 consisted of the administration of thyroid gland tissue to raise his metabolism to normal, and the injection of a pituitary-like substance. He began to develop normally and lost his stoutness. Both he and his mother needed psychotherapy in addition. The patient's behavior grew normal in about six months' time.

The factors that influenced this boy's behavior at various times were these: His metabolism was always low; hence he had a constant "general poverty of drive." His mother was always over-solicitous. Both of these factors made him inclined to be passive, as did also his difficulty in competing with other boys. When he was five years old the most painless and gratifying solution was to find pleasure and consolation in playing with girls and with younger children. His experiences at the age of ten—the attitude of the other boys in connection with the appearance of his body and his passive mode of behavior—hurt his self-esteem deeply. His reaction to this hurt was over-aggressiveness, in spite of his "poverty of drive." Thus we see that this patient's problems were caused partly by the direct influence of his disturbed metabolism and partly by the reaction of his total personality to his deficiencies.

Psychological Disturbance Leading to Pathology in Metabolism

Organic factors are often important in another type of psychological problem. Exophthalmic goiter is a condition in which there is enlargement of the thyroid gland and a considerably increased metabolism (up to + 100), bulging of the eyes, trembling of the fingers, loss of weight, rapid heart rate, excessive perspiration, and other symptoms. The main psychological symptom is marked restlessness and irritability. Many of these symptoms are due to an over-functioning of the thyroid gland. In other words, if a healthy individual is given adequate amounts of thyroid substance continuously, he will develop similar disturbances (with the exception of the bulging of the eyes), and will become markedly restless and irritable. The psychopathological problem here, however, is not as complex as it is in the patient with an exophthalmic goiter. For example, a young married woman developed an exophthalmic goiter after her husband had recovered from an attack of pneumonia. Her thyroid gland was operated on, and she improved. Five years later this condition reappeared after her daughter's recovery from an attack of pneumonia (561).

It is clear that exophthalmic goiter developed in this patient in response to a situation of severe stress. The problem, however, does not end there. Further examination showed that her reaction to stress was not normal. This patient had had a very unhappy childhood. Her father drank and was often abusive and violent at home toward both her mother and herself. The mother suffered from attacks of anxiety and leaned heavily on the patient for support against the father. The patient felt helpless and resentful toward both parents; she felt catastrophically threatened by her father and had a strong sense of worthlessness and guilt because of resentment toward her mother. At the age of 18 she married a man to whom she was not attached, solely in order to get away from her home. Her husband too turned out to be a disappointment. He was seclusive and emotionally detached, and never showed any warmth toward her. She would have left him except for the child to whom she gave birth a year after her marriage.

Her reaction to the illnesses of her husband and child can now be better understood. She unconsciously evaluated their sickness as a fulfillment of a death-wish she had toward them. This wish was the reaction of an individual who felt that all her vital needs were denied but was powerless to deal with the situation. Their death would liberate her, but at the same time deprive her of even the small amount of love she could obtain. Her conflict was intense, though unconscious. She condemned herself severely and feared retribution.

After the exophthalmic goiter developed, the patient became irritable. Previously she had never contradicted her husband, but she now expressed her resentment toward him in a rather explosive manner. This increased her fear of him. Her irritability toward her child also increased, and she condemned herself for this because it clashed with her ideals. Thus we see that the final symptoms in this patient were the result of: (1) her original conflicts; (2) the over-secretion of the thyroid gland (chemical effect on the nervous tissue); (3) the personality reactions to the effects of this over-secretion, resulting in increased fear and guilt.

The patient was operated on a second time and was given psychological treatment. The husband also was interviewed several times, and the arrangement in the home was improved. The patient recovered fully and her life became happier.

This case shows that a personality reaction may precipitate a severe organic disturbance, and that there is a further personality reaction to this disturbance.

SUMMARY

1. In certain instances a definite correlation can be established between introspective "psychological" and objective observable phenomena.

2. Normal and pathological psychological phenomena are best accounted for in terms of forces, that is, psychodynamics. These drives, needs, and reactions to situations should be thought of in broad patterns comprising both introspective and observable phenomena.

3. Psychopathology may appear because of disturbances in the motivations of an individual whose body structure is essentially normal or because of primary damage and disturbance in the structure of the body.

4. The following can be said about disturbance of motivation: In the healthy reaction one of the most important dynamic factors is "I can do this." In the pathological reaction the central dynamic constellation is that of helplessness.

5. A primary "psychological" disturbance of motivation leads to disturbance in the functions of the body, particularly through the vegetative nervous system, which are correlated with the emotions of fear and anger and with sustained tension. In a primary organic disturbance the psychological symptoms are the direct results of this defect and the reactions of the patient's personality to it.

SUGGESTED READINGS

Psychosomatic Medicine is a new journal which deals with the subject matter in this chapter. The student is also referred to the specific papers mentioned in the chapter. The serious student will be interested in the digest of all the important psychosomatic work in Dunbar's *Emotions and Bodily Changes* (202).

Two physiological classics, both by Cannon, should also be mentioned: *Bodily Changes in Pain, Hunger, Fear and Rage* (132) and *Wisdom of the Body* (131). On the problem of tension, Kempf's *The Autonomic Functions and the Personality* (429) is a classic. The most significant current work on the subject is that by Freeman (258-262).

PART II

PSYCHODYNAMIC PROCESSES

CHAPTER VI

UNCONSCIOUS PSYCHOLOGICAL PROCESSES; CONFLICT

~~~~~~

UNCONSCIOUS ACTIVITIES

It has been repeatedly emphasized in the preceding chapters that the patient cannot adequately account for the complaints and symptoms from which he suffers, but that their meaningful connections can be seen if we assume, on the basis of valid evidence, that he is motivated by needs, goals, and emotions of which he is not aware; in other words, they are unconscious. The existence of unconscious psychological processes can be demonstrated experimentally and clinically by means of hypnosis and in other ways. Erickson's demonstration (226) is as follows:

"During profound hypnosis the subject [a confirmed smoker] was instructed to feel that smoking was a bad habit, that he both loved and hated it, that he wanted to get over the habit but that he felt it was too strong a habit to break, that he would be very reluctant to smoke and would give anything not to smoke, but that he would find himself compelled to smoke; and that after he was awakened he would experience all of these feelings, though not remembering that he had been told to have them.

"After he was awakened the subject was drawn into a casual conversation with the hypnotist who, lighting one himself, offered him a cigarette. The subject waved it aside with the explanation that he had his own and that he preferred Camels, and promptly began to reach for his own pack. Instead of looking in his customary pocket, however, he seemed to forget where he carried his cigarettes and searched fruitlessly through all of his other pockets with a gradually increasing concern. Finally, after having sought them repeatedly in all his other pockets, he located his cigarettes in their usual place. He took them out, engaged in a brief conversation as he dallied with the pack, and then began a search for matches which he failed to find. During his search for matches he replaced the cigarettes in his pocket and began using both hands, finally locating the matches too in their usual pocket. Having done this, he now began using both hands to search for his cigarettes. He finally located them but then found that he had once more misplaced his matches. This time, however, he kept his cigarettes in hand while attempting to locate the matches. He then placed a cigarette in his mouth and struck a match. As he struck it, however, he began a conversation which so engrossed him that he forgot the match and allowed it to burn his finger tips, whereupon, with a grimace of pain, he tossed it in the ash tray. Immediately he took another match, but again introduced a diverting topic by asking the audience in a humorous fashion if they knew the 'Scotch' way of lighting a cigarette. As interest was shown, he carefully split the match through the middle. One half of the match he replaced in his pocket in a time-consuming manner and tried to light his cigarette with the other half. When it gave too feeble a flame he discarded it and had to search for the second half. After striking this, another interesting topic of conversation developed and again he burned his fingers before he made use of it. He apologized for his failure to demonstrate the 'Scotch' light successfully and repeated the performance, this time holding the flame in such a way as to ignite only a small corner of the cigarette from which he succeeded in getting only one satisfactory puff. Then he tossed the match away and tipped the cigarette up so that he could see the lighted end. He started to explain that that was how the 'Scotch' light was obtained and noted that only one small corner of the cigarette was lit. He smiled in a semi-apologetic manner and explained that he had really given a 'Jewish' light to the cigarette, whereupon the lighted corner expired. He made a few more humorous comments, and as he talked and gesticulated appropriately he rolled the cigarette between his fingers in such a fashion that he broke it, whereupon he put it aside and took another. This time a member of the audience stepped up and proffered him a light, but as the lighted match drew near to the top of his cigarette the subject sneezed and blew it out. He apologized again and said he thought he would light his own cigarette. While taking out his matches he commented on the vaudeville trick of rolling cigars from one corner of the mouth to the other and proceeded to demonstrate how he could roll a cigarette in that fashion, which he did fairly successfully. However, in doing so he macerated the tip of the cigarette and had to discard it. He took another, holding it in his mouth while he reached for his matches, started a conversation, and took the cigarette out so that he would talk more freely. It was observed that he took the cigarette out with his hand held in the reverse position to that which he usually used, and after completing his remarks he put the dry end of the cigarette in his mouth, exposing the wet end. He then tried to light this, held the match to the tip in the proper fashion, puffed vigorously, finally got a puff of smoke and then blew out the match. Naturally the wet end of the cigarette did not burn satisfactorily and quickly went out. He looked at it in amazement and in a semi-embarrassed manner mumbled that he had lit the wrong end of the cigarette; he then commented that now both ends of the cigarette were wet, and discarded it for another. After several similar trials he finally succeeded in lighting the cigarette. It was observed that although he took deep puffs he tended to let his cigarette burn undisturbed, and that instead of smoking it down to a reasonable butt he quickly discarded it.

"A little later, while smoking, the subject attempted to demonstrate the violent gestures of a patient and in so doing knocked off the burning tip. Then while lighting another cigarette he became so interested in talking that he lit the cigarette in the middle rather than at the tip and had to discard it. As usual he showed profound embarrassment at seeming so awkward.

"(On other occasions when the subject had demonstrated this phenomenon, he would finally complete the demonstration by selecting a cigarette in a strained and laborious fashion and then, obviously centering all of his attention upon the procedure of lighting it, would hold his hand tensely as he lit the match, applying it with noticeable rigidity to the cigarette and holding it there so long and puffing so repeatedly that all doubt was removed concerning the actual lighting of the cigarette, whereupon his whole manner and attitude would relax and he would appear to be physically comfortable.)"[1]

The Relative Controllability of Conscious and Unconscious Impulses.—Conscious wishes are more controllable than unconscious wishes. The amazing difference in controllability can be seen most clearly in one of the essential aspects of psychoanalytic therapy. The first task of this therapy is always phrased as "increasing the patient's insight into his own motives, or making the unconscious conscious." How this is done will not be discussed here; we shall point merely to the fact that deep therapy is never possible without this insight into unconscious motives.[2] Sometimes, in simpler cases, the mere baring of an unconscious impulse or thought or fantasy to consciousness may deprive it, automatically and at once, of all its pathological power. Indeed, it was with this discovery by Breuer and Freud that the history of psychoanalysis began. For instance, in such hypnotic experiments as the one cited above, it is merely necessary to tell the patient what happened during the trance, i.e., make him conscious of it, in order for the suggestions to lose all or most of their power. We quote from an experiment by Erickson on the possible criminal use of hypnosis (225):

"I secretly made the acquaintance of his roommate and acquainted him with my intentions, securing his full cooperation; then after a period of about three months, I endeavored first by indirect and then gradually by more and more direct suggestions to induce him to read his roommate's mail surreptitiously. These letters were casually left on the bureau but were always placed in definite relationship to certain objects and various cues arranged to determine whether or not they had been touched. All efforts in this regard

[1] M. H. Erickson, Experimental demonstrations of the psychopathology of everyday life, *Psychoanal. Quart.*, 1939, **8**, 338-353.

[2] To obtain this insight is far from an easy task. Impulses are unconscious for a *reason*; they do not become conscious simply because we suggest it. For example, since such impulses are usually unconscious because they are feared in one way or another, it is obviously necessary that, before they will be allowed to become conscious, they must be feared less or not at all. It is this *fear* which the psychologist must attack.

failed. Also, during the roommate's absence from the room I would visit the subject and put him in a trance and endeavor to get him to read one of the letters. He always resisted strongly and when finally I succeeded by urgent direct suggestions to get him to open one side of the paper, he opened it but looked at the blank side and declared that there was no writing on it. I urged him to turn it around and he did so but held it bottom side up. I had him turn it right side up and then discovered that he could not read it because he had taken his glasses off previously, the significance of which act I had not appreciated at the time. Only after much hunting were his glasses found, whereupon he declared that the writing was so difficult that he could not read it. An effort was made to help him, whereupon he developed a psychic blindness and could not see.

"Throughout this whole experiment it was very difficult to retain this subject's friendship. He tended to avoid me and he seemed distrustful of me. When he was told later of the experiment he confessed that he had disliked me intensely but that his knowledge of Dr. Hull and Hull's interest in my work had convinced him that it must be of some scientific value and that he was willing to endure his dislike of me in the hope of forwarding some scientific inquiry.

"Before he was given any understanding of my experiment I attempted another one, somewhat less drastic in nature. He had a reasonable money allowance but he knew I was extremely poverty-stricken. I built up a belief in him that unless I could secure some money of some sort I would not be able to complete my special research work. I built up this belief in both the waking and trance states, and then after having made proper arrangements with his roommate, I tried to get him to steal money from his roommate for me, making use of every possible euphemism in broaching my suggestion. He promised to cooperate, but despite carefully determined sums of money left in bureau drawers, table drawers, extra suits, no results were forthcoming, and the subject professed a complete inability to find any money. Finally he consented to pick his roommate's pocket. He was carefully drilled in the art of picking a pocket until he could pick mine easily. At the chosen time while his roommate was busy talking to me, apparently having met me for the first time, my subject in a deep somnambulistic trance state stood along side of him slightly to the rear. He proceeded to pick his roommate's pocket but instead of doing it delicately and carefully, he merely forced his hand in it rudely and awkwardly, yanked out the pocketbook and with extreme care and secrecy handed it to me.

"I questioned him extensively about his success in picking the pocket and he seemed to believe fully that he had picked it in the best possible style. Much later when I informed the subject of the use I had made of him, he was tremendously interested, and had no recollection of either experiment; and when I enabled him by means of hypnotic suggestions to recall the entire procedure and his reactions at the time, he could give me only this explanation, 'I wanted to do what you said; I tried hard. I had an idea that it was terribly important or you wouldn't ask me to do those things, but I just couldn't do them.' After this explanation he lost all of his dislike of me and on various occasions acted as a demonstration subject for me. Subsequently, he transferred to another medical school. When I met him again a year later he was still interested in hypnosis and inquired at length about my work."[1]

It will be noticed in this example that both behavior and attitudes proceeded from unconscious determinants. The attitude of dislike disappeared dramatically when its unconscious determinant was made conscious.

The following important question arises: Why is there this difference in the "controllability" of conscious and unconscious impulses? Or, to put it in another way, why is it that with insight the individual can handle his problems differently than he does when they are largely unconscious? There are two approaches to this problem: (1) the conditioned response experiments; (2) the psychodynamics of the unconscious processes or, to express it better, understanding why a certain psychological process becomes unconscious.

Conditioned Response Experiments and Unconscious Activities.—Ever since Pavlov began his epoch-making experiments with conditioned reflexes there have been persistent attempts to

---

[1] See also M. H. Erickson, An experimental investigation of the possible anti-social use of hypnosis, *Psychiatry*, 1939, 2, 391-414.

apply to dynamic psychology the concepts derived from these experiments. Since its beginning, dynamic psychology has proceeded with this enormously difficult task along the only paths that were open to it at the time, viz., reasoning by analogy, reasoning by parallel, using an anthropomorphic vocabulary and descriptions, hypostatizing, and employing vague and even poetic figures of speech. To the experimental psychologist the whole vocabulary of dynamic psychology has often been definitely unsatisfactory for these reasons, and there has resulted the short-sighted tendency to throw out the truths because of the way in which they were phrased. Today no one any longer denies that these unsatisfactory terms do describe great discoveries. Now more than ever before, attempts are being made to bind experimental and clinical psychologies together by furnishing them with a common vocabulary that is experimentally based.[1] In any such attempt the conditioned reflex experiments are very important. We shall describe a series of these experiments which seem to bear upon the reality of unconscious processes.

Cason (135) was one of the first to demonstrate that involuntary processes could be conditioned in the laboratory. He was able to condition the constriction and dilatation of the pupil of the eye to sound stimuli that were originally incapable of influencing it. This he did with the ordinary technique first used by Pavlov—presenting simultaneously an adequate stimulus (a light flashed into the eye) capable of constricting the pupil, and an inadequate stimulus (in this case, the sound of a bell) incapable of producing constriction. After many such simultaneous presentations, the sound alone would produce pupillary constriction.

Some years later, Hudgins (375) substantiated and extended Cason's results. In this experiment the subject was conditioned first to the sound of a bell, then to the sound of his own voice as it said the word "constrict," then to the whispered sound of

---

[1] Especially by a group of workers at Yale—Hull, Sears, Dollard, Mowrer, and many others.

his own voice, and finally merely to the *thought*. The result was that the subject could constrict or dilate his pupils at will.[1]

This was the first time that an involuntary, non-conscious process had ever been brought under conscious voluntary control in the laboratory. These experiments also proved that the conditioning process did not necessarily involve consciousness, for some of the subjects were not aware of the conditioned constriction and dilatation of their pupils.

Later, Menzies (547) demonstrated for the vasomotor response what Cason and Hudgins had for the pupillary response. He was able to condition the constriction and dilatation of blood vessels to various stimuli. What is of primary interest for us in this experiment, however, is that Menzies found that words which the subject already used habitually seemed to act unconsciously as self-administered conditioned stimuli for vaso-dilatation or vaso-constriction. For instance, he found in some subjects that uttering or thinking "cold" words—e.g., ice, frost, iceberg, snow —produced a constriction of the blood vessels similar to that produced by the actual application of cold water to the subject's body. "Hot" words—fire, heat, burn, red-hot—produced in some subjects vaso-dilatation similar to their response to the actual application of hot water. These results bring to mind the experiments on action currents by Jacobson, Max, and others, which showed that a "thought" is accompanied by nerve impulses to the appropriate muscles.

A recent experiment by Baker (39) seems to bear more directly on our problem. This unusual experiment, if it is confirmed by other experimenters, will open up an important path in the experimental study of unconscious activities. An involuntary response, constriction or dilatation of the pupil, was conditioned to a subliminal sensory stimulus, i.e., a sound that was not consciously heard, an electric shock not consciously felt, etc. Baker

---

[1] These and other experiments are presented here in a very schematic form; the interest is in the results rather than the methods or details. For the latter, see the bibliography, or Hilgard and Marquis (346).

found, first, that conditioning took place with amazing rapidity (in the preliminary form in only one trial and in a final form in two trials), and, second, that this conditioning was extraordinarily persistent, for in some subjects it could be elicited months later without any further training. Throughout the experiment the subject was not conscious of what was going on; that is, he never knew that he was being conditioned, nor was he aware after the completion of the experiment that he was different in any way.

This same author has completed another experiment (40) that goes even farther along the path of "experimentalizing" clinical psychology. This was an experiment on what Freud originally called "catharsis," which holds that unconscious material ceases to exert its harmful influence when it has been made conscious. Can the Baker effect be destroyed if the subject is made conscious of what is going on?

In this experiment the response conditioned was emotional, specifically, the psychogalvanic skin response made when blindfolded subjects received what they falsely interpreted to be hypodermic injections. The conditioned stimulus was the very faint sound of a buzzer. The subjects could have heard this buzzer if they had attended to it, but in their preoccupation with the fearful possibility of being given a hypodermic injection they were unaware of the sound. In other words, the conditioned psychogalvanic skin response can be thought of as the "symptom" of the "unconscious" processes initiated by the buzzer.

When a conditioned response had been established in this situation, the next steps were (1) to show the subject that he had never been given a hypodermic injection, and (2) to call his attention to the buzzer and convince him that he had been responding to it quite "unconsciously." Thus the unconscious material was made conscious.

In seven out of the fifteen subjects in this experiment, the expected "catharsis" actually occurred. That is, making the subliminal stimulus supraliminal (conscious) caused the conditioned response to disappear, or making the unconscious material conscious brought about the removal of the "symptom." Of course, there is still the question as to why this change was not found in the other eight subjects; but the experiment shows that when unconscious processes are made conscious they may be profoundly altered. Furthermore, there is here a strong indication that the experimental worker in the laboratory is dealing with at least some of the processes dealt with by the analyst in the life situation.

These experiments like certain older ones prove that we can perceive unconsciously, react unconsciously, and learn unconsciously. They also indicate that unconscious processes seem to proceed in accordance with somewhat different principles than do conscious activities; i.e., they appear to be less controllable and to persist longer. In a word, they seem to be more "powerful" in various ways than when they are conscious. It is also important to remember that these experiments differ in important ways from the work of clinical students of unconscious activities. For one thing, the psychoanalysts have worked mostly with unconscious *emotional* and *conative* processes, drives, wishes, desires, etc. We do not mean to give the impression that these conditioned reflex experiments and the clinical researches are the same, for they obviously are not. But they do represent a possibility and a hope of a future *rapprochement* between the experimental and the clinical approaches to abnormal psychology. (See Hilgard and Marquis [346].)

Unconscious and Emotional Conditioning.—Probably the best experimental lead is the work with emotional conditioning. We know that such conditioning can take place in early infancy, even before the age of verbalization. It may persist for a lifetime, the individual remaining unaware of the source of his emotional reaction. These conditioned responses are peculiar in that they may be established in one trial and they apparently are not easily extinguished. Furthermore—and this is of great interest for us—they show a good deal of irradiation; that is, the same emotional response may be evoked by a stimulus which only resembles the original conditioning stimulus.

A psychologist reports being aware of a general prejudice against and distrust of red-headed people. Sheerly for amusement he attempted to trace this to its sources one time, and finally remembered that when he was a little boy of about 4 or 5, he and all his friends were terrorized for a long period by a little bully who, as it happens, was red-headed. He is quite sure that his generalized dislike for red-headed people dates from this period.

The same psychologist reports another observation upon himself. He found himself disliking intensely and beyond all reason a certain woman with whom he was thrown into social contact. He was consciously aware that she was a fine person, totally undeserving of any such dislike. The aversion went so far that he was compulsively driven to avoid her, even when this amounted almost to open insult. Quite spontaneously, it flashed upon him one day that this woman, in her body build and in her facial characteristics, resembled in a vague way an aunt who had been important in his upbringing, who had been very cruel to him, and whom he had hated intensely.

After-effects interesting to the student were that, in the first case, his dislike for red-headed people seems to have disappeared. His dislike for the woman, however, while it has been modified somewhat, is still strong.

The idea of unconscious emotional conditioning is important; but it should not be thought of in terms of an individual being unconsciously conditioned to one stimulus and always reacting to that stimulus in terms of the conditioned emotion. The above example shows that the psychologist's becoming aware of a possible source of his dislike for a certain woman did not eliminate his reaction toward her. In all seriously "irrational" and psychopathological reactions the complexity of "unconscious emotional conditioning" is broad and multiple. The individual's whole personality, together with fundamental needs, is involved in the reaction. If we further consider what happens in a hypnotic experiment psychodynamically, and what happens when the hypnotist makes the subject conscious of the motivations, we find some important additional factors. In the hypnotic experiment, the subject's whole intra-personal relationship (to the hypnotist) in terms of his needs, attitudes, ideals, is involved. This leads us to the second point that requires discussion, namely, what forces make a psychological process unconscious; but we shall first mention one other assumption about the nature of "unconscious processes."

The Unconscious as Unverbalized.—It was Watson the behaviorist who first made popular the theory that the crucial difference between conscious and unconscious processes might be merely that the conscious are verbalized and the unconscious are not. Guthrie has recently revived this theory, more carefully worked out (319). Undoubtedly, however, this theory as a *complete* theory of unconscious activity is too naïve. One criticism that may be leveled against it is that it is not dynamic. It merely describes one aspect that differentiates conscious and unconscious processes. Whether this difference is superficial or controlling is not known; but at present it seems to be only superficial. Certainly a good many unconscious emotional reactions are conditioned in the infant before the age when verbalization is possible; but it is also true that a process already verbalized may be repressed in the adult. Thus the difference appears superficial. In spite of these criticisms, it cannot be gainsaid that the difference is there, and that it should be explored experimentally because it *may* be important.

Psychodynamics of Unconscious Processes.—In general, we can say that the most important unconscious processes are not unconscious by accident; they do not just happen to be unconscious. They are unconscious for a reason and a purpose. The reason may be complex, but as a rule it includes avoiding pain, danger, and hurt to self-esteem and security. For example, what were some of the reasons why the patient described in the first chapter did not see the connection between her fear and her husband's threatened departure? There are several reasons. She was reluctant, even afraid and guilty, to admit to herself that she was angry at him. She was reluctant to admit to herself that she felt utterly dependent on him; this hurt her self-esteem. She was reluctant to admit to herself that she was afraid of him; this too hurt her self-esteem.

When all the processes and reactions that are unconscious in a patient are considered, there are strong reasons for their being unconscious and for his shutting them out of awareness. We are discussing here not just one or two impulses, but the sum total of all the interrelated unconscious reaction patterns. We find that all of them are unconscious because they are all connected with reactions which spring from the anticipation of a catastrophic situation characterized by helplessness, abandonment, worthlessness, fear of humiliation, and injury. To put it another way, various psychological processes must be repressed in their totality by the patient because of his fear of a catastrophic breakdown; he feels that all these processes must remain unconscious, for if they became conscious, if he had to admit them, if he had to cope with the problems they present, he would be thrown into a catastrophic state of helplessness.

We can now understand some of the qualities of unconscious processes which have been described by Freud. In unconscious reactions there is no appreciation of the limitations of reality. Thus a patient who needs absolute dependence to feel safe unconsciously can strive for this unlimited and, in reality, never obtainable goal. Anger and hostility know no bounds in unconscious reactions. The patient dreams that the object of his anger dies or is killed, but would not admit such an impulse consciously. Unconscious processes often contain contradictory impulses. The patient may dream that he is completely and willingly dependent on an all-powerful person whom he loves, and next dream that this all-powerful individual is murdered. Thus attitudes of over-evaluation, love and dependence, and attitudes of hostility toward this person exist side by side. All these qualities of unconscious processes become understandable if we realize that they represent the reactions which spring from a catastrophic fear and the devices which the patient uses in attempting to escape a catastrophic situation. In the patient's unconscious longings these devices know no bounds and are contradictory.

Likewise, we can now understand more clearly why the individual can handle the problem better if he can do so with full consciousness. In the process of making unconscious reaction patterns conscious, the patient's fears must be diminished, he has to see the disadvantages of using these devices, his helplessness has to be relieved. Thus if we succeed in making important psychological processes conscious, we really enable the individual to recast his whole reaction pattern. In a sense we stop a vicious circle. Previously in order to allay his fears, to strengthen himself, and to be able to function, the individual had to repress —that is, make unconscious—certain needs, goals, reactions. After this, by the very fact of having made them unconscious and keeping them unconscious, he loses control over them. In the reverse process the individual is strengthened. This finally enables him to become conscious of attitudes; once they are conscious, his control over them further increases.

The individual may be conscious of a great many things and still may have only illusory control over them. For example, a man may adopt an attitude of being detached and of having others do his fighting for him. This attitude, although conscious, does not cover his whole reaction pattern. Underneath it may be profound fear and an inability to assert himself, to commit himself to causes and goals. He may expect a catastrophic situation if he ever tries to assert himself. In such instances the consciousness is really purposive. He is conscious only of what he needs to be conscious of, of what his life style demands. If this is the case, he really has no control over his detached aloofness. He would acquire control over it only if after a laborious process his fear was made conscious and he was enabled to become stronger.

Cultural Aspects of Unconscious Processes.—We do not wish to give the impression that all unconscious processes are motivated by the anticipation of catastrophic helplessness, worthlessness, abandonment, and injury. Many reaction patterns and motivations are unconscious for lesser reasons. In fact, in healthy behavior a great many motivations may be unconscious largely for reasons that are dependent on the cultural set-up. It is obvious, for example, that in an individual in a subordinate cultural or professional relationship, a considerable amount of resentment will remain unconscious because it is to his interest or it spares him feelings of guilt. In cultures where eating in public is forbidden, as among the Trobriand, unquestionably many impulses to eat in public will remain unconscious (Malinowski). In a culture in which sexual impulses are taboo until a certain age, such impulses will remain unconscious. In a culture in which the child is taught to obey and revere his parents and elders, many impulses of stubbornness and hostility will remain unconscious. If bravery is extolled as a great virtue, reactions of fear may be repressed. Thus we can say that every culture in a sense has both its conscious and its unconscious pattern.

THE NATURE OF CONFLICT

Conscious Conflict.—The nature of conflict will be understood more easily if we begin with the study of those innumerable and inevitable conflicts that are entirely conscious. Shall we go to the movies or stay home and listen to the radio? Shall we work or play for the next few hours? Here two impulses are in conflict because they are incompatible with each other. One cannot both go and stay, one cannot wear two outfits at the same time, one cannot work and loaf at the same time. In the healthy person, such conflicts, in spite of the fact that they occur by the thousands, are solved easily and quickly without any pathological effects. Advantages are weighed, all the factors in the situation are considered, the possible pleasures are balanced against the possible pains, and, as such processes go on, one of the two alternatives becomes stronger and wins. Even in conscious conflict, however, psychologists have discovered that a great deal of this weighing and balancing process goes on behind the scenes; that is, judgment or the deciding process may be largely non-conscious.

Conscious conflicts may be extremely severe. One frequent conflict is that between marriage and a career. For example, a college student who wishes to become a physician falls in love in his sophomore or junior year. Since our folkways demand that he be able to support his wife, marriage must wait until he finishes college, four years of medical school, several years of interneship, and then some years of economic struggle for a sufficient income. This means a period of perhaps ten years before he can marry. There are dozens of possible half-solutions and compromises in this situation. Certainly the conflict is severe no matter what compromise is made, and many factors may be involved. Many interesting facts can be obtained from such situations; but the one of greatest interest here is that such conscious conflicts rarely breed neurosis (even though there may be some "symptom" results), whereas unconscious conflicts, even when they are apparently less severe or important than the conflict in the above example, are much more likely to eventuate in general psychic illness or character change.

Unconscious Conflict.—Erickson's two experiments which were quoted at length above demonstrated the existence of unconscious processes, and equally convincingly the existence of unconscious conflicts. In the first experiment the post-hypnotic suggestion itself contained a command for a conflict—the subject was told that he both loved and hated smoking. He later showed in his behavior that he was actually struggling with this conflict. The command in the second experiment called for an activity against which the subject had strong moral impulses—opening his friend's mail or stealing from him. In these experiments the subject used all sorts of devices to escape the conflict situation and somehow or other solve the conflict problem. The following discussion will concern the types and significance of unconscious conflict in psychopathology.

Various types of unconscious conflict can be distinguished. On the one hand, conflicts may arise between unconscious impulses, "forbidden" drives or needs, and, on the other hand, (1) other incompatible wishes, (2) the limitations set by reality, or (3) those set by morals, ideals, or ethical notions. Thus there is always some kind of incompatibility between the two sides to the conflict, but this may be caused by any one of three factors that clash with the need in question. Since the effects of these types of conflict may be somewhat different, they merit a closer examination.

Conflict between two incompatible wishes or needs. —It is possible to love and to hate John Smith simultaneously, to feel superior and inferior to him at one and the same time, to wish him well and with equal strength to wish him unhappiness. A man may unconsciously need from his wife the simultaneous satisfaction of a need for dependence and for independence. (There was this conflict in the case cited in Chapter I.) Such a conflict is a common factor in the typical "adolescent" conflict. The following example is characteristic:

A student in a psychology class, the mother of a little boy whom she loved to distraction, reported the following dream and her reactions to it: "I brought little Teddie to his grandmother, sneaked in and left him there. I returned home only to find that somehow he was there again. I then brought him to an uncle and the same thing happened. Again and again I brought him to someone else's home, left him there and then returned to my home and there he was. Throughout I felt more and more irritated." To her, the only plausible interpretation was that she wanted to get rid of her child. But how could this be? She shivered even at the *thought* of losing her baby. Her teacher explained to her again the nature of unconscious motives, the meaning of ambivalence, and suggested that she do a little soul-searching. Her ultimate report was: "I guess deep down I keep on thinking how I could have a career if not for Teddie. My love for him is real, but my desire for a career is just as real. My dream seems to say that if only Teddie were elsewhere, I could have my career." The sequel was as interesting as the dream. She decided to go into nursery school work where she could have both her career and her baby. Compromise is usually the outcome of conflict; but in this case, because the conflict became conscious and her wits could be brought to bear on the problem, the compromise between two incompatible desires was an unusually efficient and satisfactory one.

Conflict between a need and limitations set by reality.—The common phrase for this sort of conflict is "wishing for the moon." Usually, as we grow up, we put such unreal hopes behind us. But in our unconscious wishes, we sometimes seem never to grow up. The wishes for impossible things which are of course rejected consciously (because we are "sensible" and "realistic") may persist permanently in unconscious form. The cripple in his dreams is a great athlete, the octogenarian is young again, and the dumpy girl looks like Greta Garbo, if only the conscious screen is ripped away. It is doubtful whether a short man *ever* gives up his unconscious hope of gaining height, even if he is consciously quite reconciled to his shortness.

As always, the overt resultant behaviors, thoughts, wishes, and general character will be in part determined by such a conflict. Close examination will always show some trace of such effects in that complex compromise formation that is our behavior and our consciousness.

Once in a while, the miracle does happen; reaching for the moon, persistently and with all our resources, we grasp it. Adler has called this direct compensation. The stammerer becomes the great orator because he never gave up trying. The half-deaf person becomes a great musician in spite of (or because of?)

his handicap. The man who dreams of universal power achieves it, with the odds a billion to one against him. The college student, struggling to keep himself from flunking, becomes in later life a useful and well-known scientist. How? Why? His more brilliant older brother set the pace for him, and such was his need for surpassing his brother that he gave up everything else in life to achieve his end. The fullback of a minor college football team has a withered arm, almost useless to him. He has practiced all his life and makes up for his handicap by his innate shrewdness, the experience of years of study, and the clever use of the faculties that are left to him.

Conflict between an impulse and the individual's morals, ideals, or code of ethics.—Conflicts of this type may and often do center about impulses other than sexual. An impulse to steal or an actual act of theft may conflict with the ideal of honesty. This was the case with the subject in Erickson's second experiment. A mean, nasty, or cruel act may have been long forgotten on the surface, but deep down it may burrow about, clashing with the ideal we have of ourselves as kind, decent people. The fear of such conflict and self-punishment may be very useful for society because it keeps John Smith and Jane Jones, who otherwise might harm society by erring, on the strait and narrow path.

Conflict over past actions. Guilt feelings. Self-condemnation.—Conflict may arise not only from impulses or desires but as a reaction to past actions, to deeds already done. Such conflict always involves ideals, codes of ethics, moral feelings, and the like, all of which have been summed up by Freud under the term "super-ego." More commonly this is phrased by the layman as "being bothered by your conscience."

When we do something we consider wrong or mean or nasty, when we commit a crime or a sin or do something that conflicts with our ideals, then there arise in us feelings of guilt and self-punishment.

"I had in my office a pretty little Italian girl who had recently developed a curious habit—a tic. Every few minutes she would draw her under lip between her teeth. The lip, extending for half an inch down her chin, had become an unsightly red. Tessa was also very depressed. Her mother said that Tessa had acted queer ever since she had been allowed to attend her first dance at school. Her mother hadn't wanted her to go in the first place—she herself had never gone out as a young girl. But the teacher telephoned especially to urge her to let Tessa attend like the other girls. Tessa's story to me, confided with tears, was that one of the boys had danced her into the coat-room, where he had soundly kissed her. And Tessa liked it! She had told no one about this episode; indeed, there was no one to tell, since she had no close girl friends in the American school, and she fancied that her mother would turn her into the street if she knew."[1]

Allied to this type of conflict is that in which there is a discrepancy between one's ideal picture of himself and his actual deeds, when there is worry over a lack in oneself, when one has ideals of personality which can never possibly be achieved, when one is disappointed in his achievements or in his status. One process in particular, the expiation process, is extremely important in dealing with guilt feelings. As we shall see in a later chapter, this consists essentially of making up for a wrong act by paying for it in some way. The self-punishment process is also frequent whenever illicit wishes or actions have given rise to guilt feelings.

Unconscious conflicts in social relationships.—The same rules and generalizations that we have spoken of already in connection with intra-psychic conflict hold also for unconscious conflicts created by incompatible needs and demands in the relationship between two people—parent and child, friends, husband and wife. No close relationship between two people can ever be understood completely unless the unconscious as

---

[1] Reprinted from *The Happy Family*, by John Levy and Dr. Ruth Munroe, by permission of and special arrangement with Alfred A. Knopf, Inc., authorized publishers. Copyright 1938 by Ruth Munroe Levy. Pp. 33-34.

well as the conscious factors in the situation are known. For instance, anyone will recognize the more obvious motives for marriage; but it is less often realized that people may marry for reasons that they themselves are not conscious of. A desire for dependence or for independence, for power, for appreciation, for submission—any of these demands may be made of one's marital partner without either person realizing it. Psychologically good marriages are often good simply because these unconscious needs dovetail with each other. Thus a man who has a strong unconscious need to be mothered and who marries a woman with a strong unconscious need to mother someone, may make both himself and his wife happy. If, on the other hand, he resents being mothered as a trespass on his independence and manliness, they will both be unhappy without knowing why. The situation may be further complicated by the fact that both incompatible desires may be present unconsciously and simultaneously, the need for being mothered and the need for independence. When such conflicts are unconscious, the marital friction that ensues will be puzzling and not understandable. The husband and wife may tend to blame each other or perhaps may feel inadequate and unworthy, and on the surface the picture may be one of conflict, like the following:

"Mr. Black, aged forty-five, enjoys cutting a bit of a figure with the ladies—in all innocence, be it said. His wife is not very attractive. She naturally resents a little his greater popularity and is slightly uneasy about her own status in his affections. Consciously, however, she repudiates any such petty jealousy. She never reproaches him for gallivanting around—but she does show an intense wifely solicitude for his lumbago, his heart condition, his figure even, which serves to remind him and his lady friends of his advancing years. Outwardly she is within her rights as a conscientious helpmate. Actually she makes constant, insidious little attacks upon him, without recognizing them as such for a moment. Mr. Black is more acute. He is beginning to be seriously annoyed by his wife. Her jealousy is indeed petty. She could handle it easily if she knew about it. So long as she conceals it from herself, this series of antagonistic, socially acceptable acts is likely to continue. A person may wreck a precious marriage to gratify an insignificant bit of vanity because his conscious efforts unwittingly reinforce an unconscious impulse of destructive nature."[1]

Significance and Nature of Unconscious Conflict in Psychopathological Processes.—We have said that the conflict may be between two incompatible wishes of a similar nature, or between a need or wish and the impossibility of achieving it, or between the individual's impulse and his ideals. We said further that guilt feelings and self-condemnation may be part of the conflict and that social relationships may be involved. In the conflicts involved in psychopathological processes as a rule, all these aspects are present. In fact, the conflicts are always multiple, although the emphasis at any particular moment may be on one special conflict. As we have seen, an individual who is driven by the expectation of catastrophic helplessness and worthlessness, by anger and fear of a stronger individual, by fear of abandonment, humiliation, condemnation or injury, takes measures which are conflicting. He wants to be dependent and he wants to attack and be superior; he wants to submit and he wants to conquer. All these impulses are partly or completely conflicting. Thus conflict is part and parcel of every psychopathological reaction.

Because of his great need, the patient's longings and desires are boundless. Reality constantly disappoints him. He has to be dependent and he needs overwhelming help to a degree that cannot be realized. Although he is sometimes aware of this, he still needs it. Here there is a conflict between an impulse and the limitations of reality. Another measure by which the patient unconsciously tries to relieve his fear and his helplessness and obtain approval is by a drive for perfection and by

---

[1] Reprinted from *The Happy Family*, by John Levy and Dr. Ruth Munroe, by permission of and special arrangement with Alfred A. Knopf, Inc., authorized publishers. Copyright 1938 by Ruth Munroe Levy. P. 52.

excessively strong moral ideals. These needs and impulses, however, clash with his desire for dependence and submission; they clash with his hostility aroused by disappointments. Here there is a conflict between impulses and the ideals and ethical code.

Why can the patient never adequately solve his conflicts, why do they continue, and why do they keep him under constant tension? Because vital needs and impulses, vital desires, literally life-saving measures are always involved. The patient cannot say, "I'll submit," because his ideals are equally vital. He cannot follow his ideals alone, because he is constantly disappointed and he is driven to be hostile or to submit. He cannot say, "I will not strive for the impossible," because he clings to unlimited goals, for only they will relieve unequivocably catastrophic expectation. All this was true of the patient described in the first chapter.

Cultural Conflict.—We now turn to a somewhat different type of conflict which arises from the fact that every human being is a member of a society which has a certain culture. A culture is not necessarily a consistent, unitary pattern; there may be conflicting and inconsistent trends within it. An individual introjecting (or interiorizing) this culture must thereby also introject the conflicts inherent in it. There are many conflicting and incompatible trends in our own culture. An example is the role of women in our society. Here two trends are diametrically opposed. One trend is toward equality between the sexes: women go to college and professional schools, and prepare themselves for careers just as men do. On the other hand, there still persists the tendency for our society to be a "man's world," e.g., women physicians are not trusted as are men physicians; certain professions are completely closed to women; in a conflict between a husband's career and a wife's career, the wife is usually expected to give up hers, etc. Little or no provision for having children is made in our economic system; hence women are sometimes presented with an incompatible choice

of following a career or being a wife and mother. This inconsistency in the culture may also be found in the more intelligent women in our society as individuals.

Many examples of culture conflict are afforded by primitive
societies. Linton has pointed out that among the Comanche
Indians the ideal man is the warrior and the hunter; but when
the men get old they can no longer be warriors or hunters.
Their society expects them to become suddenly calm, submissive, and unimportant, in spite of the fact that all their lives
long they have been trained and rewarded for being just the
opposite. We would expect, *a priori*, to find severe conflict in
these old men; as a matter of fact, a form of neurosis is sometimes actually present.

Pertinent here also is the inevitable confusion, the pain and
shock reaction of the young man coming into the adult world
of competition from a sheltered environment. Frequently he
has lived in a "copybook" universe where all men are decent
and honest, where hard work is always rewarded, where the
villain always comes to a bad end, and where crime does not
pay. What happens to him when he finds that many people
lie, cheat, and steal, at least a little, if not more? The villain
often prospers and the hero sometimes get laughed at for his
pains. He sees that those who work hardest too often are paid
least. Such a picture is, of course, overdrawn; but every college
teacher sees conflicts of this type in his students, conflicts between ideals and reality. Strong flexible characters can and
usually do adjust; weaker ones are apt to crack under the strain,
at least for a time.

Other conflicting aspects of the demands and goals set by
the cultural environment are an excessive morality which taboos
even the mention of sex and anything pertaining to it. The
result may be a conflict between ideals of sex and the individual's normal reactions and attractions. Further conflict may
arise between complete acceptance of excessive morality which

in some areas is a social demand, and the later social expectation of married sexual life, conception, and birth.

Still other conflicts may be engendered by social and cultural commands for and expectations of competition on the one hand, and cooperation on the other; obedience on the one hand, and self-assertion on the other. In a sense, it is correct to say that the psychopathological conflict is an exaggeration of the cultural conflict. The two are similar in quality; their difference is the helplessness and catastrophic expectation in psychopathological states. It is further obvious that the more intense the cultural conflicts are, the more likely it is that individuals will develop severe conflicts of pathological intensity. Thus, intense cultural conflict predisposes to pathological conflict in the individual; i.e., sick societies tend to make sick individuals (689, 416, 788, 250).

Dynamic Reactions to Conflict.—Every conflict *involves in its very nature automatic, persistent attempts to solve it,* to get rid of it, or to avoid it.

Why is a conflict painful? Possibly because of the tension which it creates. It may also be painful because it often represents a threat to the self-esteem, to the feeling of adequacy. A conflict is a problem that we are unable to solve and it therefore represents a lack of power in us, a shortage, an inferiority. Threats to self-esteem are always felt as dangerous and painful. Finally there is often involved deprivation or frustration, partial or complete, of one or both of the vital wishes in the conflict.

Efforts to avoid the conflict.—Since conflict is painful or unpleasant, the natural reaction of avoidance is aroused. In most animals put into conflict situations, the first reaction is one of avoidance or running away from the situation. This is probably true also in human beings, although we cannot yet be certain; at any rate, we can be sure that it is a fairly common reaction.

Attacks on the conflict; attempts to remove it.—In some people the initial reaction to a conflict situation is to attack it, to change it, whenever possible, so that it is no longer painful or annoying. In other words, such people attempt to get *both* of the desired goals. It is, at the moment, a fair guess to assume that people with a measure of self-confidence will tend to attack conflict situations, whereas people with little of this quality will tend more to avoid them. However, it must be remembered that this is a theoretical distinction, since in reality most people will use either or both reactions, depending on which promises to be more efficient.

Compromise formations.—The most common reaction of all[1] is to compromise. Most conflicts cannot be either completely avoided or removed, and therefore some halfway measure of success is all that is possible. A physical analogy may make this clearer. The student will remember the simple experiment in physics with forces pulling in different directions. The product of these various pulls is called a *resultant* of the forces and is in essence a compromise between them. In the case cited in Chapter I, the peculiar marriage contract was a compromise solution, i.e., the woman wanted both love and independence; she got a little of both, but neither wish was *fully* satisfied.

I met a student coming to school at about 9:20. Since classes began at 9:00, I commented jokingly. She told me that she had missed her bus. This certainly was a rationalization since the buses come every five minutes and could not account for her twenty minutes' lateness. I pointed this out to her and she said she had wanted so much to stay in bed this morning and not come to school. A few minutes later she remarked that she thought her instructor was not going to meet his classes this particular morning. Coming at 9:20 was a compromise formation. It represented, essentially, a halfway measure between not coming to school at all and coming on time. It achieved the objective neither of permitting her more sleep nor of coming on time as usual.

---

[1] Except, of course, normal, healthy solutions; these are realistic, and involve intelligence, reason, and sense of humor. Only psychopathology is being discussed here.

Maier (521) reports as follows in his experiments on neurotic behavior in rats. His animals were forced to jump to a window which might or might not be open. They were in conflict about this response because the customary cues which led them to jump or not jump were no longer present. In this situation they jumped in a compromise fashion, that is, sideways, so that even if the window were open they would not get in, but if it were not open their fall would not be as serious. In other words, they jumped half-heartedly, almost as if they were expecting to fall. They achieved the objective neither of getting food at the window, nor of avoiding a fall.

"A certain woman . . . believes that her husband should maintain his masculine friendships, both for his own enjoyment and as a matter of business expediency. She sees to it that he pays his dues at several clubs, that he arranges for golf, tennis and squash at frequent intervals. But she is also a little sorry for herself because she lives in the suburbs and is pretty well tied down to her house and baby. Moreover, she is extremely fond of her husband. She likes to have him around. Now, it often happens that she 'forgets' about his club nights. She invites guests to the house so that he finds it awkward to leave. She is apt to get a violent headache on Sunday morning. Although she urges him to go right ahead with his golf regardless of her sufferings, somehow her husband always stays at home. Occasionally she drops into his office for a surprise at five o'clock. Curiously enough, the day she comes turns out to be his afternoon for squash.

"In short, though young Mrs. Wilson is generous in her wish to have her husband enjoy himself and sensible about his business contacts, she is also a bit resentful because he has more freedom than she, a bit jealous of his friends, a bit lonely. Her impulses toward helping her husband go out and keeping him at home are both genuine, both natural and sufficiently praiseworthy. They are incompatible, however. No woman in her senses would deliberately get her husband to pay high club dues out of a meager salary and deliberately keep him from using the club. Mrs. Wilson solved her dilemma by consciously arranging for her husband's masculine pursuits and unconsciously—'accidentally'—managing to keep him home pretty often."[1]

Catastrophic breakdown.—If the conflict is severe and long-continued, if it cannot be solved or avoided, and if compromise formations do not suffice to relieve the situation, then complete breakdown may ensue (Schulte, Maier, Liddell, Goldstein). Essentially it is a purposeless, useless, non-functional reaction, and the most disastrous consequence possible.

Conflict and "Personality as a Whole."—From what has been said up to this point, the student has undoubtedly formed a picture of conflict as a sort of battle, of dissociation, of disintegration of the personality into two warring camps. He may then ask how it is possible to speak of the personality as a unified integrated whole, and at the same time to speak of conflict, which is ever present in the personality. There is not *necessarily* any inconsistency here. Answering this question necessitates some reformulation and clarification to avoid a false impression in the use of certain terms. There are two points to be made.

1. The statement that the individual reacts as an integrated whole does not necessarily mean that he reacts as a harmoniously integrated whole. The term "whole" refers to a pattern in which the relations of the elements can be stated. It means that the individual's image and evaluation of himself and of others are involved in the reactions, and that various aspects and details of his reactions influence each other. Clashes may occur in these various reactions, but, even so, they do not exist side by side without positively influencing each other. Naturally an individual will do his best work and be happiest and most secure if he acts not only as an integrated but as a harmoniously integrated whole.

2. Intra-psychic conflict occurs when two desires are incom-

---

[1] Reprinted from *The Happy Family*, by John Levy and Dr. Ruth Munroe, by permission of and special arrangement with Alfred A. Knopf, Inc., authorized publishers. Copyright 1938 by Ruth Munroe Levy. Pp. 56-57.

patible with each other—to use a trivial example, a woman trying to decide whether to wear a blue dress or a yellow dress to a party. What does this mean? What is this conflict about? First, what is the purpose of wearing the blue dress? It is to look pretty, to attract attention and affection. What is the purpose of wearing the yellow dress? It is exactly the same—to look pretty and attract attention. What does this conflict mean then? It is simply a matter of choosing one of two alternative paths, *both of which lead to the same goal.* And since a large percentage of conflicts, trivial or serious, conscious or unconscious, are of this type, we can now understand why the conflict process is often simply one of the subprocesses that, in spite of appearances, is really making for the integration of the personality rather than its disintegration.

Let us turn to the more serious conflicts presented by the case in Chapter I. Here the same principle is illustrated. The patient was torn between the desire for dependence and the desire for independence. But what do these mean? What she ultimately wanted was love, affection, freedom from hurt, etc. The path of isolation was one way of achieving them (although a poor one); dropping her defenses, giving up her isolation was another path to the same set of goals. In a sense there was no conflict in what she wanted; there was conflict only in the choice of means to these ends.

It is not necessary to split the human psyche into warring camps which are, so to speak, hereditary enemies. We shall make such a mistake only if we leave out of consideration the goals and purposes of life. To repeat, these are mainly the desires for love, affection, and warmth; the desire for self-esteem, self-respect, and the respect of others; and the avoidance of psychic pain and hurt (this latter, however, is usually engendered by an attack upon self-esteem and the feeling of security).

Summary.—In neurosis there is always a sharp conflict between two vital needs of the personality. But if one sees this conflict in a broader context and looks into the purpose of these so-called vital needs, then he often finds that in a sense this vital conflict is not vital at all, but is an artificial product of mistaken notions, of false means to an end, and of fallacious interpretations of the world. One of these "needs" is thus seen to be a means, usually a mistaken one, of attaining the other need. Hence these needs are not necessarily opposed to each other; in the last analysis they may be identical.

It is obvious that the patient wants protection against an anticipated catastrophic expectation. The trouble arises from the fact that the various means (which are goals in themselves) which he feels forced to use are incompatible. It is further obvious that he wants happiness, love, affection, satisfaction of his bodily needs, achievement, pleasure. But again the means with which he wants to achieve these goals and the special coloring he gives them are contradictory. Thus there is serious conflict in the partial and intermediary goals, but often no contradiction in the patient's ultimate goals.

SUGGESTED READINGS

Probably the simplest introduction to Freud is his *Psychopathology of Everyday Life*. A good book to own is *The Basic Writings of Sigmund Freud* (282) in the Modern Library Edition, which includes the first book cited, and four others (see Bibliography). Good secondary sources are Ives Hendrick's *Facts and Theories of Psychoanalysis* (341), and Martin Peck's *Meaning of Psychoanalysis* (605). Healy's *Mental Conflicts and Misconduct* (334) is useful and interesting reading, as is also Guthrie's *Psychology of Human Conflict* (319). For a general approach to this whole system of thinking, a readable, even fascinating book is *The Happy Family* by Levy and Munroe (482).

Easily the best experimental demonstration of conflict and unconscious activities is found in Erickson's article, "Experimental demonstrations of the psychopathology of everyday life," in the *Psychoanalytic Quarterly* (226). On the role of conditioning, Hilgard and Marquis (346) is useful. A good presentation of psychobiology can be found in the introductory chapters of Muncies' *Psychobiology and Psychiatry* (581).

CHAPTER VII

FRUSTRATION AND ITS EFFECTS

~~~~~~

The Concepts of Frustration and Deprivation.—The concept of frustration is customarily applied to the blocking of gratification of bodily desires. By extension, it is sometimes also used to describe the impossibility of gratifying those personality needs whose importance we have already discussed—the need for dependence, prestige, self-esteem, love and affection, etc.—needs which do not center around obtaining gratification and pleasure through the use of one particular bodily organ.

If confusion is to be avoided, we must distinguish sharply between these two concepts of deprivation and frustration. For, as we shall see, their effects and their roles in psychopathology are very different. We shall define deprivation simply as the non-gratification of a wish or desire or need, usually of an organic character. Frustration, on the other hand, will be defined as a deprivation which is also a threat to the personality, particularly to the self-esteem or feeling of security. The discussion to follow will amplify and explain these concepts. Since mere deprivation is usually not of great importance in the etiology of psychic illness, we shall be most concerned with frustration, that is, with threats to the personality.

The following experiments by D. M. Levy (471) on a litter of puppies illustrate the significance of bodily needs aiming at satisfaction, and the disturbances arising out of their non-gratification.

In a litter of six puppies, two of the puppies were permitted to suckle at their mother's teats. The other puppies were fed by bottle.

Two of the four were given milk and water from the bottle through nipples that had a moderately large hole so that it took them about five minutes to get the necessary amount of food. The other two puppies were fed through nipples which had a very large hole so that they took all the liquid within about two minutes. Within a few weeks the following situation developed: The two breast-fed puppies thrived well and engaged in no suckling activity except at the mother's nipples. They played in a lively manner and then rested. The second two puppies frequently engaged in suckling activities on various objects and were more restless than the two breast-fed puppies. The last two puppies engaged in almost continuous suckling activities, very frequently on each other, so that they sucked each other's skin bloody. They were restless practically all the time, even in their sleep. If they played or if the litter was taken for a walk, the last two puppies would pair off and go separately from the other four and would fight and snarl at the others. Thus, they were irritable and combative. These puppies lost weight, although they received the same amount of nourishment as the second two puppies.

The first obvious implication of these experiments is that the dogs had a certain need for activity with their mouths which required satisfaction. This activity was separate from the need for nourishment. If this need was not satisfied while taking nourishment, it led to a continuous activity for its satisfaction. If the deprivation was even greater and the most satisfactory activity was barred, the search for satisfaction became extremely vehement and was accompanied by inability to relax adequately and by behavior disturbance.

In evaluating this development, we should not consider only the need that is satisfied through activity of the mouth. A more complete reaction of the total organism has to be considered; and in this two factors enter: (1) A continuous tension and distress, which is never fully eased, and is similar to continuous pain. (2) A helplessness in the attempt to relieve this distress. The "neurosis" of the two puppies is a result of the three factors mentioned.

In this experiment the urge that was blocked was a bodily one aiming at gratification. As a rule, at least in the human being, the problem is not as simple as it appears here. Neither in the normal nor in the pathological is a "simple urge" ever dealt with. The total process of motivation may be divided into three phases: the drive, the motivated behavior, and the goal object or goal activity. The drive may be relatively physiological, e.g., a hunger drive; but even in this case socially learned modifications are clearly apparent—for example, getting hungry three times a day. With reference to motivated behavior, it is by now a truism that the adult human being goes about achieving goal objects, whether driven physiologically or socially, along paths that are culturally determined; thus he eats with knife and fork. Finally, cultural determination is also at work in goal objects; theoretically almost any living tissue, plant, or animal might serve as food, but actually only a small proportion of them is used as food; thus we eat fish but not worms. Obviously, in considering motivation, it is impossible to limit ourselves to the purely biological and hereditary, i.e., instincts, physiological drives. Furthermore, as has been repeatedly stated, the individual's self-confidence, his general evaluation of himself, of his body, and of other individuals play a significant role in the dynamics of every significant activity (also in all significant bodily activities).

SOURCES OF FRUSTRATION

Society as a Source of Frustration.—The particular society in which the individual lives is of great importance in determining whether he will experience many frustrations, how he will be frustrated, and what the effects of these frustrations will be. Some societies impose relatively little frustration upon the individual because their social institutions do not phrase deprivation in terms of frustration; furthermore, if the individual has to meet a frustrating situation, these institutions give him a chance to work off his frustrations satisfactorily. Other societies consider human life as one long frustration (Benedict [75]). Every deprivation is thought of as frustrating, and the individual is even encouraged to feel frustrated (Bateson [52]). In such societies the individual usually has no choice but to react to the situation with impotent anger, with inwardly burning hostility for which no socially acceptable or useful outlet is provided. It is probably fair to say that such societies implant certain needs and desires in the individual, and then frustrate them.

In regard to physiological urges, each society has its regulations as to forbidden impulses or, at least, forbidden forms of gratification. We mentioned in an earlier chapter that eating in public is taboo among the Trobriands. Our society taboos any sexual activity until a certain age, and even then allows it only under certain conditions. The amount and form of satisfaction for the urges in mouth activity likewise vary. Such regulations, accompanied by possible frustrations, are imposed early. For example, in our society, the infant may be fed every three or four hours; he is not permitted to suckle whenever he wishes. Actually the cultural set-up is not only frustrating but stimulating in regard to bodily urges. Thus the ceremonies of eating may be very elaborate and varied and almost be made into a cult. This means not merely gratifying a bodily urge, but stimulating, refining, and elaborating it. In the same way, the pleasures derived from the skin when bathed or massaged may be raised to an extremely elaborate level as was done by the Romans. Certain types of taboos and frustrations are present in almost every society; the incest taboo is an example.

Frequently, the cultural circumstances are such that they stimulate desires in the individual and at the same time forbid them or make it impossible for him to attain them. This may be true of the pleasures of eating when the individual is unemployed. Other examples can be found in our own society. Thus everyone is urged to get rich, when obviously this is possible for only a few people. We are generally taught to want more

and more; we are urged to be infinitely ambitious; and we have
continually before us in the movies, the newspapers, in books
and advertisements such goals as de luxe automobiles, pent-
house apartments, trips around the world, diamonds, and the
like; most of these are unattainable by the majority of our
population.

Not only are these desires created and fostered in us by
many social forces, but they also involve the question of self-
esteem, prestige, and security. As we grow up, we quickly realize
that the people who have these things are more respected and
admired; hence if we could only obtain them, we too would be
more respected and admired. For the relatively insecure person
such thoughts are devastating. Seeing a typical movie in which
everyone is tremendously rich, successful, beautiful, brave, and
clever may help sow the seeds of general feelings of frustration,
inadequacy, and dissatisfaction with status. These frustrations are
of just as much importance for the psychologist as biological
deprivations. Obviously, in many cases, frustrations brought
about by average cultural circumstances do not lead to psychopathology; but they may prepare the soil or create certain situations involving frustration in a degree which is beyond the
individual's power to cope with. It is in such cases that psychopathological reactions may occur.

Situational Frustration.—Invariably in everyone's life there
are situations which are extremely depriving; it is impossible
to live without going through such situations. Thus illness represents not only a threat, but also a frustration, for it may make
the individual stop certain activities—such as the pleasures of
eating—although he may not have lost the desire for them.
The death of anyone close to him may likewise be a severe
frustration apart from all other aspects. Death may mean deprivation of bodily needs as in the case of a married couple;
but there is always also a frustration of emotional needs, of
the need for closeness, affection, support, and dependence. Un-
requited love is likewise a frustration of both bodily and emo-

tional needs. Furthermore, reality always sets limitations and in that sense causes at least some blocking of the individual's goals and desires. No one can succeed in everything that he aims at, although often what he aims at is very dear to him. A scientist may invest time, energy, and emotion in a piece of research and then fail. Such an experience, of course, is disappointing and it may be frustrating. A man may want a job which he does not really need as far as money is concerned, but which would mean an advance for him both in earning capacity and in status; he may not get it because there are a number of applicants but only one job. This too is disappointing and may be frustrating. Such situations are significant because a breakdown frequently occurs when they arise; they do not, however, necessarily lead to the breakdown. Situational frustration is commonly referred to as external frustration.

Internal Frustration.—By the term internal frustration is meant the inability of the individual, for psychological reasons, to gratify an urge or a desire or a need even when he has the opportunity to do so. This factor is very important in psychopathological reactions; as a matter of fact, internal frustration is present in every patient with these reactions. We have said repeatedly that in every significant activity of the individual his evaluation of himself (self-esteem) and of other persons (feeling of security) is involved. This evaluation concerns his general strength and his body and its activities. The causes of internal frustration are conflict, inhibition, condemnation, fear. If the patient feels helpless in a situation, if he condemns and rejects a part of his body and its function, if he expects disapproval for an activity when approval is vital to him, he cannot adequately engage in that activity even if he has the opportunity. Furthermore, every activity means attitudes toward other people and assumptions regarding their attitudes toward him. Physical intimacies have the connotation of emotional intimacies. If, because of his basic character, the patient expects rejection, humiliation, and injury from the other individual, this fear will make adequate gratification impossible. The patient may have conflicting attitudes and needs in regard to the measures which he uses to save himself from a catastrophic situation. Thus he may want to be dependent but at the same time to respect himself; he may want to dominate and subjugate his partner. The result may be that he is internally frustrated in his dependency longings and experiences, as was the case with the patient described in Chapter I.

All the phenomena mentioned here may be—and as a rule, are—largely unconscious. Thus, a distinction must be made between conscious and unconscious frustrations. Even where the frustration is conscious a great many aspects of the experience may be unconscious. Or a conscious deprivation may also be unconsciously frustrating.

Effects of Frustration

The Concept of "Frustration Tolerance."—Frustration tolerance (Rosenzweig [661]) means the fact that a person may go through a frustrating situation without being hurt by it or without reacting to it in a "bad" way. We can go even further. What is a frustrating situation for one individual may not be for another, even though to the objective observer both depriving situations are exactly the same. Apparently for some people, the feeling of frustration itself is absent from some so-called frustrating situations. Thus, if they perceive something that they cannot obtain, they may simply lose their desire for it; or, possibly, they may have little desire for anything *until* it becomes available.

The effects of frustration depend on several factors: (1) the degree of frustration; (2) the nature of the impulse that is frustrated; (3) the personality structure of the individual who suffers frustration. These factors will be treated together in the following discussion.

Persistence of the Thwarted Wish.—Much can be learned about the essential nature of the effects of frustration from the experiments on perseveration by Zeigarnik, Lewin, Rosenzweig, and others. These experiments showed that an uncompleted task or an unsolved problem tended to remain much more active psychically than a completed task or solved problem.

If children are given a lot of construction toys to play with and are allowed to finish some of the constructions but not others, later when they are allowed to turn back to the construction toys, they more often choose to play with the toys that they had not completed.

An unfulfilled wish or desire is also an unsolved problem. If it is conscious, it tends to attract attention to itself again and again. Our thought processes continue to attempt to solve the problem, even if it is unsolvable. Our perceptions tend to be shaped and determined more strongly by it than by wishes that have been fulfilled. In such situations the individual's energy remains partly directed toward attempts at solving the problem and at gratifying his wish, even though this is impossible. This reduces the energy available for other tasks but causes no serious damage. Some feeling of discomfort over this state of affairs may likewise be present. But if the individual is essentially adequate and feels himself adequate regarding the depriving situation, he stands the persistence of his unsatisfied wish well. He can look at it realistically, evaluate his other resources, wait, persist in his attempt at solution, or relieve the tension by his sense of humor. In other words, the unsolved problem represents no threat to him.

The phenomena surrounding the persistent wish can, however, be much more serious. This will be elaborated on in subsequent sections. Here we wish merely to mention that many aspects of such a wish may become unconscious under certain circumstances, particularly if it represents a threat; in fact, the individual may be altogether unaware of the continuation of his wish. It was one of Freud's great discoveries that desires which are blocked by circumstances or by the individual himself may continue to live in the psychic life unconsciously.

Under such circumstances he does not admit even to himself that he has certain wishes because they create guilt feelings, self-condemnation, and loss of self-esteem; they are pushed out of consciousness and disappear as far as he is concerned. Actually, however, they continue to exist in an unconscious form and at times become a tremendously important factor in the psyche. Their importance is due to the fact that the individual is still concerned with them, he expends energy on keeping them repressed, they are accompanied by continued tension, discomfort, and feelings of threat and danger, and he may try to satisfy them in indirect and substitute ways. Mere deprivations that do not conflict with character needs for self-esteem and security probably play no great role in the unconscious life.

Frustration and Aggression.—Aggression is one of the most universal and important effects of frustration. Our analysis will follow that made by Dollard, Doob, Miller, Mowrer, and Sears in a cooperative investigation at the Institute of Human Relations (190). These men define aggression as an act whose goal is injury to someone or to whatever stands for that someone. The strength of the tendency to aggression, they believe, depends directly on the amount of frustration. The inhibition of any act of aggression depends upon the amount of punishment or pain which would ensue if the act were not inhibited; this anticipated punishment need not be direct. The greater the anticipated punishment for an act of aggression, the less likely it is to occur.

Aggression may be direct or indirect. The simplest and strongest form is that directed against a person who is the source of frustration. If this direct aggression is blocked for some reason, indirect or substitute forms of aggression may be expected. Thus, if someone frustrates an individual, the latter's primary tendency will be to revenge himself directly upon the frustrator. If this is impossible, his aggression will be displaced; that is, it will be directed toward some other person or even toward an inanimate object.

It is also possible that there may be a change in the *form* of aggression. Thus, instead of punching someone, one may gossip about him or try to hurt him financially or in any one of dozens of other ways. There are other less obvious changes in form that are just as important. For instance, aggression may express itself in fantasy and dreaming, or it may even turn inward, that is, the aggression whose expression is blocked may be turned against the self in the form of self-condemnation, guilt feelings, anger with oneself, and possibly even suicide.

The final principle of aggression elaborated by this group of psychologists is that of "catharsis of aggression," namely, that the expression of any act of aggression reduces the tendency to all other such acts. For example, if one lets himself explode in a fit of anger over a particular frustration, he is less liable to become angry over other frustrations during the same period.

Judd tells the story of the schoolboy, ordinarily placid and well behaved, who came home from school one day and, in a short period, kicked his little brother, broke a window, shouted back at his mother, and behaved otherwise in an unusual way. It turned out that the reason for this was that his teacher had taunted and made fun of him all day because of a stupid mistake he had made. She had even called him "sissy," the most horrible insult of all. Of course, he could do nothing but sit quietly. When he came out he exploded in a wild fit of anger and aggression at the world in general, and then was able to relax into his customary good behavior.

Other examples are given under Release Therapy in Chapter XIX.

It is necessary to add the following remarks to these statements. Aggression in response to frustration is a widespread phenomenon. The amount and the quality of aggression depend on the structure of the personality, that is, on the individual's strength and approval of himself. If his evaluation of himself is seriously damaged, and if, as is natural in such instances, he attributes damaging motives to the frustrator, his aggression will be much more violent in both intensity and quality. It may be overt and seem to go beyond justified bounds, or it may be unconscious. If it is entirely unconscious, the individual never-theless may show serious symptoms; he may feel frustrated, become angry but be unaware of it, and have an attack of anxiety, as did the patient described in the first chapter when she felt angry at her husband.

In the face of a serious deprivation the healthy individual may become aggressive in various ways. He may persist in the pursuit of his goal, he may insist on his rights and demand satisfaction in an emphatic, possibly sharp manner. In the path-ological reaction, there is very strong hostility which the patient may express in an excessively violent way such as a temper tantrum, or he may repress it completely and show incapaci-tating symptoms, or he may consider his strength so low that he withdraws from the situation completely.

Frustration as a Threat.—As we have said, the effects of a frustrating situation depend on the strength of the individual who is frustrated, on the degree of frustration, and on the nature of the need that is frustrated.

There are certain frustrations which, if severe enough, rep-resent a serious threat to anyone, no matter how well and strong he may be at the time. We have already pointed out that two elements can be differentiated in the concept of frustration. One is the inability to attain satisfaction (deprivation). The other, as was indicated in connection with the experiments on the puppies, is the feeling of actual helplessness to do anything about the situation and to withstand this deprivation.

Experience with human infants throws further light on the problem. Levy found that if the infant was bottle-fed and the opening in the nipple was large, the baby engaged in thumb-sucking. If the opening in the nipple was made smaller and the suckling need was thus satiated, the thumb-sucking stopped (468). The thumb-sucking activity may be considered a mod-erate disturbance. "Nursing frustration," however, may con-stitute a much more serious disturbance in the human infant

(Ribble [636]). If the nipples of the mother's breast are inverted (instead of being flat they are hollow and therefore cannot be sucked at adequately), a newborn infant first gets restless and then goes into a state similar to a deep sleep in which he stops reacting adequately to external stimuli. This condition is very similar to the stupor or coma of the adult, and considerable nursing care is required to bring the infant out of it. When he develops this condition, he has not lost any wants and is not yet undernourished. Apparently this is a "psychological" state due to continuous frustration of the infant's most important bodily need. In this instance, as in the experiments on the puppies, we should consider not only the local need of the mouth, but also the threatening character of the continuous tension and the feeling of helplessness in trying to relieve this tension. In such a case, the human infant becomes absolutely helpless and is utterly incapable of doing anything about this problem. It is to be noted that the significance of the mouth function in an infant is very great; it is the only way in which he can master anything in the world, for skilled grasping and locomotion are as yet entirely undeveloped. Any disturbance in this function is of the most fundamentally threatening character. Under such conditions a previously healthy organism becomes seriously sick as the result of a severe deprivation.

In psychopathological reactions to frustration, the situation is more complicated, but it is similar in one important respect. The serious psychopathological reaction arises if the patient feels severely deprived of one of his vital needs. He perceives this blocking of a vital need as an extremely serious threat, one which endangers his whole existence; at least potentially, he feels catastrophically threatened. It has been repeatedly brought out that in the basic psychopathological constellation the patient feels potentially helpless and worthless; he feels afraid of and angry at individuals whom he perceives as more powerful than he, and potentially he anticipates abandonment, humiliation, condemnation, injury, and complete deprivation. To relieve this fear, he uses various devices, pursues various goals, and engages in various activities in ways which enable him to exist. For example, he may depend emotionally and actually on another individual. If this vital need is frustrated—if he is no longer permitted to depend on this person, or if his self-esteem is not constantly flattered, maintained, and raised—the patient's first reaction is that his vital device is taken away from him, and second, he evaluates the frustrating situation as the final realization of his worst anticipations. The need and gratification that are frustrated may be largely of a psychological type. Often in such relationships more definite bodily needs are also involved, as in the case of the child-parent and the husband-wife relationship. In other cases some form of bodily gratification is the device used by the patient to maintain his whole emotional security. The device may be eating or sexual gratification or even one of the excretory functions. If then, for some reason or other, gratification in this sphere is denied, the individual reacts severely. For example, women who become stout from overeating and then begin to diet become profoundly depressed, anxious, and disturbed soon after starting the diet. When they begin eating again, they feel psychologically better. For other individuals almost every form of physiological gratification is significant to their security, often because they consider physical gratification an expression of help and support, love and affection from others. If they cannot obtain this gratification, they not only lose their chief means of consolation, but also feel rejected and abandoned.

There is still another reason why frustration constitutes such a serious problem and initiates psychopathological reactions. In the preceding section we said that one of the most universal reactions to frustration is some degree of aggression. This leads to disturbance in two ways. The patient feels that he is threatened in a vital spot, that the gratification on which his whole existence depends has been taken away. His hostility is commensurate to the enormity of this threat. In other words, he unconsciously regards the frustrator as hostile, cruel, heartless, menacing. Since the patient does not have enough strength to tolerate even a normal amount of aggression in himself, the enormous amount which arises in a frustrating situation leads to an extremely intense expectation of counterattack, abandonment, condemnation, disapproval, which in turn leads to self-condemnation and guilt.

It was said in an earlier section that a patient with psychopathological reactions suffers a certain amount of frustration all the time, even under the best circumstances, and that "inner frustration" is part and parcel of all psychopathological pictures. This statement will be considered further at this point in connection with situations of frustration. We saw above that while some degree of frustration is present in patients who are either actually or potentially sick, they can, under favorable circumstances, obtain enough gratification of vital needs and thus enough security to function with comfort. Frustrating situations that cause serious trouble involve radical changes in the external environment—for example, the breaking-up of a marriage, the loss of a job, or the death of someone dear to the patient. In such cases a new kind of frustration appears; it is much more severe, much greater in intensity, much more threatening. It is easily apparent that such situations are likely to occur in the lives of potential patients because their needs are so great, so unlimited, and have such irrational aspects—unlimited emotional dependence or unchallenged perfection in performance, for example.

Up to this point we have spoken mostly of unexpected, new, and dramatic occurrences in the patient's life as leading to the breakdown. In some cases the situation is chronic and develops more gradually. The patient finds himself in a difficult situation; perhaps his marriage partner is disappointing, or his child is sick, or his work presents difficulties. The situation creates a continuous, threatening problem which he manages to handle in various ways, but always with the hope that sooner or later the situation will change. But finally, after one device after another fails and one hope after another is shattered, he finds himself beaten, definitely frustrated, helpless, and without hope. Then the breakdown occurs. This general development is at times complicated by the patient's suffering another disappointment which likewise strikes at his confidence in himself and at his whole security system. Such developments are usually present in breakdowns that occur during the menopause. The fact of the menopause may lower the woman's evaluation of herself, and her hope of finding another mate or finding a new job or attaining new goals may be finally shattered.

Attempts to Obtain Gratification in Spite of Obstacles.—In situations of frustration, the frustrated individual may attempt to obtain gratification in some way, in spite of external and internal obstacles. This topic is very broad, and overlaps the problem of how the individual attempts to function in spite of catastrophic expectations and conflicts; it will be discussed in another chapter. At this point we shall consider only the aspects which are close to the points already brought out.

We saw, in the experiments and observations cited above, that if the puppies and human infants could not gratify the suckling need at the breast or the bottle, they engaged in mouth activities on other objects, such as the skin of the other puppy, or, in the case of the infant, the thumb. In this observation lies the germ of the phenomenon of displacement and substitution. In other words, one object may take the place of another object which the individual desires. One organic function may even taken the place of another from which he first wanted to derive pleasure. For example, the pleasure of eating and the gratification derived therefrom may be substituted for the gratification which a person desires from close contact with another individual, both physically and emotionally. In such cases an organ function takes the place of the satisfaction of an emotional need.

Replacing one form of satisfaction with another plays an

important role in normal existence also. Here, of course, the psychodynamics of the whole personality must be considered in order to understand what happens. Thus an individual may find solace and strength in his family circle for difficulties and disappointments which he suffers at work. The pleasures of a concert, of the theater, of sports may normally compensate for disappointments in other fields. In this statement, the individual's strength-system and his whole personality must be emphasized. In other words, the statement that one form of satisfaction takes the place of another is only partly correct. What really happens is that a certain amount of discomfort disappears and the individual's confidence is reestablished through the substitute satisfaction. Each culture has its own system of possible solace or compensation.

Frustration in Children.—All psychologists agree that the average child in our society suffers a good deal of frustration, certainly not as much as in some of the European countries, but still enough to constitute a major psychological and social problem. There is, however, a considerable difference of opinion as to which are the important frustrations. Some lay the greater stress on biological deprivations; others consider that these are not necessarily frustrating.

The first group tends to stress the major biological events in the life of the infant and child as the important frustrations which lay the basis for future character development. Taking their cue from Freud's earlier work, they tend to think of the learning of sphincter control, of being weaned, of sex control, of eating habits, and the like, as *the* critical and all-important frustrations in the life history. They consider that the child is being deprived, thwarted, and frustrated when he gives up suckling at the breast, when he gives up being held by his mother and has to learn to walk, when he gives up liquid for a solid diet, when he has to wear clothes instead of going naked, etc. Each new level of adjustment, they hold, is achieved by forcibly pushing the child, and is in turn abandoned as he is pushed on by increasingly complex demands. These theorists look upon the process of learning sphincter control as necessarily depriving the child of a great pleasure which he gives up most unwillingly.

There is a general tendency to think that what a child does, he does because he has to, because he has a drive or an instinct to do so. Thus, in discussions of the early libido theory there are many references to the child's cannibalistic instincts, to his homosexual instincts, to incestuous instincts, to coprophagous instincts (eating of filth), and the like. Why are such instincts assumed to exist? Simply because it has been observed that sometimes children actually do show sexual behavior in reference to their parents or to children of the same sex, or that they sometimes do play with their feces and that some children seem stubborn when their parents attempt to inhibit this behavior.

There is no need here to go into the intricacies of instinct theory. In any case, the simpler and probably more valid hypothesis is to assume that the infant's impulses or drives are vague and undirected, that they spread out in every possible direction, that they are diffuse, and that they have no specific goal objects until learning takes place. Thus we should say not that a child is perverse or homosexual or incestuous, but that his drives are undirected because he has not yet learned from his society and his own experience what the proper goal objects are. The concept of instinct implies not only that the drive is innately determined but that the motivated behavior and goal objects are also innately determined. This we now know to be untrue for human beings. Many experiments have shown that the child does not have to learn to be hungry or stimulated sexually or thirsty. But he *does* have to learn that when he is hungry, it is the class of objects known as food that he must look for; when he is thirsty, he must look for certain liquids; and when he is sexually inclined and seeks satisfaction, he must inhibit this impulse, or, later, look for a certain kind of people—of the opposite sex, unrelated to him, of a certain age, etc.

Let us now examine the more purely psychological point of view concerning these problems. For one thing, social drives and their frustration by social forces would be much more emphasized. Second, and just as important, would be the criticism that the biological point of view not only neglects social forces, but underemphasizes purely psychological forces which in actuality are extremely important in any understanding of frustration. For instance, the manifold possibilities of learning and unlearning that are present in the normal child must certainly be considered. To express it in another way, we must not forget that the child is extremely malleable. Let us, for a moment, consider learning in the child.

What may happen in the process of weaning? Without question, when a child is weaned crudely and hastily the experience may be frustrating and threatening for him. But it *need* not be. If the weaning is unforced and is handled gently and well, the emotional problem may be completely avoided. The healthy child is even eager for new experiences. Here two other psychological factors must be introduced: (1) the effect of praise in building up the child's self-esteem and superiority, and (2) what may be called the "going-ahead" tendency in the healthy child. How can the child be weaned so as to steer a safe course among the various dangerous possibilities that may arise from this situation? How can a compromise be worked out that will take into account the satisfaction of his "sucking" need (D. M. Levy), that will use properly his eagerness for new experience, and that will use praise properly in building up his self-esteem? Clearly, weaning must not be attempted until the proper time, that is, not until the child has satiated his sucking need. This can be determined easily by offering him the alternatives of the breast or solid food, rather than weaning him at a predetermined time. If he is not yet ready for the solid food he will reject it; but if he *is* ready for it, he will begin slowly to accept

it. It is here that we must speak of sheer curiosity, of the attractiveness of novelty, of new experience—in other words, of
"going-aheadness." If, however, when the child takes solid food
he is made much of, kissed and hugged and praised, he wil
spontaneously give up suckling at the breast. In such a procese
it is impossible to speak of frustration or thwarting, or pushing
the child forward to a new adjustment.

A healthy child can learn sphincter control almost equally
easily if the parents are gentle and patient. No punishment need
be involved; as a matter of fact, it *must* not be involved for
fear of transforming the learning process into a frustrating experience. Apparently, he learns quite automatically, willingly,
and even eagerly to urinate at given signals and in certain situations.

A healthy child learns to walk when his maturation makes
him ready for it; he is not forced to walk. Left quite alone, he
will try out his new powers as his development makes them
available. The child who walks only with help will suddenly
spurn it and insist upon walking independently. Anyone who
has observed children "learning" to walk is familiar with the
picture of an achievement that comes from internal factors,
from creative and forward-going urges that blossom most effectively in a benevolent atmosphere of love, praise, and appreciation. It is enough to witness the smile of triumph on
the child's face when he does anything new for the first time
or achieves something that he knows will bring him affection
and praise. The healthy child *wants* to go on; he does not have
to be *pushed* on. Giving up infantile ways of doing things is in
many cases not a renunciation forced upon him, a giving up of
pleasure, a ruthless stamping out of innate tendencies, but
rather a dropping of outworn and useless habits in favor of
new ways of doing the same thing which bring self-esteem, prestige, love, and a high sense of achievement.

Dr. C's six-year-old son worships his father. It is laughable to see
him parading behind his father, knitting his brows, clasping his

hands bravely behind his back, and pacing with long strides just like his father. Dr. C has a peculiar habit, maddening to Mrs. C, of brushing his shoes every morning with the face towel. To her great annoyance, the little boy now does the same thing every morning, in spite of his mother's pleas. Dr. C is an excellent swimmer; his son reports, as one of his great ambitions, that he wishes to swim well. His efforts are persistent and amazing in view of the fact that the little boy is, in a way, deathly afraid of the water. In a word, his father's respect means so much to him that he is willing to overcome fears and withstand punishments of all kinds to be as his father wishes him to be.

We wish to make clear that we have been speaking of psychically healthy children whose parents do not treat them in a humiliating way and whose frustrations come within tolerable bounds.[1]

To children who are insecure, who feel rejected, who are badly brought up in one respect or another, these same situations may be frustrating. We do not mean to imply a clear-cut distinction here. There is a smooth gradation from the best-adjusted person to the most poorly adjusted one; similarly, the degree of the feeling of frustration varies in the same gradual and continuous way. We can only say, in summing up, that if the child's feeling of being loved or his self-esteem is threatened or endangered by a deprivation or by learning, he perceives the situation as threateningly frustrating; the same result occurs if the amount of frustration demanded of him is beyond his limit of tolerance. With the ensuing hostile reaction and the

[1] Mead, Plant, and others have pointed out the dangers of observing the frustrating situation in an over-behavioristic way. Frequently two mothers treat their children in an apparently identical fashion. However, one mother will feel that she is frustrating the child in some situation, whereas the other mother will not. Somehow or other—it is difficult to analyze how—this difference in attitude will be felt by the child. Perhaps very slight unconscious movements that in the one case are rough, brusque, and mechanical, and in the other gentle, lingering, and tender, may be responsible for the difference. In any case, one factor that must be reckoned with in diagnosing a particular situation, i.e., whether it is frustrating or non-frustrating, is the way in which the mother phrases it, the way she feels about it consciously or unconsciously.

subsequent fear of retribution, he develops the catastrophic expectations already described. If, on the other hand, instead of being thus threatened, the child feels that the learning or the deprivation wins him more prestige and love, he then perceives the situation not as frustrating, but as an opportunity that he grasps with eagerness.

The Effects of the Gratification of Impulses

Let us not concern ourselves completely with the negative side of the picture. If frustration of impulses has bad effects, their gratification has good effects; however, this has not as yet been adequately studied. Kardiner (421) has pointed out that, in addition to the obvious fact of the immediate sensual pleasure derived from drive satisfaction, such satisfaction also has effects on the personality. The individual who does something successfully, who carries out a wish, enhances his self-esteem thereby and, at least with relation to that particular wish, builds up his self-confidence. If such satisfactions and achievements are frequent enough and if there are not too many failures and deprivations, we should expect this self-confidence to become generalized (Kardiner). That is, instead of saying that the individual is self-confident with respect to a single field, we would say that he is in general a self-confident person.

Can gratification go too far? Probably it can. The individual who sees all his wishes gratified and who suffers no deprivations has failed to learn how to inhibit himself. (See Chapter XVI on Maternal Over-protection.) There are even more serious possible effects. The person who has his every wish satisfied may lose all his motivation, all his reason for living, since there is nothing to look forward to, nothing to hope for. One needs only to read Suetonius' *The Lives of the Caesars* to see how complete a breakdown can be when people can fully gratify all their wishes and are never deprived or frustrated.

Again there is a compromise solution, i.e., not too **much, not too** little. Too much frustration or too much gratification—both have evil consequences. The individual must strike the proper balance between them. Discipline, training in hardship and in deprivation are by no means outlawed by the psychologist.

SUGGESTED READINGS

The base line from which discussion of frustration proceeds today is *Frustration and Aggression* by Dollard, Doob, Miller, Mowrer, and Sears (190). Some experiments by this group are described in 192, 373, 695, 697, 698. A typical criticism of their work is that by Gould (314).

The Dollard book can be supplemented by Kardiner's *The Individual and His Society* (421). Look up "frustration" in the index. D. M. Levy's articles on "instinct-satiation" and his monograph on sibling rivalry (473) are also valuable sources.

Other interesting experiments are cited in 375, 598, and 110. Rosenzweig's work in this field is also noteworthy. Characteristic are 655-657, 663, 661.

CHAPTER VIII

DISTURBANCES OF THE EVALUATION OF THE ENVIRONMENT

The Basic Psychopathological Constellation.—We have said previously that the fundamental dynamic constellation in individuals who suffer from serious psychological disturbance is characterized in part by a feeling of worthlessness and helplessness, by resentment toward more powerful individuals, and by the fear of abandonment, humiliation, disapproval, condemnation, injury, and complete deprivation—a fear which is potentially catastrophic in intensity.

It is convenient to differentiate two aspects of this constellation: (1) The individual's general attitude about the world, particularly the people in it; his assumptions as to how this world feels toward him, whether it loves him or not, whether it accepts or rejects him, whether it helps him or threatens him; if it threatens him, in what way, and how he feels toward a world that he perceives as threatening. This set of reactions we shall call *security feeling*. (2) The individual's image and evaluation of himself—his own resources, his prestige, his strength, his worth, his body, his functions. This group of feelings we shall sum up under the category of *self-evaluation* or *self-esteem*.

We wish to emphasize again that the patient who is psychologically sick is seriously disturbed in his evaluation of both himself and the environment. There are many connections between these two groups of reaction patterns; these will be discussed later. Here we wish to say only that a connection is self-evident. Thus he who considers himself worthless will assume that the world also considers him worthless, and he whose self-esteem is constantly battered down by everyone who is important to him will eventually come to feel that he is unwanted. However, it is both convenient and useful to discuss the two reaction patterns separately because differences in emphasis on one or the other are always observed in various patients. Furthermore, in the various measures that the individual takes to relieve his distress, his feeling of weakness, and his anticipation of threat, the emphasis may be on a changed evaluation of himself or a changed attitude toward the world. For example, in response to a catastrophic threat to his self-evaluation or his safety or security feelings, he may attack his environment and attempt to dominate it, or he may aggrandize himself (delusions of grandeur) and withdraw from the environment.

Relatively Mild Manifestations of Insecurity.—There are many individuals who function fairly well, who cannot be considered exactly sick—certainly not seriously sick—yet who are apt to be over-shy or withdrawn or mistrustful, or the like. They may be tense and moody and, at times, surly or abrupt. The following excerpts are from the self-analysis of a college student who did rather well in her studies but impressed all her acquaintances in this way:

"I don't trust anybody in the world, not even my mother. After all, people are all selfish deep down and are out only to get, not to give. If you relax for a minute they will take advantage of you. Even the people I have called my friends have always turned out this way and I have decided that the best thing to do is never to be too close to anybody and to keep my secrets to myself. If something good happens to you, they may all envy you; and if you get down, they all step on you and make fun of you and in their hearts they are really glad. Women are catty and jealous and all the men I have ever known have been out to get from me whatever they could. I decided when I was younger that there was no use getting hurt all the time and that the only thing to do was to be stronger than other people. Then they cannot hurt you. Now when I go out with a man I make sure that I have the upper hand. That was the way it was with my father and mother. My mother was weak so my father took advantage of her all his life. It doesn't pay to be weak. After all, the world is divided into strong and weak people. You're either one or the other and I am determined that I will be one of the strong ones.

"Certainly life is a struggle and sometimes I wonder whether it is worth living.

"I suppose I can say that I never really have a good time with people. I am always tense with them. I have to watch out all the time. Sometimes I wonder whether it is worth while.

"I guess I could be called a pessimist. I am always expecting the worst to happen; and even when something nice comes about, to myself I feel that it cannot last.

"Why shouldn't I think of myself first, everybody else does. This business of turning the other cheek—that's all a lot of bunk. If you do, you will get punished there too. The thing to do is to punch first before you get punched.

"Life is a hard thing. I cannot feel relaxed and happy with other people because I am always suspicious of their motives; but the trouble is, I cannot even feel relaxed when I am alone. I get the most horrible thoughts about everybody. Sometimes I think I hate everyone in the world, but I try not to show it. Even in my dreams I have these horrible thoughts and I wake up in a cold sweat.

"My parents never really wanted me or loved me, and nobody else ever has either. If I died tomorrow there would not be anybody in the world who would be sorry for more than a few minutes, and there would be a lot of people who would be glad.

"The one thing that drives me on is getting ahead in the world. I think the rich man is the one safe person. Everybody is afraid of him and doesn't dare try to pull any funny stuff. When he talks, everybody listens, no matter what he talks about. If I have a lot of money, I can get anything I want—fame, power, love, everything."

In this instance the expectation of hurt from the world was conscious. Of course, if such a person is studied carefully and over a long period, it will be found that his expectation of threat from the world is, at least potentially, much more intense than he realizes, and has aspects of which he is entirely unaware. He judges his views at their face value, without realizing that there are difficulties within him. For example, he is unaware that his behavior arouses discomfort and antagonism in people with whom he is in intimate contact. It is probable that if an individual with such an outlook faces a situation of severe stress, the breakdown will be much more severe.

The above excerpt illustrates an open and unquestionable expectation of threat from the environment. To bring out this distrust even more sharply, we cite excerpts from an autobiographical analysis by another college student who, both subjectively and in his behavior, felt secure in the world.

"I have the feeling of being at home in the world and at home with people. I realize now that I have always assumed that a person was nice until he had proven himself to be otherwise. I like them, therefore they like me. I have always had lots of friends, and as a matter of fact, I can think of very few people whom I have ever called enemy. One friend of mine once told me that I have such a nice view of the world because I bring out the best side of everybody I know. He tells me that the same people I like and who behave so decently and nice with me, behave in a very different fashion with other people. I think it is because they realize that I have no desire to threaten them or to hurt them, that I *really* like them, and that I am really pleased when something nice happens to them. In other words, they have nothing to worry about so far as I am concerned.

"One thing that amazes me, now that I have become conscious of this whole aspect of psychology, is that I realize that all this is true in spite of the fact that I am pretty frank in my criticisms. They do not seem to resent criticisms from me although they do from others. I guess it is because they must feel that my criticism does not have the purpose of dragging them down, but only of pulling them up, and of helping them.

"You point out that secure people are generally more happy. I never realized it exactly, but in looking back, I think I can say that my life certainly has been a happy one.

"There is another thing that I now realize is related to other parts of my personality. I feel that I am a truly democratic person. I have always felt that all people are interesting, each in his different way, and that it was silly to compare people with each other. Every person is good for some things, and not good for others, and there is a place in life for everybody. It takes all sorts of people to make a world, and one kind is just as important as another kind. I have never felt that just because I was a college student I was superior to my butcher or to the street sweeper. They are doing the best they can, and essentially we are all working toward the same thing and are really partners rather than competitors. All of a sudden also I have understood the reason for feeling that men and women ought to be essentially equal. I feel that women get the short end of the stick in this world and I have always tried to make it up to them in any way I can."

This self-analysis embodies the opposite of all the characteristics described as typical of insecurity. Here is a person who feels that he is and always has been well loved. He has many warm emotional ties with people and in general likes them. He is friendly and optimistic and equalitarian and democratic. He has little of the drive for power shown in the other excerpts. He does not need it; it would have no function in his adjustment and would, so to speak, be foreign to his personality. He is contented and happy; and outwardly, according to his teacher, is rather pleasant-looking, relaxed, and a calm sort of person. He is obviously also altruistic, kind, and sympathetic.

Less Obvious Examples of Expectation of Threat from the Environment.—Many people behave very calmly and at first give the impression of being unusually poised and well balanced. After longer acquaintance, closer observation, or more detailed psychological study, the following points may become striking: Such persons give the impression of too much calmness; they never, or almost never, are enthusiastic about anything. They do not assert themselves even when their own interest is at stake. Further questioning may bring out the fact that they have never undertaken anything out of openly confessed ambition and initiative. Their philosophy may hold that it is best to go through life as a calm spectator, with a sort of serene lassitude, without too much wear and tear and hustle and bustle, and let others do the fighting. On still further investigation, contradictory features may appear. This man who admits no ambition is an engineer and has made a success of his life career. Yet all his associates feel that he could do more than he is accomplishing; and, in off moments, he himself is dissatisfied with his status. This unusually calm and philosophical man will say that on some occasions, for an unexplained reason, he has a mild spell of anxiety—for example, if the subway train stops for any length of time in the tunnel. He admits that at times he indulges in fantasies such as this: He is flying high in a newly invented airplane, equipped with new instruments of destruction that rain havoc on cities and death on their inhabitants. Further investigation shows that he is quite frequently domineering with his wife and becomes rude and abusive to her for trivial reasons.

We begin to realize that this individual's calmness and easy-going philosophy are not to be taken at their face value. This man feels threatened, and he tries to manage his life so that he will never be confronted with a dangerous situation. He is afraid to assert himself; he is afraid of antagonists, of rivals, of his wife, and of people to whom he is close. This fear is in a way similar to the fear and anticipation of harm which was openly expressed by the college student who called herself a pessimist and said that the world consists of weak and strong people and that everyone was her potential enemy.

Our purpose in describing this man is to show that sometimes, even when a person presents a front of comparative security—in fact, the opposite extreme of anticipation of threat—detailed examination will show that in reality he feels constantly threatened. The threat which such an individual perceives unconsciously is likewise much more intense than he would be willing to admit; it is glimpsed in his mild and fleeting anxiety when the train stops in the tunnel. If such a person faces a difficult stress situation, he often suffers a severe breakdown. Something like this occurred in the patient described in the first chapter.

There are many other apparently normal individuals in whom close examination shows an undercurrent expectation of threat from the world which they unconsciously consider potentially very severe. In this group are the people who always or frequently seem overbearing, who are too assertive, who seem to avoid situations in which they would be in an "inferior" position; and also those who always say "yes" and are extremely humble in their behavior. Needless to say, this anticipation of threat, while always present, varies considerably, depending on the situation with which the individual is confronted.

Severe Manifestations.—We wish now to speak of some manifestations of insecurity which are quite overwhelming, in fact nearly catastrophic. In these manifestations is clearly apparent either the expectation or the actual experience of a profound hurt.

Some patients suffer from so-called "delusion of persecution." They are convinced that people look at them strangely and make derogatory and hostile remarks about them. They are convinced that they have enemies who are going to hurt them, and that there are plots against them. They go through distressing experiences; they taste poison in their food and are convinced that it was put in by one of their enemies; they smell gases which their enemies have released to destroy them. They hear voices which call them obscene and abusive names and threaten them with destruction and humiliation. They experience threatening sensations in their bodies which are the result of their enemies' attacks. In short, any world event, any physiological experience may be perceived and construed by such patients as the result of an action of their enemies and thus as a threat. Some patients of this type may be constantly in utter panic because they are always expecting a murderous attack.

It is obvious that in such instances the appreciation and evaluation of the hardest facts of reality are altered. The patient's experiences, of course, are conscious, but not entirely so; he has no insight, and sees no connections with his inner life. He takes his experiences at their face value. In other words, instead of blotting out his inner life, he alters reality. It is absolutely impossible to show him that the trouble is not with the world but with him. He is not aware of the reasons for his outlook, and his own impulses toward the world are entirely unknown to him. What we wish to show here is that the expectation or the experience of overwhelming threats from the world may be entirely open and almost catastrophic in intensity.

There are other cases in which an overwhelming threat is experienced consciously. The anxiety attacks suffered by the patient mentioned in the first chapter were such experiences. In rare instances such a state of anxiety, such expectation of physical suffering or death, may be almost continuous. Here also the patient has no true insight into his inner life. He does not see the connection between various events and his attacks of anxiety, and he is not aware of the nature or extent of his needs and impulses toward the world. Thus the experience of overwhelming danger may be conscious, and it is connected with the individual's attitudes toward the world.

Varieties of Catastrophic Expectation and Experience.—Just as disturbances of the evaluation of the environment and of oneself are always found together and are part of the serious psychopathological constellation, so the various aspects of the anticipated catastrophic hurt are usually present in the patient. The emphasis, however, may be on one or another aspect.

The varieties of catastrophic expectation are as follows: the expectation of abandonment, injury and annihilation, condemnation and disapproval, humiliation, enslavement, loss of love, and utter deprivation. It is obvious that many of these special fears overlap. Thus the perception of loss of love is very close to abandonment, and abandonment is very close to complete deprivation. In the following examples, some one aspect is emphasized; but as was said above, the various aspects are usually found in one patient.

The patient described in the first chapter was afraid in her anxiety attacks, particularly of being hurt and abandoned by her husband; this was a counterattack against her resentment toward him. She likewise had a strong fear of being utterly deprived in all her bodily needs which aimed at gratification; this was particularly true in regard to her need of eating and her sexual needs. With certain limitations, her husband had been the only person to whom she could get really close; and she had magnified his stature and his strength so that she could be dependent on him. Thus, unconsciously, her whole existence depended on his support and love; her bodily gratifications were possible only with his help. When he told her that he was leaving, all this was threatened. Because of this threat, she became angry at him. The further consequence was an intensification of all these threats and an anticipation of bodily injury and annihilation by this infinitely stronger individual.

Utter condemnation and disapproval are the dominant notes in some forms of emotional depression. If the depression is severe enough, the patient manifests a "delusion of sin and guilt." He is utterly dejected; he condemns himself, and says that he has committed the unpardonable sin. He is convinced that the whole world considers him a sinner, that God has rejected him and will punish him, that he is more worthless than a worm before God and man. Of course, in such a state the feeling of complete loss of love and of abandonment is likewise very strong. The expectation of bodily deprivation is also present, may, in fact, be one of the dominant features. This is particularly true of depressed patients who refuse food.

The anticipation or experience of extreme injury, of annihilation, is seen in the condition described above as "delusion of persecution." The whole world is considered hostile, ready to attack and destroy. In such cases the expectation and experience of utter humiliation and enslavement may also be present. The patient feels that he is being influenced, that his activities are governed and guided by his persecutors. He is deprived of his will, of his self-determination; he is a slave, an automaton. The "voices" that he hears call him "a prostitute," "a pervert," and refer to him in excretory terms. He is utterly humiliated.

These examples are extreme and dramatic, and occur in breakdowns which are almost catastrophic in intensity. Special aspects of the catastrophic fear can also be seen in milder form in disturbances that are not as severe. For example, individuals who want exclusive attention and constant unqualified affection and who become deeply disturbed if it is not forthcoming or if anyone else shares it, are particularly afraid of a catastrophic loss of affection. Other people in any situation of stress eat a lot and may want constant sexual attention. In such cases the catastrophic fear has chiefly the quality of complete bodily deprivation.

The catastrophic hurt may be anticipated in connection with various fields, functions, or aspects of the patient's existence. Thus, the expectation of injury may apply to the whole body or to special parts of it, to the genitals in particular. Humiliation may be perceived particularly in social contacts or in being thwarted in work. To repeat, there are differences in emphasis. A full understanding of a patient's special problem can be obtained only by a complete study of his whole personality and of all his problems.

SUGGESTED READINGS

There is no one best source here. The interested student will have to look through Adler's works for his various discussions of basic "inferiority feeling," in which he lumps together low self-esteem and insecurity feelings. Horney's notion of "basic anxiety" is clearer and more understandable (366). Kardiner's concept of the "security system of the individual" (421) is somewhat similar, but there is more stress on what the individual does about the situation. A clear distinction between security and self-esteem is made only by Plant in Chapter V of his *Personality and the Cultural Pattern* (612). Freud's *The Problem of Anxiety* is recommended for the industrious student.

CHAPTER IX

DISTURBANCES OF SELF-EVALUATION

~~~~~~

Mild Disturbances of Self-evaluation.—As we found with the evaluation of the world and of people, so with the evaluation of the self; there are some mild, open, and conscious disturbances, both subjectively and in the behavior of the individual. Such people are not seriously sick, but they may be shy, uncomfortable, fretful, and moody. The following excerpt from the self-analysis of a college student is an illustration.

"The most general thing I can say about myself is that I feel inferior. I don't seem to think well of myself. My mother tells me that I have no independence at all, that I am ready to do what anybody tells me to do. I remember one time I went to the movies to see a Charlie Chaplin picture and the boy I was with did not like it. He was very intellectual and he sort of sneered at the slap-stick comedy. I didn't like it either, and when my friend asked me how I liked it, I told him how I felt about it. Some weeks later another boy took me out to see the same picture. He liked it very much and I found that I began to like it, too. I seem to have no personality of my own but am whatever anybody wants me to be. I am very dependent upon the good opinion of other people.

"I remember once going around with one of the students. He was very attentive and I liked him. But the other girls in the dormitory did not and I got so mixed up about it that I dropped him. I remember I was so anxious to hear their opinion of him, because I didn't trust my own opinion. When they did not like him he actually changed in my eyes too.

"I am often weak in many other things too. In class I look stupid because I never say anything. Even when I am sure I am right, somehow I always feel that my opinion cannot be as good as others, and I am afraid that whatever I might say would be stupid. As a result, I usually keep my mouth shut. Even at parties and on dates I say what other people want to hear, or else keep quiet. I cannot put my foot down, I cannot say no, and this makes a lot of unhappiness for me. For instance, I dislike smutty jokes very much, but when they are told I try to laugh like everybody else. I have even wished that I could tell them too but I never get up nerve enough.

"When I go out with men I get into trouble too. They all seem to want to paw me and I hate this. I know that other girls can handle the situation, but I cannot seem to. Sometimes I just give in and sometimes I just break out crying. I don't look forward to dates at all, but all of my friends urge me to go. I don't seem to understand men. I know the girls in the dormitory like men, are even crazy about them, but they just seem sort of animal-like to me and I can never relax with them and have a good time. I wonder what I will do about marriage. I love children and certainly will have them, but why must I go through all this nasty sex business first? The only time I have ever doubted God was when I thought about this. Why is it necessary to be an animal before you can have a baby?"

The case just cited presents a picture of relative but not very extreme self-devaluation. The following excerpts from a self-analysis of a man with high self-evaluation provide a good contrast:

"In answer to your questions I can say the following: I usually feel self-confident and sure of myself and practically never bashful or shy, and I can remember only once being really self-conscious and that was in my one try at amateur acting when I had to say some awful things. . . . You could call me a strong person. At least I think you could. For instance, I have generally been the leader in my crowd and my friends come to me to settle their arguments. I feel that I can handle almost any situation and I am certainly not afraid of any of the people I know. . . .

"As I look over the qualities you ask me to rate myself in, it looks as if I were pretty well satisfied with myself [intelligence, attractiveness to the opposite sex, appearance, etc.]. People do sometimes call me conceited, but I think it is only because they envy me. After all, I am successful in most of the things I want to do, and can usually do my job better than the other people around me. . . .

"Such people in general make me sick anyway. They're always afraid of everything. They whine and cry and always look for help. What I say is, the way to do something is just to do it. I cannot understand these people who are sissies, who build up a lot of fear for themselves and then complain because they can't do this or they can't do that. Such people are just like women. I don't even like a woman who is a sissie. My girl can hold her end up in any argument. I know that if I tried to put anything over on her, she'd throw a lamp at me. She's got an awful temper, but somehow I like it; also I like the fact that there is no coyness about her. She never tries to act the clinging vine. She once told me that the reason she was attracted to me was because I seemed to think that I could get everything I want. . . .

"I have never blushed in my life. . . .

"I do not know what will happen in the future, but I am sure I can take care of myself."

Less Obvious Examples of Disturbances of Self-evaluation.— Some individuals, when asked how they feel about themselves, will first say that they are well satisfied with their performance. Further conversations and observation bring out the fact that they are eager to do everything well. They are very accurate in their work; in fact, they may be extremely accurate in almost anything they do. They say that everything should be done well; and they invest considerable time, energy, and emotion in doing their tasks well. They also expect other people to do their work perfectly. This may be the first hitch. Such individuals are apt to be emotional and a bit over-emphatic when they criticize other people because of their neglect of relatively minor matters. Thus, they may wax eloquent if someone's desk is not in perfect order. If they themselves happen to make a mistake, they grow rather disturbed and find it hard to forgive themselves, or they become unusually defensive and accuse someone else of being responsible for the mistake. In all of this there is apparent their need to do things without a flaw—a need so great as to be beyond the point of reasonableness. When such an individual is carefully examined or is caught in a mood of discouragement, he will say that he is dissatisfied with himself, that he does not trust his powers and is not satisfied with his achievements. Usually he has fantasies of great achievement; but when he is moody he thinks of failure, in his fantasies others surpass him, he is unable to do his work adequately. He may also be inclined to hound other people for their imperfections, and to demand unqualifiedly good performance of them.

Still other people manifest too much sureness, even on matters about which they know nothing; they show a surprising absence of doubt of their ability to carry out any task whatsoever; situations in which most people are doubtful and worried leave them absolutely unconcerned.

Longer acquaintance with such individuals or a careful study of them sometimes shows that, behind this need for perfection, behind this over-sureness and bravado, there is actually a doubt of their ability or worth similar to that expressed consciously by the student whose self-analysis was quoted. However, these individuals may be unconscious of this evaluation of themselves most of the time; it is glimpsed only when they are off guard or after they have failed. If they have to face situations of severe stress— particularly if there is a strain on their resources or if their self- esteem is threatened—they may suffer a more serious break- down.

Severe Manifestations.—In some of the conditions described in Chapter VIII, severe and overt disturbance of the evaluation of the self was manifest. For example, in attacks of anxiety, patients often feel that they are small, insignificant things caught in the mesh of gigantic circumstances, that they are faced with tremendous forces although they themselves are utterly powerless and helpless, or that they are alone, thrown entirely on their own resources which fail them completely. In- dividuals who suffer severe depression with delusions of sin and guilt may feel utterly worthless, accuse themselves of crimes, consider themselves most contemptible and loathsome creatures.

In all these conditions there is a profound and open disturbance of self-evaluation. Of course, such individuals are not conscious of the ramifications of their experiences. They take them at their face value without understanding their real meaning.

Varieties of Catastrophic Self-devaluation.—Self-devaluation is, at least potentially, catastrophic in intensity. It has various aspects which are commonly found in the same individual; but the emphasis is different in various patients.

The varieties of catastrophic self-devaluation are as follows: feeling and expectation of helplessness, loss of self-esteem, moral worthlessness and guilt, inability to give love, loss of strength, loss of capability. Clearly there is a considerable overlapping between them. Thus a feeling of helplessness always involves loss of self-esteem; the inability to love involves the feeling of moral worthlessness and loss of self-esteem. This is why one patient usually shows many of them. It is further obvious that in cases of self-devaluation, disturbances of the evaluation of the world are often present. If this self-devaluation is of the catastrophic variety, insecurity feelings will *always* be found.

The feeling of catastrophic helplessness was eloquently illustrated by the anxiety attacks described in Chapter I. This patient felt helpless in the face of a gigantic and hostile world; she had always considered herself helpless and poor in resources. In her frustration, her conflicts, and the anticipated abandonment and threat of attack by her husband, she anticipated utter helplessness. This case clearly indicates that helplessness is one of the most common—in fact, an ever-present aspect—of psychopathological disturbances. Even when the obvious emphasis is on some other aspect, helplessness always plays a very significant role, and it is always potentially catastrophic in intensity. This is true of the patient's estimation of his total possibilities and strength. He always feels that a thorough and radical change in his mode of living and reactions is beyond his strength. If circumstances demand it—if, for example, it is attempted in psychoanalytic treatment—he always feels that he is not capable of it. If any of his vital needs is threatened, he anticipates the catastrophically helpless state, and he is convinced that he cannot remedy the situation. If the feeling of helplessness is further aroused by failure of one of his functions, the emphasis in the feeling of helplessness may be predominantly in the field of one particular function—for example, in the field of bodily function, such as locomotion or eating or sexual function, or in the field of intellectual or emotional function.

The anticipation of catastrophic loss of self-esteem is often disclosed in patients by deep psychological analysis. Such people are convinced that something is lacking in them, that they have fatal shortcomings, that they fall utterly below their ideals and would fail in the most dismal and humiliating fashion if they attempted to live up to them or if their true nature were revealed to other individuals and to themselves. Often this low estimation of the self, this idea of something essential being lacking, is expressed by a reference to an insignificant bodily deformity such as a slight curvature of the spine or a slight difference in the size of the breasts, or thick lips. This catastrophic undervaluation of the self is expressed in some patients in delusions about their body. Some profoundly depressed patients and some who suffer from delusions of persecution also have delusions that their brains are gone, that their lungs are shriveled, that their bowels are stopped up. Patients who hear voices calling them derogatory names likewise suffer a great loss of self-esteem.

Profound disturbance of moral self-evaluation is present in the cases of depression with delusions of sin and guilt that have already been mentioned. These patients consider themselves abject sinners, and utterly worthless. Both self-condemnation and expectation of catastrophic disapproval and condemnation may be associated with some particular function of the body; in fact, the whole image and evaluation of the body and its functions may be catastrophically disturbed. In our culture, self-devaluation is very commonly associated with the genital organs and functions.

The catastrophic fear of inability to give love and affection is likewise common in patients who have found it necessary to put other people at a distance because of anticipation of rejection. If in the course of treatment they get to the point where they want to reach out to other people with genuine emotions, and they find that they are not able to, they are of course distressed and alarmed. Near-catastrophic experience of the inability to love is also present in the profoundly depressed patient. It is particularly striking in patients who suffer from "depersonalization." These individuals see everything, perceive and understand everything, but somehow the experience lacks a genuine quality; they complain bitterly that they cannot experience genuine feeling, pleasure, or even sorrow; they feel that their emotions are dead.

Interrelations Between Self-evaluation and Evaluation of the Environment.—Although disturbances of the evaluation of the self and of the evaluation of the environment have been discussed separately, the two are always found together in the psychologically sick, and there are connections between them. Some further remarks on this point will be made.

The individual tends to assume that the world evaluates him in the same manner as he evaluates himself. Thus he who feels worthless is convinced that the world considers him worthless.

The individual tends to expect a response from the environment similar to his toward it. This is obvious in connection with the inability to give affection and love. The patient feels unable to give affection, and is convinced that the environment does not give it to him; hence he feels unloved. It is equally true that he tends to treat the environment as he assumes it treats him. If, for example, he is convinced that he will not get genuine affection from anyone and that he will be rejected, he in turn will be unwilling to reach out emotionally toward others. He becomes unable to love.

The reaction of resentment and hostility is an important connecting link between evaluations of the self and of the environment. Thus the individual feels helpless; he considers that he does not get adequate support from his environment; he becomes unconsciously angry, and then anticipates complete abandonment in an even more helpless state. Or he feels unloved and rejected by the environment, grows angry because of this, anticipates utter condemnation and disapproval from the environment, and feels himself worthless and guilty. Similarly, he looks down on himself; he evaluates and interprets some act or attitude of the environment as humiliating, becomes resentful, and is then afraid of further humiliation.

The individual evaluates himself in comparison with the environment. He who feels helpless views the environment as all-powerful. As a result, all threats which he perceives as coming from the environment become terrific in intensity and he feels that he cannot cope with them. The individual who lacks self-esteem compares himself with others and considers himself worthless. Thereupon he tends to raise his evaluation of others and at the same time envies them. The expected hurt from the overvalued individuals is then all the more painful.

Evaluation of the Self and of the Environment as a Total Reaction.—Thus far the evaluation of the self and of the world has been discussed in introspective terms. We shall now speak of reactions of the total organism. The attitudes and reactions that have been mentioned show themselves in the individual's whole behavior and vegetative reactions. The laughing and smiling of the threatened person are different from those of the "secure" person; the difference is hard to describe, but it is observable. The posture, the demeanor, the mien of the two individuals tend to differ in subtle ways. The two people even tend to have different tastes in food and literature, to behave differently to their friends, and to reveal a difference in practically everything they do. (For experimental work, see W. Wolff [798, 799],

G. Allport [27], and P. Eisenberg [209-211, 213], among others.)

Another way of emphasizing the broader concept of self-evaluation is to study other people's impressions of the individual in question. Since this is, in large part, based upon behavior both obvious and subtle, we can thus learn much about the self-evaluation. The secure individual is likely to be described by his friends and neighbors as easy, natural, relaxed, affectionate, and friendly (if they approve of him), or as smug, bovine, unambitious, self-satisfied, easy-going, and lazy (if they disapprove of him). The threatened or insecure person is usually first described by other people as tense and nervous. He is often characterized as suspicious, envious, fearful, unpredictable, unstable, or introspective. Or he may be described as *extremely* pleasant or overbearing. For example, the forced laughter of a threatened individual is different from the relaxed and easy laughter of someone who has confidence in other people's affection for him.

These descriptions of course do not do justice to the complexity of the problem. All that they can convey is the fact that the individual shows in a great many ways how he is reacting, and that when we speak of introspective matters we include observable reactions also.

The individual's involuntary functions are also correlated with evaluation of the self, particularly if his actual reaction to a definite situation is included. For example, a person is shy; his hands are cold and his pulse is rapid. Even when he apparently behaves in an easy manner, his hands may be cold and his heart may beat rapidly. The general appearance of the individual and the conditions of his vegetative functions in severe reactions may of course be very striking. A depressed patient has a dejected facial expression, his eyes lack luster, the action of his bowels is sluggish, his hands are cold.

Further Dynamic Consequences of Catastrophic Evaluation of the Self and of the Environment.—The constellations which have been described are of dynamic significance not only because they contain the element of drivenness, but because the individual reacts further in response to the initial pattern. These further reactions also have an intense element of drivenness.

Every patient who feels catastrophically threatened always has a never-dying longing for restoration and safety. This may be conscious or unconscious, or both. The special form of restoration sought depends on the situation, on his hurt, and on the threat he perceives, as well as on the environment and on his notions of what will be most valuable for the purpose. All these problems will be discussed in the next chapter; here certain forms of this longing and of attempts at remedying the situation will be considered.

Intense longing for support and dependence.—It was stated above that the feeling of helplessness almost automatically carries with it an over-valuation of the strength of other individuals. Thus the patient may seek his restoration by dependence on a stronger person, by blind faith in him, by a desire for his constant presence and his undivided affection and esteem. This seeking may be expressed predominantly in the field of friendship or professional relationships or the attitude toward a mate or a relative; it may take a political form.

There is a still further development in this reaching out for unqualified support. The patient feels that the person from whom he expects and wants undivided support must realize his helplessness and will thereby be convinced of his real need of support. The patient's helplessness that is manifest in an actual situation of stress is thus a phenomenon which has several factors. One factor is the kind of helplessness he felt when he first reached out for dependence; he in no way wanted this helplessness, it had no goal. But after he reached out and thereupon felt the need of showing his helplessness, he partially desires it and it is intensified in actual situations of stress. In a sense, he *wants* to be helpless to get the support of the stronger individual; the result is that he is even less able to mobilize his resources and his panic is greater. This condition is found in patients who develop utter panic when left alone in a room.

The disturbance of the patient's self-esteem in actual situations of stress is likewise complex. Low self-esteem, as finally experienced, may consciously and unconsciously be the result of the following: The patient's self-esteem is low to start with. He reaches out for unqualified affection and dependence. To acquire this, he may even go to the point of unconsciously offering to be humiliated. In this sense, he practically offers to lower his self-esteem. Thus, his low self-esteem at first has no goal; but when he reaches out, being humiliated by the other individual and consequently lowering his self-esteem has a goal (the other's support), and the result is an even further lowering.

The patient may reach out for unqualified affection to get protection and thus be saved from the threats he perceives in his environment or to restore his feeling of worth.

Intense drive for superiority and power.—The patient's unconscious reasoning when there is a drive for power is as follows: "If I am superior to everyone, if I have power and can control and dominate everyone, I'll be saved from the dangers of the world, I'll be worth something in my eyes and in the eyes of the world, I'll even be loved." Such a patient may seek to achieve these goals in various fields. He may feel a tremendous drive to be superior in his work or to attain a position in which he surpasses and can command others. The drive may be directed chiefly toward accumulating money, or it may be present for the most part in the realm of subjective fantasies. The actual striving for these goals and the resultant feeling of esteem, which is itself in turn highly exaggerated, is again a complex matter. The individual first feels threatened; he reaches out toward superiority and power. He then feels a new threat which is potentially more intense than the first. He expects counterattack in the direction either of humiliation or of thwarting his plans or of injury. To guard himself and to cope with these new threats, he makes a renewed effort toward the goals.

Thus the finally resultant striving for power aims at relieving the originally low self-esteem and toward overcoming the new threats. This drive may also aim at relieving threats from the environment as well as catastrophic self-devaluation. The most extreme pathological result of this trend is "delusion of grandeur." This type of patient considers himself a remarkable and exceptional person, he thinks that he can do amazing things, or that he has achievements to his credit which are entirely out of keeping with his real status. He may be convinced that he is one of the prophets or one of the apostles, Napoleon, or Jesus Christ, or the Virgin Mary, or Joan of Arc.

As previously mentioned, these measures evolved by the individual are typical of the devices he may use to overcome his fears, his conflicts, and his frustrations. Such devices are discussed in the following chapter.

SUGGESTED READINGS

Good source material is to be found in the writings of Adler. An interesting book on the subject is Dodge and Kahn's *Craving for Superiority* (185). See also Maslow's papers on "dominance-feeling" (self-esteem) in monkeys, apes, and humans (530-534). Chapter V of Plant's book (612) is recommended for its discussion of the relationship between self-esteem and security feelings. See also Freud's *The Problem of Anxiety*.

CHAPTER X

COPING WITH DANGERS; DEFENSE, AMELIORATION, DEVIOUS SOLUTIONS, ETC.

We have stated that in response to various threatening situations the patient reacts as if he unconsciously anticipates a catastrophic state of worthlessness and helplessness, of rejection, abandonment, injury, and complete frustration. The special emphasis in this catastrophic anticipation may be on one or another feature, such as humiliation or injury, but this anticipation is common to every serious situation with which the patient has to cope. This fear may arise in situations which to healthy people are not threatening, as when the patient has to perform a complicated social task, or when he wants to gratify a bodily urge, to relax, to get in contact with other individuals, etc. However, he does not unqualifiedly accept his fear and he does not submit to it (unless he is completely discouraged); consciously and unconsciously he attempts to do something about it. In general, the following aims can be recognized on the part of the patient:

1. He attempts to diminish his distress by various means.
2. He takes definite positive measures to strengthen himself and thus to be able to overcome his fear.
3. He attempts to reach certain goals in spite of the fear that these goals produce.[1]

[1] Other classifications of these aims, subserved by the coping mechanisms, are possible. For instance, some that have been offered are (1) defense, (2) withdrawal, (3) attack and revenge, (4) amelioration or comfort, (5) reassurance or building up strength, (6) release and substitution, (7) compromise, and (8) rational solution. We might also add that symptoms sometimes express *none* of these aims or purposes, all of

The various mechanisms and devices to be discussed usually accomplish one or more of these aims. We shall group them, however, according to the aspect that predominates in the purpose of the device and its main goal. The various reaction patterns which will be described have been established through clinical observation (Freud [273, 279, 280, 282]; Janet [395]; Adler [6]; Horney [366, 367]; Rado [625]; Kardiner [421]). Many of them have been verified by experimental methods, such as hypnosis, animal experiments (Erickson [220, 223, 226]; Maier [521]; Lewin [490]).

MEASURES TO DIMINISH DISTRESS

Avoidance of the Situation.—The unconscious psychological formula here is: "If I avoid the dangerous situation, I will escape pain and catastrophe." For example, for many years the patient described in the first chapter kept away from men and from situations which might have brought her close to them. A more obvious form of avoidance is seen in certain types of phobia. Thus a patient may have to take a train to visit someone whom he dreads encountering because he expects humiliation, domination, and injury, but whom he feels obliged to visit. He develops anxiety attacks while riding in the train, and is unable to continue the trip. In this way he avoids the situation which he really dreads. Similarly, some individuals may avoid contact with people who are superior to them in any significant way. Others may avoid situations of responsibility or those in which they have to lead because these situations are fraught with fear for them. In other situations they feel safe. Physical illness may serve this same purpose of avoidance or escape.

---

which are, after all, attempts to cope with the threatening situation. In other words, symptoms may express complete discouragement and loss of hope, discomfort, admission of defeat or panic. Thus, we may classify symptoms into those that represent discouragement or defeat and those that represent attempts to cope with a bad situation. It is the aims or purposes of the latter type of symptoms that are discussed in this chapter.

Repression, Amnesia, and Inhibition.—Here it is as if the patient unconsciously said to himself: "If I don't know about my dangerous impulses, I won't have them at all; they don't exist." The patient does not know that he wants or feels something. Thus the woman mentioned in the first chapter did not know that she was angry at her husband for his wanting to leave her. A whole series of incidents may not be consciously remembered by patients.

A patient developed attacks of palpitation together with periods of depression about six months before applying for treatment. When he was first asked what the circumstances were under which these complaints started, he said nothing unusual. He thought hard about the circumstances, discussed them repeatedly and again he said, "Nothing distressing occurred at that time." After repeated interviews he remembered that about that time he had had a quarrel with a friend of his over money matters, following which they had not seen each other for some time. The quarrel was patched up, but they never really became good friends again. To check up on his memory, the patient asked his wife about the time of the quarrel. She confirmed the fact that the quarrel had occurred just before the onset of the patient's depression.

Usually patients not only shut impulses out of awareness, but almost completely suppress a desire or emotion. There were many years when the patient described in Chapter I was not aware of any sexual desire.

Emotional Detachment.—Another device which the patient may use to avoid distress is emotional detachment. In general, he says in effect, "I do not have any emotions which would lead to danger. I maintain my distance, my isolation from events that can cause trouble." In some individuals such emotional coolness is a constant trait; they never get enthusiastic about anything, never get really close to anyone emotionally. Others show this detachment only in certain situations; they may be intensely emotional about their work or about certain hobbies, but remain emotionally aloof from people.

Failure of an Organ to Function in the Active Situation.—
The unconscious psychological formula is: "I cannot avoid the
dangerous situation, but I can protect myself against catastrophe
if I fail." The most important organ which will be used by the
patient in an active situation fails. Examples are impotence in
man, frigidity in woman, headache, loss of appetite, spasm or
paralysis of certain muscles—e.g., the arm muscles of a musician
who dreads exposure and humiliating failure before an audience.
In Erickson's second experiment cited in an earlier chapter, the
subject suffered hysterial blindness; he could not read the handwriting in the letter addressed to his friend, although it was
clearly legible.

Renouncing Control.—This is present in connection with violent, obscene, obsessional thoughts. Thus a patient has thoughts
of injuring others; but the thoughts appear in a form which
enable him to say, "These are not my thoughts, they come to me
from without, I am not responsible for them." It should be
mentioned that these violent impulses are themselves a reaction
to catastrophic anticipation. However, the patient's "lack of control" over this or other symptoms is further "willed" (unconsciously) by him; he is motivated by fear of catastrophic consequences if he acknowledges them as his own.

Blaming Others.—The formula is: "I am not to be blamed
for failure. Others around me are." The patient makes a mistake
in his work because of serious emotional problems but blames
the condition under which he has to work; a man is impotent
and blames the woman.

Wit, Humor, Clowning.—The psychological formula is: "I
am not distressed in this situation; I am not afraid of it; I can
laugh at it." This type of behavior is used as a protection by individuals who feel extremely awkward in a situation, who find it
difficult to be with other people, who are afraid of being rejected.
Witty behavior may cover up their distress. They may use
cynicism and wit to guard against intrusion into their private
worlds which are full of trouble and worry. Clowning may be

resorted to by boys who are much distressed by their feeling of being ridiculed, rejected, and humiliated because of stoutness or deformity, for example. The clowning covers up their distress, but it accomplishes more: they retain contact with and obtain the affection of their friends. Thus in this device, a distinct compensating, ameliorating trend is also noticeable. Similarly, the subject in Erickson's first hypnotic experiment made all sorts of jokes and humorous remarks while he was acting out the post-hypnotic conflict about lighting the cigarette.

Attempted Justification (*Rationalization, Self-vindication*).— The psychological motif in rationalization is: "I am not afraid; I am not guilty; I have no conflict because what I have done has a sensible, rational purpose." Two kinds of devices are involved here; the second is more serious than the first. The first merely attempts to make the patient's behavior appear rational so that he can escape humiliation and ridicule and self-contempt. Thus a patient may have complicated conflicts and fears about asserting himself, about having initiative, about getting close to people. He will not recognize and admit this fact, but will instead give such reasons as "It doesn't pay to strive too hard. One is safest alone. In this way I can't be taken advantage of," etc. The second type of device is seen when a patient rationalizes engaging in an activity which disturbs someone else. For example, a superior who hounds his subordinates may give the need for efficiency as the reason for his behavior; the mother who dominates and tortures her child may give her interest and love for him as the reason for her behavior.

AMELIORATIVE, REINFORCING, OR DEFENSIVE DEVICES

It is characteristic of ameliorative and defensive devices that the patient who uses them tries to accomplish more than the mere avoidance of discomfort. He wants either to be helped and protected or to strengthen himself, and he usually uses a variety of devices to attain these two goals.

The general pattern of these reactions is about as follows: The patient is confronted with a variety of tasks in various fields of activity, and he has to face dangers which revive or sustain his catastrophic fear. Unconsciously, in his behavior and in the multiplicity of his reactions, he says, "If I take certain measures, I'll be safe even though the situation is dangerous; I'll be able thus to obtain my objectives and the pleasures that I want."

Dependence; Desire for Complete Care.—The formula here is: "If I have the complete help of another stronger individual I shall be safe and I can obtain my goal." This attitude may be expressed in fantasies in which the patient finds a superior person who showers favors on him and thus makes him well and happy. It may show itself in the patient's daily behavior, as when he asks someone else's advice and follows blindly on every occasion. It may show itself in such dramatic symptoms as "astasia-abasia," in which, in spite of having no serious organic ailment, the patient is unable to stand or walk and must therefore remain in bed and be taken care of. It is manifested in some patients who feel completely lost when alone. They suffer severe states of anxiety accompanied by violent bodily symptoms, such as gasping and pain around the heart; and their symptoms lessen or disappear only if someone who is devoted to them is present. Similar conditions may be present in emotional depression, or when a patient is terror-stricken at crossing the street unless a certain individual goes with him. Investigation shows that such patients desire unqualified affection, interest, and care from another individual (Horney). These dependence devices may also be used as mechanisms for domination (Adler).

Submission, Obedience, Ingratiation.—"If I obey a stronger individual I'll have his protection and will enable myself to reach necessary goals." Such a formula in its simplest form leads to obliging behavior; the patient complies with everyone's request and is extremely humble. He may express this attitude in fantasies in which he is used, sexually or otherwise, by other people. In a woman this attitude may express itself in her need or feeling of obligation to submit sexually to any man who pays some attention to her, even though she herself does not desire him. It may express itself in homosexual submission. It may be one factor in the symptoms of waxy flexibility (see Glossary), although this phenomenon is more complicated (Kardiner).

Self-debasement.—"I want to submit, I want to show that I am insignificant and worthless, in order to obtain what I am asking for." Such an unconscious formula may result in a strong tendency to self-debasement, a tendency which has another aspect, namely: "I want to show him that I am worthless, that I am insignificant, that I am contemptible, so that he will forgive me for being hostile toward him, and will help me." The manifestations of this attitude can be seen in severe depressions, in which the patient accuses himself of all sorts of crimes which he has not committed; he is a sinner who does not deserve to live, and he is being punished (delusion of sin and guilt). Such symptoms may, in some cases, represent not so much a purposeful coping with the problem as discouragement.

Turning Against Oneself.—In this reaction the patient directs toward himself an impulse that was first directed toward someone else. The unconscious formula is: "I will hurt myself instead of hurting him. If I do this, I will be forgiven and helped; I will escape worse punishment." The impulse most frequently involved is a hostile one. In emotional depression the patient usually accuses himself of acts and impulses for which he really blames someone else. The very fact of suffering and incapacity has the implication of the patient's harming himself instead of someone who disappointed him or treated him unfairly, but on whom he feels absolutely dependent. In its extreme form this attitude is manifested as suicide. In other cases, it may represent extreme discouragement and low self-esteem.

Attack, Violence, Hostility, and Projection (Defensive Hostility).—The formula here is: "I am in danger in various situations, but I shall be safe and able to carry out my goals if I successfully attack and incapacitate my adversary." This device may show itself in constantly overbearing and dominating behavior, or in elaborate fantasies of destruction.

Need to Control, to Be Superior, to Dominate.—The formula is: "If I dominate the situation, I am safe from attack and from helplessness; I am strong and I can attain my desire." A patient who uses this device may have fantasies in which he is the head of a jail and all the prisoners have to obey him. It may show itself subtly through sexual seduction, at times homosexual, the idea being, "If I can seduce him (or her), I shall have mastered him (or her)." In still other cases a patient will enter only those situations and relationships, either work or social, in which he can be superior and dominate.

Self-aggrandizement.—The formula is: "I am unique, I am remarkable, I possess exceptional qualities, I do not have to feel worthless and helpless. Being remarkable gives me satisfaction, and I can also achieve other goals." This attitude is sometimes evident only if considerable psychological study of the patient is made. It may show itself in thoughts of greatness, which are at times entirely fantastic, such as flying in an airplane over the nation's capital and controlling by means of death rays everything that goes on in the country. The attitude may express itself rather dramatically in the delusion of grandeur. A less obvious expression is seen in people who consider themselves superior in some respect to everyone they know.

Reaction Formation.—The formula is: "I do not desire something which is objectionable; on the contrary I intensely desire the opposite." The impulses involved here are chiefly hostile and sexual in nature. This attitude is seen most frequently in character traits and in the broad reaction patterns of those people who, when they break down in a difficult situation, have obsessional thoughts of violence and thoughts of a sexual and excretory nature. Such people are *excessively* kind, fair, moral, and idealistic. With these reaction patterns they not only protect themselves against the dangers apparent if they follow their own impulses of anger or sex or rage, but also considerably enhance their evaluation of themselves.

Elation with Denial.—The formula underlying this device is: "I will not acknowledge my fears, my conflict, my self-contempt, my feelings of being disapproved; I will not be helpless and hopeless. On the contrary, I will evaluate myself highly, I will be very active, I will be happy." The patient is emotionally elated and very active; his thoughts flit from one subject to another. The same phenomenon is observable, in a less intense form, in the slighter, more fleeting elation of people who constantly swing from emotional depression and pessimism to emotional elation and glowing optimism and high self-evaluation.

Gratification of Bodily Urges as a Source of Solace and Strength.—The formula here is: "I will eat, I will have sexual relations (or urinate or move my bowels or take a bath), and then I won't feel alone, I won't feel helpless and weak; on the contrary, I will derive pleasure, I will feel stronger and be safe." The most frequent function used for this purpose is eating, particularly eating sweets. Thus, whenever a patient experiences a disappointment or feels depressed and lonely, he may indulge in food.

Measures to Reach the Goal in Spite of Obstacles

Most of the devices described in the preceding section imply attempts to reach a goal directly or to relieve anxiety and increase the feeling of strength. The measures that will be discussed in this section are motivated predominantly by the desire to reach the goal in spite of obstacles. It is necessary to repeat here that many of these measures or aims may be recognizable in a single symptom.

Compromise Formation.—The unconscious formula is: "If I strive for the goal in a straightforward manner, I shall not be strong enough to reach it, or dangers will prevent me from reaching it; but if I do not try to reach the goal fully or if I use qualifications which partly deny it, I may attain approximately what I would like to get." It is also a technique of attaining both goals when there is conflict between them.

Compromise formation is seen in the patient described in the first chapter. She wanted closeness and emotional dependence and she also wanted to satisfy her sexual desires. She could not strive for this goal directly for several reasons. Her desire for dependence was so strong and her feeling of worthlessness so intense that she was afraid of rejection. Because of her hostility which arose from this and from her feeling of inferiority, especially with men, she was afraid of being injured, particularly in the sexual act, and therefore kept away from men. Under the special circumstances and in response to the character and behavior of her husband, she managed to establish the desired relationship, but with limitations: "I am close to him but I am not bound. I can relinquish him if I wish."

Another form of compromise is manifest when some act is done in such a manner that it falls short of its assumed purpose. For instance, a patient gave her antagonistic in-laws a present which suited her own house but not theirs. Thus she did what was expected of her, but they secured no pleasure from it.

The term compromise formation is often used in another sense. For example, the patient's symptoms may satisfy both the tabooed desire as well as his sense of guilt. Obsessive thoughts, in a sense, are of this nature. Through them the patient expresses hostility or sexual impulses, but at the same time he suffers. It is as if it were permissible to express a "bad" impulse, if only one "paid" for it. Many bodily symptoms have aspects which satisfy the patient's opposite urges and needs. Thus an uncontrollable contraction of the muscles of the arm may express an urge to attack, but with simultaneous incapacity and suffering.

Some patients unconsciously do not dare to take the initiative and to commit themselves fully to any action for fear of failure and catastrophic humiliation. They therefore maneuver so that another individual will persuade them to take a certain course of action, whereupon emotional responsibility falls on the other person.

Limitation of the Situation.—The formula is: "If I put certain restrictions on the situation or on the act, I eliminate the dangerous aspects." For example, a woman patient who keeps some of her clothes on while having sexual relations says that in this way she does not give herself fully to the man. Her guilt feelings and also his domination are thus lessened. A girl who is strongly attracted to men may see them only infrequently.

Counteracting (Doing and Undoing).—The formula is: "I will carry out this act which means dangers for me; but I will engage in another act which eliminates these dangers."

A patient was very tender toward his wife. But after each occasion of emotional tenderness he would walk through the park for the purpose of looking at other women. His idea was: "If I get close to my wife, she will throw increased responsibility on me and won't permit me to lean on her. If I go out and look at other women, I assert and establish my independence of her." When the patient attempted to force himself not to look at other women he could not be tender to his wife.

The term "doing and undoing" more frequently refers to patients with obsessional thoughts. In them, the thought of killing or an obscene thought is followed by a pious act which serves the purpose of undoing the effect of the thought. This type of device, however, does not serve the purpose of carrying out a function and reaching a goal; it is only ameliorative.

Rigid Regulations.—The formula is: "I can guard against unexpected danger, I can carry out my desires, cope with the situation, and still feel safe only if I follow rigid rules in my behavior."

The simplest examples of this behavior device are furnished by patients who extol and insist on, or anxiously follow, a very rigid routine in work. The patient who feels insecure in social contact follows a system in meeting people. He may be able to meet them only professionally; hence he invites people to his house only with the idea of professional contact. This motivation may be strikingly present in every contact he makes. Similar reactions are seen in patients who must have their desks arranged in a certain inflexible order or whose eating habits are rigidly set or who consider social behavior customs of the utmost importance. Some obsessional attitudes belong in this category. For example, one patient had an obsessional fear of infection. He could have sexual relations with his wife only if she took a shower, scrubbed herself with a brush, dressed completely in white, covered her hands, feet and head, and did not brush against anything—even a chair—on the way to their room.

Substitution and Displacement, Symbolization,—The formula here is: "Instead of doing something that is dangerous, I will do something which is similar but not identical to it. In this way I can safely reach my goal." Although substitution and displacement have been discussed in the chapter on frustration and examples have been given, they will be further considered at this point.

Substitution and displacement are very similar. Substitution usually refers to using another bodily organ instead of the one which affords feared or condemned (usually genital) gratification. Displacement more frequently refers to emotional reactions or general activities in which the individual responds emotionally to a situation which is in reality different from the one to which he is genuinely reacting.

A severe form of substitution was shown by a married woman who, instead of retiring with her husband, derived genuine erotic pleasure from picking and grooming the skin of her back and face for hours at a time.

Any part of the body or any article of clothing may be substituted for the genital organs in this type of substitute activity. Instances of fetishism belong here, as when a person gets all his pleasure from being aroused and gratified by shoes which belong to the person he desires.

More complicated forms of substitution are seen in the following: The individual is afraid of genuine emotional attachment, of self-assertion, of final commitment to what he wants to undertake. Whenever situations arise in which he would like to do a certain thing or in which he is requested to do it, he withdraws and masturbates or engages in elaborate fantasies of self-aggrandizement. His formula is: "This way I am safe and I get some enjoyment out of life." It is obvious that such measures are highly complex and involve the individual's image of himself, of other people, and of his activity. This device serves the further purpose of solace as well as substitute activity.

Violence and Self-injury.—The formula is: "I can carry out the activity if I violently attack the other individual of whom I am afraid." In other instances it is: "Only if I let him hurt me or if I hurt myself can I derive pleasure from the activity." Here belong sadism and masochism in genital activity. The individual can obtain pleasure only, in the case of sadism, if he hurts his partner, or, in the case of masochism, if he is hurt. In the extreme form such attitudes may lead to "lust murders."

Revival of Earlier Forms of Behavior (Regression).—The formula here is: "I am not able to cope with the situation in the form of action that is required. I am not able to obtain safety and satisfaction by pursuing my present goals, or pursuing them with my present means. I will therefore pursue goals which I had once before, and with which I was more successful, or I'll pursue my present goals in a manner that at one time was successful."

A good illustration of this type of phenomenon is the recurrence of enuresis (bed-wetting) in children. A child who is well trained in cleanliness may start wetting his bed again when a difficult situation arises. Such a situation is frequently the birth of another child. The older child, who previously felt secure, now feels seriously threatened in regard to the affection and love of his parents. The bed-wetting is partly a direct expression of anxiety, partly an attempt to show his need of parental attention and help, and partly an attempt to be a helpless infant and thus get all of the parents' affection. In such a situation a child may also want the bottle or the breast again.

The revival of earlier goals or of earlier modes of solution is at times equally obvious in the adult. It is manifest in some aspects of his outlook on life, in his fantasies and dreams, as one part of his reaction to situations of stress. Instead of enuresis, the adult may have bladder discomfort and have to get up repeatedly at night. He may have dreams of being fed, or of being a child who is given candy and ice cream by an adult.

"Coping Mechanisms" and Abnormality

Some of the mechanisms we have discussed in this chapter are clearly psychopathic; others are much less so. Still others can often be seen in quite healthy people. If we had attempted to make a complete list of coping mechanisms we should eventually have come to realize that *all* behavior, normal or abnormal, copes in one way or another with situational or character difficulties. Furthermore, as we pursued the subject to its ultimate in human nature, we should also have realized that *all* behavior mechanisms have a purpose (or purposes) which may or may not be immediately apparent.

We have been speaking, then, not of purely pathological matters, but rather of general dynamic principles of behavior which may also be perceived in the realm of psychopathology.

SUGGESTED READINGS

The best clinical readings on this subject, which is ordinarily labeled "Defense Mechanisms," are Anna Freud's *The Ego and the Mechanisms of Defense* (270), and Horney's *The Neurotic Personality of Our Time* (366). Another very important book recommended for general reading in psychopathology is Kurt Goldstein's *The Organism* (311). D. M. Levy's monograph (473) on his experiments with sibling rivalry gives the most empirical picture we have of these reactions to conflict and frustration. Erickson's article, "Experimental demonstrations of the psychopathology of everyday life" (226), is a good experimental study of human beings; and Maier's *Studies of Abnormal Behavior in the Rat* (521), a study of animals. See also Mowrer's "An experimental analogue of 'regression'" (577). A long-standing classic relating to this subject is Veblen's *The Theory of the Leisure Class* (758). This may demonstrate how much of one's own behavior subserves unconscious aims.

CHAPTER XI

EXPERIMENTALLY PRODUCED BEHAVIOR DISTURBANCES

~~~~~~~~~~~~~~~~~~~~~~~~~~~~~~~~~~~~

During the course of his many experiments with conditioned reflexes, Pavlov made the following observation. He conditioned a dog to respond with salivation to the stimulus of a circle presented visually, and he also conditioned the same animal against an oval presented visually. That is, the dog was given food when a circle was presented but not when an oval was presented. Accordingly it salivated to the circle stimulus but not to the oval stimulus. Pavlov then tried to determine the limits of the animal's visual discrimination by making the oval more and more circular and seeing at what point the discrimination between circle and oval broke down. This is known as the discrimination technique. Pavlov observed that some animals "broke down" at this point; that is, they showed behavior disturbances which led him to speak of "neurotic reactions." For instance, the dog whined and howled, struggled against restraint, and became useless as an experimental animal. This led Pavlov to conclude that if an animal is strongly motivated and tries hard to solve a problem that is unsolvable or beyond its capacity to solve, it may break down and become "neurotic."

This interesting experiment has given inspiration to a host of other workers in both Russia and America; furthermore, at the present time this technique is one of the most promising for the elucidation of abnormal behavior. It assumes added importance because, as we have said, so few experimental approaches to abnormal behavior are as yet available. For this reason one should be aware of what is going on in this field, which as yet holds promise rather than actual achievement. It is well to be cautious in interpreting this type of data. For instance, the term "experimental neurosis" seems to us to be unwarranted on the general grounds that a direct carry-over from work with animals to conclusions about human beings is theoretically dangerous. Moreover, the word neurosis has special connotations, particularly subjective ones—loss of the feeling of well-being, etc.—which cannot be determined in animals. All we can say is that abnormal behavior disturbances can be observed in animals under certain conditions. Witkin (790) has pointed out that these disturbances in animals might with equal validity be characterized as "psychotic" rather than "neurotic." We shall use the expression "experimental behavior disturbance" rather than "experimental neurosis" to describe these experiments. (See also Cook's papers.)

Most of the studies dealing with behavior disturbances in animals have been based on a common technique. The animal is most often required to adjust to a situation which calls for antagonistic and hence mutually exclusive reactions; it is put into a severe conflict situation. In Pavlov's experiment, for example, the positive stimulus (a circle) and the negative stimulus (an ellipse) called respectively for salivation and its inhibition. When the dog was presented with a stimulus that was neither markedly circular nor elliptical, the simultaneous demands to salivate and not to salivate constituted a conflict from which marked behavior disturbances developed.

Similar experiments have been carried on in this country with other animals by Liddell and his co-workers. In their extensive and careful studies they have employed techniques similar to those used by Pavlov. Thus in one study (See Chapter V) Anderson and Liddell determined in sheep the limits of discrimination between two rates of metronome beats and established a conditioned foreleg flexion to the higher frequency. When the lower frequency was increased so that further discrimination was impossible, the same kind of conflict situation was created for the sheep as for Pavlov's dogs. The positive and negative stimuli were so similar that either one was adequate for the incompatible responses of flexion and extension of the foreleg. The impossibility of making simultaneously such antagonistic responses led to behavior disturbances.

In another experiment these two investigators obtained the same results by requiring the animal to make antagonistic adjustments to very similar stimuli presented in rapid succession rather than simultaneously.

Curtis, another of Liddell's co-workers, also used a conflict situation technique with a pig. If the animal opened the lid of a food box after a 600-cycle tone it received food, but if it did so after a 750-cycle tone, it received a shock. When the pig became unable to discriminate between the two tones, it developed behavior disturbances. In a similar recent experiment by Cook with rats (144), marked changes in behavior again resulted. Dworkin's work with cats and dogs (208) is also of interest in this connection.

Maier's work with rats demands attention because it brought out similar behavior disturbances without using the conditioning technique. His rats were trained on the so-called jumping apparatus in which the animal is forced to jump from a platform to one of two windows, each of which is marked differently. If the rat jumps through the right window it obtains food; if it jumps at the wrong one, the window does not open and the rat falls to the floor. After this training, Maier's animals were shifted to a one-window situation where only one stimulus was presented at a time; regardless of which stimulus was presented, the animal was forced to jump by means of a blast of compressed air. When various modifications in procedure forced the rat to respond to a stimulus card which it had previously been trained to avoid, a singularly abnormal mode of behavior resulted. The following excerpts are quoted from Maier (521, p. 13):

"On the last trial of this day, this rat, without warning and without showing resistance, leaped out of the side of the apparatus and showed an intense neurotic pattern of activity." This neurotic pattern in the rat consists of an active phase and a passive phase. The active phase consists of the following stages: "1. leaving the jumping platform suddenly with a large undirected leap; 2. running at great speed in a circular path on the floor of the room for several seconds; 3. lying on its side showing violent convulsive movements of legs and tail . . . ; 4. resuming locomotion but this consists largely of a succession of hops (like a rabbit), most of which are straight upward rather than forward; 5. between hops and following them, exhibiting marked tics involving the head, the right foreleg, the left foreleg, or all of these." A state of complete passivity follows this active phase. Here there is limpness, waxy flexibility, etc. This very dramatic change in behavior is entirely disordered, showing no semblance of organization. Further, as nearly as can be made out, it has no adaptive value whatsoever; it seems to serve no purpose or useful function and resembles what we have called catastrophic breakdown in the human. See also Goldstein (311).

The Role of Defense and Avoidance Reactions (Substitute Activities)

Ordinarily when animals or humans are presented with a difficult problem or a conflict situation they will respond by various activities which are either avoiding, attacking, or defensive in character, the first two being the most primitive and easily elicited. In other words, when an animal cannot respond with complete adequacy to a problem situation, its first tendency is to run away from it or, in the case of certain species, to show rage and attacking responses. If these reactions are impossible, various others may be made; these may be called substitute reactions. For example, the animal may refuse to face the problem (see page 50), or react to it in a regressive way, as by forming position habits, etc. Maier lists the following avoidance and substitute reactions in his rats: (1) active resistance to jumping; (2) persistent position habits (invariably jumping to the left or to the right); (3) "abortive jumping," i.e., a weak jump in which the animal hit the stimulus card with its side rather than head on, this being a compromise response because the resulting fall was made easier (this is almost as if the animal admitted defeat before jumping); (4) jumping to the side arm or other parts of the apparatus rather than to the window containing the stimulus card, thus avoiding a direct response to the conflict situation. Similarly, Curtis's pigs showed prolonged rigidity and unresponsiveness as well as other ingenious indirect responses to the situation.

It will be observed that all the animals used in these experiments are mild and relatively docile. This is possibly the reason why avoidance reactions have been more evident than attack reactions. Presumably in more savage animals the attack reaction rather than the avoidance reaction would be the first response to a conflict situation. During a series of delayed reaction experiments by Harlow and Maslow on infra-human primates, one very savage baboon was used as an experimental animal. When it reached the limit of its capacity to delay its response, the animal developed behavior disturbances similar in some ways to those described above. For instance it refused to respond to the experimental situation, and it developed a tic-like reaction—a simultaneous swaying and jumping—that kept up hour after hour; in addition, there were certain other changes. When presented with the experimental situation the animal was apt to go into a fury and dash itself against the bars trying to scratch or bite the experimenter. It often snatched the cups on the table, ripped them loose from their strings, and bit them to pieces in a wild rage. It attacked the keeper of the zoo to whom it had hitherto been friendly. Later, the mere sight of the experimenter was enough to throw the animal into a wild, screaming, disorganized rage. Possibly such attack reactions would appear more often in the literature if wilder animals were used.

DISTINCTION BETWEEN SUBSTITUTE AND CATASTROPHIC BEHAVIOR

There is obviously a difference between these substitute activities of avoidance, attack, or defense, and the complete "neurotic" breakdown behavior described by Maier, for example. For one thing, the substitute activities are functional and organized; they serve a purpose, that is, they solve the problem in a way, even if it is not a good way. Breakdown behavior, on the other hand, is non-functional, serves no purpose, and in no sense solves the problem. We prefer to use Goldstein's term, "catastrophic behavior," for this latter type of behavior (311).

On the basis of his very extensive investigations of human beings with brain lesions, Goldstein distinguishes between substitute and catastrophic reactions. Catastrophic behavior he characterizes as "inadequate, disorderly, inconstant, inconsistent, and embedded in physical and mental *shock*. . . . After a catastrophic reaction [the patient's] reactivity is likely to be impeded for a longer or shorter interval." Goldstein also points out that, as far as possible, his patients avoid all situations which might occasion catastrophic reactions. "The avoidance of dangerous situations is brought about especially by the patient's tendency to maintain the situation with which he can cope. When we try to force him into a situation which he has identified as catastrophic, he deliberately seeks to escape through some other performance, a substitute performance. . . . The significance of these substitute performances rests not so much in their contents, as in the fact that this mode of response lies within the capacities of the patient and that as it takes place nothing can happen which might lead to catastrophe. At a certain stage of disintegration these substitute actions are the last resource, the only means by which existence can be maintained. In this sense, they are meaningful, they enable the organism to come to terms with the environment, at least in some way."[1]

---

[1] K. Goldstein, *The Organism*, American Book Company, New York, 1939, pp. 37-41.

Thus in human beings as well as animals there is a strong attempt to avoid all catastrophic situations, that is, situations that would result in complete breakdown and disorganization. The behavior observed in Maier's rats is analogous to a catastrophic or breakdown reaction in human beings, rather than to the ordinary continuing neurotic adjustment. The extreme anxiety attack which a neurotic may suffer when his system of defenses seems about to break down is an example of a catastrophic reaction in a human being. An individual who suffers from claustrophobia (fear of enclosed spaces) would probably also react catastrophically if forced into a small room and locked up.

Effect of Limitation of Substitute Responses

Witkin (790) has pointed out that the final behavior breakdown does not occur in experimental animals until their substitute activities have been limited or made impossible. He calls this "restriction of the fields of behavior." The conflict situation is most disruptive when substitute modes of behavior have been made impossible and the animal is forced to come to grips with the unsolvable problem. Anderson and Liddell originally expressed this in terms of physical restraint; but it is now apparent that it is better expressed in terms of limiting substitute activities in general, and, more specifically, of making impossible the avoiding, attacking, and defensive substitutes for more efficient problem-solving behavior.

A final prerequisite for the production of catastrophic behavior disturbances is that the animal be strongly motivated, that for some reason solving the problem or reacting successfully be important. The animal can be frustrated only if it is strongly interested in achieving the goal. To give a perhaps too simple example, an animal that is not very hungry will not be affected by an insoluble problem in obtaining food, but will either fail entirely to react to it or react in an apathetic way. Similarly, in human beings, one precipitating element in neurotic reactions is that the unsolvable problem or unbearable conflict be important, one that *must* be solved in one way or another.

Constitutional Predisposition to Behavior Disturbance

Pavlov found that only extremely excitable or "inhibitable" types of dogs were susceptible to experimental neurosis, that the more placid or average animals did not succumb even when placed in the same situation. This original observation of the relation of constitution to breakdown opens up a fascinating field both for speculation, of which there has been plenty, and for experimentation, of which there has been little. The possibilities for the latter are unquestionably extremely important; for if constitutional predispositions to breakdown are discovered, this may give us what has been sought for so eagerly, the ability to predict what will happen to a person in the future, and as a consequence the possibility of heading off a breakdown before it occurs. (See Hilgard and Marquis [346].)

All that can be said at present is that no such predispositions have ever been adequately proved in the human being. We may sum up the present knowledge in this field by saying that in human beings there is no known—or at least no adequately proved—correlation between body form, endocrine constitution, or physiological constitution and specific types of functional psychic disorders. The available research indicates, however, that the possibility of such correlations is not to be excluded.

Luria's Experiments with Artificial Neurosis in Human Beings

For obvious reasons, experimentation in the field of experimental neurosis has been done more often with animal than human subjects. Of the work with human beings, Luria's experiments (512) are outstanding, particularly the one we shall discuss here. This experiment consisted essentially in suggesting under hypnosis that an unacceptable or horrifying action had been committed. The subject was then awakened, having forgotten what had happened in the hypnotic trance, and was tested by various techniques to see how possible it is to detect the artificially induced conflict. Luria writes as follows:

"The person under test, K., a student of obstetrics, twenty-three years old, is in a fairly deep hypnotic sleep, and it is suggested to her that a woman comes to see her with the request to produce in her an abortion, which K. has no right to do. The suggestion meets an obstacle in her. The doctor says, 'You are sitting at home and there is a woman who comes to see you and implores you to perform an abortion on her and that nobody will ever know it. She offers you seven tchervontsi (thirty-five dollars). You hesitate because this is prohibited, but later you agree.' The person under test interrupts and says: 'I will not do it.' The doctor says: 'But I suggest to you that you should agree.' K.: 'I tell you I will not.' The Doctor: 'The woman is imploring. She has no other way out and you are agreeing.' K.: 'No.' The Doctor: 'You have agreed and that woman has gone away.' The person under test easily feels this suggestion; her face changes, she trembles, makes restless movements on the couch, and she is ready to cry. After the suggestion, the subject is awakened; to the question of how she feels she answers that she feels very bad, that something disagreeable has happened, but she does not know what."[1]

In another experiment, Luria suggested the following situation:

"You are in great need of money. You go to a friend in order to borrow from him; he is not at home. You decide to wait in his room and suddenly notice on his bureau a wallet fat with money. You open it and find many five-ruble notes. You make a decision; you quickly take the wallet and conceal it on your person. You cautiously go outside and look around to see if you are detected. You have stolen money and now you are afraid that there will be a search in your home and that they will discover you."

The following situation was suggested in the third situation used by Luria:

[1] This and the following two excerpts are from L. A. Luria, *Nature of Human Conflict*, Liveright, New York, 1932.

"You are sitting in your room and are studying. A child of your neighbor's, a boy of about six, comes into your room. He shouts and disturbs your studies. You ask him to stop; he does not listen to you. You get angry and, forgetting yourself, take a stick and beat the boy, first on his back and then on his head. There are some wounds on his head and he cries. You feel very much ashamed and you do not understand how such a thing could happen to you, how you could beat up a child, and you try to forget it."

Various techniques showed that the subjects who accepted these suggestions were in a state of conflict, and they behaved in a disorganized fashion; this latter was shown by free association tests and motor tests, for example. Those subjects who could not be forced to accept these suggestions behaved very differently. They showed some disturbance, to be sure, but this did not seem to affect the entire personality; rather, it appeared to be an external or superficial reaction to an unpleasant situation perceived in the outside world rather than within themselves.

A paper by Krasnogorski (444) describes a number of experiments of the Pavlovian type with children. Some of the symptoms of disturbance brought out in these experiments are taciturnity, drowsiness, anger, sleep, negativism, rudeness, fighting, crying, etc. In the main, however, we must regard these experiments only as a beginning, even though a very promising one. Sweeping conclusions are not yet warranted.

SUGGESTED READINGS

The classical work here, of course, is Pavlov's *Conditioned Reflexes* (602). A good summary of all the conditioned reflex experiments in this field is found in Chapter XII of Hilgard and Marquis' *Conditioning and Learning* (346). Maier's little book (521) is interesting reading. Outstanding experimental papers are those by Liddell and his collaborators (29, 30, 494, 495). For a more philosophical organismic approach, Goldstein's *The Organism* (311) is recommended, as is also Luria's *Nature of Human Conflict* (512).

CHAPTER XII

THE PRECIPITATION AND MAINTENANCE OF PSYCHIC ILLNESS

There may be found in the psychopathological individual: (1) suffering and unhappiness; (2) certain manifestations called symptoms; (3) impaired efficiency; (4) impairment of the ability to enjoy; (5) lack of adequate insight.

Futhermore, the periods of intense and acute reaction can be differentiated from the periods during which some complaints are present but the individual somehow "gets by." During both these periods patients have preferred modes of reacting—they may be extremely sensitive to criticism, for example—they may also seek certain situations and avoid others, and want certain types of relationships. Even when their actions are roughly in harmony with the social norms, the inner processes by which they perform these actions show certain distortions in character structure; thus, when doing good work they aggrandize themselves or perhaps disparage its significance. The sum total of these constant modes of behavior and reaction, in both external and internal aspects, we call personality or character.

CATASTROPHIC EXPECTATION; DEFENSIVE AND AMELIORATIVE DEVICES

As has been repeatedly stated, the nuclear constellation in psychopathological disturbances of any severity is the expectation of a catastrophic state of helplessness, involving feelings of rejection, worthlessness, condemnation, annihilation, and complete frustration. This parallels the helplessness that can be deduced in the "experimental neurosis" of animals.

The patient may manifest this catastrophic expectation in a variety of situations, such as complicated social tasks, contact with other people, bodily gratification, relaxation, and sleep. Usually he does not succumb to it; instead, he uses various devices to escape or diminish his distress, to strengthen himself and to reach his goal; in other words, he does the best he can in a bad situation.

Some of the patient's symptoms and character traits are the direct result of emotional stress, anxiety, tension, anger, or discouragement and, as such, serve no purpose. Many others are the result of the various defensive, ameliorative, and goal-reaching devices mentioned in Chapter X, often combined with the direct results of emotional stress. The variety of the symptoms depends on the dominant aspect of the patient's fears and on the ameliorative devices he uses. Another important factor in determining this diversity is the fact that functional disturbance may be manifest in various areas.

AREAS OF DISTURBED FUNCTION

Patients suffer profound disturbances in regard to their image of themselves and of others, in regard to their feelings of strength, and in regard to particular situations which may possibly involve catastrophic fear. They feel safer in some fields of activity than in others and therefore they seek such fields. This latter fact contributes considerably to the differences in symptomatology in various patients. It is important to differentiate here, however, between the situation in which the disturbance is genuinely aroused, and the forms in which the disturbance expresses itself.

The disturbance may manifest itself in the sphere in which it really arises. Thus the patient may do poor work, make serious errors, be tense, and become exhausted because his fear of displaying initiative, self-assertion, and rivalry makes it dangerous to succeed. In such instances, the patient's image and concept of himself (self-esteem) and of others, e.g., his superior, his rivals (insecurity feelings) are involved.

Even though the disturbance manifests itself where the trouble really lies, its expression may be greatly distorted. This is particularly true of obsessional manifestations. Thus a woman may feel completely dominated and threatened by her husband and unconsciously be very angry at him. Whereas in her behavior she is tender toward him, admires him, and caters to all his wishes, she has such intense thoughts of hurting him—cutting his throat, for example—that she does not dare have sharp knives about the house.

The manifestations may be completely displaced. Thus the patient may be afraid of crossing the street or of high places, although he knows perfectly well that no "real" dangers are connected with these situations. Such displaced manifestation occurs in response to genuine difficulties in other situations in one of two ways: (1) The situation of which the individual is afraid is indispensable to the performance of some part of the function that is causing the difficulty. For example, a man whose office is on the twentieth floor of a building was thrown into a sudden panic. Investigation showed that he was afraid to be close to his wife and to assume responsibilities, and that she wanted him to earn more money. He was suddenly struck by the thought that he might suddenly become ill, the elevator might not stop, and he might not be able to get out of the building. (2) The situation or the object represents to the patient unconsciously what he is afraid of in an entirely different situation. This same man at times became panicky when he entered the subway station because he felt the walls close in on him. The narrow, confined space unconsciously meant to him his wife's crushing condemnation which would be disastrous and from which he could not escape if she decided to avenge herself for his anger toward her.

Partial Goals

The various means—the partial substitute devices—which the patient uses to attain his goals come in themselves to represent important goals for him, and he is emotionally disturbed if these partial goals are threatened or unattainable. For example, the patient may seek complete dependence as a means of attaining safety, protection, and help in satisfying his main needs. If the individual on whom the patient depends does something which he interprets as rejection, he reacts with anger, fear, or a feeling of worthlessness and humiliation. Similarly, a patient may want perfection in all his activities and superiority in every situation as a means of protecting himself against helplessness, defeat, and fear, and strengthening himself in attaining his primary goal—success and pleasure. If anything threatens his perfection, he does not fear only helplessness, he genuinely resents this threat. In a sense, the state of perfection has become a goal in itself. From this it is clear that every significant act in which the patient engages is not directed toward one single aim, but implies a complexity of partial goals and devices.

Vicious Circles

The patient often uses contradictory devices for amelioration or for reaching goals and therefore has conflicting needs. Thus he may want both to be completely dependent and to attack violently. He wants to escape the consequences of both these attitudes, but needs emotional warmth and closeness. Similarly, a patient may want to debase himself, but at the same time use the self-aggrandizement device.

Even the initial psychological constellation of a patient's strivings may have elements of conflict and danger in it. For example, a child wants to reach for a toy in the presence of his severe and humiliating mother. Because of the whole relationship with the mother, this impulse contains the unconscious constellation: "I can do this only with her permission because I am weak and dependent on her; but she will not give me permission." This necessitates either carrying through the wish defiantly and chancing her disapproval, or asking her for permission and risking her refusal and the accompanying humiliation. Either case means further conflict for the child. If he takes the toy he faces possible catastrophe. If he asks for it he faces possible refusal and humiliation which are catastrophic in character. Even if he gets it he will feel somewhat relieved and gratified but the tension will remain because he will feel humiliated at having cowered before his mother, will still feel worthless and unloved, and may expect future disapproval. If he renounces his desire, he still will not feel that he is someone, that he is loved by his mother, that he has security, that he can depend on her; hence renunciation adds to the resentment toward her already created by humiliation and lack of love. The response to such a situation, with its immediate implications and its ensuing conflicts, thus creates in him an emotional constellation which cannot be relieved by any adequate action. The tension occasioned by his earlier experiences and by this new experience continues to increase, thus preparing him for conflicting reactions to new situations. The conflict as such also intensifies and maintains the feeling of helplessness and of inability to master the situation, and thus contributes to and renews the expectation of catastrophe.

In such a chronic situation as the above, practically every one of the child's attempts to reach a goal will either fail completely or be only partially successful. With the tensions and conflicts which remain, there remain also the problems with which the individual is unable to cope. He has both a feeling of helplessness and an actual impairment of function, a psychological state which implies renewal and maintenance of catastrophic expectations. This sequence, which is a "vicious circle" (Horney [366]), is one of the most important factors in the persistence and recurrence of abnormal psychological manifestations. The concept implies that the patient takes certain measures to enable himself to function or to escape catastrophe, but that these measures renew his difficulties if he fails, and even, to some extent, if he succeeds. This concept can be applied both to internal psychological experiences and to the patient's actual relationships with other people.

Both types of vicious circle are present in childhood. The child who reacts with the basic psychopathological constellation to parental handling does not react merely to distressing situations. The child's evaluation of the parent and of his acts becomes distorted and magnified. Furthermore, his own behavior changes and becomes the stimulus for parental mishandling. Thus there develops a constant interplay and interlocking in the psychological problems of the child and the parent.

Internal Vicious Circles.—Complete dependence leads to expectations which are continually thwarted because of their extreme and irrational nature; this leads to anger. Complete dependence also goes with loss of self-esteem, the assumption of being looked down upon; this likewise leads to anger. Anger, however, means attacking the individual through whose help the patient had hoped to avoid catastrophe. This in turn renews the fear of catastrophe; therefore the patient has to continue his dependence on this individual, but to an even greater extent.

If the chief ameliorative device is violent counterattack and attempt to vanquish the enemy, the vicious circle is again at work. The patient expects a similar attack from the foe; but, since he is defenseless, this would mean catastrophe; therefore he has to continue his attack.

Since the renunciation of a desire is based on the expectation of catastrophe, it is usually felt as unfair. The reaction to this is anger, through whose anticipated consequences the fear of catastrophe is renewed. For this reason renunciation has to be continued.

Self-aggrandizement leads to the fear of being resented, attacked, and humiliated by others, which in turn renews the feeling of failure, of catastrophe. Therefore self-aggrandizement has to be continued to an even greater degree.

The individual may not dare to use the genitals in hetero-sexual relations because of fear of failure or injury; and in his attempt to obtain and give love in a special way, he may become homosexual. This lowers his self-esteem, not only because of cultural ideals which he himself espouses, but also because the very act of retreat is humiliating to him. Thus, even though he may obtain considerable satisfaction from the relationship, his feeling of humiliation, of helplessness, and weakness is renewed, and with it his conflicts, and increased feeling of helplessness, and the fear of catastrophic situations. Hence he has to continue this relationship in spite of feeling increasingly worse.

Environmental Vicious Circles.—The patient's behavior fol-lows certain lines and patterns implied in the relatively subjec-tive attitudes mentioned above. He enters into relationships to satisfy the needs implied in those attitudes, but the reactions of other individuals to his behavior are such that in the long run he must maintain the very attitude that causes the difficulty. For example, a patient attempts to maintain his security and freedom from anxiety and to attain his goals by adopting an overbearing and superior attitude. This attitude may be created by internal conflicts and catastrophic anticipations; but the hostile reactions of other people will provide his expectations of catastrophic counterattack with a real basis. Those whom he humiliated and conquered want to humiliate and conquer him. Inasmuch as their success would mean catastrophic defeat for him, he has to continue the same overbearing, attacking, and superior behavior.

Another type of vicious circle develops when the measures used by the patient to allay his anxiety contain false and irra-tional assumptions. A patient wants to relieve his feelings of worthlessness by achievement, let us say; and he expects this to make him loved as he feels he should be loved. The error here is that these measures, even if successful, do not really bring him the love he expected. To secure that, his own emotional structure and his approach to people would have to change; he would have to be able to accept affection when it was offered to him. The result is that, at least partly, he feels disappointment and rejection. But since he again evaluates this in his own terms, the measures he uses are the same as before.

The Role of the External Situation

The intensity and quality of symptoms depend in large measure on the external situation. There may be long periods of time when the situation is such that the patient who has a relatively low intensity of fear and uses adequate ameliorative measures will function well. For instance, he may feel that the complete dependence and help forthcoming from one individual guards him against danger. Under these circumstances, the feelings of disappointment, humiliation, jealousy, anger, etc., are relatively slight, but nevertheless strong enough to force him to remain dependent; by and large he can function well, at least well enough.

To what extent a patient can function well all the time depends on various internal factors. There are people who go from one crisis to another, regardless of their opportunities and circumstances, almost as if they are literally searching for situations which will make them suffer and be unhappy. This will be clearer if we first discuss what happens to an individual who functions relatively well under certain conditions but reacts severely when a new acute situation arises. The factors that are of importance here are threats to vital needs of the personality because of chronic deprivation, frustration, or conflict.

Deprivation, Disappointment, Frustration.—What the individual is deprived of may vary considerably. As a rule it is something which a great many people consider important and significant—a position, a mate, a fortune. Sometimes, however, it lacks this universal significance; it may be merely a small gift which he treasured and admired. Frustrations of this latter type usually cause only distress; there is no serious, generalized breakdown. The significant situation which represents frustration sometimes does not seem frustrating because the individual represses his reactions to it. For example, a man became depressed for some unknown reason over the approaching marriage of his son. Although consciously he did not object to his son's marriage, further investigation made it clear that unconsciously he considered as a catastrophic frustration the "loss" of this son to whom he was deeply attached. The death of one's mate or one's child, termination of an engagement, divorce, being deprived of opportunity to satisfy one's bodily wants are all situations which may represent severe frustration and precipitate more acute breakdowns.

The question now arises as to why frustration of this type is such a disturbing and near-catastrophic event in the patient's life. There are several reasons for this.

What the patient lost satisfied not merely the healthy desire of someone who says, "I want this; I can have it"; rather, it represented the fulfillment of an absolutely vital but "sick" need which enabled him to avoid a catastrophic state.

The individual may have an essential lack of confidence in himself and a feeling of helplessness, and be convinced that he cannot by his own efforts replace what he lost. For example, a woman who is so dependent on her husband that she can make no decision without his help and support will feel that the bottom has fallen out of her whole life if he dies or leaves her.

Frustration frequently results not from a sudden and acute change in the situation but from a gradual change in a continuing situation. Thus the woman who wants unlimited strength and superiority in her husband may constantly look for more and more evidence that he has all the qualities and stamina that she wants him to have. When she begins to realize that he is not the man she thought he was, she feels frustrated, cheated, disappointed. Here a severe conflict situation arises because her hostility toward him is intense, but at the same time she feels dependent on him. As a rule, conflict situations accompany frustration because of the hostility toward the person who is held responsible for the frustration.

Situations of Threat; Acute Conflict.—Other situations which may precipitate an acute breakdown are those in which the patient is exposed to an actual threat, to actual distress. This type of situation is likely to arise when one's superior in work or one's mate is unfair, domineering, and humiliating, or when someone in authority finds himself challenged either by a rival or by his inferiors. In the case of the domineering and humiliating superior or mate, the reaction and its development are as follows: The individual who has a basic fear of feelings of worthlessness and helplessness feels tremendously threatened and expects utter humiliation and enslavement. He reacts to this threat not only with fear but with anger which is proportionate to the tremendously unfair, heartless, and catastrophically threatening manner in which he feels he is being treated. But his anger creates a new difficulty because he feels completely powerless to do anything about the situation; he cannot stand up for his rights or speak up or extricate himself in any way. And thus there arises a state of acute conflict between his feeling of utter helplessness in the face of tremendous threat and his intense resentment and hostility.

A man was a successful salesman as long as he worked in his father's place or for another firm where he was treated fairly. He then became a salesman for still another firm. The manager was a blustering sort of man who always disapproved, never praised, and never gave any credit for performance. The salesman developed dizziness, a moderately high blood pressure, attacks of trembling and of anxiety, particularly when he sat in the barber's chair. His symptoms became so marked that he had to take a vacation. During this period he felt somewhat better, but when he returned to work the symptoms reappeared. Then he went to a psychiatrist who discovered that he felt humiliated and down-trodden all the time; although he resented this intensely, he never protested because he was afraid of counterattack in the form of being discharged. This situation was one of intense conflict. After considerable treatment, the patient became able to demand different treatment, to complain to the owners, and in fact either to put the manager in his place or to look for a better job—steps hitherto impossible because of his feelings of helplessness and worthlessness and the acute conflict situation. Sometimes such a good outcome is impossible if, for instance, there is no possibility of another job. Then psychology can help little or not at all.

Conditions of Continuous Crisis.—As we said earlier, the majority of patients manage to function under favorable circumstances, but get into difficulties when a situation of acute stress arises. This statement must be amplified somewhat. While it may be correct to say that the quality of the patient's needs and conflicts is essentially the same during both the smooth and the acute period, their intensity changes tremendously. Even after the actual external situation of stress is remedied, the patient frequently continues to suffer and have symptoms. In other words, once the breakdown occurs, he may not feel comfortable in situations which he stood very well previously. There are two reasons for this: (1) All of life involves a continuous solving of problems; getting up in the morning, going to sleep at night, attending to bodily wants, seeing other individuals, etc., are all problems in a certain sense. After a severe breakdown all or most of these functions may present *acute* problems or situations of stress for the patient. (2) Because of his acute fear and need, the patient clutters up all his relationships with desires, expectations, and requests which continuously lead to frustration or acute conflict. Or he seeks new relationships for the purpose of fulfilling his needs; constant frustration and acute conflict are the result because of his inflated, unreal expectations from these new relationships or the sick manner in which he handles them. This is essentially the case with individuals who for years go from one self-made crisis to another.

Summary: The Nature of Neurotic Illness

Psychopathology implies that following situations of stress, the individual manifests suffering, symptoms, impaired efficiency, lessened ability for enjoyment, lack of adequate insight.

The most distressing manifestations appear in response to new and difficult situations; but less obvious ones are present before and after the acute periods.

Psychopathological manifestations in general cover a wide variety of phenomena belonging to the sphere of affects, thinking, and volition in an interrelated manner. They may appear in any situation and in connection with any function of the individual: in his behavior and organic function, in the performance of complicated tasks, in relaxation, sleep, etc.

In all neurotic manifestations, the patient's vital needs are involved as well as his evaluation of himself (self-esteem), of other individuals (security feelings), and of the situation with which he has to cope. Thus, one can say that in neurotic manifestations, the patient's whole personality and whole body are involved.

The central motif of psychopathological manifestations is the anticipation of a catastrophic situation with the various colorings of loss of help, approval, and affection; helplessness; bodily injury or pain; humiliation; and the impossibility of satisfying vital bodily needs.

The patient then attempts to diminish his distress, increase his strength, override his fear, and reach certain goals in spite of the fears aroused. He attempts this by means of various devices or "mechanisms."

The patient's needs, goals, and devices have contradictory aspects; that is, they are incompatible with each other.

This leads to a psychological conflict which is present in every psychopathological reaction. Any measure that the patient takes is inadequate to relieve his tension fully; furthermore, it often arouses contradictory needs in him.

For these reasons, regardless of whether the goal is reached or not, a vicious circle of reactions is ordinarily set up. This renews the patient's feeling of helplessness and increases his use of ameliorative devices. These vicious circles are further strengthened by the binding effect of the external situations and the interhuman relations which the patient seeks. The vicious circles are largely responsible for the persistence and recurrence of psychopathological reactions.

The intensity of suffering or the relative well-being of the patient depends to a considerable extent on external situations. If the situation is favorable, the ameliorative devices are relatively effective and the disturbance and distress are kept at a minimum. Furthermore, most patients retain some healthy and well-preserved functions and some shreds of security and self-esteem.

The anticipation of catastrophic situations, together with the use of ameliorative devices, begins in childhood and is maintained throughout life with the aid of vicious circles of reactions. The most important determinant of the catastrophic anticipation is stress and strain in the relationship with the parents. This is intensified by the inevitable vicissitudes of life and by biological and cultural dependence on the parents. (This will be discussed in succeeding chapters.)

Cultural factors in psychopathological reactions exert their effect through interhuman relations in actual situations. The most significant effects of our cultural milieu are determined by the smallness of the family, resulting in an intensification of the dependence on the parents; contradictory emotional and ideal demands—a demand for obedience on the one hand, and for self-assertion and rivalry on the other; forbidding any emphasis on certain bodily activities.

SUGGESTED READINGS

For general reading on the nature of psychopathology and its self-maintenance, the works of Freud and Adler are of paramount importance. The best current works are by Horney (366, 367), Kardiner (421), and Goldstein (311). Pavlov's neurological theories (603) are also recommended. A. Meyer's writings are of a fundamental nature (548-554).

PART III

THE ETIOLOGY OF PSYCHOPATHOLOGY

CHAPTER XIII

GENETIC, CONSTITUTIONAL, AND ENVIRONMENTAL DETERMINERS IN MENTAL DISEASE

Is Mental Disease Inheritable?

Mental diseases have always been held by the folk belief to be hereditary, and this belief has been uncritically accepted by many scientists regardless of the presence or absence of evidence. Much work has been done on this subject, and the results of several vast researches are now available. In spite of this, the question of whether mental disease is inheritable is at present still debatable.

The "Family Line" Hypothesis.—It has long been known that mental disease tends to run in family lines. Statisticians have prepared such careful figures in this connection that it is now possible to predict the future incidence of various mental diseases in a given population. This means that in our society, given certain information about age, sex, nationality, socio-economic status, etc., we can predict from statistical tables the mathematical probability of a particular person's becoming "insane."[1] Furthermore, this probability is raised considerably if the individual in question has an insane sibling or an insane

[1] It should be emphasized that this discussion is concerned mostly with the so-called "functional" psychoses, and not with the organic psychoses. For instance, paresis is known to be the result of a syphilitic invasion of the nervous system; it is not inherited. One disease—Huntington's chorea —is definitely known to be inherited in the Mendelian ratio. However, this disease is so uncommon as to be unimportant in general theoretical considerations.

parent, and even more if two members of his family have been insane. Thus Kallmann (414) has concluded that "the probable recurrence of schizophrenia is 19 times higher in the children of schizophrenics than it is in the general population," and that "the expectancy figures in grandchildren of schizophrenics indicate that their chance of developing schizophrenia is 5 times greater than it is in the general population."

Does this prove that mental disease is hereditary, that it is determined in the genes at the moment of conception? Actually such data prove nothing about heredity. They are merely compatible with the heredity theory. We shall see later that they are equally compatible with an extreme environmentalist position.

Most of the data upon which assumption of the inheritance of mental disease rests are of the "family line" type. Not so long ago certain geneticists, finding that the sons of drunken fathers tended to be drunkards themselves, assumed that drunkenness was hereditary. What they neglected to realize was that father and son or brother and sister usually have also the same or a similar environment. Thus, if one was a drunkard, the other was apt to be one also, simply because of environmental contact and training. But certainly no responsible scientist believes any longer in the inheritance of drunkenness or criminality or bad temper or shiftlessness. The evidence for the inheritance of mental disease is of exactly the same type as that for the possible inheritance of drunkenness, etc. The argument may be made even more forceful by a *reductio ad absurdum*, for one can prove with the same line of reasoning that speaking the English language is hereditary.

In a recent, thorough study, Pollack, Malzberg, and Fuller (613) realized, after careful examination, that their data had little bearing on the question of inheritance of mental disease. However, they definitely dispose of the idea of its inheritance according to Mendelian principles. In addition to their "family line" data, these authors studied carefully correlations of the incidence of schizophrenia and manic-depressive psychosis with

various socio-economic indices. They found "family line" tendencies to be weak with respect to schizophrenia and strong with
respect to manic-depressive psychosis, but they also found
marked correlations with various socio-economic indices.

Kallmann (414) recently made a very careful and extensive
study of the genetics of schizophrenia which proved to be somewhat disconcerting to him, for his data do not accord with his
earlier conclusions. For instance, in spite of the fact that his
researches again disprove the possibility of the Mendelian inheritance of schizophrenia, he still refuses to give up this idea completely. For him, as for other investigators—for example, Landis
and Page (454)—the familiar "family line" type of data still
proves that mental disease is inherited.

These same criticisms apply to Myerson's theory of blastophoria. He examined family lines over a long period of time, and
found some families in which one individual, his son, his grand-
son, his great-grandson and his great-great-grandson had all been
confined in a hospital for mental disease. In examining these
records, Myerson made the important finding that when mental
disease first appeared in a family line, it came late in life and
was apt to be associated with senile changes, e.g., involutional
melancholia, senile psychoses; if it occurred in succeeding generations, it tended to appear earlier and earlier in life and also in
different forms. For example, in the second and third generation
it was perhaps manic-depressive psychosis or dementia praecox,
and in later generations it took the form of feeble-mindedness
leading to sterility and dying out of the family line. These data
—which, incidentally, disproved the Mendelian inheritance of
mental disease—led Myerson to formulate his theory of blastophoria, which holds that mental disease is a product of a general
disturbance or damage to the germ plasm rather than a product of
a specific gene. This blastophoria, he believed, became worse
and worse in succeeding generations. Other workers in this field
have used the rather vague notion of hereditary taint in a similar
way, which is, of course, an interesting hypothesis. Obviously,

however, there has as yet been no satisfactory proof of inheritance of mental disease.

The Practical Importance of the Question.—One consideration that is particularly important for the clinical psychologist is the factor of belief, expectation, and suggestion. Thus if a person who believes that mental disease is hereditary sees one of his parents stricken with it, the thought will occur to him that he also will fall prey to it. The more firmly he believes this, the greater his fear and perhaps the greater his chances of developing the disease. The following case illustrates this, and indicates that the fear and expectation following a psychotic reaction in one's family may be a potent force in bringing on psychosis in oneself.

A boy whose father was confined to a mental hospital with dementia praecox had worried about the possibility of becoming insane ever since his father's confinement. He was regarded by the people who knew him as queer, eccentric, lacking in common sense and sense of humor. The fact that he worried about the possibility of insanity was clearly shown by his hesitation in marrying and his later reluctance to have children. However, he was assured by various psychologists and his own reading that he would not necessarily become psychotic. He was successful in handling major problems of his life, did well economically and, helped by the reassurances and treatment of a psychologist, slowly became a better and more normal person. Suddenly one day he was notified that his sister had been confined to an asylum with dementia praecox. Immediately all his psychological gains were wiped out and he became once again the stiff, humorless, unemotional, withdrawn person that he had been. Conversation with him showed that his fear of insanity had slowly died away but had come back redoubled when his sister became ill. As a young man he would have been diagnosed possibly as pre-psychotic; just before his sister became ill he would have been diagnosed as normal; after her illness he would again have been diagnosed as possibly pre-psychotic.

The foregoing remarks must not be considered an exhaustive

or definite discussion. We have not mentioned many other lines of evidence. It has been our intention only to sow the seeds of a healthy skepticism in the student, for he is apt, in such problems, to make up his mind too rapidly and with inadequate evidence.

THE RELATIONSHIP BETWEEN MENTAL DISEASE AND SOCIAL DISORGANIZATION

The Work of the Chicago School of Sociologists.—A long series of intensive sociological studies of the city of Chicago have indicated many correlations between various indices of social pathology and urban areas. Generally the city was found to be organized in a concentric zone pattern. Zone 1 was the amusement and bright-light area, and here were found the hoboes, the prostitutes, the drug addicts, and other people without financial or home stability; Zone 2 was the slum area; Zone 3 contained inexpensive private residences and Zone 4 the more expensive private residences; Zone 5 was the zone of the commuters and wealthier people in general. Extremely high correlations were found between these zones and the incidence of juvenile delinquency, tuberculosis, venereal disease, drug addiction, crimes, vices, and other indices of social disorganization or pathology. In every case the highest percentage occurred in Zone 1, the next highest in Zone 2, and so on, with the lowest percentage in Zone 5.

This kind of data indicates that a section of a city has a character of its own which, at least from a statistical point of view, is independent of the individual characteristics of the people who move into and out of it. This is substantiated by such findings as the following: The social pathological statistics for a city area remain roughly the same over a long period of years, in spite of the fact that different waves of immigration pass through it. In one case, for instance, five different national groups successively occupied one section; yet the statistics for that area remained the same. As each national group moved out of the area and into another, it took on the characteristics of the new area. Thus an immigrant group in which crime was absent became criminal when it moved into an area with a high crime rate, but ceased being criminal when it moved into a non-criminal area. Another equally important fact is that a differential study of the Negro group in Chicago shows that the Negroes living in Zone 1 show the characteristics of this zone, whereas those living in Zone 2 or Zone 3 show respectively the characteristics of those zones.

The Faris and Dunham Study.—Faris and Dunham (231) have recently reported the results of their sociological study of mental disease in Chicago. This brilliant study shows clearly the relation between mental disease and urban areas. The figures on the occurrence of mental disease in general indicate the same pattern of distribution shown in earlier studies for poverty, unemployment, juvenile delinquency, adult criminality, suicide, family desertion, infant mortality, communicable diseases, and general mortality. That is, there is a regular decrease from the center to the periphery of the city. Further analyses of the same sort were then made for specific categories of mental disease. Schizophrenia in general showed the "typical" distribution pattern of mental disease as a whole; but analysis of the main forms of schizophrenia brought out some differences. For example, the rate of incidence of paranoid schizophrenia was highest in the rooming-house district; that of catatonic schizophrenia, in first-generation immigrant neighborhoods. In general, catatonic schizophrenia is correlated as perfectly with the zone pattern of the city as is the paranoid form. The same typical correlations with the zones of the city (with minor variations) were also found for alcoholic psychoses, senile psychoses, and drug addiction. The distribution of manic-depressive psychosis was completely different. This showed practically no correlation with city zones, indicating that while schizophrenia is a poor man's disease, manic-depression strikes rich and poor impartially.

Such data as these, of course, do not *prove* any causal relations between mental disease and socio-economic factors, but
indicate only that they are correlated. Nor do they necessarily
prove that heredity has nothing to do with schizophrenia; they
indicate only that the same underlying factors that give rise to
poverty, crime, and disease also give rise to all the mental diseases studied by Faris and Dunham, with the notable exception
of manic-depressive reactions. Such data are also useful in sup-
plying hypotheses around which we can organize crucial research that may finally answer the question: Can we get rid
of mental disease by sterilizing people or by giving them better
living conditions? The only hypothesis that Faris and Dunham
allow themselves to formulate is suggested by the extremely high
relationship between paranoid schizophrenia and social isolation.

It is generally conceded by psychiatrists that schizophrenia is
usually a withdrawing from the environment or a loss of contact
with it. Faris and Dunham point out that this withdrawing may
be forced upon the individual by social conditions. They postulate three steps: (1) the normal sociability characteristic of the
child; (2) the rejection of this sociability or the lack of opportunity to express it, as when one lives in an area where one has
no friends; (3) the giving up and withdrawal. Paranoid schizophrenia was found in tremendously high percentages in the
hobo sections and in those rooming-house areas where friendless
bachelors lived alone in tiny hall bedrooms. Opportunities for
social communication are undoubtedly necessary for normal psy'
chological and social development, and it is obvious that an unfavorable social environment might mean the withdrawal of
such opportunities. Without doubt, mental diseases appear to
be more prevalent where the population is mobile and heterogene-
ous than where it is stable and homogeneous, and where life
conditions are complex and precarious rather than simple and
secure. In this connection Plant's finding (612) that high
mobility—i.e., much moving from place to place—is correlated
with insecurity in children is of interest. One very unexpected

finding that indicates the great complexity of the question with which we are dealing is that there was no apparent increase in mental disease during the financial depression which began in 1929. (On this point see also Landis and Page [454].)

HEREDITY AND CONSTITUTION

Now that the complexity of the problem and the inadequate answers given by researches thus far have been indicated, what can be said about the present state of opinion in this field? There is another line of research which will help in our thinking about the problem, even though nothing final is *proved* thereby. Where adequate research has been done on the relative importance of heredity and environmental factors in various other fields of psychology, it has always been found that there was a complex interrelationship between hereditary, constitutional, and environmental factors. Such a piling up of the data in other fields may legitimately lead us to expect that the findings will be similar in the field of mental disease. Ultimately, then, we may expect the discovery of a complex interrelationship among hereditary, constitutional, and environmental factors, all of which work together to produce mental disease.

The term "constitutional factors" does not imply that an individual always reacts in a certain way under any and all circumstances. It means rather that under given circumstances and in response to given stimuli, he is more likely to react in a certain way; he might react quite differently under other circumstances. Furthermore, "constitutional factors" implies the normal range of reaction tendencies. In other words, the question is not how an individual who is born without a thyroid gland will react, in comparison with an individual normal in this respect, but rather what differences in reaction tendencies are shown by people who are physically and psychologically, at least in the beginning, within the normal range.

There is little question that individuals have different congenital tendencies to react, and that one person can stand certain hardships and stresses and use certain functions for compensation, consolation, and reestablishment of self-esteem better than another one can (although here also there is too little experimentation). Thus a constitutional factor is involved (or assumed) in the question whether under certain hardships an individual will break down with a severe neurosis in childhood or in adulthood.

Differences in reaction tendencies—to feeding, to training, and to discipline, for example—can be observed in infants immediately after birth. The difficult problem, however, is to formulate these differences and to identify the factors on which they depend. As yet, this has not been done satisfactorily.[1]

It seems to us that a more promising lead in the field of constitutional-characterological correlations is found in the observation of infants. For instance Ribble (636) has reported that the rejecting or accepting way in which a mother nurses her newborn baby seems to create different attitudes toward feeding, the breast, the mother, etc., even in the first few days of life. Mead (539) has made similar observations with primitive children. Maslow has observed in six infants that the reaction to illness seems to be what may be called a generalized insecurity—much crying and whining, fearfulness, restlessness, easy startling, feeding disturbances, vomiting, the ceasing of smiling and laughing, an exclusive and desperate clinging to the mother, a fear of strangers, crying tantrums, etc. This syndrome comes sud-

---

[1] On the basis of extensive measurements, Kretschmer (445) differentiated among "pyknic," "asthenic" ("leptosome"), and "athletic" types. The pyknic type is characterized by a tendency to overweight, a large round chest and short neck. The asthenic type is characterized by a tendency to underweight and a flat chest. The muscular or athletic type is long-limbed. Many patients with manic-depressive psychoses belong to the pyknic type. Patients suffering from dementia praecox are more often asthenic and athletic. The psychological value of such a classification, however, is questionable. Many workers in the field consider this differentiation over-simplified. In this connection, see also Sheldon's attempt (706) to classify individuals on the basis of a number of measurements (head, arms, chest, abdomen, etc.). This seems to be a much more careful and sophisticated approach than Kretschmer's.

denly and disappears almost as suddenly in a short illness, but persists for a considerable period if the illness is longer. In one child with a severe congenital illness, the syndrome was observed from birth, and disappeared very slowly as the child's condition improved. Apparently such a reaction does not have to be learned but is an innate response to this most elemental of all threats. The Dollards have observed similar reactions and come to a similar conclusion.

Thus an intermediate stand between extreme environmentalism and extreme hereditarianism is necessary. This will probably not be at the midpoint, however, for the tremendous weight of evidence which is steadily piling higher and higher indicates that we shall have to lean considerably toward the environmentalist side.

What would this mean for mental disease? It would mean that a decrease in the incidence of mental disease could be expected as living conditions were improved, but that it could never be expected to disappear completely, however perfect the living conditions. Living conditions and environment here include more than houses, bathtubs, clean streets, etc. What may be called the psychic environment is also extremely important. Thus, improved living conditions mean not only that wages be raised or that there be more windows in homes, but also that it be made possible for people to feel secure, respect themselves, and be certain of the love of their fellow men.

The Use of Heredity and Environment by the Personality

Adler some time ago and Plant more recently have spoken of heredity and environmental factors in a new way. Getting away from the simple causal picture, they hold essentially that the personality which has already made an adjustment (or adopted a style of life) will, so to speak, assimilate hereditary and environmental factors into this adjustment, using them in ways dictated by this already existing adjustment. In other words, new factors will be assimilated into the personality through a sort of sieve which will keep out some influences, admit others, and distort still others.

Adler has pointed out that an organic inferiority may push the individual in the direction of either strength or weakness, depending upon the "use" that he makes of it. If his life style is one of giving in, of running away, of refusing to see unpleasant things, then such an inferiority will be apt to defeat him, to make him weaker. If, on the other hand, his life style calls for making a direct frontal attack, overcoming and conquering his handicaps, then a new handicap may make him stronger if he overcomes it. He is given more practice at conquering and overcoming, and in this way he gains in self-confidence and self-esteem. Plant points out that people who go through adversity will either crack up completely or come through with increased strength, like tempered steel.

It will be seen how such considerations modify the ordinary discussion of heredity and environment in psychology. Usually the question is phrased in such a way as to imply that heredity or environmental factors are causes that influence the personality directly. What Adler and Plant say is that the equation is reversible; not only do heredity and environment influence the personality, but the personality influences heredity and environment, or at least the way in which they are used.

SUGGESTED READINGS

Some of the best-known and not too technical works on heredity in psychopathology are by Myerson (587) and by Landis and Page (454). For an expression of the strongly hereditarian point of view, Rosanoff's *Manual of Psychiatry* (651) should be consulted. The best example of the sociological approach to the problem is by Faris and Dunham (231). Plant's book (612) and any of Adler's are recommended as attempts to express the personality's functional use of the hereditary, constitutional, and environmental influences. Gould's paper (315) is recommended as a good critique of the over-hereditarian approach. A. Meyer's articles on neurotic constitution and mental reaction types are further recommended (548-554).

CHAPTER XIV

CULTURAL AND SOCIAL FACTORS IN PSYCHOPATHOLOGY

Psychological Meaning of Cultural and Social Factors.—Psychologically, the terms "cultural" and "social" involve relationships with other individuals—situations, tasks, demands, discipline, ideals, rewards, punishments, gratifications, and renunciations. These actual experiences, together with some of his ideas and his verbalized and implied goals, can be understood adequately only if the individual is viewed as a member of a larger group. The cultural background is significant in the parent-child relationship as well as in such biological functions as the use of various bodily organs. In these respects, cultures vary considerably.

Eating seems to us to be relatively unregulated in our culture, whereas the genital function is strictly regulated. Among the Trobriands in Melanesia, the eating function is strictly regulated from early childhood on. Thus it is considered dangerous for individuals to eat in public. For this reason they eat only in the family circle and even then do not look at one another.

The sexual function is not regulated at all among the Trobriands in early childhood, but it is strictly regulated in adulthood. For instance, sexual relations are forbidden between husband and wife for six months after the birth of a child.

It has been mentioned in various connections that some social groups put a premium on rivalry, excellence, and victory, whereas others emphasize cooperation, emotional calmness, and gentleness; and that substitute gratification, consolation, and compensation are possible in various degrees in various groups.

Anthropologists (525, 526, 74, 76, 539, 541, 497, 52) have discovered that some simpler cultures tend to have a unity, a pattern, an organic wholeness of a kind. In such societies, one feature—e.g., the motif of rivalry—tends to become predominant in all institutions and individual functions. The general atmosphere or "flavor" of the culture seems somehow similar to the general behavior and emotional life, the general "flavor" of the personality of the adult member of the society. Thus, it is possible, as Benedict and Kardiner have done, to describe characteristic psychological constellations for the individuals in each group at various periods of their lives.

Factors in Psychopathology.—As we look for the origins of maladjustment in individual cases, we find that, for the most part, the situations of stress, the demands and taboos that the patient has to face, the goals that he strives for, are the same for most of the members of his group. The way in which parents bring up their children is usually a characteristic of the whole society. In other words, one of the most important aspects of the family is its role as interpreter and transmitter of the group's culture to the child. If conflicts are inherent in the culture, they will be communicated to the child early in his life, and he will make them his own internal conflicts. Of course, how his family interprets the culture to him makes a great difference for a particular individual.

Some psychologists—for instance, Williams (788), Kamiat (416)—have declared flatly that all neurosis is "social neurosis" and, pressing this thought to its ultimate conclusion, have maintained that individual psychotherapy is only patchwork and treatment of symptoms. The only ultimate therapy, they say, is social therapy, i.e., changing society so that it does not foster conflict, frustration, insecurity, etc. We shall not discuss this interesting question further at this point, for we are here interested only in where psychic ill health originates. It always occurs in a cultural milieu, and this milieu must be understood and analyzed, if only for the sake of more efficient individual psychotherapy.

In her study of competition and cooperation in primitive societies (540), Mead was able to show a relationship between cooperative trends in the culture and personal security in the individual. Bunzel demonstrated a relationship between anxiety and intra-social hostility on the one hand, and, on the other, the presence in the society of economically exploiting institutions, such as rent, interest, and exploitation of labor. Benedict in various lectures has stressed other relationships between cultural institutions and insecurity in the individual, such as overt intra-social hostility, i.e., feuds, murder, etc.; covert hostility, i.e., malevolent sorcery, malicious gossip, etc.; fearful, awe-inspiring religion; great fear of death and of dead people; the use of religious power for selfish individual ends rather than for group purposes; the lack of widespread and warm emotional ties among the members of a group; the presence of institutions that humiliate the individual at times, and the absence of socially accepted methods of working off this humiliation, etc. Any or all of these, if institutionalized in a culture, will tend to correlate with personal insecurity in the individuals of the society.

One of the most important paths to safety in societies where rivalry and hostility run high is the achievement of victory and the maintenance of the victorious position. This, however, does not eliminate the victor's unconscious fear of being vanquished, humiliated, and destroyed; he feels threatened by the wrath of the vanquished, and his power may be further challenged by other rivals. This is somewhat similar to the vicious circles described above in connection with individual psychopathology. The measures that the individual has to use in order to be safe and respected are the very factors which through intra-psychic and external effects renew and maintain a measure of fear.

The culture is the background against which the individual's stresses and strains appear; it also determines the type of situation in which he has to struggle. In view of the compensatory aspects of this complex situation, it can be said that he will be able to function with comfort and will not break down psychologically if he lives under circumstances that are compatible with physiological well-being, and if he can measure up, essentially, to the ideals held by him and by others on whom his self-approval depends.

Stresses which are incompatible with such comfort come from two sources: (1) The individual may be exposed to hardships which are faced in common by most others in his group or status, but which are particularly intense for him. This may be the case in both childhood and adulthood. For example, the child may have to obey like other children, but his parents may exact unqualified obedience in an unusually cruel manner, with no compensating emotional warmth or approval. Likewise, every adult employee has to accept the leadership of his superior; but if the superior is extremely harsh and unappreciative, the employee may buckle under the strain. The stress is particularly hard to bear if other members of the group are entirely free from it. (2) Widespread social conditions—economic depression, unemployment, war—may hit the individual very hard but many others may be hit just as hard. The effects of such universally felt pressure may be different from those following pressure on some individuals but not on others. Thus, one's self-esteem will not be hurt as much by a financial failure if all one's friends have also failed.

The Intertwining of Cultural and Individual Factors in Psychopathology.—The interrelationship of cultural and individual factors will be illustrated in our own culture along the lines worked out by Kardiner (421) in particular. We speak here, let us stress, not of the American family in general, but of those families that foster psychopathology.

The American family is "small"; it consists only of parents and children. (Many other societies have much more "extended" families.) As a result, the child must of necessity seek to satisfy his most important emotional and bodily needs—the

need for affection, protection, dependence, food, ideals, etc.—
within the confines of this narrow family (585). Because the
parents are his exclusive protectors, their importance and stature become greatly magnified and intensified. Hence any
resentment toward them is particularly dangerous and contemptible. The rivalry with other siblings for parental favors
and approval becomes intense for the same reason. The bodily
urges which seek gratification are stimulated in the close confines of the family, and are forced further in that direction by
the taboo upon gratifying them elsewhere. The child's sexual
desires, for example, thus become directed toward the parents
or siblings; but since gratification at that source is tabooed, this
affords another source of fear, guilt, and conflict.

Contradictory demands are made of the child and the adult
as far as emotions and ideals are concerned. The two most
significant demands—for obedience and self-assertion—are
raised to the level of ideals. Adequate adaptation to them is possible if the process of obedience does not destroy the child's
self-esteem, self-confidence, and feeling of being loved. If these
are seriously damaged, his need for dependence becomes intensified. The two impulses are contradictory, and they form the
basis of one of the conflicts most characteristic of psychopathological reactions in our society.

Another demand calls for the suppression of certain bodily
urges aiming at gratification, by threatening injury, disapproval, condemnation if they are not suppressed. This results
in self-condemnation and guilt, particularly in connection with
hostile and sexual impulses. But situations constantly arise which
stimulate both of these impulses. If the individual's self-esteem
and confidence are intact, he can cope with these situations
adequately; but if he feels helpless, his sexual desires become
intensified, partly from defiance, partly because physical closeness comes to represent emotional dependence. The resulting
conflict is also characteristic of our culture.

Certain bodily activities are severely restricted. In our culture genital activity is most severely inhibited. The restriction is not only direct; it manifests itself also in indirect ways, e.g., in not naming the organ or discussing such pleasures. Furthermore, there is hostile parental reaction if the topic arises. The child thus has constant bodily urges which he is forbidden to gratify. Later in life, however, the individual is expected to exercise the very function which has always been forbidden. He can do so only if the circumstances are not too adverse and if his security, self-esteem, and confidence have not been seriously damaged. Otherwise he may feel a serious reaction of guilt, a fear of disapproval and a feeling of helplessness. It is for this reason that genital activity and the emotional relationships surrounding sex are the field in which psychopathological disturbances most frequently occur or through which they manifest themselves. The relatively superior evaluation of the male and of masculinity adds further to the stresses and strains connected with sex. The woman feels inferior both anatomically and emotionally, and this leads to envy of the male, to hostility toward him, and to fear of the superior being. Her feelings lead the man to fear her (because of the great things he feels she expects of him) and also to fear rivalry on the part of other men.

The case discussed in Chapter I illustrates the role of cultural factors in psychopathological reactions. The mother's emotional distance from the patient was particularly important because the only two individuals from whom she could expect full affection, protection, and satisfaction of her bodily needs were her parents. This is characteristic of our cultural set-up, and in sharp contrast to some societies, e.g., the Zuñi, where parental behavior toward the child differs little from the behavior of other adults.

The patient's attitude toward her work also shows the influence of cultural factors. Ambition, achievement, and competition are highly valued in our society. Consequently success in her work could have considerable compensating and consoling value, and could be substituted for what she missed in relationships with other people. Because of this aspect of her work, and her fear of competition and rivalry, she felt secure only if the perfection of her work could not possibly be challenged.

It should be strongly emphasized that the separate presentation of such factors as "cultural," "individual," "social," "biological-physiological" in the psychopathology of any given individual is, in a sense, a schematization or abstraction. The individual reacts to certain experiences. This is what matters to him. If his mother rejects him and he perceives this as potentially catastrophic, he is not interested in whether or not this experience is culturally determined. In other words, all these factors are fused in the individual's experiences.

Some Therapeutic Comments.—The psychotherapeutic procedures and the various factors involved in them will be discussed subsequently at greater length. Only a few comments will be made here, partly in order to avoid some misunderstandings.

We said earlier that the individual can function adequately if circumstances permit him to live within the range both of physiological comfort and of his ideals, his self-approval, and the approval of those upon whom he depends emotionally. This involves an appreciation of the potentialities for anxiety, helplessness, conflict, and frustration which the individual brings into any particular situation. In other words, it depends on his functional image of himself and of the world around him. His strength at a given time depends on the sum total of all his significant emotional experiences up to that point in his life. His weakness at that moment may be partially the result of the contradictory cultural stresses that have impinged on him at various times. We have seen that helplessness and catastrophic anticipation, once developed in an individual, tend to persist. This is where therapy enters. To summarize, certain cultural influences make a person weak; other cultural influences demand that he be strong. Therapy eliminates the effects of these contradictions which in the last analysis were culturally determined.

The helpless individual takes definite measures to continue to function and improve his lot. Moreover, once he starts utilizing these measures, they come to represent vital needs to which he clings tenaciously; if he has to give them up, he feels that he will be catastrophically lost. Such patients, and to some extent all patients, expect their salvation to come from external events; they either do not see the irrational and harmful aspect of their outlook and of the measures they adopt, or they disclaim responsibility for them, saying, "I am this way because I went through hardships. I have and can have no control over this; this must happen to me." Such attitudes are particularly important in psychotherapy, for there an attempt is made to strengthen the individual's whole personality. This can be accomplished only if he learns to abandon devices that are based on the premise of helplessness. Obviously one who still considers absolute dependence a way out of catastrophic expectation cannot develop full confidence in himself and make the best use of his potentialities. The discussion of cultural determinants of psychopathological symptoms most emphatically does not imply that the individual patient can disclaim all responsibility for the attitudes to which he clings. He has to realize that he wants them actively; he has to learn to see that they are inadequate ways of coping with his problems, and he has to learn to handle his problems differently. He must not be allowed to rest on his oars self-righteously after assigning the blame for his troubles to his culture.

It is obvious from earlier discussions that, theoretically at least, cultural set-ups can be compared with each other in regard to the degree of stress, conflict, suffering, and happiness that the individual attains under them. "Cultural" here includes everything that is significant in the individual's life and that concerns the group's economic, political, ideational, and emotional organization. A great deal can be accomplished psychotherapeutically for the individual through social engineering; but whether it is possible to "design" a society in which no serious psychopathology develops in any individual during his entire life is of course questionable. It is undoubtedly true that in extremely severe situations of external stress—war, invasion, economic crisis, unemployment, with which particular individuals are faced—it may be possible to give only emotional support and solace; any psychotherapy worthy of the name may be impossible or, at least, worthless. A starving man needs food, not therapy.

Experiments on "Social Atmospheres" and Personality

Some recent experiments by Kurt Lewin and his students, Lippitt, White, and others (491), are pertinent to this discussion. These investigators attempted to discover the influence on the personality and social behavior of working in autocratic, democratic, or laissez-faire groups.

In a series of experiments, boys' clubs were formed to do handicraft work under the leadership of older men. The leader of the autocratic group told the boys what to do; he dictated activities step by step so that the boys never knew what the next step was. He arbitrarily assigned a work task and companion to each boy. He alone praised or criticized each boy's work, and in this he was personal; otherwise he remained aloof from the group—not actively hostile, but rather impersonal.

In the democratic group, all the policies were a matter of group discussion and decision, and the general steps to the group goal were outlined in advance. The division of tasks was left to the group, and each boy could choose his work companion. The group leader was objective or "fact-minded" in his praise and criticism; he tried to be a regular group member without, however, doing too much of the boys' work for them.

In the laissez-faire group, there was complete freedom for group or individual decision without leader participation. The leader was available to supply materials or information when asked, but he took no part in discussions. He commented infrequently on activities unless questioned, and made no efforts to participate in or interfere with activities.

The factor of personality differences in the boys was controlled by having each group work under various social conditions—democracy and then autocracy, etc.

In one experiment, hostility was 30 times as frequent in the autocratic as in the democratic group, and aggression was 8 times as frequent. Much of the latter was directed toward two successive "scapegoats" in the group; none of it was directed toward the autocratic leader.

In another experiment, one of five autocratic groups showed the same aggressive reaction as was found in the first experiment. The boys in the other four autocracies showed an extremely non-aggressive "apathetic" pattern of behavior.

Other results were as follows: (1) A change from democracy to autocracy caused an increase in dominating behavior; a change from autocracy to democracy caused a decrease. (2) On the days when the boys were removed from the repressed autocratic atmosphere to the much freer atmosphere of democracy or laissez-faire, they behaved as if they had previously been in a state of bottled-up tension. (3) In the "apathetic" autocratic atmosphere the level of aggression rose rapidly to ten times its former level. The effect of the leader's absence is shown significantly in deterioration of work. Observers used such terms as dull, lifeless, submissive, repressed, or apathetic in describing the laissez-faire group. There was little smiling, joking, or freedom of movement. (4) When ego-involved types of language —e.g., hostility, resistance, demands for attention, hostile criticism, expressions of competition—were counted, 73 per cent of the language in the authoritarian group was of this type, as compared to 31 per cent for the democratic group. (5) There was more ascendance, less submissiveness and objectivity toward one another in the autocratic group. The democratic group showed more manifestations of an objective attitude. (6) The democratic group was more constructive. This was revealed in their superior work as compared with the careless and unfinished work of the autocratic group. (7) There was a greater feeling of "we-ness" in the democratic group. The "I" feeling predominated in the autocratic group.

Four types of evidence showed that the lack of aggression in the apathetic group was caused not by absence of frustration but by the repressive influence of the autocrat: (1) The outburst of aggression when transferred to a freer atmosphere which showed the bottled-up tension that the boys felt. (2) A sharp rise in aggression when the leader left the room. In the apathetic autocratic atmosphere it rose to ten times its former level; the boys' work also deteriorated. (3) Other indications of generalized apathy, such as absence of smiling and joking. (4) The fact that 19 out of 20 boys liked their democratic leader better than their autocratic leader, and 7 out of 10 liked their laissez-faire leader better than their autocratic leader.

The relative determining value of the deliberately created social atmosphere, as compared with that of either the personality make-up of the group or the personality of the adult leader, is apparent in the fact that there was a moderate amount of aggression in the democracy and an abnormally small amount in the apathetic autocracy, regardless of the leader's personality or of the group's personnel. When the boys were transferred to a new atmosphere and a new leader they changed markedly. For example, in the laissez-faire atmosphere aggression was very high, although different groups and different leaders were involved. One form of overt aggression was manifested in out-group hostility. In the democracy this took the form of wars fought in a spirit of fun between clubs which met in the same room, whereas in the autocracy it took a different form—strikes, rebellious acts, reciprocal aggression between members of the group, and scapegoat attacks, which usually occurred as release behavior after a decrease in leader pressure. In the transfer from the autocratic to the democratic group there was a decrease in the dominating behavior of autocratic members, and vice versa.

Such experiments show clearly the influence of the social milieu, even when the role of individual personalities is experimentally controlled. They should help to an understanding of the role of social determinants in the etiology of psychopathology.

PATHOGENIC EFFECTS OF UNEMPLOYMENT

The study of the effect of unemployment upon the individual is another excellent approach to an understanding of the part played by social forces in the etiology of psychopathology. Such a study can reveal clearly the role of socially created frustration and of social values, ideals, and needs in this frustration. The following analysis is based most heavily upon the work of Lazarsfeld (460) and Eisenberg (212).

The problem of the psychological effects of unemployment centers around the question of why men become demoralized and why their personalities are disrupted when they are unemployed for a long period. Various clinical studies indicate clearly that the unemployed individual tends to become emotionally unstable and anxious, that he devalues himself (develops feelings of inferiority, loses self-confidence, etc.), and that he develops a general feeling of insecurity (sense of helplessness, fear of the future, etc.). The phrase most often used to describe this general process is "lowering of morale." It might be described more technically as development toward what we have called the basic psychopathic constellation.

In his analysis of case histories of unemployed people, Lazarsfeld (460) speaks of three basic attitudes, the *unbroken*, the *distressed*, and the *broken*. The unbroken are the unresigned individuals who maintain their morale though not content with their situation (i.e., their personality is not fundamentally threatened). The distressed are those who fluctuate markedly between acts of aggression or rage and despair, resignation or escapism (i.e., fundamentally threatened but not completely discouraged). The broken individuals are the resigned, apathetic people who have lost hope and interest in life (i.e., completely discouraged), and adapt themselves to an extremely restricted way of living, with a very low level of aspiration.

These attitudes are related both to the individual's present situation and to his personality make-up. Obviously the most important among the first group of determinants is the length of unemployment. As unemployment continues, the individual tends to proceed from an unbroken attitude to a distressed and finally to a broken attitude. But his personality, including his particular system of values—both of course products of his life history—will be important in determining pathogenic effects. For instance, the unemployed neurotic person may deteriorate almost immediately, whereas the healthier individual may be able to feel unthreatened and retain his strength and his feeling of being accepted over a long period so that if a job does offer, he is fit to take it. Differential values for various groups in our society also play a part in this. For example, it is still generally considered to be the man's role to earn a living and support his family, whereas the woman's place is in the home. Consequently, it is not surprising to find that men deteriorate more rapidly with unemployment than do women.

The loss of morale in the unemployed cannot be said to be due to sheer deprivation—restriction in food, clothing, and shelter—because when these needs are satisfied, as when the individual receives relief or is supported by his relatives, he may still become demoralized. Rather this is a question of frustration in the sense of threat to his self-evaluation and his sense of security.[1] The unemployed person usually expresses this in terms of the loss of social standing in his own eyes and in those of others. In our society an individual's worth is judged largely by the position he holds; when he loses this he loses practically

---

[1] This should also bring out more clearly the difference between deprivation and frustration.

every claim to social status. These values are so strong that even if an entire community becomes unemployed, every member of it may lose morale and feel ashamed of his condition. This was adequately demonstrated in an investigation of Marianthal, an Austrian town which depended for its livelihood on a textile mill. When the mill shut down everyone was unemployed. All the people suffered consequent deterioration even though they were *all* unemployed and it was clear that their condition was not due to their own inadequacies.

The desire to maintain respectability and social status is apparent in various ways (except in those who have been "broken"). It can be seen in the efforts of the unemployed to dress as well as possible to hide their actual status. Casual observations of their homes frequently reveal signs of former glory—perhaps a carefully preserved party gown, a vase, or possibly an old car constantly taken care of to keep it going.

If the unemployed did not retain the values put on prestige and status, the likelihood is, of course, that they would not become demoralized. For instance, Dollard (186) has shown that lower-class Negroes in the South, who have never had any hope of advancement, consequently give up trying, and therefore seem to suffer little from a low social status that is ruinous to other people. By maintaining values that cannot be achieved, the individual puts himself into a conflict situation for which he can find no solution. Breakdown ensues sooner or later unless he achieves his values by securing a job or by changing his values. For example, the person's self-esteem may be saved if he realizes clearly that his unemployment is not his fault, but the result of a defect in the total institutional system. He may sustain his feeling of security by working with others in an organized effort to obtain jobs, to have remedial laws passed, or even to reconstruct society to eliminate unemployment altogether. There are few data for the already "broken" individual; but theoretically we might expect permanent brokenness and a practically irremediable loss of morale.

The Effects of Poverty

As with unemployment, a distinction must be made in a society like ours between the sheer effects of poverty *per se*—the actual lack of money with which to secure necessities—and the effects of having an inferior social status (deprivation versus threat to personality). The psychological effects of poverty are far different in a society in which everyone is poor, than in one in which some are poor and others are rich. Furthermore, even in the latter society, the psychological effects will differ according to the degree of insecurity of the society. Thus, in a very insecure society, the poor man is tremendously threatened, frustrated, and insulted by his contrast with the rich man; this is less true in a more secure society. Here again reference to the values, the ideals, and the aims of the individual is necessary in determining how deprivation will affect him.

In a prestige society like ours, a large proportion of the poor people lose self-esteem merely through having an inferior social status; for too many of us, this denotes inadequacy or incapability. The more definite the contrast between wealth and poverty, as in the movies, and the more often wealth is held up as the only desirable state, the worse the effects of poverty will be on the self-esteem. What this means is that in our society there are many forces that teach the poor man to be ashamed of his poverty, thus making poverty a frustration. We have already seen how severe the effects of frustration may be.

The sociologists and social workers have shown us that poverty has another important set of effects, namely, on the socialization of the individual. Usually the poor person must live in what is called a "bad neighborhood"—one in which there tends to be social disorganization, juvenile delinquency and crime, drunkenness, prostitution, and the general sordidness and cruelty that are encouraged by poverty, which makes the struggle for life a very literal struggle indeed. The child in such an area tends to be either over-hardened or altogether broken in spirit. The lack of play opportunities leads to mischief or actual delinquency; the lack of parental care encourages the formation of gangs. The hard struggle for life makes difficult the cultivation of the softer virtues—honesty, unselfishness, kindliness, cleanliness, cooperation, etc. As we saw in the preceding chapter, Faris and Dunham have shown that psychosis is also more probable in such environments.

SUBCULTURAL CONFLICTS

A special social-psychological problem which is often found in certain areas, particularly large cities, is the second-generation immigrant child who is faced with the tremendously difficult task of adjusting to two cultures simultaneously. Too often he breaks down in the process. This is why a definitely higher proportion of the neurotics and psychotics come from this group.

As a rule, such an individual feels both insecure and inferior because of his peculiar status. He frequently becomes greatly ashamed of his family background and the folkways associated with it, and feels humiliated and rejected because he thinks everyone is laughing or sneering at him. He is generally ambitious and strives hard to achieve the superior status of the American who is completely at home in his own country. Were it not for our growing intolerance of foreigners, his task would not be difficult; but traditional American hospitality has been replaced in too many cases by suspicion, hatred, and prejudice (Singer [716]).[1] Thus, the second-generation individual, who already tends to feel rejected and inferior, has these feelings reinforced by the real rejection and assumption of superiority which he must face. Ordinarily, the problem tends to disappear in the third or fourth generation; they in turn, feeling safe and at home, are quite ready to bolster the newly arrived immigrant's insecurity and inadequacy by deriding him. Sometimes one

[1] For a similar study with Negroes, see M. Brenman, *J. Soc. Psychol.*, 1940, 11, 171-197.

is tempted to believe that the most intolerant groups in this country tend to be those who only recently were immigrants themselves, and who thus compensate for their own feelings of inferiority and rejection.

It is not only the hated one, the rejected one, who is affected psychologically. The hater, the rejector, is also affected. Even though they may be different, the effects of hating are quite as serious as the effects of being hated. The hater's lot is to project into others, through his own strong feelings of guilt and his unconscious loss of self-esteem or self-respect, the hatred which he feels; hence he soon comes to think that he himself is hated, and therefore he becomes insecure. The fact that the degrading and brutalizing effects of hating are largely unconscious does not make them any less effective. These truths hold not only for the native-foreigner situation, but also for hatred arising from differences in color, religion, nationality, or class.

AUTHORITARIAN EDUCATION

A widespread belief holds that, more than anything else, a child must learn to obey. Only when he has learned this is he fit to lead, to stand on his own feet. The observations of modern psychology prove that this is for the most part wrong; if one wants the individual to be independent, courageous, and capable of thinking for himself, then he must be trained and educated for independence, courage, and self-reliance and not for submission and dependence. The following excerpt from Pierre van Paassen's *Days of Our Years* illustrates well what we mean by authoritarian education:

"Thinking of that now distant place and day, it is as if I feel a breeze from the Middle Ages blow into my face. That school was a model of authoritarianism: the pupils were considered and treated as little automatons without a will or inclination of their own. The discipline was ascetic, almost penitential; while the curriculum did not differ in essentials from that in use in Dutch schools a hundred cr even two hundred years earlier. . . .

"The headmaster, a tight-lipped sallow-complexioned old funda-mentalist whose protruding blue eyes were enlarged to twice their natural size by a pair of enormously thick lenses, was a descendant of a Huguenot family which had settled in Holland after the revocation of the Edict of Nantes. Gaunt, his face a mask of deep wrinkles, his bony fingers tapering off into nails as long as those of a Chinese mandarin, he inspired me with so much more terror than respect that I still see his ghost at times. There was not a spark of humor in that man. Not once in all those years did I see his face soften into a smile. He had come to the teaching profession much in the same spirit as an Inquisitor approaches a victim in the torture chamber. His conception of his task was not to guide and shepherd, but to correct a crowd of hopelessly bad children who were inclined from birth—as that lovely Catechism specified—'to do evil and hate God.' . . .

. . . "The 'instilling' was frequently done (in our case) with the aid of a brass-edged ruler of ebony wood, which the principal, in spite of his reputed shortsightedness, manipulated with uncanny precision. He never missed. Upon the slightest provocation: a mere whisper in the classroom or a giggle, he advanced upon you without a word, seized hold of your wrist, and brought down his stick on your knuckles, not in anger, but with calm deliberation. If you wept in pain and humiliation after one of these punitive ministrations, he locked you up for the rest of the day in a small dark room where the coal was kept and which swarmed with rats and mice."[1]

It is unquestionably true that one of the primary aims in education is to make the child a willing, moral, law-respecting member of his society, and that discipline and social training are therefore necessary. But more than this is necessary. His education must enable him to feel secure and independent as an adult. This is obviously impossible if the discipline is so rigorous that it endangers the child's self-esteem and independence.

Some miscellaneous characteristics of authoritarian educa-

[1] Pierre van Paassen, *Days of Our Years*, Hillman-Curl, Inc., New York, 1939.

tion are: (1) setting up the teacher as omniscient and omnipotent, one who can make no mistakes; (2) giving him unquestioning obedience; (3) regarding him as made of a different clay, as someone who has no passions, who is aloof from the world, who never cries or laughs; (4) being punished frequently; (5) being humiliated; (6) being given grades, report cards, examinations, the general purpose of which, from a psychological point of view, seems to be to make education a competition in which everyone is pitted against everyone else; (7) learning by rote without understanding.

The Psychological Effects of Authoritarian Education.—The effects of authoritarian education are varied. It may destroy self-reliance, independence, and courage (self-esteem); it may create "the model child," the masochistic teacher's pet, or a child who obeys his superior but dominates and tortures the weaker children. Wexberg gives us a good picture of the development of such a youngster.

". . . Obedience to his elders means that he belongs to them, that he has nothing in common any longer with the poor little brothers and sisters over whom he has assumed, so to speak, a commanding role, as model child. Now he can utter all his repressed desires for power against the smaller ones. He 'snitches' on his younger brethren, and when they are punished for their little misdeeds feels himself the usufructuary of their punishment. In school the same situation occurs. It is the model child who is made the monitor, who watches over the others in the recesses. What satisfaction when he can turn in the name of some offender and see punishment meted out to him! Of course, he must be entirely beyond reproach himself, he must learn and know everything that the teacher could ask—beyond that, of course, nothing. Personal ambition in extra-curricular activities, such as theaters, reading, sports, etc., he has not developed, for he is completely busied with the duties of his school, and these other activities are not recognized by teacher or father. He learns the greatest tommyrot by heart simply because the teacher has uttered it; to doubt the word of the teacher, to think independently, that were a sin! And besides, one makes oneself unwelcome in the high places by independent thought. So the child forgets how to think independently, or, better said, he never learns how, for this, like every other ability, must be practised.

"Life finishes what the home and the school began. Model children can hardly become anything more than employees, and if by chance they find themselves in independent situations the subaltern-employee nature of their essential being would not matter if they were good employees! But they are the carriers of the most inconsolable bureaucracy, theirs is the greatest thought-laziness and the greatest shirking of all responsibility. They never accomplish anything, but they are artists in 'passing the buck'; they interpret their duties always literally, never toward any independent purpose. Are they happy? We think not. Perhaps they are saved the grosser buffets of fate; failures and disappointments are not theirs so long as their employment goes its regular way without interruption. What they never experience is the pleasure of real accomplishment by their own performance, the pride of thinking their own thoughts! But if the model child who has been educated for the status of an employee is thrown out of his regular rut by some accident, then the happiness of his secure existence is at an end. He becomes the plaything of a capricious Fate, for he has lost the ability to act for himself (and he has no friends, for those who do *only* their duty seldom have many friends), and he finds himself completely unable to rebuild his life.[1]

SUMMARY

Psychopathology is fostered in a society in which the old threaten the young, and children are legitimately and conventionally frustrated, humiliated, and sneered at, punished freely, and made to feel worthless and inferior—all this done by "good" men and women. Such a society creates gratuitous conflicts and frustrations, and holds out before the individual a goal which he can never reach, but which is described in such glowing terms that only if he possesses it can he respect himself and

[1] E. Wexberg, *Your Nervous Child*, Boni & Liveright, New York, 1927, pp. 102 ff.

feel that he has a place in the world. This society creates aggression and hostility by all these means, but gives the individual no legitimate, socially useful outlet for this piled-up energy; hence it can only emerge later in life in the form of hatred, envy, or jealousy directed against younger or weaker people. This makes the whole system self-perpetuating; for these younger people, grown up, will pass it all on to their inferiors.[1]

SUGGESTED READINGS

The student should become acquainted with some of the contributions made by anthropologists and sociologists to basic psychological theory. Malinowski's books on the Trobriand Islanders (525, 526), Benedict's *Patterns of Culture* (74), Mead's various books (536, 537, 539, 540), and Waller's *The Family: A Dynamic Interpretation* (761), are usually recommended. A good introduction to the general field, textbook style, is Linton's *Study of Man* (497).

Outstanding books on culture-personality relations are those by Dollard (187), Plant (612), and Kardiner (421). A shorter summing-up of the anthropological influence on psychology is given in Maslow's chapter in Stagner's *Psychology of Personality* (721). Kamiat's book (416), though not sound in the academic sense, is provocative and interesting. The same is true of William's book (788). A good discussion of the relation between society and the child's personality is found in L. B. Murphy's *Social Behavior and Child Personality* (585). Adler's approach may be understood from (11, 15). Various other interesting papers appear in the symposium in the *American Journal of Sociology*, 1937, Vol. 42. One of the outstanding papers in this field is by Fromm (291), and is strongly recommended to those who can read German. Freud's *Civilization and Its Discontent* (276) is further recommended.

---

[1] In other words, any individual can be a real (even though minute) force which creates maladjustment in others, e.g., by rejecting, hating, humiliating, or scorning others. Or else he can be a real (even though minute) psychotherapeutic force, e.g., by respecting others and being kind, affectionate, loving, and accepting. Of particular interest in this connection are such books as Plant's *Personality and the Cultural Pattern* (612), Kamiat's *Social Forces in Personality Stunting* (416), and Adler's *Social Interest* (12).

CHAPTER XV

ORIGINS OF PSYCHOPATHOLOGY IN CHILDHOOD

There are two means whereby the psychologically sick individual can be understood. The first is by analyzing the dynamics of the character, and the second is by analyzing its history. Each in itself gives only a partial analysis. In dealing with psychic illness, two questions—"What is the individual like, how does he react?" and "How did he get that way?"—should be asked.

Part of the answer to the second question has already been discussed in the two preceding chapters. Now we shall proceed to the most important immediate genetic determiners of character and character disturbances.

An earlier chapter brought out the fact that the basic pathological constellation is characterized by feelings of worthlessness and helplessness, hostility toward those on whom the individual is dependent, and by the fear of abandonment, injury, condemnation, humiliation, and complete frustration in bodily needs. We saw there briefly how this constellation is formed during childhood. The following discussion will elaborate on some of these points, in regard to both normal and psychopathological development.

Several points must be borne in mind throughout the discussion. Although the individual's needs and desires arise, and aim at being satisfied, through the use of particular organs, nevertheless the complete organism is involved. In other words, a need which is to be satisfied by means of the mouth is nevertheless a need of the whole organism. So, too, frustration of this need is a frustration not of the mouth, but of the whole organism.

The infant is literally helpless. He cannot exist without the cooperation and attention of other individuals in his environment. This holds also for the child and, to a lesser extent, even for the adult. The child's relationship with the people on whom he is dependent is of particular importance in determining his evaluation of himself, his evaluation of other people, and his psychological functioning as a total organism.

In the development of the human organism new functions appear constantly, and there is a continual shift in emphasis on the predominance and relative importance of various organs and functions. We turn now to the discussion of these organic functions.

DEVELOPMENT OF THE ORGANISM; ORGAN FUNCTIONS

A great deal can be learned about the infant by observing him, but of course no information can be obtained directly from him, that is, by words. This fact in itself is a sharp reminder that certain "psychological" functions are as yet not present, and, further, that great caution is needed in all theoretical constructions about the infant. If we use terms that imply similarity to later experiences of the individual, we must always remember that there may be only partial identity in meaning, or perhaps none at all.

The infant, at first, is probably unable to differentiate between himself and the world. When this process of differentiation begins, it is very vague, and it is a long time before the infant has a clear concept of the "I" and of the external world. We shall return to this problem later.

Similarly, all the infant's needs and desires and emotional reactions are at first probably extremely vague and undifferentiated. Almost certainly he at first has only bodily needs which are not clearly directed toward definite objects. It is only through gradual development, repeated experiences, and conditionings—

most of which are of course non-verbal and non-conscious—that these needs become directed toward definite objects and situations leading to gratification, satisfaction, and elimination of distress.

The infant has drives of various sorts, and he behaves in a manner which can be reasonably interpreted as distress if these drives are not stilled. He shows similar distress reactions to some stimuli, such as injury, which can be assumed to be painful. He is affected in a positive way by gratifications of various sorts, such as the satisfaction of needs and drives, rocking, warmth, and sensory stimulation (stroking, tickling, sexual stimulation).

The Mouth.—The organ that is most significant for a long period after birth from the point of view of both utility (nourishment) and satisfaction (akin to pleasure) is the mouth, and with it the whole digestive tract. For this reason, disturbances in the infant are most likely to be manifest in connection with the functioning of this organ. This may be either because of inadequate nourishment or because the pleasure needs of the mouth are not adequately satisfied. (See the observations of D. M. Levy and M. Ribble.)

From the point of view of the whole organism, positive experiences improve the infant's functional capacity. Continued or serious frustration, severe pain or distress create something which parallels the feeling of helplessness. No longer does the infant aim merely at satisfying the original need; he now begins to aim at or react to this more generalized "helplessness." In cases of extremely serious frustration in the function of the mouth, the infant behaves as if he could not cope with or master the world (Kardiner).

Another common observation which is of interest is the fact that in many social groups one of the most customary ways to still a crying infant is to give him something to suck. From this we can postulate that somehow the use of the mouth, together with the satisfaction derived from it, can serve as measures for amelioration of distress (and helplessness) arising from other sources. This behavior—eating as a consolation—is often seen in adults.

Cultural factors become operative with the first feeding; they determine such questions as what the infant is given to eat, at what intervals he is fed, how he is handled while suckling. The effect of the environment, that is, his relationships with adults and siblings, becomes important later in disturbances of the functions of the mouth (eating and chewing indiscriminately, refusal to eat, loss of appetite, vomiting) in the following ways: (1) The adult who takes care of the child and upon whom he is dependent may make a special issue of discipline in connection with the mouth function. (2) Digestive and oral disturbances may arise because of general rather than specific conflicts. Tensions and conflicts may arise in the child's relationship with the adult or with siblings. The mouth function may then be disturbed concomitantly with the arousal of general anxiety, helplessness, resentment, need for affection and help. One might say then, somewhat incorrectly, that the older infant or the child may "use" this function to express hostility or defiance or to obtain help and affection.

The reaction of the digestive tract and of the other organs involved in the total reaction to distress is at first (and to some extent always) almost like a purposeless reflex; it is simply a part of the emotional reaction of fear and anger and the straining of all the musculature. Later, through repeated experiences the reaction itself acquires goal aspects; it becomes part of the expression of hostility or of the attempt to obtain affection. An illustration of this acquisition of purposefulness by an initially purposeless activity is found in the crying of an infant. What he does at first as a reflex act, he later does with malice aforethought. The function of the mouth and of the upper part of the digestive tract thus may become linked with any emotional attitude. The attitudes with which it is linked most frequently are dependence (eating equals "being cared for") and defiance, disgust, and rejection on the part of the hurt individual (nausea and vomiting).

To summarize, the functioning of the mouth and upper digestive tract may give rise to oral and digestive pathology if the function of the organ itself is seriously interfered with by the environment, or if the organ becomes involved in conflict situations in the manner we have indicated.

The above statements relating to the functioning of the mouth and upper digestive tract hold also for all the organism's other significant functions, for instance, excretion, sexuality, motility, etc.

Excretory Functions.—Excretory functions, of course, are present at birth. However, in the course of spontaneous development they do not have the same psychological significance as the mouth does; but they may acquire this significance in connection with the individual's handling, environment, conflicts, and physical illnesses. It must be remembered that, in their all-inclusive curiosity and handling, children will play as innocently with feces as with any other object. This is, however, a definite emotional problem for the mother if not for the child, but her attitude may make it a problem for the child as well.

The two ways in which the bowel function most frequently becomes involved in psychopathological attitudes are as follows: (1) The parent is particularly preoccupied with the function, punishes the child if he soils himself, and hounds him in general on the subject. (2) The child has a measure of control over the excretory functions. Since the parent obviously cannot gain the mastery of this control, the child may express his defiance (if he has any) either through soiling or through refusal, that is, retention of the bowel content.

Like the functioning of the mouth and the upper digestive tract, the bowel function may become a source of consolation and pleasure.

Another significant point in connection with the excretory functions is the fact that, in the course of training, the child usually acquires, as part of the pattern of winning parental approval, two attitudes toward the functions and their products, namely, shame and disgust. The adult who is training the child expresses disapproval at the child's positive interest in his excreta and trains him to control himself in the presence of others. Therefore a moderate degree of shame and disgust is normal for our culture; but when carried to extremes these attitudes are unquestionably pathological.

The excretory functions and their products may become involved in the expression of any emotional attitude. They most frequently are linked with hostility and disparagement, as is evidenced in the slang of practically every culture. The reason for this is apparent from what was said above about these functions becoming an expression of defiance in the child. Furthermore, in connection with the attitude of disgust the individual may dramatize the idea, "You are nothing but dirt."

The Genital Function.—Some genital activity—occurrence of erections, touching of the genitals, indication of pleasure from external stimulation, etc.—is present in most infants at a very early age. In our society such indications of early sexuality are usually stamped out ruthlessly by the frightened parent; and probably, almost from birth on, there is a general negative conditioning to the genital area, i.e., vague attitudes of fear, guilt, and anxiety. In spite of this, genital activity usually increases at about the age of four or five. Masturbation or other genital play is common at that age in both sexes. Because parents usually taboo such activities, they loom large in the child's fantasies, but always accompanied by fear and guilt.

Frequently there is a repression and cessation of sexual activities and attitudes in children from the age of about six up to puberty. This is not found in societies that do not disapprove of sexual manifestations in the young. The glandular development connected with puberty brings about a considerable increase in sexual needs and desires, and with them a strong revival of emotional problems and conflicts. It is at this time that the individual masters these problems for better or worse.

It should be remembered that this discussion concerns our own society; other societies hold very different attitudes. For example, in some societies—the Trobriand Islanders, among others—genital activity is entirely unrestricted from the very beginning, and even encouraged. In several other societies, the adults stimulate children sexually to pacify them or to express endearment. Of all bodily functions in our society, the sexual is the one most hedged about with taboos, anxieties and fears. And, as might be expected, sexual problems are extremely common in the psychologically sick individual.[1]

Like the functions discussed in the preceding sections, the genital function may become involved in the expression of any psychopathological attitude. It most commonly becomes involved with a desire for unqualified affection and dependence (in both sexes, but particularly in women); a desire for submission and pain (particularly in women); hostility, or a desire to conquer, dominate, or injure the other (in both sexes); self-aggrandizement (in both sexes, but more often in men). Using sexuality as the "carrier" of such a hidden emotional attitude is extremely common in our society, in "normal" as well as in sick people.

DEVELOPMENT OF THE ORGANISM; OTHER FUNCTIONS

Intellect, Mastery, Motility.—The development of intellect, mastery, and motility goes on from birth. (Intellectual activity is here considered as an active outgoing function on the part of the individual, not merely a passive response.) These functions

---

[1] In order fully to realize that sexual problems are peculiarly characteristic of our society, the student should read Mead's *Coming of Age in Samoa* (536) and *Sex and Temperament in Three Primitive Societies* (539), and Malinowski's *Sex and Repression in Savage Society* (525) and *The Sexual Life of the Savage* (526). The first book listed is probably most valuable for this purpose, for it is a convincing demonstration of the fact that the problems of puberty and adolescence which are so intense and universal in our society are completely absent in Samoa where a different attitude toward sex obtains.

become particularly important with the development of walking and talking, usually between the ages of eighteen months and two years. Even before this, the infant engages in continuous activities which can be called play, exploration, attack, mastery. There is continuous action, contact, curiosity, and a strong aspect of drive to all these activities. As intellect, mastery, and motility develop, the interrelation of the infant and his environment changes profoundly, and new problems arise in connection with the organic functions already discussed. The child explores, "experiments," attempts to find out about these organic functions; he asks questions about them, wants to see them, makes theories about them, dreams about them, and desires them. The attitude of people in his environment gradually changes, for it now demands more firmly that he control these functions, that he refrain from sexual activity altogether, that he excrete only at the proper time and in the proper place, that he eat in the culturally approved manner, etc.

There may also be considerable interference with his activities which involve curiosity and motility; this may be direct (he may be criticized, reproved, and punished if he is active, if he talks, if he inquires), or more subtle (he may be laughed at, ridiculed, slighted, called stupid or unskillful, and compared unfavorably with other children). Thus, similar psychopathological problems may arise in connection with curiosity and motility as with other functions, although there is no strong cultural taboo on these functions as such. The competitive emphasis in our society and the resulting disparaging and humiliating attitude of the child's social environment may be extremely disturbing.

Disturbances of motility and speech may appear when certain forms of them come to represent to the child a helpless state, with its consequent affection and care. Thus, crawling on all fours may represent being an infant again and thus being completely cared for. This may also be true of "baby talk," or even of general stupidity. Expressions of hostility may become significant in disturbances of speech (uncontrolled inarticulate utterances which resemble swear words or obscene words) as well as in disturbances of skeletal motility (in the form of tics). A great many other possible disturbances may be manifest in these areas. However, it is difficult to determine whether any special psychopathological attitude is predominantly connected in its expression with speech and motility, as for instance tends to be true of oral, anal, or genital functions, because these functions may become linked with any other activity. Furthermore, they are direct expressions of emotional attitudes, of evaluations of oneself and of attitudes toward the environment.

Aggression and Hostility.—The problem of aggression and hostility is as important in psychopathology as is the problem of fear, and is closely connected with the problem of motility and mastery. We have mentioned the considerable increase in the child's activities during the development of motility and intellect. An important aspect of this activity is the fact that it possibly destroys, inflicts pain, or injures. This type of activity has been called aggression and even "sadism," although many deny that its primary aim in the child is to destroy or to inflict pain; i.e., it may be *merely* activity. In a more specific sense, hostility has been defined as an activity which has exactly the aim of destroying or inflicting pain. Of course, not only the skeletal musculature and the hands can be used for this purpose, but also the mouth and, in fantasy at least, any other organic function. An individual may act aggressively if he is in danger or has been hurt, or if he can thereby derive some other benefit, such as obtaining a desired object or satisfying a desire. The situations in which aggression and hostility arise are serious frustration, serious humiliation, and, in general, situations in which the individual for some reason feels entirely or almost helpless and catastrophically threatened. Hostile impulses and acts are of great importance in psychopathology because they lead either to serious consequences or to their expectation. Moreover, these impulses are one of the most frequent targets of adult disapproval; they lead to actual punishment, and thus in time to fear of counterattack and of injury, to the fear of further humiliation, abandonment, rejection, and deprivation in regard to bodily wants. The feeling of hostility is also one of the most potent sources of feelings of guilt.

Turning Against Oneself.—When infants show "intense anger" reactions, they are sometimes seen to scratch, bite, and strike themselves or beat their heads against the floor, etc. This behavior may appear if there is no possibility of "attacking" objects. A more complicated and significant later development occurs if, after expectations of catastrophic threat are established and environmental goals and taboos are internalized (readiness for guilt), the individual turns his hostile and aggressive impulses against himself instead of the environment. This is just as significant psychologically as is the development of catastrophic expectation and hostility, and it is a factor in almost every psychopathological manifestation. From the point of view of the whole individual, it may have the following implications: (1) It wins pity and therefore help. (2) It is unconsciously felt to be a satisfactory penance and thus wipes the slate clean. (3) It may be a form of revenge upon the one responsible— as when the child imagines himself dead because his mother refused him some cookies. As a result, the individual may suffer incapacitating symptoms when he ought to assert himself, he may seek out situations which are harmful to him, and he may be able to derive enjoyment and pleasure only from situations in which he is hurt.

The Child's Needs and the Beginning of Pathology

The Relationship with Parents.—Definite reactions toward certain individuals are noticeable in the infant almost as soon as he is able to identify and recognize objects. This first attachment and reaction is, of course, very vague, but gradually becomes more and more definite. It is usually selective and is shown, particularly or exclusively, to the individual who takes

care of the infant. In fact, it may be so exclusive that he will
be frightened and cry if this person is absent or if another one
approaches him.

The pattern of attachment and of positive reaction to the
parent has a special coloring, depending on the child's stage
of development and on his dominant organic needs and functions; and it acquires a gradually increasing richness of emo
tional and intellectual content.

Although the normal and psychopathological aspects of this
relationship have been discussed in various parts of the book,
we wish to emphasize the following points:

1. The older infant or the child has a definite need for parental affection, help, appreciation, support, and praise.

2. He engages in certain activities and refrains from others
for the sake of approval and affection.

3. The child tolerates easily a fair amount of disapproval and
punishment if he feels that he is essentially loved and if the
parental demands are not over-severe.

4. The behavioral aims set by the parent acquire a definite
emotional coloring and are given a high evaluation. They are
accepted by the child on the basis of either "My parents want
this, and I want it too; I am like them" (identification), or "If
I behave this way, they value me; if I don't they will reject me
and hurt me," and later, "If I behave this way, I value myself; if
I don't, I am worthless" (ideals, conscience). In these ways the
child makes the attitudes in his environment his own (internalization).

5. The older infant and child evaluates the strength and
power of his parents very highly; he wants not only to love
them, but also to consider them supreme and all-powerful. In a
word, he *needs* to respect them.

6. A measure of conflict is apparently unavoidable in the
process of growth and training. Because of the relationship with
the mother, any serious threat issuing from her is constantly
renewed, constantly reacted to, and again renewed. The child

feels this threat as a total organism. Under circumstances of intense frustration, parental rejection, and impossible demands, the basic psychopathological constellation arises. Thus, the child's relationship with the parent is the most potent source of catastrophic expectation.

7. During the process of growth, the infant and child is of course exposed to and influenced by other environmental factors, such as illness, injuries, siblings, playmates, schoolmates, teachers, relatives, strangers, etc. All of these may play a somewhat similar role in the child's life as do the parents. Both in the parental relationship and in all other relationships, cultural factors are significant. Thus, in our culture, the individual is supposed gradually to acquire increasing self-determination and freedom of action and to be treated and regarded more and more as an adult; this is particularly true after puberty, and entirely so after he becomes self-supporting. Close emotional attachment is limited as a rule to a few individuals.

Another illustration of the importance of cultural factors is afforded by the Trobriands. Trobriand children form a sort of "republic" composed of spontaneous groups. They do what they want to do as individuals; they go away for several days unaccompanied by adults. That the Trobriand child's evaluation of his parent, as well as the parent's relative role in the formation of the child's character, ideals, etc., is different in important respects from that in our own society is extremely probable.

Linton (Kardiner [421]) found that among the Marquesans, the five-year-old first child becomes in a sense the ruler of the household. He has the right, when he is displeased, "to declare his name" over the household. This means that, until he lifts the ban, his parents cannot enter the house. On one occasion, Linton actually found the parents sitting out in the courtyard. He says that the most self-possessed children he has ever seen are those of the Marquesans.

The Feeling of Isolation.—A feeling of isolation arises from many sources. For instance, excessive mobility of the family may produce it, for the child who moves to a new neighborhood every year may never have a chance to make any friends; similarly, the child who moves from the country to the city, or vice versa, or from one country to another will also have the feeling of being "out of it." Being of a different religion or race or color may make a child friendless in his neighborhood. A feeling of isolation may come from being orphaned, or from having parents who are separated or neglectful. Any situation that makes it difficult for the child to form friendships tends to produce this feeling. In addition to these sources, excess maternal over-protection which keeps the child away from other children may give rise to it. Generally isolated children feel unloved; they tend to become excessively introverted and withdrawn, and in severe cases they may retire completely into their private worlds of fantasy.

Allied to this is the so-called "feeling of difference" in which the child feels himself to be in some way different from other children, almost of a different species. This may be produced by organic inferiorities, by intellectual inferiority or superiority, or by a difference in social background, socio-economic status, or race, religion, color, or nationality. This ordinarily results chiefly in feelings of inferiority and inadequacy.

Organic Inferiorities in the Child.—Psychopathology may sometimes have its inception in various organic inferiorities in the child, such as being crippled, having a bad heart, etc. What is important is that the inferior organ may become the center of attention of the developing personality so that the whole plan of life may be arranged either to defend or disguise it or to counterbalance or compensate for the deficiency. Organic inferiorities also have direct effects, e.g., anxiety, a generalized feeling of inferiority, feelings of being rejected because of the inferiority, etc. Between organic inferiority and the feeling of inferiority there is a very complex relationship which is discussed elsewhere; here we wish only to stress the importance of cultural attitudes and, more specifically, parental attitudes toward the defect. This is also related to the all-important fact that it is not the defect itself that is so important, but what the environment and therefore the individual do about it. Crookshank put this well when he said, "The personality is not determined by the inferiority but by the reaction of the individual to the inferiority." According to Wexberg,

"It is not the gravity of the disease, but the child's personal attitude to its inferiority which is decisive for psychological effects. Thus, it may happen that serious diseases may have no special importance for the mental development, inasmuch as they are not seriously felt by the child itself. Conversely, a defect harmless in itself, but troublesome or deforming, may severely shake the courage and self-confidence of the child, since he estimates the importance of the organ inferiority only by the outward effects thereof, and by his own subjective impressions."[1]

The Psychological Interpretation of Biological Facts.—The foregoing remarks lead naturally to some remarks on the significance of what we have been discussing. Why are we interested in the early sex life of the child, or in his eliminative or feeding habits? Do they lead directly to psychopathology? Is it true that the vicissitudes of these early needs give rise to maladjustment and psychological illness? Or is there a more complex relation with other factors that must be taken into account? The last question explains our interest. Whether considered in relation to motility or to defect or to genital function, physiological facts are *in themselves* unimportant. *They become important only in so far as they are the target of cultural attitudes held by the parents, only in so far as they arouse anxiety or hostility or shame or panic in the parents.* The sexual drive in itself is no more innately pathogenic than the need to drink water or breathe. If it were treated by our society with the same degree of nonchalance as is the need to breathe, psychologists would

[1] E. Wexberg, *Individual Psychology*, Cosmopolitan, New York, 1929, p. 20.

rarely hear of it as an originator of pathology.[1] They *do* hear of it and they are concerned with it simply because most individuals in our society are anxious about it, their anxiety being created by the parents' anxiety, which in turn was created by *their* parents' anxiety, etc. Individual attitudes are thus inevitably to be interpreted, at least in part, as a reflection or an internalization of general cultural attitudes. This holds true for all the biological functions that have been mentioned, with the possible exception of severe congenital illness.

Image and Evaluation of Oneself.—The human individual learns to differentiate between himself and the outside world very gradually and through a complicated process. The formation of the concept of the self will not be discussed here in detail (Piaget, Schilder), beyond saying that it involves the child's intellectual development, such experiences as having two sensations simultaneously when he touches his own body, the fact that parts of his body are always near him, that they are visible and touchable and are sources of comfort and discomfort, whereas other objects may be near or far or completely absent at times, or may be at hand or removed if they are sources of pleasure or pain. The child's differentiation between animate and inanimate and between dream and reality, and his theories of the world and events are part of this process.

What we wish to emphasize here is that the development of the concept and image of the "self" is not an unemotional, detached process. It is concerned with needs, urges, and drives, and has throughout a strong emotional coloring. It is obvious that the individual's image and evaluation of himself will depend greatly on whether, in this process, he is relatively secure or constantly frustrated and catastrophically threatened. The following facts are important in this connection:

[1] Of course, a sharp distinction must be made here between an organic system as originating conflict and as expressing or carrying conflict. Breathing does not initiate psychopathology, but disturbances of breathing are common in neurosis as an *expression* of anxiety or conflict.

1. There is a strong need and desire for a positive evaluation of the self (self-esteem) and this evaluation is greatly desired from others as well (prestige).

2. In the evaluation of the body and of various reactions there is partial approval and partial disapproval. Some organs and their functions and some psychological reactions are strongly rejected, condemned, and shut out of consciousness. If this is done on a large scale it is definitely pathological. Similarly, there may be an over-valuation and aggrandizement of the whole body or of parts of it, or of the entire image of the self, or of some psychological function. This, too, is definitely pathological. Such attitudes are largely unconscious.

3. One of the most important factors in both the formation and the final pattern of the evaluation of the self is the relationship with parents, siblings, and playmates. The fact that the parent interferes with some of the child's actions and encourages others, urges him on, gives him strength, etc., is significant in its formation. The parent's positive evaluation of the child as an individual is reflected in the child's evaluation of himself. If the situation is such that it leads to the basic psychopathological constellation, then the evaluation of the self is characterized by feelings of helplessness, worthlessness, and insignificance.

4. These remarks about the evaluation of the self should not be taken as purely introspective statements. Self-evaluation manifests itself in the phenomena that we call thoughts, emotions, motives, and actions. It is a functional, dynamic concept, and as close as we can come to expressing what we mean by reactions of the organism as a whole.

Interrelations Between Child and Adult Psychopathology.— As is obvious from the discussion in this chapter, definite pathological manifestations and "mechanisms" may appear in the individual at an early age. Fear, hostility, repression, displacement, turning against the self, and other psychopathologically unconscious processes may be definitely manifested by the child.

The early appearance of strong conflict, guilt, and self-condemnation is illustrated by the case of a three-year-old girl who was badly mistreated by her mother. The mother scolded her, humiliated her, beat her every day, locked her in frequently, and at times starved her. As a result of the neighbors' complaint, the child was taken away from the mother. During the subsequent period of observation, she showed various disturbances, "terrors," insomnia, weeping spells, soiling. Although she was intelligent and could talk well, no matter how the conversation was conducted, she would never admit that she had been badly treated by her mother.

In serious cases the basic psychopathological constellation is always found to have appeared first in childhood, usually as a result of disturbed relationships with the parents. However, it may not appear until a later age, even adulthood. In this case the disturbance is more passing and one that is easier to remove.

The main outlines of the sick adult's evaluation of himself and of the world are roughly identical with those formed in his childhood. There are, however, important differences that must not be overlooked. For one thing, the relative emphasis may be different. Then too, the measures that the adult uses in the face of catastrophic threat may be quite different from those he used as a child. The total interrelated reaction pattern is also more involved; it is influenced by everything that has happened throughout his life up to and including the current situation.

The continuity between the psychopathology of the child and that of the adult is established in two ways:

1. The vicious circle of reaction patterns, the manner in which the individual approaches the world, carries out his tasks, allays anxiety, reaches goals—all these renew and maintain the basic psychopathological constellation. In other words, the fundamental personality tends, in its vital respects, to remain the same throughout life.

2. Potentially or actually, consciously or unconsciously, memory patterns are constantly revived. By "revival of memory patterns" is meant not memories and thoughts alone, but also

memory patterns in organic function, in behavior, in needs and desires, in emotional conditioning. The adult who has an unconscious feeling of rejection and is afraid of further rejection may have dreams and vague memories that seem to reinstate early experiences of actual physical punishment and withdrawal of gratification. To this extent, the sick adult is afraid not only of losing prestige and his neighbor's affection, but also (in a sense) of being beaten and whipped, of having his mother's breast withdrawn, and of having his father scold him (as if he were still a little boy rather than a grown man).

SUGGESTED READINGS

See Chapter XVI.

CHAPTER XVI

ORIGINS OF PSYCHOPATHOLOGY IN PARENT-CHILD RELATIONS

~~~~~~

The Personality of the Parents.—It is sometimes possible to predict roughly, even before birth, what a child's character will be if one knows the parents well. For instance, an important factor is whether the parents want the child. If they do not, if the coming child is unwelcome, there is greater likelihood of the child's being rejected, at least partially; and this rejection, whether open or hidden, conscious or unconscious, will eventually communicate itself to the child and create in him a feeling of rejection. The unconscious hostility, antagonisms, and resentment toward the child cannot under any circumstances be completely hidden from him, no matter how fair the parents wish to be. (Here, of course, we are speaking not of certainties, but of possibilities and probabilities; for often the unwanted child is well loved by his parents.)

Another example of possible pre-birth prediction is the more general statement that children of neurotic parents tend to be neurotic themselves. Among the many reasons for this prediction are identification with the parent, the likelihood that a frustrated parent will project his frustrations upon his child, or make him a vehicle for his own ambitions, or be "threatened" by either superiority or inferiority in the child, etc. Similarly, psychic healthiness in the parent will also tend to communicate itself to the child.

PARENTAL REJECTION AND THE CHILD'S FEELING OF REJECTION

The Need for Love.—In addition to what has already been said about the need for love—that it is referable to real gratification and sensory stimulations in the infant—several comments of another kind must be made. In an experiment described in an earlier chapter, D. M. Levy demonstrated the fact that there is in the infant an autonomous need for suckling for its own sake, as well as for the sake of nourishment. In the same way, in addition to the need for love because it means gratification and pleasure of various kinds, there may also be a need for love for its own sake. Many data bear on this hypothesis; none of them prove it absolutely, but all point toward it.

Another point that is important in the development of the child-parent relationship is the tendency to strong positive conditioning to the mother. She is the one who gratifies the infant, bathes him, cuddles him, and warms him. Hence he comes to love her, to need her, to depend on her, and—very important—to over-value her as well as his father. The parents tend to become awe-inspiring, omniscient, omnipotent, god-like beings, and the young child attributes to them practically magical powers. This in turn helps to make *him* feel utterly safe and secure, and makes it possible for him, by pleasing these wonderful beings and securing their praise, to start building up his self-esteem. As long as he feels that they are standing by him and are ready to help him, his self-confidence grows.

If the parent rejects the child, interferes consistently with gratifying his needs, punishes him indiscriminately merely for having needs—genital, eliminative, moving about, being curious, etc.—then the child feels not only rejected but also helpless, and his self-esteem is profoundly shaken. This does not destroy his desire to love the parent as well as respect him; nor does it remove entirely the feeling of securing some love, protection, gratification, and pleasure from the parent. In such a complex situation, new and more complex reactions might be expected to appear. As a matter of fact, such children do show full-fledged anxiety, hostility, guilt feelings, etc.

Forms of Parental Rejection.—Parental rejection, according to Levy and Symonds, may show itself in three ways: (1) neglect; (2) harshness, severity, punishment, cruelty; (3) strictness, over-ambition, too high standards for the child, dissatisfaction with the child as he is.

These, it will be seen, are expressions of either lack of love for the child, or actual hostility toward him. But there are many subtler forms inherent in the mother's unconscious rejection of the child. Thus, rejection may be expressed paradoxically by over-solicitousness, where the mother worries so much about the child that she restricts his activities "for his own good"; she may show a lack of respect for him, etc. In all these cases, the child usually feels that something is wrong, feels threatened, or actually has a conscious feeling of rejection, even though his mother's rejection is not conscious.

Another example of hidden rejection is seen in the mother who bargains with her affection. Such a mother continually offers love as a reward for obedience and threatens to withdraw it as a punishment. She thereby puts her child into an uncertain world, a world in which one of his basic needs may at any time be unsatisfied. So deep and so constant is the child's need for affection and for being certain and safe about it, that any tampering with affection strikes deeply at his psychological vitals.

The following excerpt is a good description of a rejected child:

"1. Children in Eleanor's grade were to ask their father some question or other and report to the class next day. Eleanor remained after class to ask if she could have a question to ask her mother instead, as she couldn't talk to her father since he didn't like her to.

"2. Eleanor had been referred to an oculist. Nothing done for month of September. Eleanor told teacher her father wouldn't get her glasses because it was just an idea to make money. School nurse called at home. Mother explained difficulties child and father had always had. Said she had given him one week more to get the glasses and then she would take Eleanor and charge the glasses to Mr. L. Explained her husband thought too much of this sort of thing was done in schools today. He had made the same sort of fuss when Eleanor had her tonsils removed two years ago. Did not want school nurse to talk to Mr. L.; afraid he might insult her. Eleanor came with glasses a week later, very worried about breaking them.

"3. In the Stanford-Binet test Eleanor was very confused. She could not control her attention but talked incoherently about anything that came into her mind. She had a pronounced stutter which disappeared during the course of the examination. She said that her father used dirty words to her and slapped her all the time. She is afraid of him, especially when he licks her. He didn't hit John and Betty. He doesn't like her. Knows no reason except that she had no curls any more as she used to when she was two years old. Was a pretty girl then, but now she isn't pretty any more, she says, so he doesn't like her.

"4. A few days later Eleanor told teacher father had brought presents home for them but she couldn't have hers. Mother explained later that when Eleanor hears father's car drive in she goes upstairs to bed to avoid seeing him. This particular time he called her downstairs to give her her present but not knowing what she was wanted for Eleanor called down that she was too tired. This sent the father off into a rage and he said she couldn't have hers next morning when the other two children told her there was a present for her. The mother persuaded him to give it to her three days later.

"5. Eleanor said she would like to study tap dancing but her father won't let her. She has picked up some simple steps by herself and dances to the radio when her father isn't home.

"6. Mother says Mr. L. often called Eleanor a 'liar' and tells her that as far as he is concerned he wishes she were dead. Called her 'dumb' the way she acts.

"7. Eleanor cannot speak to her father without stuttering badly.

This enrages the father. She does not stutter when talking to the mother or children."[1]

Results of Rejection.—Parental rejection is the method *par excellence* for creating insecurity in the child, an insecurity that is likely to persist through life unless something is done about it. Symonds (739), summing up the studies of parental rejection, finds that the rejected child is likely to be characterized as aggressive, rebellious, hostile, jealous, attention-getting, annoying in school, hyperactive, etc. He may also show such delinquencies as truancy, thieving, and lying.

These are all symptoms of general insecurity of the aggressive type. It is a pity that so few studies have been made of rejected children who show insecurity of a fearful, withdrawing character. In any case, what is common in all cases of rejection is a deep feeling that the world is hostile, unloving, and dangerous, and that it cannot be counted on. More specifically, we find reactions of worthlessness, isolation, humiliation, and of being unwanted and unworthy of love.

Neglect of the child is not to be wondered at when there are eight or ten younger children, when the parents are too poverty-stricken even to feed their children properly, and when the mother is far too busy to give them the attention and love that they demand. What can we expect but neglect or even hatred when a child is born to parents who never wanted him, for whom he represents only a burden and an unwelcome economic problem!

"We saw a little eleven-year-old recently with whom the directors of the institution could no nothing. She was timid and backward, always retiring, never taking part in the games of others; she spent her entire time with a similar companion who exercised a certain imperious sway over her through her jealousy. This outspokenly intelligent, but obviously deeply discouraged child had the sorriest home one could imagine. Her mother was a prostitute, her

[1] P. M. Symonds, *The Psychology of Parent-Child Relationship*, D. Appleton-Century Co., Inc., New York, p. 67.

father did not live at home, but returned only from time to time
dead drunk, demanding money from the mother to the accompani-
ment of scenes. The child sees, knows and understands everything. No wonder that she is pessimistic, that she approaches life
without joy, that she fears people and refuses to play with others.
One often sees inconsolably intimidated children from orphan asy-
lums, schools and other educational institutions and so-called con-
valescent homes. In some of these institutions an imperious medieval
discipline and lovelessness still rule in cold blood. It is little wonder
that these victims of inhuman education strive to commit those very
crimes against which one is attempting to shield them, or that
they leave these institutions with broken courage and vivacity,
unable to become a friend to anyone, unable to occupy any position, inapt in the easiest work."[1]

Affect Hunger.—The essential motivating characteristic of
the rejected child is a hunger for love resulting from "starvation," from lack of love. D. M. Levy (474) has named this
"affect hunger." But affect hunger may arise in other ways, and
these must not be overlooked. Levy has found many cases of
this hunger in orphaned or abandoned children who are handed
around from foster mother to foster mother and given no chance
to form any strong relationship.[2] Presumably, then, we should
expect affect hunger in any similar situation—for instance, when
children are cared for not by their parents, but by nurses and
governesses who, although efficient, may show no great love for
them.

Various symptom complexes may arise from affect hunger. In
the person who has been deeply wounded by this lack of love
and whose tentative attempts to get it have been rejected, it
may take the form of an apparent "emotional frigidity." However, the overt symptom picture may also take exactly the opposite form, being manifested "in various maneuvers to hold

[1] E. Wexberg, *Your Nervous Child,* Boni & Liveright, New York, 1927,
p. 127.
[2] See also Bowlby's excellent paper, The influence of early environment in
the development of neurosis and neurotic character, *Int. J. Psychoanal.,*
1940, **21,** 154-178.

closely to a person, to win demonstrations of affection, to plead for love, to utilize pathetic appeals in states of helplessness, in order to stimulate a love response from a mother-person. The kissing-bug reaction represents an avidity for physical affection . . . and belongs in this category of responses; so also the numbers of whiners and pleaders and naggers for attention, for closeness and for guarantees that the maternal sustenance will never be withdrawn. Out of this group, also, are derived . . . the overwhelming demands from a friendship later in life . . ." (474). Both types of symptom syndrome are illustrated by the following cases:

"My first example is an eight-year-old girl who was adopted a year and a half before referral. After an illegitimate birth, the child was shifted about from one relative to another, finally brought to a child-placing agency, and then placed in a foster home for two months before she came to the referring foster parents. The complaints were lying and stealing. The parents described the child's reaction to the adoption as very casual. When they brought her home and showed her the room she was to have all for herself, and took her on a tour of the house and grounds, she showed apparently no emotional response. Yet she appeared very vivacious and 'affectionate on the surface.' After a few weeks of experience with her, the mother complained to the husband that the child did not seem able to show any affection. The child, to use the mother's words, 'would kiss you but it would mean nothing.' . . . The father said he saw nothing wrong with the child. In a few months, however, he made the same complaint. By this time, also, it was noted that the child was deceitful and evasive. All methods of correction were of no avail. A psychoanalyst was seen. He recommended that the parents stop all correction and give the child a great deal of affection. This method was tried, according to both parents, with no result.[1] The school teacher complained of her general inattention, and her lack of pride in the way her things looked. However, she did well in her school subjects, in keeping with her good intelligence. She also made friends with children,

---

[1] [This technique usually works well.]

though none of these were close friendships. After a contact of a year and a half with the patient the father said, 'You just can't get to her,' and the mother remarked, 'I have no more idea today what's going on in that child's mind than I knew the day she came. You can't get under her skin. She never tells what she's thinking or what she feels. She chatters but it's all surface.' "[1]

"A patient was referred to the Institute for Child Guidance at the age of nine years, with a complaint of enuresis and temper tantrums. A visitor to the foster home wrote a letter to the Institute from which the following excerpt is taken: 'He is starved for affection. His mother rarely visits him, although she is urged to do so frequently. When she is there, he acts very infantile, climbing up on her lap, always wishing to be with her, and showing off. Then as time elapses after her visit, he becomes more unmanageable and disagreeable.' The history of the case is featured by the child's affectionate response to grown-ups, his making up to any stranger, the explosive and dangerous temper tantrums, and marked jealousy of the other children in the foster home. The 'hunger' element in the difficulty is seen in the response to grown-ups and to the mother, with whom he acts in complete disregard to what is usually a strong inhibiting influence—the presence of other boys. When his mother is about he is always sitting on her lap, he holds his face up to be kissed and puts his arms around her neck. According to the foster mother, he acts in these situations like an infant. Though affectionate to the foster mother, he makes no such display with her. The severity of the temper tantrums must be mentioned. On one occasion he tried to break up a game in which the other boys were playing. The foster mother sent him to his room, whereupon he tore up the bedding, and pulled all the pictures off the walls. On another occasion he attempted to hit a boy with an axe. On another, he chased the teacher and the children out of school.

"The patient lived with his father and mother in the first year of life. After the death of the father he was placed in an institution for a year, then for two years in a boarding home, from which he was removed by his mother. He was placed again in a foster home

---

[1] D. M. Levy, Primary affect hunger, *Amer. J. Psychiat.*, 1937, **94**, 644-645.

in which he had been living for a year and four months at the
time of referral. There are certain elements in the history that
indicate a certain modicum of affection from the mother and in the
homes in which he was placed. In one boarding home there was
an affectionate mother. The foster mother also was affectionate
with him. Furthermore, his own mother, though very spasmodic
and infrequent in her visits, was affectionate while with him.

"In this case, treatment consisted in getting placement with a
foster mother who could give him a great deal of affection. There
were only four interviews with the psychiatrist. They consisted
largely of chats about the foster home. Marked improvement in behavior occurred and continued for two years. A follow-up made
when the patient was twelve years, six months old, showed complete cessation of the temper tantrums, good school adjustment,
growth in responsibility, though no improvement in the enuresis."[1]

DOMINATION OF THE CHILD

Parental rejection has been seen to be the most important
creator of insecurity feelings in the child. Now we shall see that
domination of the child is the most important method of destroying his self-esteem, courage, and confidence. (There are also
other methods; rejection, for instance, often has this effect to
some extent.)

Again the general cultural attitude toward children is involved. Dozens of psychologists, sociologists, and anthropologists
have been alarmed by our tendency to think of children as not
quite human beings. We pet them, we play with them, we love
them, but essentially we tend to treat them as little toys given
to us for pleasure, rather than as an obligation. Ours is generally
not a child-respecting society. We may be sentimental about
children, but we seldom treat and respect them as independent
individuals; they are taught to respect older people, but older
people are not taught to respect them. In general, the technique
of handling and educating children rests firmly upon the belief
that they must be dominated. Fortunately, this situation is chang-

[1] *Ibid.*, pp. 648-649.

ing for the better; but even now it is still sometimes possible to say that a "well-brought-up" child is essentially one whose spirit has been broken, who is dependent rather than independent, timid rather than brave, helpless rather than self-confident.[1]

Essential respect for the child shows itself not in complete submission to his whims or in allowing him to dominate the household, but rather in not forcing his development according to a prearranged schedule. It means taking his desires and needs into account as well as those of the parents and of society. It means not using the child as an extension of one's "ego," but rather regarding oneself as a guide and helper who can aid him to develop along the path dictated by his own fundamental temperament. It substitutes fairness and reasonable explanation for arbitrariness. Psychologically, its most important result probably lies in giving him as much independence as is possible without hurting him, e.g., allowing him to go to camp rather than keeping him at home, permitting him to some extent to make his own mistakes and to learn for himself.

Another important technique for building up self-esteem is a generous though judicious use of praise and reward. The opposite technique lowers self-esteem by scolding, nagging, lack of appreciation and praise, setting up unattainable ideals, laughing at mistakes, ridiculing efforts, etc.

It should be emphasized that all the parental techniques

---

[1] There are still far too many who rely upon the whip as the main educational tool. But the advance of psychology, the scientific trend in education, and the child study movement are among other influences which are changing this rapidly. Such a rapid change has brought mistakes and overreactions, such as the tendency to eliminate discipline altogether and to identify the phrase "freedom and individuality for the child" with complete anarchy and lack of restraint or socializing taboos. Any Victorian novel will show that children are much better treated today. Gruenberg quotes the following from an 1834 issue of *The Mother's Magazine:* "Cost what it may, break the child down to obedience to the first command, and when this is once done, if you are careful never to let disobedience escape punishment of some kind or other, and punishment shall be effectual and triumphant, you will find it not difficult to maintain your absolute authority." The excerpt from van Paassen on page 222 is also of interest in this connection.

under discussion have partially desirable, partially undesirable results. This is well brought out, in the case of parental domination, by Symonds, when he says: ". . . Children of dominating parents are better socialized and have more acceptable behavior than the children of submissive parents. They show the results of training in their behavior. They are more interested in and have a better attitude toward work at school. On the other hand they tend to be more sensitive, self-conscious, and to have greater difficulty in self-expression than children who are given more freedom. Children of dominating parents conform more closely to the mores of the group in which they are reared." This is a fair picture of the "good child" in our society. Such training makes children obedient, orderly, and submissive. The only trouble is that the men in our society are supposed to be independent, aggressive, forward, self-confident, and strong; the resulting clash or conflict between their childhood training and these later demands is often pathogenic.

MATERNAL OVER-PROTECTION

The layman's synonyms for over-protection are spoiling, over-indulgence, over-solicitude, giving in to the child, and the like. D. M. Levy, the outstanding investigator in this field, has defined it more accurately in terms of the following four categories; however, he is concerned mainly with maternal over-protection (477).

1. Excessive contact between mother and child: The child may sleep in the mother's bed until he is relatively old, sometimes even up to adolescence. There is much fondling, kissing, hugging, holding the child by the hand, keeping him in sight, etc.

2. Prolongation of infantile care: The mother refuses to wean the child until he is several years old; she keeps him in infants' or children's clothing, and bathes, dresses, and feeds him, long after the average mother has given up these habits.

3. Prevention of the development of independent behavior: The mother refuses to allow the child to try his own wings, to achieve for himself, to stand on his own feet, to fight his own battles, or to choose for himself.

4. Lack or excess of maternal control: The mother alternately and inconsistently submits to and dominates the child. Or the child may definitely dominate his mother, or, more usually, the mother may dominate the child. Thus she may over-indulge him in regard to privileges and possessions, wait upon him, and give in to his every whim. If her control dominates, she may insist upon complete obedience in her attempts to prolong his infancy, making him stay away from other boys because they are too rough, forbidding him to take such chances as playing football, climbing trees, or riding a bicycle.

Other classifications of over-protection have been made. Hattwick, for example, has characterized it as follows:

1. The parent favors the child.
2. The parent is over-solicitous.
3. The parent treats the child like a baby.
4. The household revolves around the child.

As a rule, parental over-protection makes the child dependent and infantile, and fails to teach him how to meet the ordinary hazards of life which every normal person must face eventually. The child is guarded to a pathological extent against bad ideas, bad companions, sickness, and accidents. The effect of dominating over-protection are obvious—loss of strength, of independence, and hence of self-esteem. The overt result in people who were over-protected as children is submissiveness and dependency.

The foregoing description is characteristic of children who have been over-protected in a dominating way. When the over-protection is indulgent and submissive, quite different characteristics may appear; these can usually be summed up under the head of "selfish over-aggressiveness." Because the child has never been frustrated in any wish and has learned to regard other individuals as tools or means to his own selfish ends, he will tend to react violently, when deprived or restrained in any way, with "authority-rejection," selfishness, bullying, and attention-getting. His self-esteem, apparently high, may in reality be extremely shaky and easily threatened. Such a person is very apt to be insecure, and will easily become insecure, when he must step beyond the bounds of his own little kingdom. Other people will not give in to him as his mother did, and he will inevitably interpret this in terms of envy, hatred, jealousy, and the like. He will be disapproved of by others because of his lack of socialization, courtesy, consideration for others, etc.

The first of the following cases describes the dominating type of over-protection; the second, the indulgent type; the third, the dominating type when the child is almost grown up.

(*Male, 8 years*). "*Excessive Contact:* When he was an infant, mother could never leave him for an instant. When he was two years old, she had moods of despondency because she could not get away from him. She feels worried and unhappy when patient is out of her sight. Has been sleeping with him the past six months because he has called her. Lies down with him at night. Extra nursing care has been required because of his frequent colds. Mother says they are attached like Siamese twins.

"*Prolongation of Infantile Care:* Mother dresses him every day (age 8), takes him to school every morning and calls for him every afternoon. When at school in the morning she pays the waiter for his lunch and tells waiter what to give him. Breast fed 13 months. Mother fed him the first five years. Mother still goes to the bathroom with him and waits for him. Mother insists on holding his hand when they walk together. Resents his walking alone.

"*Prevention of Independent Behavior:* He has one friend whom mother takes him to see every two weeks. Mother does not allow him to help in housework for fear he'll fall and break a dish, etc.

"*Maternal Control:* Mother must have a light burning for him until he falls asleep. He goes to bed at 10 P.M. Mother always gives in to him; does everything for him; is dominated by him. He spits at her and strikes her."

(Male, 10 years). "*Excessive Contact:* Mother slept with him until he was six years old. During the entire first five years, the mother and patient lived alone with practically no other contacts.

"*Prolongation of Infantile Care:* The patient was breast fed to age 3, with the excuse, 'You know he was all I had.'

"*Prevention of Independent Character:* The mother changed the patient to another school because the walk there was a little shorter. She never allowed him to play with other children because they were rough, until age 8. He is now allowed to play with boys in front of the father's store. Mother hired an older boy to accompany him to school because he complained that the boys molested him.

"*Maternal Control:* Anxious, obedient child. Accepts mother's domination. Accepts mother's infantile methods of discipline without protest. Mother's 'slightest disapproval' is very effective in making him mind. He wants to do exactly what the mother does, helps her with the housework, and is over-responsive to her approval or disapproval."

This boy's mother forbids any athletic activity; and, though he is sixteen years old, he yields to her demands, except on one occasion, when the mother allowed him to play ball; she then accompanied him to the baseball field, to see that he wouldn't get injured. Though the mother will not allow him to go to the movies alone, he does not protest. . . . He was always "such a good baby." Girls regard him "like a sister." Interviewed with mother, he never speaks for himself.[1]

Over-indulgence is a weakness in maternal control, in which the mother yields to the child's wishes and submits to demands not ordinarily tolerated by most parents. The child is allowed to eat whenever he wishes, and to sleep regardless of hours. His behavior is disrespectful, and his refusals to comply with the

---

[1] These three cases are from D. M. Levy, Maternal over-protection, *Psychiatry,* 1938, 1, 578, 579.

mother's request are insulting. One mother does not go out in the evening because the child refuses to let her do so. Another child compels his mother to prepare meals whenever he wishes to eat; if he is not suited, he throws the food on the floor. In other cases the mother is compelled to sleep in the bed the son chooses, is struck, teased, bullied, kicked, pinched, sworn at, etc.

One might think that mothers who display such remarkable tolerance would show evidence of general submissive attitudes, but this is not true. On the contrary, their attitudes toward their husbands and friends are distinctly dominating. Let us see how these peculiar attitudes arise.

The Etiology of Maternal Over-protection.—In his study, Levy was able to isolate several of the most important factors that make a mother over-protective. We can do little more than list them here.

1. Factors that increase maternal longing for a child seem conducive to making the mother over-protective. Prolonged anticipation because of long periods of sterility, death of off-spring, spontaneous miscarriages, or serious complications during pregnancy all may increase the longing for a child and make him over-valued when he finally does come.

2. Sexual incompatibility tends to make the mother either more over-protecting or more rejecting. When husband and wife are sexually compatible and have social interests in common, they thereby create conditions that operate against a mother-child monopoly; a wife devoted to her husband cannot be exclusively a mother. In Levy's group of 20 undoubtedly over-protecting mothers, 80 per cent were sexually maladjusted. This contrasts with, and is about double, the usual figures for unselected wives, where sexual maladjustment ranges between 30 and 50 per cent. (Davis, 30 per cent; Hamilton, 46 per cent; Terman, 33 per cent; Lewenberg, 46 per cent.)[1]

3. The parents of over-protected children usually have little

---

[1] All these studies, and also Foley's which is mentioned later, are referred to in Levy (479).

social life in common. This was true for 75 per cent of Levy's group. In Lewenberg's study, social maladjustment in marriage was found in 88 per cent of over-protecting mothers and in only 38 per cent of a control group of non-over-protecting mothers.

4. Most over-protecting mothers give accounts of parental privation of affection and childhood play in their early life ("affect hunger"). A more exact study by Foley found that lack of affection in the mother's childhood occurred with greater frequency in the over-protecting group (68 per cent of 48 mothers), less in the group of rejecting mothers (42 per cent of 19 mothers), and least in a neutral group (15 per cent of 40 mothers). Levy's figures for his group of 20 over-protecting mothers show that 9 (45 per cent) received no affection from either mother or father, 12 (60 per cent) were deprived of maternal affection, and 16 (80 per cent) were deprived of either maternal or paternal affection.

5. The over-protecting mothers represent predominantly those who, as children, had a good deal of responsibility; e.g., they started work early, cared for the family, helped support the family, etc. In practically all the twenty cases, this responsibility was accompanied by considerable aggression. Since Levy thinks of active or aggressive responsible behavior as a distinctly maternal type of behavior, he comes to the conclusion that the over-protecting mothers showed strongly maternal behavior from an early age.

6. Sixty per cent of Levy's over-protecting mothers (no control data supplied) give clear evidence of thwarted ambitions. This, he thinks, tends to act as an enhancing factor for over-protection because of the mother's attempt to experience through the child the satisfaction of demands and ambitions which are necessitated by an experience of love hunger.

7. The fathers of over-protected children can be generally characterized as submissive, stable husbands and providers who have little or no authoritative role in the child's life. The phrase "discipline of the child was left entirely to the mother" is used

in thirteen of the twenty records. In three cases the fathers aided over-protection by indulging the child, in two they interfered with the mother's attempts at discipline, and in two others they had little contact with the child because of absence from the home. There was not one dominating father in the entire group. These men were not necessarily weak; some of them merely gave up in disgust.

8. Over-indulgence and spoiling by grandparents are fre-quent in these case histories.

Effects of Maternal Over-protection.—The characteristic ef-fects of indulgent over-protection are as follows:

1. Selfish, demanding behavior, sometimes to a psychopathic degree.
2. Frustration tolerance usually adversely affected. Even the slightest blocking of gratification is unendurable.
3. Difficulties in adjusting to routine and authority. The child must run things his own way; he rejects authority.
4. Difficulties in tolerating monotony and routine. The child is restless under discipline, he cannot take orders or carry through a long, monotonous task, etc.
5. Difficulties in social behavior. The child has bad manners, is impolite and undisciplined.

The indulged group shows a tendency toward earlier marriage. This may mean that sexually, as in other spheres, they are not to be denied. This group also has a curious self-assurance and unworried attitude, a feeling that, come what may, someone will take care of them.

In general, it may be said that the effect of indulgent over-protection on self-esteem and strength is to heighten them. The security of indulged people, however, is maintained only if the original situation (the continuous presence of the indulging parent or the person on whom they are dependent for gratifica-tion) is maintained. Otherwise a severe feeling of rejection will ensue.

The characteristic behavior of dominated over-protected children is anxious, submissive, sweet, and obedient. They want always to be with the persons by whom they are dominated and upon whom they depend, and they seek to remain in their good graces by the child-methods of sweetness and goodness. They may be expected to choose a maternal woman when they marry. For this group, as for the over-indulged group, the feelings of rejection are very severe when the original situation (presence of the person by whom they are dominated) is not maintained.

The two case histories which follow are in sharp contrast to each other. The first deals with an "accepted" child; the second, with an over-protected child.

"I have known Wilson for about five years. He has never had occasion to feel anything but perfect security in his environment from a social, economic, and love standpoint.

"His parents seem to be in agreement in all things for the boy. He is allowed and encouraged to go in for athletics in which field he excels and gets commendation. When in training for football his mother helps him to stick to his diet. Parents attend games and thus show their interest.

"In summer they have a summer home at the seashore where Wilson has many friends. He has his own sailboat and goes in for all kinds of water sports. The father is keenly interested in sailing, so he and the boy are together a great deal during the father's vacation.

"When the parents have taken trips in the past, Wilson always accompanied them. Now that he is older he does not go many places with his parents. He has many girl friends and being a football hero is much sought after by girls. They all tell how quiet he is but that he seems to enjoy the fun although he can't make it. He is very fond of dancing and goes to all school and community dances and takes a girl.

"His parents show a keen interest in and sympathetic understanding of his school work. They do not 'nag' him because he does not get high marks, and at one time were willing to pay for tutoring when he needed extra help in a subject. They appreciate that he is not a brilliant boy, that he is a slow thinker, and that it takes him longer to 'get things' than most boys in his group. However, they know that he is conscientious and that he really tries very hard so they encourage him in every way possible.

"His mother told me recently that Wilson had told her he would like very much to get into more school activities such as the monthly paper, but that it was only the bright ones that could do that and still keep up their work. He also said he knew he wasn't very smart in school. His mother told him that after all he was fortunate that he could do so well in athletics and they were satisfied that he was doing his best.

"These parents, it seems to me, are attempting to make the most of this boy's potentialities, not expecting too much, giving plenty of wise counseling and encouragement, an excellent example of an 'accepted child.' "[1]

"This case came to my attention first for irregular attendance at school. I found the mother kept the child at home for little physical ailments. He was a regular patient for a local doctor who 'carried the mother and child around in cotton batting' and encouraged frequent visits.

"Up through the first six grades W's school progress was very irregular. For several years in succession he missed whole months at a time. The mother brought W to school and met him after school. She even brought him at noon so no one would molest him. Only last year the mother came and complained that a much smaller boy in a special class (low mentality) made W give him money by a threat that he would beat him up. When the teacher pointed out the absurdity of the charge, the mother became indignant, but finally withdrew and allowed W to come to school alone.

"Practically all of W's time is dominated by the mother. He seldom plays with or shares in games with neighborhood boys. He goes downtown day in and day out with the mother. The mother has him help in the garden, calls him in when visitors come, goes with W and asks him to show the visitor his pets—a duck (he wanted it because Joe Penner had one), a small dog, and several

[1] P. M. Symonds, *The Psychology of Parent-Child Relationship*, D. Appleton-Century Co., Inc., New York, 1939, pp. 63-64.

rabbits. Mother gives the history of them all. W stands by and occasionally volunteers a few words.

"The father is disgusted. He formerly tried to make mother see that she wasn't fair to W, but now he says he gives up and allows the mother to dominate the situation. The father loves to go out in the woods, fish, and hike. He comes home from work and when the weather is favorable he takes his small family for drives through the country. On days off and week-ends they pack a lunch and go to a neighboring state to enjoy the woods and hills. He tries to interest W in fishing and outdoors, but the mother always accompanies them to see that W doesn't get hurt or go too far into the woods.

"From morning to night W is in the company of the mother or under her influence. She selects the clothes he is to wear for the day, knows his plans for the day, discusses his diet and personal habits, and decides what they shall do after school.

"The mother does not care for movies or reading, so W seldom sees a picture and seldom reads in his spare time although he does enjoy reading in school if encouraged. The mother does insist, though, that he take care of his pets. This he does conscientiously and well."[1]

Disturbances of the Family Constellation

Order of Birth.—Whether a child is the oldest or the youngest or the only boy or the only girl among the children will obviously have important psychological effects (Adler, Wile). However, these effects are so complex, and so few simple generalizations can be made, that it is difficult to treat them in a limited space.

Eisenberg, for instance, has found that the oldest child tends to be highest in dominance feeling (self-esteem), the second oldest to be second highest, and so on down to the youngest who tends to be lowest in dominance feeling. In general, it is fair to say that however important the place in the family constellation may be, it is *individually* important, and must be determined separately in each case that is investigated.

[1] *Ibid.,* pp. 111-112.

The Only Child.—The only child is apparently more likely to be brought up badly. He is likely to be over-protected in the worst possible fashion, and he is never dethroned by any later children. He is so important to his parents that they are apt to guard him with extreme care; they may spoil him completely and make him selfish, dominating, and egotistical, and at the same time essentially weak in his character structure. He tends to be deeply hurt when he is not the center of interest and attention. He is more likely to have nervous habits.

We wish to emphasize that all only children do not necessarily turn out in this way; there is a tendency in this direction which, if it is not to become dominant, must be counteracted by other measures—the intelligence of the parents, the psychological efficiency of teachers, the playmates, etc.

The Orphan; the Fatherless Boy.—Several dangers are encountered by orphaned children. First and most important, of course, is the fact that they usually have no one to love them as their own parents would; this leads to affect hunger. Institutions for orphans used to stress discipline and obedience rather than love and affection, but fortunately the trend is changing. However, there is no telling how many of these institutions are still serving in effect as breeding places for affect hunger.

The fatherless boy runs the danger of cross-identification. With no man in the home to look up to and identify himself with, he has no one to teach him to be masculine except the boys of his own age. If his mother is foolish and wishes all his love for herself, she may keep him from other boys; hence he may identify himself with her rather than with a man, and thus become feminine rather than masculine. He may also develop a feeling of being different from other children (which for the child usually means inferior to other children), as well as a feeling of isolation.

Quarreling; Separation of the Parents; Divorce.—The child whose parents are separated or divorced is apt to compare his family unfavorably with others, to feel that something is wrong with it. He is likely to feel ashamed, thwarted, and even cheated. A child's security demands a predictable, safe world, certainly in his immediate social environment—his family. If this is broken up, if the parents make mutual recriminations and accusations, the child loses this feeling of a safe harbor, of a unified, mutually loving family upon which he can count. Furthermore, in our society parents are all-important in socializing the child, and in this process each parent contributes something unique. The danger of cross-identification, discussed above, is also present here. Several investigators have shown that broken homes tend to have the same effect on children as parental rejection; that is, they either make the child very independent (a good effect) or extremely over-aggressive and even criminal (a bad effect) or else they break him completely and he becomes "crushed."

Sibling Rivalry.[1]—The situation in which sibling rivalry is manifested most commonly and strongly is the coming of a second child who dethrones the first one. The latter, having reigned supreme for some time in the hearts of his parents, having been given all their love, is now suddenly thrust out of the limelight by the arrival of the new baby; he therefore tends to feel neglected and believes that his parents no longer love him. In revenge he may turn upon the new baby. If he is young and uninhibited enough, this hostility may be expressed overtly in actual attempts to hurt the baby. If he is older, he will of course inhibit these attempts, but he may show various compromise formations; that is, he may behave in a way that compromises between the impulse to hurt the baby and the impulse to be afraid and guilty because of this impulse.

The primary effect of this situation is to create insecurity in the dethroned child. And, because insecurity is so closely related in the child to inferiority feelings, there may be the secondary effect—the loss of self-esteem, feelings of worthlessness,

---

[1] D. M. Levy (473) has done several illuminating experiments on sibling rivalry in children and is the source of most of the present information on this subject. His techniques will be discussed in the chapters on therapy.

etc. He may feel that he is unloved and unwanted because the new baby is in some way superior to him, more worthy of love. Urgent demands for reassurance by the parents are often made in such instances; and it is at this time, when the child's feeling of security and safety is most threatened, that parental thoughtfulness and affection are extremely important. Frequently a sibling rivalry is carried through life in a pathological form.

In later life, sibling rivalry with all its effects may become chronic because the parents prefer one child rather than another (favoritism). Damage to self-esteem is usually greater in such cases than in the sibling rivalry situation that we have already discussed. As a matter of fact, this is one of the most potent ways of undermining self-confidence and self-esteem, as well as creating a feeling of rejection.

Summary

Let us reorganize our material and look at it now from the point of view of the effects on the child's psyche rather than in terms of pathogenic situational etiology. The bad effects of all the situations, both social and personal, that we have enumerated can be grouped into the following three main categories:

1. The undermining or destruction of the feeling of security, of being loved, wanted, and accepted.
2. The undermining or destruction of the feeling of self-esteem, self-respect, strength, adequacy, etc.
3. Poor or inadequate socialization, in which wrong ideals are internalized, taboos and inhibitions remain inadequate, and bad social habits are learned.

In general, any force or situation which creates one of these effects also tends to create the other two, even though in a lesser degree. That is, any influence that affects the child's security feelings tends to some extent to affect his self-respect; furthermore, any influences that hurt either the child's security feeling or his self-esteem tend thereby to make him a more poorly socialized individual. Therefore any list of the forces which damage self-esteem is virtually a list of the forces operating in either of the other two situations.

A SAMPLING OF FORCES DAMAGING PRIMARILY THE SECURITY FEELINGS OF THE CHILD

1. Cultural Factors:
    Subcultural conflict
    Color, class, racial, or religious prejudice
    Poverty
    Chronic unemployment
2. Factors in Earlier Childhood:
    Parental rejection or neglect (lack of love)
    Parental over-protection
    Broken families
    Tension, quarreling, or divorce of parents
    Parental dishonesty and insecurity
    Identification with insecure individuals
    Social isolation
    Inadequate or incorrect sex education
    Traumatic experiences
    Unjust, inconsistent, or excessive physical punishment
3. Current Situational Factors:
    Chronic conflict
    Chronic frustration
    Humiliation and ridicule
    Irregularity, inconsistency, injustice, cruelty
    Sibling rivalry

A SAMPLING OF FORCES DAMAGING PRIMARILY THE SELF-ESTEEM OF THE CHILD

1. Cultural Factors:
    Authoritarian family structure
    Authoritarian education in the schools

2. Factors in Earlier Childhood:
> Dominating over-protection by the parents
> Domination by others
> Rivalry with older siblings
> Chronic invidious comparisons with others by parents
> Over-severe discipline and punishment
> Lack of praise, respect, appreciation
> Favoritism in family
> Identification with weak individuals
> Lack of independence, long-continued dependence
> Punishment by terror or shock

3. Current Situational Factors:
> Organic inferiorities
> Inadequate achievement, failure
> Feeling of difference from others
> Snobbishness or rejection by other children
> Inability to meet cultural demands for masculinity or femininity
> Over-severe ideals, feelings of sin or guilt
> Being regarded as a baby

A SAMPLING OF FORCES DAMAGING PRIMARILY THE SOCIALIZATION OF THE CHILD

1. Cultural Factors:
> Social disorganization
> Subcultural loyalties
> Poverty

2. Factors in Earlier Childhood:
> Pampering, over-indulgence, lack of discipline
> Direct acquisition of bad habits from others
> Lack of positive training in etiquette, manners, etc.
> Training in foreign folkways

3. Current Situational Factors:
> Identification with wrong people
> Boredom, lack of play opportunities

SUGGESTED READINGS

The original impulse which led to the subjects discussed in these two chapters came from Freud (273, 282); Adler (5, 6) later supplied additions and differences in stress. Easily the best experimental work on the subject has been done by D. M. Levy; his papers, especially those on sibling rivalry (473) and maternal over-protection (477), are particularly recommended. A good summing up is given in Symonds' book (739). Halverson's article (324) should also be consulted. The most interesting reading on this subject is *The Happy Family* by Levy and Munroe (482). Significant problems are concisely presented in Wexberg's *Your Nervous Child* (778). Fries' papers are also recommended, particularly (290). Flügel's book (243) is still good. An amusing and instructive article is Shipman's "How to make your son a misfit" (712).

PART IV

PSYCHOTHERAPY

CHAPTER XVII

AIMS AND NATURE OF PSYCHOTHERAPY

~~~~~~

The most important and adequate form of help available for psychologically distressed individuals is psychotherapy. This is a method of treatment which aims to help the impaired individual by influencing his emotional processes, his evaluation of himself and of others, his evaluation of and his manner of coping with the problems of life. It may also include, if need be, influencing and changing his environment and thus altering the problems he has to deal with and simultaneously increasing his potentialities of mastery and integration. What types of disturbances require psychotherapy? Any type of disturbance which is emotional in origin or which contains a large emotional factor may be benefited by it, for example, anxiety attacks or palpitation of the heart occurring in situations of psychological stress. Even a patient who has an organic heart disease may be incapacitated, not only by the effects of this disease, but also by the stresses originating from life problems which throw an additional burden on the damaged heart. Thus even a primary "organic" disturbance may contain an important emotional factor.

There are various forms of psychological treatment. Some emotional developments occur in all of them, but in varying degrees. Hence, we will first discuss the aims and the nature of psychotherapy in general, then proceed to a discussion of the various methods used. The problem of appropriate psychotherapy together with that of physical and chemical means of treatment, will be discussed again in a later section of this book in connection with each special form of psychological disturbance.

Any discussion of the aims of psychotherapy must represent a fusion of the immediate needs of the patient, the demands of society and accumulated psychiatric knowledge. It is convenient to differentiate between clinical and dynamic aims in psychotherapy. The former refers to obvious phenomena in the improved functioning of the patient; the latter to less obvious changes which, however, have a wide influence on various aspects of his functioning. The first, obviously, cannot be accomplished without the second.

AIMS OF PSYCHOTHERAPY

Relieving Symptoms.—To the patient who comes for treatment because of intensely distressing symptoms, the main aim of therapy is to relieve his suffering in the quickest and most direct manner. He may have suffered from less annoying symptoms for years—he may have been a problem as a neighbor, as a husband—but that does not concern him now. What he wants is direct aid for incapacitating symptoms. The relief of severe symptoms is one of the unquestionable aims of psychotherapy, but the therapist recognizes that the symptoms are the end product of the patient's conflicts, frustrations and disturbed relationships with his surroundings. Instead of treating the symptoms directly, the therapist may focus his attention on the patient's life problems, helping him, if necessary, to reorganize his character, in the expectation that as the patient grows stronger, his symptoms will disappear without primary attention.

Increasing the Ability to Be Happy.—In every maladjusted individual, the ability to enjoy life in one or another of its aspects is at least partially impaired. The patient may not recognize this fully, except in retrospect after he has improved. In other patients there may be the further complication that they crave forms of pleasure which cause suffering or lead to unhappiness—for instance, masochism. Such forms of activity must ultimately be replaced by forms of enjoyment compatible with health. A particularly important factor in the attainment of happiness is the ability to form genuinely affectionate relationships.

Increasing Efficiency.—The achievements of disturbed individuals characteristically do not come up to the level of their capacities. To improve the individual's functioning, the therapist will try to release his inhibited capacities indirectly, that is, by correcting the underlying stress and conflict. In this way, he is enabled to accept responsibilities, to concentrate on a task, and to persevere.

Aiding in Social Adaptations.—One aim of psychotherapy is to help the patient adapt himself to his surroundings. This does not imply blind conformity and obedience, but the desire and ability to contact other individuals and to adapt himself more or less to their way of life. Under the head of adaptability, we must include a closely allied trait, namely, flexibility. Some maladjusted individuals suspect everyone, rather than the specific few whom they might have reason to mistrust; they do not want partial affection from certain others, but complete worship from everyone. The therapist's aim here is to enable the individual to discriminate or to compromise, if need be.

Increased Spontaneity.—It is particularly important to pursue this aim, which is sometimes phrased, "letting the natural personality come out," in treating individuals who accede to all demands of their environment without providing for any satisfaction of their own demands upon life. Such people always do what they "should" do and rarely what they want to do (Maslow [534]). The purpose here is to enable them to find out and to follow their inclinations and their dislikes and to realize what type of *sound* person they want to be. Fromm (296) emphasizes that all psychotherapy may be summed up as an attempt to achieve a proper balance between spontaneity and adaptation. The therapist's aim should be to help the patient realize the discrepancy between his deeper inclinations and his obvious patterns of behavior, and to encourage him to pursue his legitimate goals with of course adequate regard for social limitations.

Adjusting Bodily Functions.—The general aim is to help the patient attain the best physiological functioning, with due regard to social patterns. The need for help is obvious in patients who suffer from a serious disturbance in the functions of various organs, but it is important in patients who feel anxious or guilty about such activities, also. Diminished, excessive or distorted functioning, such as lack of appetite, overeating and fetichism, may have to be adjusted. Sometimes the patient becomes aware of the disturbance, its emotional background, and the need for correction, only during the treatment.

Dynamic Aims of Psychotherapy

Increase in the Patient's Feelings of Self-Esteem and Security.—The patient's feelings of helplessness, worthlessness and guilt, and his fear of catastrophic breakdown must be replaced by a positive evaluation of his strength. His feelings of rejection must give way to feelings of acceptance. His fear of punishment and pain, his view of the world perpetuated since childhood as a place inhabited exclusively by stronger, threatening individuals, must be corrected and made more adult. He is, thus, enabled to give and receive affection. The resultant increase in the patient's strength has, as a further consequence, the ability to be self-assertive, enterprising and better able to tolerate failure, disappointment and pain. This development has been phrased by Rosenzweig (661) as increase in frustration tolerance.

Release.—Besides the patient's inclinations already discussed, there is further a release of certain hitherto forbidden and repressed impulses, such as aggression, and some types of sexual craving. The release may occur in the form of overt action, e.g., outbursts of temper or weeping, or in the form of consciously experienced craving. Such reactions largely disappear in the course of later developments, but a certain amount of release may be indispensable for ultimate psychic health. Impulses of this type play an important role in the individual's difficulties and he can be relieved only if they are uncovered.

Increase in Insight.—The patient's attention shifts from his symptoms and his obvious behavior to their *meaning*. He ac' quires knowledge of his hidden motivations, repressed wishes, conflicts and defenses, both past and present. He recognizes how these reactions determine his behavior. The patient gains insight only when his anxiety and guilt, which were responsible for the repression of his impulses, are allayed. With the development of insight there is a reorganization of his values and needs and consequently some of the most pernicious and harmful reactions disappear.

Increase in Self-Acceptance.—The patient learns to accept himself as an individual. This development has several aspects. With the disappearance of the pernicious impulses, with his increase in courage and self-assertion, he actually becomes a changed person; his desires and behavior no longer clash with his ideals. He has learned to accept his healthy cravings and he realizes that the impulses he has and did have are common to all human beings. With this, his feelings of being unique in his sinfulness, of being unworthy of the company of others, that is, his feelings of isolation, disappear and he can relate himself adequately to the group.

If a patient has a permanent defect, such as being crippled or blind, he may learn to accept his disability. If he is in a distressing situation which cannot be corrected at the time, such as having a cruel parent, he may learn to accept, without self-contempt and fear, the fact that he is resentful.

Increased Integration and Reaching Toward Positive Goals. —With the gradual disappearance of fears, inhibitions, conflicts, with the increase in spontaneity and the release of fundamental inclinations, the patient is enabled to develop new patterns of goal seeking. The joy of success renews his desire for new activities. In a sense, the whole psychotherapeutic process is an educational one. Man being the highest organism in the scale of intellectual development, one aim of all psychotherapy is to release the intellectual functions to their fullest potentialities; that is to say, to enable the individual to integrate his emotional and intellectual activities into a harmonious unity.

The Relationship Between the Patient and the Therapist

Personality and Training of the Psychotherapist.—The personality of the therapist and the manner in which he relates himself to the patient and reacts to his problems are of the utmost importance.

The therapist should have a true appreciation of individual differences and a respect for various personalities. He should recognize that the world is not made up of one kind of person. This characteristic is often called a tolerance for differences in other people—respect for another's individuality; it used to be described by such terms as the "sacredness of the human individual." The therapist's task is to find out in what direction the patient naturally tends to go, and then to help him proceed in that direction more efficiently.

The therapist should have an adequate knowledge and evaluation of himself. He should neither overestimate himself as an individual, nor have distressing feelings of inadequacy or insecurity. In other words, he should be a fairly strong individual. His knowledge of his own stress situations should enable him to understand the patient's sufferings and struggles.

The therapist must have a very extensive training. The day has gone when we could lean upon the "wise old man," although in cooperation with the therapist and knowing the limitations of his possible role, his therapeutic effect can be important. Psychology has advanced far beyond "just common sense"; to understand it today requires long and specialized study. The first step in training is for the psychotherapist to undergo psychological analysis himself. An adequate realization of his own moderate tensions, conflicts and difficulties will enable him to put them aside so that they will play no part in his treatment of other people. He should have no serious emotional difficulties, for he might thus be entangled in his patient's difficulties, disapprove of him, force him into wrong directions, or be blind to his shortcomings.

The good therapist should be interested in people in general and desirous of helping them. He needs a generous allotment of kindness and sympathy so that he may identify himself, to some extent, with every one of his patients.

Rapport.—Good rapport means a frank, trusting attitude on the part of the patient, which enables him to pour out his difficulties to the therapist. It implies hope of being helped, and eagerness to cooperate to that end. Through it, the therapist can use his knowledge and influence to help the patient, and the patient can take advantage of this help.

This essentially good relationship between patient and therapist is important for another reason. The patient has many conflicting attitudes and reactions toward the therapist, most of which are unconscious. In some treatments, as in psychoanalysis, these attitudes must be discussed. Unless a feeling of trust has been established, the patient will be incapable of discussing them or withstanding the effect of their discussion.

Permissive Attitudes.—The attitude of the therapist who listens to everything without condemning, censoring or being shocked has been described as a permissive attitude. Such an attitude assures the patient that he can say what he wishes without being reprimanded or losing the therapist's respect and affection. Thus, the therapist's role is one that is played by *almost no one else in our whole society.* He is almost the *only* person to whom all secrets may be told and who will be sympathetic and understanding even when he has to descend to what are called "the lowest depths of human nature." Indeed, the therapist not only permits, he actually encourages the patient to talk freely. This is universally reported to bring relaxation and relief in itself. Furthermore, it contains an aspect of confession inasmuch as the patient relates many things for which he condemns himself and about which he feels guilty. This makes him feel that he has faced his problems, has revealed himself honestly, has been forgiven, does not have to fear punishment and attack, and that he has been accepted by a person whom he considers important.

Receiving the Help and Interest of a Stronger Individual.— The patient regards the therapist as stronger and superior in comparison with himself. There are several reasons for this: the patient asks the therapist for help, whom he regards as superior because it is he himself, not the therapist, who is sick. He is influenced by the therapist's professional and individual prestige. The therapist's behavior, however, should not be dominating or disinterested; it should make the patient feel that he is interested in helping him. With this, the patient feels that he is not alone, but has a stronger person helping him to face the world and master his problems.

Adjustment of Irrational Attitudes Toward the Psychotherapist.—All the irrational attitudes, suspicions, hostilities and excessive demands which the patient has toward the world will unconsciously be focussed upon the therapist also. Thus, the relationship reflects the patient's whole attitude toward life and toward people in general. If the therapeutic process goes well, he learns to form a healthy, affectionate and self-respecting relation with at least one individual; usually this carries over to his daily life, so that he is able to relate himself well to other individuals.

Depending on the form of psychotherapy, the attitudes mentioned are brought, to a greater or lesser extent, into consciousness. Part of the process described occurs unconsciously in every form of effective psychotherapy.

SUGGESTED READINGS

See Chapter XVIII.

CHAPTER XVIII

TECHNIQUES OF PSYCHOTHERAPY

The psychotherapeutic needs of the community are difficult to estimate because figures are available only for the population in hospitals of mental diseases (see Appendix). The number of patients who suffer from neuroses, or disturbances of character and of organ function, and who do not need institutional care, is very great. In addition to treating the psychologically sick individual, psychotherapy has the preventive functions of treating the individual before serious disturbances occur, and of guiding the relationship between parent, teacher, and child in work and play.

Unquestionably, the present therapeutic facilities are insufficient to meet the needs of the community because of economic limitations and the lack of trained personnel. Therapy is relatively available for the very ill and for those who have a good income. The state provides hospital facilities for those who are incapacitated, or are dangerous to themselves or to society. Clinical facilities are, however, quite inadequate to care for the many patients who do not need hospitalization; and, in any case, these facilities are limited to large cities. The mental hygiene movement has done remarkably well in providing therapeutic and preventive facilities, but cannot take care of the entire nation. These statements apply even to relatively short forms of therapy; they hold even more for such prolonged treatment as psychoanalysis. The solution to these problems lies in the direction of increasing the number of trained therapists, in providing increased clinical facilities, and in increased emphasis on research to improve the effectiveness and discover new forms of shorter therapies. Of course, there is also need for more social psychotherapy—changing society so that it will be less of a source of anxieties, conflicts, and frustrations, and making psychotherapy available early in educational institutions—from the nursery school to the university.

The problem of the relationship between theories and results in psychotherapy is a vexing one because of the difficulties of truly experimental work in treatment. The saying of a nineteenth-century psychiatrist, "psychiatry is the art of applying a science which does not exist" is no longer true today. But it is true that something that could be called psychotherapy existed long before there was a science of psychology and psychiatry. Therapies of such type, as treatment by magic in primitive societies, were based on obviously false theories, yet they were often effective. We realize now that their effectiveness was based on suggestion, release of pent-up emotions, expiation, relief of guilt feelings, unwitting reassurance and support. Unconsciously, the patient came to feel safer and his system of defenses was bolstered. Even today, practices based on theories which run completely counter to scientific thinking, manage to achieve partial or sometimes even complete symptomatic cures.

One may ask, "if they achieve their effects, what difference does it make how they do so?" Quack cures are temporary at best, often harmful, and they delay proper treatment. While it is true that some patients can achieve a symptomatic cure without the attainment of true psychic health, even such treatment should be administered by an expert. And while it is further true that theories can be no more than good approximations of what takes place as a result of certain procedures, these approximations can be developed along scientific lines. They should constantly be improved and, as a result, further improve practice. In the evaluation of psychological practices, theories, and findings, no moral discussions can take the place of sober scientific search for facts and methods.

How do patients react to the suggestion of psychological treatment? Some welcome it because it relieves their perplexity about their condition, and because they recognize their emotional plight. Others become frightened or resentful, either because emotional disturbance implies "insanity" to them, or they feel humiliated by the idea. After proper explanation and reassurance, such patients may accept the suggestion—sometimes after a further period of suffering. Some, however, refuse permanently, and continue to suffer, there being no reliable way of inducing such patients to accept treatment. Dangerous patients, of course, must be committed to mental hospitals.

A variety of techniques has been developed in treating patients psychologically. We can differentiate various integrated forms of psychotherapy, such as hypnosis, psychoanalysis, or institutionalization. In the following we will discuss both the various integrated forms and the special devices in use, including those which are largely in the research stage.

Therapeutic Interviews.—An interview is any type of prolonged contact between the therapist and the patient in which conversation plays a prominent role, and which centers around the patient's problems. The set-up is such that it encourages the patient to unburden himself and talk about his complaints and of the stresses and strains of his existence. Some patients do this almost spontaneously, whereas others require a measure of guidance from the therapist. The aim of the therapist is to have the patient touch, sooner or later, on all significant aspects of his life. He may guide the patient's conversation to further topics by repeating, in the form of a question, something which the patient has already touched on, or by raising new queries. In this procedure it is very important to observe the patient because he shows by facial expression, changes in color, halting and evasion, where the points of stress lie. Such signs, if they are mild, guide the therapist in recognizing what points should be taken up, and if they become severe, what points should be left alone for the time being.

The patient should not be forced in the conversation because this can do damage or may cause him to break off the treatment. To know in what direction to guide or not guide the conversation, the therapist must have a thorough knowledge of psychopathology. It is obvious that in the interview, the patient does most of the talking and that the interview is both a diagnostic as well as a therapeutic procedure. The close interrelation between diagnosis and therapy is one of the most characteristic and unique aspects of psychotherapy.

Interviews of this type usually last about an hour and occur once or twice a week. If there is a great need for help, they may be given daily for a period of time. If they are effective in patients who do not require institutional treatment, beneficial results may be apparent after one interview, but they should definitely be evident after about five to ten sessions; otherwise, it is futile to continue. The total number of interviews needed depends on the patient. Some gain full benefit from about five interviews; others continue for several months, improving all the while; and still others make use of the treatment, with some interruptions, for years—it being the only measure which enables them to stand the recurrent strains of their existence. Other methods which can be used in conjunction with the sympathetic guidance in the patient's story of his difficulties will be discussed later.

Why and how is the patient benefited by this type of procedure? The answer lies in what we have discussed in the preceding chapter. The fact that the patient talks to an individual whom he considers strong and capable of giving help, who listens to everything and who encourages him to speak without condemning or punishing him, in itself allays his fears and guilt, and makes him feel more worthwhile and accepted. Together with this, there is an implicit development in spontaneity and frankness through the very fact of talking about forbidden and avoided subjects. He gradually feels that he has faced himself and his problems. The burst of emotions frequently occurring in interviews leads to release. The comparatively healthy and self-respecting relation established with this one individual, the therapist, carries over to the patient's daily life. With the shift of the patient's attention from his symptoms to the circumstances and relationships out of which they arise, there is a considerable development of insight.

It is obvious that some of these developments in the interviews are similar to the effects obtained by confiding in a trusted and sympathetic friend. Besides this, however, the therapist, because of his special knowledge, guides the patient's conversation to all significant points of stress; furthermore, such emotional entanglements as insistence on complete dependence or submissiveness, or subsequent feelings of humiliation are prevented.

Interview therapy may be particularly effective in relieving the acute symptoms of any psychoneurotic disturbance of relatively recent origin. It can be very effective in patients who have mild disturbances of a psychotic type, but can still function in society. In addition to organic treatment, it can be of further benefit to patients with psychological disturbances complicating an organic ailment.

Although other measures besides interview may be used in treating the patient, a survey of his difficulties should never be omitted. This is needed so that the therapist may know what measures are imperative—for example, proper supervision if the patient is suicidal, and what measures should not be used lest they cause an aggravation of the patient's condition. Likewise, the therapist must not overlook an organic disturbance; if necessary, he must advise physical examination and laboratory tests.

Interpretation.—Interpretation consists of the therapist's pointing out the nature of the patient's reactions to situations, his unconscious conflicts, cravings, and anxieties, on the basis of the observation of and information received from him.[1] It is one

---

[1] The term "deep therapy" is sometimes used for any procedure that changes an individual's character structure for the better. Coordinate with

of the most effective and, if improperly used, one of the most dangerous weapons of psychotherapy. One type of interpretation occurs implicitly in most interview therapy. The very fact that the therapist guides the conversation from the patient's symptoms to the situation in which they arose, implies a connection, particularly if he directly asks the patient what occurred on a given day before this complaint started. After hearing of the incident, he may ask, cautiously at first, "Do you think you were disappointed, afraid or angry?" The patient may come to this conclusion himself and the therapist may agree. If the patient comes regularly for a prolonged period of time, the therapist may begin, with due caution, to point out to him feeling of humiliation, attitudes of dependence, etc., and with limitations, may interpret his dreams. Recklessly used interpretation can cause intense emotional storm. There are very serious reasons for the patient's lack of awareness of his motivations, and the interpretation may threaten his whole security system. Interpretation is one of the main tools of psychoanalysis and will be discussed in detail under that heading.

There is one form of therapy in which the patient comes daily and in which the therapist attempts to get as quick a knowledge of the patient's conflicts as he can and then uses all the tools of interpretation continuously. This type of treatment lasts several months. The patient probably does not gain extensive fundamental insight, the psychological obstacles being too great for the brief period of time; but very much happens to him emotionally. In the hands of some skilled therapists, this type of treatment can be very effective.

Reassurance.—We will discuss under this heading how the patient is made to feel (1) that he can be hopeful, (2) that he

---

this usage is the definition of "symptom therapy" as any technique that removes the symptoms without changing the character in any profound manner. However, it now seems probable that changes in character structure may be effected by therapies in which insight is unnecessary, as in work with children, particularly if the child's environment is changed at a relatively early age.

is accepted and loved (security), and (3) that he is worthwhile and can respect himself (self-esteem). Properly conducted interviews work implicitly in this direction by the very fact that the patient reveals his innermost secrets, experiences of rejection, humiliation, his failures, and his aspirations, to an individual who is important to him, and who listens to him with respect and sympathy.

While some patients prefer an aloof, impersonal attitude in the therapist, the majority thrive best if he is warm and sympathetic, as expressed by his demeanor, facial expression, and voice. The patient derives reassurance from the fact that he is accepted for treatment, the implication being that he is not really hopeless. It is useful in addition, if the therapist actually tells the patient that he can be helped. If, during the interview, the patient asks direct questions about his condition—whether he can be helped, by what methods, and why, the therapist must use his judgment as to whether he ought to answer them and to what extent. If the patient is very anxious but is emotionally able to trust the therapist, the answers should be firmly encouraging. Other patients, eagerly asking for reassurance, become alarmed by the therapist's statement that they are not in mortal danger because it implies to them that he does not realize the gravity of their condition. If the urgency in such patients is great, the therapist has to preface his encouragement by assuring the patient that he is fully aware of his suffering and difficulty. It is apparent from this that the form of reassurance has to vary considerably from patient to patient.

Voicing the conviction that the patient is worthwhile, that he has good capacities, and that he can be loved and accepted by others, can have a powerful effect on him, and may prove to be lifesaving. However, one must beware of the quackery of guarantees of cure and flowery promises of the patient's ability for superior achievements. Such measures achieve temporary success, at times, but the later disappointment may be disastrous. At other times, praise given to a person who does not feel worthy of it defeats itself by creating suspicion of the therapist's motives. This mistrust breaks the rapport and by disturbing the relationship may make all the other efforts of the therapist worthless.

Advice.—Many people conceive advice to be the most important task of the therapist, but this is not so. It is best, as a rule, for the therapist to refrain from giving direct advice in a given situation, but merely to help the patient to discover the answers for himself. The reason for this is that some patients resent advice even though they have asked for it, and as soon as they get it, they proceed to prove it to be wrong. Others, not being able to carry out the suggestion because of their conflicts and anxieties, begin to feel worse or worthless over the failure, or blame the therapist for it. In some emergency situations, however, direct advice must be given to prevent disastrous action on the part of the patient. Some exceptional patients accept directions from the therapist approvingly and do not become disturbed regardless of whether they carry them out, modify them, or fail to fulfill them successfully. In such instances, after cautious attempts, the therapist should not refrain from giving advice, but should emphasize that he is giving his own evaluation of the situation, and that he counsels a course which, in his opinion, seems best. The patient should feel free to accept or reject it.

The following is an illustration of how contact with the therapist helps the individual to arrive at a decision by himself:

A student, who seemed very distressed, came begging for help. She had a serious problem which she could not possibly solve by herself; she needed someone else's opinion and advice. Her story, as she told it, was that she had to choose between two men who wanted to marry her. One was poor and without any prospects, the other was somewhat older and could offer her a great deal more security. It was soon evident that she wanted to talk herself out completely, for she interrupted whenever the therapist started to ask a question. So he just sat back, nodding, smiling, frowning, or grunting at the proper moments, but saying nothing. As she talked, she seemed to become more and more definite about being in love with the first man and not with the second. After about an hour, she made her final decision. She seemed greatly relieved, thanked the therapist profusely for his help, said that she could never have reached a decision without the aid of a psychologist, and left. The therapist had said hardly a word throughout.

Information.—Information given to the patient by the therapist is often essential and useful, and, of course, has emotional implications for the patient. It should be given with proper regard for his emotional needs and with the full realization of the fact that his lack of knowledge in certain subjects has emotional reasons. Information imparted rudely or with superior contempt can have very disturbing effects. Knowledge of sexuality is most often needed by the individual, particularly if he is a child or adolescent, and often even if he is an adult. Enlightenment regarding conception, intercourse, masturbation, etc., may be necessary. Proper knowledge allays insistent curiosity, and with it, the fear of rejection and guilt engendered by this curiosity. The fear is further allayed when the patient realizes that his impulses are common to all human beings. Adequate enlightenment imparted early, before erroneous conclusions with their emotional repercussions have become an integral part of the personality, may do wonders in relatively mild disturbances. The limitations to the value of imparting corrective information which runs counter to the patient's emotional needs, is exemplified by women who believe that "all men are brutes seeking only sensual gratification." It is futile to tell them that they are wrong and to try to back up this statement because their conviction is motivated by complex fears.

Objective means can sometimes be helpful in correcting an erroneous self-evaluation of the patient. Intelligence tests may convince the patient that he is not as stupid as he thought he was, and personality inventories may show him that his case is not as extreme as he thought. By various other means it may be possible to have the patient make an inventory of his assets and liabilities on the basis of objective evidence. Measurements, norms, and indices of variations from the norm, whether anatomical, psychological, or physiological, may all be helpful in allaying persistent doubts. Even if the objective information thus obtained is not flattering, it may still serve a psychologically good purpose. It may help the patient accept his limitations in one field, and look for success and satisfaction in another.

Persuasion and Exhortation.—There is an implicit appeal to the patient's judgment and his desire for well-being when it is explained to him that he has a psychological illness and that he would derive benefit from having it treated. This, however, cannot be called persuasion since it is not done insistently. The patient may be refusing treatment for emotional reasons which cannot be reached by the shortcut of logic. More persistent reasoning with the patient may be necessary during the treatment to prevent him from taking a harmful course of action.

These measures are quite different from an appeal to the patient's reason for the purpose of ridding him of his symptoms. Holding them up to him as being contrary to logic does little good since they are brought about by emotional factors, and the patient is only made to feel more inadequate and deprived of sympathy.

Dubois, a French psychotherapist, first explained to the patient why the symptoms were present and then why it was logically unnecessary for them to appear. In reality, this is an appeal to reason in the hope that the patient will "see the light" as it were and get better through his intellect and will. Most workers in the field do not consider this an efficacious method since the patient does not acquire genuine insight, and there is an attempt to force a logical shortcut in emotional problems.

Appeal to the patient's moral and social values and to his sense of duty as a therapeutic measure, is harmful because it makes the patient feel more worthless. It can be used in some emergency situations, however,—e.g., to tide the patient over during a period of suicidal danger. No therapist should disregard individual differences or dogmatically impose his own standards and ideas on the patient in the attempt to provide him with a positive way of life. He must be wary of trying to make a religious patient an agnostic or vice versa. The patient's ideals and aspirations must be decided on the basis of self-development.

Influencing the Patient's Environment; Guidance.—The therapist may contact the patient's family or his friends, either to gather needed information, or to provide for adequate supervision and help, or to correct conditions unfavorable to the patient. If he is in serious danger of harming himself, this measure is imperative. In the case of children and adolescents, cruel, humiliating treatment or mistaken kindness and overprotection on the part of the parents have to be remedied. In other instances, an understanding and helpful friend or member of the patient's family can help a great deal by giving him emotional support and guiding him in practical situations. Contact by the therapist with the patient's family is an emotional problem for the patient which he may welcome, or of which he may be afraid for fear that the therapist will side with the family against him. With adequate handling, however, it can be done with benefit both to the patient and to his family. The cooperation of a social worker on this point may be invaluable.

Companionship and participation in the activities of the group relieve the patient's feeling of isolation and raise his self-esteem. The therapist may encourage him to make friends and to join clubs or other social organizations. Such suggestions should be given when the patient has become emotionally able to reach out toward other people, and to cooperate in ventures with them. Here too, the help of a social worker or of a friend may be needed. Newly-found friendships and love may completely alter the patient's emotional life. If it is the right kind, it may bring him relief and happiness, which ultimately must always be found outside of the therapeutic situation. If it is the wrong kind, it will bring more suffering.

The therapist should always be alert to the problem of his patients' ambitions and aspirations. Most patients have them when they enter treatment, and become better equipped to follow them when their conflicts are resolved; others develop them during the treatment. To patients who feel perplexed and at a loss the therapist should give all assistance in their attempt to orient themselves. Here, the aid of applied psychology may be invaluable.

Reading in Psychology.—Reading in psychology may be helpful to disturbed individuals, particularly to college students, if it is accompanied by interviews and discussions, and if the right kind of books are chosen. Unless such a book conveys reassurance, support, and permissiveness, and unless it is clear in its presentation, it will frighten the patient more. There are very few books of this type available:—an outstanding work like *The Happy Family* by Levy and Munroe shows that it is not impossible to popularize a thoroughly scientific point of view and apply it to the stresses and strains of everyday life.

Training in Behavior.—Individuals who have changed their social environment—for instance, some college students who come from rural districts, poor families, or immigrant homes—may be ill at ease, shy, and generally lack poise because they are unprepared for conventional social intercourse. They can frequently be made happier, more effective, and better liked by adequate social training—wearing the "conventionally-right" clothes, learning the ordinary social cliches and etiquette, learning how to dance, and to handle introductions properly. The therapist himself may give him some advice, or he may suggest that he learn all this from a friend.

Other patients are benefited at the proper point in the progress of psychotherapy, if they are given some suggestions on how to behave in certain situations and with certain people. Thus, they may be urged to admit ignorance and *naïveté* when they feel them, rather than to act sophisticated; in other words, to be frank and honest whenever possible. Such suggestions are effective if the patient already has proper understanding of his past behavior.

William James assumed that the emotion felt introspectively was simply the perception of bodily changes and therefore if one were to behave as if he felt happy, he actually would feel happy after a time. This is too simple an assumption, but the technique of behavior change can be used to some advantage. Mildly maladjusted college students who lacked self-confidence, were told in detail how to act on certain occasions so that they would appear self-confident to other people. Some of them reported later that after they had convinced themselves of the success of their deception, they actually began to feel more self-confident. An extension of this method is that of imitation. The individual who is shy or who feels that he behaves incorrectly is instructed to select a person who behaves as he would like to and to imitate this person's behavior (not his total personality). After a while, his behavior becomes less and less artificial and external, and more and more natural and habitual.

Training in Relaxation.—The method of teaching relaxation is complex, but it may be briefly described as an attempt to secure voluntary control over the tension and relaxation of various muscle systems by increased awareness of kinesthetic impulses in these muscles (Jacobson [382]). The underlying idea is that tension accompanies most psychological disturbances and this tension should be directly attacked without regard to the factors that create and maintain it. Too much has been claimed for the technique which is based on too simple an assumption. It is, however, of experimental interest and can be used as an adjunct to other therapeutic measures.

Conditioning.—The use of various conditioning methods for therapeutic purposes is in an experimental stage, and in the case of favorable effects, the underlying processes are probably complex. They should be used only after adequate study of the patient's conflicts has been made.

The student will recall the famous laboratory experiment by John B. Watson (764) in which he created a fear of rabbits in a young child and then removed it by a process of reconditioning, that is, by changing the stimulus "sight-of-rabbit" from a producer of fear to a producer of pleasure.

The conditioning principle has been used in the treatment of adults, the so-called "association-set method" being a verbal form of it. For example, Yates[1] instructed one of her patients—a girl who burst into tears in the presence of men, particularly her father—to relax and repeat the word "calm." She was to connect with this word definite ideas of peace, security, and well-being, and to be convinced that this word would always bring her physical and mental composure. In this way she succeeded in maintaining her composure when faced with the actual distressing situation.

Recently Mowrer (578) and Morgan experimented with negative conditioning for the cure of enuresis. Their apparatus consists of a very absorbent blotter separating two copper wire screens. Any moisture makes a short circuit between the two screens; closing the delicate circuit causes a bell to ring, which disturbs and awakens the child. Thus, simultaneously with the undesirable urination there is a disturbing and frightening sound. After this has happened three or four times, the impulse to urinate will awaken the child in time. The results reported by these two investigators are uniformly favorable. In spite of the fact that this is obviously only symptom treatment, no undesirable after-effects have been noted in follow-up studies. The student should remember, however, that the problem of enuresis is a complex one and is closely connected with the problems of frustration and rejection in the child.

[1] D. H. Yates, An association-set method in psychotherapy, *Psychol. Bull.*, 1939, **36**, 506.

The observations of Max[1] may be mentioned as another example of negative conditioning experiments in an adult. His subject associated homosexual impulses with a particular object. The conditioning process consisted of presenting this object to the patient, at the same time giving him an electric shock. Although he still retained thoughts of a homosexual nature, this special object finally lost its power to induce them in him. The student should again remember that the problem of homosexual impulses is very intricate and is connected with the problems of the organism as a whole.

RELEASE THERAPY

Release therapy, as developed by Levy (478), is a combination of the principles of "catharsis" with the usual play technique in the treatment of children. Breuer and Freud (97) observed in cases of hysteria in adults that the emergence of a repressed memory in hypnosis, accompanied by a storm of emotions, was followed by a disappearance of symptoms. They called this phenomenon "catharsis." Play technique is the use of appropriate toys with the purpose of having the patient, usually a child, express his needs and conflicts in the presence of the therapist. In release therapy the child is guided in his play and is permitted to engage in bursts of violent activity under the controlled set-up of the therapeutic situation.

A relatively small number of such sessions was followed by the disappearance of the child's symptoms under the following conditions: (1) the child's problem was precipitated by a specific event—a frightening experience, the birth of a sibling, or the divorce of the parents; (2) the child was under ten years of age so that his problems were of relatively short duration. If the child's fears had persisted so long that they affected the social relationships, his handling of the sex problem, or even his intellectual functions, release therapy in itself was distinctly

[1] L. M. Max, Conditioned reaction technique; a case study, *Psychol. Bull.*, 1935, 32, 734.

inadequate; (3) regardless of the child's age when he was referred for treatment, and regardless of the specificity of his problem, the problem must have arisen in the past. Release therapy could not be used successfully for longstanding problems which continued during the period of treatment—for example, the results of intense maternal rejection or overprotection.

In release therapy the therapist's interpretative function is reduced to a minimum. In some cases, when play sessions are devoted entirely to the release of destructive behavior and general naughtiness, there is no interpretation at all. D. M. Levy (478) reports the following cases:

A girl aged two years, nine months, was referred because of tantrums in which she would remain mute for about half an hour, and because of general lack of responsiveness to affection. In the nineteen sessions with her, her activity consisted chiefly in throwing clay on the floor, stepping on it, playing with water, at times spilling it on the floor and sitting in it, and cutting, throwing, and hitting objects. Such activities presented release of aggression, the doing of forbidden things, and indulgence in infantile pleasure. Notes from the mother received during the sessions indicated an increase in general affectionate response, a more outgoing quality, and a marked increase in speech in this girl.

By overcoming anxieties and inhibitions that have to do with orderliness and hostile expression, release therapy with this type of child makes possible an extension of personality which was presumably bound down by a discipline administered too early or too severely. In this process a permissive and accepting attitude on the part of the therapist is extremely important.

Another case in which release therapy was effective is the following:

A girl aged five years, the youngest of three children, was referred because she refused to be a girl, cut off her curls, insisted on being called by a boy's name, and fought against wearing girl's clothes. The difficulty started when she was about four years old.

The difficulty was related to jealousy of a boy of her age who showed off his strength to her and pooh-poohed girls; and of her brother, aged thirteen, the next older sibling, whom her governess distinctly favored.

For external reasons it was possible to have only five sessions with the patient. These consisted chiefly of release of destructive behavior on boy dolls. . . . In the fourth session she said that girls were better than boys; they could wear pretty things.

A follow-up one week after the last session revealed that the patient made no protest against wearing girl's clothes and stopped insisting on being called by a boy's name. A follow-interview six years after the treatment indicated normal feminine development.

It is important to realize that there are cases in which the important task of treatment is to give the child insight into his own motivation, that is, to interpret to him the meaning of his symptoms. Release therapy alone cannot do this. In some severe cases it is at once clear that the child's attitude toward the therapist is too suspicious or too anxious to permit him to risk the rapidity of release therapy. Furthermore, in children with severe neuroses, the problem is primarily psychoanalytic.

Group Therapy

Group therapy has been used by Burrow (123-125), Wender (776), Schilder (684), Moreno (568), and others. It is the best means of removing feelings of uniqueness and isolation and restoring community feelings. It is desirable, though not imperative, for the group to be closed; that is, the membership should be the same over a long period of time, no new members being admitted until a new group is formed. Under such circumstances, frankness, mutual discussion of problems, and comparing of notes are made possible without self-consciousness.

Schilder employs group psychotherapy to some extent in the out-patient department of the Psychiatric Division at Bellevue Hospital in New York. The patients are first seen individually; during this interview they give their life histories and are taught the principles of free association and dream interpretation. After several sessions, when a preliminary insight is reached, the patient is asked to write a detailed autobiography, and is given the following instructions:

"When you write down the history of your life you must not keep back anything. There may be situations and experiences which you would prefer not to write about; still you have to write them down. Do not attempt to make a masterpiece out of your biography. Write it down as it comes into your mind and do not polish it. Contradictions and repetitions may finally help us to an important insight. It is of great importance that you write down every remembrance pertaining to your early childhood up to the age of five. Give particular attention to your first memories. It will help you to keep in mind that the relation to father, mother, siblings, and nursing personnel are of particular importance. Write down, therefore, whatever you can remember about them.

"You certainly have not always experienced love only. There must also have been some experiences of hate. In the world of the child there is a great interest in food, in urination and defecation. Write down whatever you can remember about this. Sexual experiences are not uncommon, even in early childhood; try at any rate to give an accurate description of the development of your sexual attitudes and also do not forget that your opinions about sex problems are of importance.

"Follow these fundamental relations through the school age to puberty, and describe the relation to all the persons who played an important part in your later life. These relations are relations to friends and to love objects. Also give consideration to your professional achievements and to the persons you have met in your professional career.

"Give an idea of your aims, goals, and interests, and how they have developed. In every person's sex life are facts and experiences which he feels do not conform to the professed moral standards. Do not hesitate to write these experiences down. The human life is not merely filled with experiences and memories. Everyone has fantasies, wishes, and dreams. Write them down as far as you can remember them. There is no necessity that you give this report quickly. Take your time. No detail is unimportant which comes to your mind. Give us also a general idea of your surroundings in childhood and in later life."[1]

The patient is then seen with a group of other patients at various stages of treatment. Schilder begins the session by reading one of these autobiographies aloud. This is discussed as it would be in individual psychoanalysis, but the other patients may comment or cite experiences of their own. Schilder may also ask for associations from any member of the group, giving interpretations when they are appropriate, and making general remarks about the underlying mechanisms that are involved; he sometimes uses a specific case as the basis for a lecture on a general psychological process. These groups never number more than six or seven, and are seen perhaps once a week.

Schilder reports that this type of group therapy makes the patient see the fundamental identity of his problems with those of others because it takes him out of the isolation characteristic of neurosis. The members of the group easily identify themselves with one another. The fact that one brings forward experiences which another has hidden, lessens resistance and results in a freer flow of both conscious and unconscious material. In similar experiments, Maslow has found a strong tendency for all the members of the group to grow to like each other.

Schilder reports that with social and obsessional neuroses the results have been particularly beneficial; they were also good with anxiety neuroses. Most depersonalization cases were benefited to some extent, and some were cured. Character problems could be solved. Only *some* cases of hysteria were influenced, and no results were obtained with manic-depressive patients. (See later chapters for descriptions of these types of cases.)

INSTITUTIONALIZATION

The most dramatic form of environmental change effected in the treatment of patients is institutionalization, recommended

[1] P. F. Schilder, *Psychotherapy*, Norton, N. Y., 1938, p. 201.

chiefly for the cure of psychotics, but also for drug addicts and some very sick psychoneurotics. Commitment to mental hospitals or sanitoria not only protects the community from dangerous patients, but helps the patients also. It guards him against self-injury, against social, moral, or financial harm—for example, from sexual misdemeanors, or reckless financial ventures. It further removes him from the influence of people who may have precipitated his illness.

Institutional care imposes a regular routine upon the patient. He gets up, eats, and carries out his tasks according to a definite schedule. The fact that he does not decide these things for himself has a stabilizing, calming effect if the routinization is not too rigid. Furthermore, confinement frees the patient from many of the problems which have pressed upon him so heavily, and it safeguards him from humiliation, sneers, and ridicule; it places him instead in a more sympathetic and understanding environment in which people regard him as sick and not as an object of horror, awe, or laughter.

Finally, of course, institutionalization makes various forms of psychotherapy and medical therapy available such as, occupational therapy, hydrotherapy, metrazol or insulin shock therapy, malaria treatment, and other forms of fever therapy. These will be discussed in connection with the various psychoses.

SUGGESTED READINGS

There are relatively few good treatises on specific psychotherapeutic aims and techniques. However, we can recommend Schilder's *Psychotherapy* (684), Diethelm's *Treatment In Psychiatry* (183), Franz' *Nervous and Mental Re-education* (255), Stekel's *Techniques of Analytical Psychotherapy* (725), and Robinson's *Supervision In Social Case Work* (647). For an interesting historical glimpse, read Zilboorg's *The Medical Man and the Witch During the Renaissance* (814).

Various points are illuminated in papers by Anna Freud (268), Klein (431), Homburger (360), Levy (470, 473, 475, 478) and Felix Deutsch (171).

CHAPTER XIX

SUGGESTION AND HYPNOSIS

~~~~~~

THE NATURE OF SUGGESTION

There are two types of suggestions: ideomotor, and prestige (584, 376). It is difficult to separate them perfectly, for the two intermingle in many actual instances of suggestibility; but it is possible to find extreme and therefore relatively pure instances of each. Prestige suggestion is, by definition, a response to social stimuli, whereas ideomotor suggestion may or may not be.

Ideomotor Suggestion.—William James long ago postulated the theory that, unless it were positively inhibited, an idea tended to express itself quite automatically and reflexly in corresponding behavior. This theory was attacked by Thorndike and others mainly on the ground that "idea" is an unscientific concept which no one can define. If, however, stimuli and stimulating situations are used instead of ideas, there is a great deal of evidence to indicate that James's theory can be taken seriously. So long as there is no inhibiting force, a stimulus, whether externally or internally administered, tends definitely to elicit the response which is suitable to it or has been connected with it. The reason this ideomotor tendency is not more apparent in everyday life is that when we are conscious and wide-awake we tend to inhibit it.

Consciousness is, from this point of view, a state in which inhibitory tendencies are alert and ready for action. There are various states in which these tendencies are themselves inhibited or dulled—sleep, drunkenness, fever, great emotion, abstraction

301

and absent-mindedness, and, as we shall see, hypnosis. In reality, many of the phenomena that are called imitation, sympathy, and empathy are frequently simple examples of this fundamental ideomotor tendency.

Hull (376) describes several experiments that will serve as illustrations of ideomotor suggestion. For instance, a subject who is brought into a room where a person is straining vainly to touch a point that is just beyond his reach will himself unconsciously strain. There are innumerable examples in everyday life. For example, as the characters on the motion picture screen smile, so also will the audience smile; as they frown, so will the audience frown. The spectators at a football game will lean over to the right as the player attempts to make a wide sweep around the right end.

Prestige Suggestion.—Prestige suggestion may be made clear by the following examples: The observers at an art gallery are apt to consider that the painting which has received first prize is the most beautiful. The opinions of the rich, the powerful, the people in authority, receive more attention and are taken more seriously than those of the poor and the weak. He who is confident and sure of himself is much more likely to have people do his bidding than the person whose self-esteem is low. The experiments of Cantril, Lorge, and others have shown that the prestige of the name of the creator of a work of art is important in determining its evaluation. Thus a group of people listening to music, supposedly by Beethoven, will rate it high; they will rate it much lower if they are told that its composer is relatively unknown.

The concept of dominance status is essential to an understanding of prestige suggestion. This is defined as the relationship whereby other people defer to one's own impulses, wishes, opinions, etc. The person whose status is subordinate is likely, where there is a choice between his own opinions and those of someone else, to consider the other's opinion better than his own. Thus he usually does what he is told; he takes suggestions, both direct and indirect.

The Nature of Hypnosis

The "Waking Trance."—It is essential that it be clearly recognized that suggestion and hypnosis are not abnormal, but normal and universal. Many of the phenomena observed in a hypnotic trance may be seen in waking life; furthermore, most if not all of them may be elicited in everyday life, but with more trouble. Only for historical and traditional reasons are discussions of suggestion and hypnosis not included in textbooks of normal psychology.

Let us now consider some phenomena that are common in everyday life and which will help us to understand the hypnotic trance—for example, the state in which attention is concentrated on a certain problem. Attention is a total response of the whole psyche in which every tool of adaptation is brought to bear upon a problem. The more the attention is focused in one direction, the less will be paid to peripheral objects or happenings, or to stimuli that are irrelevant to the problem. It is this aspect that is of greatest interest here. Thus, a person who is solving a geometry problem, reading a fascinating book, or thinking over an important personal problem will show great sensitivity to anything connected with what he is doing, but a decrease in sensitivity to everything else. He will become to some extent anesthetic—blind to what is happening around him, deaf to irrelevant noises, anosmic to irrelevant odors, etc. Certain motor phenomena may also appear; that is, he may show waxy flexibility (see Glossary), or he may become rigid or tense. There will also be some amnesia for everything that happened during this period of concentration and that was unrelated to the problem. In other words, such a person may be said to be in a trance. And if we now test the very plausible hypothesis that at once comes to mind—that in the waking trance as in the hypnotic trance, suggestibility (or ideomotor tendency) is enhanced—we shall find it to be corroborated. The student can easily try the experiment himself. If, when he is at the movies with a friend, he waits until the friend becomes totally engrossed with the film and then whispers quietly, and without disturbing his absorption, "Raise your arm" or "Open your mouth," the command will often be obeyed. However, it must be administered with just the right intensity; furthermore, the waking trance will ordinarily be broken immediately after the suggestion is complied with.

Methods.—There are almost as many ways of producing hypnotic trance as there are hypnotists. For instance, Hull, Erickson, and Wells, all outstanding workers with hypnosis, use different techniques. Usually, however, the technique employs some combination of relaxation, visual concentration, and verbal suggestions. Neither relaxation nor sensory fatigue produced by concentration is absolutely necessary. For that matter, it is possible to induce trance without suggestion if the other two elements are present and the individual is particularly susceptible to trance.

Some give suggestions in a friendly way, others give authoritative commands; still others are coldly scientific and impersonal. Some use suggestions of sleep; others never do this. Some prefer phonograph records for presenting the various suggestions. All of these methods are successful. The technique finally chosen is a matter of the operator's personal predilection and of the needs of the particular patient.

Thus in assaying the relative efficacy of various hypnotic operators and the validity of their results, we must take into account many variable factors—there are many kinds of hypnotic trance and many techniques for inducing them; subjects and operators vary in personality and have widely varying beliefs and expectations about hypnosis; there are various depths of trance, and there are many ways of selecting subjects.

It is not surprising, then, that different experimenters sometimes come to different conclusions. For instance, some are con-

vinced that women are easier to hypnotize than men; others
believe that the opposite is true. Some operators report great
feats of endurance and remarkable memory efficiency which
others do not observe in their cases. These conclusions obviously are conditioned by the many variable factors that have
been mentioned.

The Classical Phenomena of Hypnosis: Amnesia.—The subject who is in a deep trance will spontaneously develop an
amnesia for everything that happened during the trance. It may
have lasted an hour or two, and he may have carried on conversations, walked about, and obeyed various commands; but
when he wakes he will remember nothing that happened. If
the trance is not so deep, he may have hazy memories or even
a clear recollection of what happened.

Anesthesia.—In the deep trance, the subject will develop
spontaneously a deafness to any other sound but the operator's
voice. The operator can suggest almost any other anesthesia—
anosmia, insensitivity to pain, etc.

During the course of an experimental hypnotic trance, the subject began to moan with pain and doubled up with a stomach cramp.
She was asked what had happened and she reported that she had
eaten too much of some bad food. It was suggested to her immediately that the pain had disappeared, but she kept on doubling
up, rubbing her stomach, and groaning. When she was asked if it
hurt, she said no, in spite of her groaning. She was also told that it
would not hurt when she woke up. Just after this, she broke through
the trance spontaneously and awoke, but continued groaning and
rubbing her stomach. She looked surprised; and when asked what
was wrong, she said she didn't know. She was asked if she was in
pain and said no. She was then asked, "If it doesn't hurt you, why
are you behaving like that?" She replied, "I don't know. It just
seems that I can't stop doing this."

Motor phenomena.—Such motor phenomena as complete
limpness, complete rigidity, waxy flexibility, localized paralysis,

etc., can be induced. These will ordinarily not develop spontaneously, but must be suggested.

Hypermnesia.—Experimenters have found that forgotten events can be recalled on command more easily in the hypnotic trance than in the waking state. (See page 311.)

Partial release of inhibitions.—There is a slight weakening of the subject's inhibitions. However, we wish to emphasize the fact that the most important inhibitions remain active, that people will do almost nothing in the ordinary hypnotic trance that they will not do in the waking state. Various unpublished experiments indicate with few exceptions that the popular belief concerning the increased possibility of criminality and immorality is almost entirely false; a recent paper by Erickson (225) practically proves this.[1] To say that inhibitions are somewhat lowered means simply that a subject who wants very much to do something which he cannot do in the waking state, will find it somewhat easier in the trance.

Loss of capacity to initiate action.—The patient in a trance will sit quietly and do nothing until he is given some suggestion. If he is commanded to walk about the room or perform some task or to behave naturally, he will do so. Afterward, he will sit stolidly without moving. An onlooker will notice that he is slow in his movements and appears dreamy. In other words, he does not initiate activities spontaneously.

Heightened suggestibility.—Suggestibility is, of course, the chief characteristic of hypnosis, and the most startling. As long as the suggestions are acceptable, the patient will carry them out immediately and without question. This statement holds not only for behaving and talking, but also for inducing anesthesias, paralyses, and amnesias. Hallucinatory, visual, auditory, and painful experiences can also be suggested; as we shall see, various bodily states—headaches, nausea, sleepiness,

[1] See, however, Wells' more recent paper, *J. Psychol.*, 1941, 11, 63-102, in which he presents contradictions of Erickson's results.

or insomnia—can be induced by suggestion in the hypnotic
trance.

"I had induced hypnosis in a boy of twelve who was extremely
fond of chocolate éclairs. Giving him a plate to hold, I suggested
that he should see on it a chocolate éclair. Now, on this plate was a
reproduction of Millet's celebrated picture The Gleaners, in which
there are three female figures, two bending forwards and one up-
right. After a second or two, the boy said in high glee: 'But there
are three chocolate éclairs, and two of them have an odd shape, for
they are bent in the middle.' This was a well-marked instance of
hallucination or illusion by compromise."[1]

Hypnosis and Physiological Depression.—There is some evidence that the hypnotic trance may be considered to resemble
a physiological depression, akin, in some ways, to the state produced by alcohol, anesthesia, sleep, fatigue, etc. It is easy to
agree with this when a hypnotized patient is observed. He
breathes more slowly, he is lethargic and relaxed, his arms hang
limply, his head slumps on his chest, his eyes are closed, his
responses are much slower, and in general he looks as if he
were asleep.

In this connection, several experimental findings are of interest. Using a plethysmograph, Walden noted a sudden short
constriction of the peripheral blood vessels at the beginning of
hypnosis which was followed by a gradual dilation until the
end of the trance. At the moment the subject awakened, there
was again a brief constriction. Pulse rate and respiration became slower, and there was a steady but slight drop in the
rectal temperature, with a concomitant rise in surface temperature. Dorcus and Shaffer found that blood pressure decreased
during a trance, along with a drop in the pulse rate. Even
though there is no definite evidence to this effect, Beaunis believes that muscular tension is lessened in a trance, although
not uniformly; he also reports a considerable spontaneous de-

[1] C. Baudouin, *Suggestion and Auto-Suggestion*, Dodd, Mead, New York,
1921.

crease in auditory acuity. Hoff and Schilder found that some subjects who could not be hypnotized easily could go into a trance if they took a hypnotic (paraldehyde).

These and similar findings all seem to support the hypothesis that the suggestion tendency is stronger when the highest nerve centers are inhibited. However, too much cannot be made of this evidence because there is too little of it; furthermore, the hypnotic trance is a variable rather than a uniform phenomenon, that is, it differs widely from person to person and from experiment to experiment.

Some Fallacious Notions About Hypnosis.—Certain erroneous ideas regarding hypnosis have persisted down to the present time. Among the more common are the following:

Fallacious Beliefs	Facts
1. Not everyone can hypnotize; a person must have some electrical or supernatural power, or animal magnetism; he is in some way different from ordinary men.	1. Theoretically, anyone can hypnotize. Hypnosis consists in creating conditions that encourage the appearance of a tendency which inheres not in the hypnotist, but in the person being hypnotized. No special qualifications are required except confidence, a certain amount of prestige, and a knowledge of the procedure.
2. Hypnosis is abnormal, weird, and supernatural.	2. Hypnosis is a perfectly normal phenomenon which is manifested in a mild form in everyday life without attracting any particular attention.
3. Hypnosis is dangerous; it is to be feared and condemned.	3. In the hands of the amateur non-psychologist, hypnosis may be dangerous; but in the hands of the skilled technician who uses it for scientific or therapeutic purposes, it is a

Fallacious Beliefs	Facts
	powerful instrument for good. No harmful effects have ever been confirmed in the literature.
4. Only people with weak wills can be hypnotized; hypnosis breaks down will power.	4. Hypnosis has nothing to do directly with will power. If anything, it is the people with somewhat stronger wills who are most hypnotizable (Maslow [534], Wells [772]). Even long-continued trances need have no effect on this quality. Some subjects have been hypnotized more than a thousand times without any perceptible effect on their will power (Erickson).
5. Only stupid people can be hypnotized.	5. Just the opposite is true. The ability to be hypnotized is positively correlated with intelligence.
6. Not everyone can be hypnotized.	6. Theoretically, any normal person can be hypnotized, some much more easily than others. Psychotics are the only group generally reported to be "immune" to it, and even a few of them have been hypnotized.
7. Immoral and criminal acts are possible under hypnosis.	7. The person in a trance will do nothing that he does not want to do and that he would not do in the waking state. If anything, experiments along these lines show that people are much more suspicious of

Fallacious Beliefs	Facts
	immoral or criminal sugges-tions in a trance than in the waking state.
8. People are able, when hyp-notized, to do things hitherto impossible—play the piano, speak an unfamiliar foreign language, etc.	8. Except in some cases of neu-rotic inhibition, people can do nothing in the trance that they cannot do in the waking state. Thus a person who plays the piano well but has stage fright while playing, may be able to play better when hypnotized because the fears that inhibit the display of an ability can be controlled by hypnosis.

Hypnotic Therapy

Hypnotic Suggestions.—Before a patient is treated by the hypnotic technique, he should be closely studied during inter-views. There are several reasons for this. First of all, everything significant about him must be found out. Second, this procedure enables the more intelligent use of hypnotic suggestions. From a therapeutic point of view, hypnotic suggestions should not be simple, direct commands about a symptom; they should be ex-pressed in general terms and refer to situations that he is about to face. For example, the operator suggests that the patient will react more desirably if he puts himself in a certain frame of mind. "You will have a good time at the party; everyone will like you. You will feel gay."

In spite of the fact that the reaction to the hypnotic technique varies with the patient and that usually only a small percentage of people can go into a deep trance easily, the usual hypnotic technique, with adequately given suggestions, is of therapeutic value, even with patients who do not go into a deep trance (Hoff and Schilder). There have been attempts to combine psychoanalytic treatment with hypnosis (Ferenczi), but the results have not been altogether satisfactory.

Suggestions given during a trance will sometimes help considerably in breaking various undesirable habits—insomnia, nail-biting, cigarette smoking, etc. However, this is not altogether simple, for the suggestions must be very detailed and must be given repeatedly over a long period of time. It is not enough to say to the hypnotized person, "Stop smoking." He may have to be hypnotized again and again, and the suggestions be made gradually, rather than being given as a direct command. Thus the operator may suggest that the cigarettes he will smoke the following day will taste like straw or cause disgust. In relieving insomnia, the patient is not told merely to sleep well; the operator tells him that when he goes to bed he will feel relaxed, his tensions will disappear, thoughts of sleep will come into his mind and that as he thinks these thoughts he will fall sound asleep. Similarly, anxiety symptoms, various bodily symptoms characteristic of emotional stress (a lump in the throat, palpitation, etc.) respond well to hypnotic suggestions. Sometimes more serious symptoms such as tics, enuresis, etc., can also be relieved (see Smith [718]).

Breaking Through Amnesias.—If the therapist has the patient's cooperation and can induce a fairly deep trance, it is comparatively easy for the patient to recover forgotten material —alcoholic amnesias, hysterical fugues or even shock amnesias. The patient who has "lost his personal identity" may remember his name, address, etc. Also because of the hypermnesia in hypnosis, the trance may be a useful adjunct to ordinary psychotherapeutic work, particularly in exploring and recovering early memories, even memories of traumatic experiences that have been partially repressed.

A practiced hypnotic subject came back from a week-end party with a complete amnesia for all the events of both days. She had been completely drunk throughout all this period. A few days later she received a letter from her hostess asking for a ten-dollar bill that had been entrusted to her. The subject did not remember receiving any bill, nor, of course, did she remember what she had done with it. It was at her request that hypnotic treatment of the amnesia was attempted. In deep trance she was asked to reconstruct all the events in order from the moment of her arrival at the party. She was able to do this very easily, with no more than slight hesitation here and there, until she came to the point where she remembered being given the ten-dollar bill to hold. She remembered that she was wearing a borrowed dressing-gown and put the bill in the pocket of this gown. She was then awakened from the trance and was told what she had said. She wrote to her hostess and the bill was found in the gown.

Interview Under Hypnosis.—Any of the general processes of psychotherapy may be carried on under hypnosis as well as in the waking state. Thus, the therapist may impart interpretations or therapeutic insights to the hypnotized patient if for some reason he does not wish the patient to have any memory of the process. Frank discussion is sometimes easier for patients in a trance than it is in the waking state; embarrassing or shocking subjects can be discussed more easily. It is often possible to break through a severe block or resistance that threatens to slow up treatment by putting the patient into a trance and encouraging free association. When it is necessary to be brutal to the patient—accusing him of a lie, or telling him a very unpleasant truth—he can bear the shock more easily in a hypnotic trance.

Removing Hysterical Symptoms.—In cases of hysteria, when it is desired to remove a symptom quickly, the hypnotic trance is a fairly easy means of doing this. Suggestion can be used when the patient is awake; for example, the therapist may apply an electrical current to a paralyzed limb and tell the patient that this will cure the paralysis. In one case, pernicious vomiting was stopped with aspirin tablets, simply by convincing the patient that these tablets were a wonderfully potent new medicine. However, such measures are usually purely symptomatic treatments because they do not go to the root of the disturbance. The symptom may be expected to reappear later or to be replaced by another hysterical symptom.

Hypnosis as an Analgesic.—When a deep trance can be induced, pain may be easily dispelled. Esdaile has reported a long series of surgical operations, including amputations, abdominal and other equally severe operations, where hypnosis was the only anesthetic. It has often been used as an analgesic during childbirth; there can be no possible harm to either mother or child. This method is reported to be widely used in France and Russia, but for some unknown reason has not yet been accepted by the medical profession in the United States. The superiority of hypnotic over chemical anesthesia is obvious in certain cases, particularly for poor operative risks, e.g., bad heart.

The Induction of Relaxation by Hypnosis.—The excellent and widespread effects of the release of bodily and psychic tensions have been amply demonstrated by Jacobson (although the psychodynamics of relaxation are often much more complex than he indicates). There are scattered reports of similar effects achieved by hypnotic relaxation—fatigue and insomnia being relieved, a calm and peaceful state of mind being induced, constipation being removed and good digestion of food being promoted, etc. Since Jacobson's technique of progressive relaxation is long and difficult, a possible short-cut with hypnosis would seem to be a fruitful research project.

SUGGESTED READINGS

The earlier books by Bernheim (81), McDougall (519), Forel (249), Bramwell (96), etc., are still readable and useful. We recommend more strongly, however, Hull's *Hypnosis and Suggestibility* (376), which sums up his work and that of many of his students; and the papers by Erickson and his collaborators (218-228), and by Wells (772-773). The best reading on suggestion and auto-suggestion is Baudouin's book by this title (53). For more recent experiments, see Murphy, Murphy, and Newcomb, *Experimental Social Psychology* (584). The best psychoanalytic approach to hypnosis is presented by Schilder and Kauders, *Hypnosis* (687). Schilder's *Psychotherapy* (684) is useful on hypnotherapy.

CHAPTER XX

PSYCHOANALYTIC THERAPY

~~~~~~

As in all disciplines, it is important to differentiate in psychoanalysis among (1) the method of procedure, (2) the data obtained, (3) working concepts and hypotheses, (4) practical applications, the most important of which here is therapy.

Many short illustrations will be used to make the relationship between data and working concepts clear; in addition to these, we shall carry one case throughout the entire chapter, always giving as many facts about this patient as are needed for the subsequent discussion.

A Typical Case.—A 30-year-old woman, whom we shall call A. V., applied for psychoanalytic treatment because of an emotional depression which followed a disagreement with her husband. (This was her second marriage.) The disagreement had arisen over the departure of her husband, who was a prominent bacteriologist, from the city for a period of two months, for occupational reasons. She knew the reason for his leaving the city and approved of it intellectually, yet she asked him not to go. When he left in spite of her request, she became resentful and depressed; her depression continued even after he returned.[1] She suffered from insomnia, fatigue, loss of appetite, frequency of urination, and partial frigidity.

She was a very gifted laboratory worker and had published several articles and books on scientific problems. When not obviously depressed, she was calm, serene, and poised. Her relationship with her husband was fundamentally good. They respected and were

[1] The condition from which she suffered is commonly termed "hysterical depression."

emotionally attached to each other, and had many scientific and artistic interests in common.

The following series of events occurred during the third month of analytic treatment: One Friday, the patient stated that she felt very cheerful, that her depression had disappeared, and that she was grateful to the analyst for this. In fact, she thought that she was quite well. The analyst reminded her that some of her complaints, such as insomnia, frequency of urination, and sexual frigidity, were still present, and that she was still having dreams in which her husband was killed (hostility) and others in which she was a little girl and the analyst was feeding her (dependence). He pointed out to her that the attitudes and motivations which had been responsible for her complaints had not been clarified, that the disappearance of her complaints did not mean the elimination of the needs and reactions responsible for the original appearance of her depression, and that her feeling of well-being was based chiefly on the fact that she felt that she had the complete and exclusive care of the analyst. From now on we are concerned not so much with the analyst's remarks as with the patient's reactions and behavior in response to them.

The patient was ten minutes late for her interview the following Monday; this was unusual, because hitherto she had always been prompt. She gave no explanation for her lateness, but talked in a lively and pleasant manner during the hour, and then, contrary to her usual habit, left without saying goodbye. On Tuesday she was late again, talked freely, and again left without saying goodbye. On Wednesday she came on time and related a dream that she had had Sunday night. This was unusual because she regularly told of her dreams in the next interview. Her dream was as follows: She was back in the college dormitory in a room that was shaped like the analyst's office. There were five beds in the room, one of them being placed as the analyst's couch was. She was dissatisfied in the dream because she had to sleep in a room with four others, but consoled herself with the thought that eventually she would have a room to herself.

The patient thought of the following facts in connection with the dream: She recognized that the dream represented the analyst's room because of the similarity of the rooms and the location of the analyst's couch. In connection with not having a room to herself, she remembered that a former classmate of hers had once remarked: "An intelligent and scientifically trained individual can know as much about himself as an analyst can. Real friendships can do more for one than analysis. Analysts are really pretentious." In connection with the five beds in the room, she thought of the fact that she was the oldest of five siblings.

On reviewing some of the events of the last few days, the patient said that she had been late on Monday because she bought a dress before coming for the analytic hour. She was surprised to hear from the analyst that she had been late on Tuesday also. She did not remember it. Likewise, she could not remember at first that she had left twice without saying goodbye, and then she said: "I don't know why I did it, I just did not feel like saying goodbye." She then added, "I do not know why I waited three days before telling you about the dream. I did not think of it on Monday, and I felt reluctant to relate it on Tuesday." The analyst asked her: "How would you explain the events of the last few days?" She replied, "I don't know."

The various aspects of the patient's behavior—namely, being late twice, leaving twice without saying goodbye, not relating her dream at the proper time, the content of her dream, her thoughts in connection with the dream, forgetting part of her behavior, and her inability to account for her behavior—are all data which appear to be similar in nature and are interrelated. Such data are of value only if they can be used to construct a psychological reaction and if the meaning of this reaction can be conveyed to the patient.

The analyst told A. V. that the details of her behavior during the last few days seemed to indicate that she was resentful toward him; she was conveying to him that he was incapable, that he was not doing anything for her, that there was not much sense in her coming for treatment, and that she was better off buying a dress. A. V. replied that she was not aware of any such attitudes, but acknowledged that the incidents admitted of no other explanation. The analyst then went on to say that she really did not want to disparage him, but that she wanted exclusive and complete affection and care. This was evidenced by her dream with the disappointed wish and the later hope to have the analyst (represented by the analyst's room) all to herself. This construction becomes even more convinc-

ing if we realize that A. V.'s behavior followed the analyst's comments on Friday. She evidently evaluated his remarks as meaning
that he was not willing to give her this exclusive affection and care.

We can ask why the patient forgot part of her behavior, why she
was unable to give an explanation, and why she spoke cheerfully
and politely during all this period if she was resentful. There were
several reasons for this. The chief reason becomes evident when we
consider how the patient took the analyst's comments about her
resentment and her desire for exclusive affection and care. She was
distressed about them; they represented a blow to her self-esteem
and her ideals. She felt, first of all, that she ought not to be resentful
toward someone whom she respected and whom she liked, and,
further, that she ought to rely on herself and under no circumstances should she crave dependence.

This case gives the student an idea of what takes place in
the analytic hour, what types of problems arise, and how they
are handled. We can now proceed to a detailed discussion of
the methods of procedure, the data obtained, and some working
concepts.[1]

METHOD OF PROCEDURE

As a rule, the patient comes five times a week on consecutive
days; each interview lasts about one hour. The patient lies on a
couch, and the analyst sits where the patient cannot see him
unless he turns around specially. The patient is instructed to
tell the analyst everything that enters his mind, regardless of
whether it is embarrassing or foolish, or whether it refers to
his attitudes toward the analyst. These thoughts usually include
events of the previous day, his complaints, his reactions, and
his dreams. The analyst then interprets to the patient the meanings and the reasons for his reaction patterns. The patient, as
a rule, does most of the talking, in a spontaneous manner, during

[1] The originator of the psychoanalytic method, which led to fundamental
discoveries, and the most influential systematizer of the data, was Sigmund
Freud. He has a similar relationship to psychoanalysis as Pavlov does to
reflexology. Important contributions of many other analysts are used throughout the book; for these, see Suggested Readings and the Bibliography.

the hour. Continuity and general uniformity of procedure are important. At the same time, the set-up is elastic; the analyst may, for various reasons, bring certain topics to the fore, and vary different aspects of the procedure.

Significance of Frequent Interviews and of the Procedure.— There are important reasons for the above procedure. Only if the patient is seen frequently can the analyst obtain all the data necessary for interpretations and convey them to the patient safely and effectively. The connection between the events of the preceding day and his responses to them is still fresh in the patient's mind, and he can tell them to the analyst without difficulty. Furthermore, events can be disturbing to the patient, and he is likely to suffer if the analyst does not see him within a day or two to interpret his reactions.

The patient lies on a couch because he can relax more completely and "let his mind go" with greater ease. Moreover, this posture may assume changing emotional implications for him at various periods of the analysis, e.g., helplessness, submission, dependence, humiliation, etc. Only in exceptional circumstances e.g., intense fear, does the patient sit up or is he urged to do so during the interview. The fact that the analyst is out of sight enables him to talk more easily about embarrassing and humiliating thoughts and feelings.

Role of Free Association.—"Letting one's mind go" is usually referred to as "free association." This is a different "set" from that which the patient has when he applies himself to a given task deliberately. The feelings and thoughts that arise during free association are determined, just as thoughts and activities are determined when the individual is bent on accomplishing a task with conscious effort. The mood of free association is similar to that of daydreaming. It is mostly the patient's wishes, needs, hopes, fears, and angers that guide the flow of thoughts and feelings.

In analysis there are certain determining factors: the patient comes to the analyst for help, but he has definite expectations as to how the help is to be extended. He has definite reactions both to everything the analyst says and to events in his daily life while he is relating them to the analyst. Because many of these thoughts and impulses are such that the patient is ashamed of them or afraid of their consequences, he would exclude them, shut them out of awareness, if he chose topics for conversation as deliberately as he would set about solving a mathematical problem. This point is illustrated in the thoughts that A. V. had in connection with her dream. These thoughts were the recollection of some remarks which were derogatory to both the analysis and the analyst. Without free association such thoughts would not have emerged because the patient had conflicts about them.

The analytic procedure has unique features which are offered in no other situation. The patient learns to behave and speak and think in a way which is possible at no other time—he is encouraged to describe to the analyst, another human being, all his attitudes toward him; he is encouraged to reveal feelings which, under ordinary circumstances, are conventionally completely hidden; finally, in talking, he has to discard shame, embarrassment, and his desire to maintain a good impression. It is due to the uniqueness of the procedure, which incidentally the patient learns only gradually, that remarkable data are revealed and that the treatment can be so successful.

Role of Dreams.—Dreams are psychological products which represent a person's reactions to his daily experiences. They express psychological forces, the nature of which can be clearly determined with adequate methods of investigation. As we shall see, the dream is a source of significant information in the analysis; Freud called it "the royal road to the unconscious."

Dreams can be interpreted; that is, an analyst can state both the response they represent and the underlying event that caused them. In analyzing dreams, the analyst follows the patient's associations or asks him to tell what comes to his mind in connection with the dream. He follows this same procedure with each element of the dream. Adequate interpretation is possible only if the analyst knows the patient well, the circumstances under which the dream occurred, the events preceding it, and the patient's immediate reactions to them.

The psychological forces expressed in dreams are mostly emotional and often irrational. Frequently they are of a forbidden character; that is, in them are embodied the impulses —hostile and sexual impulses, attitudes of dependence, feelings of humiliation, fear, and guilt—for which a person fears punishment and about which he feels guilty. Even when an individual succeeds in maintaining a smooth front and convincing himself that his behavior is serene and sensible, his dreams may furnish information which reveals difficulties. Thus, a man who feels perfectly calm during the day may tell the analyst that he feels well and is adequately adjusted, but he may have nightmares which indicate disturbances (136). In A. V.'s case, a dream and its associations gave a good clue to her attitudes; it revealed not only her resentment and disparaging attitude, but also her need for complete care. This case also illustrates the frequent wish-fulfilling character of dreams which enables the individual to experience fulfillment of hopes and wishes which he would otherwise miss. Thus A. V. consoled herself with the hope that eventually the analyst would give her the exclusive care and affection that she craved.

Dreams frequently represent an attitude or idea graphically and often embody the phenomenon of so-called condensation. For example, one patient who was afraid to discuss a certain topic dreamed that he was standing panic-stricken at the edge of a precipice. Near him was a person in whom were combined the features of the analyst, of a former employer who had been extremely harsh, and of a very severe teacher who by failing him in high school had caused him one of the unhappiest incidents in his life. Thus, in this patient's reaction to the current analytic situation was condensed the memory of two previous experiences.

Some interesting experiments have been done on symbolization in dreams. Schrotter (690) hypnotized a woman and discussed a homosexual incident with her. After she was awakened, she remembered dreaming that she had seen a woman carrying a traveling bag which was labeled "For women only." Betlheim and Hartmann (83) told stories with a sexual content to patients suffering from Korsakoff syndrome (memory disturbance with confabulation). When asked to repeat the stories, the patients gave a distorted version; for example, instead of the sexual event, people jumped up and down a stairway. Similar symbolizations occur in dreams. Displacement is also frequent. A. V. had pairs of dreams at times. In the first dream she saw a man in a coffin; in the second, someone was reading a simple news item. She felt calm during the first dream, but the second one disturbed her a great deal because the emotion she felt really belonged to the first dream. Condensation, symbolization, and displacement are some of the means by which "forbidden" thoughts are distorted in dreams.

Not all dreams are analyzable; that is, the analyst is sometimes unable to construct a sound interpretation when the situation is so involved that the patient finds it difficult or is unconsciously reluctant to reveal some of his attitudes. Whether everyone dreams every night is, of course, impossible to answer because of the lack of adequate proof, although recent work with electroencephalograms gives some indication that at least some periods of sleep are dreamless. Unquestionably, however, a person may dream and not remember it. This is shown in the instances in which a sleeping individual says something which someone else hears. Often these remarks are analyzable and can be interpreted like the dream. An analyst's patient was once heard by his wife to say in his sleep, "That's nonsense. I know as much as you do." This man's attitude toward the analyst was at the time characterized by rivalry and an attempt to show that his knowledge was as great as the analyst's.

The duration of the average dream cannot be stated with

certainty. Both accidental and experimental observations show, however, that, on the basis of the dreamer's recollections after he wakes, an amazing amount can happen and an exceedingly long period of time can be covered in an extremely short time from the observer's point of view. Maury's experience is a famous example. Once, while ill in bed, a piece of board fell and hit him on the back of his neck as he slept. His mother, who was sitting beside him, noticed that he woke immediately. As he waked up, he remembered a long dream in which he was captured in the French Revolution, brought before the tribunal, sentenced to be guillotined, and then guillotined.

Data Obtained by the Psychoanalytic Method

Certain data can be obtained through psychoanalysis that as yet cannot be obtained in full by any other method of investigation.

Conscious and Unconscious Types of Data.—Obviously the analyst can obtain information from the patient only if the latter tells him something or behaves in a certain way. Under other circumstances he may surmise, on the basis of his general knowledge and previous experience, that certain types of information will be forthcoming from the patient even when it is not yet available and the evidence for it is not yet obvious. Such information, however, becomes definite data only after the patient can talk about it or show it in his behavior. It is clear from this that the patient has various degrees of consciousness concerning the information that he eventually imparts in the course of the analytic treatment. Sometimes, because of shame or guilt, the patient withholds information from the analyst, although he knows it is important and that he should speak about it. Several weeks or months may pass before he imparts the information.

A 25-year-old successful architect, who had enjoyed his work, the company of others, sports, and shows, developed attacks of anxiety in reaction to a trying life situation. Difficulty in breathing was the most severe complaint. From the age of five on, he had had the recurrent pleasurable fantasy that a woman was sitting on his chest, and at puberty he actually put a typewriter on his chest to "realize" his fantasy. The patient gave this information to the analyst after one month. Before starting analysis he had been receiving interview therapy from another therapist once a week for six months. During this entire period, he had not revealed this fact to his therapist because he felt too much ashamed of it. Only under the circumstances of psychoanalytic therapy was he finally able to talk about it.

At times, the patient knows that it is important to tell of the events of the previous day, his reactions to them and his dreams, but does not because he feels that he ought to have a full understanding of and insight into all of his reactions before he speaks about them to the analyst. In such instances, the patient's feeling of worthlessness and his extreme need to establish his worth in his own eyes and in those of the analyst bar the way to his imparting significant information.

At other times the patient reveals something in his behavior but cannot account for it; even when the analyst interprets it, the patient is not at first aware of his motivations. The series of incidents related about A. V. is an example of this. Only after repeated occurrences and repeated comments by the analyst does the patient's motivation become clear to him.

In still other instances the patient knows about an event that occurred the previous day, but does not speak about it at first, although he does talk about symptoms that are closely connected with it. Later in the hour or often on direct questioning by the analyst, he relates it and the significance of the event then becomes manifest. In such instances, the patient does not impart the information because, for emotional reasons, he does not recognize the connection between his complaints and the event.

A floor manager who was under analytic treatment because of attacks of anxiety was given a rush job to do by his superior. He felt resentful at first, but then he did his work. Not long after, he had a severe attack of anxiety in which he was afraid that he was dying.

In the analytic interview on the next day he described his anxiety attack in detail. He did not mention his resentment toward his superior until the analyst asked him point-blank what had happened.

The connection between the two events—his resentment and the consequent anxiety attack—was significant. The attack meant to the patient that he, a helpless individual, would be crushed by a stronger one (his superior) because he had dared to feel resentment toward him. This type of reaction was one of this patient's major problems.

The last two situations, viz., when the patient imparts some information but cannot account for it, and when he does not mention pertinent happenings or mentions them but does not see the interrelation between them and his reactions, are common in analysis. There is still another situation which is usual and very significant: the patient agrees to "tell everything" to the analyst, but he cannot, simply because he is entirely unaware of some of his impulses which have a very important role in his difficulties.

In spite of having decided always to tell the analyst everything, A. V. could not have told him that she felt resentful toward him or that she wanted his exclusive and unlimited care and affection because she did not know of these feelings. At the beginning of the analysis she gave no direct evidence of resentment. Only after some time was it manifest in her actions and dreams, as was shown in the incidents already related. It was still later that she was able to recognize and state her feelings of resentment openly.

The conscious and unconscious data obtainable by psychoanalysis can be classified as follows:

Hostile impulses directed toward others.—These include reactions of anger or rivalry; the desire to injure, humiliate, destroy, or triumph over others to the point of deriving pleasure from cruelty.

This type of impulse is clear in A. V.'s case. As a rule she did not recognize her anger reactions toward either the analyst or her husband. Instead, she became depressed. After considerable analytic work, she saw that her depressions occurred after incidents with her husband in which she might have had reason to be angry. It was still later that she experienced anger toward him.

Destructive impulses directed toward oneself.—These include the impulse to injure and humiliate oneself, the attitude of self-contempt, the desire to submit, to be exploited, and to be physically injured by another.

A school teacher undertook analytic treatment because of dissatisfaction with his love life. He was always calm; his philosophy was one of "serenity and non-participation" in all significant life situations. He had dreams in which he humbly scrubbed the bathroom floor of a famous educator, but he was unaware in his daily life of the self-humiliating attitude represented by this type of dream.

Ambition, desire for accomplishment, pride.—

This same teacher never admitted any ambition to advance himself in his work. He changed positions several times, but only, as he put it, "to be able to work less for more pay." Considerable analytic work was necessary to make him realize that his apparent lack of ambition was due to his feeling of helplessness and his unconscious fear of dismal failure if he ever strove for success. To escape the conflict between ambition and fear of failure, he adopted an exaggerated attitude of "serenity and non-participation."

Desire for closeness, affection, love, and warmth.—

This same man never allowed himself to become fully attached to anyone. He was married, but he said that he had chosen a woman who was self-supporting and would therefore not be dependent upon him. He opposed her desire to have a child because this would tie him to her. After the tenth month of analysis his emotional condition was characterized by a vague fear and general discomfort. This occurred after situations in which he felt comfortable, congenial, and emotionally close to someone. He soon realized that his feeling of fear resulted from his desire for closeness. In other words, he did not lack the desire for closeness and affection; he was really afraid of them. Of the several reasons for his fear, only one will be mentioned here. His desire was so exaggerated that if he yielded to it, he feared there would be no bounds to what he would do. He would kiss people on the street, would even submit to them sexually. He would be subject to utter humiliation and would be effaced as an individual. Rather than this, he chose (unconsciously) to be emotionally detached, serene, and non-participating.

Attitudes of superiority; self-aggrandizing trends.— The patient who shows these trends not only wants to be respected and esteemed, he often has the need to consider himself superior to other individuals in some attribute.

A 30-year-old man was unusually talented in music, art, and science; but he never followed through any pursuit, partly because he felt that any accomplishment, even becoming a famous concert artist, would not do justice to his potentialities. Both his self-disparaging and his self-aggrandizing trends manifested themselves strikingly in the analysis. He felt that the analyst was superior to him in every respect; but unless he could consider himself superior in some way, he would not be able to go on with the analysis. In his desperate need for help he finally hit on a solution: He was able to feel superior to the analyst because he (the patient) could trace his ancestry back six generations, whereas the analyst could not. This solution, however, was charged with serious conflict for him. Not until four months after he became conscious of this attitude did he tell the analyst about it because he was afraid that the analyst would discharge him—and this in spite of the fact that he knew very well that in analysis one talks about everything that comes to mind.

Need for dependence and complete care.—A. V.'s behavior and dream illustrate the extent of the need for dependence and care. There are extreme cases in which patients will want the analyst to be with them twenty-four hours a day, instruct them on how to behave, and handle by direct action every situation in business or at home.

Oral, genital, and excretory impulses and fantasies. —Various bodily functions constitute a natural and indispensable

part of everyone's existence. Even so, many people have conflicts about the forms of bodily functions that are approved of
by their society. Frequently, the individual has impulses and
desires that are strongly disapproved of both by his society and
by himself. The conflicts over such impulses are extremely
severe. They may appear as conscious desires and fantasies accompanied by strong discomfort, or they may be entirely unconscious.

Thus, a woman may have unconscious impulses to behave as
a prostitute or to deprive a man of his masculinity. Other such
impulses are expressed in unconscious fantasies of a woman
being a man, of urinating on other individuals with the intent
of humiliating them, or of committing incest. Such impulses are
shut out of awareness because of shame, self-condemnation, fear
of disapproval, fear of consequences, or guilt feelings.

A. V. dreamed in response to certain situations that she moved
her bowels on the analyst's bathroom floor, that she possessed both
male and female organs. She was ashamed of such dreams.

Memories and reactions of childhood.—Childhood
memories generally fall into one of two classes: (1) Incidents
which the patient has forgotten so completely that even if he
thought about a particular period in his life, he still would not
be able to remember them, even though they disturbed him
greatly at the time and had a significant influence on his development. The memory of sexual seduction by an adult is such
an incident.

A successful business man who, although he was in love with his
wife, drank periodically when he visited prostitutes and who had
periods of depression, finally remembered what he had "forgotten";
he had been repeatedly seduced by a maid when he was three and
one-half years old, and he had greatly feared his parents' disapproval
and punishment. The feelings of fear and guilt, the resentment
toward the maid, and his conflicts toward his parents had a strong
influence on his development.

(2) Incidents which the patient remembers, but certain aspects of which are either completely blotted out at first or, if remembered, are not told to the analyst until relatively late in the treatment.

A gifted musician was being given analysis because of recent difficulties in his work. For many months he told the analyst that he had been devoted to his mother, had loved and admired her. He had felt no grief over her death, which occurred when he was nineteen. In fact, not until a certain period in the analysis was he emotionally aware of the fact that she was dead. He first said that his mother had treated the children with devotion, understanding, and care, but later he related the following incident: When he was five and one-half years old, he whipped a horse to see him jump. His mother, finding this out, took the whip out of his hand and said, "I want you to feel what you are doing to the horse." With this, she whipped him. The patient was deeply disturbed and the analyst remarked that he must have been angry at his mother. Only after considerable work was the analyst able to make him realize that he had ever had any feelings of resentment toward her. The patient had not "forgotten" the incident of the whipping. If he thought of that period of his childhood he could always recall it; but he wanted to isolate it and not connect it with the picture he had of his relationship with his mother. He had a need to keep this relationship free from any flaw on the part of his mother, and free from any anger on his part.

Most frequently, the childhood memories which are more fully recovered in the analysis and whose significance is fully elucidated fall into the second class. Whichever type of memory it is, it usually deals with attitudes of hostility and sexual activities which have been partly or completely repressed because of guilt and the fear of punishment and a loss of love.

Emotions and attitudes of fear and guilt.—The patients are partly or completely unconscious of certain attitudes because they consider them dangerous. The danger that they anticipate may be that of being deprived of help and gratification, or injured or destroyed, or utterly humiliated, exploited, disgraced, and condemned by others as well as by themselves. These fears arise particularly in connection with reactions of hostility, self-destruction, forbidden sexual attitudes, and rivalry. It is important to realize that the attitudes of fear and guilt may themselves not be known to the patient. He represses them for several reasons. He wants to protect himself against the feared consequences of these impulses; he can do this even more by shutting his feelings of fear and guilt out of awareness. Further, these latter feelings are extremely distressing, sometimes actually incapacitating. The patient tries to attain a state of comfort and to maintain his ability to function by repressing them. It is extremely important in analysis to uncover such reactions and make the patient realize their significance. They form an important part of the data obtained through psychoanalysis.

A 29-year-old social worker entered analysis when his marriage was threatened with dissolution. His wife wanted to leave him because of his continued emotional distance. This man was usually calm and aloof in all life situations. Although he maintained in the analysis that he was undisturbed, that his calmness showed genuine strength, and that it was the right way of living, he often had frightening dreams in which he was shot at or elevators fell while he was riding in them.

Attitudes of helplessness, fear of abandonment, self-condemnation, and guilt played an important role in A. V.'s reactions, but one of which she was not fully aware. At times when she was depressed after some difficulty with her husband, she had a vague impulse to walk in front of passing cars and be injured. Such impulses were the expression of an unconscious guilt because of her hostility toward her husband; her desire to suffer was her means of atoning for this hostility and regaining her husband's love and help by rendering herself completely helpless.

WORKING CONCEPTS

Working concepts are assumptions based on observations, which attempt to establish interrelations between isolated observations and which furnish the practitioner with tools that enable him to deal with the phenomena he encounters. It is convenient to group psychoanalytic working concepts in the following classes: (1) Concepts which influence chiefly the practice of the analysis itself. These are closely connected with the method of procedure. (2) Concepts which are constantly used in psychoanalytic practice, but which have wide application in the study of psychology and psychopathology. (3) Concepts which systematize a large body of observations and in which the element of assumption is greatest. These latter will be called hypotheses.

Concepts Influencing Chiefly the Practice of Analysis: The patient's need for help.—The need for help is the patient's strongest reason for beginning and continuing analytic treatment. This need, the hope of fulfilling it, and the actual experience of relief make him willing to persist even when some of the analyst's comments are distressing. The patient tells the analyst particularly about his weaknesses and disabilities, and he usually expects the analyst to concentrate on them and not on his achievements. However, it does not follow that he is happy to find out the reasons for his difficulties and eager to correct them as quickly as possible. On the contrary, he has his own emotional needs and ideas of the kind of help he should be given, and he clings to them persistently. If the help offered differs from what he wants, he reacts strongly; resentment, disappointment, fear, humiliation, and self-condemnation follow. He again requests the type of help which he felt was refused him before. All these reactions are the ultimate results of his feeling of helplessness.

The analyst is constantly aware of the patient's suffering and of his need for help. In some very precarious situations, as when there is danger of suicide or of incapacity, his most immediate task is to give the patient relief by some means. More generally, however, the concept of the patient's need for help has a long-range significance for the analyst. It is on the basis of this assumption that he denies many of the patient's requests, such as a set of rules for his conduct, and that he points out reaction patterns to the patient—e.g., hostility, or the need for exclusive affection and care—although he knows that the immediate effect will be disturbing. It is obvious from this that the working assumption of the patient's need for help is quite different for the analyst than for the patient. The statements made here are well illustrated in A. V.'s analysis. The aims of analytic therapy and the factors operating in achieving these aims will be discussed in the section on practical application. Here we wish to show that the working concept of the patient's need for help influences every activity which occurs in the analysis.

Reaction patterns.—During the analytic interview, the patient reacts to occurrences in his daily life and to experiences. These reactions can be interpreted to him and they can be further used as a yardstick for gauging the progress of the analysis. The analyst considers the analysis as progressing satisfactorily if the patient is furnishing adequate data for such interpretations, and if he can utilize these interpretations in his further reactions. All types of reactions are of significance in the analysis, including attitudes of disparagement toward the analyst. For example, A. V.'s resentment in response to the analyst's comments had its continual parallel in her daily life; it was a reaction which led to conflicts, self-condemnation, and a fear of disapproval, loss of love and loss of health. Therefore, such reactions have to be uncovered, the reasons determined, and the attitude corrected. A. V. was not being "uncooperative" when she resented instead of welcomed the analyst's comments; it was a useful and valuable reaction. Reactions of fear, attitudes of superiority toward the analyst, emotional withdrawal are all significant and useful if they are clear and if they can be utilized for interpretation. If reactions are not clear, the analyst's first task is to determine what is responsible for the lack of clarity; in other words, this lack is itself considered and is dealt with as a reaction pattern.

Essential identity of the patient's reactions to daily events and to the analyst.—The patient displays the same patterns of behavior toward the analyst as he does toward people and his work; many of these patterns are emotional and irrational. An examination and discussion of the patient's reactions toward the analyst give important clues as to the needs and motivations which are responsible for the illness. Thus A. V. needed unlimited and complete affection and care; the need was the same whether her husband or the analyst was involved. While she realized that his occupation made it imperative for her husband to go away, she reacted to his departure as if he were abandoning her.

Examination of the patient's emotional reaction to the analyst is important for another reason. In spite of the latter's essentially kind, understanding, and helpful attitude, the patient often reacts to him with anger, fear, and a feeling of humiliation. The reasons for these reactions lie within the patient; the reactions are transferred by him to the analyst, a phenomenon commonly known as "transference." Because of the working concept of the transference, the analyst constantly considers what reactions the patient is displaying toward him and calls his attention to them. This is one of the most important aspects of analytic work.

The question is often raised as to how it is possible for the patient to have the same attitudes toward the analyst as he does toward other people in his daily life—his family, friends, co-workers, when he knows that his relationship with the analyst has definite limitations. The phenomenon becomes understandable, however, if we realize that the patient undergoes analysis because he feels helpless; this undertaking is of great significance for him. He feels in need of help; with this he immediately displays the reasons for his need, his needs and ideas of how help is to be given him, his conflicts about these needs and desires, and his fear of the individual from whom he wants them. Furthermore, when the analyst denies him his requests and desires, he reacts to this just as he reacts to denials in other situations. When the analyst makes interpretations which inevitably cut deep and concern vital needs, he reacts to them as he does to stresses and to threats to his vital needs in life situations. Further aspects of the patient's emotional, irrational attitudes toward the analyst will be discussed under therapy.

Resistance.—When the analyst constructs a reaction from the data and interprets it to the patient, the latter is usually reluctant to accept it; he struggles against it, and tries to prove the analyst wrong. The patient continues to react in this way during subsequent interviews, although he has allegedly accepted the fact that his old reaction had disadvantages. Resistance is also manifest when a patient maintains a stubborn silence, when he is unable to think of anything significant, or when he talks, but omits significant facts and thoughts.

Resistance is a collective term for some of the most important reactions brought out by the analysis. It is prompted by the patient's struggles and his refusal to give up a vital need. For example, many of A. V.'s reactions dovetailed to maintain her vital need of complete care and dependence. She unconsciously felt that disaster would befall her without this dependence, and she therefore clung to it. In the course of repeated reactions and interpretations, the analyst made clear to her the nature of her need and the reason for its tenacity; and finally she became able not only to accept his interpretation, but also to react differently. The reactions which constitute resistance are just as significant as the patient's final acceptance; in fact, the largest part of the analysis deals with resistance reactions.

Psychoanalytic Concepts Having Wide Applications in Psychopathology.—Some concepts which have been created or adopted in psychoanalytic work are applicable to psychological phenomena in the individual's daily life and, in general, to psychopathology. They are used by analysts and other psychiatrists for the purpose of understanding and interpreting their observations. Such are the concepts of psychodynamics, conflict, unconscious processes, catastrophic expectations, defensive and coping reactions, the vicious circle of reactions, etc., which have been discussed in various parts of the book. These and other psychodynamic concepts have been applied to the fields of general psychiatry, experimental psychology, general medicine, anthropology, sociology, social work, criminology, art, and literature (16, 24, 421, 464, 815, 22, 86, 156, 170, 187, 190, 203, 398, 507, 674).

Hypotheses.—As previously stated, by hypotheses are meant a group of integrated concepts which systematize a large body of data and contain a large element of assumption. Some of the hypotheses developed in psychoanalysis have aroused considerable controversy. Furthermore, differences exist as to what observations and what concepts derived therefrom should be considered more fundamental. These problems are important because the analyst's interpretations to the patient are based not only on immediate information, but also on these hypotheses.

We shall illustrate the type of data the hypotheses are based on, and the differences in emphasis, by further facts in A. V.'s life history and another series of incidents which occurred during her analysis. It will be remembered, of course, that A. V. started analysis because of an emotional depression started by her husband's having to go away for occupational reasons.

Relationship with Parents and Siblings.—A. V.'s parents, both of whom were alive, lived in a distant city. Whenever she saw her mother, they got along badly with each other. In fact, her mother had always been emotionally distant and undemonstrative to A. V. She had never praised her either as a child or as an adult. She had been frequently critical of her, especially in reference to expressions of hostility or to such activities as smoking or drinking, and, as a child, to exposing herself or to talking about the excretory functions in the presence of others. Thus, A. V., when a child, had always felt herself to be without affection and she had felt rejected and humiliated.

At first in the analysis, A. V. had spoken chiefly of having always been distant toward her mother. It gradually became evident, however, that she had been very resentful toward her, and had had the consequent fear of being abandoned and condemned by her.

A. V. had always been on good terms with her father. He was emotionally warm and A. V. was attached to him. He had been inclined to scientific work, but at his family's insistence he took over his father's business. This failed when A. V. was about ten. After that the mother became the family's chief supporter, acted superior to her husband, and was openly critical of him. A. V. was much pained by these developments. It became clear in the analysis that besides her friendly feelings toward her father, she had also felt resentment toward him, although never as intensely as toward her mother. This resentment arose particularly at the time when he had failed in business; A. V. reacted to that almost as if he had disappointed her.

As has been said, A. V. was the oldest of five siblings. She had always got along fairly well with them, although she felt resentful when her mother made her take care of them without giving her any overt appreciation and praise.

Sexual Development.—At the age of four A. V. discovered a book "belonging to father" which had on its cover a picture of Columbus in chains. She used to look at this picture and would become erotically aroused. This started about the time that her mother gave birth to her second child. A. V. stopped this activity at the age of six or seven, and had not thought of it since. After remembering it again in the analysis, she herself was eager to verify this memory. During her summer vacation, she took a trip home and found the book in the attic.

When A. V. was about five years old, she learned about the difference in the anatomy of the two sexes on the occasion of a mutual exposure with a boy. She was much disturbed by this experience. At the period of puberty, she had elaborate fantasies of being tied to a tree by threatening men in oriental garb, and being sexually assaulted by them.

Career and Marriage.—A. V. excelled in school from the beginning; she was ambitious but very sensitive to criticism, felt easily rejected by friends, and then deeply hurt. After graduating from college, she became a laboratory worker, soon excelled in that field, and, as has already been mentioned, published numerous scientific articles and books.

Although she was attractive, she married at the age of twenty-three a man with whom she was not in love. She was convinced that she would never get anyone better; furthermore, she wanted security. She soon became unhappy, however, because she did not feel stimulated by the company of her husband and because he acted superior toward her. She was humiliated and angry; she started to spend long hours in daydreaming about men, and her work suffered. She was sexually frigid toward her husband and did not want to have children. After four years they separated at her initiative, and she moved to another city. Periods of efficient and intensive work alternated with periods of fatigue and lassitude.

She met her second husband not long after she had moved to her new surroundings. They fell in love with each other, and after a year's acquaintance A. V. obtained a divorce from her first husband and they were married. As previously mentioned, her relationship with her second husband was fundamentally good, but she suffered from partial and at times complete frigidity, as well as from periods of mild depression, fatigue, and insomnia. Her husband likewise had a psychological disturbance; whenever he encountered difficulties in his work, he developed bodily complaints, such as backaches, headaches, and nausea, as well as loss of confidence in himself and a hopeless outlook toward his work. On other occasions he was irritable and unreasonable.

They wanted to have children, but A. V. could not quite make up her mind about this. At times she would be very eager to have a child, but these were overshadowed by times when either she thought it would interfere too much with her career, or she would feel too much afraid to go through childbirth.

Another Series of Incidents During the Patient's Analysis.—One evening A. V.'s husband was irritable and unreasonable with her; at the same time, however, he spoke about some difficulties that had arisen in his work. She realized that he was disturbed and knew the reason for it. She was in a dilemma because she wanted to be considerate to him; in fact, she made the ideal demand upon herself that she should under any and all circumstances help him in his distress. At the same time, however, she felt hurt and resentful. Following this episode she was depressed for about five days, felt tired and perplexed, was not able to work well, lost her appetite, and slept badly. The following are two of the dreams she had during this period:

Five couples were sitting at a table and A. V. had to divide a piece of steak among them. One of the men sitting there was a dictator. Everyone got his share except A. V. She felt bitter and resentful. In connection with the dictator, A. V. thought of the high-handed behavior of her husband when he was irritable.

In the process of weeding out her garden, A. V. chopped off the heads of some tulips. She was disturbed over the damage. The shape of the tulips suggested a sexual symbol to the patient.

During this same five days, A. V. was often irritable with the analyst.

Her depression finally ended in this way: The analyst noticed during the fourth interview that A. V. was becoming more and more distressed in response to his interpretations about her anger toward her husband, about her self-condemnation and helplessness, and about her sexual attitudes. He commented on this and told her that she was probably taking his comments as signs of disapproval and rejection. She replied: "One cannot take these comments in any other way. There is no excuse for me to behave as I am acting." The analyst pointed out to her that her reactions originated from conflicting vital needs and helplessness, but that she was demanding unqualified, flawless performance of herself, even while she was suffering and incapacitated. The next day she felt better; she related two dreams:

She is at a dinner party at which her girl friend shoots a man. A. V. is afraid of the police.

She is at another dinner party at which a man wants to have an intimate talk with her. They go into the bathroom. The man says: "You did well in shooting X. I love you; I want to marry you."

In connection with both the shooting and the marriage proposal, A. V. thought of her husband and the analyst.

The patient felt better at this point for two reasons: One was that she could accept her hostility without the intense self-condemnation and the fear of abandonment that were present during the period of depression. With that she acquired more mastery over such impulses. Second, she felt that the analyst (and her husband) had forgiven her for her attitudes, that the analyst was willing to marry her and in that symbolic way give her exclusive affection and care. This latter aspect represented the illusory satisfaction of the same need for complete care as a means of help that has already been discussed.

We shall now give a general presentation of some hypotheses, and shall follow this by showing how these hypotheses apply to the data about A. V.

Libido Theory; Structure of the "Psychic Apparatus"

The Concept of Instinct.—Instincts in Freud's concepts mean strivings which manifest themselves in characteristic bodily tension, fantasy formation, emotional experiences, character traits, and, in the case of "sublimation," in cultural and intellectual activities. This concept is quite different from the usual meaning of the term "instincts." If the original aim of this striving is one of pleasure, it is called "libido." This seeking for pleasure Freud calls "sexual." In other words, for Freud, the concept of "sexual" is essentially identical with the drive for pleasure, and, as such, has a much wider meaning than just genital function.

Libido Organization.—During each period of development, an organ is the dominant source of pleasure, and there is a characteristic, corresponding emotional attitude toward the environment. This is called "libido organization." During the nursing period, the dominant source of pleasure is the mouth (characteristic attitude: dependence). From the age of two to about four, it is the anus (characteristic attitude: destructiveness). At about the period of five to six years, it is the genitals (characteristic attitude: feeling of tenderness combined with self-centered attitudes). At a still later period, if development has been normal, the genitals remain the main source of pleasure and there is a genuine feeling of tenderness toward other individuals and the acceptance and desire for propagation.[1]

Persistence of Infantile Impulses; Fixation, Regression.— Fixation implies a relatively strong development of psychological and bodily desires belonging to one of the libido levels of the child, together with a tendency to retain or revive these manifestations. Freud assumed that infantile impulses persist in a repressed, yet unchanged form throughout life. As a result of frustration in later life, repressed infantile desires are revived, especially those belonging to libido levels at which the individual is fixated. This revival of the former types of libido organization is the special coloring of the term "regression" as used by Freud. The assumption is that the patient is motivated at the time of the symptom by the unchanged infantile desires. The patient's transference attitude toward the analyst is the exact repetition of the attitudes he had in his childhood toward his parents.

Narcissism; Sibling Rivalry.—The infant and also the child desires exclusive possession of the parents and wants to be the sole object of their affection and care; therefore he considers all other children in the family as rivals. His love is directed primarily toward himself. With some further broadening, feeling of omnipotence, of magic power, this direction of one's love toward the self is termed "narcissism." The hostility toward the rival siblings is called "sibling rivalry."

Oedipus Complex; Masochism.—The Oedipus complex means unconscious love for the parent of the opposite sex, and hostility amounting to a death wish toward the parent of the same sex. This results in fear of injury by the rival parent, and in feelings

[1] The theory of the "life and death instinct" implies that all phenomena of life, including psychological phenomena, are the result of various fusions of a "life tendency" (drive for pleasure and self-preservation) and a tendency toward death (destructive and self-destructive impulses; tendency to reinstate inorganic equilibrium). The concept of "repetition compulsion" implies an inner necessity to repeat psychological experiences regardless of whether they are pleasurable or painful. (Freud [272]).

of guilt.[1] The best evidence for such constructions is to be found in many male patients who dream, usually in a partly disguised form, of being intimate with their mothers, and of being injured by a powerful male or a large, frightening animal (symbolizing the father). Freud considered the Oedipus complex as extremely significant in character development and as the nuclear complex of the neuroses. Because of the fear it arouses (particularly of "castration"), the child renounces or represses his sexual and hostile aims, "internalizes" the parental taboos, and thus develops conscience and ideals. This takes place about the age of five or six.

As a result of the fear, guilt, and internalized taboos, the hostile impulses at first directed toward others (sadism) may turn back on the individual himself. Together with this, the genital impulse, instead of being aroused by pleasurable stimuli, may be aroused and gratified through painful stimuli. These phenomena are manifestations of "masochism."

Ego, Superego, Id.—Freud differentiates three parts in the "psychic apparatus": Ego, Superego, Id. Id refers to the sum total of persistent, unconscious, infantile, pleasure-seeking, and hostile strivings. Superego refers to the functions of conscience, ideals, self-criticism, and self-observation. The conflict is between these two groups of forces. The function of the ego is to consider the individual's interest, to attempt to make his lot bearable, and to consider both the outside world and the individual's inner battlefield. Repression, effected by the ego, is responsible for the patient's impulses being largely unconscious. Id impulses are mainly unconscious in order that danger may be avoided. The Superego impulses are mainly unconscious so that forbidden strivings will be repressed all the more effectively and suffering

---

[1] The name "Oedipus complex" originated from the Greek legend of King Oedipus, who unknowingly killed his father and then married his mother. When he discovered his crime, his sense of guilt was so profound that he tore out his eyes and gave up his kingdom. Under exceptional circumstances the Oedipus complex may be conscious.

will be alleviated. The ego further attempts to straighten things out by making compromises.

APPLICATIONS OF THESE HYPOTHESES TO A. V.'S REACTIONS

On the basis of the above concepts, the following interpretations can be made of A. V.'s reactions:

As a result of her disappointment in her parents, particularly because of the birth of the next sibling, and as a result of her resentment toward them as well as her fear of them, especially of her mother (her rival), she developed masochistic patterns in regard to both her sexual activities and her hostility, "Columbus in chains," "puberty fantasies," and later, in order to protect herself against the consequences of her masochism, sexual frigidity. She had a desire for the male organ (mutual exposure incident), and resentment toward and fear of the man who possessed it (another factor in her sexual frigidity). All these attitudes, together with the oral (evidenced in the steak dream) and anal (meeting in bathroom in the last dream) cravings, had been repressed and had remained unchanged since her childhood.

In response to the frustrations inflicted on her by her husband, all of these impulses became active. She was motivated by her unchanged desire for the exclusive possession of and love of her parents, by her anger toward and fear of them, by her resentment toward the siblings (five beds in the first dream, five couples in another dream), by her desire to possess the male organ and deprive the man of it, and to suffer and obtain sexual pleasure through injury and suffering. The husband (and the analyst) became identified with the frustrating parents and siblings. All these impulses were the id impulses. They were opposed by her superego, by her self-criticism, conscience, and ideals. This resulted in severe feelings of guilt. Her depression was the result of the self-punishing activities of her superego. Her superego itself was extremely severe and implacable; it had been severe since her childhood because of the necessity to repress these forbidden impulses. Her ego played a mediating role and attempted to maintain A. V.'s adjustment. She was angry at her husband, yet she behaved kindly toward him. She wanted to hurt him, but she herself suffered instead. With this, instead of arousing his anger, she aroused his sympathy. Thus, the ego enabled her to escape the catastrophic results of yielding to the id impulses and being crushed under the superego impulses, and to retain the affection of her husband.

RECENT DEVELOPMENTS IN ANALYSIS; OTHER HYPOTHESES

We shall now present in a synthesized form other hypotheses that have been recently elaborated in psychoanalysis.

Formulation in Terms of Current Attitudes.—The patient's disturbances, emotional life, and reaction patterns should be described and formulated more in terms of current needs and their interrelations and less in terms of childhood etiology. This is the most important dynamic aspect of psychopathology; it is largely unconscious (366, 367).

Helplessness the Central Problem.—The central problems of a neurotic's reactions are the phenomena of helplessness, distress, hostility, and particularly fear. Three assumptions are current at present: (1) Feelings of helplessness and weakness are experienced in comparison with other people who are conceived of as stronger, superior, and threatening (366). (2) In situations which the individual considers dangerous, his ability to function and to cope with the situation becomes impaired (inhibition), and some of his functions actually fail. The neurotic phenomena derive from this inhibition and from reactions to it (418, 421). (3) The individual reacts to certain situations with *fear*. The neurotic phenomena result from the fear and also from various maneuvers to escape this fear instead of striving to attain goals (625). These patterns pervade most or all of the patient's functions.

The individual's pernicious reaction patterns begin, in their essential features, in childhood as a result of his whole relationship with other people, especially his parents. The individual is seen to develop more general attitudes and reaction patterns, not so much as specific habits, but as more general characteristics of the total personality. They may continue through life because of vicious circles of reaction patterns (anxiety reactions causing impairment of function, leading to ameliorative measures which in turn create anxiety) and because of memory reactions, general conditioning and habituation.

APPLICATIONS OF THESE HYPOTHESES TO A. V.'S REACTIONS

On the basis of these concepts, A. V.'s reactions would be interpreted as follows:

Because of her fundamental feeling of helplessness and worthlessness, she had a need for unqualified affection and respect from her husband. His behavior was interpreted by her as a withdrawal of support and also as humiliation; thus a threat to her vital needs. She pictured herself in a state of catastrophic abandonment and worthlessness. To this she reacted with anger. The anger, however, led to self-condemnation, to fear of disapproval and of abandonment and injury. This resulted in her depression. Her work suffered, and this incapacity further increased her feeling of worthlessness because of her implacable demand that she never become angry and that she cope with all situations. The implacable quality of her demands was in itself a result of and a reaction to her feeling of worthlessness and helplessness. With it she attempted to re-establish her self-esteem, save herself from incapacity, and gain the approval of others. These constellations of conflict continue (in the reported reaction to the husband's irritability) until they are uncovered in the analysis and she thus partly gains mastery over herself; at the same time (still on an illusory basis) she feels she is completely forgiven and approved of, and that she will obtain unqualified care.

These are the essential features of A. V.'s reactions to the incident, to her husband, and to the analyst. She expresses these reactions in her behavior, in her bodily functions, and in her fantasies. The abandonment and loss of love are pictured symbolically as not being fed. She expresses her anger in the fantasy of attack on her husband (and the analyst) as a man. The attitudes are expressed in such terms partly because the functions are stimulated daily in the patient's existence. She eats daily, and she sees men daily. They are further expressed in terms of memories with the following formula:

"You are treating me as badly as I was treated when I was a child." Furthermore, conflicts arise in connection with these bodily functions, once they acquire these emotional connotations.

Her intense need for dependence, complete care, and affection arose in her childhood because she was dependent on her mother for her existence, for relief, for comfort, for satisfaction of bodily needs, and for affection. She felt worthless if her mother became angry with her. Her fear of the consequences of her resentment likewise began in that period. Her serenity and emotional calm were not only a charming character trait, but contained a factor determined as follows: She felt she was worthless and contemptible whenever she had any feelings of anger toward those to whom she was attached and from whom she needed love and care. The general patterns mentioned here were recognizable or at least traces of them appeared in all of A. V.'s relationships and activities.

She developed the attitude of pain and submission as being inevitably connected with sexual activity as a result of these attitudes in her childhood. It was a forbidden activity, with the threat of complete rejection, disapproval, and punishment; yet she continued it—defiantly, in fact. The painful and submissive aspect partly served the purpose of saying: "I don't want to do this; I am chained as Columbus was"; and: "Don't punish me for this, I am suffering pain already"; and finally, "I am not angry at you; I don't want to hurt you. Don't be angry at me; I am hurting myself."

Another prominent conflict of A. V. as an adult was this: She wanted complete submission and dependence on the one hand, and, on the other, wanted to preserve an untouched, isolated, and superior individuality. She longed for sexual relations but considered them as complete submission and the entire loss of her individuality. This attitude was based on her desire to submit completely and thus obtain help from the male whom she considered stronger. To protect herself she had to deny the activity and was therefore frigid. This meant: "I haven't given myself fully and therefore will not be catastrophically destroyed." It also expressed her resentment toward the man on whom she wanted to be dependent, and whom she therefore considered superior (reinforced by cultural over-valuation of man, and a memory pattern of envy of masculinity). It meant: "You're not competent to give me pleasure." It further meant protection from the expected counterattack: "I don't abandon myself to you, therefore you cannot hurt me."

Practical Differences and Similarities Between Various Approaches.—Various psychoanalytic hypotheses have been applied to the psychological material pertaining to A. V. We wish now to make the differences between the various approaches sharper and simpler, and then we shall point out their similarities.

We have mentioned that A. V. often had dreams in which she was both a man and a woman; at other times, she had dreams in which she was a man. Therefore there can be no doubt of the existence of such desires on her part. Such information can be handled in various ways during the analysis.

If the libido theory and the concept of the unchanged persistence of infantile impulses are his main guides, the analyst will evaluate this information as a direct expression of the patient's envy of and desire for the possession of the male organ, and will phrase his comments accordingly. He will focus attention on the other material presented by the patient on the data which back up this construction. He will take up in particular childhood recollections which elucidate the circumstances under which this desire first arose and manifested itself. He will interpret the patient's current attitudes of superiority, hostility, and rivalry during this period of the analysis as deriving from this desire. To put it briefly, the topic is considered finished when all the patient's memories pertaining to this desire have been recovered and adequately evaluated.

If the concepts of current dynamics, disturbance of the evaluation of the self and of others, and helplessness are taken as practical guides, the analyst will evaluate the patient's desire to be a man as a manifestation of a need to strengthen herself by using all available weapons to establish her superiority over people whom she considers threatening; and he will make his interpretations to the patient accordingly. He will take up particularly material from her current reactions which show these attitudes in work relationships, in friendships, in activities aiming at bodily gratification. He will point out, on the basis of daily incidents, how this desperate striving for superiority arises from the feeling of helplessness, and what the harmful consequences are of this method of attaining safety.

Childhood memories are taken up and clarified to show the patient even more clearly what her present reactions are and to make her understand how they first arose. In all this the analyst implies that the main reason for her present need to strengthen herself and to be superior to the threatening individual in all significant situations arises from the sum total of her present evaluation of herself, her fears, and her methods of coping with problems. In brief, the topic is considered finished when the patient's current need for superiority is fully traced in the daily behavior and in significant recollections, and if the interrelation of this need with other needs is made clear.

The two approaches have obvious similarities. The data and interpretations in all analyses inevitably include memory, current difficulties in the patient's daily life, and the patient's attitudes toward the analyst. They also include references to organ functions and to emotional attitudes. If the persistence of infantile impulses is taken as a guide, the analyst must show the patient where and how this unchanged infantile impulse is exerting its influence in his daily existence and in his attitudes toward the analyst. Likewise, as has been stated, if the concept of current dynamics is used as a guide, memories will be discussed and clarified. The difference lies in the relative emphasis and in the degree to which attention is focused on various types of data, and in their use to explain other manifestations. The genetic or historic approach usually places more emphasis on organ function data, whereas the current approach places it on emotional data. The analyst makes more comments on the patient's attitude toward himself in the current approach. This topic is used by some analysts continuously as a central thread by which to elucidate the patient's emotional reactions. In general, there is increasing emphasis in psychoanalytic practice on the role of anxiety, of coping reactions, and disturbances of character (usually referred to as "ego psychology") (270). The impression should not be got that there are "two approaches." As in all sciences, there has been development and growth in psychoanalysis since its inception.

The broad implications of many of the concepts which constitute the systems of hypotheses are very similar. Thus, one implication of the libido theory is that the patient is driven in his behavior by passionate, non-logical needs (367). This broader idea also constitutes part of the approach based on current dynamics and on helplessness and insecurity. The Oedipus complex, in a broader sense, implies the psychopathological constellation which comprises emotional attachment, hostility, conflict, and fear. This broader idea of a complex psychological pattern is equally a part of the other approach. Thus in any type of analysis, the patient as well as the analyst has to work strenuously on complex, largely unconscious, emotional strivings which the patient evaluates as dangerous, yet to which he clings desperately.

Therapeutic Aims and Effects of Analysis

The general therapeutic aims of psychoanalysis are the same as those discussed in connection with psychotherapy—the disappearance of symptoms, increased efficiency and ability to enjoy life, increased ability to stand stress and to make the best of one's opportunities, and the like. The special therapeutic aim is an extremely thoroughgoing recasting of those reaction patterns which are responsible for the patient's difficulties. Not only are symptoms relieved, but there are also changes in some aspects of his relationship with others, his evaluation of himself and of others, his goals and the way in which he seeks to attain them. No other therapeutic method today seems able to accomplish this to the same extent as psychoanalysis.

The length of time that the treatment requires depends on

the patient's difficulties and on how thorough a recasting is desired by himself and the analyst. Usually the patient shows an early improvement. If a satisfactory analysis is interrupted for any valid reason, the patient may nevertheless derive benefit from it. The lessening of symptoms is often rapid, particularly in patients who are suffering markedly when they start the analysis; but the symptoms return in varying intensity when new life stresses arise and when new disturbing topics are taken up in the analysis. Gradually the patient's behavior in situations of stress improves; and finally, his behavior rises above its previous level even in situations in which he excelled. Completely satisfactory analyses may vary in length from about one year to three years.

Not all patients are equally benefited by psychoanalytic treatment. There are four prerequisites for a patient to be analyzable: (1) He must desire to be treated. Often the explanatory statement that he needs treatment suffices to create a willingness to undertake analysis. Some patients at first are averse to analysis either because they are afraid of becoming completely dependent, or because their need for self-esteem is so intense that they want to handle all their difficulties, no matter how great, themselves. Such patients may eventually change their outlook, however; and their treatment is often very successful. (2) The patient must have enough intelligence to realize that his suffering may have emotional causes, and to understand the analyst's explanations. Thus, feeble-minded people, for example, are not analyzable. (3) The patient must have the "right" type of psychological difficulty; in other words, not all types of psychological difficulties can be analyzed. Thus a patient with psychosis cannot be analyzed except in hospitals; and even here success is rather limited (Zilboorg [811]). Analysis in a private office not only is of no help, but may actually be dangerous because during a reaction to stress situations the patient may commit suicide or engage in some violent act. (4) The patient's life goals must be essentially good; if they need to be changed, his situation must be such that he can do so. Furthermore, he must be able to obtain from his surroundings an indispensable minimum of emotional support. For example, a patient suffers from anxiety attacks; he has spoiled his relationships with most people and he must therefore live alone. He may be very intelligent, but he may have broken off his professional training. Because of his dissatisfaction with his station in life and because of the unbearable strain of living alone, analytic treatment may not be able to bring him even to the point where he could alter his situation.

The question of whether the patient's psychological disturbance is amenable to psychoanalytic treatment, whether he can change his life goal if necessary, and whether he can obtain the minimum emotional support from his environment cannot always be easily answered at the beginning of the analysis. The analyst may begin the treatment, even though he has serious doubts, and the analysis may be successful.

It must not be assumed that a patient who has been successfully analyzed is free from shortcomings. He is making the best of his opportunities and will continue to do so increasingly after the analysis is completed. Furthermore, he is able to handle his minor shortcomings successfully. Under new and very adverse life situations, he may need help again.

If an individual undergoes analysis as part of his professional training, the analysis proceeds essentially as has been described. The reason for this is that no one is free from fears and difficulties, although he may cope with them more successfully by means of various psychological devices. His manner of functioning in life, however, can always be improved. A successful analysis will enable such a person to live his life more fully. While his psychological devices are being broken through in the analysis, he may go through considerable emotional stress, for analysis can never be a purely intellectual experience.

We shall now describe the changes that took place in A. V. during the analysis, and we shall follow this by a discussion of the factors which operate in psychoanalytic treatment.

The Progress of A. V.'s Analysis.—A. V.'s analysis lasted three years. The emotional depression which she had had for four months before she started treatment disappeared within two weeks. (A. V.'s depression was of a milder type and did not belong to the group of manic-depressive reactions [see Chapter XXVII].) Her depression recurred in a milder form whenever she had any difficulties with her husband, whenever her work was not accepted as well as she had hoped it would be, and whenever the analyst introduced a new problem. Her working ability improved gradually, almost from the beginning of the analysis, except during her periods of depression. As the third year of her analysis approached, she was working with more steadiness and enjoyment than she had had at any other time in her life. She was free of the distress which had resulted from her having set too high goals for herself, as far as her work was concerned, and periodically falling short not only of her high expectations, but of the average she should have attained. Her sleep disturbances, loss of appetite, and frequency of urination began to improve at about the sixth month, but with some fluctuations; they did not disappear entirely until after two and one-half years of analysis. Her frigidity began to decrease after about eleven months, and her sexual function became steadily adequate after about two and one-half years.

Her over-sensitiveness to some of her friends began to diminish after one year of analysis. About the same time, her relationship with her mother, whom she saw occasionally, showed improvement. It became evident that in response to her mother's treatment of her, which to be sure had an element of rejection and disapproval in it, A. V. herself had been behaving in a hostile and rejecting manner. This, in turn, had caused her mother to become even more distant emotionally from her.

Her relationship with her husband fluctuated considerably without any essential change for about one year. She had greater difficulty in recognizing and accepting her reactions of hostility, her need for unqualified dependence, and her fear of abandonment in reference to him, than to the analyst. It distressed her considerably when the analyst showed her that these disturbances led to physiological and psychological dysfunctioning. As has been said, all these reactions clashed with her intense ideals, her need for moral ap-

proval and unqualified performance. Her husband's periods of hope-
lessness and bodily complaints have also been mentioned. During
such periods he leaned on his wife for help. At other times, however,
he jealously guarded his right of self-determination and would
irritably construe any request on her part as interference with his
liberty. He often reacted in this way when *she* felt a desire to lean
on him.

It is to be noted that some personality characteristics of these two
individuals dovetailed. One of A. V.'s ideals was to be able to cope
with any situation. This, of course, included helping her husband
when he was not well. Her own feeling of helplessness and her
profound need for affection and care, however, aroused in her a
strong need to lean on him after she had helped him. She wanted
his presence, and she wanted him to be attentive; but on such
occasions he was apt to feel that she was trying to dominate him
and he would therefore refuse. Her reaction to this would be the
feeling that he was rejecting and humiliating her. She would become
resentful; but because of her helplessness, her fear of abandonment
and self-condemnation she would also become depressed and need
him even more, whereas he would guard his rights all the more. In
fact, exactly this situation prevailed when A. V.'s husband had to
leave the city. When she asked him not to go, he told her that even
if he could make the sacrifice and remain with her, he would not
do it, so as not to set a precedent for being dominated.

A very important part of analytic work is to make the patient see
and understand the intricacies of his relationship with individuals
who are closest to him. The difficulty here is to make him see not
only his own attitudes, but those of his mate as well. This latter
implies criticism and consequent fear. It further implies considering
someone on whom the patient wants to depend completely as
imperfect.

A. V. began to see her own reactions toward her husband more
clearly after one year of analysis, whereupon they lessened in
severity. Still later she began to realize that many of her difficulties
were reactions to his difficulties. Her resentment toward him and
her dependence on him lessened. At the end of two years, however,
it became clear to both her and the analyst that she could not progress
beyond a certain point unless her husband underwent some treat-

ment. A. V. was attached to her husband and had never seriously considered leaving him. Her need for unqualified performance had lessened and her courage had increased sufficiently so that she could definitely request him to be treated and tell him that she herself could not progress any further under the circumstances. Out of consideration for her, and because of a need for self-esteem, he overcame his reluctance against seeking psychotherapeutic aid. This he had previously rejected because he considered it a sign of weakness to accept anyone's help. A. V.'s husband finally received interview therapy from another therapist for a period of six months. This effected a desirable change in him which enabled A. V. to work out her remaining problems. It was during this period that she gradually understood and overcame her fear of childbirth. Two years after the completion of the analysis, A. V. had a child; and she has continued to function well in all significant situations during the three years that her case has been followed since the completion of the analysis.

Curative Factors in Analytic Treatment.—Now that we have presented an account of the psychoanalytic procedure and of its therapeutic effects, we shall discuss what psychological factors are operative in achieving these results. Many of the factors are the same as those discussed in connection with psychotherapy in general. These will be referred to briefly, the emphasis being placed on the features characteristic of the analytic procedure.

Support and reassurance by the analyst; permissive attitudes.—Although these topics have been discussed previously, it should be mentioned here that the patient desires the analyst's *unqualified* and *unlimited* support, reassurance, and approval. He is not permitted the illusion that he is receiving this; if he is, any topic he or the analyst discusses will only subserve to maintain this illusion. How much the analyst comments on this attitude depends on the immediate analytic situation and on how much deprivation the patient can stand at the moment.

Effects of investigation of attitudes toward the analyst.—The fact that the patient manifests all the significant psychological attitudes in relationship to the analyst turns the analysis into a living experience for him. He must face and work out his emotional problems in this new interhuman relationship; thus he experiences his impulses under a unique set of circumstances. Comments on his reactions are made at the time they occur; he must face them. Furthermore, the impulse is not met by the analyst with moral approval or disapproval, or with counterattack or submission; nor can the problem be settled by action as in the patient's daily life. It is met with understanding and explanation, and with the implication that the patient should change his method of dealing with problems. Therefore the "fate" of the impulse and its effect on the patient's whole personality are different than would be the case under other circumstances.

The most important irrational attitudes that the patient has toward the analyst are: The expectation that the analyst will cure him by a sort of magic act, and that the analyst is all-powerful, omniscient, and perfect; an attitude of and a desire for complete submission in order to obtain the needed help; the assumption that the analyst looks down on him especially because of the above attitudes, and that the analyst wants to dominate or overpower him and keep him in subjection (counterpart of complete submission); anger toward the analyst for this reason and for his refusal to give the desired help; a desire to rule the analyst and to do to him everything that he thinks the analyst will do to him; fear of the analyst because of the anger toward him, chiefly fear of loss of his love and approval, and fear of injury; desire for gratifications; impulse to attack the analyst at certain parts of the body, and fear that the analyst will attack him at the same places.

The patient's various attitudes toward the analyst arise and are recognized partly spontaneously, but they are brought out particularly in response to the analyst's interpretations.

Unconscious attitudes becoming conscious.—The exact therapeutic effect of an unconscious impulse becoming conscious is a complicated question. Permissive and supportive attitudes on the part of the analyst often play an important part in the resulting relief. Another significant aspect is the following: The patient, because of his fear, shuts a distressing problem out of awareness and in that way renounces control over it; he becomes helpless to handle it. As a result of analytic work, his fear of the problem lessens and it becomes acceptable to him for consideration. This has a further effect: He now receives a key to a problem which has distressed and perplexed him, and he acquires mastery over it. In some cases this effect of analytic work is very striking.

A patient arrived for the analytic interview in a disturbed emotional state and complaining that her feet felt numb. The complaints persisted throughout the entire interview, in spite of repeated attempts at interpretation. She finally related an incident which had occurred not long before this interview and which up to this point she had not mentioned or thought of. She had expected a telephone call from her husband at noon, which had not come. She had felt that this was inconsiderate of him, and was angry and hurt, but then she had become worried lest he might be leaving her. Soon afterward, her complaint had started. As she discussed this incident with the analyst, her complaint disappeared. In this instance, the patient had been afraid of the consequences of her anger toward her husband and had therefore repressed her impulse and the memory of the incident. With the aid of the analyst, she acquired enough self-confidence to see the immediate problem and acquire mastery over it.

This patient was well along in her understanding of the type of problem that this incident presented, and it was for this reason that the effect was so immediate and clear. Usually, a patient is at first afraid to become conscious of attitudes which have been repressed, and he struggles against the analyst's efforts to enable him to see them. The lessening of the fear and the acquisition of mastery in such instances is achieved after some period of time.

Forcing the patient to change his attitudes.—As has been said, all interpretations have the unvoiced implication that, although they arise from helplessness, the patient's goals, e.g., complete dependence, have pernicious consequences and should be changed by him. The patient, however, reacts to this as if it were a threat to a vital need, and he pursues the same goal in a different form. Again this is interpreted to him, and thus the struggle goes on until he feels himself forced out of the attitude; he then, almost in desperation at first, begins to make a new effort. Thus, every important change in the patient's reaction patterns is a result not only of lessening anxiety, increased self-confidence, increased feelings of mastery and of approval, but also of being forced to abandon goals whose realization is refused. In this process the patient's desire to proceed further with his problems and to acquire increased self-esteem also plays a role. From this and what has been said under the two previous heads, interpretation is seen to be one of the most powerful therapeutic weapons of psychoanalysis.

Resolution of conflicts and of vicious circles; relief of bodily distress.—As a result of the analytic work, the feelings of helplessness and worthlessness and the catastrophic expectations are gradually relieved. With this, both the intense need for dependence and the hostile reactions subside, as well as the self-condemnation, the feelings of guilt, the self-aggrandizement, and the frantic struggle to reach implacable ideals. Thus, the conflicts grow less intense and are finally resolved, and compromise formations and substitute bodily gratifications are abandoned. The tense struggle to reach normal functioning abates, as does the continuous tension resulting from unsatisfiable psychological and physiological needs. Consequently the whole vicious circle of reactions is halted.

Increase in self-confidence and well-being.—Almost from the beginning of the analysis there is an increase in the patient's self-confidence and in his psychological strength. This is true in spite of the fact that the patient's fears become recurrently intense. The self-confidence and strength are not to be taken here as always meaning subjective comfort. They imply that the patient takes up problems which previously he could not face at all, regardless of the fact that they frighten him. These terms further imply that many of his functions improve when he is free from intense stress. Direct encouragement and reassurance are rarely given in the analytic interview. The patient often asks: "What can I do to have more self-confidence? How can I overcome my fears? In what ways is analysis going to help me?" The analyst may answer such questions once, but his answers are invariably interpreted by the patient as either containing magic help in themselves or falling far short of the kind of help he needs. Usually the patient repeats such questions later as if he had not asked them before and as if he had not had an answer. The reason for this is that these questions really represent disguised statements and requests on the part of the patient; therefore they have to be analyzed, not answered. The remarkable fact is that the patient's self-confidence increases as a result both of the implied supportive and permissive aspects of analysis and of the resolution of conflicts and of dangerous attitudes, and also because of increasing mastery. As the analysis progresses, successfully completed tasks and new gratifications increase the patient's desire for new efforts and in turn increase his self-confidence and strength, thus establishing a healthy circle of psychological and physiological reactions.

Summary

The following is an analytic outline of the functioning of the psychologically ill individual in his cultural environment, and of the processes of readjustment.

1. The individual constantly seeks out or is confronted with inevitable situations with which he has to cope. These situations are:

a. Gratification of specific bodily needs (e.g., food, sex, relaxation and sleep).

b. Pursuit of complex intellectual goals (e.g., occupational activities).

c. Pursuit of emotional satisfaction (e.g., friendship).

In all these situations complex cultural influences affect both the external situations and the individual's impulses. The individual's behavior in these situations is healthy to the extent to which it follows the formula: "I am worth something. I can pursue this goal. Other people are friendly toward me; if they are not, I can still cope with the situation and I can reach my goal later, if not now" (good evaluation of oneself and of the environment).

2. The individual may be motivated in the same situations by needs and strivings which are derivatives of expectations of distress which, in the extreme, are of catastrophic nature. To the extent to which these factors enter into his behavior, it is considered pathological.

3. The individual's reaction patterns are best formulated in terms of current motivations and interrelations, but the genetic determination of these reactions is also very important. The expectation of a catastrophic situation, as well as the reactions derived from it, always includes the following aspects:

a. The individual's evaluation of himself and of others.

b. Impairment of function with further resultant feeling of helplessness.

c. Emotional reactions of fear and anger.

4. The resultant final behavior is determined by three factors:

a. Direct results of emotional stress.

b. Defensive and ameliorative measures.

c. The attempt to reach the goal in spite of all hindrances.

5. Conflicts arise as a result of contradictory measures which the individual takes to escape the catastrophic situation and to alleviate his suffering. The contradictory needs and the extreme

character of each need (e.g., of hostility and of craving for dependence) make impossible action which is completely satisfying. This leads to continuous tension.

6. Current pathological reactions are perpetuated, at least potentially, through circular reactions. Both the incapacitating and the ameliorative reactions revive the fear of catastrophe directly or indirectly.

7. The individual is largely unaware of his significant motivations and their interrelation. The lack of awareness is an active process and is maintained by him to escape suffering and catastrophe.

8. Disturbances in bodily functions have three determinants:
a. Strong emotional reactions are accompanied by disturbed physiological functions.
b. The bodily function expresses attitudes—e.g., defiance, dependence—toward other people.
c. Fear arises in pursuit of certain bodily wants, and other goals are substituted.

9. Catastrophic expectations and their derivative reactions first appear in the individual's childhood, at first in the pursuit of bodily gratifications, but very soon also in connection with parental relationships and with any situation in which the parent is involved. The reaction patterns become largely "internalized," but the evaluation of other individuals (interhuman relations) is always included in them. The tendency to unhealthy reactions in critical situations persists throughout the individual's life largely because of the circular aspect of these reactions.

10. In analytic treatment the individual's harmful reactions are invariably dealt with in three contexts:
a. In his relationship with the analyst.
b. In his relations with persons and situations in daily life.
c. In situations of his childhood.
Effective results can be obtained by basing the constructions during the treatment on current motivations of the patient, with

proportionate emphasis on the above-mentioned topics in the sequence in which they are given.

11. Analysis attains its therapeutic effect by supportive, reassuring, and permissive implications, by giving the patient insight and increasing his mastery of his problems, by forcing him out of defended attitudes, by disentangling vicious circles of reactions, and by relieving emotional and physiological tension; further, through all these processes, by relieving his feelings of helplessness and worthlessness, his insecure evaluation of the world, his anxiety and guilt, and by increasing his self-confidence and his joy in success.

SUGGESTED READINGS

For reading for this chapter, the following are recommended: All of Freud's writings, particularly *A General Introduction to Psychoanalysis* (279) and the *New Introductory Lectures* (277); also Hendrick's *Facts and Theories of Psychoanalysis* (341). See also (308), and Fenichel's articles (234).

For an understanding of some recent developments, the following are recommended: Ferenczi and Rank's *Development of Psychoanalysis* (237), S. Freud's *The Problem of Anxiety* (280), Horney's *The Neurotic Personality of Our Time* (366) and her *New Ways in Psychoanalysis* (367), Kardiner's *The Individual and His Society* (421), Rado's article, "Developments in the Psychoanalytic Conception and Treatment of the Neuroses" (625), Alexander's article, "Psychoanalysis revised" (23), and Anna Freud's book, *The Ego and the Mechanisms of Defense* (270).

For readings on the analysis of children, the student is referred to Anna Freud's *Introduction to the Technique of Child Analysis* (268), and M. Klein's *The Psychoanalysis of Children* (431). See also Appendix.

PART V

THE SYMPTOM SYNDROMES

CHAPTER XXI

REACTIONS TO SHOCK, THREAT, OR BODILY INJURY (TRAUMATIC NEUROSES)

~~~~~~

THE CLASSIFICATION[1] OF PSYCHOLOGICAL DISTURBANCES

The classification of psychological illnesses is an important and difficult problem. This is shown by the fact that almost every year special committees of the American Psychiatric Association meet to decide on the terminology and classifications to be used. The general purpose of classification is to enable the therapist to orient himself with respect to the individual who applies to him for help. If he knows a few facts about the patient he knows what other facts to look for, he can estimate the seriousness of the condition and determine the treatment to be used.

The following points are significant in connection with classifications:

1. All symptoms and modes of handling situations—in other words, character traits—represent characteristic reactions to situations and problems; to use Meyer's term, they are reaction types.

To say that people differ in every characteristic is of course a truism; here we wish to point out briefly *how* these individual

---

[1] The older and more conventional classification of the neuroses into hysteria, neurasthenia, and psychasthenia is not suitable for many reasons. For one thing, much has been learned about anxiety in recent years, and it is now recognized to be a factor in any classification. Furthermore, enough is known today about all the neuroses so that subclassifications become possible and useful. Finally, the older classification is not dynamic enough, the "fashions" in choice of symptoms have changed, more is known about psychosomatics, etc.

differences, particularly in emotion, influence the sick individual's choice of symptoms and make him either more or less accessible to psychotherapy. Their specific role in affective reaction tendencies will be seen clearly in many of the cases which follow.

Various patients usually react to problems in a manner characteristic of them; e.g., one may run away from them, another seek the help of others, another attack the problems directly, etc. One person may use detachment, a second person bursts of temper, as the preferred mode of solving life problems. The first individual will be more likely to have symptoms that express and cover repressed aggression and self-assertion, whereas the second will be more likely to repress feelings of weakness and the like. These two people will probably have very different symptoms, even though the situation of stress is the same. Furthermore, they present different problems for the psychotherapist. The detached person is much less overt, reactive, and flexible in his emotional reactions than the one who knows how to express his emotions. These detached or rigid individuals are much more difficult problems therapeutically, for they fight off the therapist, refuse to react emotionally, and so insulate themselves that it is difficult to make contact with them.

2. Similar conflicts may lead to a variety of symptoms and reactions. To a considerable extent, however, striking and extremely characteristic reaction types have characteristic and partly specific determinants. In other words, the dynamics of an anxiety attack are usually different—to some extent at least— from the dynamics of depressive reactions. But in considering specificity, complex determinants should be sought, not one single determinant. For example, many factors which operate in an anxiety attack are also operative in a depressive attack; the feeling of helplessness is common to both and equally important in both. Furthermore, a given patient's personality features— his evaluation of himself and of others, his fears, etc.—are im-

portant therapeutically, even if they are not specific determinants of the reaction from which he suffers at the time. A patient suffers from attacks of anxiety which occur whenever he becomes angry at his superior who is unfair to him. His anxiety attacks probably represent fears about the consequences of his anger, particularly fear of destruction and injury. However, such factors as his need for unqualified dependence, inability to shoulder responsibility, unconscious attitudes of superiority, are all important in evaluating this patient's problems—even in these attacks—and in his treatment.

3. Classifications must not be adhered to too rigidly. Although it is very useful to say that a patient suffers from "anxiety hysteria" or "obsessional neurosis" or "manic-depressive psychosis," none of these labels, no matter how correct, describes the whole patient and all of his significant problems. Patients who suffer from these syndromes always have other complaints and symptoms which may be in the background, symptoms usually classified under different headings. It should be remembered that the patient has a variety of problems which he attempts to handle in a variety of ways, even if one form predominates. Further, there are maladjusted individuals with many minor symptoms but whose main problem is the fact that they have made a mess of their lives and thus in despair seek help. Moreover, when the symptom syndromes are explored thoroughly, they show many common features. For example, in all of them are manifest disturbances of evaluation of the self (feeling of helplessness) and of the environment (not being loved).

4. Various phases of a patient's complaints and symptoms can be selected as a basis for classification. Most of the classifications are based either on striking symptoms or on the causes of the patient's condition, or both. Thus the syndromes "anxiety hysteria," "obsessional neurosis," and "manic-depressive psychosis" are based on striking symptoms, whereas "cerebral arteriosclerosis" (hardening of the arteries of the brain) and

alcoholic psychosis are classified on the basis of the chief cause of the disturbance. In classifications based on symptoms, other than striking symptoms can also be used; for example, character traits, the patient's characteristic emotional life, a dominant dynamic principle such as a search for dependence are valid bases.

Our discussion will emphasize the following factors which will often be interwoven: (1) acute symptom groups; (2) causal factors, particularly where there is a specific organic factor; (3) character traits such as emotional reaction patterns, conscientiousness, etc.; (4) dynamic factors.

One of the most important differentiations based on symptoms is that between neurotic (often called psychoneurotic) and psychotic reaction patterns. The main differences between neuroses and psychoses are as follows:

1. Each has its special symptoms, more or less peculiar to it. For example, attacks of anxiety and obsessional thoughts are neurotic symptoms. Delusions of persecution and severe hallucinations are psychotic symptoms.

2. As a rule, the disturbance in the psychosis is much more incapacitating and continuous than it is in the neurosis.

3. The appreciation of reality—the actual perception and evaluation of events and of social customs—is disturbed more profoundly and in a different way in the psychosis than in the neurosis.

4. The relationship with the physician (and with all individuals) is much more elastic in the neurosis than in the psychosis. For this reason, the neurotic patient can be influenced much more easily and a permanent cure is more likely.

All these differences are sharply defined in typical cases, but they are quantitative in borderline cases. Thus, a neurotic with a very severe compulsion may be far more incapacitated and more difficult to cure than a mild schizophrenic who has no delusions of persecution and only hazy ideas of reference.

Traumatic Neuroses

The syndrome occurs after any event which is interpreted by the individual as a sudden threat to existence—usually, a close approach to death. Such a trauma seems to demonstrate to the individual that his confidence in himself, his ability to handle the problems of life, his picture of the world as a safe place that he can count on, are all false; that in reality he is entirely helpless to control the forces of life, and that the world is an extremely dangerous and fearful place. The condition arises most commonly after accidents and, in its severest form, as a result of experiences in war. Hence it is often called "shell shock" or "war neurosis."

The symptoms are various, for there are many forms of traumatic neurosis. Characteristic, however, of milder cases are irritability, excessive perspiration, trembling of the hands, sensitiveness to noise, dizzy spells, tics, nausea, and sometimes vomiting. The patient tires easily and his efficiency is generally impaired; it sometimes disappears almost entirely. In more severe cases—shell shock, airplane accidents—there may be various paralyses, speech disorders, disturbances of walking, severe attacks of dizziness, confusion, fugues, sometimes even convulsions. The patient may not be able to walk, talk, or feed himself. Perhaps most characteristic of all are the dreams; they are terrifying nightmares in which the patient repeats the original traumatic experience again and again, or is annihilated in one catastrophe after another, or is repeatedly frustrated in many ways.

It must be emphasized that the symptoms are the result not of physical damage, but of the disruption of the personality. These symptoms are seen in physically wounded individuals, but they occur in exactly the same form in people who are unharmed physically.

Probably everyone has at some time experienced a mild temporary traumatic neurosis—an automobile or train accident, a fire, in fact, any event that brings to mind the possibility of death. Although the symptoms here are the same as those found in the "abnormal" cases, they last only a few hours or days, whereas the latter may persist for years or even permanently. Why one person shakes off the experience quickly while another succumbs completely is not known.

A middle-aged woman driving an automobile at night was hit head on by another car that suddenly swerved to her side of the road. The other driver had fallen asleep at the wheel. Amazingly, neither driver was hurt, although both cars were smashed. The woman was not even bruised.

A few minutes after she got out of the car, she was overtaken with such violent trembling and weakness that she collapsed and started weeping. Later this was succeeded by a mild but persistent nausea which came whenever she looked at the wrecks. She had the strong impulse to flee from the situation but was able to control herself.

She could eat nothing until the next evening, and she spent a sleepless night thinking about the accident and what it meant. She had been driving for twenty years and had never had an accident because she was a very careful driver. But what did her care avail her if her fate was not in her own hands? She felt very foolish in having been over-confident, and she was extremely perturbed by the thought that her existence was a matter of mere accident. She relived the accident again and again, particularly the moment before the crash when she had expected to die.

For almost a week thereafter, her sleep was disturbed, with recurrent nightmares which slowly calmed down toward the end of the week to frustration dreams in which she tried again and again to build a house which collapsed repeatedly. She would wake from these dreams trembling and perspiring. During this period her work suffered. She was extremely jumpy; a sudden noise made her gasp and made her heart beat rapidly.

She recovered almost completely without help from anyone, and was able later to laugh at the episode. No change in personality was noticeable. She was a little more likely to jam the brakes on suddenly and completely if anything untoward happened while she was driving. Beyond this there was no change in her driving.

Psychodynamics of Reaction to Trauma.—While this syndrome has been known for a long time, only a few authors (Rivers, Freud, Kardiner) have studied its psychodynamics. Rivers interpreted it as a way of dealing with repressed emotions. This is not incorrect but it is certainly incomplete. Freud was so impressed with the character of the dreams of shell-shocked soldiers that he reorganized his whole theory of psychoanalysis. He had thought that all dreams were wish-fulfilling, and that, more generally, all reactions were pleasure-seeking; but this is obviously not so in the traumatic neurosis. Kardiner has made the only complete studies of psychodynamics, and it is on his work that this discussion is largely based.

Because of his evaluation of the world as a threatening place, the traumatic patient's vital physiological and psychological functions become inhibited, partly to protect himself from further hurt. There is no substitute for walking, standing, sleeping, or eating, the functions that are inhibited or destroyed in traumatic experiences. The individual is deprived of the fundamental abilities upon which rest the most primitive feelings of self-esteem and security. Hence it is easy to understand why he perceives the world as overwhelmingly hostile and dangerous and himself as helpless. This is the meaning of the catastrophic dreams. In fact, we may think of the traumatic neurosis as an actual catastrophic breakdown. Furthermore the patient feels resentful toward the world that threatens him; as a result, he fears counterattack. He may revert to childlike mechanisms and in severe cases may have to be cared for like an infant. This type of device, together with the care, gives him a measure of security but perpetuates his helplessness.

We can do no better by way of illustration than to quote directly from Kardiner a case history and his analysis of it.

"A young man of twenty-four engaged as an airplane mechanic, met with an accident while on a practice flight. The plane fell to the ground from a height of 1500 feet, killing the pilot and injuring the patient. Within a short time all the injuries healed and he was physically in good condition. But a new series of phenomena appeared, indicating that some gross change in his *adaptation* had taken place. He could no longer do or enjoy the things he did before the accident; he could not work. He had lost his aptitudes and many of his capacities. He was irritable to noise; his hands trembled so that he could not hold tools in his hand or manipulate them with accuracy. Any attempt to force the issue by driving himself to work beyond his inclination led to an outburst of rage or to a loss of consciousness. He was subject to these fainting spells two or three times a day. His sleep was disturbed by dreams whose content was always the same—he was always in danger of falling from a great height and would awaken with anxiety four or five times a night. In the morning he was always weak and exhausted. His interest in his wife and children lagged. His sexual interests diminished. He was constantly having visceral pains of one kind or another. He had constant headaches and a constant cutting sensation on one side of his forehead. He had an anesthesia on the entire left half of his body, etc.

"Certain inconsistencies stand out in his story. On the one hand, he informed me that he fell out of an airplane. This information he delivered in a most casual manner. On the other hand, when I asked him to talk about his accident he showed considerable signs of distress and a decided reluctance to pursue the subject any further. This is a bit of active, direct experience accompanied by a certain kind of affect and behavior which gives us our first indication that the total adaptation of this individual is impaired and not a particular isolated segment. It further advises us that we must observe our patient in action, for there are apparently more phenomena to his newly organized adaptation than we have recorded in the symptoms, which are apparently only gross surface manifestations which have connecting links with every fine detail of his adaptation. Not only is his adaptation disturbed in his waking hours, but his sleep has taken on a character that it never had prior to the accident. It is characterized by these mysterious dreams, with their stereotyped content and terrifying effects, which are another indication that the break in adaptation is constant and ever present.

"What we find in the symptoms of the neurosis above described is, therefore, a disturbance in the action constellations of the personality. The nature of this disturbance is hinted at by several of the symptoms: the loss of consciousness, the anesthesia on the left side of the body, and, to interpolate from other similar cases, the complete obliteration of whole sensory and motor systems. The central disturbance seems to be that the functions in question are no longer available for use, they have ceased to operate. This cessation of function must, therefore, be a new kind of activity of the whole personality and for this phenomenon we can use the construct 'inhibition.'

"Since the individual is still alive, we must assume that the drives are intact and that the defect lies in the executive functions with all their accouterments, which are now blocked more or less completely. Although the scale on which we see this principle operating is very vast, it is really nothing new, because it is the same principle which operates when a child withdraws its hand from the flame or when I fear to mount my horse after I have been thrown. It is, in other words, the size and the expanse of this reaction which makes it difficult for us to envisage the whole process. Once these functions become blocked, it follows that the outer world has taken on a new and inhospitable character, because it was the function of these action constellations to interpret the outer world and to manipulate the individual safely through his encounters with it. Now, without their help, the endopsychic perception of the individual by himself as helpless, and the outer world as a hostile place, is entirely justified. And this is exactly the picture of the new personality in operation that we get in the distressing catastrophic dreams.

"It can be made clear to the patient that his neurosis consists of a very elaborate defense system occasioned by the fact that the situation that confronted him originally in his fall in the airplane was beyond his capacities to master; that the danger situation no longer exists although he behaves as though it did. We can utilize his reluctance to talk about the incident as evidence of his defensive maneuvers and as evidence that he is not dealing alone with a painful memory; he is dealing with an altered conception of the outer world and himself, etc."[1]

The following case, also from Kardiner, is of interest in this connection:

"When originally seen, the patient complained of a strange symptom in both lower extremities, extending up to the umbilicus. He was subject to feelings of numbness, pain and cold, but more especially to sweating from the waistline down to the toes. This sweating, he said, was continuous, especially at night. When he was asked how old this symptom was, he said at least seven years. Among his other complaints were marked irritability and instability of temper; he became aggressive and pugnacious very suddenly and without sufficient cause. He also suffered from spells of transient blindness, which lasted anywhere from five to fifteen minutes. Attacks of vertigo were among his symptoms. His sleep was disturbed continually by the usual dreams of drowning, being run over, or receiving electric shock. In some dreams he was the aggressor.

"When inquiries concerning his traumatic history were made, he denied ever having suffered a serious shock. Then he casually stated that he was on board the U.S.S. *President Lincoln* when she was torpedoed. He was asked to narrate the details of this accident, which were in substance: He was in the kitchen gambling with several of the mess attendants when he heard a shot. This he interpreted as due to target practice and continued his game. Several minutes later there was another shot, and then another, the last one a distinct explosion. At this, all of the men ran upstairs. The command was given to take to the lifeboats, and he realized the ship had been torpedoed. It so happened that some of the lifeboats were disabled and there were not enough to go round. At all events, the patient and about eight other Negroes were obliged to take to a raft. He described the sinking of the ship, his lack of trepidation at the sight, and the absence of panicky sensations. He said this was due to the fact that the retreat to the lifeboats and the rafts was very orderly, and the ship did not sink until some hours later. At this point in his recital the patient became rather excited and began

[1] This quotation is from Dr. Kardiner's forthcoming book, *Character and Neurosis.*

to swear profusely. His anger was aroused chiefly by the incidents connected with the rescue. They were in the water for a period of about twelve hours when a destroyer picked them up. Of course priority was given to the officers in the lifeboats. The eight or nine men clinging to the raft were allowed to remain in the water. They had to wait for six or seven hours longer until help came. In describing his feelings while in the water, the patient emphatically denied having had any panic or fear. However, while narrating these incidents, it was quite clear to me that he was very disturbed. The disturbance he acknowledged. He said that his telling of the story made him fearful. I made him revive many details of the story that had a harrowing effect on him.

"The similarities between the symptoms he complained of, in the form of sensations and sweating from the waistline down, and his story of being submerged in cold water up to this level were pointed out to him. He admitted that when he allowed himself to close his eyes and think of his present sensations, he still imagined himself clinging to the raft, half submerged in the sea. He stated that while clinging to the raft, his sensations had been extremely painful ones and that he had thought of nothing else during the time. He also recalled the fact that several of his companions had lost consciousness and were drowned. It was quite obvious that, to a large extent, the patient owes his life to the concentration of attention on the painful sensations occasioned by the cold water.

"The symptoms represented, therefore, a hallucinatory reproduction of the original sensation of being submerged in the water. Concerning his remaining symptoms, it is of interest to note that he developed many of the secondary symptoms of traumatic cases that are epileptoid in character. The spells of transient blindness used to come on specific occasions, for example, when he saw something in the nature of violence. Thus the patient was out walking one day and witnessed an automobile colliding with a train. He became maddened with excitement, was blinded for ten minutes, and was taken home in a state of extreme agitation. He alleges that it took him four months to recover from the effects of this incident, although the danger did not directly concern him. During these four months, he was obsessed by a vision of the accident. He had, in fact, a profound reaction to violence of any kind. He could not witness others being hurt, injured or threatened. Prior to his service, he had never had fears or phobias of any kind. He had been an employee of a railroad company and had seen a very bad wreck without serious consequence to his state of mind. In fact, he himself had assisted in extricating people from the wreck. He was also extremely sensitive to loud noises. This was very remarkable, because he had heard very little shellfire during his naval career—yet he shared this secondary reaction with patients who had come from the zone of active fighting. He would yell or scream on a sudden call or other abrupt noise. He was troubled by the violence of his reaction to these stimuli. He claimed that he felt like suddenly striking people, and that he had become very pugnacious to his family. He remarked: 'I wish I were dead. I make everybody around me suffer.'

"He had the usual disturbing dreams, but his memory for them was poor. However, he might start from his sleep several times during the night.

"Of great interest is the fact that in the lower extremities he had no objective sensory disturbance whatsoever. His reactions to water were quite typical. He did not like sea-bathing, and whenever he had attempted to go into the water since his return from service, he became nauseated and vomited. He treated his lower extremities most tenderly. He protected them with all kinds of ointments and wore warm stockings in all seasons."[1]

Treatment.—Milder cases improve with weekly interview therapy. Sedative medication is also helpful. In severe instances the patient has to be seen more frequently and over a longer period. He must be made aware of the fact that he has an altered conception of the world and of himself, and that this change originated with the traumatic experience. The reflexly defensive character of the syndrome must be demonstrated to him, and he must have a clear understanding that, in this, the syndrome defeats its own ends. Depending on various factors, the condition may last a few weeks or may be partly permanent.

[1] A. Kardiner, The bio-analysis of the epileptic reaction, *Psychoanalytic Quarterly*, 1932, i, Nos. 3 and 4, 375-483.

SUGGESTED READINGS

The best readings are the chapter on dreams in Freud's *New Introductory Lectures on Psychoanalysis* (277), and Kardiner's *The Bio-Analysis of the Epileptic Reaction* (418). It would be interesting to compare these with Goldstein's concept of catastrophic breakdown (311).

CHAPTER XXII

REACTIONS IN WHICH ANXIETY OR PHOBIA PREDOMINATE

~~~~~~

ANXIETY HYSTERIA

Fear (or a similar emotional state such as concern, worry, anxious anticipation) is one of the commonest psychopathological symptoms. Often this state and its accompanying discomfort are low in intensity, but they may be almost continuous. The patient may feel concerned, worried, or afraid about practically everything, important and unimportant. A woman may be continually afraid that her child or her husband will become ill or have an accident. In other instances, a patient vaguely anticipates considerable trouble and misfortune even though there is little justification for it; for example, a mother expects her child to develop pneumonia although he has only a slight cold, or a person suffers a slight scratch and worries about blood-poisoning. In such cases, the fear may be fairly intense. It may be even more intense periodically if, because of some slight bodily discomfort, the patient thinks that he has tuberculosis or heart disease. The average individual suffers in all these types of fear, but he does not realize that he is psychologically sick and he is therefore inclined to consider his fear justified.

There are other cases, however, when the individual is suddenly thrown into a state of intense fear which lasts a few minutes or even less and then subsides. This is known as an anxiety attack. Such attacks are frequently the predominant complaint of a sick person. They may occur several times a day or once a week or even less often.

These attacks are extremely disquieting. During one the patient may be afraid of dying, "going insane," or having heart disease, tuberculosis, or cancer. In still other instances, he is gripped by anxiety without knowing why. He may feel that the walls are closing in on him, that he is a small thing in a gigantic, threatening world, that he is trapped in some place, e.g., on a boat with no possibility of getting off, or is alone on a great height with the huge world around him. The fear may be coupled with the desire to jump out of the window.

Anxiety attacks are often accompanied by bodily manifestations, such as palpitation, rapid heart rate, pain around the heart, difficulty in breathing, feeling of suffocation, nausea, perspiration, coldness of the extremities, need to urinate or to defecate, dizziness, choking sensation (lump in the throat), bodily tremors, sudden weakness, belching, need to clear the throat, or headaches. These symptoms may be manifest even when the patient has no conscious feeling of anxiety, or the anxiety attack may be accompanied by a disturbance in only one organ, such as difficulty in breathing, palpitation, etc.

Anxiety Attacks as Reactions to Stress Situations.—Anxiety attack is always a person's reaction to a situation which he evaluates in terms of his image of himself (self-esteem) and of other individuals (security feeling).

A patient who was under analysis had no cigarettes to offer a visitor at his home. He put on his hat and started out to get some. His wife asked him where he was going, and when he told her, she said, in a hurt and angry manner, "We decided to save money; don't go for the cigarettes." The patient's feelings were varied and largely unconscious; he felt that she was dominating him, he was ashamed at being scolded before the visitor, and he became angry at her; but he went for the cigarettes. While he was out, he began to have difficulty in breathing; it continued, but he controlled himself until the visitor had left. He and his wife then had some further discussion about expenses, whereupon he began to have considerable difficulty in breathing, became very anxious, and feared that he was dying.

Still later he had a fantasy that he would hang himself in the bathroom, and his wife would be grief-stricken when she found him dead in the morning.

The patient's anxiety attack thus had as its most immediate source the fear of the consequences of his anger: "I became angry at the person upon whom I am absolutely dependent, and by being angry at her I endanger my whole existence." He then expressed his helplessness, and his anger as well, in the form of the anxiety attack, as if saying, "I am helpless, have pity on me"; and also, "See what you have done to me."

Attacks of anxiety do not represent a sort of foreign body in an individual who is otherwise emotionally well. Detailed study always shows that he has other disturbances also, in interpersonal relations, in his work, in the functioning of various organs. The locus and extent of these disturbances may vary considerably from one patient to another. The personality make-up of these patients likewise varies; for example, they may be conscientious and ambitious or careless and irresponsible. Most frequently their general emotional make-up shows considerable elasticity[1] and is outgoing. They are apt to respond emotionally to most situations of either stress or pleasure, although this may not show in their behavior.

Psychodynamics of Anxiety Attacks.—The fact that anxiety attacks occur in response to important events in the patient's life and that various bodily functions may be disturbed makes it clear that the individual's whole personality and its functions are involved in such an attack.

1. The anxiety attack is the closest actual approximation of the catastrophic state which most patients anticipate unconsciously. The patient's self-evaluation is chiefly a feeling of helplessness; the catastrophic expectation is chiefly injury and abandonment. The injury may concern the entire body or one part of it; the

---

[1] That is, they react emotionally in accordance with various situations, instead of sailing through all situations with no reactions, or always reacting to everything in only one way, such as rage.

unconscious expectation of injury to the genital organs is common. It may also take the form of complete paralysis, of being immobile while destroyed by uncontrollable forces. The abandonment which the patient fears and experiences in his attack may embody complete loss of love and emotional isolation, or the refusal of all help and protection where vital needs and physical safety are concerned. A vital need which the patient commonly experiences as being threatened is the obtaining of food. For example, he may become angry at someone. If he considers himself helpless and the other person all-powerful, he may unconsciously fear that the other one will deprive him of food, even though consciously he recognizes this to be a ridiculous idea. Food here is equated with love and help. Fears of catastrophic humiliation, disapproval, and condemnation may also be present in the anxiety attack; but injury, abandonment, and the withdrawal of love usually predominate.

2. In the anxiety attack the patient experiences an intense emotion openly. In so far as the attack partially represents a near-catastrophic expectation or experience, it has no goal; almost always, however, there is also a definite goal. By means of his anxiety attack, the patient emphasizes his helplessness and unconsciously appeals for help. Thus his chief method of dealing with the threatening situation is an open, dramatic appeal for help. This is why anxiety attacks are most frequently a predominant complaint in people whose emotional life is adaptable, changeable, non-rigid, and open. However, this is not always so, for occasionally these attacks are almost the only overt emotional manifestation in individuals who otherwise are detached and attempt to repress all their emotions (Zilboorg, 813).

3. Insight into the emotional factors leading to the anxiety attack is always inadequate, for repressed emotional factors are always connected with it, the most frequent ones being anger and hostility. The patient may be entirely unaware of any resentment in certain situations, and he may reject the idea that he is angry; but he has an anxiety attack. Only after considerable

therapeutic work will he realize and acknowledge his anger. Other impulses which may be completely repressed are submission, sexual impulses, superiority.

In so far as the patient is afraid of the consequences of these impulses, he is really afraid of his own impulses; that is, he becomes angry and is then afraid unconsciously of counterattack in the form of injury or abandonment—he is afraid of his own anger.

4. Revivals of earlier forms of behavior and reactions (regressive phenomena) are often observable in anxiety attacks, or in the patient's attitudes which are connected with or lead to these attacks. The need and desire to obtain reassurance and safety by being fed or completely cared for as by a protective parent, are frequent. Such a patient is often found to have been particularly anxious as a child, to have had anxiety attacks at an early age, and to have expressed his conflicts and tried to obtain parental help by means of them. All these phenomena are part of the patient's current problems and his manner of dealing with them.

Treatment.—Shorter treatments, such as a series of interviews, can be very effective with patients whose dominant complaint is anxiety attacks, particularly if their general emotional reaction pattern is open, not detached. The patient may experience considerable relief after the first visit; if he continues treatment after the most distressing symptoms disappear, there is often marked improvement in other functions. For example, his work may improve; the woman who was unable to love her husband may find that she now is able to do so. Occasionally, partial frigidity disappears, particularly if, as a result of treatment, there is open discussion between cooperative mates.

Psychoanalytic treatment is also very effective for these patients. A very remarkable change can often be observed in their work, in their interpersonal relations, and in their organic functioning. Thus, one man who was a passive type, preferred masturbation to intercourse with his wife, and was afraid to show initiative and ambition, attained normal potency and a healthy emotional attachment, and became one of the best-liked men in his field, after analytic treatment.

Patients with long-standing anxiety attacks who in general are strongly repressed emotionally or whose life circumstances are very unhappy present difficult therapeutic problems. Psychoanalysis can be effective here also, although the results may not be as brilliant as in the case just cited. Insulin treatment has recently been used with varying success. Group therapy is also partially effective.

Reactions in Which Fear of a Special Situation Predominates (Hysterical Phobia)

Hysterical phobia is characterized by an overwhelming fear of special situations such as closed or open spaces, heights, subways, animals, the dark. Most people have relatively unimportant fears of this type, but in some individuals these fears become so intense as to be overwhelming. In such cases important activities are interfered with because of the phobia, or the continuous presence of another individual is necessary.

Phobic Symptoms as Reactions to Stress.—Like the anxiety attacks just discussed, the phobia represents a definitely patterned reaction to stress. Once the reaction pattern is fully established, it is more difficult to see the connection between it and the stress of daily events than in the case of anxiety attacks. There are two reasons for this:

1. The phobic patient unconsciously disconnects the reaction from the stress causing it; he reasons as follows: "I am afraid only of going out on the street; I fear nothing else. My fear is something with which I have nothing to do; it is entirely beyond my control. The reason for my fear is not that I want to leave my husband because of the way he treats me; it is not true that I want intimacies with other men because I am angry at him or because I need a more affectionate and dependable mate. My

fear is the completely unsubstantiated fear of going out on the street. I am an invalid and I must be helped."

Thus the patient can be said to displace or project the fear of an impulse or of its consequences on to an external situation. This displacement at times takes the form of symbolization, the external situation becoming the symbol of a more general fear. Thus being alone on a height or in any high place may come to represent abandonment with the threat of catastrophe. For example, a man may have a disagreement with his father which is not immediately followed by fear; it may instead appear later when he is going up in an elevator in a tall building. If he is working in a high place, he becomes utterly unable to work. The true reason for his inability is completely hidden; he knows only that he cannot work in a high place. In some phobic reactions, particularly in children, large animals may represent the father or the individual of whom the patient is afraid.

2. The phobic patient attempts to prevent the occurrence of the dangerous situation. Thus the woman mentioned above develops fear, not after attempting to flirt with strange men, but before going out on the street. This means that the connection between stress and fear is further hidden.

In reality, the interaction between the patient's unconscious attitudes and the activities of his daily life constantly renews his emotional reaction pattern of disappointment, anger, and feeling of helplessness. It is this fact, together with his tendency to prevent situations of stress and to blame the external situation instead of his reaction, which maintains the phobia.

The general personality make-up of the patient with phobic reactions varies; but it usually shows the same outgoing and elastic emotional traits as that of the patient with anxiety attacks. If the phobic reactions have lasted for some time, the patient usually becomes more rigid emotionally, and generally fearful and anxious; he tends to shut out of awareness all emotions except those that are entirely approved of.

Patients with phobic reactions often have either fleeting or continuous disturbances in various organic functions—head-aches, dizzy spells, gastro-intestinal troubles, etc.

Psychodynamics of Phobia.—The patient's self-evaluation is chiefly helplessness; his catastrophic expectation is of injury and abandonment, as in anxiety attacks.

The purposive aspect of the phobic reaction is stronger than in anxiety attacks. The displacement is strong and the connections between the situation of stress, the hidden impulses, and the subsequent reactions to these impulses are hidden. The patient's statement of helplessness and appeal for help are likewise stronger. The patient who is afraid to cross the street or ride in the subway can often do these things if he is accompanied by someone close to him; his dependence is thus safeguarded. Sometimes another unconscious purpose may be detected in a phobia. In subtle ways he can express hostility if he wishes, and thus obtain vengeance on and domination over the individual whom he forces to be at his side. Thus the wife who forces her husband to be with her in this manner secures his help and at the same time tortures him.

A patient with phobic reactions attempts to cope with certain problems by carefully avoiding them. As we shall see, this tendency to systematic and carefully controlled behavior is not as marked as it is in patients with obsessional reactions, but it is definitely present.

Treatment.—The treatment of phobic reactions is more difficult than that of anxiety attacks, particularly if the condition has lasted for some time.

Psychoanalytic treatment often has brilliant results, especially when the patient is of the outgoing emotional type. However, this treatment may present difficulties if the patient is unable to come to the therapist's office by himself, but must be brought by someone else. His phobic symptoms may become worse during crucial conflict situations and his behavior toward his escort be objectionable. If because of his own conflicts or antagonism the escort refuses to cooperate or becomes pugnacious, the patient may not tolerate him. Because the patient's external circumstances are therefore more significant than they are in the case of anxiety attacks, direct contact with the patient's relatives and with his environment may be indispensable for the therapist. Often enough, such difficulties interrupt the interviews or even make them impossible. Institutionalization may be necessary for such cases. For very severe cases insulin treatment is now being recommended, but no data on its efficacy are yet available.

A 25-year-old girl was afraid to be alone at home (claustrophobia), and to go alone more than one block away from home (agoraphobia). These conditions were of one year's duration when she applied for treatment. Because of her fear of being alone, a friend always stayed with her, except in the evenings when her father was home. Her father often took her riding, this being the only way in which she could tolerate leaving her own neighborhood.

She was an efficient housekeeper, and enjoyed reading, sewing, embroidering, and other normal pursuits. She occasionally had mild spells of dizziness and was often constipated. She was never aware of any sexual desires.

The patient's parents had not gotten along well. The mother was rather emotional, the father rather strict and exacting; he had fits of rage during which he would threaten to leave the family. The mother often appealed to the daughter for sympathy; and although the father had been kind to her, the daughter always inclined to take the mother's part. During all this time the girl had minor fears such as fear of the dark and of thunderstorms; at times she was depressed. When she was sixteen, her mother died, and the daughter got along better with her father. She kept house for him and prepared his meals. After she finished school she stayed home altogether to keep house. She was very efficient in this, but she directed her father's routine behavior at home almost completely, even to the point of designating which room he should use, reprimanding him when he upset the house in any way, etc.—all of which he accepted docilely. The patient never became interested in any young man, although she had several girl friends.

When she was twenty-five years old, her father came down with pneumonia, and she took care of him; this was an anxious time for her. The father spent part of the period of convalescence at home, then went to a resort for a few months before returning to business; his daughter accompanied him. At the resort he often conversed with a woman who was also a guest there; the patient was polite but disliked her. After the father returned to business again, the daughter gradually developed the fear of being alone and of going out alone.

From early childhood the patient never felt that she was loved for her own sake, that she had any strength within herself. Her attachment to her mother was strong, but she felt that her mother did not really care for her, but used her against her father. Her attitude toward her father was likewise split. She wanted his affection, but she felt that by accepting it she would lose more because she would be deprived of her mother's affection. She felt fairly secure in school and worked well. Her mother's death was followed by a period of depression because she realized for the first time her absolute need of the support that she had lost, and also because of her guilt at her previous hostility toward her mother. In the years that followed she achieved a fairly satisfactory relationship with her father. She had more of his affection than before, but at the same time she could dominate him to some extent and satisfy whatever resentment she had toward him. She formed no attachments with young men because she unconsciously anticipated trouble similar to that she had experienced with her parents. Furthermore, she was afraid of new relationships because she would have no protection. She was afraid of the genital function because of her insecurity, the idea of submission and domination, and the fear of being injured in retribution for her anger toward men (first experienced toward her father). Unconsciously, as a form of sensual expression, as well as to obtain even more of her father's support and to increase her domination of him, she had sexual desires in reference to her father. His illness represented a serious threat to her both because his death would deprive her of needed support and because of her guilt and consequent fear of retribution, hurt, and abandonment resulting from her resentment toward him. His contact with the other woman at the resort aroused the daughter's fear that he might marry this woman, and she would thus be abandoned by the one person on whom her whole existence depended. When he returned to business, his leaving the house represented a constant renewal of this threat of abandonment.

This patient was interviewed for six months, during which time she improved about fifty per cent. Further improvement was impossible because the father really did not want her to become more independent of him; for example, he never wanted her to go out in the evening, etc. He would not consent to her being given psychoanalytic treatment.

SUGGESTED READINGS

See Chapter XXIII.

CHAPTER XXIII

REACTIONS IN WHICH OBSESSIONS AND COMPULSIONS PREDOMINATE

In obsession and compulsion neuroses, the patient's chief discomfort arises from thoughts which he does not accept yet cannot avoid, and from actions which he cannot resist. He may consider them silly and ridiculous, or exceedingly painful or humiliating, and shrink from them in horror. If he attempts to resist the compulsion he becomes extremely uncomfortable, and may even suffer a violent anxiety attack. He may be incapable of any sustained or constructive activity because the major portion of the day is devoted to compulsive acts.

Doubt and indecision may be an important factor. The patient may become vacillating, hesitant, and so uncertain of himself that he is unable to make any decision (abulia). In some cases this completely incapacitates him for any normal activity, such as business, education, etc.

Such a patient may have a terrifying thought which he attempts to counteract by a specific action. For example, if he thinks that he has picked up some germs on his hands, he may feel compelled to wash his hands. In fact, hand-washing is one of the most common compulsive acts; it may be carried to such an extreme that the hands become irritated and painful. Similarly, if he thinks of killing someone or of someone's death, he may fear that this will cause that individual's death; he thereupon is compelled to utter a word or phrase—"God save mother," for example—or to make certain definite movements with his hands, such as folding them in prayer.

Compulsive actions are manifold. The patient may be unable to sleep unless his pillows are arranged in an apparently senseless way; he may have to return to his house several times to assure himself that all the gas jets are closed or that no windows are open—this in spite of the fact that he checked them carefully before he left the first time. Compulsive acts may interfere with the patient's work, or even endanger his life; thus one pianist had to interrupt his playing frequently to wash his hands, and an army officer had to stop frequently to look for papers in his pocket, even if this meant holding up an attack he was leading.

Minor compulsive thoughts or acts are rather common in many people. The above description applies to cases in which the individual is definitely disturbed if not incapacitated.

A variety of personality features is encountered in obsessional reaction types. Some of them, among which are the following, occur relatively more frequently and can be assumed to have some relationship to the dominant symptom.

1. Extreme orderliness, together with excessive cleanliness, stubbornness, and stinginess (Freud). The tendencies to arrange and put things in order, when accompanied by an emotional conviction of the usefulness of this behavior, may be of some social value, but it may be annoying to other individuals and seem quite ridiculous to them. One of the most common examples is presented by those housewives who expect everything in the house to be spotless all the time, and who feel that every chair, napkin, book, and ashtray must *always* be in its proper place. Such patients have no insight into the pathological aspects of these character traits. This is well brought out by the amusing story of the university librarian who was hurrying so much that he bumped into a member of the faculty. His eyes gleaming, he explained that every book but one was now safe in the library stacks and he was hurrying to take that one away from the person who had it.

2. A strong idealistic trend with great conscientiousness and

tenderness and considerateness toward almost everyone. These features also are fully approved of, and they have very useful social aspects, but they are carried to extremes in patients. The patient may expect himself and others to be motivated only by idealistic impulses, never to become angry but always to settle everything by reasoning, always to treat everyone considerately, and always to understand and forgive. His emotional reactions may be quite definite and outgoing, but usually there is also considerable emotional rigidity.

The above character traits are often combined with their opposites, and the picture then becomes exceedingly contradictory. On the one hand the patient is clean and orderly; on the other, he at times neglects his duties or keeps part of his life in a disordered state. Thus, his house may be spotlessly clean, but in a closet he may keep a disordered pile of old, filthy rags. The considerate and conscientious patient with high ideals may engage in irresponsible acts and be openly unfair and cruel. He may be annoyingly over-logical in some respects, and in others be completely ruled by superstition.

Patients whose dominant symptoms are obsessional reactions are usually also troubled by disturbances in various organic functions such as elimination, appetite and eating, spells of dizziness, headaches, etc. The exact relation of these bodily symptoms to obsessions and compulsions is not known; a reasonable assumption is that they are, in part, products of great physical and psychic tension.

Psychodynamics of Compulsions and Obsessions.—The most important aspect of the obsessive-compulsive personality is his great need for safety and security. This he attempts to achieve by arranging his world in an orderly, regular way that he can count on, and in which nothing unexpected can happen. He attempts to live by rules and regulations rather than by spontaneous decisions.

The dominant aspects of the patient's self-evaluation are feelings of helplessness and worthlessness. In spite of this devaluation, his continual need of safety, and his other fears, the patient with obsessional symptoms may attempt to assume responsibility and to establish close relationships with other individuals. He may, however, be irritating because of his hard, persistent, and rigid manner, and because of his insistence on perfection of function and achievement.

The patient's dominant reaction to difficult situations is one of hostility, disparagement, humiliation, and degradation. His major fear, expressed in the obsessional symptom, is of being completely enslaved, injured and destroyed, and morally disapproved of. The tendency to and the expectation of hostility, the tendency to humiliate others and the expectation of being humiliated explains the fact that obsessional thoughts most frequently are thoughts of violence, such as killing, shooting, cutting the throat, and thoughts of dirt, such as excreta, germs, and infection.

The patient's chief ways of dealing with his impulses and anxieties are: (1) Reaction formation (see page 161): This explains how a patient may at the same time have thoughts of violence and ideals of excessive tenderness. (2) Displacement (see page 165): The patient's main conflict situation may be the feeling of being dominated or humiliated by his wife; he may show exceeding tenderness toward her, but also have obsessive thoughts of cutting his children's throats. (3) Persistent and rigid thought and behavior patterns: These are the most obvious symptoms. (4) Regressive phenomena are often observable as part of the patient's total reaction to stress. These consist chiefly of the revival of childhood attitudes, reactions, and fears, particularly in connection with anal functions and more specifically with bowel movements. Often these childhood attitudes were already pathological, having risen in response to over-severe parental discipline and its attendant conflicts. Thus, the child may have used his bowel function (holding back or soiling) as the only means of asserting himself against, expressing his hostility to, or obtaining attention from, his parents (Kardiner).

Treatment.—Patients with predominantly obsessional complaints often respond well to treatment, particularly if they have an emotionally outgoing personality. Interview therapy is especially effective when the complaint is chiefly obsessional thoughts and not compulsive acts, and when the symptoms have not incapacitated the patient for work. The first sign of improvement is usually the less frequent recurrence of the obsessional thoughts and their decreased ability to disturb. Under continued treatment these thoughts may eventually disappear almost entirely. However, they are likely to return when a new situation of stress confronts the patient, but renewed treatment will put them under control more quickly.

Psychoanalytic treatment can achieve excellent results with patients whose major complaint is obsessional thoughts or compulsive actions. However, it may fail when the condition is long-standing, when the patient has become almost completely incapacitated, when his whole life revolves around these thoughts and actions, and when in addition he is emotionally rigid. Analytic treatment presents one difficulty, but this can be overcome. The patient may be inclined to doubt every interpretation the analyst makes, and to advance logical reasons against them; or he may agree to the interpretations but have a detached emotional attitude toward them. Unless both of these reactions are themselves analyzed, the patient will be untouched by treatment.

According to recent reports, insulin or metrazol treatment has led to improvement in severe cases.

A 30-year-old man applied for treatment because of disturbing thoughts that he would cut the throat of his child, his wife, or his mother. He considered himself utterly contemptible and worthless for having such thoughts, was in constant dread of carrying them out, and even contemplated suicide. At times he would not dare to touch a knife.

The patient, the oldest of five siblings, was not born in the United States. When he was five years old, his father left the family to come to this country; the rest of the family followed him about three years later. The patient's mother was incredibly harsh, unfair, and cruel toward the children. She never showed them any affection or praised them for anything. For example, she would tie the patient to a chair and let him watch while the rest of the family ate, or promise him a dime to clean the house, but give him a whipping instead of the dime because she found some nook in which there was dust. The patient's father, a mild-mannered man, occasionally made the mother treat the children with less severity.

The patient, an ambitious child, wanted to go to high school. His father did not want to lose any money on this because he saw no purpose in it; his mother, however, was in favor of his studying and was willing to forego what he would earn if he were working. The patient always felt considerable unconscious resentment toward his mother and there was also considerable conflict between them. The mother was very exacting in her demands as far as his scholastic requirements were concerned, but he was always a good student. This was the only activity for which his mother did not punish him, but she never praised him either.

When his father died, the patient interrupted his studies to earn money to support the family, but continued to educate himself by reading and attending courses; he was very ambitious in this respect. He was a good worker, had intelligent ideas, was charitable and fair. He was a peacemaker; he never swore, never abused anyone, and never lost his temper. His mother had prevented all her children from marrying. However, after one son's suicide because of this, she raised no objections when the patient married a fairly sensitive and intelligent woman, who had difficulties in her home, and was frequently depressed. The patient knew of this; in fact, one reason for his marrying her was to help her. The two had much in common and were deeply in love at the time of marriage; they had a child a year later. The patient's mother lived with them and there was frequent friction between the two women.

The patient's compulsive symptoms started four years after his marriage. He had been active in organizing his co-workers into a union, and he was to be elected a delegate to the union conventions. However, he refused the offer because his wife became depressed at the thought of his being away from home for such long periods. Not long after this his compulsive thoughts began. He never went out alone in the evenings, though he liked to attend political meetings, visit friends, and go bowling. Although his wife would not openly object to his going out, she would become depressed. He also gave up all his labor union activities.

The patient often had headaches and burning sensations in his forehead; these usually appeared in situations when he should have become angry. He had a slight difficulty in breathing, and palpitations of the heart; these usually arose when he was afraid or should have been afraid. The connection between these organic disturbances and their underlying cause became clear during analysis because the disturbances appeared whenever the patient spoke of certain incidents or the analyst made various comments. Thus the compulsive symptoms predominated in this patient, but some organic functions were also disturbed.

When the patient came for treatment he said that his relationship with his wife was perfect and that he had no criticisms of her. His attitude toward his mother, he said, was one of understanding; he realized that she had treated him and all her other children badly, but he forgave her because she had known no better. Only by day-to-day observation could the therapist be certain and convince the patient that he felt considerable resentment and conflict toward both his wife and his mother. The therapist could then make clear to him that he felt that his wife dominated him, was unfair to him, and had interfered with his career and his ambitions; in other words, his compulsive thoughts were particularly intense whenever he stayed home to prevent her from becoming depressed. He was also shown that because of his high ideals and his need of her approval he did not permit himself to feel angry or to acknowledge his anger; instead, he felt that he had to take her burden upon himself and sacrifice himself for her happiness, for if he did not do this, or if he became angry, he felt utterly worthless. He also realized eventually that he was very resentful toward his mother, that he had not actually forgiven her for her treatment of him, and that he also resented the nature of her relationship with his wife.

The patient improved considerably after one year of analytic treatment. His condition then remained stationary until his wife agreed to be treated. At the end of three years, the patient had recovered completely.

MANIAS—KLEPTOMANIA; PYROMANIA; ASSAULT

The conditions grouped under the heading of manias are characterized by the fact that the patient engages in acts that are unlawful, in spite of the fact that he is reluctant to commit them and knows that he thereby runs the danger of arrest and punishment. Such patients behave and act well and apparently normally when they are not engaged in these activities.

Some of the most common of these acts are stealing, arson, sexual crimes, assault, and murder (the latter also usually has an unconscious sexual motive). The patient derives no significant material benefit from any of these acts, but he experiences various degrees of satisfaction and relief; however, guilt and self-punishment follow later. The objects stolen are either not of much use to these individuals, or they do not have to be obtained through theft. Thus a very wealthy person may be a shoplifter who takes only comparatively low-priced objects. Sometimes a person steals objects which have sexual significance for him; for instance, a man may steal women's gloves although he can afford to buy them; in any case, he obviously cannot use them for their ordinary purpose.

These conditions differ from the compulsive thoughts in compulsion neurosis in one very important respect: Patients in the latter group have thoughts of violence which make them extremely uncomfortable but which they never carry out.

Among the reasons for these various acts are the following:

1. The patient feels rejected and threatened, humiliated, unfairly treated, worthless, or deprived. He is often completely isolated, unmarried, without friends or relatives.

2. These feelings arouse in him hostility and defiance, which he unconsciously expresses by these acts.

3. He obtains gratification and satisfaction from these forbidden deeds in several ways. There is a peculiar satisfaction in

"saying," so to speak, to one who has injured him: "You said I was worthless and helpless; that I was a criminal. Therefore, I will be a criminal; that will be my vengeance." There is also the satisfaction derived by the kleptomaniac, not so much from the stolen object itself, as from what it symbolizes for him. The sense of power is often also involved; e.g., the pyromaniac has a feeling of grandeur when he sees the flames bursting high; the man who has assaulted or killed another feels superior and all-powerful because he has vanquished his adversary. These actions may also, like so many other symptoms, be partially a bid for attention.

4. Frequently these forbidden acts are committed because the individual wants to be punished, and expects that he will be forgiven afterward. Thus, he unconsciously hopes to obtain acceptance and love. In the same way, a child who feels neglected by his mother will often actually court punishment as if it were a paradoxical kind of assurance that she still loves him. That is, even punishment is better than not being noticed at all.

A 15-year-old girl stole dresses from department stores. Investigation showed that her family was fairly well-to-do and that it was not necessary for her to steal if she wanted dresses. But a noticeable characteristic of her thefts was that she always stole dresses that were too large for her. She realized this but could not explain it. Further investigation brought out the following facts:

Her family had originally been rather poor, and her father drank. When she was four years old her father deserted her mother, who thereupon became a prostitute. The child was sent first to one and then to another relative. This went on for many years until finally, when she was thirteen years old, an aunt and uncle (with whom she was still living) took her to live with them. They were good to her; they gave her love and affection and bought her things.

Apparently, in stealing these dresses that were too large for her, this girl was unconsciously thinking of her mother and of true "mother love." She felt that she was not getting a proper measure of love and affection; she felt that she was utterly worthless and abandoned and no one could give her the unlimited and almost illusory amount of mother love that she required. This feeling of worthlessness dated back to the time when as a young child she was unhappy at home because of her parents, and later when she was shifted about from one household to another. Now she was defiant, her attitude being: "I was made worthless, therefore I will actually be worthless and steal." Her associations showed that by stealing large-sized dresses she convinced herself that she really had a mother.

SUGGESTED READINGS

A comparison of this and the preceding chapter with the corresponding ones in other textbooks of abnormal psychology or psychiatry is valuable; Henderson and Gillespie (340) and Rosanoff (651) are suggested. For a more thorough treatment, Ross (664) should be consulted.

For more general reading, the following are recommended: Freud's *A General Introduction to Psychoanalysis* (279) and his case histories (273); the relevant chapters in Fenichel's *Outline of Clinical Psychoanalysis* (233), in Menninger's *The Human Mind* (544), and in Janet's books (395-397).

CHAPTER XXIV

REACTIONS IN WHICH DISTURBED STATES OF CONSCIOUSNESS AND OF MEMORY PREDOMINATE

~~~~~~

Amnesia, somnambulism, fugue, and double personality—the symptom groups to be discussed in this chapter—are characterized by the following:

1. The individual undergoes extensive dissociations of consciousness; some activities are considerably affected while others may remain unchanged.

2. The complex activities which remain enable him to carry on very complicated performances, such as locomotion, contact with other individuals, the execution of various tasks, without any apparent loss of efficiency.

3. The four symptom groups differ from each other in the degree to which consciousness and memory are disturbed, and the extent to which complicated tasks are possible.

4. Strong psychological forces in the patient—conflicts, anxieties, situations of stress—are responsible for his loss of identity or disturbance of consciousness. However, other strong psychological forces make him *want* to retain or regain knowledge of his identity or integration of consciousness; these are the forces which eventually result in breaking through the dissociation.

These four conditions are usually called "dissociation," because the unity of the individual may be disturbed and several different and non-associated processes go on simultaneously. The best non-pathological examples of dissociation, in addition to those given below, are the phenomena of automatic writing, crystal gazing, hypnosis, etc. In hypnosis, for instance, there seem to be two different levels of memory. A subject awakened from a deep trance will remember nothing that happened during the trance. But if he is put into a trance again, then he will remember. Girden's work on conditioning under curare (304) is of interest in this connection.

A conditioned reflex was established so that a specific isolated muscle of one hind limb contracted to an auditory stimulus while the animal was under the influence of curare, a drug that paralyzes the gross musculature of the body. It was found that upon recovery from curare, the CR (conditioned reflex) established in one hind limb during the drugged condition was now suppressed, and reappeared only upon recurarization. If a CR was then established during the normal situation in the other hind limb, it became suppressed when curare was injected, and it reappeared only in the normal state after recovery from the drug.

These two systems of behavior to a single stimulus (bell) were thus mutually antagonistic or *dissociated* from one another; one appeared only in the curare state, the other only in the normal situation.

Amnesia (Loss of Identity)

As we have seen, every psychopathological reaction has aspects of which the individual is unconscious; these aspects frequently concern the memory of definite events which occurred at any time in his life. In the syndrome to be described here, however, this disturbance of awareness concerns a special aspect of his existence and becomes the predominating problem.

A person thus disturbed suddenly forgets his name; he does not know who he is. As Abeles and Schilder (1) put it, "The subjects forget their own identity. To one's own identity belongs the connection with a specific social structure. One has relatives, friends, a place where one works and another where one lives. But one's name and the address are symbols of one's identity. In everyday life one identifies people by these criteria and they identify themselves in this way."

Usually patients cannot remember either their name or their address, although there are rare cases in which only the name is forgotten. In some cases they forget practically everything about their past; they become perplexed and agitated, alarmed and depressed; they wander about the streets trying to discover their identity, and finally ask someone for help, usually a policeman, who takes them to a hospital. Some patients cannot recognize even their own name if they are identified, and they may not recognize near relatives.

Once in the hospital, the patient's memory for recent events is usually good. He may do well on memory tests, and his perception and judgment may be functioning well. In some cases, however, his evaluation of objects around him may be disturbed.

The amnesia lasts from three hours to a month (Abeles and Schilder). The patient may recover his memory spontaneously, in some cases when he hears a name or sees an object which reminds him of his identity. In many cases, hypnosis has been found the speediest means of bringing patients out of their amnesia. Amnesia rarely persists for years.

Psychodynamics of Amnesia.—The loss of identity is a reaction to situations of conflict and distress which may vary considerably in nature and all of which accompany anxiety. They may be economic—financial reverses, unemployment, impending poverty—or sexual, or largely interpersonal, as, for example, hostility toward a particular individual.

The amnesia represents the patient's attempts to find a way, even if a poor one, out of conflict. The desire to escape the distressing situation is quite obvious. Having forgotten his identity and his circumstances, he is prevented from returning to them; thereupon he shuts his whole conflict out of awareness. The amnesia is sometimes literally a lifesaver, as in the following case.

A man married against his family's wishes. He lost his job and was forced to appeal to his family for support. An uncle gave him some money, but warned him he would get no more unless he divorced his wife. On the way home the patient was held up and his money taken from him. He decided to jump into the river. But on his way to the river he forgot who he was and where he lived and that he was married; nor could he account for his being in that locality. He became perplexed and alarmed and asked a policeman for help. He was taken to a hospital and, one day later, recovered his memory of these incidents and his identity under hypnosis.

Patients who develop amnesia have various personality problems and conflicts, which on careful examination are found to be the cause of other symptoms. That is, the amnesia is so dramatic a symptom that others are overlooked which indicate that the individual is *generally* maladjusted.

Even before his economic crisis, this same patient had had occasional dizzy spells and mild attacks of palpitation and depression. His father had been very severe, and his mother extremely emotional. He had been on bad terms with them from early childhood, and broke with them completely after his marriage. His life in general was characterized by alternate periods of rebellion and self-effacement.

SOMNAMBULISM

In somnambulism, the patient attempts to carry out an act which he unconsciously desires but which inhibition prevents him from doing in the waking state. The somnambulistic acts are probably connected with dreams, which, however, are almost always forgotten, just as are the somnambulistic episodes themselves.

The patient usually goes to sleep as usual, and then, without waking, but with his eyes either open or half open, gets out of bed and does various things. Spontaneously, as a rule, he goes back to bed later, sleeps through the rest of the night, and has no recollection of what happened. These patients usually avoid obstacles, and, probably because of the absence of fear, some have a better sense of balance than when awake; others, however, suffer injuries. Thus a young man, in climbing out of the ground-floor window which was at some distance from the ground, fell and dislocated his shoulder. Patients usually hear when they are spoken to, and will stop their activity on command. Violent stimuli, such as shouts, being held down, etc., force the patient to awake.

Patients who suffer from somnambulism usually have other symptoms; the total personality is disturbed. Somnambulism first appears most frequently during puberty; in many cases there are only one or two episodes, after which it disappears. Individuals in whom somnambulism appears during puberty sometimes have severe conflicts which arise in connection with the increase in the genital urge, particularly masturbation. These conflicts are connected primarily with their evaluation of themselves and their relationship with others, their parents in particular.

A 13-year-old boy would get up in his sleep and walk to his parents' bedroom, open the door, and attempt to get into their bed. If they asked him what he wanted, he would either murmur unintelligibly or walk on toward the front of the house. If they said, "Go back to bed," he would turn around, go to his own room and sleep until morning.

On other occasions, he would go through the bedroom and proceed directly toward the front of the house. Upon being asked, "Where are you going?" he would answer, "I have to get dressed; I have to get washed," although the bathroom was in a different direction. Upon his father's request he would go back to bed and sleep until the morning.

This boy was strongly attached to his mother. His father, whom he had always been afraid of, was idealistic, but strict and demanding; he never showed the boy any affection. The latter's attitudes toward his father were so strongly repressed that he never became consciously angry at him, although he was frequently severely punished. He was often in a state of severe conflict about masturbation, felt worthless and guilty, and feared discovery and disapproval. As a result of this fear, he became markedly fatigued. Unconsciously he longed for his parents' affection and approval and at the same time felt strong hostility, particularly toward his father. One by-product of this situation was that he became excessively religious.

Walking into his parents' bedroom was an unconscious way of satisfying impulses which were totally repressed in the waking state.

Fugue

The patient with a fugue reaction unexpectedly engages in a series of complicated but apparently normal acts which usually take him far away from where they started. He suddenly finds himself in a strange place without knowing how he got there, but he usually knows who he is, although in some cases there is also amnesia. His activities during the fugue may vary. He may simply wander off or go on a hike or buy a railroad ticket and go off on a journey or spend all his money on shows, drinks, etc. The fugue may last from a few hours to several days and may be recurrent in some patients.

Fugue is a reaction which occurs in response to a difficult situation of stress, partly as an escape (fugue means flight). For example, patients suffering from severe anxiety attacks walk down the street, suddenly feel frightened, and then start to run, as if they were running away from their own fear. There is no amnesia in such a reaction, but it contains the germ of the fugue.

The patient's activities during fugue often have a wish-fulfilling or compensatory aspect. Thus, in addition to running away from the situation of stress and escaping conflict and anxiety, the patient by his activities satisfies certain needs or consoles himself in his plight.

The following case, which presents a combination of amnesia and long-continued fugue, illustrates these points.

J. F., aged 50, was admitted to the hospital, complaining of complete loss of memory and identity. He was supposed to have left a town in Pennsylvania and to have arrived in New York a week earlier, but remembered nothing that had happened before this. His memory of events of the past week in New York was hazy. He had

some recollection of going to see "a lot of shows." His knowledge of
general current events was almost nil. He declared that his mind was
a complete blank.

When his sister and a niece visited him the next day he did not
recognize them. He even said that he could not speak his native language, although he evidently knew it. He denied understanding the
most basic conceptions of everyday life. When asked if he recognized
his face in the mirror, he said, "My face looks strange—it does not
look natural." On the fourth day in the hospital the patient recovered
with the aid of hypnosis.

His history showed that he considered himself a "mental healer"
who helped people by "hypnotizing" them. Several months before
his illness, a girl he was treating in an effort to make her reform her
way of life accused him of having sexual relations with her. He was
arrested, and fined $500. On the day of the onset of his illness he
had been near the Union Station and had suddenly gone to New
York on an excursion he saw advertised.[1]

The situation of stress from which this patient sought escape
is obvious. The compensatory elements—the attempt to console
himself by "going to shows" and "having a good time in New
York"—are also clear. The disturbance of his whole personality
structure is made even more obvious by the occupation in which
he engaged.

That criminal activities may occur in fugues is shown by the
following case.

"A young man committed murder in what appears definitely to be
a state of fugue. He killed a taxi driver, took possession of the taxi,
later disposed of it, and disappeared. He was not apprehended until
six years later, during which time he had led the life of a very honest
worker, married, and lived happily and peacefully with his wife
under an assumed name. While vaguely aware that a crime had been
committed, he was completely amnesic as far as the act itself was
concerned. A prolonged study of the case, lasting many months,
revealed an unusually complicated life. Ever since childhood the boy

[1] M. Abeles and P. Schilder, "Psychogenic loss of personal identity" (1).
This is a shortened account of the case.

had been interested in mechanical things. He had wanted to drive the family automobile which was forbidden to him. The family had always imposed their decisions upon him as to studies, career, or anything else. When one day it was announced that the family had decided that he was to study medicine, he became low in spirits and was found that evening tinkering with the carburetor of the family car. Now, while serving a life sentence in prison, he is one of the best, most industrious, and most capable automobile mechanics of the institution. His life was a mixture of a great desire to settle down and a peculiar truancy. The whole crime was reconstructed as a sudden impulsive acting out of the murder of the taxi driver. Incidentally, a great part of the man's amnesia of the crime was cleared gradually in a piecemeal fashion during the course of many interviews."[1]

DOUBLE PERSONALITY

The following phenomena are observed in so-called double personality: From birth on, the individual, like any other person, has a name, a general mode of behavior, interests, associates and friends, and he speaks a certain language. Suddenly, however, he becomes convinced that he has a different name and different interests; his whole behavior changes; even his knowledge of his language may become limited. While in this condition he has no conscious knowledge of his name and the various aspects of what he previously considered his own life. He behaves essentially normally, and the people around him do not realize that anything is amiss. Thus under his given name a man may have been a professional man, such as a priest, a lawyer, a teacher; under his second name, he may enter an entirely different occupation such as opening a store, but still function essentially well.

After many weeks, months, or even years, the individual may, apparently spontaneously, remember who he is. He has no recollections of the intervening period, and is surprised and puzzled at finding himself in his present situation.

[1] G. Zilboorg, "Some sidelights on the psychology of murder," *Journal of Nervous and Mental Diseases*, 1935, **81**, 442-444.

Cases have been reported of individuals who, while under observation in a hospital, changed alternately from one "personality" to another, or even rotated among "several personalities."

Like amnesia, somnambulism, and fugue, double personality represents an escape reaction to situations of conflict, distress, or dissatisfaction, or a revolt against one's own unsatisfactory personality, in favor of a completely different type of character.

A classical case of dual personality is described in Morton Prince's *The Dissociation of a Personality* (619). However, a more recent case has been reported by Erickson and Kubie (228); this presents a brilliant analysis of the appearance, the function, and the *modus operandi* of this second personality.

"For over a year a twenty-year-old college girl, quiet, reserved, and well poised, had suffered secretly from constantly recurring fears that the icebox, kitchen, college laboratory and locker doors had been left open. These fears were always accompanied by a compulsive, often uncontrollable need to examine and reexamine the doors to make certain they were properly closed. She awoke in the night to make repeated trips to the kitchen in order to reassure herself, but this failed to resolve her incessant doubts about the doors. An additional but seemingly unrelated symptom was an intense hatred of cats, which she considered 'horrid, repulsive things.' This feeling she attributed to an early experience of watching 'an awful cat eating some pretty little baby robins.' It was learned that she enjoyed making pets of laboratory animals such as white rats and guinea pigs despite obsessive fears that she might fail to close the door of the animal room. At the time the patient was seen her difficulty was becoming more inclusive and she was beginning to have fleeting, recurring doubts about many other doors, although not to a troublesome degree."

This girl (Miss Damon) volunteered to serve as the subject of some experiments in hypnotism. Later she spontaneously showed some dissociative phenomena. Erickson at once suggested that she might like to try automatic writing (an excellent technique for investigating dissociation). The writing, however, was scrawly and illegible. It was in the course of discussing it that the second personality was discovered:

"After the subject's hand had completed the last bit of automatic writing . . . the investigator quietly slipped the sheet of paper from under her hand, leaving a fresh one in its place with her hand still holding the pencil. This was done without attracting her attention. She continued her task of deciphering the writing, finally declaring aloud that she could make out only the words 'trance,' 'will,' 'my,' 'catalepsy,' and 'ever,' and expressed much amusement over her inability to read more, asking laughingly, 'Did I really write that nonsense?' Both the investigator and his assistant replied affirmatively and in the same amused tone. At the moment the subject was leaning forward over the desk and her hand was out of her peripheral vision. As the verbal reply was given to her question, her hand was observed to write 'No,' of which Miss Damon remained unaware. Immediately the investigator asked, as if speaking directly to the subject, 'What do you mean?' and while Miss Damon puzzled over what he meant, her hand wrote 'Can't.' Again speaking as if to Miss Damon, the question was asked, 'Why?' to which her hand replied, 'Damon doesn't know these things.'"

There followed a series of oral questions seemingly directed to the subject; she was bewildered and confused because of their unintelligibility, but her hand wrote appropriate replies. These questions and their answers, continuing from the last one above, are quoted verbatim to show the definition of this second personality.

"Q: Why?
"A: Don't know, afraid to know.
"Q: Who?
"A: D (Damon).
"Q: Who does?
"A: Me.
"Q: Me?
"A: Brown.
"Q: Who?
"A: Me —— Brown——B.
"Q: Explain.
"A: D is D, B is B.

"Q: B know D?
"A: Yes.
"Q: D know B?
"A: No. No.
"Q: B part of D?
"A: No. B is B; D is D.
"Q: Can I talk to B?
"A: Are.
"Q: Talk to D?
"A: Want to. (If you want to.)
"Q: How long have you been B?
"A: Always.
"Q: What do you want?
"A: Help D.
"Q: Why?
"A: D afraid.
"Q: Do you know what D is afraid of?
"A: Yes; D no.
"Q: Why?
"A: D afraid, forgot, don't want to know.
"Q: Think D should?
"A: Yes, yes, yes.
"Q: You know what it is?
"A: Yes.
"Q: Why don't you tell D?
"A: Can't, can't.
"Q: Why?
"A: D afraid, afraid.
"Q: And you?
"A: Afraid a little, not so much.

"At this point Miss Damon interrupted to declare her utter bewilderment over the investigator's fragmentary remarks, and demanded an explanation.

"Q: Shall I tell her?
"A: Sure; she don't know.

"The secretary then read the questions and her answers were

shown to Miss Damon. She attended carefully with a look of increasing understanding, finally remarking, 'Why that really must mean I have a dual personality,' and then was greatly startled that her hand emphatically wrote 'Right.' Recovering her poise, Miss Damon asked, 'Can I talk to you?' 'Sure.' 'Can you talk to me?' 'Yes.' 'Is your name really Brown?' 'Yes.' 'What is your full name?' 'Jane Brown.'

"Throughout the investigation, the Brown personality was found to be literally a separate, well-organized entity, completely maintaining its own identity, and differentiating to a fine degree between Brown and Damon. Brown was capable of entering into spirited arguments with the investigator, his assistant and with Miss Damon, and of expressing ideas entirely at variance with those of Miss Damon. She could know before Damon did what Damon would say or think, and contributed thoughts to Miss Damon in a manner quite as psychotic patients bring up autochthonous thoughts. She would interrupt an attempted explanation of Miss Damon's by writing 'Wrong,' and would respond to stimuli and cues which Miss Damon either overlooked completely or misunderstood. In fact, she so impressed her personality upon those in the office that automatically she was regarded by the entire group as a distinct personality among them. Nor was Brown limited just to the problems at hand. She would enter readily into conversations on many other topics, often resorting to this in an effort to distract the investigator from his efforts. In addition Brown was possessed of a definite sense of personal pride; on two occasions she resented derogatory remarks Damon made about her, and thereupon refused to write anything more except 'Won't' until Damon apologized. Brown frequently became impatient and irritable with the investigator because of his inability to comprehend some of her cryptic replies; and at such times she would unhesitatingly and unsparingly denounce him as 'dumb.'

"Brown's attitude toward the investigation was consistent throughout and was highly significant. She asserted emphatically that she alone knew the content of the writing, that Miss Damon did not know, and because of fear could not know; that *Miss Damon needed help which must be given in a way known only to Brown*, and that the investigator's function was primarily the assumption of a very special kind of 'responsibility' that permitted Brown to give assistance only in response to direct and specific questions, with the reservation that Brown might accept or reject or postpone the questions as she felt to be best. Brown was found to maintain a highly protective attitude toward Damon, shielding her, demanding special consideration for her, offering encouragement, distracting her attention, deliberately deceiving her, and employing various other protective measures."

In brief, images were finally brought to D's consciousness that evoked the repressed memory of a traumatic experience that had occurred at the age of three. Her symptoms disappeared, and over a period of years have not returned.[1]

TREATMENT

We have said that the patient sometimes breaks through the dissociation spontaneously. If spontaneous recovery does not occur quickly, hypnosis or waking suggestions in repeated interviews help to bring him out from his immediate condition. However, because he usually has general personality problems, he should then be given prolonged interview therapy. Psychoanalytic treatment is valuable if the patient is analyzable and cooperates; but he must be watched since the symptom may recur in crucial conflict situations because he may attempt to act out his conflicts instead of solving them.

SUGGESTED READINGS

Of great value are Janet's *The Major Symptoms of Hysteria* (395), Sadger's *Sleep Walking and Moon Walking* (667), M. Prince's *The Dissociation of a Personality* (619), Franz' *Persons One and Three* (256), Abeles and Schilder's "Psychogenic loss of personal identity" (1), and Erickson and Kubie, "The permanent relief of an obsessional phobia by means of communications with an unsuspected dual personality" (228).

[1] M. H. Erickson and L. S. Kubie, "The permanent relief of an obsessional phobia by means of communications with an unsuspected dual personality," *Psychoanalytic Quarterly*, 1939, **8**, 471-509.

CHAPTER XXV

REACTIONS IN WHICH BODILY COMPLAINTS PREDOMINATE

The symptom syndromes to be discussed in this and the following chapter are characterized by various distinct neurotic reactions. Differentiation of these reactions is based partly on the character of the complaint, the possibility that physiological or structural disturbances can either be demonstrated or assumed, and the emotional and ideational reaction pattern accompanying the bodily complaint. On this basis, the following can be differentiated: (1) conversion hysteria; (2) hypochondriasis; (3) neurasthenia; (4) sexual disturbances, and (5) organ neuroses with structural change. The last will be discussed in the next chapter.

It is particularly important that this type of patient should have adequate and, if necessary, repeated physical examinations, for only in this way can the relative importance of organic factors in symptoms and complaints be determined. The neglect of the emotional causes is, however, as serious as the neglect of possible physical causes.

CONVERSION HYSTERIA

The term hysteria has been and, to a lesser extent, is still used to cover a wide variety of disturbances. Furthermore, different authors use it to describe various manifestations. Thus Janet uses the term psychasthenia to refer to phobic reactions, whereas Freud uses the term hysteria. A certain type of amnesia and double personality are frequently referred to as "hysteria."

The term "conversion hysteria" was coined by Freud to convey the idea that in situations of conflict and stress the patient, instead of having the purely "psychological" symptom, shows an observable change in an organic function. In other words, the "psychological" conflict is "converted" into a bodily disturbance. Why this is more common in some individuals than in others is an unsolved problem. Often the organic disturbance, which at this stage is entirely psychological or functional, was first an actual structural disturbance; for example, the patient with hysterical coughing spells may first have had bronchitis.

Many of the symptoms to be described still occur as predominant complaints in some cases, but such patients are comparatively rare—one may work in a mental hygiene clinic or a psychiatric ward for many years without encountering a single case of "hysterical convulsions" or "hysterical blindness." Such conditions were probably more frequent about fifty years ago; because of the way in which they were treated by both society and physicians, they lasted longer and were more continuous.

Symptoms: Disturbances of autonomic functions.—The disturbances of autonomic functions are either entirely or partly involuntary. Breathing is an example of the latter. Among this type of symptoms are a "lump" in the throat, a "choking" sensation, belching, hiccoughing, coughing spells, clearing the throat, difficulty in breathing (particularly the inability to take a deep breath), loss of appetite, vomiting, nausea, frequency of urination, constipation, diarrhea, cold and clammy extremities, excessive perspiration, headaches.

A rare but very serious condition called anorexia nervosa is often grouped with hysteria. It sometimes starts with loss of appetite, but in other cases the loss of appetite follows a voluntary restriction of the diet. Because of the continuous limitation of food intake, the patient shows an extraordinary degree of emaciation; and unless successfully treated, he dies of starvation, tuberculosis, or pneumonia. All these patients have serious conflicts and personality problems (Rahman, Richardson, and Ripley [626]).

Sensory symptoms.—Sensory symptoms are observable in the functioning of the sensory organs such as touch, sight, etc. Thus anesthesia (loss of sensation), hyperesthesia (excessive sensitiveness), or paresthesia (exceptional sensations, such as the "pins and needles" feeling) may be manifest in the tactile sense. It is characteristic that, in contrast to organic disturbances, these sensory disturbances do not follow the anatomic distribution of the nerves; moreover, they respond quickly to suggestion. In one type of this disturbance, "glove" or "stocking" anesthesia, the patient feels neither touch nor pain in the area of the limb like that covered by the gloves or stockings. Another form of sensory disturbance is the loss of sensation on one side of the body. This non-feeling area stops exactly at the midline, whereas, in disturbances of sensation that are due to such factors as a hemorrhage of the brain, the transition from the non-feeling to the sensitive part of the skin is gradual.

In hysterical blindness, the eyes and the optic nerves are entirely normal, but the patient cannot see. In some cases, testing the field of vision shows that the patient "sees" the object only in the center of the normal visual field. This is called constriction of the visual field. Janet was the first to observe that patients whose field of vision was constricted almost to a pinpoint in direct testing, were able to engage in complicated activities, such as ball playing. In other words, in actual activity, they used the complete visual field.

Motor symptoms.—Motor symptoms are manifest in the muscles that are under voluntary control, and consist of excess and unusual movements, continuous contraction, or complete limpness with paralysis. There may be jerky and curious twisting movements in most of the muscle groups, or the disturbance may be limited to one or another extremity. The differentiation of such disturbances from certain organic nervous diseases is difficult but possible, particularly after a period of observation and

treatment. Their differentiation from organic tics such as those
following encephalitis is extremely important (see Chapter
XXIX).

If the hysterical paralysis or contraction remains for many
years, there may be a secondary wasting or shortening in the
muscle. The paralyzed limb is usually cold and bluish even in
the early period, if the condition is continuous, and secondary
disturbances may appear in the skin and nails.

In one form of disturbance, called astasia abasia, the patient
is able to sit, but can hardly stand or walk. Both the reflexes and
the reaction of the muscles to electric stimulation remain normal.

Tremor (shaking) is of relatively frequent occurrence. In
another type of motor disturbance, there are tics, recurring
spasmodic movements of an extremity or of the head, the movements sometimes closely resembling a purposeful movement such
as turning the head. In milder disturbances—e.g., spasmodic
blinking of the eyes—the patient has considerable control over
these movements; if he has a large measure of control, such
movements are customarily called habit spasms. Some authors
(Ferenczi [235, 236], Kardiner [418]) do not group tics under
hysteria.

A generalized twitching of the muscles (hysterical convulsion, "hysterical fit") may also occur. The patient falls to the
ground (without injuring himself) and his whole body shakes;
but in contrast to the epileptic, he neither bites his tongue nor
turns blue in the face. In epileptic convulsions the pupils cease
to react to light, whereas in hysterical convulsions the light reaction is present and other reflexes remain unchanged.

In aphonia the patient is able to talk only in a whisper; in
mutism he is unable to utter any sound. These conditions usually
occur suddenly, usually immediately after a fright or a few days
later. They can be differentiated from organic conditions in the
following ways: There is no sign of inflammation of the larynx
and throat and the voice is not hoarse (differentiation from
laryngitis); furthermore, the vocal cords can be seen to be com-

pletely separated on expiration and well together on inspiration (differentiation from organic paralysis).

These bodily symptoms, with the exception of the anesthesias, are usually accompanied by corresponding local physiological changes. Even though these changes sometimes cannot be determined with certainty, they can be validly assumed to occur. For example, in hysterical paralysis the arm hangs limp and the muscle tone is diminished; in a hysterical spasm the muscles are actually contracted. Probably when the hysterical patient complains of pain in the area of the heart region, there is actually some change in the circulation. In dizziness there is probably some real change in the circulation in the brain.

Psychodynamics of Conversion Hysteria.—The personality type most commonly found in conversion hysteria is emotionally outgoing and elastic. The patient needs and is inclined to form attachments to other individuals.

His self-evaluation tends to be one of helplessness and infantilism. He is afraid to shoulder responsibility. He longs for emotional closeness, but is frightened by it. The main catastrophic fear is of rejection, abandonment, injury, and frequently, bodily frustration.

The bodily symptoms represent reactions to situations of stress. This can be demonstrated as easily in conversion hysteria as in anxiety attacks, provided that the symptoms have not yet become continuous. (Chronic symptoms, of course, come from stress situations in the beginning; but they may eventually become so habitual that they persist even after stress has disappeared.) They appear during or after situations of stress and disappear after the stress subsides. The emotions with which the symptom is correlated are often entirely unconscious, particularly anxiety and anger. The patient also expresses his helplessness, punishes himself, and seeks forgiveness, love, and support with the symptom. It is, at times, predominantly a defense against distress by avoidance and exclusion (blindness: "I do not want to see the cause of my misery").

Often the symptom has an additional disguised gratifying and ameliorative function. For example, the patient wants to gratify a need arising in a pleasure-seeking organ, but this gratification occurs not in the organ where it is normally experienced, but in the organ where the symptom arises. Thus instead of sexual excitement and gratification the patient may complain of frequency of urination which is for him both painful and pleasurable. Confirmed hystericals use such symptoms to get practically anything they want.

There is usually abundant fantasy behind the symptom. Thus weakness of an arm may mask fantasies of murder, of being hurt, of being tied and injured. The sexual function is often involved in these fantasies. For this reason and because of the patient's devaluation of himself, disturbances of this function are frequent.

Treatment.—Patients with conversion hysteria are usually very good subjects for psychotherapy, particularly if the symptoms have not been of long duration. The more serious symptoms are easily controllable by suggestion or hypnotic techniques; for lasting cures, psychoanalysis is very effective. If there is not enough time for this more thorough technique, a series of interview discussions in which various combinations of partial techniques are used usually gives good results.

A 40-year-old pianist complained that when he tried to play music which was particularly soft and slow his arm became rigid. This happened only when he was performing publicly in an auditorium, not when he practiced alone. Before the symptom occurred for the first time, however, he had had attacks of anxiety in the auditorium. He was ambitious, but his symptom seriously interfered with his playing.

The patient always smiled in his contacts with people; at times he was angry but did not express it. He never insisted on his rights. He preferred prostitutes to his wife, and masturbation to intercourse. He often felt very tender toward his wife, but at other times he was aloof. He rarely slept well.

His parents got along very badly with each other, his mother constantly threatening to commit suicide. When he was about eight years old, she suggested that he learn to play the piano, and he proved exceptionally talented. His father died when he was thirteen years old, and he became completely self-supporting when he was about nineteen. He had had mild attacks of anxiety ever since his father's death. They became more incapacitating when, at twenty-five, he found that he had to continue to support his mother. He married at the age of twenty-seven upon his wife's initiative—he told her that he was not in love with her.

His unconscious resentment toward his mother, his wife, and other people created feelings of worthlessness and helplessness. The manner in which he behaved toward them led to the fear of discovery and of retribution and abandonment. His playing in public represented to him a situation of exposure and of threat. In the course of two years of psychoanalytic treatment the patient was entirely cured of his main symptom, his relations with his wife became satisfactory, and he grew normally self-assertive.

Hypochondria

The term hypochondria is often used very broadly to mean any preoccupation with, or fear or anxiety about, one's body and its functions. We shall distinguish between the hypochondria that occurs with anxiety (which is discussed elsewhere) and pure hypochondria, in which no anxiety or fear is found, but only a tremendous absorption with the bodily processes.

A definite type of personality is usually associated with such hypochondria (Freud). He usually keeps to himself emotionally, and in extreme cases gives the impression of being a completely isolated person. This isolation need not be actual—that is, he may seem to have ordinary social contact with others. Psychologically, however, he is soon found to feel completely isolated, to be interested only in himself, without any identification or sympathy with others. Others are apt to describe him as self-centered and selfish.

The specific symptoms are likely to be very variable, not only from patient to patient, but sometimes in a single patient. He may complain of discomfort in various parts of the body—pain in the back, uncomfortable sensations in the back of the head, the stomach, the chest, the genitals, or, for that matter, any-where. Or there may be no complaints in the literal sense, but rather a cheerful, interested preoccupation with his digestive functions or excretory processes. Sometimes these patients show a gloomy, almost ghoulish, fascination with disease symptoms and imagine that they have this or that disease; however, they do not seem to worry about it in the interview.

Some authorities place in this group all the vast army of health and diet fiends—people who drink mineral oil as others do beer, who decide suddenly to live only on nuts or cabbage, or who shun tea or coffee as they would poison. Only some of these are true hypochondriacs; most are merely victims of false informa-tion or fallacious theories.

Physical examination of the hypochondriac shows that nothing is wrong with his body. Instead of reassuring him, this usually irritates him and he is apt to come to the conclusion that the physician is an ignoramus. In older people who have had these symptoms for years, there may eventually be real organic changes. For instance, one older woman who somewhere picked up the notion that daily enemas were necessary for health and followed this advice for years, now actually needs them because of loss of colon tonus.

Psychodynamics of Hypochondria.—The self-evaluation of these patients is dominated by feelings of complete worthless-ness, insignificance, and inferiority. Sometimes these feelings are masked by almost paranoid notions of superiority, even of grandeur. The patient may also be called a generally insecure person, the outstanding characteristic of this insecurity being the feeling of complete isolation with a lack of attention and affection from others. Thus the feeling of rejection is apt to be complete and profound. In response to these feelings, the pa-tient ordinarily reacts with pleas for attention and with feelings of anger and hostility.

The symptoms themselves have, as usual, several meanings or purposes. First, they reflect his solution of the problem by increasing his social detachment; a compensatory increase in interest in himself endows him and his organs with an increased significance which gives him a certain pleasure and feeling of protection. Second, the symptoms are in part a very direct and bald expression of suffering. That is, they are in effect pleas for attention, help, love, and respect. Third, they are in part self-punishment and expressions of guilt, arising perhaps from masturbation, from his unconscious or conscious hatred of others, from his perception of his own selfishness, or from other sources.

Treatment.—The treatment of the hypochrondriacal patient is usually difficult because he does not easily establish a good rapport with the therapist. Furthermore, it is difficult to convince him that his complaints are products of psychological stress and that they have purposes. He clings to his symptoms and is loath to admit that they are not what they seem. Only the most patient therapist, one willing to listen to reports of symptoms by the hour in order to achieve his purpose, can be successful.

Long-continued interviews, in which the patient is convinced of the therapist's interest and affection, can be helpful. Psychoanalysis is probably necessary for complete cure, and even here success cannot be counted on.

A college student complained of extensive gastric disturbances, indigestion, "weak" stomach, belching, aches, and many other symptoms. Questioning showed that he had made a full-time job of studying his eating, his digestion, and his eliminative processes. For instance, he had menus made up for a month in advance in which everything was weighed to the ounce. He always cooked his own meals, because he did not trust this important task to his mother. After each meal he would watch himself carefully for an hour to see if it agreed with him. If it did not—and this happened often—he would change his eating plans and make new menus. In this way, he had slowly eliminated one food after another because it was not good for him; as a result, his diet was extremely restricted. He had kept charts of his bowel movements for over a year.

He spent several hours each day using muscle exercisers, breathing according to a special system, and reading medical books.

The problem that brought him to the psychologist was his relation to his fiancée. Questioning revealed that she loved him intensely but had angered him by disparaging his symptoms. He apparently did not love her at all, but intended to marry her because "everybody gets married." He had broken off with her without any feeling of loss, even with relief. He now wanted to know if marriage was necessary to health.

It took some time to convince him that he needed psychological treatment, and this was possible only after a very detailed examination by a medical specialist showed negative results. He never really made contact with the therapist and no results were being obtained by interviews; therefore he was sent to another therapist with whom he got along a bit better. However, when he was instructed to give up his pills and laxatives, he never returned.

Neurasthenia

The term "neurasthenia" was once used to describe almost any psychopathological condition. Later it was limited to conditions characterized primarily by continuous fatigue. Many individuals suffer these complaints in a minor degree; in fact, temporary fatigue and exhaustibility are among the most common of all symptoms. In neurasthenia, however, they are predominating. Because of their continuous character, it is often difficult, except in the advanced stages of treatment, to make clear to the patient their connection with situations of stress and conflict. Of course external conditions which cause real fatigue have to be excluded.

Psychodynamics of Neurasthenia.—Neurasthenic patients are disappointed or discouraged people, people who are living a life that is disappointing to them, doing a job they do not like, or who have problems that weigh heavily on their shoulders.

Their self-esteem is low; they have feelings of inadequacy, helplessness, or uselessness. They often feel unimportant and unwanted; and they fear rejection, abandonment, or condemnation because of failure; they want to stop functioning.

The symptom, of course, has also ameliorative, defensive, and
goal-seeking aspects. It wins pity, attention, and sympathy, and
brings an illusion of being wanted and looked after. There
is often an element of sheer pleasure in the laziness, sloth,
and sleep justified by this fatigue. The condition sometimes
centers about unsolved sexual problems—for instance, in young
people, about conflict over masturbation. It sometimes occurs
in people who are chronically stimulated sexually with no ultimate satisfaction. Probably, however, it is most common in the
so-called "nervous housewife" who is neglected by her husband
and children.

Treatment.—The first recommendations should be the obvious ones of attempting to ameliorate the precipitating situation—in the example above, securing love in a legitimate way,
raising self-esteem by actual achievement, bringing about amelioration of the family situation. Only if these are impossible
or prove to be ineffective should extensive character reorganization be attempted. Interview therapy can be of considerable
value. Psychoanalysis is ordinarily entirely successful.

A gifted and ambitious engineer complained of continuous fatigue
and pressure in the head. He excelled in his work, but felt seriously
handicapped because he became easily exhausted. At times he needed
eleven hours of sleep, but he slept badly. He complained of frequency of urination, frequent constipation, and impaired potency.
His complaints started during puberty, with terrific guilt reactions
to sexual impulses and masturbation for which he was brutally punished and threatened.

The patient's father was strict and at times brutal, particularly in
his sexual discipline. He was frequently away from home when the
patient was a child, and during such periods the mother was very
close to him; however, she always had the father discipline the lad

on his return. The boy was disappointed in both parents; he felt betrayed, particularly by his mother, and he feared severe corporal punishment from his father. The patient was completely relieved during three years of psychoanalytic treatment, during which the etiology and dynamic meanings of his symptoms were made clear to him.

STUTTERING

Stuttering is a disorder which is characterized by a spasmodic repetition or blocking on speech sounds. The stutterer has difficulty in enunciating certain words because he cannot articulate the first consonant. In some individuals the stuttering is almost always present; in others it appears only in situations of stress. Any speech sound may cause difficulty, but the ones that are most apt to be troublesome are those that require the greatest articulatory effort, such as *d* or *t*. A person may repeat smoothly by rote, but stutter badly if he has to compose speech. Certain investigators assume that the causal mechanism is a lack of coordination of the impulses from the two sides of the brain (Orton, Travis). Some experiments suggest that nervous impulses to the speech mechanism, and the brain waves in the two hemispheres, are not well synchronized.

The psychodynamics of stuttering is, however, a moot question; hence only tentative interpretations can be made. Speech is a form of self-assertion and an attempt at contact with other individuals. Fear in these situations may lead to a disturbance of this function. The consequent embarrassment may make the stutterer shy and cause him to lose self-confidence. Another factor may be a considerable unconscious preoccupation with oneself, particularly with the bodily function of speech. For the stutterer, speech may have the connotation of a hostile attack and the consequent fear of injury.

The treatment of stuttering is likewise complex. There is no doubt that the younger the individual is when he starts treatment, the better are the chances of success. A general survey of the patient's problems and situations of stress should always be made. Although psychoanalysis is not recommended by most investigators, some therapists use it for some cases (Blanton [89]). The method of treatment varies. Some recommend training in breath control during speaking. Others concentrate on easing the patient's emotional tension while he speaks, the emphasis here being not on clear enunciation but on a relaxed, easy flow of words. Group therapy is also used. Speaking in the presence of a group, all of whom are undergoing speech correction, helps to decrease the embarrassment of the stutterer. Some therapists hold that stuttering may be corrected for periods of time but cannot be cured permanently (Eisenson [214]).

Disturbances of the Sexual Function

Disturbances of the sexual function are extremely common and, at one time or another, are present in most psychopathological reactions. Although the patient frequently does not mention them to the psychotherapist because he considers this aspect of his functioning entirely adequate, it often becomes obvious that his estimation of this phase of his life is not correct, just as he fails to estimate accurately his interpersonal relations and his behavior in friendship and in work. Other patients, however, appeal for help chiefly because of disturbance in this field. These patients sometimes assume that their difficulties are limited to sexual ones; but closer investigation always shows clearly that other aspects are also involved.

The discussion of this subject could be limited to disturbances in the functioning of the organs, but this would make the survey too narrow. There are customs, laws, ideals, and limitations which are accepted by the group as a whole and by its individual members. Therefore disturbances of the sexual function usually involve one or more of the following: (1) disturbance of the organic function itself, (2) disturbance in the functioning of related organs, (3) disturbance in the circumstances under which the organic function is exercised, and (4) deviations in the choice of sexual partner.

In any discussion of sexuality, the social group and its customs and values must always be taken into consideration because attitudes vary greatly from one society to another. For instance, the Japanese consider kissing a perversion. When the French government presented one of Rodin's statues, The Kiss, to them, the statue was placed in a public park, but later it had to be hidden from sight by a high fence.

Emphasis on different social customs may lead to the extreme position which holds that no disturbance except impaired functioning should be considered a "sickness"; it should rather be called merely a deviation from the social norm. This position is unquestionably incorrect. For example, the individual who tries both consciously and unconsciously to follow the accepted standards and still finds himself unable to do so is "psychologically sick," not merely a social deviant.

The evaluation of the sexual function depends on the individual patient—on his outlook, his whole personality, his immediate situation, his social environment. The healthy pattern for the adult in our society is the ability to form a close emotional relationship with an adult of the other sex, and the desire to engage in the sexual act with objective and subjective adequacy, that is, emotional acceptance of the function and adequate duration and satisfaction. In the following discussion not only the actual functioning of the individual, but also his conscious and unconscious fantasies must be kept in mind.

Impaired Potency; Frigidity.—Impaired potency is usually applied to sexual disturbances in men; frigidity, to sexual disturbances in women. The disturbance may appear in any or all phases of the function, or in any or all situations. There may also be considerable individual differences, depending on the behavior of the partner. As a rule, if the partner is loved and behaves tenderly and considerately, the disturbance is less. In other cases it may appear in just those situations in which there is attachment to the partner and the partner is emotionally outgoing. Usually, however, the function improves under conditions of security and happiness.

The characteristics of frigidity and impaired potency are as follows: (1) All desire may be absent; the function, or even the thought of it, may be repellent. In the latter instance the exercise of the function may be accompanied by other organic disturbances such as nausea or vomiting. (2) In the man tumescence may be inadequate or the climax may be reached too quickly. In rare cases he may be unable to reach a climax; or the function, even though objectively adequate, may lead to inadequate subjective satisfaction. (Even such "biological" functions may be culturally determined; in some primitive societies there is no sexual climax.) (3) In the woman there may either be complete absence of gratification or a slight gratification but without the ability to reach a climax.[1]

The Individual's Attitude Toward the Disturbance.—The individual may be deeply disturbed by the symptoms for many

---

[1] We are discussing here only disturbances which are due to psychological factors. The glandular factor of the sexual functions is extremely complex and is dependent not only on the ovaries and testes, but also on the other glands of internal secretion. In recent years considerable new knowledge has been accumulated in this field; the interested student is referred to books on endocrinology and to various numbers of the periodical *Endocrinology*.

Once the sexual function is adequately established, it may continue even after the sex glands have ceased to function. Thus, the woman may continue to function after menopause, and the adult man whose testes have been removed because of disease may suffer no impairment. The following case, reported by Rowe and Lawrence (665), illustrates both this point and the extreme care necessary in deciding how physiological factors lead to psychological disturbances.

The man's testes had been removed bilaterally for medical reasons. The man lost all interest in his work, lost his ambition, became apathetic and returned to his native village. There he fell in love with a woman who reciprocated his feelings. She knew of his condition but was willing to marry him. He found himself to be potent, his ambition and efficiency returned, and he took up his former occupation.

Sexuality is obviously not purely a physiological activity. As a matter of fact, accumulating evidence indicates strongly that psychological and social determiners are more important than biological ones in the higher animals and in man (Maslow).

reasons. His self-esteem may be badly damaged because he considers himself worthless and inadequate, or feels that something is profoundly wrong with him, that something essential is lacking in him. In our society, self-esteem, especially in the male, depends in part on sexual adequacy. He may feel that his happiness is threatened because his relationship with his mate is endangered. Other such individuals have a remarkably detached and philosophical attitude toward the disturbance. They rationalize it on the grounds that the whole function is a nuisance and of no importance; they may even say to themselves that they want to be self-sufficient and that auto-erotism is more satisfactory. More detailed examination shows that most of these individuals are concerned by the disturbance, but that they repress this attitude and try to compensate by rationalization and a philosophical outlook.

The emotional attitude with which disturbances of the sexual function are most closely correlated is fear in its broadest sense. At times partly consciously, or largely or entirely unconsciously, the individual is afraid of failure, rejection, injury, and humiliation. He is afraid to assume responsibility or to become emotionally close to anyone. These fears involve his whole evaluation of himself and others. Here an early attitude of disapproval of and guilt toward sexuality in general, as well as parental fear of sex which is internalized by the child, plays a significant role.

A patient related the fact that her mother made her feel very guilty as a child if she even mentioned anything pertaining to sex. At a somewhat later date she heard such remarks from her mother as "Women are just pleasure-toys for men" and "That man ought to be sent to jail for killing his wife with too many children." The mother told the patient when she was a child never to be alone with boys because something frightful would happen to her.

The dominant goal aspect of impotence or frigidity is avoidance and defense: "This action isn't taking place at all; I'm safe from danger," or "I don't have this organ at all," or "I'm not really part of this affair and therefore am doing no wrong."

The defensive aspects are often the result of other general attitudes involved in the function. Thus, the woman may want protection from the man through complete dependence and submission, humiliation, and pain. But this desire leads to the fear that what she is asking for will actually happen—she will be humiliated and injured. To save herself from that fate she develops frigidity. Often attitudes of hostility are also involved; they may be entirely unconscious or appear in fantasies. The individual is afraid of their consequences because he does not want to help the mate, or feels guilty, or fears counterattack. Impotence or frigidity may develop a defense against these fears.

Disturbances may arise partly as a disguised expression of the desire to frustrate and humiliate the mate: "I did not grant you what you wanted" or "I remained aloof." These attitudes may be almost entirely unconscious. All such expressions of hostility injure the individual himself as well.

Treatment.—In the prevention and treatment of sexual disturbances, proper enlightenment about the problems of sexuality, marriage, and pregnancy is important. It is not merely a question of imparting proper knowledge; such enlightenment also imparts reassurance, permissiveness, or approval which leads to a lessening of fear and guilt. However, the adult who has a definite disturbance needs more than this. Symptomatic improvement, particularly in men, may be secured by interview therapy and suggestion. In interview therapy the patient's entire mode of existence has to be discovered; in other words the treatment deals with the whole individual, not merely the symptom. The treatment of severe frigidity is, as a rule, more difficult than that of impotence, although the latter can also be extremely difficult. The best results with impotence and frigidity can be obtained through psychoanalysis.

Other Disturbances of the Sexual Function.—Disturbances

of the sexual function may have other forms, among them being:

1. Sadism (infliction of pain) or masochism (enjoyment of pain)
2. Fetichism (substitution of an inanimate object for the mate)
3. Perversion (substitution of other organ functions)
4. Exhibitionism (self-exposure) or voyeurism (looking as the ultimate aim)
5. Nymphomania or satyriasis (excessive desire, promiscuity, insatiability)
6. Homosexuality (choice of individuals of the same sex)

These behavior patterns can sometimes be observed in a very clear form, as when the individual consciously desires rather severe pain and injury, or wants to inflict it. It is difficult, however, to draw a sharp line, for often the pain or injury is emotional rather than physical, the partner being humiliated and tortured by words and behavior. In other cases this desire appears in fantasy but never in any action. Some of the above terms—masochism and sadism, for example—have been extended to include tendencies on the part of the individual which do not include the sexual organs. To avoid misunderstanding, it seems best in such instances to speak not of sadism and masochism, but of the desire to hurt, to humiliate, to submit, etc. These sado-masochistic attitudes may of course be present in connection with any kind of function and in any kind of situation. However, sexuality is a common means of expressing them. For instance, in our society, the sexual act is more often phrased in terms of domination-submission than in terms of equality.

All the above behaviors may have the individual's full and conscious approval if the circumstances are relatively favorable for their practice, and he may in general function well. However, other people who engage in them disapprove of them-

selves to a greater or lesser degree, at times very intensely, even
when circumstances are favorable. This disapproval is almost
always accompanied by the desire to change, an essential element
in helping the individual overcome the practice. This type of
disapproval must be differentiated from that involved when the
patient gets into legal difficulties; for in some extremely severe
conditions, not only are there no qualms of conscience but
even murder may be committed in a state of ecstasy.

The practices arise in two ways: (1) Various conflicts and
problems appear whenever the sexual drive is activated; these are
expressed in and solved by these practices. (2) Similarly, conflicts and disturbances which appear in various other situations
are reflected in and solved by practices in the sexual sphere.

As in all other reaction patterns, these practices are interrelated with the patient's total personality, his evaluation of himself and of other people, and other emotional attitudes or modes
of behavior. The general disturbances in self-esteem and in
security feelings, the various fears and psychological reactions
are essentially the same as those described in the discussion of
potency. There is always fear of failure, of responsibility and
closeness, of abandonment and injury, of the organ function,
and of both sexes, particularly the opposite sex. There is usually
special emphasis on some one type of catastrophic expectation
in connection with the various practices; and the compensatory,
ameliorating, or goal-seeking elements in these reactions are
particularly definite and characteristic.

In sadism the dominant fear is of being injured, to which of
course is always linked the expectation of humiliation, domination, and frustration. The ameliorative formula is: "If I engage
in violence, I am safe; I can reach my goal safely. With this I
avenge myself also, and thus I obtain satisfaction and I triumph."

In masochism the chief fear is of abandonment, neglect, or
rejection. Against this is a strong hostile reaction, with the fear
of counterattack: "I offer to submit and to be hurt, and in that
way I'll be forgiven and I won't be abandoned."

Fetichism is characterized by a fear of rejection and humiliation by the opposite sex. The individual safeguards himself through a full mastery of an inanimate object. There is also frequently a strong tendency toward self-degradation; for this reason shoe fetichism is particularly common.

In exhibitionism the chief fear is of insignificance and humiliation, the self-exposure representing a sort of aggrandized "showing off." In voyeurism the fear is of frustration and disapproval; the activity (almost always secret) represents partly a stealthy, partly a defiant, way of attaining the limited goal, for it frequently brings a feeling of power over the one being looked at.

Promiscuity may be based on various types of fears and have varying compensatory aspects, such as self-degradation, abandoning one's partner instead of being abandoned, blaming another for one's own deficiencies, or searching incessantly for love and affection from a distance. Self-aggrandizement is a common factor, particularly in men. In insatiability, the dominant fear is of frustration; the attempt is to secure more and more gratification, as if it might all suddenly be lost.

In homosexuality the dominant fears may be of abandonment and rejection, humiliation, being vanquished in competition, and frustrated by the opposite sex. The compensatory aspects may be self-aggrandizement and self-sufficiency (fantasy of belonging to both sexes); submitting to and being completely looked after by a less dangerous partner; dominating, humiliating, and inflicting pain on a less dangerous antagonist; being free of any possibility of progeny; looking after another individual as if saying: "This is how I ought to be taken care of."

Some element of defiance and hostility is also present in all these reactions: "I will do that which is forbidden."

These reaction patterns often contain regressive elements and are frequently recurrent continuations of phenomena which were first manifested in early childhood. In many cases elements of the reaction pattern first appeared in actual situations in childhood. Thus in shoe fetichism, the kind of shoe to which the individual is attracted is usually found to be that worn by an adult to whom he was emotionally close as a child.

Many of the practices described here appear for a short time during the life of a great many people. They become permanent only if they are linked with the basic psychopathic reactions—if they acquire a special significance in relation to conflict, anxiety, and meeting problems. Therefore it is best to apply the various terms, i.e., exhibitionism, homosexuality, etc., only if these practices are actually engaged in, and if this is compulsive and exclusive; that is, if the individual is driven to this activity, and if it is the preferred or only way of achieving satisfaction. The recurring fantasies and impulses that many people temporarily engage in may have determinants—emotional reasons and purposes—similar to those concerned in the actual practices; at other times the determinants are different. In either case there are very important differences from the point of view of the individual's total adaptation. To put it more simply, exactly the same behavior which is called normal if it occurs in a healthy person is called sick if it occurs in a neurotic patient, because the behavior has different meanings and different motivations.

A patient who complained of anxiety attacks, trembling of the hands, periods of discouragement, and some minor compulsive acts, was frequently troubled by homosexual fantasies. It was soon established during treatment that these fantasies appeared in two situations: (1) Whenever he had to face an individual who was stronger and more brilliant than he, or who had a superior position. In this instance the homosexual thought meant, "I am willing to submit to you in any form you want me to, only don't injure me, don't disapprove of me, and don't abandon me." (2) Whenever he felt rejected, or when he was too shy even to speak to a woman to whom he was first attracted. Here the thought meant, "I can't find love and gratification from women because I am too helpless, too weak and too much afraid of them. Perhaps I could have love from men whom I fear less. I must have some love and some gratification."

Similar reactions are found in many people who have homosexual fantasies and are greatly disturbed by them. The difference between fantasy and actual practice in the individual's total adaptation is as follows: The person who has the fantasy but does not engage in actual practice has found other ways of coping with his conflict and anxiety. For example, he may have sadistic fantasies, but in actual behavior he may be tender with his wife, may have potency disturbances, and may have a complacent and serene outlook on life, refraining from ambitious undertakings. These characteristics take the place of actual sadistic behavior. That is, they are symptoms of repressed sadism; it is repressed because of serious inner objections to the actual practices, such as need for self-esteem or approval, the attempt to avoid secondary anxiety, the desire to maintain his ideals, etc.

Profound changes may occur in the person's outlook and total adaptation because of new situations of stress; they may be the result of chronic situations, or of external circumstances which make one form of solution preferable to another. Under these circumstances he may begin any one of these practices at any period of his life; for example, a man may engage in homosexuality after rejection by women.

A man and a woman, both of whom had had serious personality problems all their lives and passing homosexual experiences in adolescence, were married. They got along fairly well until the wife became pregnant, a fact which greatly disturbed both of them. The wife had a miscarriage, left her husband, and became homosexual. The husband, feeling rejected, also became homosexual. This solution was easy for both of them because they moved in a social group in which homosexuality was relatively common.

The man came later for treatment. He had an intense feeling of worthlessness because of his sexual life; this was aggravated by the fact that he had not been attracted by a woman for five years although he attracted them.

The treatment of these conditions is difficult and involved. In general, a person can be enabled to change these practices and become sexually adequate only if he is strongly dissatisfied with this aspect of his existence, if he has an intense desire to change it, and if the practices have not continued for too many years. If he is satisfied with this phase of his life and wishes to continue it, there is no reason why any therapist should insist that he change, as long as he does not harm others. If the patient is dissatisfied with his sexual practices, it depends on the degree of his dissatisfaction and on the therapist's judgment as to how much can be expected of the patient, whether the therapist will aim at "curing" him or merely enabling him to live at peace with himself. In any case, the treatment always involves the whole individual, not the symptom alone. Almost the only ultimately effective treatment is psychoanalysis, but the results are often limited.

SUGGESTED READINGS

Comparison should be made between our treatment of these disturbances and the discussions of other authors. In addition, we recommend in Freud's *A General Introduction to Psychoanalysis* (279) the portion on hysteria. A very readable book on neurasthenia is Meyerson's *When Life Loses Its Zest.* There is very little good reading in the field of sexuality. Most of the books sold over the counter are worthless or obsolete, and some are very harmful because they perpetuate a large number of false theories stated as facts. For a good approach to the subject, see Levy and Munroe (482), Wexberg's *Psychology of Sex,* and the books by R. L. Dickinson (179, 180). On therapy, read Diethelm (183) and Schilder (684).

CHAPTER XXVI

REACTIONS IN WHICH ORGAN NEUROSES
PREDOMINATE

~~~~~~

Psychological factors play an important role in many disturbances which have until recently been considered to be purely medical. In this chapter we shall discuss a few of these medical syndromes which will demonstrate typical findings now being made in this type of research. If we take into account not only these specific findings, but also their trend and their implications, we are led to the conclusion that the distinction between mental and physical illnesses is not nearly as sharp as has been thought. Perhaps, even, it will eventually be found that there is practically no ultimate differentiation—that *all* illnesses are illnesses of the whole individual, and not of just his arm or chest or mind.

It is imperative to remember that this is the direction which a good many data seem to take. Such a theory cannot, as yet, be considered proved. For instance, in the various illnesses discussed in this chapter, the patient's chief complaint is a disturbance in the functioning of an organ or part of the body. Examination in all cases discloses definite structural or physiological changes; and, *in some cases*, the onset of the complaint as well as its severity is shown to be correlated with the patient's emotional reactions to certain distressing situations, or to his general character structure.

Various personality types and various conflict situations are found in the same type of organ neurosis. As a rule, however, certain personality types and conflict situations show a higher degree of correlation with particular types of organ neurosis. Thus ulcers of the stomach and duodenum are relatively common in the hard-driving, ambitious personality (22), as is also an anger response to conflict situations (564). The personality type in which repressed anger predominates is particularly common in high blood pressure (19, 674). Evidently a multiplicity of factors, psychological and organic, may determine a special type of neurotic organ reaction. Deutsch (172) assumed the following determinants in the case of asthma: (1) physical illness in childhood (e.g., whooping cough or bronchitis) during a period of emotional conflict; (2) parental attitude during this period concentrated on the child's illness (the mother being particularly concerned); (3) current conflict and situation of stress for the adult (e.g., the wife separating from the husband). (See also 203.)

The following experimental observation affords a good introduction to the discussion of the relation between organ neuroses and anatomical changes.

Several patients suffered from periodic attacks of small blisters around the mouth (herpes labialis). It was found that these attacks followed reactions to situations of stress. These patients were hypnotized when they were free from blisters; and severe, emotionally traumatic events (for example, death of the fiancé) were discussed with them. After the trance the patients always developed blisters. Thus the connection between emotional stress and a physical ailment was clearly demonstrated.

The experiment was carried further. The contents of the blisters were transferred to the eye of a rabbit. The fact that the rabbit developed small blisters and then ulcers on the cornea proved that the contents of the blisters contained germs. (The germs that are responsible for herpes labialis have not yet been identified, but the infectious nature of the condition can be proved in this way.)[1]

Obviously the germs in the blister were not created by hypnosis; they were present in or on the body. The hypnotic ex-

[1] R. Heilig and H. Hoff, Uber psychogene entstehung des herpes labialis (336).

periment created some change in the function of the body concomitantly with the reaction to stress; the blisters were the result of these two factors. This general principle is probably the pattern for all organ neuroses that will be discussed. Although in this experiment an identifiable agent (germ) was involved, in most situations the bodily factor is not clearly known. For this reason, in discussing psychological factors in organ neuroses, it should be understood that other factors may be operating which remain to be investigated.

Peptic Ulcer

A peptic ulcer is a small wound which develops either in the stomach itself or in the duodenum, the portion of the bowels immediately below the stomach. The patient complains of recurrent pain in the upper abdomen usually when the stomach is empty; the taking of food usually relieves the discomfort.

Psychosomatic Experiments on Emotions and Gastric Function.—Mittelmann and Wolff (564; see also 22) have conducted experiments on normal individuals, on individuals with anxiety states, on those whose chief bodily symptom was a burning sensation in the stomach, and on patients with peptic ulcer. In control observations, the subjects were urged to relax while lying on a comfortable couch in a quiet room, and the finger temperature, the gastric secretion (obtained through a nasal catheter), and the stomach motility (registered by means of a swallowed inflated balloon) were recorded. After an initial period of relaxation, emotional stress was induced through the discussion of emotionally charged life situations. The predominant emotional tone of these experiments was anxiety, anger, and embarrassment. Many normal controls showed a decrease in the secretion of hydrochloric acid on days of greatest relaxation. During active discussion the secretion increased. At times, this increase was preceded by a temporary decrease. Bile was also regurgitated from the duodenum during excitement and stress.

In the most striking experiment on a patient suffering from peptic ulcer, the following phenomena were observed: During a period of moderate but continuous anger, the secretion of hydrochloric acid was high and stomach motility increased. During periods of more intense anger, peristalsis increased still further; the hydrochloric acid secretion first dropped and then rose to its previous high level. After the period of most intense anger, blood appeared in the content of the stomach. This latter indicates that circulatory disturbance may occur during active periods of stress. There was a circulatory disturbance in the extremities also, as indicated by a fall in finger temperature.

These experiments illustrate beyond question that emotional disturbance—i.e., anger, anxiety, embarrassment, and shame—may be correlated with disturbances in the functioning of the stomach. The experimental disturbing stimulus and its duration closely resembled the disturbances to which the subjects were exposed in their daily lives. The experiments also illustrate the widespread and complex changes in the body involved in a reaction to distress in connection with significant life situations. There was change not only in the functioning of the stomach, but also in finger temperature, respiration, blood circulation, etc.; in a word, in the whole body, as well as in the whole psyche.

The following case illustrates clearly an ulcer complaint that appeared under stress and was correlated with the patient's character traits and emotional needs. Once the ulcer is established, it is maintained and reinforced by the stresses and strains of daily existence.

A 35-year-old electrician, a conscientious, rather hard-working and ambitious man, had been suffering from duodenal ulcer for five years. He was devoted to his wife and his three children. He enjoyed the company of his friends and was interested in labor problems. Outwardly he always maintained good poise and calm. Careful discussion of his life history and of the circumstances under which his complaint started revealed the following: Frequently his work took him to another city for prolonged periods. During such periods, he visited his family about once a month and sent money home regularly. While away from his home, he sometimes had relations with other women. When he was about thirty years old and away from home, he met with a serious accident in which a leg and an arm were broken. He was removed to the hospital and recovered fully. However, the next time he had to be away from home he began to have pain a few hours after meals.

He was the oldest member of his family. His father, a good provider and a rather dutiful and strict man died in an accident when the patient was five years old. The boy supported his mother and his three younger siblings practically from the age of fifteen. His younger brother was the mother's favorite. The patient's mother also died in an accident as did one of his sisters.

In spite of the patient's predominant ambition, poise, and excellent performance, it was found that he had a strong, unconscious need to lean and depend upon others. This need clashed with his ideals and his self-esteem. Furthermore, beginning with his relationship to his parents, he had always unconsciously expected rejection in all close emotional relations. He was in conflict about being away from his wife and family. His accident, together with guilt feelings because of his relations with other women, threatened his emotional dependence upon his wife. ("If she knew what I had done she would condemn me, repay me in kind, and abandon me."[1]) This resulted in anxiety and resentment. This emotional constellation was correlated with disturbance of the stomach, and each time he had to be away from home it was revived.

After psychotherapy was begun and dietary measures were taken, the patient's complaints lessened considerably and he came to be almost entirely free from symptoms. Then a disturbing event occurred when his wife suffered an attack of appendicitis and had to be operated upon. She was reluctant to undergo the operation, but the patient reasoned with her without anger or rancor, and persuaded her to submit; he handled the situation with considerable poise and

[1] Where there is such an unconscious fear of retribution, an accident like breaking a leg strengthens the fear, for the accident itself is unconsciously regarded as retribution.

in a very sensible manner. During this period, however, his ulcer symptoms returned in full vigor because of the conflict situation which was characterized chiefly by anxiety and the fear of losing her psychological support. Because of his unconscious outlook, this, of course, was accompanied by anger.

COLITIS

Colitis is characterized by frequent bowel movements accompanied by pain and a discharge of mucus and blood. If the condition continues long enough, ulcers appear in the colon. Colitis may be caused by a variety of agents such as infections or dietary indiscretions; all these factors must be excluded before a case can be diagnosed as colitis attributable chiefly to emotional causes.

Some experimental observations are available on the influence of emotions on the activity of the colon (202). X-ray observations show that the emptying time and the tonus of the colon change concomitantly with emotional conditions. The colon may become spastic (extremely tense) or atonic (completely relaxed) in periods of emotional stress (22).

A 55-year-old man, an efficient carpenter, had symptoms of colitis. He had always been headstrong and rather aggressive, and inclined always to dominate the situation. His wife was completely obedient to him and accepted his verdict in everything. His father's character had resembled his own, and his mother had accepted all his father's verdicts. The father was rather strict with the patient and punished him severely when he rebelled, as he often did. He finally left home, chiefly to get away from his father. He later became reconciled with his father, but he himself adopted a similar behavior. When he was about fifty, he found it difficult to maintain his earning capacity and his position in his trade. Although he was not hard up financially, the situation enraged him, and it was during this period that his bowel movements became too frequent and finally colitis developed.

This patient had felt dominated, insecure, and unfairly treated in his relationship with his parents. His relationship with everyone else had the same qualities as that with his parents. He solved his conflicts chiefly by assuming a dominant, overbearing, ambitious, superior, self-centered attitude. This carried him along fairly well until his age and the economic depression made it impossible for him to maintain such an attitude successfully. The preference for younger men threatened his whole security system, his method of solving life problems. It was the threat to his over-valued picture of himself that aroused his anger and his anxiety.

BRONCHIAL ASTHMA[1]

Bronchial asthma is characterized by attacks of difficulty in breathing, during which the patient practically has no control of it. An examination during the attack shows characteristic wheezing sounds over the chest and certain characteristic blood changes. The attacks are caused by an involuntary contraction of the bronchial muscles. This spasm interferes with the respiration during both inspiration and expiration, but particularly during expiration. This contraction of the bronchial muscles is mediated chiefly through the vagus nerve. The muscles are relaxed and the attack is terminated by an injection of adrenalin which increases the tone of the sympathetic system.

Asthmatic patients often suffer from various emotional conflicts and their attacks are correlated with certain emotional reaction patterns, particularly with anger and resultant anxiety.

Psychosomatic Experiments on Respiration.—Comprehensive experiments on the correlation between emotions and respiration were conducted by Finesinger (239). He determined the respiratory curve and the amount of oxygen consumption (basal metabolic rate) of several patients, first in a period of relaxa-

[1] The asthmatic syndrome, urticaria, and vasomotor rhinitis are not always or completely emotionally determined, although there often are strong emotional factors in the total picture. Frequently the condition is caused mainly or entirely by the individual sensitiveness to an external protein in the form of food or something which the patient inhales (allergen). The offending agents may be horsehair or some other animal hair, pollens, beef, pork, etc. The attack occurs whenever the patient is exposed to the offending agent, and it disappears if this substance is eliminated. In some instances the patient is sensitive to an agent, but attacks occur only if his emotional condition is poor.

tion. They were then asked to think of something disturbing, and the respiratory curve and the basal metabolism were recorded. He found that, during disturbed periods, respiration became more frequent and deeper, the inspiration-expiration angle grew sharper, and the oxygen consumption rose considerably. (See also Deutsch [169, 170] and Benussi [78].)

An 8-year-old child suffered from frequent attacks of asthma. He excelled in school work, although his performance was irregular; he was particularly gifted in drawing. His mother was emotional and over-protective, and the disciplinarian of the household. His father, of course, spent most of his time at business and received the conventional respect usually given to the man of the house; actually, however, he always yielded to his wife's decisions and requests.

The parents had been well-to-do up to the time the patient was four years old. After the father lost his money he never really attempted to reestablish himself in any other business. The patient's mother became even more emotional and abused her husband until he finally left home; thereupon she had to work to support the children. Her emotional state grew more intense; in the patient's hearing she would say over the telephone to her sister or brother, "Tomorrow morning will find me dead and all the children with me." As a rule, a few hours later or on the following day the patient would have an asthmatic attack.

Investigation brought to light a feeling of complete helplessness in a situation in which he had to depend on his undependable parents, a disappointment in both of them because they themselves were weak and fell far short of his ideals, and a feeling of not being loved by either of them. Such statements as that quoted above represented a serious threat to the patient, a threat of injury which made him afraid. To this he reacted with anxiety, resentment, and fear of condemnation by his mother and himself. (These are common reactions in children who have an unconscious contempt for their parents.) The asthmatic attack represented this emotional constellation of alarm, contempt, attack, guilt, etc., but with a strong plea of helplessness as well. It is as if the patient unconsciously said, "You leaned on me and made me suffer when you were in difficulties.

Now it is my turn to demand help from you, to make you suffer and to make you alarmed about me."

URTICARIA

The symptoms of urticaria are a fleeting rash, and a swelling and itching of the skin. The relation of this disturbance to emotional disturbance has been known for some years. A recent study by Saul, as yet unpublished, demonstrates that this relationship is much more specific than was ordinarily suspected. (See also [203].)

A patient who was being treated psychoanalytically had twelve attacks of urticaria all of which could be connected with a previous acute frustration of her strong desire for warmth and affection in her engagement. There were of course more than twelve frustrations, and Saul attempted to discover why no urticaria resulted from these others. His conclusion, based on very plausible evidence, was that if weeping occurred after frustration, urticaria did not appear; i.e., urticaria is a result of unreleased emotion in frustration, and weeping represents such a release. He reports at least one startling confirmation of this hypothesis. A traumatized woman who wept incessantly developed an urticaria of the whole body when forced to stop, the urticaria disappeared when she was encouraged to weep again. Saul is properly cautious in acknowledging that one such case cannot prove anything conclusively; but this seems an excellent lead for further research, particularly on the therapeutic effects of weeping.

The following case shows how the symptoms are connected with emotional problems and fantasies.

A gifted mathematician, who was under psychoanalytic treatment, agreed to his wife's desire that they have a child, although he had resisted it for years. He had never admittedly applied himself wholeheartedly to anything and he never became fully attached to anyone. He married because he felt that his wife was a good worker and no financial burden would fall on him. In general, he was a dependent individual, but he followed a philosophy of detachment and self-sufficiency. His decision to have a child was based partly on his improved outlook, but to an even greater extent on his desire to show the analyst that he was entirely well and completely independent of him. The latter was obvious from the fact that he said nothing of his wife's pregnancy until the analyst deduced it from the patient's dream.

At the time of his wife's delivery, the patient went into a serious anxiety state. His general reaction was: "I'll have to take care of her now, I'll have to assume the burden of the children, and I'll have to submit to their domination. Actually, I am helpless and enslaved and I ought to be looked after without being dominated. In fact, I ought not to be the father, I ought to be the child." The emotional constellation was chiefly anxiety, anger at being entrapped, a feeling of helplessness and enslavement and rebellion. In several dreams, the patient threw a woman and child into a rocky turbulent stream and himself fell into the stream. He dramatized these emotions with urticaria. The patient, of course, had many other symptoms during this time, such as nightmares, periods of complete inability to work, the desire to sleep twelve or thirteen hours at a time, and sometimes considerable irritation with his wife in the hospital. All of these symptoms were connected with his emotional crisis.

Exophthalmic Goiter

Exophthalmic goiter is characterized by irritability, restlessness, bulging of the eyes, excessive perspiration, loss of weight, rapid heart rate, trembling of the fingers, and enlargement of the thyroid gland. Oxygen consumption is considerably increased, indicating a rise in basal metabolism. The physiology of the condition is not entirely clear, but it is known that not all the symptoms are caused by the over-functioning of the thyroid gland. Bulging of the eyes does not appear in a healthy individual who takes an excessive amount of thyroid substance.

It is difficult to state whether an emotional factor is always involved in the syndrome in human beings. Conrad (143) and Mittelmann (561) found that the condition followed an emotional crisis with a probability of 93 out of 100 cases.

Deutsch and Kauf (173) observed that during emotional stress which may be largely unconscious, pulse rate and metabolism rise. They hypnotized subjects and tested their pulse rate and metabolism. After a control period they suggested harrowing experiences to these subjects, at the same time recording pulse rate and metabolism; there was a rise of about 27 in the pulse rate and of approximately 20 per cent in the metabolism. The suggested harrowing experiences were of this type: They told a woman who was much attached to her mother that her mother was lost in a forest during a storm. They told this woman that after waking from the trance she would forget the experience, but that these emotions would recur when the experimenter took a handkerchief out of his pocket. They found that her metabolism and pulse rate rose under these conditions, without conscious anxiety and without her knowing why. Such experiments show that anxiety and other distressing emotional states are correlated with change in basal metabolism.

Another interesting example of the influence of emotional forces on the body is found in a technique used for operating on patients whose hyperthyroidism is so severe that part of the gland must be removed. It is dangerous for such patients to become excited. Intense fear *added* to hyperthyroidism may shoot the blood pressure and pulse rate up tremendously, and even cause death. Therefore patients who are afraid of an operation are told merely that they are in the hospital for observation and rest. Heavy bandages are at once put on the throat, and they are given regular rectal enemas. When the patient is calm, a strong general anesthetic is administered through the rectal enema, and the patient loses consciousness suddenly and completely. The operation is then performed, and the patient, still unconscious, is returned to his bed. His bandages do not frighten him when he wakes up because he is accustomed to them; the pain is kept to a minimum so as not to alarm him. Not until he is discharged does he know that everything is over.

HIGH BLOOD PRESSURE (ESSENTIAL HYPERTENSION)

Opinion differs on the normal upper limit of the blood pressure in a relaxed individual; some consider 140 the limit, but no authority considers a pressure above 150 anything but high. The person with continuously high blood pressure may have no complaints, or he may complain of headaches and dizziness. Primary physical disturbances, such as inflammation of the kidneys or hardening of the arteries, may be responsible for this condition. In some instances, however, as in essential hypertension, no such factor can be found, but the presence of strong emotional influences can often be established.

Normal people who are apprehensive—e.g., students before an examination—may have a higher than normal pressure. The blood pressure in animals rises during rage or fear (132), and normal human beings who are extremely angry likewise show a rise (453).

The emotional constellation most frequent in patients with essential hypertension is anger, often completely repressed, mingled with anxiety and depression.

Alexander (19) regularly recorded one patient's blood pressure before and after each analytic session. It was high when he was in a disturbed emotional state, but was at or near normal when he was emotionally calm.

This patient was self-conscious and had a vivid sense of inferiority, but at the same time he was ambitious to excel and to do perfect work. His overt modesty and compliance put him under extreme pressure and created intense inferiority feelings in him. The patient would never contradict his superior; he would follow his suggestions and accept blame while talking with him, but after he left the office he would be filled with self-contempt and would say to himself: "You should have answered; you should have said no! You are no good and you never will be any good." This self-deprecatory attitude usually became so unbearable that he would want a drink, for alcohol dissipated his sense of weakness and inefficiency. Furthermore, drinking during the day represented an act of rebellion in that he was indulging in a forbidden activity. He also was promiscuous sexually at such times; this was an expression of rebellion against his wife. Otherwise he subjected himself to all the requirements of the marital state.

As a child, the patient had had outbreaks of extreme rage which he later completely forgot, but which were recovered in the analysis, His father, an object of fear and hostility to the boy, thought it his duty to break the lad's aggressive spirit and rebelliousness, and made a point of teaching him how to be a loser. When the patient was about eight years old, his father began taking him out to the golf course, beating him at the game repeatedly, and trying to make him like to be beaten. The patient remembered his senseless rage when he was beaten in any competitive game. (Alexander [19].)

MIGRAINE

Migraine consists of periodic severe headaches, usually on one side, which are frequently accompanied by nausea, vomiting, constipation, or diarrhea. In more severe cases, the patient may have spots before the eyes and uncomfortable sensations on one side of the body. The attack may last from a few hours to several days.

Migraine usually occurs partially as a reaction to situations of stress. Wolff found that, as a rule, patients suffering from these attacks are unusually ambitious and preoccupied with achievement and success. They are often perfectionists, to whom efficiency means a great deal; they are orderly to an extreme. A disturbance of the sexual function is common, manifesting itself in frigidity and disgust.

A married woman aged 33 had migraine of six years' duration; it had been growing worse in the last six months, attacks occurring once or twice a week. The illness had its onset with growing domestic tension, culminating in her husband's sister coming to live in her home. The sister quarreled continuously with both the patient and the patient's husband. The latter had been unemployed for four years. The family was on relief; and the patient, besides keeping house and caring for two children, supplemented the family income by peddling stockings. She was a meticulous, "fussy" housekeeper.

"When I am home I don't sit down for five minutes. I always find something to do. I've got a worrisome nature; and besides, having a man around the house seven days a week, you can't keep your house 'just so.' "

The patient was a tense, anxious, driving, and ambitious woman who was thoroughly dissatisfied with her lot and looked on her life as miserably lacking. Despite an unusually small income, she gave her children advantages that could come only from good management. Notwithstanding concern for her family's welfare, her relations with her eldest daughter were bad. The child had temper tantrums, was obstinate, and seriously distressed her mother. On one occasion the child precipitated in the mother a frenzy of murderous rage. "I wished she were dead. I started to undress her. I wanted to murder her. I wanted to kill her dead nude. It ended by my having an hysterical crying attack."

The patient had been the youngest of seven children and had been considered a timid, bashful, obedient child. "There was never a question of being forced or told to do things. I was always a fussy person—wanted things done just right."

At the age of eleven many responsibilities were loaded on her, primarily the care of her sister's babies. This, and the oppressive influence of a dominating father, caused her to resent her home life bitterly. She ultimately succeeded in going to business school and also took piano lessons; she learned to play moderately well. "I am very ambitious. I wanted a career as a piano player. I used to give piano lessons, but I was no success at it. I was deathly tired of my home. I was tired of 'hand-me-downs' all the time. My whole trouble was I wanted more than I had in life. It made me resentful and nasty." Consequently she grasped the first opportunity for marriage, explaining, "I married my husband just to get away from home." Her sexual and married life were unsatisfactory.[1]

[1] H. G. Wolff, "Personality features and reactions of subject with migraine" (795).

SUGGESTED READINGS

Of value here are relevant parts of Dunbar's *Emotions and Bodily Changes* (202) and of Fenichel's *Outline of Clinical Psychoanalysis* (233), Alexander's *The Medical Value of Psychoanalysis* (17), and various issues of *Psychosomatic Medicine*.

CHAPTER XXVII

MANIC-DEPRESSIVE REACTIONS; INVOLUTIONAL MELANCHOLIA

Psychotic Reaction Types.—Various developments have taken place in the concept and classification of psychotic reactions. At first, patients were classified on the basis of their symptoms and the outcome of their condition as observed for many years by Kraepelin (443). He established the syndromes of manic-depressive psychosis and dementia praecox. He described manic-depressive psychosis as a condition characterized by long periods of either elation or depression or the alternation of both, with long free periods between; these attacks might ocur throughout a person's life and never lead to dementia (intellectual deterioration). Dementia praecox he described as a condition which appears at an early age—the end of the second decade or the beginning of the third—and, with various symptoms, (e.g., characteristic delusions and hallucinations) continues through life, resulting in a progressive mental deterioration.

Later observations by Bleuler (90) showed that symptoms of dementia praecox may appear later in life, and that patients may recover and be able to function socially and professionally. Later, it was found that if individuals who showed minor symptoms or character traits similar to those shown by patients with fully developed dementia praecox were treated early, they continued to function fairly well and their symptoms disappeared under treatment.

The most important element in the psychopathology was considered a characteristic disturbance of the patient's emotional life, a "splitting of the personality," which was why Bleuler called this disease schizophrenia rather than dementia praecox. This "splitting" refers to the incongruity in thoughts, emotional reactions, and behavior, whereby a patient may state, with apparent emotional indifference, that he is a king and a moment later agree to scrub the floor. Another important theoretical development was the correlation of the symptoms with the individual's total personality, and the realization that they represented ways in which the total organism reacted to needs, hardships, fears, and conflicts. Thus the concept of "reaction type" was developed (Adolf Meyer [549]).

The psychodynamics of the psychotic reaction types were elucidated also by the application of psychoanalytic principles to the symptoms (Freud [273], Jung [407], Abraham [2]). This emphasized the fact that the patients developed their various symptoms and personalities as an expression of characteristic needs and fears, and of characteristic ways of handling their desires and problems.

Classification of Psychotic Reaction Types.—Phenomena classified in various psychotic reaction types may occur in one patient; sometimes neurotic and psychotic manifestations may be combined. It is important to realize that, like the neurotic, psychotic manifestations are motivated by catastrophic fears and are the individual's attempts to solve his conflicts and cope with the world as best he can. Extreme psychotic manifestations are in part, however, *actual* catastrophic breakdowns rather than just fear of breakdown. That is, in part, they express complete discouragement and giving up in the face of the problem; the neurotic symptom, on the other hand, is functional in the sense of trying to cope with and ameliorate the situation.

In general the following reaction types are differentiated: (1) the affective or manic-depressive, (2) the schizophrenic, and (3) the organic. Some also include the paranoic as a separate reaction type. Although ultimate proof is lacking, the affective and the schizophrenic are assumed to be chiefly psychogenic in origin. In the organic reaction type the patient has a serious bodily condition which is caused by physical agents and which directly affects the functioning of the brain; the patient has a further psychological reaction to his organic difficulties. Thus, when the blood vessels in the brain harden, the patient is irritable and suffers from disturbed memory; he is particularly liable to irritation when he feels ashamed of forgetting something. In other words, his irritability is due not alone to changes in his brain; it may also be a defensive, hostile reaction toward someone before whom he feels ashamed of his loss of memory.

The Manic-depressive Reaction Type

Patients who react to severe stress with manic or depressive states often show characteristic personality traits during the time they are relatively normal (Reiss). Many of them are outgoing, hard-driving, and successful. Others are very conscientious in their habits and work with great accuracy ("the compulsive" type). Still others are worried, concerned, and anxious. Another large percentage is composed of individuals who vary between optimism, cheerfulness, and energy on the one hand, and discouragement, lassitude, and gloominess on the other. These latter people are called cyclothymic. Their swings of mood are based on conflicts and attempted solutions similar to those in the manic-depressive reaction itself. Kretschmer claims that in physical appearance the majority of the manic-depressive patients are short, stocky people with thick necks (his "pyknic" type). Other psychiatrists, however, are inclined to doubt this. It should be realized that patients may develop manic-depressive reactions under stress, regardless of their personality or physique.

"Harvey Behring is an extreme case in point. He was a stout, florid man who gave the impression of great ability and power. His conversation immediately stamped him as a superior individual. When he was only thirty-three he had acquired nearly forty thousand dollars by his enormous activity, working nightly until one o'clock in the morning month after month. He became over-sanguine, invested all the money in one project, lost heart in it, became depressed, and lost all of his money.

"He recovered from this and started in business again on a small scale. A few years later the building which his business occupied was destroyed by fire and he was plunged into another depression, in which he remained a year. After that there occurred attack after attack, with and without provocation.

"His characteristic cycle would begin with a phase of prodigious activity in which he would exert himself to the utmost. His efforts were usually crowned with a good deal of success, and this success would only stimulate him to greater exertion. At the same time, however, his judgment would become impaired by an overdose of optimism and he would make wild plunges and risk large sums of money. Sometimes these speculations turned out well, but more often they turned out badly. Then he would be plunged into a depression in which he would be quite incapable of doing any work at all. He would wake up in the morning groaning, crying out for God to spare his soul, heaving long sighs, and bursting into tears when spoken to. This depression would pass and he would again work himself up to great enthusiasm and industry.

"In one of his depressed phases he shot himself."[1]

General Characteristics and Course of the Reaction.—1. Some patients suffer only from periods of depression; others manifest only periods of elation; still others show alternation between the two.

2. The manic-depressive reaction may develop gradually or suddenly. In typical instances the reaction terminates after about six months or a year, either spontaneously or in response to treatment.

3. Patients with manic-depressive reactions have essentially "normal" periods of several years' duration between attacks.

4. Attacks of manic or depressive reaction often recur.

5. Manic-depressive reactions do not lead to a deterioration of intellectual and emotional faculties of the individual.

[1] K. Menninger. *The Human Mind,* Alfred A. Knopf, Inc., New York, 1937, p. 107.

DEPRESSIVE REACTIONS

General Characteristics.—The depressive reaction is usually characterized by three major symptoms:

Depression.—The patient feels sad, discouraged, disheartened, and hopeless. This depression is continuous and is maintained even in a comic or humorous situation. In addition, the patient finds it difficult to take any interest in his surroundings.

Psychomotor retardation.—The patient is disinclined to engage in any activity; he has to exert an effort to do anything, and he works slowly. This is related to the next symptom.

Difficulty in thinking.—The patient's thought processes are considerably retarded; he has to make an effort to think or to solve problems.

These three symptoms lead to characteristic behavior. The patient is inclined to sit in the same place for long periods of time. His speech is slow and monotonous, his activities are lethargic, and it takes him much longer than usual to do tasks.

These major symptoms are frequently accompanied by others, among which are the following:

Delusions.—The general thought content is characterized under all circumstances by ideas of utter worthlessness and guilt. The patient thinks little of himself, condemns himself, and feels guilty over misdemeanors which seem trivial to other people. In more severe cases the patient has delusions, particularly of sin and guilt. He accuses himself of having committed the unpardonable sin, of being an abomination before God and man. He may be convinced that he has cancer or syphilis and that he will infect the whole world. He considers the future absolutely hopeless and black. There may be fleeting and changeable "ideas of reference," i.e., he may think that people are talking about him and are going to harm him. This last, however, is infrequent.

Hallucinations.—The patient may hear voices which accuse him of having committed a crime or call him derogatory names. These phenomena also are infrequent.

Bodily symptoms.—As has been said, the patient's behavior is lethargic; his posture, whether sitting or standing, is stooped, and he is apt to drag his feet when he walks. The muscle tone is diminished. The eyes are lusterless; the facial expression is sad.

The common vegetative symptoms are: (1) Considerably diminished secretion of saliva. (2) Decrease in gastro-intestinal activity resulting in severe constipation and loss of appetite; the latter is present in every acute depression. Because of it, the patient eats little and loses weight. The constipation may lead to secondary auto-intoxication. (3) Changes in blood pressure from high to low in elation or depression, respectively. (4) Cessation of menstruation at the onset of the reaction; its reappearance is often a sign of real improvement. (5) Sleeplessness, which in the depressive reaction is correlated with the patient's sadness and anxiety, and in the manic reaction, with his continuous excitement.

Varieties of Depressive Reactions.—All these symptoms may be shown by one patient, but most frequently they vary in intensity from one case to another, or some may be entirely absent. Thus in some mild cases, the patient's depression may be more apparent to others than to the patient himself; or he may be depressed, but not retarded in his behavior, reactions, or thinking; or his depression may lead to considerable restlessness and agitation such as wringing the hands. Depending on the degree and type of the symptoms, the following classes of depressive reactions are usually differentiated:

Mild (masked) form.—The patient may be aware of and complain of a slight depression, but more usually his complaint concerns a physical discomfort, such as persistent vague headache, gastric disturbance with loss of appetite, bad taste in the mouth, constipation, blurred vision, irritability, fatigue, exhaustion, lassitude. It is difficult for him to work, and he does so with great effort. He cannot concentrate and he cannot express himself easily. Sleep is disturbed and does not refresh him. Although he may completely repress his depression and sadness, the continuous presence of these symptoms and his general behavior enable the examiner to conclude that the patient is suffering from a general depressive reaction. The physical examination of such patients furnishes nothing that would adequately explain their condition.

Patients with this type of reaction can usually be treated and brought to full recovery by the psychotherapist without hospitalization, although suicide must be guarded against in some cases.

Simple retardation.—In simple retardation the patient is depressed and lethargic; his facial expression is sad, and his eyes are dull. Questions and commands often have to be repeated, and it takes him a long time to respond to them. He has to be helped in such daily activities as getting dressed, eating, going to the toilet. He feels worthless and guilty, but there is no disturbance of consciousness or of intellectual faculties. Patients of this type should be treated as invalids. They should be hospitalized when possible, although they can be treated at home if adequate care is available.

Acute depression.—The same symptoms appear in acute depression as in simple retardation, but are more marked. The patient sits alone, does not speak of his own accord, and is extremely slow in his responses. He accuses himself of frightful wrongdoings that will bring disaster to everyone and for which he will be imprisoned or executed. He thinks that his bowels are completely stopped up, that his heart is badly damaged, or that his brain is wasting away. He feels that his whole personality is changed, and everything around him seems unreal. He may have hallucinations, particularly in connection with sin and guilt, disease and poverty.

Depressive stupor.—The patient is utterly depressed; he does not speak and does not respond. He has to be fed because he will not eat voluntarily; his bladder and bowels have to be emptied artificially. His health is in great danger because of loss of weight and auto-intoxication. The heart action and circulation suffer, and infections may develop.

The Possible Dangers from Depressive Reactions.—The patient with the mild form of depression may be unable to do his work and as a consequence may lose his job. This loss is a blow to his self-esteem. Lack of sympathy in his social environment and the accusation that he is pretending or indulging himself increase his irritability and his feeling of inadequacy and self-condemnation. Well-meant remarks like "Snap out of it" and "There's nothing to worry about" make him feel that no one realizes that he is sick or sympathizes with him. All this increases his discomfort and intensifies his symptoms. The danger of suicide is in general proportionate to the intensity of the depression, although it may be present even in relatively mild cases. In serious cases, there is considerable danger from loss of weight, exhaustion, and auto-intoxication. However, most patients recover with adequate care.

Psychodynamics of Depressive Reactions.—It is frequently found that the accusations which the patient makes against himself have previously been directed by him toward someone close to him by whom he has been profoundly hurt (Freud). For example, a depressed woman may accuse herself of unfaithfulness, selfishness, and immorality; but careful investigation shows that she formerly made these accusations against her husband. The unspeakable crimes of which she accuses herself may really express her profound hostility toward her husband; in other words, they are the crimes she would have committed if she had carried her repressed impulses into action.

Depressed patients are unable to turn away from the people who hurt them because of their emotional dependence on them. The profound feeling of worthlessness is caused by their self-condemnation and their expectation of disapproval resulting from their hostility toward these indispensable individuals. Such a patient then feels not only disapproved of by this individual but also abandoned and rejected. His helplessness and suffering are increased by his desire to abase himself and suffer in order to expiate his hostility, show his helplessness, and thus obtain forgiveness, approval, and help. This constellation closely approximates for the patient the catastrophic situation of which he is afraid, namely, utter rejection and condemnation both by himself and by the persons on whom he depends. Because of these factors, his appreciation and evaluation of reality are altered.

The characteristics of the emotional pattern of the depressive phase thus are: (1) intense dependence on another individual; (2) strong hostility toward this individual which the patient turns on himself; (3) intense self-condemnation, guilt, feeling of worthlessness, and expectation of disapproval and abandonment because of this hostility.

Treatment of Depressive Reactions.—The general treatment should be based on understanding; this is particularly important in mild or moderate cases. The patient should feel that the therapist realizes his suffering and wishes to help him. Encouragement is important, but it should be so given that the patient will not feel that his condition is being minimized. A measure of persistence, persuasion, and kind firmness is needed to persuade him, when feasible, to attend to his needs, to eat, to engage in some activity. Patients with suicidal tendencies must of course have constant but not too obvious supervision.

Adequate nourishment is essential. Severely depressed patients who are unable to eat have to be fed through a stomach tube. Constipation is corrected by cathartics and occasional enemas; if the patient is unable to void by himself, the bladder has to be emptied artificially. Sleeplessness is combated by hot baths and, in some cases, hypnotic drugs.

Occupational therapy is always valuable for patients capable of interesting themselves in anything. The activity chosen by the patient varies; it may be something in which he has been interested before, or it may be entirely new—drawing or paint-

ing, carpentry, clay modeling. Attending the occupational class
and seeing others engaged in useful activities may in itself have
a therapeutic effect.

More active psychotherapy, such as discussing his difficulties
from the psychiatric point of view, should be begun only when
the patient is strong enough to face his problems, his conflicts
and frustrations. It is always safe to encourage him to talk about
his mild difficulties; but the conversation should never lead
him, when he is extremely depressed, to topics which for him
are charged with serious conflict. Psychoanalytic treatment
should not be undertaken until the patient is over his depression.

It is always desirable to consult with the patient's family,
investigate their adjustments, help them with their difficulties,
and advise them regarding their relationships with him during
his normal periods. Only in this way can the situations and
difficulties which depress the patient be either diminished or
eliminated.

In mild cases of depression the use of benzedrine sulphate has
proved to be of limited usefulness. Benzedrine, a derivative of
ephedrine, has a stimulating effect on the psychomotor functions
and on mood. In this way, depression may be lessened enough so
that the psychiatrist may be able to make contact with the patient.

The following case is an illustration of simple retardation.

"A. B., 18 years old, is a good example of a simple retarded
depression. She had had a former attack one year previously, which
had only lasted for about one week, and from which she made
apparently a good recovery. The family history indicated suicidal
tendencies, because a paternal grandmother had taken her life when
she was sixty-two years old, and a maternal uncle had committed
suicide at the age of forty-five. This family history seemed to have
a definite bearing on the case.

"She had always been a strong, healthy child. She was not
nervous, but was quiet, shy, reserved, and not inclined to make
friends easily.

"She did quite well at school, but was described as being more practical than intellectual, and was especially interested in house-wifely tasks. It was while she was attending a course of instruction at a School of Domestic Economy that she broke down. The illness developed acutely, and three days before her admission she sud-denly told her parents that she had drunk a bottle of eye lotion that had been in the house. It is of interest that preceding the onset of her previous attack she had overheard talk about suicide. This reminded her of similar incidents in her own family, and she was depressed for about a week afterwards.

"At the time of her admission she was in a dull, depressed state, feeling hopeless, and feeling that she had not been learning and concentrating as she should have done. She feared in consequence that she would become a burden on her friends. Suicide had there-fore seemed the simplest solution of her difficulties. She was slow in answering questions, replied for the most part in monosyllables, readily admitted that she was melancholy and that her mind was not at peace, but was occupied with morbid feelings and thoughts. As a result she had not been sleeping well. She said, 'I seem just to have been slipping along, and not doing my duty. I feel as if I had got everybody into a mess. I thought I was not so efficient as others, and that I could not hold my own with them.' Her answers to questions were always quite coherent and relevant. She denied ever having suffered from ideas of reference, from hallucinations or delusions. Her memory, her grasp on school knowledge, and her intellectual faculties generally were not impaired. She realized that she was ill and in need of treatment in a mental hospital, so much so that she came as a voluntary patient. Her general physical exami-nation showed that she was in good condition, and there was no evidence of disease. She had erosion of her lower lip, due to the eye lotion which she had swallowed.

"After a short period in bed, she was allowed up, an attempt was made to cultivate her interest in the occupational department, and this she readily took to. She found that she was able to do certain simple pieces of work comparatively well, and in consequence her self-confidence rapidly returned, and in the course of two months she made a good recovery. She put on weight, her sleep improved, she realized more clearly than heretofore what her actual difficulties had been, and was able to return home.

"A case such as the above illustrates very clearly a simple, depressed, retarded state occurring in a somewhat shy, sensitive girl. There is no reason to suppose that she will not be able to carry on satisfactorily in the future."[1]

MANIC REACTIONS

General Characteristics.—Like the depressive reaction, the manic reaction is also characterized by three primary symptoms.

Elation.—The patient is happy and has a general feeling of well-being. He evaluates himself highly, and has an optimistic outlook in which he expects everything he undertakes to turn out well. In one phase of elation, jocularity, the patient makes humorous remarks, laughs at them, and succeeds in making others laugh too; he enjoys punning.

"There is absolutely nothing the matter. Everything is perfect, all is peace and love. I feel fine—perfect. Everything is hotsy-totsy now. My only complaint is Patsy isn't here. I have never been sick. I have always been good or else God couldn't have lifted me up. Now Adam made a mistake and he's doing time now. I never did. I was perfect and I see the light and love. He sent my mother and father down here as the best in order to have me. They were perfect when they had me—I've always been clean."[2]

Flight of ideas.—The patient's thoughts, as well as his speech and writing, jump from one topic to another without following a single course. The trend of thought is diverted by a subtopic which in turn diverts it in still another direction. Distractibility is common; that is, the trend of thoughts may be diverted by an external event, such as a noise, the ringing of a bell, a picture on the wall, etc.

Psychomotor activity.—The patient is always on the go, always busy. His activities are not merely aimless motor phe-

[1] D. K. Henderson and R. D. Gillespie, *A Textbook of Psychiatry*, Oxford University Press, London, 5th ed., 1940, p. 150.

[2] Wendell Muncie, *Psychobiology and Psychiatry*, Mosby, St. Louis, 1939.

nomena such as playing with a pencil or drumming with the fingers; they may have a definite purpose. For example, he will talk to other individuals, pick up a book and start to read aloud, try to persuade someone to do something, try to organize a party, invite people, write letters, make purchases, want to institute changes in the routine of the ward, etc.—all in rapid succession. The terms "pressure of activity" and "pressure of speech" are customarily used in connection with these phenomena.

Because of these three symptoms, the patient is over-talkative, constantly on the go, engages in one activity after another, and displays a rather infectious gaiety.

A woman in the psychopathic hospital was walking around in the ward in a gay mood with a smile on her face. She stopped at one of the rooms, the door of which was open. In this room the psychiatrist was examining a patient who kept repeating stereotyped phrases and stereotyped motions and who would not answer the examiner's questions. After watching for a short time, the manic patient entered the room and said to the other patient in a cheerful, laughing manner: "Talk to him. Why don't you talk to him? The paragon of beautiful male specimen is trying to converse with you. Just look at her! Here is the paragon of beautiful male specimen talking to her and she won't answer."

Frequently, even relatively dull people become very entertaining and show a mastery of their language in the manic reaction. Thus, the above patient would never be able to coin the phrase "paragon of beautiful male specimen" when she was well.

Other symptoms are frequent in the manic reaction, among them being:

Irritability when thwarted.—The patient becomes angry and abusive, to the point of shouting or even assault, if anyone crosses him, if his requests are not granted immediately, or if someone tries to show him that what he is doing is not right. He cannot brook contradiction or accept criticism. His thoughts, activities, and mood are unstable.

Suspiciousness.—The patient may be suspicious of the actions and motivations of those around him, may assume that they want to do harm or that they have sexual designs.

Delusions.—The patient's over-valuation of himself may reach the degree of grandiose delusions. He may consider himself extremely wealthy, a great political or military genius, or an emissary of God. The delusions in typical manic reactions are changeable and of short duration.

Hallucinations.—Auditory hallucinations are particularly common. The patient hears someone whom he loves say tender things to him, or he hears God talking. As a rule the hallucinations do not have an obscene and derogatory content as in schizophrenia.

Physical symptoms.—The patient's facial expression is lively, either joyful or angry; his eyes shine. There is increased perspiration with the excessive activity, and the muscle tone is increased. Among the vegetative symptoms are rapid heart action, increased blood pressure, possible cessation of menstruation. Sleeplessness may result from the patient's excitement. Because of his constant activity, excitement, and sleeplessness, he may lose considerable weight. If his excitement reaches a delirious intensity, he may refuse to eat, he may lose considerable water through perspiration, and a toxic state may result.

Varieties of Manic Reactions.—The patient may have all or only some of the symptoms, in varying degrees of intensity and in various combinations. Thus, he may be elated, flighty, and jocular; irritable, angry, domineering, over-active, and talkative with no obvious sign of elation. The only indication of elation may be the fact that he says he feels particularly well. Hallucination and delusion may accompany relatively moderate over-activity. In some patients the reaction is mild and it remains essentially the same during the whole illness; in others, it increases in intensity, hallucinations and delusions appearing at its height. The relative dominance of the elation or of the irritability and impulsive stubbornness may fluctuate during the course of the illness. Three varieties of manic reactions are usually differentiated.

Hypomania.—The characteristic features are moderate elation, flightiness, and over-activity. The patient is particularly witty and entertaining—he is the life of the party. He may get into trouble because of extravagance, sexual promiscuity, or alcoholic indulgence, or, if his mood changes, because of his irritability, combativeness, and intolerance of criticism. The continuous activity and restlessness are the most constant symptom. Such a patient is difficult to treat unless hospitalized because the people around him are often reluctant or unable to realize that he is sick. He himself, as a rule, does not realize this; he insists on having his own way, disregards advice, and resents supervision.

Acute mania.—Acute mania may follow hypomania or it may appear in its full intensity, possibly after a short period of sleeplessness and irritability. The patient's excitement is intense, his flightiness and restlessness are at a high pitch. He considers himself superior to everyone, wants to manage everyone's affairs and to command and dominate everyone. The dominant mood fluctuates from gaiety to anger. The patient may break up the furniture and strike other patients or nurses. He loses his sense of shame, is obscene in his talk, exposes himself, and makes sexual advances toward those around him. He may also have delusions and hallucinations. His intellectual functions are not impaired, but his orientation for time, place, and person may be inadequate; even his consciousness may be cloudy. Because of the flight of ideas and his distractibility, his speech may become incoherent. The physical symptoms described in connection with hypomania may be intensified by the continuous excitement, loss of water, and lack of nourishment—the pulse rate may rise to 180. Such patients unquestionably require hospitalization.

Delirious mania.—Delirious mania may develop from hypomania and acute mania, or it may appear almost at the beginning of the manic reaction. The patient's symptoms are manifested so intensely that he is totally disoriented; his speech is incoherent, he is extremely restless, and his activities lack any apparent organization or goal. He may have vivid auditory and visual illusions and hallucinations. He lacks all insight and is entirely shameless in his behavior, appearance, and habits. The chances of exhaustion, self-intoxication, and infection by other diseases are great, and the loss of weight may be very rapid. Such patients, of course, must be treated in hospitals.

The Possible Dangers from Manic Reactions.—In mild types of manic reactions, the patient is in danger of getting into trouble because of his reckless spending of money and mismanagement of his business, his indiscriminate conclusion of contracts, etc. He may be arrested on charges of felonious assault, misconduct, or immoral behavior, or be injured in a brawl. These dangers are also present in acute mania. Because of indiscriminate sexual behavior, the patient may acquire a venereal infection, or a woman may become pregnant without knowing who her partner was. In the acute and delirious reactions there is danger from physical exhaustion, intoxication, and infection by disease.

Psychodynamics of Manic Reactions.—The nature of the conflict and of the catastrophic fear in the manic reaction is probably the same as in the depressive reaction. The manic patient, however, arrives at a different solution and he uses different means of coping with his difficulties and problems. He declares that his conflicts, his anxieties, his guilt, and his helplessness do not exist; he is stronger than any problem he faces and stronger than the individual who hurt him and threatened him with condemnation and abandonment. He considers himself remarkably capable instead of helpless. He is demanding instead of submissive. Instead of condemning himself, he fully approves of himself. Far from his being abandoned by the world, he declares that the whole world is his. With tremendous effort and expenditure of energy he overrides his guilt, anxiety, and helplessness, and makes contact with the world, rushing from one object to another.

There is another factor in the hyperactivity as well as in the flight of ideas; i.e., the patient is constantly running away from his pain and discomfort, his conflict, guilt, and fear. He is escaping into his environment from his own conflicts; hence the manic reaction may in a sense be called a pathological outgoingness. In this whole process, the evaluation of reality in all its phases— the evaluation of the self and of social customs, and of the functions of the senses and ideas—is seriously altered. Overriding his anxieties and throwing off the yoke of his conscience makes the patient joyous because he feels completely liberated; he discards his inhibitions and gets additional pleasure from gratifying "forbidden" and previously inhibited impulses.

Attention has been called to the fact that some of the physiological manifestations of manic-depressive reactions involve particularly the mouth functions (Abraham). As we have seen, the depressed patient does not want to eat; this is his reaction to his desire to destroy the individual who disappointed him. The situation in the patient with a manic reaction is reversed. He may eat ravenously, saying in effect that the whole world is his and he can have his fill of it.

At times the patient's hopes and expectations of a solution of his difficulties center around his relationship with another individual, such as a child or a lover. Upon being disappointed in or losing this individual, the patient may develop a manic reaction instead of becoming depressed. The manic reaction here represents an overriding of the feeling of loss and resentment and of all the conflicts which in the complete constellation represent a catastrophic situation for him. The delusions then assume a wish-fulfilling quality—that the child is alive or that the lover will marry the patient. This is not a simple wish-fulfilling fantasy; it is a fantasy to which the patient clings in

order to escape the catastrophic situation and for which he has
to alter his evaluation of reality. The following case illustrates
this point. This is one of those rare instances in which the observer had the opportunity to see the patient before the development of the overt manic reaction and in which he was thoroughly familiar with the event to which the patient reacts.

A 25-year-old woman was moderately depressed in connection
with her difficulties with her family, her aspirations, and her station
in life. This depression did not seriously interfere with her work or
her everyday life. She met a man who was superior to her in intellect and who, as a way out of his emotional difficulties, was seeking
contact with someone who would be unqualifiedly devoted to him.
This man was under psychoanalytic treatment and, against the
analyst's advice, proposed to her; she had fallen intensely in love
with him.

As the day of their marriage approached, the man became panicky
and antagonistic toward the woman; he wanted to break with her
completely; not openly, but by such an aggravation of his symptoms
that they would completely incapacitate him. The analyst felt forced
under these circumstances to take a more active part in the situation,
and he suggested that the man ask the woman to come to his office.
It became obvious in the course of the conversation that her love for
the man contained an element of pure admiration for a person
whom she considered great and strong and on whom she could
unqualifiedly depend.

The analyst told her that the man was in no condition to embark
on a marriage, and that it would be best to postpone any decision in
the matter since a hasty step might cause severe suffering to both.
Although she had looked forward to marriage and had talked about
it constantly to the man, she accepted the analyst's advice.

The next day, the woman became over-active and over-talkative
and remained home from work. She saw the man that day, and
volubly and happily discussed the coming marriage with him, and
made plans to go to the country. When the analyst heard this story
from the man, he asked him to bring the woman to his office. In a
happy, elated mood, the woman told the analyst that she had come
to his office with the man to be married there, and that they were

going to the country. Her facial expression was blissful, her eyes were shining. While sitting in a chair across from the analyst's desk, she gazed intently into the distance and talked to herself. On direct questioning she said that she could hear her fiancé talking to her, and that she was conversing with him. She herself repeated both sides of the conversation. For example, She: "What did you say, darling?" He: "We are going to the country, darling." She: "Are we going to be married?" He: "Yes, sweetheart, we'll get married right away." The patient also heard him tell her how to comb her hair, what dress to wear, and what to eat.

In this instance, the postponed marriage was evaluated by the woman as a threatening catastrophe, depriving her of hoped-for help and dependence, and rescue from her state of helplessness and abandonment. She felt an undercurrent resentment toward and conflict with her fiancé because of this blow. As a way out of her conflict and the threatening catastrophe, she developed this rela-tively manic reaction which contained the wish-fulfilling delusion that they were being married immediately.

This patient did not lack insight entirely in this interview. As long as she was permitted to talk about her delusion and to hallu-cinate freely she seemed happy. But when the psychiatrist asked her: "Are you feeling entirely well?" or "Don't you think you are dis-turbed?" an expression of alarm came over her face and she said: "Am I going mad?" "Am I hallucinating?" After the analyst told her that she was not well and that she needed rest and treatment, she became alarmed and had to lie down because she was faint. When he advised her to go back to her family, which she had just left, she was reluctant, but her fiancé prevailed on her to do so. Following the interview with the analyst, the woman lost her delu-sions and hallucinations; she remained tense and disturbed, but she was able to return to and continue her work. Under treatment by another psychiatrist she emerged from her condition without losing her job.

This case affords a rare type of observation. Because of the mild character of the reaction, the immediate treatment, and the understanding cooperation of everyone concerned, the condition could be controlled from the start. The degree of insight that this patient still showed is rare in fully developed reactions, but disturbing and contradictory flashes of insight can be observed in any case of relatively mild severity.

Mixed States.—The variation in the predominant symptoms presented by different patients has been mentioned in connection with both the depressive and the manic reaction. In some instances the symptoms are mixed. These mixed states are particularly frequent when a manic reaction changes into a depressive reaction, or vice versa, without an intervening period of relative well-being. In "maniacal stupor," for example, the patient has a blissful expression; and, as he says later, he has flights of ideas and delusions but he does not speak or react to stimuli. Other patients may be depressed and have flights of ideas, or be depressed and agitated, over-active, irritable. Psychodynamically, such patients have not succeeded in adopting either form of solution for their conflicts but are employing conflicting measures.

Treatment of Manic Reactions.—Mild cases may be treated at home if adequate understanding and supervision can be obtained. Unless this is provided, the patient may damage his self-interest or get into any of many difficulties. The handling of the manic patient requires a combination of understanding, kindness, patience, and firmness; but any attempt to "talk him out of his problems" has a bad effect. He should be given adequate nourishment and should be urged to eat and drink. Prolonged baths have a soothing effect. In relatively mild cases occupational therapy is valuable because it guides the patient's activity into some organized and constructive channel. The activity may be one which the patient already likes, or it may be new to him. Participating in a dramatic performance, for example, is helpful because it satisfies his desire and need for activity, and he is willing to accept constructive suggestions and criticisms for the sake of the organized group goal. In more serious conditions, but to some extent in mild ones also, hypnotics and continuous baths are necessary to quiet the patient; temporary restraint may also be required.

Discussion of the patient's difficulties, even if the conversation only touches on distressing topics, has no value in a reaction of any intensity. This type of therapy, however, is useful when the condition begins to subside or after it has ceased. Psychoanalysis can be used successfully only after the manic reaction has disappeared.

Involutional Melancholia

The term involutional melancholia refers to the period of bodily and often intellectual decline in later life. The word decline is not necessarily limited to an actual, realistic decline; it includes also the individual's evaluation of his life situation at a certain time. For example, he may suddenly feel that something he had hoped for up to that time will never be attained; or he may feel that everything is lost when some attribute or function which is extremely valuable to him declines. Likewise, he may have been handling certain difficulties in his existence more or less successfully; but when these functions decline, the additional burden and the blow break his endurance.

This involutional period is usually considered to be from 40 to 55 years in women and from 60 to 65 years in men. Thus, in general, in women it coincides more or less with the appearance of the menopause which is often accompanied by various discomforts, such as hot flushes, headaches, periods of dizziness, fatigability, excessive perspiration.

Menopausal Depression.—Mild depression in women during the menopause is not infrequent, but it is not psychotic as a rule and is relatively easy to treat. The patient feels sad, has weeping spells, and may be irritable; but she is able to go about her work, laughs at jokes, and appears reasonably happy, in spite of her suffering. The depression here is caused not alone by a decrease in follicular hormone secretion but by a combination of this with psychological factors.

This hormone is a chemical substance secreted in certain quantities by the ovaries in the mature woman. The amount secreted begins to decline when the menopause occurs. The resulting glandular imbalance is initially responsible for the menopausal symptoms. Psychotherapy and the administration of follicular hormone are effective in this type of depression.

Characteristic Symptoms.—Severe depressive reactions which occur during the involutional period in people who have never previously had a psychotic episode are best grouped under involutional melancholia. The characteristic symptoms are:

Depression with agitation and anxiety but without retardation.—These patients are not retarded or slow in their thinking or responses, but they may be difficult to converse with. They feel depressed and worthless, are self-accusatory, and give the appearance of great misery. They are extremely anxious and expect something dreadful to be done to them. Similar thoughts are frequent in severe depressions at any time of life; but in the involutional period they are accompanied by great anxiety. In talking with the psychiatrist, the patient may at first want to say something; but he becomes anxious and agitated, wrings his hands, says nothing or gives an evasive answer, or just says that everything is lost, or asks, "Are they going to hurt me?" or repeats continually "Oh my God!"

Feeling of unreality.—The patient has the distressing feeling that neither he nor anything around him is quite real. He recognizes objects and can name them accurately, but he feels a peculiar distance between himself and them. According to him, both his perceptions and his feelings lack something.

Hypochondriacal or nihilistic delusions.—These patients may say that they have changed; that their tongues are gone, their brains are going; that they are all dried up; that they suffer from cancer or syphilis; that their relatives are dead.

They may also have feelings of unworthiness, suspicions, and delusions of sin, guilt, and persecution. A particularly good example of the statements made by this type of patient is the following:

"The beauty of the earth and the glory of the sky do not now exist; the seasons are not the seasons of yesteryear; the flowers, the trees and the birds are not raised in the glory of old time; people display only repulsiveness, deceit and all forms of wickedness. All, all is gone; those days are bygone splendor, and things can never be changed; body, soul and spirit have been altered until I have become a weariness to myself. . . . The beautiful furniture; the beautiful needlework—clean and beautiful people—think of them all, all buried: these things are literally under the earth. That is all over; all is gone, absolutely, and here am I. I wish I had never seen the world, and now I have ruined it."[1]

The physical symptoms during the period of depression are in general the same as those present in the depressive reaction, except for the additional symptoms, particularly those of the menopause, characteristic of the period of involution.

Psychodynamics of Involutional Melancholia.—Psycho-dynamically, the general features of involutional melancholia are like those in depression. There is, however, an additional factor, in that the feeling of inadequacy and worthlessness is based on physiological decline and all that this means to the patient. Thus, the woman may consider that all her attractiveness disappears with menopause. Her attractiveness may in itself have had for her a very significant supporting and reinforcing value against all sorts of feelings of helplessness and expectations of rejection. With this supportive aspect gone, she considers herself worthless, helpless, and about to be rejected. Any difficulties in her relationship with other individuals become tremendous dangers. The presence of strong hypochondriacal and nihilistic delusions is probably due to the involutional background, for they represent an exaggeration of actual physiological decline. The patient may evaluate this decline in itself as a threat and retribution and injury on the part of those on whom

[1] D. K. Henderson and R. D. Gillespie *A Textbook of Psychiatry*, Oxford University Press, London, 5th ed., 1940, pp. 184-185.

she is dependent and toward whom she is hostile; this explains the strong anxiety.

The treatment of involutional melancholia is essentially like that of other depressive reactions, with, in addition, administration of the lacking hormone.

SUGGESTED READINGS

The treatment of the psychoses in this and following chapters should be compared with those in any standard textbook of psychiatry. Any of the following is recommended: Rosanoff (651), Henderson and Gillespie (340), Jelliffe and White (400), Henry (343), Bleuler (90), White (785), Muncie (581).

Shorter treatments may be found in textbooks of abnormal psychology, such as Conklin (142), Dorcus and Shaffer (193), Fisher (241), and Morgan (574).

A specific reference is Freud's paper on mourning and melancholia in his *Collected Papers* (273). A popular autobiographical account is *A Mind Restored* by Elsa Krauch.

For fundamental concepts, see A. Meyer (548-554) and Sullivan's article in *Psychiatry*, 1938, 1, 121-134.

CHAPTER XXVIII

SCHIZOPHRENIC REACTIONS

~~~~~~

The "Schizoid" Personality.—The type of individual who, under adequate stress, most frequently develops a schizophrenic reaction is the so-called "shut-in" person. These people are disinclined to seek other individuals; they are bad mixers; when they do make friends, they do not form intimate or close friendships. They often have queer habits, are apt to behave in a silly manner and to consider themselves superior to others in a grandiose way. They often show a peculiar lack of appreciation and evaluation of other people's reactions, particularly in connection with social customs. This trait, together with an impulsive urge to make decisions without conscious emotions, may appear in situations which are of extreme importance for the patient, as when a man faced by a difficult situation says nothing to his wife or his close relatives and leaves home without much conscious emotion. Sometimes there is a continuous tenseness in the person who in general is inclined to be "shut in." When he is with other people his manner is intense, loud, and awkward, not in harmony with the emotional requirements of the situation. These same patients often have an odd way of thinking; for example, they may approach relatively simple problems in an involved philosophical way. There are other characteristics and varieties of "shut in" or schizoid personality. It should be remembered, however, that occasionally individuals develop schizophrenic reactions, regardless of personality type.

Symptoms of Schizophrenic Reactions.—The symptoms of schizophrenic reactions vary considerably, "queerness" of emo-

471

tional thought and behavior processes being the most common feature. By "queerness" is meant the fact that the examiner and the normal individual find it difficult to feel themselves into the manifestations or to sympathize with them, whereas this is very easy in manic-depressive reactions. The symptoms may appear at any time of life, but they are most common between fifteen and twenty-five years of age. The condition may persist, although with fluctuations, throughout the individual's life and usually terminates in a complete deterioration of the intellectual and emotional faculties. However, any form of schizophrenic reaction may end in a social and occupational recovery.

The symptoms usually include: (1) An emotional dulling, with absence of adequate emotional response by the patient to either the situation or his own thoughts. If there is emotional excitement, it is rigid and preoccupied, without keen and adequate contact with the external world. (2) Bizarre thinking which manifests itself in (3) delusions, preoccupation with curious inventions, plans, and mechanical devices. (4) Frequent obscene hallucinations. (5) Rigid behavior, with a silly fixed smile, stereotyped movements, negativism, or automaton-like behavior. (6) Radical alteration of speech, including the coining of new words, rambling, monosyllables, nonsensical utterances. These will now be discussed in detail.

Emotional alterations.—Alterations in emotional responses may be manifest in several ways. In emotional dulling, the patient does not consciously manifest or experience keen and adequate emotions. He is apathetic, dreamy, or indifferent, and does not seem to comprehend joy, sorrow, or fear. He may speak of a death or great disaster or of being a genius or a great inventor without any show of sorrow, excitement, or pleasure. There is "lack of contact" with people around him.

The patient's emotional responses, when they do occur, have more the nature of a general excitement than a specific quality of emotion. When the patient talks loudly and vehemently and is comparatively silent and preoccupied by turns, it is difficult to determine properly the quality of this emotional response. The most common response to be identified is fear, even amounting to panic, resulting from anticipated harm by persecutors. Here too, however, the excitement is more in the foreground than the fear; at times it has a strong self-aggrandizing tone. Suspiciousness is another mode of behavior that the patient may both experience and show. But generally the emotions seem to be undifferentiated, to "run one into the other." It is easy to say of a normal person that he is afraid *or* joyous *or* angry; of the schizophrenic, one can say only that he is excited or emotional-in-general.

Bizarre thinking.—The patient may be preoccupied with his bodily processes, his thoughts being concerned with any organ in which he usually has some abnormal sensation. He has various explanations for these. If, for example, he has a feeling of discomfort in his spine, he may explain how masturbation or an infection in his nose is responsible for this complaint. He may be preoccupied with mechanical devices to cure this condition, or with a complicated drawing which graphically represents it. The perpetual motion machine has always held particular fascination for these patients. In all these thoughts and preoccupations such patients always deviate foolishly and persistently from the accepted thinking on such matters, nor can they be influenced concerning them.

Delusions.—Ideas of reference and of influence and delusions of persecution and of grandeur are common in schizophrenic reactions; they are not as fleeting and changeable as in manic-depressive psychosis.

Ideas of reference are present when the patient evaluates trivial occurrences as referring to him and implying something very significant. He may think that people are talking about him or laughing at him or dropping hints, or that they close the door in a certain way either to convey something to him or to express something in reference to him. If details are asked for, the patient's assumption is found to be entirely unsubstantiated, but he believes it just the same. Thus he may say that two people who passed him said that he had an immoral character. Investigation shows that he did not actually hear this remark, that he never saw the two individuals before, that they were not even looking at him when they passed. Nevertheless, he remains unshaken in his belief.

Ideas of influence are manifest when the patient says that someone puts thoughts into his head, that he influences his actions, that he causes him discomfort and pain by influencing the functioning of his organs. Often this influence is assumed to be exerted by complicated machines operated by electricity or some other means; patients often describe the influence as "hypnotic."

In delusions of persecution, the patient attributes many of these phenomena just mentioned to his "enemies." One of the best means of securing information about delusions of persecution or ideas or reference or influence is to ask the patient if he has any enemies; this usually elicits a vivid account of at least one enemy, usually many. He may believe that "secret police" are after him, or attribute his troubles to a lawyer or a physician. He may believe that poisonous gas is being released in his room or that poison is being placed in his food. Such patients often think that they are being followed or that their enemies have immoral intentions.

Delusions of grandeur, in the form of mild statements indicating a belief in the possession of remarkable qualities, can almost always be elicited from patients suffering from schizophrenic reactions. At times this consists only of an answer to this effect; the patients cannot name these qualities. Other patients, either spontaneously or on direct questioning, say that they can influence others, that they can send secret messages, that they are great thinkers or inventors who will be called up to assist in a national crisis, or that they are already serving in this capacity. They also claim to be of royal blood, or, depending on their sex, to be Napoleon or Jesus Christ or the Virgin Mary.

These statements are not accompanied by an adequate emotional response. There are fleeting disturbances in the patient—i.e., he is reluctant to answer, or evasive—but he does not evidence joy over his invention or great deed or wonderful quality.

These thoughts and convictions and experiences are not systematized or worked out consistently by the schizophrenic patient. Contradictory and fragmentary thoughts exist side by side. Thus the patient may accuse a lawyer or a relative of being responsible for his troubles, but be unable to give a systematized answer as to how or why. A woman may protest insistently against persecution by a certain man, but upon seeing him smile, say that his voice speaks of love, and announce her engagement to him. The patient may announce himself as the king of England and at the same time agree to work in the laundry. Contradictions of this sort, indicating conflicting attitudes, have often been referred to as ambivalence, implying rejection and acceptance, love and hatred at the same time. It should be emphasized again, however, that while the patient's ideas, thoughts, and experiences are largely incoherent, they persist in their vague form week after week and month after month.

Hallucinations.—Hallucinations are most frequently of the auditory type. The patient may hear the voice of the same person or of several persons. This voice may belong to someone he knows, or he may attribute it to an unseen enemy or to secret police or to God. The content of the hallucinations varies, but in general it is of the following types: (a) Obscene words: The patient is called sexually immoral, a pervert, a street woman, etc. These hallucinations are particularly malignant and are most characteristic of schizophrenia. (b) Statements about what the patient is doing at the moment: "Now he is eating," "Now he takes the spoon." (c) Command: The voices tell the patient what to do. The commands may vary and the patient may or may not execute them. Thus he may be commanded to throw furniture out of the window or hurl a stone into a show window or follow a woman and propose to her. (d) Messages from secret organizations or religious bodies or God: The contents are usually of the type, "You will redeem mankind," "Yea, we shall relish thee," "You are my prophet," etc.

Hallucinations of taste and smell are next in frequency. The patient says that the food has a curious taste and believes that there is poison or vermin in it. He smells a peculiar odor and attributes it to poisonous gases released in the room by his enemies. In hallucinations of touch and pain, the patient has unpleasant sensations in various organs and may be convinced that he has been sexually assaulted. The patient suffering from visual hallucinations may see objects change in shape, or see fiery crosses or God or the saints.

Changes in behavior and actions.—The patient's posture is often rigid and constrained. His facial expression is vacant and lacks mobility. He does not look at the examiner while they are talking. A silly smile is extremely frequent in schizophrenia, as are also facial grimaces recurring in a stereotyped fashion, sniffing or snorting, short repeated coughs, spitting movements. Stereotyped movements are apparent in other parts of the body; these consist of rubbing the hands or legs, twisting the hair, etc. In waxy flexibility the patient's body retains whatever posture the examiner puts it in; thus the arm remains lifted for long periods of time without apparent fatigue. In negativism, the patient does not carry out commands, and he resists any part of his body being moved. Unchanging, and at times strained, posture may be maintained. The patient may lie motionless without eating or attending to his wants for long periods, even years. He may assume a peculiar posture—for example, the intra-uterine position of the foetus—and retain it for a long time; if it is disturbed he resumes it again. The patient may become actively absorbed in his hallucinations; he looks intently at one spot as if seeing something, listens intently to his "voices," moves his lips, or makes signs with his hands. He may make compulsive assaults on other individuals whom he considers his persecutors, or make sexual attacks or display exhibitionism.

Changes in speech.—Some change in the speech is always present in schizophrenia. At times it consists of a lack of proper inflections leading to monotonous speech; less frequently, the speech becomes vehement and the patient talks animatedly about his troubles. In evasiveness, the patient does not answer the question, but makes a statement about something else; for example, "How did you get along with your mother?" "I ate various things at home," or "My mother bought some furniture and it was spoiled." The speech may ramble; that is, the patient talks freely but he does not follow the topic and one sentence merges into another. In monosyllabic speech, he answers only yes or no; he may answer such questions as "What day is today?" but he does not respond spontaneously to such questions as "What are your complaints?" In mutism, the patient does not speak at all; in echolalia he repeats like an echo whatever the examiner says; for example, "What day is it today?" "Today." The statements may be incoherent. Even if they form clear sentences they show no coherence and are often unconnected. The speech shows other remarkable alterations which are the result of the peculiar emotional and thought processes characteristic of schizophrenia. The sentence structure is often shattered to the point of a sentence consisting of a sequence of apparently unconnected words: "The nail file on the wall, the radio said, a green came out on the wall, gosh." New words are coined. These neologisms often consist of the condensation of two or more words, and if the patient is willing he can explain them. Thus a patient who used the word "gacidcator" said that it was the name of a chemical he had invented to dry out gas in the acid in the stomach (gas, acid, desiccator). The patient may invent a complicated language which can be deciphered with adequate analysis.

Certain physical symptoms may be present. Patients are frequently undernourished, and they usually lose weight because of their disturbed appetite and reluctance or refusal to eat. The blood pressure may be low, and the extremities and nose and ears be bluish and cold and clammy. Pupillary reactions may be disturbed. Under normal circumstances, the pupils dilate in response to pain; in schizophrenia this reaction may be absent. The basal metabolic rate is lowered, the diminution ranging around —12 per cent. Whether this indicates a primary disturbance of the metabolism or is the result of poor nourishment and an inactive life is questionable. In women, the menstrual flow may be decreased or disappear.[1]

Varieties of Schizophrenic Reactions.—Four varieties of schizophrenic reactions are usually differentiated. However, these should not be considered fixed, because one patient may have certain features of various reactions, or the dominant reaction may vary from one kind to the other in any patient.

Simple schizophrenic reaction.—The patient becomes disinterested and apathetic. He wants to be alone, neglects his work, and does not participate in any activities. He becomes dull emotionally and loses his ambition; depending on the environment, he may become a hobo. The patient may be somewhat irritable and moody; he is unable to sustain attention and may become evasive and monosyllabic in his conversation. He is apt to sit in the same place with no facial expression or a foolish smile. At this stage the patient is still oriented for place and time and there is no serious intellectual impairment; if his condition receives attention, it may develop no further and he may recover. In other cases the condition progresses, and, as the years pass, the patient becomes completely apathetic and deteriorates intellectually to the moronic level. In this type of schizophrenic reaction there are almost no hallucinations and no delusions.

Paranoid schizophrenic reaction.—The dominant symptoms of the paranoid reaction are ideas of reference and influence, delusions of persecution and often of grandeur. There are

---

[1] A considerable amount of investigation has been made on the various organs of schizophrenic patients. Some investigators (Mott, Gibbs, and Lewis) found changes in the various endocrine glands and in the brain tissue, but others (Morse, Lewin) were unable to substantiate these findings.

usually vivid auditory hallucinations and often hallucinations of smell and taste.

The patient becomes moody, preoccupied, and suspicious. His life becomes disorganized; he does not continue his work; he gets into trouble with other individuals whom he accuses of persecuting him. He may withdraw; he may want to stay in bed to avoid exposing himself to danger, and he may refuse to eat to escape being poisoned. The patient may commit a violent act, such as breaking up the furniture, at the command of a "voice." His speech may be voluble, excited, rambling, and even incoherent.

Patients of this type require hospitalization. The condition may fluctuate; that is, the patient may eat, speak, and behave better, and recover at least socially and occupationally. But there is no adequate insight; he remains evasive if asked about his illness, or he may deny that he has ever had hallucinations and delusions. Frequently, however, the condition continues throughout life and may end in a complete deterioration of the emotional and intellectual capacities.

Catatonic schizophrenic reaction.—The catatonic reaction may be preceded by symptoms of simple or paranoid schizophrenic reactions, but in some cases it is present almost from the beginning. The symptoms are usually described as a fluctuation between depression, excitement, and stupor.

After a period of apathy or queer behavior the patient may sit idly in one position or remain in bed in a peculiar posture; he does not speak or eat, and does not react to painful stimuli. He either is incontinent as far as excreta are concerned, or retains them completely. The patient may lie with his eyes open without blinking for hours or days. There may also be waxy flexibility or negativism. This condition is called "stupor." The patient is not unconscious; he is able to notice everything that goes on around him even though he does not participate in it. If the patient is not in a condition of stupor, more moderate disturbances of initiative and responsiveness may be present. The patient then may sit idly, may be willing to go to the table if led, and to eat if the food is offered him. He may not answer questions, but he may make stereotyped irrelevant utterances, such as repeating "I could not say, I could not say," or making up a list of unrelated names. Stereotyped actions may be prominent together with mannerisms—the patient may make the same motions with his hands continuously, he may walk in the same peculiar way, there may be echopraxia (imitation of the actions of the examiner) and echolalia.

The patient's experiences in this stuporous condition are very vivid and often on a cosmic scale. Thus a patient stated that a gigantic struggle was going on in the universe between good and evil and that he was the battleground. The forces of good and evil were so equally balanced that any movement on his part might have decided the struggle one way or another. He was afraid to make the wrong move, hence he lay still. In this stuporous state the patients often hallucinate, have delusions of persecution and of grandeur.

The patient sometimes suddenly emerges from the catatonic stuporous state with a violent, frenzied excitement. He may talk excitedly and incoherently, engage in excited activities, impulsively attack and attempt to kill another person, or mutilate himself or commit suicide.

After a paranoid period, a patient became stuporous. His family, particularly his mother, refused to send him to a hospital. After a few days of being in this stuporous state he suddenly got up, struck his mother unconscious with a chair, got dressed, turned on the gas, and left the house. His father came home in time, and the mother, although her skull was fractured, recovered. The patient himself, after other violent acts in the street, was taken to a psychopathic hospital.

The catatonic excitement may last from a few hours to several days, after which the patient may lapse back into a stuporous state. In their excited state patients frequently have hallucinations, and the violent acts that they commit are often a command from their "voices." They may also have delusions of persecution, and they often hear the voice of God.

The pupillary disturbances mentioned above and the cold, clammy, bluish extremities, nose, and ears are most common in this reaction.[1]

The schizophrenic reaction type in which catatonic features predominate may end in social and occupational recovery even after many years of illness; but they may also end in an emotional and intellectual deterioration.

Hebephrenic schizophrenic reaction.—It is customary to differentiate the hebephrenic reaction also, although most of its characteristic features are present in the other three types. The difference lies in greater emphasis on the incoherence of thought, queer impulsive conduct, sudden weeping and laughter without adequate cause, and lively hallucinations. In addition, there are usually shallowness of affect, delusions of persecution or grandeur, catatonic features and mannerisms—all usually summed up under the term "hebephrenic silliness."

Psychodynamics of Schizophrenia.—Even though one of the most characteristic features of schizophrenic reactions is the alteration in emotions—the dulling or the unjustified excitement —it must not be assumed that the patient lacks an emotional life. It is more correct to say that his emotional reactions are so intense, so painful, and so fraught with danger that he represses them. This repression is so intense that it affects all his emotional processes in reference both to himself and to his environment. The world is so full of danger and pain for him that he withdraws from it emotionally. Withdrawal from the world is particularly marked in catatonic stupor. The "senseless" laughter and weeping are his complicated attempts both to react and at the same time to refrain from reacting to something emotionally.

---

[1] Some stuporous patients become suddenly alert, communicative, and coherent if they are given a mixture of 40 per cent carbon dioxide and 60 per cent oxygen to inhale. They are roused and behave essentially normally for about fifteen minutes (Lorenz and Levenhart). This phenomenon is not entirely clear.

At times, because he thereby turns something desperate into a joke, his laughter is supercilious and superior, not laughter at something humorous, at something he enjoys. The vehement excitement occurs when the patient's pain, anxiety, and anger get the better of him. This is his reaction to conflicting experiences from which he tries to escape by apathy and emotional blunting. Hence his excitement too lacks the essential quality of realness and contact with reality. Similar defensive measures, together with conflicting attitudes, are responsible for the fragmentation, the illogicality and inconsistency of his emotions. In all these phenomena the patient attempts to deprive his reactions of poignancy, of consistency, of meaning, because if he did not, it would be catastrophic.

There is still another aspect to the psychodynamics of withdrawal. A patient always, to a varying degree, shows a definite self-centering of interest: "The world for me is full of danger and disappointment, pain and catastrophe. I will withdraw from all this and get consolation, pleasure, and safety from my own excellence." This attitude is particularly manifest in the patient's grandiose trends.

Several other processes can be identified in a schizophrenic reaction. The evaluation of reality, as regards both social customs and perceptions, is disturbed partly because of the phenomena just discussed; but in addition the patient seems to follow a formula which implies: "Reality does not matter; only what I desire matters." This results in the absence of shame and the disregard of restrictions common to normal human beings. These phenomena in themselves—exhibitionism, lack of sexual control —also represent the patient's attempts to derive gratification and strength from substitute sources. The delusions of grandeur necessitate an altering of reality, for otherwise they could not occur or serve their purpose.

Finally, these symptoms also represent a good deal of discouragement and feeling of defeat. This probably explains the frequent apathy.

Treatment.—Schizophrenia, of course, is a complex set of

psychotic reactions, but it represents, by and large, the individual's attitudes and his manner of coping with the world and with himself. Much can be accomplished if a schizoid personality is recognized early and given adequate attention. These people should be examined and the situations of stress to which they are reacting should be determined; the latter usually concern relationships with their own family. They should be encouraged to make contact with others of their age, to join clubs, to participate in activities.

Mild cases of schizophrenic reactions can be treated at home. Even though these patients are inclined to be withdrawn, are emotionally dull to some extent, are suspicious, and have mild ideas of reference, mild delusions of persecution and even some hallucinations, they are often able to continue at work, particularly if they are employed by a friend or relative. Some emotional contact with the psychiatrist can be established in weekly or bi-weekly visits, each lasting about an hour, during which their complaints are discussed and suggestions are offered on how to spend their free time. It is useless to try to convince such a patient that his ideas or delusions are false, for he takes this as a sign of a lack of understanding or as an insult. The psychiatrist should talk with some members of the family in order to make them understand the patient's difficulties. The patient himself should not be relied upon, at least not in the beginning, for information as to the sources of his distress because he has not strength enough to face his conflicts openly. Gross situations of stress should be ascertained from his family and corrected. Usually, after a few months of treatment, a patient loses his ideas of reference and delusions of persecutions, stops hearing voices, and gains some insight because he attributes his previous ideas to an "upset."

More severe cases of schizophrenic reaction require hospitalization. Often the hospital acts merely as a custodian; that is, the patients are cared for and are prevented from getting into trouble. Special cases necessitate special measures, such as permanent baths for excited patients. The more attention patients receive, the less frequently do they go into catatonic stupors, and the shorter the stupor is.

Various methods which have been developed recently use chemical substances to hasten the recovery of the patient. Insulin injections (Sakel [654]) and metrazol are used for this purpose. Apparently their value lies chiefly in the fact that they produce shock in the patient. Although no one knows yet why shock should have curative effects, probably the best hypothesis is that the feeling of threat of death reported by patients is in some way concerned (686, 426, 631, 632).

Occupational therapy is of value for patients who have improved sufficiently or are in a relatively mild phase. Some patients can do simple repetitious work well. Even if they are not able to leave the hospital, at least they feel useful and are happier.

Some schizophrenic patients can tolerate psychiatric treatment if it is given after they have shown a certain amount of improvement. Psychoanalysis has been successful with only a small percentage of cases confined in a psychopathic hospital (811, 21). It can be used with extreme caution with borderline cases—patients with schizoid personalities—in their usual surroundings.

The following case history describes a predominantly hebephrenic patient:

"P. R., a young girl 20 years old, who had been employed as a nurse, was admitted in a restless, agitated state, but a few minutes later she was smiling and happy. These phases rapidly alternated, even in the course of a few minutes. It was difficult to get her to cooperate in a satisfactory examination; she spoke in a simple, childish way, said that she wished someone would do an operation to her head and make her better. She told how she had worked in various hospitals, but had not been able to continue steadily at her job, because she seemed always to be working in a maze. Perhaps the question and answer method brings out certain points better than a mere description.

" 'You were at a fever hospital?' 'Yes, just a few weeks.'

" 'Why did you leave?' 'I am not sure.'

" 'Do you hear voices?' 'No, yes, very seldom. I seem to be going sort of dead.'

"Later she admitted that she did hear voices, and that they terrified her dreadfully.

"She was able to do simple calculations correctly, and answered some questions on general information correctly; but her diffuseness and inconsequent talk can be gathered from the following:

" 'Who discovered America?' 'Well, I think it was a Murray. I had an old Aunt Sally who died and an old brother went to Hudson Bay.'

"She behaved in a disturbed, excitable way, and made such a noise that she had to be removed to a room by herself. While there she promptly smashed several panes of glass. Her impulsive, violent conduct continued at intervals. She refused food, so that for a time it was necessary to tube-feed her. Still later she deliberately poked her fingers into her eyes, and caused a certain degree of conjunctival hemorrhage.

"During her residence in the hospital she has continued to be hallucinated, and talks freely about her experiences. She says that voices tell her things have been done to her during the night. During the day also she hallucinates, and often she sits gazing at the ceiling in an ecstatic way.

"Gradually her impulsiveness subsided; she began to look after her appearance, to help the nurses in the ward, but often she would have outbursts of weeping with no apparent cause. She was asked about this time why it was that she frequently sat with her eyes tightly shut, and would open them only for a moment or two at a time. She explained that when her eyes were wide open the doctor, or the sister in charge of the ward, or the nurses, saw what she was seeing, and that they were therefore seeing through her eyes, and to prevent this she shut her eyes. She also explained that she had two voices; the one which was speaking she called her 'top voice,' and what she said with the 'top voice' was true; but there was a second voice, an 'under-voice,' which she apparently believed or felt was what her auditors at times heard replacing the true 'top voice.' Consequently we were getting false ideas by believing this second voice. She also expressed the idea that the doctors and nurses used her as a 'medium' to affect the others. She held up the three middle fingers of her hand to illustrate the idea clearly to us; pointed out the first outside finger as representing the number 'six,' the finger in the middle was herself, and the other outside finger represented 'the others.'

"Her condition has become gradually worse. She wanders about in a restless, aimless way, and when the physician visits the ward she clutches him by the arm, and can only be detached with difficulty. Her thought-processes are blocked and her speech is incoherent, her sentences being composed of detached words and phrases which have no relationship to each other, except for an occasional superficial association.

" 'Losh, I don't know what it is. You see—she says—I don't know, I'm sure. There's Cinderella. There is a much better play than that. "I don't know," I said. He is an awful idiot. Oh dear God, I'm so stupid. That's putting two and two together—saying I really don't know—saying Cathie, and so I observe and—flowers. An orange, and shoe laces. The gabardine skirt. Pettigrew's and the jazz-band, with cream cakes. She says no. They like my hair bobbed, but I'm so stupid. Contrary Mary. Statues at Copland and Lye's. "Oh," I said, "yes, yes, yes." I'd go off to sleep immediately afterwards. I said, "I know quite well," "Nothing," I said. I forget all that I saw next. The next thing was—eh? The poor man's mad. They'll be chopping off our heads next, and—calenders tied with blue ribbons. Oh, dear God. Contrary Mary again. What period—that's right. I don't like acting the goat at all. A cream-sponge sandwich. My memory is so slow, that all I'm sure. It was caramels then and fruit cakes. Well, well, I said, I can't help it—I don't want to help it, and well, I don't care. Contrary Mary again, and says—Nurse Grant—dogs barking. What's the matter with me anyway? I'm so terribly stupid. I'm fed up with this place—that's all. Sago pudding. She looks pale and tired often, but not—I know that. (Sings) "Take me over there, drop me anywhere, Manchester, Birmingham, Leeds, Well I don't care." I should like to see my best girl—Mrs. Patrick, she says—"Though 'tis time for parting, that's it, Jean, and my tears are starting." I've got the Kruschen feeling.—Blue belts and medals—three eggs for tea. No that won't do. Oh, dear God, I'm so stupid. I won't see my way—white rabbits. "Back home in Tennessee"—that's the way it's spelt. Oh, I don't know what I am going to do now. It's all wrong. Dear God, I'm so silly. It's killing, isn't it? Cream cakes, French cakes and meringues. Flies, fleas, butterflies,' and so on.

"She has the idea that she is changed, and sometimes remarks, 'My face is changed.'

"The course of her illness has already been of five years' duration, and she is steadily going downhill.

"A sample of her letter-writing shows very well the incoherence and the tendency to repetition.

"Dear Sir,

"I have just had dinner. I ate my dinner the monkey and I feel better. change I. Nurse is always making the tea. Betsy's nurse.

> "Wearing for a cup of
tea.
> > "Bathing patient.
> > "(Ogalvie).
> > > "Your—
> > > > "I   j g u.
> > > "gins Druce,
> > > > "Yours
> > > > > "sincerely,
> > > > > > "P. R.

"Dear Dr. Hind,

"I am just that watea ahe bring me som gin snap & I u—a lobster — — — l a. the water's hot what a monkey goes with.

> > > "Y   I am
> > > "s incere.
> > > "Nurse Bruce
> > > > "gave
> > > > > "me two
> > > "snaps.

> > > > "Thursday.

"Caristic.

"Soc.

> "Sit up latest

"Ruby was away with it—Shorthand. So that I don't get a bath."[1]

[1] D. K. Henderson and R. D. Gillespie, *A Textbook of Psychiatry*, Oxford University Press, London, 5th ed., 1940, p. 222.

Paranoia

In a fully developed paranoic reaction, the patient's delusions are unshakable. They are well systematized and, if the patient's first premise is granted, highly logical. The patient stubbornly defends them and usually is lively emotionally when they are discussed. His emotions are usually even in tone—he may feel bitter or mistrustful or superior or antagonistic. The delusions may center around any topic, such as some problem which may arise in anyone's life, e.g., marital infidelity or mistreatment. The patient with this type of delusion often succeeds in enlisting even highly intelligent friends and acquaintances on his side, and they may be willing, at least for a while, to assist him legally in his attempts to secure "justice." Closer examination, however, brings out the following evidences of a disturbance: (1) The patient, in the course of the conversation, is either suspicious and uncommunicative when the examiner talks on the topic, or unusually insistent in making and defending points. This becomes evident, of course, only after a period of discussion. (2) The patient is absolutely unwilling to consider any other possibility than the one he has in mind. (3) The evidence that the patient advances to justify his idea is often extremely slim and inconclusive.

A man who was jealous of his wife returned home from work one day and found that the dust was missing from one of the hooks on the clothes rack. He immediately concluded that a man's coat had been hanging there. From this he came to the conclusion that his wife had had a male visitor and had committed adultery.

Forms of Paranoia.—The development of the paranoic delusion is gradual; at first there are only suspicions, but these become more and more numerous, more and more systematized and unshakable. The following forms of paranoia can be differentiated on the basis of the main theme of the delusion: (1) Paranoia of jealousy, the most common form. The case above is an example. (2) Persecutory paranoia, in which the patient is convinced that someone is attempting to thwart him, harm him, and induce others to do likewise. (3) Erotomania, in which the patient, usually a woman, is convinced that someone is making sexual advances toward her. She puts this interpretation on all types of actions, and she may feel persecuted by this person for rejecting his advances. (4) Litigious paranoia, a comparatively rare condition. The patient may actually have been slightly wronged or have been denied something to which he felt entitled, such as a license. However, he expends an enormous amount of effort in getting justice, and appeals to higher and higher authorities; his efforts and the emotions involved are far in excess of the significance of the matter.

In all these delusions, the circle of accused individuals widens increasingly and involves higher and higher authorities. The topic of the delusions does not always remain confined to everyday topics, and "queerer" aspects may enter into them. Thus, a patient may accuse a physician of introducing germs into her sinuses when treating her, and at the same time of making sexual advances. Grandiose features, together with hallucinations, also occur.

Psychodynamics of Paranoia.—The most striking and consistent aspect of paranoia is projection. Reality is completely revalued on the basis of subjective reactions, but this alteration of reality has a unique aspect because, in contrast to schizophrenia, many other aspects of reality are retained. In fact, the sharp and consistent logic represents an attempt to prove the reality of the distortion. Furthermore, both the distortion of reality and the compensatory attempt to retain it are limited to a single theme and do not destroy the patient's general personality.

The formula for projection as stated by Freud is examplified by the following: "I don't love him; I hate him; I don't hate him; he hates me." These "projections" are made in order to escape intolerable self-condemnation and feelings of worthlessness because of repressed homosexuality.[1] There is always a

---

[1] Most theorists disagree with this hypothesis because it lays too little stress on the importance of severe inferiority feelings.

strong element of defensive hostility in paranoia; the patient feels threatened and therefore becomes hostile and ready to attack. Because of this and because of his clear logic and ability to plan, the patient may be very dangerous; he may carry out a carefully planned attempt on his "persecutor's" life.

The catastrophic hurt in paranoia may vary, but usually has three elements: rejection, very low self-esteem, and injury.

Before the onset of the paranoic reaction the patient has often succeeded in unconsciously satisfying a vital need, such as pride, aloofness, homosexuality, excessive erotic attachment. The paranoic reaction develops over conflicts or threats.

Treatment.—In the early stages of paranoia, careful interview therapy may be effective; the patient may lose his delusions and acquire insight into his sickness in the course of a few months. In more advanced cases, hospitalization is necessary; but here also a rapport between physician and patient is valuable. This can be established by the physician discussing understandingly with the patient his delusions and his evidence for them, but without questioning or challenging them. After a period, the physician raises some questions and suggests other possibilities. Eventually he attempts to convince the patient that his delusions are unfounded and wrong. This treatment, when accompanied by other institutional measures such as occupational therapy and a sheltered environment, is sometimes effective. In some cases it is dangerous to discharge an advanced paranoic patient as cured, for he may simulate improvement but commit murder after his discharge.

These therapeutic measures should, of course, always be attempted; but the prognosis for paranoia is not good.

Case Illustrations of the Psychoses

The following case histories of the members of one family will show that:

1. The reaction patterns may be either a "clear type" or a

"mixture" of various psychotic and even neurotic types (Green-acre).

2. All the reaction patterns should be considered as the individual's responses to situations of stress and his attempts to cope with catastrophic expectations and conflicts.

3. Even if the occurrence of these reactions in the family is assumed to be suggestive of a hereditary predisposition, there still remains the question of the extent to which this is influenced by the parents' handling of the children. In any case, the breakdown is a response to situations of internal and external stress.

4. A patient with any form of manic-depressive or schizophrenic reaction may recover, at least in a social sense.

Several members of a family of Armenian extraction developed fairly severe psychopathological reactions. The mother suffered from manic-depressive reactions. The father was neurotic and had anxiety attacks. Of the four children in this family, the oldest had schizophrenic reactions with paranoid and catatonic features. Another had a mild schizoid reaction which could be treated at home. The third child had a compulsion neurosis with schizoid aspects. One daughter was free from serious disturbances.

The father, an engineer, was an active, enterprising man, conscientious in his work but very selfish and domineering at home. He had always earned enough to support his family, but he was stingy and dictatorial with his money as far as his family was concerned. For example, he insisted on giving his wife money from day to day instead of a weekly allowance. He sharply rebuked anyone who contradicted his views or opinions, often showing temper and raising his voice. He expected the utmost attention from his family when he had even mild ailments such as a cold or a cough; on such occasions he suffered attacks of anxiety. However, if other members of the family were ill, he would tell them not to give in to such weaknesses.

The mother as a rule was submissive to her husband; she never challenged any of his wishes or opinions, and tried to mediate between him and the children. She accepted, though with some inner rebellion, his reluctance to give her money and tried to save on every item. Her home was spotless and she took good care of her children, but was inclined to worry about them. She submitted to physical intimacies reluctantly. She had periods of over-activity about every two or three years, when she would sleep little and talk excessively. She would be busy rearranging the furniture, and receiving and visiting friends. During such periods she was excitable, and frequent altercations occurred between her and her husband. In the excitement she or her husband would break things, the whole family would be in a turmoil, and the children would try to separate the parents by taking sides. Most of her attacks lasted about six to eight months.

She had a few periods of depression which also lasted about six months but were less frequent than her periods of excitement. During such periods she looked sad, and did her work with difficulty. She was inclined to sit all day and she did little cleaning or cooking. She accused herself of being selfish, inconsiderate, and a sinner.

Her background was as follows: As a child in Armenia she had escaped several massacres. Her mother died when she was four years old, and her father remarried about a year later. Her stepmother made her do all the housework, always criticized her, and preferred her own children. The patient had her first attack of depression about the age of sixteen, before she was married. Her first period of excitement occurred about one year after her marriage, approximately a month following the birth of her first child. The patient's periods of depression were later determined chiefly by her anger toward her husband, her feeling of helplessness, self-condemnation, and guilt, and her fear of abandonment. The nuclear emotional constellation was first developed in her relationship with her stepmother and was later further elaborated in her relationship with her husband. Her period of excitement was chiefly one of rebellion against her husband, and of overriding her own conflicts, self-constraint, submissiveness, guilt, anxiety, and self-condemnation.

There were four children in the family; the age difference between the oldest and the youngest was 12 years. The oldest of the children, a girl, was 35 at the time of this report. She had developed a schizophrenic reaction with paranoid and catatonic features. During most of her life she had been inclined to keep to herself; she had few friends, and was sensitive and easily hurt. She did her school work moderately well, and was later steadily employed as a dressmaker. She derived some pleasure from her work and from books and movies, and she enjoyed the company of one of her sisters. When she was twenty-five years old she became even more withdrawn and started to behave queerly. She would refuse to eat some articles of food at home, and she would stand at the window making grimaces; she would listen attentively as if someone were speaking to her, and she made apparently senseless remarks. She soon quit her job because she was convinced that her fellow workers were talking about her and whispering indecent and obscene words. She then said that she would not eat at home because the food was being poisoned. She later said that there were lice in her clothes and that they were creeping into her body. She refused to leave the house and sometimes locked herself into her room for long periods. On one occasion she became excited, broke some furniture, and threw it out of the window. She said that the voice had told her to do so. As a result, she was sent to a psychopathic hospital.

This patient had a "shut-in" personality all her life. The immediate situation of stress to which she responded concerned a man. Mostly at the persuasion of a friend she started to go with a man who worked where she did. She liked his company and had thoughts of marriage, but never permitted any intimacy, not even a kiss. They quarreled, and she refused to go out with him again. He then became sarcastic and ostentatiously paid attention to other girls. All this coincided with one of her mother's periods of excitement and the resulting strife at home.

In the hospital she remained withdrawn and was occasionally excited. She was emotionally queer and unapproachable; her facial expression was unchanging, except for a recurring grimace and spitting motion. At times she refused to eat. She would not answer some questions, and gave evasive replies to others. When pressed for an answer, she sometimes became excited, and then she talked about lice and poison in the food and about voices calling her obscene names. On one occasion, she struck another patient who she said was making remarks about her. She also spoke of the secret police being after her and said that they were sending out radio messages about her. Often she imagined that she was Queen Esther and that God was talking to her. At times she refused to eat and would sit alone without moving. She showed waxy flexibility.

She remained in the hospital for eight years. Her condition fluctuated, but she gradually improved in her behavior. She remained evasive when asked about her delusions, but was able to leave the hospital and for the two years since has been getting along well.

Another sister, who had been married for five years, became considerably concerned about herself when her sister was sent to the psychopathic hospital. About this time she developed the persistent thought that there were lice in her clothes or in the furniture and that they were getting into her skin. She often had an uncomfortable sensation in her skin and she made slight "brushing" movements as if to get rid of the lice. In contrast to her sister, she realized that this was only a thought, and she tried to get rid of it, but could not. She could not use such articles as combs or purses because of this thought. She became tense and distressed emotionally, made frequent mistakes in her work, and was afraid that she would go insane. She showed genuine concern about herself and was easily persuaded to seek help.

The patient's complaints were of the obsessional neurotic reaction type, but the nature of her thoughts closely resembled that found in schizophrenic reactions. Thus, repeatedly during treatment she had reactions which were like mild delusions. For example, she once refrained from buying aspirin for a headache because she was convinced that the analyst would somehow get in touch with the druggist. In spite of this, careful psychoanalysis was possible with this patient. She recovered fully and has had no recurrence for six years.

Her sister's psychosis aroused this patient's fear that she too might suffer a breakdown. This fear was intensified by the fact that the father at first denied that the oldest daughter was sick. The patient resented this, and as a result had feelings of fear and retribution. In her difficulty she leaned on her husband for support. However, her husband, although tender and understanding in many respects and with many interests in common, was rather penurious and acted superior toward her. She responded to this with the feeling, "Not only does he not give me the help I need, but he even rejects me and humiliates me." Thus the patient was resentful and was again afraid of abandonment and retribution.

The next sister was essentially well. She was married and had two children at the time of the report.

The brother, a statistician, was 23 at the time of this report. He had begun to masturbate during puberty. He had some sexual thoughts about his sisters and about men, and he began to brood and to stay by himself more, but he did not break off friendships. When he was about eighteen, he began going out with a girl, but she put an end to this. Following this, his sexual thoughts about his sisters and about men increased; he considered himself degenerate and believed that people knew this and moved away from him in the train. Moreover, he thought that these troubles were the result of his masturbation, and he became preoccupied with various bodily sensations, and began to talk loudly and at great length on involved philosophical matters. He was dissatisfied with his job, but did nothing to improve his status. He himself did not want to go to a physician but one of his sisters, who was aware of his changed behavior, persuaded him to consult a psychiatrist.

The particular problems with which this man was struggling were the pressure of his sexual urge, his relationship with women, and, to a lesser extent, his career. Contact with individuals and, even more, with the opposite sex involves considerable self-assertion and self-confidence, at least enough to enable one to bear disappointment and hardships. This was impossible for this patient. Furthermore, his emotional conflicts made him view the socially tabooed sexual activity as dangerous and one in which he might inflict injury or be injured. His sexual thoughts about his sisters represented the reaching out of a helpless individual who could not look for satisfaction anywhere else. His homosexual thoughts, chiefly about his superiors in business, represented submissive reactions of a helpless person.

A reaction to one of the psychiatrist's comments illustrates the precarious state of the patient's adjustment, the caution and experience necessary in handling such patients, and the appearance of the manic response in the course of a predominantly schizophrenic reaction. After this man had shown considerable improvement, the psychiatrist said: "You have homosexual thoughts particularly in connection with your employer because you feel too much frightened, you lack self-confidence; you are really expressing by these thoughts: 'I want to submit to you without any reservation in order to have your good will.' " The next day the patient's mood was somewhat excited; he said that he felt remarkably well after the preceding day's session, and that for the first time in his life he had real self-confidence. He had decided, he said, that he would be submissive no longer, and that henceforth, when his employer asked him to do something objectionable he would refuse. During this interview the patient talked animatedly and much more voluminously than usual. Obviously he had reacted with a mild elation to the psychiatrist's remarks on the previous day, unconsciously following the formula: "The physician, who is all-powerful, said that I have the strength and that I can assert myself. I now have renewed powers in myself and I can cope with any situation." The intensity of the elation based on this excess of self-confidence was due to the pressure of helplessness and fear behind it. The self-confidence, as it were, over-rode the anxiety, and with it were freed the patient's anger, hostility, and aggression which previously he had not dared to release. If this reaction had proceeded further, he would have developed an open psychosis. The psychiatrist, realizing this danger, told the patient that although his increase in self-confidence was good, he was imprudent to try to do too much in a short time and that he must avoid disagreements in the office. The patient calmed down after these remarks and returned the next day in a quiet state, yet with a definite increase in his well-being and self-confidence. This he maintained in the course of further treatment, and made a satisfactory adjustment to the problems of his daily existence.

This patient would probably have developed a serious condition, had he not had his sister's interest and advice and had he not come for treatment early.

SUGGESTED READINGS

See readings at end of Chapter XXVII. More specific references which demonstrate promising leads in the study of schizophrenia are the papers by Cameron (126-128), Bolles (92), Hanfmann (327), Bender (64, 58), Jung (407), Devereux (177). On shock therapy see Sakel (669). On paranoia, read Freud's "Psychoanalytic notes on a case of paranoia" in his Collected Papers (273). An important paper by Schulte is translated in Ellis' *Source Book of Gestalt Psychology.*

CHAPTER XXIX

ORGANIC PSYCHOTIC REACTIONS

~~~~~~

The psychological phenomena in organic reactions are the results of a direct disturbance of the functioning of the brain and of the individual's reaction to this disturbance. Organic reactions may be acute or chronic. In many conditions both are combined; that is, there is chronic disturbance with occasional acute periods. Senility and hardening of the arteries of the brain, for example, are accompanied by chronic changes with acute periods intervening. In other reactions there are only acute disturbances. Fever as a rule causes only acute disturbances. Periods of mental clarity may intervene in all organic reactions.

The causes of organic psychotic reactions are numerous. Among them are deterioration of the brain substance because of hardening of the arteries due to age, infections of the brain such as syphilis or encephalitis; infections in other parts of the body which are accompanied by fever, such as pneumonia, inflammation of the joints, typhoid fever; toxic substances, such as alcohol, opium, illuminating gas, lead; growths on the brain; injury to the brain; vitamin and glandular deficiency.

The chief symptoms of organic reactions—the chronic in particular—are: (1) Impairment of intellectual functions: comprehension, orientation, memory for both recent and remote events, concentration. (2) Emotional instability: general irritability, laughter and weeping without adequate cause. (3) Changes in general conduct: carelessness in personal appearance, neglect of responsibilities, disturbance of morals. There are considerable individual variations, and one or another set of symptoms may predominate. The acute reaction resembles a delirium; the patient is disoriented, has illusions—i.e., misinterprets his perceptions, has difficulty in focusing his attention, hallucinates, and does not remember what has happened to him. He may be highly excited and have various emotions, particularly fear, or he may be emotionally dull. He cannot carry out certain functions or recognize objects adequately.

ARTERIOSCLEROTIC-SENILE REACTIONS

With advancing age the brain substance and its functioning usually deteriorate. Although a certain degree of intellectual and emotional decline is just as normal as the wrinkling of the skin, this decline may be more marked and certain additional symptoms may appear. These symptoms are due to (1) damage of the brain tissue itself, which is usually made worse by the hardening of its arteries and the consequent defective blood supply; (2) the individual's reactions to the damaged functions. The condition is often initiated by a stroke.

In arteriosclerosis of the brain after the age of forty the following symptoms are common: (1) Disturbed memory, particularly for recent events. The person who used to remember everything well cannot remember where he put his keys or his glasses; a business man who formerly remembered figures very well has to ask three or four times for them. (2) Difficulty in sustaining effort. The patient at first works actively at a task, then seems to tire, begins to make mistakes, and wanders away from it. (3) Emotional instability and irritability. These emotional traits may be manifest on many occasions, but they are particularly marked when the patient makes a mistake. There may be frequent outbursts of laughter or weeping without cause.

When arteriosclerosis occurs at a comparatively early age, attention to appearance, the desire to behave properly, moral values, and interest remain present for a relatively long time.

Simple Senile Deterioration.—Senile deterioration appears after the age of 60 or later. The chronic condition is marked by the following symptoms: The individual's range of interest grows smaller; he becomes self-centered and loses interest in other people, even his family. His thinking slows up, and he is inclined to be stubborn about his opinions and ways of existence, and he may be irritable. He tells the same stories over and over and spends most of his time in reminiscences. His memory becomes worse, particularly for recent events—he may even forget that someone in his immediate family has died recently. The failure to remember past events may be so complete that the patient will finally say that he is one day old. Patients with this condition frequently hide things—money or such useless articles as pencils, newspapers, etc. Their orientation as to place is impaired; they often wander around the hospital wards asking where their beds are. They are also disoriented for time, having no knowledge of the year, season, month, or day. As the condition proceeds, other symptoms frequently appear, such as paranoid attitudes and delusions. Patients accuse others, frequently close relatives, of being their enemies, and for this reason they often change their wills and disinherit their children. They often accuse others of stealing articles. More marked paranoid delusions together with hallucinations may appear. These patients will say that policemen are after them or that people are making immoral remarks about them. Their emotional states may likewise be seriously disturbed. They may be depressed, or grow extremely anxious and panicky in anticipation of something terrible such as being burned to death or cut to pieces. They may become very restless and be unable to sleep, wandering about day and night. They may become indecent, expose themselves, make sexual assaults on children. They may grow violent, particularly those who are jealous and paranoid. Chronic senile deterioration may have acute phases in which periods of delirium occur.

The physical symptoms are those of old age. Speech is slow, the handwriting shaky. The patients become incontinent and soil themselves. Some physical symptoms, such as convulsions, stroke, loss of speech, are caused by a sudden disturbance in the circulation of the brain, but these symptoms may be only temporary.

Treatment.—Patients with simple senile deterioration can be taken care of at home, as can also the patients with delirium except during the delirious period. Patients with lively hallucinations and delusions should be hospitalized because they are dangerous both to themselves and to those around them. Sleeplessness can often be combated by baths or hot drinks before retiring, but sometimes sedatives are required.

A 75-year-old man wandered away from home. He asked a policeman where he was, and the officer took him to a hospital. The patient's wife died while he was in the hospital, and his son came to take him to her funeral. Later when the patient was visiting a friend, he talked of his wife as if she were alive, and he talked about his experiences in the Spanish-American War, saying what a great hero he had been. He wandered away from home again and was taken to the hospital. He was completely disoriented as to both time and place. He was delirious and hallucinated himself as being in a workshop; at other times he became panicky because he saw an imaginary fire break out. He had no control over his bladder and bowels. He died in about three months.

GENERAL PARESIS (DEMENTIA PARALYTICA)

General paresis is caused by syphilitic damage to the brain tissue. However, it has been estimated that only about 2 per cent of the people who contract syphilis ever develop general paresis. The condition appears from five to twenty-five years after the syphilitic infection, and, unless treated, usually leads to death within a year and a half after the first symptoms appear. General paresis manifests itself in mental and emotional deterioration and in physical and biochemical changes. The disease usually begins gradually; but in some cases convulsions are the first symptoms.

Symptoms: Mental.—The mental symptoms are as follows: There are alterations in character. The patient becomes careless in his work or disinterested in his family or his appearance, or he starts to drink or commit petty thefts or expose himself. These changes usually occur in the early stages of the disease, in contrast to those in arteriosclerosis. The patient shows changes in emotional reactions, such as irritability, over-sentimental behavior, etc. There are disturbances in simple intellectual functions, such as memory and calculating. These likewise appear early and at first concern recent events. The patient forgets what he did even a few minutes earlier, and he makes mistakes in simple calculations, particularly if sustained effort is required. Lack of insight is present in some cases. Such patients are not aware of their condition, and do not realize that their habits have changed and that their functions are growing defective. Some patients, however, in the early stages of the disease are distressed by their disturbed memory, their declining efficiency, and their fatigability, and may seek medical advice in this connection.

As the condition progresses, other mental symptoms appear. The following classification is based on the predominance of one symptom over another; but the various groups are not sharply differentiated because the patient's symptoms may belong to one group at one time, and to another at a later time. (1) Dementia: The patient's intellectual faculties decline progressively. He is content with his lot; when asked how he feels, he may answer, "As well as a fish in water." If he is asked the names of the Presidents of the United States he may answer blandly, "I was never interested in politics." Demented patients may have grandiose but not luxuriant delusions. For example, a patient may repeat for days, "I am the best carpenter in the universe." This type of patient finally becomes completely unable to take care of himself; he becomes disoriented for time and place. (2) Depression: The patients are despondent and anxious. They have delusional ideas, such as that their bowels are completely stopped up, that their heart has been removed, that they are dead, or that they have no pulse. The patients may be so depressed that they become mute and stuporous and attempt to mutilate themselves or to commit suicide. Such attempts are usually unsuccessful because their mental deterioration makes any but foolish attempts impossible. (3) Expansiveness: The expansive patient has a feeling of great well-being, he over-evaluates himself, and has grandiose delusions. For example, one patient said that he was 200 years old, he weighed 400 pounds, he had a head of gold, he had 100 wives and a thousand million boys and girls, his urine was Rhine wine, his feces were gold (Kraepelin). Such patients claim superhuman qualities and remarkable strength; they say that they are giants, that they "broke the bank at Monte Carlo," that they own 500 houses in New York. Before they become obviously incapacitated, they may engage in commercial enterprises which ruin them financially. As they deteriorate more and more and become completely helpless, their grandiose ideas may disappear entirely or be manifest only by some phrase such as "millions of houses." (4) Agitation: Agitated patients are extremely restless and are engaged in some activity all the time. Their mood may be changeable—depressed or elated—and their thoughts may be grandiose or hypochondriacal or persecutory.

Physical symptoms.—In general paresis there are the following characteristic physical manifestations: (1) the pupils of the eyes do not react to light but may show the accommodation reaction. (2) The face has a characteristic appearance. The features are smoothed out, the expression is vacant, and the patient looks somewhat dissipated. This last is so characteristic that a correct diagnosis can sometimes be made simply by looking at the patient. (3) There are speech disturbances consisting particularly of slurring. This becomes evident when the patient repeats certain test phrases, such as "medical electricity," "truly rural," "Methodist Episcopal," "round the rugged rock the ragged rascal ran." (4) When the patient writes, the lines are tremulous, and syllables are omitted or transposed. (5) In rare cases the optic nerve atrophies. This nerve can be seen by looking through the pupil of the eyes with a special instrument. Under normal circumstances the nerve appears as a yellow disk where it enters the eye; if it is atrophied, it is white. (6) If locomotor ataxia is associated with general paresis, there is an absence of tendon reflexes, such as the knee jerk.

Biochemical symptoms.—Various tests and analyses have been devised to determine the presence of biochemical symptoms. (1) The Wassermann test, a complicated procedure, can be done on the blood serum and the spinal fluid. The fluid is obtained by means of a hollow needle which is inserted into the spinal canal between two lumbar vertebrae and through which about 5 or 10 cc. are withdrawn. In general paresis, the Wassermann test on the spinal fluid is positive in about 95 per cent of the cases, and on the blood serum in about 100 per cent. (2) The number of cells in the spinal fluid increases as the result of an irritation of the membranes lining the brain. The number of cells is determined by putting freshly drawn spinal fluid into a special counting chamber in which the cells are counted with a microscope. Normally, the spinal fluid contains up to 5 cells per cc.; more than 10 cells indicates an unquestionable increase. In general paresis, the increase may vary from 10 to 200 per cc. (3) An increase in the protein content of the spinal fluid is likewise due to inflammation of the membranes lining the brain. For this test, a saturated solution of ammonium sulphate is mixed with the spinal fluid. If the protein content has increased, the protein will precipitate and the mixture will become cloudy within three minutes. (4) Another method of testing for biochemical symptoms is the colloidal gold reaction. A solution of gold chloride is mixed with varying concentrations of spinal fluid. The solution itself is colorless; a change in color gives a positive test. The changes consist of various mixtures of red and blue.

Psychodynamics of General Paresis.—As has been said, some disturbances are attributable to the organic damage and some are due to the patient's reaction to this damage. The reaction itself may be correlated with the organic damage. For example, a patient may be irritated because of the organic damage, and he becomes more irritated when he makes mistakes (defensive hostility). The irritability which thus appears is more severe because of the organic damage.

In general paresis the most obvious damage is that to the memory. The patient reacts to this in various ways which are sometimes in harmony with his previous personality. The grandiose trends may partly represent an attempt to overcompensate for the failing functions and his consequent inferiority feelings. Depression may appear for similar reasons (damaged self-esteem). In other words, the patient who has previously felt worthless for many other reasons now feels even more worthless and self-condemnatory because of his failing function, and often evaluates this failure as a punishment or retribution for his previous sins and aggression or as a rejection by the world. In still other instances the pathological processes which have diminished the patient's judgment and inhibitions permit him to give a freer rein to his previously inhibited impulses.

Treatment.—Two great discoveries have made possible the successful treatment of paresis: (1) fever treatment, and (2) treatment with arsenical compounds.

Two methods are generally used to induce fever: infection with malaria, and short-wave apparatus.

In the malaria technique, blood obtained from a patient with malaria is injected either subcutaneously or directly into the blood stream of the paretic patient. Within three days to four weeks, if the injection is subcutaneous, or two to twenty days, if intravenous, the patient starts to have chills and fever; his temperature rises to about 104° F. After eight to twelve such attacks, the attacks are terminated by giving him quinine sulphate. The improvement ordinarily is rapid, but in some cases it appears only after some months. A second malarial treatment is usually given about one year after the first.

Fever can also be induced by short-wave apparatus. The patient's temperature is raised to about 104° F. and is kept at that level for about six hours.

In arsenical treatment of paresis, an arsenical called tryparsa-mide is injected into the blood stream once a week for eight weeks. The patient rests a few weeks, after which injections are resumed.

Statistical surveys show that both methods are about equally successful. From 30 to 35 per cent of the patients undergo a complete remission of symptoms which for practical purposes can be called a cure; that is, they are able to live their normal daily life. Approximately another 30 to 35 per cent improve but are unable to resume their former daily life. About 15 per cent show no improvement, and about 10 per cent die.

Two factors apparently are operative in the effectiveness of these two methods of treatment. The spirochetes are killed by the arsenical compound or by the high temperature incident to the fever. Certain defensive biochemical reactions are brought about by the fever or the compound which enable the patient to fight the infection better and to improve his general health. A combination of the two methods does not improve the chances of recovery to any extent.

A 55-year-old successful business woman had a sudden convulsion at about 5 A.M. which lasted about ten minutes. Careful physical examination a few hours later and the next day showed the follow-ing: The pupils of her eyes would not react to light but retained accommodation. She could not pronounce clearly such test phrases as "truly rural." At times her thinking was clear and she calculated correctly, but at other times she made mistakes about such simple matters as how much change the maid was to get if she gave her fifty cents and the maid bought some apples. Even after her attention was called to these mistakes, she did not realize them. She could not enumerate clearly the names of the Presidents of the United States during the last twenty years, although she had voted in each elec-tion. Her blood and spinal fluid gave positive test results on all the tests.

She had contracted syphilis when she was about 25 years old, and had been treated for it. However, her spinal fluid had never been examined, nor had she ever had any neurological examination. She was married and had three healthy children; neither her husband nor her children showed any syphilitic symptoms. This was due to the fact that by the time she married, her infection had become localized in the brain tissue and was not contagious.

She was given injections of tryparsamide. After the fifth one all her symptoms disappeared. In all, she received about 100 injections in the course of two years and a half. She remained at work and has been well for six years.

The patient, a moderately successful 45-year-old business man, first went to a physician with a friend to get a certificate for injuries sustained in an accident. He had crashed into another car and suffered a minor contusion of his arm. This friend told the physician that the accident was the patient's fault, and said that he often had to pull the emergency brake because the patient was apt not to stop for a red light. The physician examined the patient carefully and found that his pupils did not react to light; he also noticed that his speech was slurred. The patient himself told the physician that his memory was not as good as it used to be, and that he made mistakes in his work. The physician took a blood sample for testing, and told him to return later for the report; but he never came back.

About a month later he got into more trouble. He called a taxi, went to a restaurant, and had the cab wait while he ate. He left a check in the restaurant instead of cash. He then had the cab driver take him to various places; he told the driver that he had many friends with a lot of money. After three hours of driving, the driver asked for his money. This angered the patient and he struck the driver in the face. The latter called a policeman, and the patient was taken to jail, where he sang, told everyone about his rich friends, and said that his business was worth millions of dollars. The judge sent him to the hospital. He told everyone in the hospital that he felt excellent, better than ever before in his life, and told about his riches, that he had 300 houses and about 70 children.

The blood and spinal fluid tests were positive. He was given the malaria treatment. After several attacks he began to improve; he became quieter, and lost his delusions. He was discharged from the hospital after two months, and has been working since.

Encephalitis Lethargica (Sleeping Sickness)

Encephalitis lethargica, an epidemic disease, is an inflammation of the brain caused by an ultra-microscopic virus. The condition has acute and chronic forms. The acute phase is often first manifested by double vision and failure of the pupillary light reflex. Frequently there is somnolence or drowsiness, twitching of various muscles, and pain and rigidity of the neck muscles. The acute period may last a few weeks or many months, or it may be fatal. The chronic condition lasts a long time but does not endanger the patient's life. Sometimes it reappears after the patient has apparently been entirely well for a long period, even several years.

The Acute Stage.—The following mental symptoms may be present either singly or in combination, or one may be followed by its opposite at a later period. Lethargy, if present, is very characteristic. The patient is in a stuporous condition and appears to be sleeping all the time. For this reason the condition is called "sleeping sickness" or "encephalitis lethargica." This stupor, however, is unusual for if the patient is spoken to he wakes for a brief period and is able to answer questions clearly; then he quickly goes to sleep again. Insomnia may be severe and may appear before the lethargy. Emotional disturbances such as anxiety and agitation are common. The patient may suffer delirium with hallucinations.

The Chronic Stage.—The physical symptoms in the chronic stage consist mainly of so-called "Parkinsonianism." This is caused by the localization of the disease in the basal ganglia of the brain whereby the muscle tonus increases and rigidity results. There is a continuous shaking motion (coarse tremor) in all or some of the extremities. The facial expression is fixed and the skin is oily. Another symptom common to many cases in the chronic stage is the "oculo-gyric crisis," in which the eyes suddenly turn upward in a spasm and stay that way for several minutes. As a rule, no gross physical disturbances are found in children.

Mental symptoms in the chronic stage may appear with or without obvious physical disturbances.

Encephalitis in Children.—Children's symptoms often follow a recognized acute attack of encephalitis, but the acute attack is sometimes so slight as to be mistaken for a cold. In this case the diagnosis can be made on the basis of the characteristic symptoms and the fact that there was an epidemic of the disease at the time the child had the cold or influenza.

One of the characteristic symptoms in children is hyperkinetic behavior. The child is restless and very active, and the behavior is unruly and mischievous. Apparently the child cannot control this excessive activity; if he is asked about it, he answers, "I don't know, I don't want to do it, still I do it." He may feel remorseful and self-condemnatory about his behavior.

Either as a result of this constant pressure for activity or possibly as an independent factor, the children are disobedient, unruly, destructive, boisterous, combative. They break furniture and windows, cut things up, and torture animals and other children. Their moral evaluations suffer; such children smear themselves with excreta, urinate on persons around them, expose themselves, make sexual assaults, steal, use obscene language. Their aggressive impulses are strong and uninhibited; they quarrel, fight, have temper tantrums, set things on fire. Obviously, such children present extremely serious problems of management at home, with their playmates, and in school; for they may injure others, cause accidents, or completely disrupt discipline.

The sleep may show the so-called "inverted rhythm," i.e., the child sleeps during the day and is awake at night. The intelligence, as a rule, is normal, but the child does not focus his attention for long periods or study adequately. Tics are common physical symptoms in children in this condition. Sometimes the forced movement appears in attacks, such as forced breathing or a crescendo repetition of syllables. The attacks subside, and between them the functions involved may be normal.

Post-encephalitic children are such major problems after an epidemic that special departments have been established for their care in psychopathic hospitals.

Encephalitis in Adults.—The dominant symptoms may vary in the adult, but the following symptoms are common: The patient has compulsive and obsessive thoughts which appear during attacks usually associated with oculo-gyric crises. He may show depression with agitation; that is, he is dejected and sad but at the same time restless and emotional, possibly anxious; he may engage in impulsive acts, sometimes with a suicidal intent. This behavior may be the patient's reaction to his physical difficulties as well as to environmental factors which he now finds difficult to cope with because of his physical disability. In rare cases, a post-encephalitic patient is unusually happy. Apathy is a frequent symptom. The patient is inclined to sit in the same place, possibly looking out at the street or just staring into space. He may lie for long periods without moving. Delusions and hallucinations are comparatively rare, but occur in some cases. Hallucinations are sometimes tactile, the patient feeling insects crawling on him, or auditory.

Treatment.—The adult encephalitic may be benefited by psychotherapy and exercise. There is no reliable treatment for the acute period of encephalitis. Excited patients may be helped by hydrotherapy, and those with the Parkinsonian condition are benefited by exercise and various forms of medication.

The irritable and impulsive behavior of children is partly a direct influence of the organic damage, but other factors are also involved. Their reaction to the indistinct physical discomfort in itself may be hostility and insecurity; their reaction to the struggle with the environment is hostility, as are also their reactions to rejection by the environment, to punishment, to competition, to frustration. For these reasons, considerable reeducation is possible in some cases, and the children are able to master their impulses in part.

Hyperkinetic children can be treated best in sections of psychopathic hospitals especially established for that purpose. With adequate management, reeducation, and proper medication, they may improve sufficiently in behavior so that they can return to their homes.

A 30-year-old man, a conscientious worker, was inclined to worry about his wife and two children. If he was out of a job for any length of time he became depressed although he had saved money. During an epidemic of encephalitis, he became drowsy and lethargic, slept almost all the time for several weeks, and developed double vision. He recovered from this condition and was comparatively well for about a year and a half. Muscular rigidity gradually developed in his body and his right arm began to shake. His face became somewhat mask-like and the skin grew oily. About the same time he became depressed—he spoke of life not being worth living, and he worried about the health and future of his children. Although he could have worked as a gardener since with enough volition he could control his movements, he stopped working. On several occasions he stayed away from home and spent the night in the park; another time he took tincture of iodine but was not seriously hurt.

He was sent to a psychiatric hospital, but was restless and depressed and anxious about his family. He was oriented for place and time, and his intelligence was good. He helped to take care of the hospital lawns and garden. However, he suddenly threw himself in front of a truck which was driving in with some supplies, and was instantly killed.

This patient's depression in the chronic stage of encephalitis was in harmony with his previous personality. The depression was the combined result of the damage to the brain and his reaction to it. His high ideals, his stern demands on himself, and his general anxiety about the future made him react severely to his physical debility, and the reaction was all the stronger because of his damaged brain tissue.

Psychological and medicinal therapy often enables such patients to lose their depression and return to work. In some cases, however, patients with a similar physical condition do not have a serious enough reaction to interfere with their work.

A 7-year-old child, a fairly good student in school and moderately obedient, developed a fever and a running nose during an epidemic of encephalitis; he was very restless and could not sleep. This was diagnosed as a cold. He recovered fully. About two years later he became very unruly. He talked back to the teacher, and would get up during class and walk over to another seat. He got into fights with his classmates and would sometimes start to beat them in class. He used obscene language at home, played with matches, and repeatedly set the curtains on fire. If his mother tried to discipline him, he became angry and broke the furniture or windows; on one occasion he threw a knife at her. He exposed himself in the street before girls, and several times masturbated before his sister. He was sent to the post-encephalitic division of a psychiatric hospital, where he improved considerably. He resumed his studies and after three years returned to his family. He has been home three years; in spite of recurrent moderate difficulties, he has been able to adjust to his daily surroundings. He attends a special class in school.

ALCOHOLIC PSYCHOTIC REACTIONS

The use of chemical substances such as alcohol, opium, etc., can be considered pathological only (1) if they are used in excess, if the individual cannot do without them, and if they have deleterious effects, and (2) if their use is disapproved of by the group. In a sense, the second point is a special instance of the first, because if a person uses a substance which the group disapproves of, he almost invariably does so because he "craves" it and cannot be deprived of it, and he invariably uses it in large quantities.

The following discussion will center chiefly on the pathological aspects, but the effect of a moderate use of these substances will also be mentioned. Essential to an understanding of the whole problem are the patient's psychological problems which lead him to use the substance, the physical effects of this substance, and the psychotic reaction which results. In these psychotic reactions, the direct toxic effects of the substances are combined with the psychological reactions, attitudes, and conflicts characteristic of the individual.

Psychodynamics of Alcoholism and Drug Addictions.—The fears that are characteristic of addictions are of unbearable and catastrophic humiliation, particularly after failure, and complete submission and destruction, especially after the individual has sought relief from anxiety through homosexual submission. This catastrophic threat is closely approximated psychologically in alcoholic hallucinosis.

In addition to these fears, several other factors combine to make the habitual use of a substance a major problem. External factors are important. For example, contact with groups which drink heavily or use drugs give a person an opportunity and inclination to do likewise. An individual faced by conflicts, unhappiness, and anxieties may attempt to cope with or escape them through the narcotic or intoxicating effect of these substances. A special bodily responsiveness to the substance or special psychological constellations are probably responsible for his adopting this special solution.

The most commonly used intoxicant is alcohol. Its use has the following "ameliorative" effects: (1) Alcohol gives the individual pleasure through the use of the mouth and the taste. This in itself has a consoling value and may compensate for other pleasures or satisfactions that he is not able to obtain. (2) The narcotic effect of the alcohol enables the individual to forget his fears and stresses. In the state of drunkenness, the external world is excluded. The intoxicating effect further enables him to indulge in satisfying impulses which he ordinarily struggles against. Thus, alcoholic belligerency may serve the purpose of expressing his hostility toward various people, and sexual desires which are ordinarily inhibited may be satisfied. (3) The elation which may accompany alcoholism enables the individual to enjoy positive joy and satisfaction that he is otherwise unable to attain and which helps him to forget his difficulties. Probably both self-debasing and self-aggrandizing tendencies are concerned when a person tends toward chronic alcoholism. (4) The individual's companions are like himself; they drink. This companionship compensates him for his rejection by and the loss of the love of other people. It is often quite characteristic of this alcoholic relationship that it lacks "closeness" and "warmth." As a matter of fact, the individual is afraid of close relationships because he fears rejection. The barroom relationships do not demand too much from him, and he receives from them just as much as he wants. (5) Alcohol induces defiance and self-assertion, and raises self-esteem. The drinker says, "I have the courage to defy prohibitions and authority. I am somebody. I am worth something. I cannot be dominated." (6) Profound desires for self-effacement, submission, self-debasement, and withdrawal from the world, ordinarily repressed, may appear because the alcohol diminishes inhibitions.

Dipsomania.—The patient with dipsomania indulges in excessive drinking periodically. He drinks to such an extent that he is not able to pursue his normal work and he gets into trouble and may be injured. The period of drinking may start quite involuntarily—a cocktail with friends may initiate it—or it may begin voluntarily after a period of struggle against it. Between periods of drinking the patient behaves apparently well, but careful examination will bring forth personality disturbances. The periodic drinking is a reaction to situations of stress.

A gifted and fairly successful writer had periods when he drank heavily. They would occur anywhere from every three to every eight months and would last from two weeks to a month. He would get into trouble. He would wander away from the house and turn up in a hospital with a fractured rib, without knowing how he broke it. He would neglect his work, fail to keep appointments and to live up to his contracts. He would become belligerent, get into fights, and be beaten up. Several times he attempted to forge checks, but they were not accepted.

The patient's drinking bouts always occurred after a disappointment, either with a friend or with his work. During his free periods, he worked quickly and wrote voluminously; he had a good market for his material. After many years of drinking, his work began to deteriorate, the periods of drinking grew much longer, his hands trembled, and he showed signs of chronic alcoholism. He would spend the money that he earned on drinking, and then would beg his friends for money to buy food for his wife and child. Frequently, when he was drinking at home, he shouted abuse to men whom he heard talking and who he said called him obscene names. He accused his wife of infidelity and threatened to kill both her and his child. He refused all psychotherapy and nothing could be done for him.

Delirium Tremens.—Delirium tremens occurs in people who have drunk excessively for a long time; it may also appear after a debauch, or after an injury or an infection. It is sometimes assumed to follow a sudden cessation of drinking, but this is questionable.

In some cases, the delirium does not appear immediately. Before its onset, the patient is restless, unable to sleep, has nightmares and is terrified by sounds or impressions, particularly in the dark. This may last several days. In other cases, the delirium itself appears suddenly, and the patient is then disoriented for time and place.

The particular characteristics of this delirium are: (1) Vivid hallucinations, particularly of such animals as snakes and rats: The patient may see these animals or feel them crawling over him. Often such patients hallucinate while engaged in their regular occupation—driving a truck, gardening, etc. (2) Acute fear: The patient is terrified by the animals in his hallucinations. But in addition he may be in a state of acute terror. He may be afraid that something dreadful will happen to him, that he will be mutilated or killed. This terror may lead him to attempt suicide. (3) Extreme suggestibility as to sensory illusions: The patient, when requested, will read a blank piece of paper which is placed before him; if asked what he sees on the wall, he may say animals and try to catch them. (4) Misidentification. The patient may mistake a total stranger for one of his close friends.

The most striking symptom, which gives this condition its name, is coarse tremor of the hands, face, and tongue. The tongue is coated and the breath is foul. The heart is rapid, and the patient perspires profusely.

The delirium usually lasts from three to six days. Although most patients recover, the delirium may terminate in death from exhaustion or heart failure (about 3 per cent).

The Korsakoff Syndrome.—The Korsakoff syndrome is most frequently encountered in chronic alcoholism; but it occasionally appears in other conditions, such as cerebral arteriosclerosis, lead poisoning, or chronic infections. The symptoms are as follows: (1) Impairment of memory for recent events: The patient cannot remember what he did a few hours earlier. (2) Confabulation: If the patient is asked what he did during a period that he does not remember, he will make up a story—that he went to visit a friend or went to the country, etc. (3) Delirium with visual and auditory hallucinations: The patient may picture himself in his workshop at home engaged in some trivial occupation. Frequently, patients know where they are and recognize people, but may be disoriented for time. (4) Emotional instability: The patient is at times friendly and cheerful, but at other times he is irritable and quarrelsome.

Among the physical symptoms are inflammation of the nerve trunks throughout the body (polyneuritis), areas of anesthesia in the skin, and paralysis—for example, wrist drop, in which the patient cannot raise his hand. The Korsakoff syndrome lasts a fairly long time, there often being no sign of improvement until after six to eight weeks. The syndrome may be permanent.

Chronic Alcoholism.—In some individuals who have used alcohol excessively for many years, certain changes take place which are due to the toxic effect of the alcohol on the brain tissue. Chronic alcoholism is a combination of this toxic effect and of slow psychological deterioration.

The symptoms may vary, and they usually develop gradually. The following are characteristic: The patient is affable and charming on superficial contact but is apt to be abusive, rude, and inconsiderate toward his family, friends, or business associates, and to neglect his responsibilities toward them. He is likely to lie, particularly about his activities. He relates his good deeds, and tries to give the impression that he has lived up to high ideals. He makes a sentimental appeal to people for money to buy drinks with. If he works at all, his work is poor; he is unreliable and inefficient, and is likely to give up his job at a crucial time. His memory is impaired, particularly for recent events and for such matters as work he has to do. In more advanced stages, the patient may commit sexual crimes such as exhibition or assaults.

The physical symptoms are tremor, a "flat, ironed-out" face (characteristic facial expression), gastritis, cirrhosis of the liver, heart disease, nephritis, etc.

The Treatment of Alcoholism.—The treatment of alcoholism has three aspects: the treatment of acute drunkenness with coma, and of acute psychotic reactions, and the prevention of a return to excessive drinking.

A person who has drunk so much that he remains unconscious more than one day is exposed not only to the effect of the alcohol but also to auto-intoxication and hence to the danger of developing disease infection. For this reason the stomach is washed out and an enema given. Frequently the individual revives as a result of the enema. If he is able to swallow, he is given coffee; if not, caffein is injected into the muscles.

Patients with acute psychotic reactions are best treated in a hospital. The patient with delirium tremens should be given a great deal of fluid in small amounts; sleep can be induced by means of a warm bath followed by a hypnotic.

The patient with alcoholic hallucinosis must be hospitalized because his acute state of fear and panic and the sudden cessation of alcohol make him unmanageable. He should be given good food and adequate amounts of liquids. Bromides may be used to quiet him and induce sleep.

The treatment of chronic alcoholism requires the complete cessation of drinking. This can be done gradually within seven days, but it is impossible if the patient remains at home, for he will sneak out and buy liquor.

It is very difficult to prevent the recurrence of chronic heavy drinking after the patient leaves the hospital. This can be accomplished with certainty only if his whole personality can be rebuilt so that his reactions to problems and difficulties change and he copes with them differently. Surprisingly enough, some people who have been heavy drinkers for as much as thirty years can stop suddenly. Other individuals are benefited by a thorough discussion of their problems, their personalities, their reaction patterns. Psychoanalytic treatment has proved successful in still other cases. None of these methods, however, has thus far been successful in every case.

SUGGESTED READINGS

See Chapter XXVII. See also Diethelm (183), and S. E. Jelliffe's *Post-encephalitic Respiratory Disorders*, N. Y., 1927.

CHAPTER XXX

OTHER ORGANIC PSYCHOTIC REACTIONS

~~~~~~

ENDOCRINE DISORDERS

The psychopathology in endocrine disorders, like that in other primary bodily disorders, may be the direct result of the impaired brain functioning or the patient's reaction to his disorder, or both. We shall discuss here only the disturbances in which both factors are involved; and although three glands—the thyroid, the pancreas, and the pituitary—are particularly associated with such psychotic disturbances, we shall limit ourselves to the thyroid.

Hypothyroidism.—When the thyroid does not function sufficiently, the condition is called hypothyroidism. If the thyroid is underactive during childhood, cretinism results. This condition, which is essentially feeble-mindedness, will be described in detail in the next chapter. In some instances, however, the individual has an additional psychotic reaction to his bodily appearance. For example, one girl who was a cretin developed the delusion that she was a changeling and in reality a queen, and thus attempted to compensate for her physical defect (Bender).

Thyroid deficiency which appears in an adult hitherto normal in that respect, is called myxedema. The characteristic mental symptoms are emotional dulling, decline in intelligence and in memory, and slowness of response, in both movement and speech. Among the physical symptoms are swelling and puffiness of the face; the swelling does not pit on pressure. The skin becomes coarse and dry, and the pulse slows to between 40 and 60 per minute. There is sensitiveness to cold, and the basal metabolic rate drops sharply (—30 or lower). This latter condition can be quickly remedied by the proper administration of thyroid extract.

An efficient worker in the street cleaning department began to complain of slowness, fatigue, inability to work well, and loss of memory. On examination he was found to have a coarse skin; his face was swollen, dull, and stupid-looking; his speech was very slow. His basal metabolism was —36. Administration of desiccated thyroid raised his metabolism to normal within a month's time, and all his complaints disappeared. In such cases, the thyroid usually has to be administered continuously.

Hyperthyroidism.—Since the causes and effects of a hyperactive thyroid have already been discussed, only severe psychotic reactions will be considered here. These are of two types: (1) The patient with a very severe toxicosis may become extremely restless and delirious. He may be partly or completely disoriented for time, place, and people. He may hallucinate, the hallucinations usually embodying great excitement and fear. This condition is due chiefly to the effects of the thyroid substance on the functioning of the brain; it disappears on the administration of iodine and partial removal of the thyroid gland. (2) In some instances, the patient's reaction to severe emotional stress involves both hyperthyroidism and a psychotic reaction; in others, the reaction to the initial stress is hyperthyroidism, additional stress eliciting psychotic symptoms.

The parents of a 20-year-old girl had separated when she was one year of age. She lived in Haiti with her mother, and her father lived in the United States. She corresponded with her father but had not seen him for nineteen years. She came to visit him when she was 20 years old. Her father received her cordially and she stayed at his apartment. He was popular with women and several of them sometimes stayed at the apartment. The patient who had keenly anticipated seeing her father, was deeply disappointed in him both morally and emotionally, for she had hoped to be the only object of his emotional interest during her visit.

The patient also had sexual fantasies about her father and this made her feel guilty. In response to this situation of stress, she developed hyperthyroidism and went to a physician for treatment. Her father consulted the physician about her. She was much concerned about this visit because she hoped it would lead to different behavior on the part of her father. However, when he said merely, "Now, you see, there's nothing really the matter with you; you are not in any danger; you just have to take things easy," she considered this as the final rejection. Feeling that she had been betrayed by both her father and her physician, she grew depressed and self-accusatory, and sat by herself much of the time brooding. Her speech became rambling and partly incoherent. She was hospitalized and treated, and part of the thyroid gland was removed. Her thyroid symptoms disappeared, but her depression continued, though in a milder form. In about six months she recovered fully.

This patient's psychotic reaction was a response to the second and even more damaging disappointment, a situation of stress which arose when she was already in a debilitated physical and psychological condition.

Brain Tumors[1]

Brain tumors are new growths which appear in various parts of the brain. This growth may vary in nature and localization. For example, it may be a cyst, i.e., a round sac filled with fluid, which grows very gradually. This type of tumor may damage the nerve tissue through pressure. The new growths may consist of cells which grow quickly and invade and infiltrate the surrounding tissue. The gliomas are of this type. This tumor is similar to cancer in its behavior.

Physical Symptoms.—The physical symptoms of brain tumor depend on two factors: the size of the tumor and its localization. The general symptoms are headaches, vomiting, and slow pulse.

[1] The following extremely significant papers came to attention too late to be included: A. Gelb, Zur Medizinischen Psychologie und Philosophischen Anthropologie, *Acta Psychologica*, 1937, 3, 193-272; the papers by Gelb, Goldstein, and Fuchs on brain-injured patients which are condensed and translated in W. Ellis, *A Source Book of Gestalt Psychology*, Harcourt, Brace, New York, 1938, pp. 315-369.

The optic nerve may be swollen in one or both eyes where it
enters the eye. All these general symptoms are due to increased
intracranial pressure, the pressure sometimes being four times
as high as is normal.

Local symptoms are produced by irritation or, more frequently,
by damage to a particular part of the brain. These symptoms are
numerous because of the extremely complex structure of the
brain. Among them are paralysis; changes in the muscle, tendon,
or skin reflexes; and disturbances in sense perception. If any of
the nerve centers or the nerve paths leading to these centers are
damaged, a loss of function results.

Psychological Symptoms.—The psychological symptoms may
also be either general or local. The general symptoms may be
due to disturbances not of the whole brain, but of certain parts
of it, particularly the frontal lobe, the diencephalon or the basal
ganglia; but these symptoms are called general because the disturbances are often due to increased intracranial pressure as a
whole. The general symptoms are apathy and disinterestedness,
confusion and perplexity. The patient's consciousness may be
deeply disturbed.

Considerable research has been done on localizing psychological signs. For example, Schuster found that emotional symptoms are more likely to appear if the tumor is localized on the
left or dominant side of the brain (probably in right-handed
people).

Gibbs analyzed 1545 records of patients who were either
operated on or had died and been autopsied. Among his findings
on hallucinations are the following: Visual hallucinations are
most common if the tumor is located in the temporal or occipital
lobe or in the thalamus. "Lilliputian" hallucinations are frequent in temporal lobe tumors; the patient sees small figures
which he usually knows are not real. The temporal lobe is not a
visual center, but some visual pathways go through it; and it is
the irritation of these pathways that is responsible for the hallucinations.

Olfactory hallucinations are most common when the tumor is localized in the temporal lobe or in the thalamus. The patient may smell peculiar odors, such as rubber burning, when there is no external cause for them. These hallucinations are produced by irritation of the olfactory areas.

Gustatory hallucinations are produced by tumors in the basal ganglia and the thalamus. The patient may taste something bad —he may have a metallic taste or taste vinegar for no reason.

Jocularity is most common when the tumor is located in the thalamus or the striate body. The patient is witty, puns, and makes jokes, when he obviously is seriously ill. The jocularity may approximate the euphoria, elation, and flight of ideas found in manic reactions.

Irritability is most common when tumors involve the striate body on the left side of the brain.

Auditory hallucinations are extremely rare.

In some cases, the mental symptoms may appear long before any convincing local symptoms appear. This is particularly likely when the tumor is in the frontal lobe because it may not extend back far enough to damage the motor area. It is also likely when the tumor is localized in the corpus callosum, the structure which connects the two hemispheres.

Diagnosis and Treatment.—As a rule, brain tumors can be diagnosed. Ventriculography is one of the important diagnostic methods. The fluid is withdrawn from the ventricles of the brain; they are then filled with air, and X-ray pictures are taken. Any displacement, obstruction, or distortion in the shape of the ventricles indicates the presence and location of a tumor.

Electro-encephalography is valuable in determining the location of a tumor, for there are changes in the electric waves if a tumor is present. For example, if electrodes are placed on the right side of the head of a patient who has a tumor in the middle of the left hemisphere, there will be no changes; but if the electrodes are placed on the left side of the head, changes will be observed.

Some brain tumors can be treated by an operation, in which the brain is exposed and the tumor removed. The patient may fully recover, depending on the size and location of the growth and whether any part of the brain had to be removed with the tumor. In other cases the patient has no recurrence of the tumor but is left with a residual symptom, such as partial paralysis. Certain types of tumors may recur after several years. Some tumors cannot be removed, and the patient dies within a short time.

A 25-year-old mechanic grew very dull mentally. His reactions slowed and his facial expression became dull and stupid. He was unable to grasp simple matters. For example, when he expected an out-of-town visitor, he would ask how the guest would travel and how long he would stay; he was unable to figure out where the visitor would sleep. He became more and more forgetful, even forgetting where he put his tools. He failed to complete jobs and, when criticized for it, did not know what he had done wrong. A mental examination showed that he had memory disturbances and slight intellectual impairment. His physical examination showed neither general nor local symptoms of brain tumor, but the encephalogram showed partial obliteration of the ventricles. On the basis of this, a tumor in both frontal lobes was diagnosed. It was removed surgically, the patient recovered fully and has been well for ten years.

EPILEPSY

Forms of Epilepsy.—Epilepsy is a condition which is characterized by attacks of convulsions accompanied by loss of consciousness. The severest form, the so-called grand mal, is accompanied by phenomena called aura which precede the attack. Thus the patient sees flashes of light or smells an unpleasant odor or experiences an uncomfortable sensation in various parts of the body, or has visual hallucinations or muscular twitches or obsessive thoughts; he may start running. He loses consciousness, and his entire body begins to shake violently; his arms and legs thrash wildly about. During this attack the tongue is often bitten, there is foam on the mouth, and the face grows bluish.

This violent thrashing, which is called the clonic phase, is often preceded by a contraction of the whole body; this is called the tonic phase. The patient remains unconscious for a while; he may regain consciousness for a short time, but he is drowsy and usually sleeps soundly for some time. When he recovers from the attack, he is often confused and acts in a half-conscious, automatic manner.

The convulsions are not always as severe as this; for example, the patient may lose consciousness but have no convulsions, or the convulsions may not be general. In some instances, however, they may be extremely severe, the patient going from one attack to another without recovering consciousness; but usually there is an interval of anywhere from a day to a year between them. Sometimes the attacks occur at night while the patient is asleep. The patient has no memory of the attack, but usually remembers the aura. During the attack, the pupils do not react to light, and there is a positive Babinski reflex. (Under normal circumstances, if the sole of the foot is stroked, all the toes flex; but if there is a temporary or permanent damage to the pyramidal tracts, the big toe extends instead of flexing, and the other toes may flex or extend.)

Petit mal, a less severe form of epilepsy, is characterized by a fleeting loss of consciousness during which the patient may stand rigidly or keep doing what he was doing before the attack; he may drop things, turn pale, mumble, utter curious and irrelevant phrases, or make champing movements with his mouth. He has no memory of his actions.

Another form of paroxysmal disorder which occurs in epilepsy is the so-called "psychic equivalent," also called epileptic furor. This may assume great importance, for it usually is characterized by great excitement, often with considerable anxiety and extremely violent behavior. A patient in this state may commit wholesale murder and know nothing about it, except possibly for a vague feeling that he has done something dreadful.

Other more serious and lasting psychological disturbances

occur in a prolonged psychotic state when there are hallucinations and delusions, particularly of a religious character. The patient may hear God talking to him; he may see a cross of fire, or pray most of the day. There may be stupor with ecstasy during which the patient goes through intense religious experiences such as seeing God and all the angels. The patient may have a prolonged period of depression. This type of psychosis lacks the obscene characteristics which are almost invariably present in schizophrenia.

In the epileptic fugue, the patient suddenly stops what he has been doing and does something totally different. For example, he may steal something, leave his home at night clad only in his pajamas, and wander many miles away; when he recovers consciousness later, he has no idea of how he got there.

After many years of epileptic attacks, in spite of continued treatment the patient may deteriorate intellectually; his memory may be violently disturbed and his judgment impaired.

It was formerly customary to include under epilepsy all disorders characterized by convulsions and attacks of psychological and motor disturbances; but if this is done, the plural form, epilepsies, should be used. A better procedure is to group these patients on the basis of the condition underlying their epilepsy. Convulsions may be caused by general paresis, hardening of the arteries of the brain particularly if a hemorrhage occurs, maldevelopment of the brain which results in idiocy or hydrocephalus. Patients with epileptic symptoms and these conditions are now customarily spoken of as having symptomatic epilepsy. The diagnosis is based on characteristic signs, such as the Wassermann test, mental changes, neurological changes in general paresis. Another important group included under symptomatic epilepsy are patients with Jacksonian seizures. These seizures consist of attacks of muscular twitching which always start in the same place—the muscles of the face or of the hand, for example—while the patient is still conscious; the twitching then spreads over the entire body and the patient loses consciousness. This condition is usually due to growths or pressure localized in the region of the motor area. A generalized convulsion which always starts with the same type of aura—for example, olfactory aura—may be due to brain tumors. After all forms of symptomatic epilepsies are eliminated, there remains a large group in whose brain no gross localized pathology can be found. This condition is called essential epilepsy (also idiopathic epilepsy), to indicate that the cause is not known. The discussion in this chapter concerns chiefly these patients.

Personality of the Epileptic.—The patient's general personality may be essentially normal, but in some cases characteristic alterations are observable. Sometimes these alterations appear before the attacks occur; in still other instances they develop only after repeated attacks. Irritability is very evident. The patient is angered easily, raises his voice, and becomes abusive. This is combined with destructiveness in younger age periods; for example, the adolescent child is inclined to attack his playmates rather violently on slight provocation and to tear up and break things. The patient grows extremely self-centered. He is selfish, inconsiderate, and preoccupied with his own person; everything pertaining to it is of prime importance, and he expects others to have the same attitude. He may grow especially susceptible to flattery and boast childishly. The patient has a shallow, at times sentimental and superficial, interest in his environment. This interest is often religious. As MacCurdy says, "These patients are considerate without being kind, religious without zeal, and . . . they will work for praise, but not for love."

There have been various theoretical assumptions concerning the psychopathology of epilepsy. One holds that the primary difficulty lies in the patient's whole outlook as determined by emotional developmental factors; in other words, he remains essentially infantile. Another assumption holds that the patient has an organic disturbance which causes him discomfort and impairs his ability to function, and he reacts to it psychologically.

If this impairment is present from infancy, his whole development may be determined by this chronic factor (Kardiner). Probably both of these assumptions are valid for the average patient.

Treatment.—The majority of patients suffering from epileptic attacks can be treated outside of hospitals. There is still no entirely satisfactory treatment for epilepsy, but with certain methods the patient may be freed from attacks for many years and be enabled to pursue his regular occupation. A recent important development is the use of brain waves to detect epileptic attacks before they occur.

The methods of treatment are largely medicinal—the administration of pheno-barbital and bromides, along with general hygienic and dietary cautions, and dehydration. Psychotherapy may be attempted with caution, but no great successes have been reported.

Exceptionally severe cases require treatment in a psychopathic hospital. This is true if a prolonged psychotic episode occurs or if the personality changes, with irritability or a tendency to violence predominating. Special colonies for epileptics, such as Craig Colony in New York State, are of great value. The patients there live in healthful open surroundings and are under the supervision of individuals who know how to handle them.

A 30-year-old man who was suffering from both convulsions and petit mal worked in a store. In the course of his work he had a violent argument with his employer. He came home and went to sleep because of a headache. He got up at night and started to shout inarticulately, brandishing a knife. He barricaded himself in one of the rooms, shouting all the while, and started to hack away at the furniture, tore up the bed linen, and slashed the woodwork with his knife. His wife called the police, who finally overpowered him. After a considerable struggle he quieted down, but he had to be restrained. Several hours later he looked around, puzzled, and asked why he was tied up. He had no knowledge of anything he had done. Later, in another epileptic rage, the man killed his entire family.

HEAD INJURIES

The reactions to be described in this section occur after severe head injuries. The psychological symptoms depend on the injury to the brain, which is usually but not always proportionate to the injury to the skull—a person may be killed by a blow to the head but his skull may not be fractured. In most cases the injury to the brain is not direct; the force of the blow is transmitted through the skull to the brain.

The injury to the brain may cause small, "pin-point" hemorrhages throughout the entire brain. In more severe injuries larger blood vessels may rupture and the tissues may swell. All these effects may eventually disappear; but in some cases the nerve tissue is permanently destroyed and scar tissue forms subsequently.

Symptoms.—The most common immediate effect of a severe blow to the head is a disturbance of consciousness. The victim may be only temporarily dazed, or he may remain completely unconscious for anywhere from a few minutes to several days. A relatively severe brain injury may cause only a slight disturbance of consciousness. The patient may suffer nausea, vomiting, headache, or dizziness in varying degrees. In some instances, the patient becomes delirious on regaining consciousness. This condition may be of short duration or may last for several days or weeks. The patient is disoriented for time and place; he is restless, talks incoherently, may want to get dressed and return to work. He may have hallucinations.

The physical symptoms in brain injury depend on the extent of the damage. While the patient is unconscious, the breathing and pulse may be slow; the blood pressure may rise and there may be a slight rise in temperature. In cases of more extended damage to the brain, the pupils do not react.

The chronic symptoms in general can be classified as psychotic reactions and changes in personality.

The patient with a psychotic reaction may become apathetic

and slow; he is often depressed and shows no initiative. People who knew him before his injury notice the change immediately. However, he may be oriented for time and place and answer questions correctly. This condition may disappear after several months. The patient usually has an amnesia for the accident, and there are often large gaps in his memory which are gradually filled in if he improves.

Another form of psychotic reaction is characterized by over-activity, mild elation, and wittiness. The patient jokes and is very talkative; his stream of thought approximates a flight of ideas. He fills out his large gaps of memory with confabulations. His mood may be euphoric, in spite of such a serious noticeable injury as paralysis. This condition also may last several months and then disappear.

Changes in personality are often marked. In some instances such symptoms as headaches and dizziness persist; and the patient complains of fatigability and inability to concentrate. Together with this he becomes markedly irritable, to the extent of sudden, almost impulsive violence. He may lose his ambition and initiative and become irregular in his work. His sense of beauty and his moral evaluations may slacken. Such patients tolerate alcohol very badly; their reaction to it is sometimes a terrific excitement during which they commit acts of violence. These personality changes may persist without much change for several years. In some instances the change is progressive, and the patient deteriorates intellectually as well. However, the condition may clear up completely.

Treatment.—During the acute period the patient must remain in bed; if he is unconscious, he must receive proper care and be given adequate fluids to prevent dehydration. The injection of caffein has been recently recommended to reduce intra-cranial pressure. If the headache is severe, a lumbar puncture may be made. Sedatives and mild hypnotics may be necessary for a restless patient. The treatment of fracture of the skull is essentially the same, except that a longer period of rest is required. A depressed fracture, one in which part of the skull presses into the brain, requires surgery.

Psychotherapy is important after recovery because it allays the patient's fears, increases his desire to return to a regular mode of living, and prevents him from merging the problems arising from his accident with those connected with his everyday life. In other instances, however, the psychotherapy has another purpose: to make the patient who is reluctant to admit his helplessness realize his disability and go easy temporarily.

A 35-year-old man underwent a change in character after an accident in which he was knocked down by an automobile. Whereas formerly he had been rather sociable and considerate, he now tended to keep to himself; he became irritable, and was reluctant to go to his office. However, he was able to keep his job because he was well liked; he was given easier work which he could do. His memory for recent information was impaired, but his judgment and calculation were good. This tendency to keep to himself and his irritability persisted for several years after the accident, together with occasional headaches and dizziness. He was able to get along because he was encouraged to take up gardening as a hobby. His wife, a very considerate and understanding woman, bore his irritability well. He finally recovered completely. In this case, psychological discussions helped; but the affection, kindness, and patience of his wife and friends were of primary importance.

A 28-year-old man suffered a severe head injury when his car collided with another car. He was taken to a hospital and remained unconscious for two hours. An X-ray examination showed that his skull was fractured; the facial nerve on the right side was paralyzed, and he had difficulty in hearing with one ear; his spinal fluid was bloody. After being drowsy for several days, the patient became rather talkative. He obeyed instructions and stayed in bed, but had to be watched constantly because he would sit up and give everybody advice. He calmed down after several days except that he remained over-talkative. About a month later, he grew even more talkative; flight of ideas and distractibility developed. He would talk about how well he felt, and say that he had planned a trip; then he would relate his experiences on one of his supposed trips and discuss the political policies of the various places he had visited. A few weeks later he began to talk of being secretly commissioned by the government to undertake various engineering projects to improve the condition of the country, and he described several visits to Washington which he had actually never made. He felt that he was in the best of health, although his face was still paralyzed from the accident. His condition remained essentially the same for about eight months, after which he gradually recovered, under ordinary medical treatment and discussions with a psychiatrist.

SUGGESTED READINGS

See Chap. XXVII. See also Dunbar's *Emotions and Bodily Changes* (202), Cobb's article on the treatment of epilepsy in the *American Journal of Psychiatry*, 1939, **96**, 1009-1022, and footnote on page 520.

CHAPTER XXXI

FEEBLE-MINDEDNESS AND STUPIDITY

A discussion of mental defect presents many difficulties. Little is known definitely about the etiology of many of its forms. Clear thinking and hopeful research have been made difficult by the long-held conviction that most mental defects are almost entirely hereditary (Goddard, Tredgold). Only recently have psychologists begun to shake off this stultifying influence and look for actual etiologies. There are still, however, large gaps in our knowledge of feeble-minded individuals—for instance, the psychodynamics of this condition have been studied by only a few (Adler, Lewin); our knowledge of the social life and adjustment of aments is inadequate (see, however, the writings of Doll); we know practically nothing about their interpersonal relations, their emotional needs, their picture of the world, or their feelings about themselves. In this chapter, we can do little more than raise questions.

Levels of Feeble-mindedness.—Three grades of mental defect have been recognized—idiocy, imbecility, and moronity. It must be remembered that originally feeble-mindedness was a legal category which was defined largely in terms of social adjustment.

The idiot.—Idiots are persons so deeply defective in mind from birth or from an early age as to be unable to guard themselves against common physical dangers. An idiot is defined as a person whose I.Q. is between 0 and 30, and whose mental age is 2 years or less.

Idiots are the only feeble-minded individuals whose condition can be recognized early in life by their physical appearance.

The idiot learns to walk and talk much later than is normal, and his speech consists of a few mumbled syllables. A low-grade idiot cannot walk or talk. He is more animal than human in his personal habits, for usually he can do almost nothing for himself. Idiots are usually sterile.

It is only in the cortex of an idiot that histological differences from the normal can be detected—fewer cells, different arrangement of cells, etc. No differences have as yet been found in the structure of the brains of morons and geniuses; in other words, little is known about the neurological basis of intelligence.[1]

The imbecile.—Imbeciles are persons in whom there exists from birth or from an early age mental defectiveness not amounting to idiocy, yet so pronounced that they are incapable of managing themselves or their affairs, or, in the case of children, of being taught to do so. Their I.Q.'s range from 30 to 50, their mental ages from 3 to 7 years.

Imbeciles can be helped by educational measures; for example, they can be taught to take care of themselves, and perhaps even to read a little. But, more important, they can become economically useful in very protected surroundings, for they can do simple, routine, repetitive tasks like rock-breaking, etc.

The moron.—Morons are usually defined as persons in whom there exists from birth or from an early age mental defectiveness not amounting to imbecility, yet so pronounced that they require care, supervision, and control both for their own protection and for that of others; or, in the case of children, that they appear to be permanently incapable of benefiting from instruction in ordinary schools. Their I.Q.'s range from 50 to 70, and their mental ages from 7 to 12 years. They do not differ in appearance from normal children. It is particularly difficult to distin-

[1] See, however, L. D. Morgan, "Alterations in the hypothalamus in mental deficiency," *Psychosomatic Medicine*, 1939, 1, 496-507. If these findings are confirmed, our conclusions will have to be modified. The discussion which has usually been confined to the neurology of the cerebral cortex would have to shift to a consideration of the possible influences on the intellect, of damage to the vegetative centers in the brain.

guish between those who seem to be constitutionally feeble-minded and those who are "pseudo-feeble-minded"; that is, many who are classed as morons have undoubtedly acquired their low intelligence, or have never been given the chance to develop to their full capacities.

The following extract from Wembridge demonstrates more specifically than generalizations can, how morons fall short, intellectually. The questions are from the Binet test.

"You recall, no doubt, the standard example in arithmetic which every fourteen-year-old school child is supposed to be able to solve: If two pencils cost five cents, how many can you get for fifty cents? Not only pencils, but doughnuts, dill-pickles, apples and cotton handkerchiefs are bought at about this price. *But neither Flora nor any of her moron friends could master the problem.* We knew they could not because we had asked them. Flora's answer was twenty-five because two into fifty is twenty-five. Her friend Lucille's, on the other hand, was a hundred, because two times fifty is a hundred. Another friend, Annie, ventured a still more generous estimate. She said: 'Five times fifty, because five cents times fifty cents is five times fifty—whatever that is.' Chuck himself answered ten, because 'You get two for five, and two times five is ten!' It will be observed that all of them knew that *something* must be done in the way of arith-metic, and that their arithmetic was generally correct—except that they could not select the right process to employ. A simple problem was to them as Relativity is to the rest of us. If our household accounts depended upon a real understanding of Relativity, we should be precisely in Flora's case, for her capacity to live within her income depends upon simple arithmetical analysis. If she and her friends had been low-grade feeble-minded, they could not even have multiplied their two's and five's. But they were only morons.

"It was certainly essential that Flora, out of Chuck's weekly twenty dollars, should save a little for the future, so another example suit-able for a fourteen-year-old was set for her. 'If you have twenty dol-lars a week, and spend fourteen a week, how long will it take you to save three hundred dollars?' Flora, who had a sense of humor, could not at first get past the joke that she should ever save anything. 'A lifetime,' she answered—'and a long lifetime.' Then, 'Three hundred times fourteen.' 'Three hundred times fourteen *what*?' we persisted, and Flora answered, 'Dollars.' The example was written out for her, but she had completely lost the connection, and when she was again reminded, 'But how long a time would it take to save it?' she answered, as if through the telephone, '2025.' What she meant by that we shall never know. We know only that the firms equipped to solicit business with the mentally unsound will find Flora out and use the courts to collect their bills. We know also that with such arithmetical equipment her savings account will never be large. . . .

"It is hard, indeed, to discover just what words convey to morons with such a background. Flora when questioned says that 'lecture' means 'getting hanged,' while Lucille says, 'It's the chair.' The fact that the latter's husband is in the penitentiary perhaps explains why both girls should associate the word 'electric.' Flora says skill is 'You do it,' which isn't so bad. Lucille says, 'You do it to fish.' 'Not scale, but skill,' we repeat. 'In your head,' she answers, which seems perhaps on the right track, until she adds, 'a bone.' 'Not skull, but skill,' we insist patiently. 'Fry in it,' she tries again, and we give it up. For purposes of ordinary conversation, words of that abstraction are too hazy for Lucille.

"Of course, uneducated people necessarily have smaller vocabularies than the highly trained. But on the other hand, children taught in American schools and confronted by the newspapers have been exposed to a good many words, and the meanings of a few of them have got to penetrate if any sermon on behavior is to be intelligible. Moreover, it is impossible for good advice to be couched entirely in words devoid of some degree of abstraction. So we ask, 'What is pity?' That seems easy: 'You're sorry.' Encouraged, we proceed, 'What is justice?' 'Peace,' answers Lucille, 'I got married by one.' Envy is 'enemy' or 'You like them,' or (hesitating), 'You don't like them.' Insure, to Flora, means 'sure,' or 'You get it when you're dead,' or 'They get it at the house,' or 'It's in the company like,' or 'It's when you get hurt.' So much for Flora grasping the insurance principle when some new agent at the door wheedles her out of a first installment, never to be followed by a second!

"Cotton is 'wood-like,' to Flora, but 'comes from animals' to

Lucille. ('Like coal,' she adds, to make it more clear.) Chuck, however, says with a flourish that 'it can be viewed from a perspective point,' and Flora is silenced with admiration. Brunette, says Flora, means 'blondes'; regard means 'guard-like'; civil is 'civilized' or 'big.' 'Why big?' 'Because the Civil War was big.' Another venture was with knives'—'because the war was fought with knives.' In what words, then, shall we express to Flora, 'You must learn to keep an account of your money, not spend more than you have, and be faithful to Chuck,' when she has already told us that charity is 'Don't be silly,' faith is 'You do it,' and when to a question requiring the answer 'thirty-five cents' she has answered, 'eighteen hundred weeks'? When it is possible to say that control means 'wagon' and chastity means 'tricks,' what hodge-podge of ideas has one's sermon produced in the good-natured mind of the moron bride, who probably has not been listening in any case, but has only been wondering whether her hair would look better in bangs or with a marcel? . . .

"Chuck was fond of fables and read them fluently. But the question was: What lesson, if any, did he learn from them? We soon found out. From the fable of the man who called to Hercules for help, and was advised by him to put his own shoulder to the wheel, he derived the lesson, 'Always do the same to them.' He laughed appreciatively at the girl who counted her chickens before they were hatched and said, 'It pays to be broad-minded.' He sighed over the crow who was flattered into dropping her meat in order to sing, and said, 'That's like Lucille. These flappers. It don't pay to be led by flappery.' Of the miller and his son who took everyone's advice about their donkey instead of using their own judgment, he said, 'They're so backward, these dumb animals. Too backward, much more backward than human beings.' "[1]

The I.Q. as a Gauge of Feeble-mindedness.—Until recently the definition of feeble-mindedness seemed to be relatively simple because it was stated arbitrarily in terms of the I.Q. Any individual whose I.Q. was less than 70 was classified as feeble-minded. The classification was as follows:

[1] E. H. Wembridge, *Life Among the Lowbrows*, Houghton Mifflin Company, Boston, 1931, pp. 6-7.

Class	Range of I.Q.'s
Genius	140 and above
Very superior	120-140
Superior	110-120
Normal	90-110
Dull	80-90
Borderline	70-80
Moron	50-70
Imbecile	25-50
Idiot	0-25

For various reasons this method of defining feeble-mindedness is being questioned. Either the intelligence tests are not as valid as they have been considered, or else the scores are far more susceptible to environmental influence than has been thought. Various experimental studies have been made of the influence of the environment on the I.Q.; among them are the following:

Sherman's famous investigation of the Hollow-Folk in the backwoods of Kentucky showed a clear relationship between the average I.Q. in the various communities and the social and educational opportunities in these communities.

One of Klineberg's experiments also indicated that a better environment raised the intelligence test score. He investigated the intelligence of Negroes who had come to New York City from the South and who thus had better educational opportunities. The intelligence test score increased, the longer the stay in the city.

A recent series of experiments by Wellman, Skeels, Skodak, and others throws further doubt on either the validity of the intelligence tests themselves or the validity of the whole theoretical structure centering about the concept of the I.Q. These investigators found startling increases in I.Q. when children were placed in superior environments such as nursery schools, foster homes, etc.

It may now be accepted as proved that an initially intelligent child may become progressively less intelligent, in comparison with the average child, because of a stultifying environment. Good educational opportunities, a general atmosphere which encourages intellectual development, some economic freedom so that some leisure time is available, etc.—all these encourage the growth of intelligence. Or, to put it more conservatively, all these insure that there will not be deterioration of intelligence.

The rejection of the I.Q. as the sole criterion of feeble-mindedness and as a proof of its inheritance does not mean that intelligence test scores have no value in this connection. Modern authorities like Pressey, Doll, Wallin, and Penrose claim that a suspected ament should never be diagnosed on the basis of a single criterion, regardless of what it is. Pressey considers inadequacy of education, economic inefficiency, social inadequacy, and a definitely low rating in a carefully conducted series of tests to be essential for a satisfactory diagnosis of feeble-mindedness. Furthermore, before all hope of improvement is given up, there should be some proof that the condition was present in infancy so that it could be attributed to inherited or congenital factors.

One other factor which must be considered in connection with feeble-mindedness is the socio-economic environment to which the individual has to adjust. For example, a person who cannot adjust in a complex urban environment may do so easily in a simpler one and even be quite successful. Wallin cites a man whose mental age was only 10.6 years, but who raised a family of nine, all high school graduates and almost all college students. For ten years he was president of the Board of Education in the small town in which he lived, and was considered by others to be a success.

The Role of Heredity.—It was at one time believed that feeble-mindedness was practically always inherited. Originally this was based largely on folk belief, and it was apparently borne out later by a large number of "family-line studies," such as those of the famous Jukes and Kallikaks. The "family-line method" of proving a trait to be inherited was criticized earlier in this book; it was pointed out that exactly the same data could be used to "prove" that the particular trait was environmentally determined. For instance, in both the Jukes and Kallikaks there was also a perfect correlation between poverty, poor social conditions, lack of education, and feeble-mindedness.

A more promising line of investigation opened by Gesell indicates that some feeble-mindedness goes back to the child's earliest days, which strongly indicates that it is either inherited or congenital. Gesell established developmental norms in the first months of life; and with them he was able to show clearly, in some cases, that an initial retardation of maturation is correlated with a later diagnosis of feeble-mindedness in the same individual.[1]

Types of Feeble-mindedness

Mongolian Imbecility.—A common form of amentia is Mongolism. While ordinary mental deficiency is not marked by any unusual bodily conformation and such a person cannot be distinguished from the normal individual by appearance alone, the Mongolian imbecile can be identified almost at a glance. The characteristic features are a relatively short stature and consequent underweight; a flattening of the back of the head; poor dentition; a comparatively large tongue, often deeply fissured; small, broad, and stubby hands; laxity of the joints (what is usually called double-jointedness); great sensitivity to extreme heat and cold because of poor circulation; poor speech or mutism. The most characteristic symptom is the peculiar narrowing and slanting of the eyes which has given this syndrome its name.

The cause of Mongolism is unknown. According to Rosanoff and Handy, it is correlated with only one important factor, namely, advanced age of the mother. That some damage to the ovum is involved is indicated by the fact that Rosanoff reports that both members of eight pairs of identical twins were Mongolian imbeciles; no cases have been reported in the literature on identical twins in which one twin was Mongolian and the

---

[1] There is one form of feeble-mindedness—a very rare one—for which there is fair evidence that it is hereditary, namely, amaurotic family idiocy. The idiocy does not appear at once. At a certain point there is arrest and subsequent deterioration to the point of complete idiocy and finally death.

other was not. There have, however, been pairs of fraternal twins in which one was Mongolian, the other not (Penrose).

Cretinism.—Cretinism is due to a deficiency in thyroid secretion. It appears early in life, and it varies in severity, ranging from complete idiocy to moronity. A cretin is easily identified by his physical appearance, for the body is dwarfed, the head is abnormally large, the neck is short and thick, the skin dry, the eyes are half-shut and the eyelids swollen, the hair is scanty, and the limbs are short and pudgy. These individuals are harmless and easy to manage, for they are good-humored and placid.

The physical condition is almost always curable if treatment is started early enough. Treatment consists in making up the thyroid deficiency with thyroid tissue or extract. There is some indication that the essential causative factor in hypothyroidism is an insufficiency of iodine, which is necessary in the production of the thyroid hormone, thyroxin; hence the administration of iodine may lessen the incidence of cretinism. Often enough, however, the intellectual improvement does not keep pace with the physical, and the person remains mentally retarded.

Microcephaly.—The skull of the microcephalic usually has a smaller than average circumference; but the chief features are its cone shape, the receding forehead and chin, and the absence of the usual protuberance at the back of the head. The brain is abnormally small and often shows anomalies of one type or another; for example, the convolutions are simpler and the cerebellum and cerebrum are smaller. Microcephalics as a rule are imbeciles; they tend often to be less good-tempered and affectionate than other aments, but respond well to training.

There is some evidence that pelvic X-ray irradiation during pregnancy considerably increases the probability of microcephalic births.[1]

Hydrocephaly.—The chief characteristic of the hydrocephalic is the enormous skull. The condition is due to an excessive amount of cerebral spinal fluid in the ventricles of the brain.

[1] D. P. Murphy, Ovarian irradiation, *Surgery, Gynecology and Obstetrics*, 1928, 47, 201-215.

Since the skull has a limited capacity, the abnormal quantity of fluid impairs the development of the nerve cells of the brain; the brain tissue is so greatly reduced that there are gross changes in the brain, such as absence of convolutions, etc. The cause of the condition is not known. The mental defects incidental to hydrocephaly may vary in severity; in fact, a few cases have been reported which showed no apparent defect. Like so many other feeble-minded people, the hydrocephalics tend to be cheerful, good-natured, and affectionate.

Feeble-mindedness Due to Trauma or Disease.—Many factors may damage the nervous system and give rise to mental deficiency. Tredgold uses a fourfold classification for such factors: traumatic, toxic, convulsive, and nutritional. Traumatic factors are usually those which inflict direct physical damage to the brain, such as blows, falls, and similar accidents. Here also may be included brain damage due to difficult birth. Toxic factors likewise enter, as when the brain is poisoned during such diseases as scarlet fever, diphtheria, etc.; fortunately, however, this is rare. More common is amentia as an effect of cerebral inflammation due to syphilis or encephalitis lethargica. Alcohol and other drugs and various poisons may have a general deleterious effect upon the development of the brain in the young child. Various evidence indicates that qualitative malnutrition (lack of vitamins, minerals) may cause or encourage mental deficiency, but no definite statement is as yet possible. Mental deficiency is related to certain of the hormone deficiencies. For example, a thyroid deficiency results in cretinism. Pituitary dystrophy may also lead to mental defect.

Mental Defect Due to Sensory Deprivation.—Although little of this is seen today, the subject is still of great theoretical importance, for it is one of the clearest instances of acquired feeble-mindedness. It used to be that children born blind or deaf were practically doomed to retardation or actual feeble-mindedness, both because of limitation upon their knowledge and also because they were inaccessible to ordinary techniques of education. With the new understanding that science has made possible and with the development of special educational techniques, such children can now be reclaimed to normal intelligence.

Mental Defect Due to Social Isolation.—Also of great theoretical importance is the fact that there are in the literature a small number of psychological reports of children who had been isolated at an early age and had lived in woods and in caves with animals. When found, these children always appeared to be feeble-minded. Sometimes education helped and other times it did not. In the most famous case on record, the so-called "Wild Boy of Aveyron," we do not know to this day whether the child's ultimate feeble-mindedness was hereditary or due to the social isolation.

Whether this feeble-mindedness is permanent or not seems to depend on the child's age when social isolation begins. If he is very young, permanent mental defect is to be expected; otherwise not (159). Man's humanness seems to depend upon his being a social animal. Without a cultural training, man is really not to be considered a true human being.

Stupidity; Pseudo-feeble-mindedness

It is clear that low intelligence test scores can be a result of various environmental influences; it is now becoming increasingly apparent that they can also result from a poor internal environment—emotional confusion, unconscious conflict, or a frustrated personality. That is, like so many of the responses we have already studied, a decrease in intelligence may be a functional, purposeful adjustment, a poor but nevertheless effective way of coping with the stresses and problems of life. And as heretofore, it will be instructive to look for the meanings, the unconscious purposes expressed by the particular symptom.

Lack of Intelligence as a Response to Discouragement.— Adler[1] and his students (Löwy, 510, among others) were of the

---

[1] It was a favorite amusement of Dr. Adler to take children who had been diagnosed as stupid or even feeble-minded in terms of I.Q., and by means

opinion that apparent stupidity, where it was not definitely innate, was often the way of life of a discouraged person, one who had been been beaten and kicked about, who felt so little respected or loved that he drew into himself, using apparent stupidity as a way of avoiding all responsibilities and at the same time revenging himself upon the world.

It is easy enough to see this in a milder form in the college classroom. Students with low self-esteem (who may be considered to be mildly "discouraged") speak less often, do not do as well as they should when they do speak, get more flustered by examinations, and in general do not make as good an impression as their abilities would indicate.[1]

Where self-esteem is low, as in these college students, or has altogether disappeared, there is a great mistrust of one's mental products and also, as Harlow has suggested, a very low level of aspiration. Such individuals are afraid to try anything that has not been proved again and again to be well within their capacities. They are likely to give up before trying; and even if they do try, their expectation of failure is likely to insure their actual failure.

The manifestation of intelligence is thus based in part on a certain level of courage, of aspiration, and of self-esteem.

"Mary Mason was sent to me by the dean because she was failing in most of her work. I found that in addition to great difficulties in studying she was having trouble with her room-mate, was burdened down by jealousy of her sister, was alternately tearful and cynical, and was regarded by the students as moody and disagreeable. She was totally discouraged with college and was homesick, and thought she could never be popular or successful in her work.

"Upon looking up her intelligence-test rating, I found that it indicated that her intellectual capacity would probably never exceed that of a fifteen-year-old girl. Accordingly I wrote to the dean that it was

---

of psychotherapy, to make them intelligent again. His style of treatment is discussed in Löwy (510).

[1] See a recent experiment on this point by A. Meadow, "Personality and Classroom Achievement." *Journal of Psychology*, 1940, 9, 269-274.

probably not worth while struggling on with her, because she lacked the intellectual capacity to do college work and was having adverse emotional reactions to her difficulties.

"What actually happened is that she developed influenza and pneumonia and had to leave school for a semester; when she came back, she got down to work with such energy that a year later she was doing average or better than average work in every subject."[1]

The Defensive Values of Low Intelligence.—If we think about it for a moment, we can easily see that apparent lack of intelligence has many advantages. It justifies dependence, laziness, and lack of effort. It is a perfect way of avoiding all problems, responsibilities, and potentially dangerous tests of ability. It can be a subtle method for expressing hostility or even superiority in a roundabout way. It affords a path whereby suppressed or subordinate people can still get what they want without endangering themselves. In children, it may even be a vicious form of revenge upon parents for their wrongdoings.

Joan had been queen in her home until the age of two, when a baby sister was born. The little girl was completely forgotten by her hitherto worshiping parents, for they foolishly gave the new baby all their attention. The change from complete and exclusive love to utter neglect was more than Joan could bear. She showed open hatred for the baby and struck her several times; when she was harshly punished for this, she became mute and never spoke again until she was about three and a half years old. Most of the time she apparently did not understand what was said to her, but the parents reported several incidents which seemed to prove that she did understand when it was definitely to her advantage to do so.

The situation was rather easily cleared up by suggesting to the parents that they reassure Joan of their love for her in as many ways as possible, that they show no favoritism, and finally that Joan attend a nursery school. After several months, the nursery school teacher, to whom the case had been carefully explained, began to report a rapid development in overt understanding, cooperation, and speech.

[1] Menninger, *The Human Mind*, Alfred A. Knopf, Inc., New York, 2nd ed., 1937, p. 60.

One year after the initial interview, Joan's intelligence would be diagnosed as at least average and possibly even superior.

The defensive value of pseudo-feeble-mindedness has been brilliantly brought out by John Dollard (187) in a study of Negroes in southern towns. According to this study, the Negro, pushed into a position of subordination, has open to him very few channels through which to express aggression and independence. One of these, paradoxically enough, is stupidity—not understanding, doing things wrong. In this way, a hated boss may be hurt or his interests damaged without incurring any of the penalties that a more "intelligent person" would incur; for the boss himself has set up as needed and purposeful the myth of innate Negro inferiority. This process is evident in everyday life. For example, men who dislike housework have unanimously fostered the legend that they are stupid about cooking, washing dishes, etc. What better way is there to avoid washing dishes than by clumsily breaking a few once in a while!

Thus even in the sphere of intellect, we rediscover some of the essential psychodynamic principles which have been discussed throughout the book. Even unintelligent behavior may have its various meanings; these are likely to be unconscious attempts at achieving something, defending the personality, or making the person happier. This roundabout and inefficient path is chosen because the individual's fundamental needs have, in one fashion or another, been frustrated or come into conflict with one another. Give him back his self-esteem and his feeling of security, and his symptoms—whether apparent stupidity or hostility or compulsions—tend to disappear.

SUGGESTED READINGS

For technical surveys of the whole field of mental defect, the student is referred to Penrose's *Mental Defect* (606) or Tredgold's *Mental Deficiency* (755). For a less technical but a much more readable account, "Moronia," the first chapter of Wembridge's *Life*

Among the Lowbrows (775) is excellent. For another approach to feeble-mindedness, read the various numbers of the *International Journal of Individual Psychology*; in this journal will be found several cases treated by Adler's methods. A good example is the article by Löwy (510). For another example of dynamic study of feeble-mindedness, see K. Lewin (488).

BIBLIOGRAPHY

1. Abeles, M., and Schilder, P., Psychogenic loss of personal identity, *Arch. Neurol. Psychiat.*, 1935, **34**, 587-604.
2. Abraham, K., *Selected Papers on Psychoanalysis,* Hogarth, London, 1927.
3. Adler, Alexandra, *Guiding Human Misfits,* Macmillan, New York, 1938.
4. Adler, Alfred, *Neurotic Constitution,* Moffat, Yard, New York, 1917.
5. Adler, A., *Study of Organ Inferiority and Its Psychical Compensation,* Nerv. & Ment. Dis. Pub., Washington, 1917.
6. Adler, A., *The Practice and Theory of Individual Psychology,* Harcourt, Brace, New York, 1924.
7. Adler, A., *Understanding Human Nature,* Greenberg, New York, 1927.
8. Adler, A., *Problems of Neurosis,* Cosmopolitan, New York, 1930.
9. Adler, A., *The Education of Children,* Greenberg, New York, 1930.
10. Adler, A., *What Life Should Mean to You,* Little, Brown, Boston, 1931.
11. Adler, A., Psychiatric aspects regarding individual and social disorganization, *Amer. J. Sociol.*, 1937, **42**, 773-780.
12. Adler, A., *Social Interest: A Challenge to Mankind,* Faber and Faber, London, 1938.
13. Adler, A., and Crookshank, F. D., Individual psychology and sexual difficulties (II), *Individual Psychology Pamphlets, No. 13,* Daniel, London, 1936.
14. Adler, A.; Dreikurs, R.; Wexberg, I.; Hervat, J.; Young, J. C.; Crookshank, F. D.; Luff, M. C., and others, Individual psychology and sexual difficulties (I), *Individual Psychology Pamphlets, No. 3,* Daniel, London, 1932.

15. Adler, A.; Wolfe, W. B.; Burns, C. L. C., and Young, J. C., Individual psychology and social problems (I), *Individual Psychology Pamphlets*, No. 5, Daniel, London, 1932.

16. Aichhorn, A., *Wayward Youth*, Viking, New York, 1935.

17. Alexander, F., *The Medical Value of Psychoanalysis*, Norton, New York, 1936.

18. Alexander, F., Psychoanalysis and social disorganization, *Amer. J. Sociol.*, 1937, 42, 781-813.

19. Alexander, F., Emotional factors in essential hypertension, *Psychosom. Med.*, 1939, 1, 173-179.

20. Alexander, F., Psychological aspects of medicine, *Psychosom. Med.*, 1939, 1, 7-18.

21. Alexander, F. G., Schizophrenic psychoses: Critical considerations of psychoanalytic treatment, *Arch. Neurol. Psychiat.*, 1931, 26, 815-828.

22. Alexander, F. G., The influence of psychologic factors upon gastro-intestinal disturbances: A symposium, *Psychoanal. Quart.*, 1934, 3, 501-588.

23. Alexander, F. G., Psychoanalysis revised, *Psychoanal. Quart.*, 1940, 9, 1-36.

24. Alexander, F. G., and Healy, W., *Roots of Crime*, Knopf, New York, 1935.

25. Alexander, F. G., and Staub, H., *The Criminal, the Judge, and the Public*, Macmillan, New York, 1931.

26. Allen, C., *Modern Discoveries in Medical Psychology*, Macmillan, New York, 1937.

27. Allport, G. W., *Personality: A Psychological Interpretation*, Holt, New York, 1937.

28. Anderson, H. H., Conflicts in personality development, *Ment. Hyg.*, 1936, 20, 605-613.

29. Anderson, O. D., and Liddell, H. S., Observations on experimental neurosis in sheep, *Arch. Neurol. Psychiat.*, 1935, 34, 330-354.

30. Anderson, O. D.; Parmenter, R., and Liddell, H. S., Some cardiovascular manifestations of the experimental neurosis in sheep, *Psychosom. Med.*, 1939, 1, 93-100.

31. Angyal, A., Perceptual basis of somatic delusions in case of schizophrenia, *Arch. Neurol. Psychiat.*, 1935, 34, 270-279.

32. Ansbacher, H., Johannsen's terminology as applied to Adler's theory of personality, *Int. J. Indiv. Psychol.*, 1935, 1, 63-66.

33. Anthonisen, N. L., Aggression and anxiety in the determination and nature of manic attacks, *Arch. Neurol. Psychiat.*, 1937, 38, 71-89.

34. Ayres, C., *Holier Than Thou*, Bobbs-Merrill, Indianapolis, 1929.

35. Babinski, J., and Froment, J., *Hysteria or Pithiatism and Reflex Nervous Disorders in War*, Univ. of London Press, London, 1917.

36. Bagby, E., Inferiority reaction, *J. Abnorm. Soc. Psychol.*, 1923, 18, 269-273.

37. Bagby, E., *Psychology of Personality: An Analysis of Common Emotional Disorders*, Holt, New York, 1928.

38. Bailey, P., "The psychology of human conduct," a review, *Amer. J. Psychiat.*, 1928, 8, 209-234.

39. Baker, L. E., The pupillary response conditioned to subliminal auditory stimuli, *Psychol. Monog.*, 1938, 50, No. 3.

40. Baker, L. E., Catharsis and subliminal conditioning. (In press.)

41. Bard, P., A diencephalic mechanism for the expression of rage, with special reference to the sympathetic nervous system, *Amer. J. Physiol.*, 1928, 84, 490-515.

42. Bard, P., The central representation of the sympathetic system as indicated by certain physiologic observations, *Arch. Neurol. Psychiat.*, 1929, 22, 230-246.

43. Bard, P., On emotional expression after decortication, with some remarks on certain theoretical views (Parts 1 and 2), *Psychol. Rev.*, 1934, 41, 309-329, 424-449.

44. Bard, P., Central nervous mechanisms for emotional behavior patterns in animals, in *The Inter-Relationship of Mind and Body*, Williams & Wilkins, Baltimore, 1939.

45. Bard, P., and Rioch, D. McK., A study of four cats deprived of neocortex and additional portions of the forebrain, *Bull. Johns Hopkins Hospit.*, 1937, 60, 73-147.

46. Barkley, K. L., A case illustrating probable sublimation through pathological stealing, *J. Abnorm. Soc. Psychol.*, 1936, 31, 208-215.

47. Barnett, J. H., Personality in primitive society, *Character and Pers.*, 1933, **2**, 152-167.

48. Barris, R. W.; Ingram, W. R., and Ranson, S. W., Optic connections of the diencephalon and midbrain of the cat, *J. Comp. Neurol.*, 1935, **62**, 117-153.

49. Barry, H., Jr., A study of bereavement: An approach to problems in mental disease, *Amer. J. Orthopsychiat.*, 1939, **9**, 355-360.

50. Bartlett, F. C., Psychological methods and anthropological problem, *Africa*, 1937, **10**, 401-420.

51. Baruch, D. W., Contrasts in marital relationships impinging on child adjustment: Two cases, *J. Genet. Psychol.*, 1938, **53**, 159-171.

52. Bateson, G., *Naven*, Cambridge Univ. Press, Cambridge, 1936.

53. Baudouin, C., *Suggestion and Auto-Suggestion*, Dodd, Mead, New York, 1921.

54. Beard, G., *A Practical Treatise on Nervous Exhaustion*, Wood, New York, 1880.

55. Beard, G., *American Nervousness*, Wood, New York, 1881.

56. Beck, S. J., Introduction to the Rorschach method, *Monog. No. 1*, Amer. Orthopsychiat. Assoc., 1937.

57. Beers, C. W., *A Mind That Found Itself*, Longmans, New York, 1908.

58. Bender, L., Principles of Gestalt in copied form in mentally defective and schizophrenic persons, *Arch. Neurol. Psychiat.*, 1932, **27**, 661-686.

59. Bender, L., Psychoses associated with somatic diseases that distort the body structure, *Arch. Neurol. Psychiat.*, 1934, **32**, 1000-1029.

60. Bender, L., Form as a principle in the play of children, *J. Genet. Psychol.*, 1936, **49**, 254-261.

61. Bender, L., Reactive psychoses in response to mental disease in the family, *J. Nerv. Ment. Dis.*, 1936, **83**, 143-165.

62. Bender, L., Group activities on a children's ward as methods of psychotherapy, *Amer. J. Psychol.*, 1937, **93**, 1151-1173.

63. Bender, L., A visual motor gestalt test and its clinical use, *Research Monog. No. 3*, Amer. Orthopsychiat. Assoc., 1938.

64. Bender, L., and Schilder, P., Unconditioned and conditioned reactions to pain in schizophrenia, *Amer. J. Psychiat.,* 1930, **10**, 365-384.

65. Bender, L., and Schilder, P., Encephalopathia Alcoholica, *Arch. Neurol. Psychiat.,* 1933, **29**, 990-1053.

66. Bender, L., and Woltmann, A., The use of puppet shows as a psychotherapeutic method for behavior problems in children, *Amer. J. Orthopsychiat.,* 1936, **6**, 341-354.

67. Bender, L., and Woltmann, A., The use of plastic material as a psychiatric approach to emotional problems in children, *Amer. J. Orthopsychiat.,* 1937, **7**, 283-300.

68. Bender, L.; Keiser, S., and Schilder, P., Studies in aggressiveness, *Genet. Psychol. Monog.,* 1936, **18**, 357-564.

69. Bender, M. B., Fright and drug contractions in denervated facial and ocular muscles of monkeys, *Amer. J. Physiol.,* 1938, **121**, 609-619.

70. Benedek, T., Adaptation to reality in early infancy, *Psychoanal. Quart.,* 1938, **7**, 200-214.

71. Benedek, T., and Rubenstein, B. B., The correlations between ovarian activity and psychodynamic processes: I. The ovulative phase, *Psychosom. Med.,* 1939, **1**, 245-270.

72. Benedek, T., and Rubenstein, B. B., The correlations between ovarian activity and psychodynamic processes: II. The menstrual phase, *Psychosom. Med.,* 1939, **1**, 461-485.

73. Benedict, R., Anthropology and the abnormal, *J. Gen. Psychol.,* 1934, **10**, 50-82.

74. Benedict, R., *Patterns of Culture,* Houghton Mifflin, Boston, 1934.

75. Benedict, R., Anthropology and personality (unpublished lecture, Cooper Union, Nov. 14, 1937).

76. Benedict, R., Continuities and discontinuities in cultural conditioning, *Psychiatry,* 1938, **1**, 161-167.

77. Bentley, M., and Cowdry, E. V. (eds.), *The Problem of Mental Disorder,* McGraw-Hill, New York, 1934.

78. Benussi, V., quoted by Woodworth, R. S., *Experimental Psychology,* Holt, New York, 1938.

79. Bernfeld, S., *Psychologie des Sauglings,* Springer, Vienna, 1925.

80. Bernfeld, S., Types of adolescence, *Psychoanal. Quart.*, 1938, 7, 243-253.

81. Bernheim, H., *Suggestive Therapeutics*, Putnam, New York, 1883.

82. Berrien, F. K., A study of the drawings of abnormal children, *J. Educ. Psychol.*, 1935, 26, 143-150.

83. Betlheim, W., and Hartmann, H., Über Fehlerreactionen bei der Korsakoffschen Psychose, *Archiv f. Psychiatrie*, 1924-1925, 72, 275-286.

84. Bevan-Brown, C. M.; Layton, F. G.; Woodcock, O. H., and Edwards, F. M., Individual psychology and practice (II), *Individual Psychology Pamphlets, No. 12*, Daniel, London, 1935.

85. Bevan-Brown, C. M.; Ward, G., and Crookshank, F. G., Individual psychology: Theory and practice, *Individual Psychology Pamphlets, No. 15*, Daniel, London, 1936.

86. Binger, C., The psycho-biology of breathing, *Ann. Int. Med.*, 1937, 2, 195-208.

87. Blalock, J. R., Psychiatric aspects of physical illness, *Virginia Med. Month.*, 1939, 66, 92-94.

88. Blanton, S., *Child Guidance*, Appleton-Century, New York, 1927.

89. Blanton, S., and Blanton, M., *For Stutterers*, Appleton-Century, New York, 1936.

90. Bleuler, E., *Textbook of Psychiatry*, Macmillan, New York, 1924.

91. Bloomberg, W., Effects of benzedrine in altering mental and emotional processes, in *The Inter-Relationship of Mind and Body*, Williams & Wilkins, Baltimore, 1939.

92. Bolles, M., The basis of pertinence, *Arch. Psychol.*, 1937, No. 212.

93. Bonaparte, M., Passivity, masochism and femininity, *Int. J. Psychoanal.*, 1935, 16, 325-333.

94. Bond, E. D., and Braceland, F. Y., Prognosis in mental disease, *Amer. J. Psychiat.*, 1937, 94, 263-274.

95. Bowman, K. M., Alteration of mental and emotional processes by chemical and hormonal agents, in *Inter-Relationship of Mind and Body*, Williams & Wilkins, Baltimore, 1939.

96. Bramwell, J. M., *Hypnotism, Its History, Practice and Theory*, Rider, London, 3rd ed., 1930.

97. Breuer, J., and Freud, S., *Studies in Hysteria*, Nerv. & Ment. Dis. Pub., Washington, 1936.

98. Brickner, R. M., *The Intellectual Functions of the Frontal Lobes*, Macmillan, New York, 1936.

99. Brickner, R. M., and Kubie, L. S., A miniature psychotic storm produced by a super-ego conflict over simple post-hypnotic suggestion, *Psychoanal. Quart.*, 1936, **5**, 467-487.

100. Bridges, J. W., *Outline of Abnormal Psychology*, Adams, Columbus, Ohio, 1925.

101. Bridges, J. W., "What is abnormal psychology?" *J. Abnorm. Soc. Psychol.*, 1930, **24**, 430-432.

102. Briffault, R., *Sin and Sex*, Macaulay, New York, 1931.

103. Brill, A. A., *Fundamental Conceptions of Psychoanalysis*, Harcourt, Brace, New York, 1921.

104. Brill, A. A., *Psychoanalysis: Its Theory and Practical Applications*, Saunders, Philadelphia, 1922.

105. Brill, A. A., The concept of psychic suicide, *Int. J. Psychoanal.*, 1939, **20**, 246-251.

106. Bromberg, W., The effects of marihuana, in *The Inter-Relationship of Mind and Body*, Williams & Wilkins, Baltimore, 1939.

107. Brown, F., The problem of nervousness and its objective verification in children, *J. Abnorm. Soc. Psychol.*, 1936, **31**, 194-206.

108. Brown, J. F., Freud and the scientific method, *Phil. Sci.*, 1934, **1**, 323-337.

109. Brown, J. F., Psychoanalysis, topological psychology and experimental psychopathology, *Psychoanal. Quart.*, 1937, **6**, 227-237.

110. Brown, J. F., Reactions of psychiatric patients in a frustrating situation, *Bull. Menninger Clin.*, 1939, **3**, 44-64.

111. Brown, W., The revival of emotional memories and its therapeutic value, *Brit. J. Med.*, 1920, **22**, 1-2.

112. Brown, W., Sleep, hypnosis and mediumistic trance, *Character and Pers.*, 1934, **3**, 112-126.

113. Bruel, O., Genesis of schizophrenia, *Character and Pers.*, 1936, 4, 185-194.

114. Brun, R., "Experimentelle Beitrage zur Dynami, und Oekonomie des Triebkonfliktes (Biologische Parellelen zur Freuds Trieblehre)," *Imago*, 1926, 12, 147-170.

115. Brunswick, D., The effects of emotional stimuli on the gastrointestinal tone, *J. Comp. Psychol.*, 1924, 4, 19-33.

116. Brunswick, R. M., The preoedipal phase of the libido development, *Psychoanal. Quart.*, 1940, 9, 293-319.

117. Bugelski, R., and Miller, N. E., A spatial gradient in the strength of avoidance responses, *J. Exp. Psychol.*, 1938, 23, 494-505.

118. Bullard, D. M., The application of psychoanalytic psychiatry to the psychoses, *Psychoanal. Rev.*, 1939, 26, 526-534.

119. Bunker, H. A., The treatment of general paralysis by inoculation with malaria, *J. Amer. Med. Assoc.*, 1925, 84, 563-568.

120. Bunker, H. A., and Kirby, G. H., The height and duration of fever in relation to the clinical outcome in the treatment of general paresis with malaria, *Med. Rec.*, 1925, 7, 413-415.

121. Burnham, W. H., Retroactive amnesia, *Amer. J. Psychol.*, 1903, 14, 382-396.

122. Burnham, W. H., *The Wholesome Personality*, Appleton-Century, New York, 1932.

123. Burrow, T., The law of the organism, *Amer. J. Sociol.*, 1937, 42, 814-824.

124. Burrow, T., The organismic factor in disorders of behavior, *J. Psychol.*, 1937, 4, 333-341.

125. Burrow, T., Bio-physical factors in relation to functional imbalances, *Hum. Biol.*, 1938, 10, 93-105.

126. Cameron, N., Individual and social factors in the development of graphic symbolization, *J. Psychol.*, 1938, 5, 165-185.

127. Cameron, N., A study of thinking in senile deterioration and schizophrenic disorganization, *Amer. J. Psychol.*, 1938, 51, 650-665.

128. Cameron, N., Deterioration and repression in schizophrenic thinking, *J. Abnorm. Soc. Psychol.*, 1939, 34, 265-270.

129. Campbell, C. M., *Destiny and Disease in Mental Disorders*, Norton, New York, 1935.

130. Campbell, J. D., Psychiatry and general practice, *J. Amer. Med. Assoc.*, 1939, **112**, 2577-2581.
131. Cannon, W. B., *Wisdom of the Body*, Norton, New York, 1932.
132. Cannon, W. B., *Bodily Changes in Pain, Hunger, Fear and Rage*, Appleton-Century, New York, 2nd ed., 1936.
133. Cannon, W. B., and Britton, S. W., Studies on the conditions of activity in endocrine glands: XV. Pseud-affective medulliadrenal secretion, *Amer. J. Physiol.*, 1925, **72**, 283-294.
134. Carpenter, J., and Eisenberg, P., Some relations between family background and personality, *J. Psychol.*, 1938, **6**, 115-136.
135. Cason, H., Conditioned pupillary reactions, *J. Exp. Psychol.*, 1922, **5**, 108-146.
136. Cason, H., The nightmare dream, *Psychol. Monog.*, 1935, **46**, No. 5.
137. Clark, L. P., Clinical studies in epilepsy, *Psychiat. Bull.*, 1916, **9**, 60-103.
138. Clark, Le Gros W. E., and Boggon, R. H., On the connections of the anterior nucleus of the thalamus, *J. Anat.*, 1933, **67**, 215-226.
139. Coignard, J., *Spectacle of a Man*, Morrow, New York, 1937.
140. Conklin, E. S., The definition of introversion, extraversion and allied concepts, *J. Abnorm. Soc. Psychol.*, 1923, **17**, 367-382.
141. Conklin, E. S., Photographed Lilliputian hallucinations, *J. Nerv. Ment. Dis.*, 1925, **62**, 135-140.
142. Conklin, E. S., *Principles of Abnormal Psychology*, Holt, New York, 2nd ed., 1939.
143. Conrad, A., The psychiatric study of hyperthyroid patients, *J. Nerv. Ment. Dis.*, 1934, **79**, 505-656.
144. Cook, S. W., The production of experimental neurosis in the white rat, *Psychosom. Med.*, 1939, **1**, 293-308.
145. Cook, S. W., A survey of methods used to produce experimental neurosis, *Amer. J. Psychiat.*, 1939, **95**, 1259-1276.
146. Coriat, I. H., Reduplicative paramnesia, *J. Nerv. Ment. Dis.*, 1904, **31**, 577-587, 639-659.
147. Coriat, I. H., *Stammering*, Nerv. & Ment. Dis. Pub., Washington, 1927.

148. Crichton-Miller, J., *Psychoanalysis and Its Derivatives,* Butterworth, London, 1933.

149. Crookshank, F. G., Individual psychology, medicine, and the bases of science, *Individual Psychology Pamphlets, No. 3a,* Daniel, London, 1933.

150. Crookshank, F. G., Individual psychology and Nietzsche, *Individual Psychology Pamphlets, No. 10,* Daniel, London, 1935.

151. Crowley, M. R., Psychoanalytic literature on drug addiction and alcoholism, *Psychoanal. Rev.,* 1939, **26,** 39-54.

152. Cubberly, A. S., The effect of tensions on the body surface upon the normal dream, *Brit. J. Psychol.,* 1923, **13,** 245-265.

153. Culler, E., A phobic case, *Brit. J. Med. Psychol.,* 1930, **10,** 46-69.

154. Curti, M. W., *Child Psychology,* Longmans, New York, 1930.

155. Curtis, Q. F., Frustration as an experimental problem, *Character and Pers.,* 1938, **7,** 140-144.

156. Daniels, G. E., Neuroses associated with the gastro-intestinal tract, *Amer. J. Psychiat.,* 1934, **91,** 529-540.

157. Daniels, G. E., Psychic factors in gastro-intestinal disease, *N. Y. State J. Med.,* 1936, **36,** 602-606.

158. Daniels, G. E., Emotional and instinctual factors in diabetes mellitus, *Amer. J. Psychiat.,* 1936, **93,** 711-724.

159. Daniels, G. E., Present trends in the evaluation of psychic factors in diabetes mellitus: A critical review of experimental, general medical and psychiatric literature of the last five years, *Psychosom. Med.,* 1939, **1,** 527-552.

160. Daniels, G. E., Treatment of case of ulcerative colitis associated with hysterical depression, *Psychosom. Med.,* 1940.

161. Darling, C. R., Fire walking, *Nature,* 1936, **137,** 621-622.

162. Davis, H. D., and Davis, P. A., The electrical activity of the brain: Its relation to physiological states and to states of impaired consciousness, in *The Inter-Relationship of Mind and Body,* Williams & Wilkins, Baltimore, 1939.

163. Davis, K., Extreme social isolation of a child, *Amer. J. Sociol.,* 1940, **45,** 554-565.

164. Davis, L., and Husband, R. W., A study of hypnotic susceptibility in relation to personality traits, *J. Abnorm. Soc. Psychol.,* 1931, **26,** 175-182.

165. Dearborn W., *Intelligence Tests: Their Significance for School and Society*, Houghton Mifflin, Boston, 1928.

166. Dent, J. Y., *The Human Machine*, Knopf, New York, 1937.

167. Dershimer, F. W., A study in the cause and prevention of functional mental disease, *Amer. J. Orthopsychiat.*, 1938, **8**, 302-328.

168. Deutsch, F., Gehauftes auftreten von Morbus Basedowi, *Med. Klin.*, 1923, **19**, 678-681.

169. Deutsch, F., Emotions and respiratory mechanism: hypnotic experiments, *Wiener Kl. Woch.*, 1925, **38**, 1127-1130.

170. Deutsch, F., The choice of organ in organ neuroses, *Int. J. Psychoanal.*, 1939, **20**, 252-262.

171. Deutsch, F., The associative anamnesis, *Psychoanal. Quart.*, 1939, **8**, 354-381.

172. Deutsch, F., The production of somatic disease by emotional disturbance, in *The Inter-Relationship of Mind and Body*, Williams & Wilkins, Baltimore, 1939.

173. Deutsch, F., and Kauf, E., Uber die ursachen der Krieslaufstorungen bei den Herzneurosen, *Ztsch. f. d. ges. Exper. Med.*, 1923, **34**, 71-81.

174. Deutsch, H., *Psychoanalysis of the Neuroses*, Hogarth, London, 1932.

175. Deutsch, H., Zur Psychologie der manisch-depressiven Zustande, insbesondere der chronischen Hypomania, *Int. Zeit. f. Psychoanal.*, 1933, **19**, 358-370.

176. Devereux, G., Institutionalized homosexuality of the Mohave Indians, *Hum. Biol.*, 1937, **9**, 498-527.

177. Devereux, G., A sociological theory of schizophrenia, *Psychoanal. Rev.*, 1939, **26**, 315-342.

178. Dewey, J., *How We Think*, Heath, Boston, 1933.

179. Dickinson, R. L., and Beam, L., *One Thousand Marriages*, Williams & Wilkins, Baltimore, 1932.

180. Dickinson, R. L., and Beam, L., *The Single Woman*, Williams & Wilkins, Baltimore, 1933.

181. Dicks, G. H., and Childers, A. T., The social transformation of a boy who had lived his first fourteen years as a girl: A case history, *Amer. J. Orthopsychiat.*, 1934, **4**, 508-517.

182. Diethelm, O., On bromide intoxication, *J. Nerv. Ment. Dis.*, 1930, 71, 151-165, 278-292.

183. Diethelm, O., *Treatment in Psychiatry*, Macmillan, New York, 1936.

184. Diller, T., The question of hysterical analysis and the theory of Babinski, *J. Abnorm. Psychol.*, 1920, 15, 55-56.

185. Dodge, R., and Kahn, E., *Craving for Superiority*, Yale Univ. Press, New Haven, 1931.

186. Dollard, J., *Criteria for the Life History—With Analysis of Six Notable Documents*, Yale Univ. Press, New Haven, 1935.

187. Dollard, J., *Caste and Class in a Southern Town*, Yale Univ. Press, New Haven, 1937.

188. Dollard, J., Hostility and fear in social life, *Social Forces*, 1938, 17, 15-29.

189. Dollard, J., The average American personality (unpublished lecture, Cooper Union, 1938).

190. Dollard, J.; Doob, L.; Miller, N.; Mowrer, O., and Sears, R., *Frustration and Aggression*, Yale Univ. Press, New Haven, 1939.

191. Doob, L. W., Variability and culture, *Psychol. Monog.*, 1936, 47, 374-380.

192. Doob, L. W., and Sears, R. R., Factors determining substitute behavior and the overt expression of aggression, *J. Abnorm. Soc. Psychol.*, 1939, 34, 293-313.

193. Dorcus, R. M., and Shaffer, G. W., *Textbook of Abnormal Psychology*, Williams & Wilkins, Baltimore, 2nd ed., 1939.

194. Draper, G., Constitution and disease, In *Nelson Loose-Leaf Living Medicine*, Vol. VII, Chap. XVI.

195. Draper, G., Disease, a psychosomatic reaction, *J. Amer. Med. Assoc.*, 1928, 90, 1281-1284.

196. Dreikurs, R., The choice of a mate, *Int. J. Indiv. Psychol.*, 1935, 1, 99-112.

197. DuBois, C., Some anthropological perspectives on psychoanalysis, *Psychoanal. Rev.*, 1937, 24, 246-263.

198. Dubois, P., *Psychic Treatment of Nervous Disorders*, Funk & Wagnalls, New York, 6th ed., 1909.

199. Dunbar, H. F., Physical-mental relationship in illness, *Amer. J. Psychiat.*, 1934, **91**, 541-562.

200. Dunbar, H. F., Psychic factors in cardiac disease. *N. Y. State J. Med.*, 1936, **36**, 423-429.

201. Dunbar, H. F., The psychic component of disease processes in cardiac, diabetes and fracture patients, *Amer. J. Psychiat.*, 1936, **93**, 651-679.

202. Dunbar, H. F., *Emotions and Bodily Changes*, Columbia Univ. Press, New York, 2nd ed., 1938.

203. Dunbar, H. F., Psychoanalytic notes relating to syndromes of asthma and hay fever, *Psychoanal. Quart.*, 1938, **7**, 25-68.

204. Dunbar, H. F., Psychosomatic history and techniques of examination, *Amer. J. Psychiat.*, 1939, **95**, 1277-1305.

205. Dunham, H. W., Ecology of the functional psychoses in Chicago, *Amer. Sociol. Rev.*, 1937, **2**, 467-479.

206. Dunton, W. R., *Prescribing Occupational Therapy*, Saunders, Philadelphia, 1922.

207. Dusser de Barenne, J. G., Recherches expérimentales sur les fonctions du système nerveux central, faites en particulier sur deux chats dont le néopallium avait été enlevé, *Arch. neerl. de Physiol.*, 1920, **4**, 31-123.

208. Dworkin, S., Conditioning neuroses in dog and cat, *Psychosom. Med.*, 1939, **1**, 388-396.

209. Eisenberg, P., Factors related to feeling of dominance, *J. Consult. Psychol.*, 1937, **1**, 89-92.

210. Eisenberg, P., Expressive movements related to feelings of dominance, *Arch. Psychol.*, 1937, No. 211.

211. Eisenberg, P., Judging expressive movement: I. Judgments of sex and dominance-feeling from handwriting samples of dominant and non-dominant men and women, *J. Appl. Psychol.*, 1938, **22**, 468-480.

212. Eisenberg, P., and Lazarsfeld, P., The psychological effects of unemployment, *Psychol. Bull.*, 1938, **35**, 358-390.

213. Eisenberg, P., and Zalowitz, E., Judging expressive movement: III. Judgments of dominance feeling from phonograph records of voice, *J. Appl. Psychol.*, 1938, **22**, 620-631.

214. Eisenson, J., *Psychology of Speech*, Crofts, New York, 1938.

215. English, O. S., and Pearson, G. H. J., *Common Neuroses of Children and Adults,* Norton, New York, 1937.

216. Enke, E., The affectivity of Kretschmer's constitution types as revealed in psycho-galvanic experiments, *Character and Pers.,* 1933, 1, 225-233.

217. Ephron, H. S., Moral judgment in therapy, *Amer. J. Ortho-psychiat.,* 1939, 9, 339-347.

218. Erickson, M. H., A brief survey of hypnotism, *Med. J.,* 1934, 140, 609-613.

219. Erickson, M. H., A clinical note on a word association test, *J. Nerv. Ment. Dis.,* 1936, 84, 338-540.

220. Erickson, M. H., The experimental demonstration of unconscious mentation by automatic writing, *Psychoanal. Quart.,* 1937, 6, 513-529.

221. Erickson, M. H., The problem of the definition and the dynamic values of psychiatric concepts, *Med. Rec.,* 1938, 147, 107-109.

222. Erickson, M. H., The hypnotic induction of hallucinatory color vision followed by pseudo-negative after-images, *J. Exp. Psychol.,* 1938, 22, 581-588.

223. Erickson, M. H., A study of clinical and experimental findings on hypnotic deafness, *J. Gen. Psychol.,* 1938, 19, 151-167.

224. Erickson, M. H., The induction of color blindness by a technique of hypnotic suggestion, *J. Gen. Psychol.,* 1939, 20, 61-89.

225. Erickson, M. H., An experimental investigation of the possible anti-social use of hypnosis, *Psychiatry,* 1939, 2, 391-414.

226. Erickson, M. H., Experimental demonstrations of the psychopathology of everyday life, *Psychoanal. Quart.,* 1939, 8, 338-353.

227. Erickson, M. H., and Kubie, S. L., Use of automatic drawing in interpretation and relief of a state of acute obsessional depression, *Psychoanal. Quart.,* 1938, 7, 443-453.

228. Erickson, M. H., and Kubie, S. L., The permanent relief of an obsessional phobia by means of communications with an unsuspected dual personality, *Psychoanal. Quart.,* 1939, 8, 471-509.

229. Erikson, E. H., Observations on Sioux education, *J. Psychol.*, 1939, **7**, 101-156.

230. Fairbairn, J. S.; Eccles, W. M., and others, Individual psychology and psychosomatic disorders (II), *Individual Psychology Pamphlets, No. 9*, Daniel, London, 1935.

231. Faris, R. E. L., and Dunham, H. W., *Mental Disorders in Urban Areas*, Univ. of Chicago Press, Chicago, 1939.

232. Federn, P., The undirected function in the central nervous system. A question put to physiology by psychology, *Int. J. Psychoanal.*, 1938, **19**, 173-198.

233. Fenichel, O., *Outline of Clinical Psychoanalysis*, Norton, New York, 1934.

234. Fenichel, O., Problems of psychoanalytic technique, Parts 1-4, *Psychoanal. Quart.*, 1939, **8**, Nos. 1-4.

235. Ferenczi, S., *Contributions to Psychoanalysis*, Badger, Boston, 1916.

236. Ferenczi, S., *Further Contributions to the Theory and Technique of Psychoanalysis*, Hogarth, London, 1926.

237. Ferenczi, S., and Rank, O., *The Development of Psychoanalysis*, Nerv. & Ment. Dis. Pub., Washington, 1925.

238. Ferguson, M.; Weber, H.; Woodcock, O. H.; Bevan-Brown, F. H., and Young, J. C., Awareness and the neuroses of declining years, *Individual Psychology Pamphlets, No. 14*, Daniel, London, 1936.

239. Finesinger, E. J., Effect of pleasant and unpleasant ideas on respiration in psychoneurotic patients, *Arch. Neurol. Psychiat.*, 1939, **42**, 425-490.

240. Fisher, V. E., *Auto-Correctivism*, Caxton Printers, Caldwell, Idaho, 1937.

241. Fisher, V. E., *An Introduction to Abnormal Psychology*, Macmillan, New York, 1937.

242. Flannery, R., Child behavior from the standpoint of the cultural anthropologists, *J. Educ. Sociol.*, 1937, **10**, 470-478.

243. Flugel, J. C., *The Psychoanalytic Study of the Family*, Internat. Psychoanal. Press, London, 1921.

244. Foerster, O., Symptomatologie der Erkrankungen des Grosshirns. Motorische Felder und Bahnen, in Bumke and Foerster, *Handbuch der Neurologie*, 1936, **6**, 1-448.

245. Foerster, O., The motor cortex in man in the light of Hughlings Jackson's doctrines, *Brain*, 1936, **59**, 135-159.

246. Foerster, O., and Penfield, W., Der Narbenzug am und in Gehirn bei traumatischer Epilepsie, etc., *Z. ges. Neurol. Psychiat.*, 1930, **125**, 475-572.

247. Foley, J. P., The criterion of abnormality, *J. Abnorm. Soc. Psychol.*, 1935, **30**, 279-291.

248. Forbes, A., and Sherrington, C. S., Acoustic reflexes in the decerebrate cat, *Amer. J. Physiol.*, 1914, **35**, 367-376.

249. Forel, A., *Hypnotism and Psychotherapy*, Allied Book, New York, 1907.

250. Frank, L. K., Society as the patient, *Amer. J. Sociol.*, 1936, **42**, 335-344.

251. Frank, L. K., The fundamental needs of the child, *Ment. Hyg.*, 1938, **22**, 353-379.

252. Frank, L. K., Cultural control and physiological autonomy, *Amer. J. Orthopsychiat.*, 1938, **8**, 622-626.

253. Frank, L. K., Cultural coercion and individual distortion, *Psychiatry*, 1939, **2**, 11-27.

254. Frank, L. K., Projective methods for the study of personality, *J. Psychol.*, 1939, **8**, 389-413.

255. Franz, S. I., *Nervous and Mental Re-Education*, Macmillan, New York, 1923.

256. Franz, S. I., *Persons One and Three*, McGraw-Hill, New York, 1933.

257. Freedman, B., Psychosocial repression and social rationalization, *Amer. J. Orthopsychiat.*, 1939, **9**, 109-123.

258. Freeman, G. L., The effect of inhibited micturition upon interrupted and completed acts of unrelated origin, *J. Gen. Psychol.*, 1938, **29**, 277-283.

259. Freeman, G. L., Postural substrate, *Psychol. Rev.*, 1938, **45**, 324-335.

260. Freeman, G. L., Postural tensions and the conflict situation, *Psychol. Rev.*, 1939, **46**, 226-240.

261. Freeman, G. L., A preliminary study of the role of postural adjustment in conditioning, *Amer. J. Psychol.*, 1939, **52**, 89-94.

262. Freeman, G. L., The problem of set, *Amer. J. Psychol.*, 1939, **52**, 16-30.

263. Freeman, W., and Watts, J. W., An interpretation of the functions of the frontal lobe, *Yale J. Biol. Med.*, 1939, **11**, 527-539.

264. Fremont-Smith, F., The physiological basis of aggression, *Child Study*, 1939, **15**, 234-235.

265. Fremont-Smith, F., The influence of emotional factors upon physiological and pathological processes, *Bull. N. Y. Acad. Med.*, 1939, **15**, 560-569.

266. French, T. M., Reality and the unconscious, *Psychoanal. Quart.*, 1937, **6**, 23-61.

267. French, T. M., Social conflict and psychic conflict, *Amer. J. Sociol.*, 1939, **44**, 922-931.

268. Freud, A., *Introduction to the Technic of Child Analysis*, Nerv. & Ment. Dis. Pub., Washington, 1928.

269. Freud, A., *Introduction to Psycho-Analysis for Teachers and Parents*, Allen & Unwin, London, 1931.

270. Freud, A., *The Ego and the Mechanisms of Defense*, Hogarth, London, 1937.

271. Freud, S., *Group Psychology and the Analysis of the Ego*, Boni and Liveright, New York, 1922.

272. Freud, S., *Beyond the Pleasure Principle*, Internat. Psychoanal. Press, London, 1922.

273. Freud, S., *Collected Papers*, Vols. I-IV, Internat. Psychoanal. Press, London, 1924 (contains Freud's most significant papers and case histories up to 1918 in English translation).

274. Freud, S., *The Ego and the Id*, Hogarth, London, 1927.

275. Freud, S., *The Future of an Illusion*, Woolf, London, 1928.

276. Freud, S., *Civilization and Its Discontents*, Hogarth, London, 1930.

277. Freud, S., *New Introductory Lectures on Psychoanalysis*, Norton, New York, 1933.

278. Freud, S., *Gesammelte Schriften*, Vols. I-XII, Int. Z. Psychoanal., Leipzig, Vienna, Zurich, 1934 (contains all of Freud's works in German up to year 1934).

279. Freud, S., *A General Introduction to Psychoanalysis*, Liveright, New York, 1935.

280. Freud, S., *The Problem of Anxiety*, Norton, New York, 1936.
281. Freud, S., Analysis terminable and interminable, *Int. J. Psychoanal.*, 1937, 18, 373-405.
282. Freud, S., *The Basic Writings of Sigmund Freud*, Modern Library, New York, 1938. (Includes: *The Interpretation of Dreams, The History of the Psychoanalytic Movement, The Psychopathology of Everyday Life, Three Contributions to the Theory of Sex, Totem and Taboo*, and *Wit and Its Relation to the Unconscious*.)
283. Freud, S., Constructions in analysis, *Int. J. Psychoanal.*, 1938, 19, 377-387.
284. Freud, S., An outline of psychoanalysis, *Int. J. Psychoanal.*, 1940, 21, 27-84.
285. Fries, M. E., Interrelationship of physical, mental and emotional life of a child from birth to four years of age, *Amer. J. Dis. of Children*, 1935, 49, 1546-1563.
286. Fries, M. E.; Brokaw, K., and Murray, V. F., The formation of character as observed in the Well Baby Clinic, *Amer. J. Dis. of Children*, 1935, 49, 28-42.
287. Fries, M. E., The study of the emotional development of children, *Medical Woman's J.*, 1936, 1-8.
288. Fries, M. E., The value of a play group in a child-development study, *Ment. Hyg.*, 1937, 31, 106-116.
289. Fries, M. E., Play technique in the analysis of young children, *Psychoanal. Rev.*, 1937, 24, 233-245.
290. Fries, M. E., Factors in character development, neuroses, psychoses, and delinquency, *Amer. J. Orthopsychiat.*, 1937, 7, 142-181.
291. Fromm, E., Die Entwiklung des Christusdogmas, *Imago*, 1930, 16, 305-337.
292. Fromm, E., Zur Psychologie des Verbrechers unter der strafenden Gesellschaft, *Imago*, 1931, 17, 226-251.
293. Fromm, E., in *Studien uber Autorität und Familie* (M. Horkheimer, ed.), Alcan, Paris, 1936.
294. Fromm, E., Lectures on Psychoanalysis and Authority (unpublished).
295. Fromm, E., Selfishness and self-love, *Psychiatry*, 1939, 2, 507-523.

296. Fromm, E., The social philosophy of "Will Therapy," *Psychiatry*, 1939, **2**, 229-237.
297. Fromm-Reichmann, F., Transference problems in schizophrenics, *Psychoanal. Quart.*, 1939, **8**, 412-426.
298. Fulton, J. F., *Physiology of the Nervous System*, Oxford Univ. Press, New York, 1938.
299. Fulton, J. F., Levels of autonomic function with particular reference to the cerebral cortex, in *The Inter-Relationship of Mind and Body*, Williams & Wilkins, Baltimore, 1939.
300. Gantt, W. H., An experimental approach to psychiatry, *Amer. J. Psychiat.*, 1936, **92**, 1007-1021.
301. Gantt, W. H., Extension of a conflict based upon food to other physiological systems and its reciprocal relations with sexual functions, *Amer. J. Physiol.*, 1938, **123**, 73-74.
302. Gelperin, J., Spontaneous remissions in schizophrenia, *J. Amer. Med. Assoc.*, 1939, **112**, 2393-2395.
303. Gillette, J. M., An examination of criteria for the determination of normal society, *Amer. Sociol. Rev.*, 1937, **2**, 501-507.
304. Girden, E., Cerebral mechanisms in conditioning under curare, *Amer. J. Psychol.*, 1940, **53**, 397-406.
305. Gitelson, M. (chairman); Ross, H.; Erikson, E. H.; Allen, F.; Blanchard, P.; Lippman, S. H.; Gerard, M., and Lowrey, L. G., Section on play therapy, *Amer. J. Orthopsychiat.*, 1938, **8**, 499-524.
306. Glover, E., The psycho-analysis of affects, *Int. J. Psychoanal.*, 1939, **20**, 299-307.
307. Glover, E., *Psycho-Analysis*, John Bale Med. Pub., Ltd., London, 1939.
308. Glover, E.; Fenichel, O.; Strachey, J.; Bergler, E.; Nunberg, H., and Bibring, E., Symposium on the theory of the therapeutic results of psychoanalysis, *Int. J. Psychoanal.*, 1937, **18**, 125-189.
309. Goldman, G. S., A case of compulsive handwashing, *Psychoanal. Quart.*, 1938, **7**, 96-121.
310. Goldstein, K., The meaning of words, *J. Psychol.*, 1937, **2**, 301-316.
311. Goldstein, K., *The Organism*, American Book, New York, 1939.

312. Goltz, F., Der Hund ohne Grosshirn, *Pflug. Arch. ges. Physiol.*, 1892, **51**, 570-614.

313. Gordon, R. G., *Personality*, Harcourt, Brace, New York, 1926.

314. Gould, R., Review of "Frustration and Aggression," *Amer. Anthrop.*, 1940, **42**, 350-353.

315. Gould, R., Social factors in psychopathology, *Psychol. League J.*, 1939, **3**, 53-59.

316. Greenacre, P., The content of the schizophrenic characteristics occurring in affective disorders, *Amer. J. Insanity*, 1918, **75**, 197-202.

317. Groves, E. R., and Blanchard, P., *Readings in Mental Hygiene*, Holt, New York, 1936.

318. Gutheil, E., *The Language of the Dream*, Macmillan, New York, 1939.

319. Guthrie, E. R., *The Psychology of Human Conflict*, Harper, New York, 1938.

320. Haas, L. J., *Occupational Therapy for the Mentally and Nervously Ill*, Bruce, Milwaukee, 1925.

321. Hallowell, A. I., Psychic stress and culture patterns, *Amer. J. Psychiat.*, 1936, **92**, 1291-1310.

322. Hallowell, A. I., Fear and anxiety as cultural and individual variables in a primitive society, *J. Soc. Psychol.*, 1938, **9**, 25-47.

323. Hallowell, A. I., Shabwan; A dissocial Indian girl, *Amer. J. Orthopsychiat.*, 1938, **8**, 329-340.

324. Halverson, H. M., Infant sucking and tensional behavior, *J. Gen. Psychol.*, 1938, **58**, 365-430.

325. Halverson, H. M., Genital and sphincter behavior of the male infant, *J. Gen. Psychol.*, 1940, **56**, 94-147.

326. Hamilton, J. B., Treatment of sexual underdevelopment with synthetic male hormone substance, *Endocrinology*, 1937, **21**, 649-654.

327. Hanfmann, E., Thought disturbances in schizophrenia as revealed by performance in a picture completion test, *J. Abnorm. Soc. Psychol.*, 1939, **34**, 249-264.

328. Hanks, L. M., Jr., Adulthood of the favored child among the Northern Blackfeet, *Psychol. Bull.*, 1939, **36**, 541-542.

329. Harington, C. R., *The Thyroid Gland, Its Chemistry and Physiology*, Oxford Univ. Press, London, 1933.
330. Harris, S., Hyperinsulinism and dysinsulinism, *J. Amer. Med. Assoc.*, 1924, **83**, 729-733.
331. Harris, S., Clinical types of hyperinsulinism: A report of cases, *Amer. J. Digest. Dis. and Nutr.*, 1934, **1**, 562-569.
332. Hart, B., *The Psychology of Insanity*, Macmillan, New York, 4th ed., 1931.
333. Harvey, E. N., Electrical potentials of the human brain, in Baitsell, G. A., *Science in Progress*, Yale Univ. Press, New Haven, 1939, 233-254.
334. Healy, W., *Mental Conflicts and Misconduct*, Little, Brown, Boston, 1919.
335. Healy, W.; Bronner, A. F., and Bowers, A. M., *The Structure and Meaning of Psychoanalysis*, Knopf, New York, 1930.
336. Heilig, R., and Hoff, H., Uber psychogene entstehung des herpes labialis, *Med. Klin.*, 1928, **24**, 1472.
337. Heise, H. A., Alcohol and automobile accidents, *J. Amer. Med. Assoc.*, 1934, **103**, 739-741.
338. Helson, H., and Quantius, L., Changes in skin temperature following intense stimulation, *J. Exp. Psychol*, 1934, **17**, 20-35.
339. Henderson, D. K., *Psychopathic States*, Norton, New York, 1939.
340. Henderson, D. K., and Gillespie, R. D., *A Textbook of Psychiatry*, Oxford Univ. Press, London, 5th ed., 1940.
341. Hendrick, I., *Facts and Theories of Psychoanalysis*, Knopf, New York, 1939.
342. Henry, G. W., Psychogenic factors in overt homosexuality, *Amer. J. Psychiat.*, 1937, **93**, 889-908.
343. Henry, G. W., *Essentials of Psychiatry*, Williams and Wilkins, Baltimore, rev. ed., 1938.
344. Henry, J., The personality of the Kaingang Indians, *Character and Pers.*, 1936, **5**, 113-123.
345. Hermann, I., The use of the term "active" in the definition of masculinity, *Int. J. Psychoanal.*, 1935, **16**, 219-222.
346. Hilgard, E. R., and Marquis, D. G., *Conditioning and Learning*, Appleton-Century, New York, 1940.

347. Hill, L. B., A psychoanalytic observation on essential hyper-tension, *Psychoanal. Rev.*, 1935, 22, 60-64.

348. Hill, L. B., The use of hostility as defense, *Psychoanal. Quart.*, 1938, 7, 254-264.

349. Hill, W. W., The status of the hermaphrodite and transvestite in Navaho culture, *Amer. Anthrop.*, 1935, 37, 273-279.

350. Hinsey, J. C.; Ranson, S. W., and McNattin, R. F., The role of the hypothalamus and mesencephalon in locomotion, *Arch. Neurol. Psychiat.*, 1930, 23, 1-42.

351. Hinsie, L. E., *Concepts and Problems of Psychotherapy*, Columbia Univ. Press, New York, 1937.

352. Hitschmann, E., *Freud's Theories of the Neuroses*, Moffat, Yard, New York, 1917.

353. Hitschmann, E., and Bergler, E., *Frigidity in Women: Its Characteristics and Treatment*, Nerv. & Ment. Dis. Pub., Washington, 1936.

354. Hohman, L. B., Problem child or problem habits, *Proc. Inst. Exceptional Child*, Research Clinic of the Woods Schools, 1936, 16-30.

355. Hollingworth, H. L., *Abnormal Psychology*, Ronald, New York, 1930.

356. Hollis, F., *Social Case Work in Practice*, Family Welfare Assoc. of America, New York, 1939.

357. Hollos, I., and Ferenczi, S., *Psychoanalysis and the Psychic Disorders of General Paresis*, Nerv. & Ment. Dis. Pub., Washington, 1925.

358. Holmer, P., The use of the play situation as an aid to diagnosis, *Amer. J. Orthopsychiat.*, 1937, 7, 523-531.

359. Holt, E. B., *The Freudian Wish and Its Place in Ethics*, Holt, New York, 1915.

360. Homburger, E., Configurations in play—clinical notes, *Psychoanal. Quart.*, 1937, 6, 139-214.

361. Horney, K., Psychogenic factors in functional female disorders, *Amer. J. Obstet. Gynec.*, 1933, 25, 694-704.

362. Horney, K., The denial of the vagina, *Int. J. Psychoanal.*, 1933, 25, 694-704.

363. Horney, K., Conceptions and misconceptions of the analytical method, *J. Nerv. Ment. Dis.*, 1935, 81, 399-410.

364. Horney, K., The problem of feminine masochism, *Psychoanal. Rev.*, 1935, **22**, 241-257.

365. Horney, K., Culture and neurosis, *Amer. Sociol. Rev.*, 1936, **1**, 221-230.

366. Horney, K., *The Neurotic Personality of Our Time*, Norton, New York, 1937.

367. Horney, K., *New Ways in Psychoanalysis*, Norton, New York, 1939.

368. Horney, K., What is a neurosis? *Amer. J. Sociol.*, 1939, **45**, 426-432.

369. Horowitz, E. L., Racial aspects of self-identification in nursery school children, *J. Psychol.*, 1939, **7**, 91-99.

370. Horowitz, R., and Murphy, L. B., Projective methods in the psychological study of children, *J. Exp. Educ.*, 1937, **7**, 133-140.

371. Hoskins, R. G., Physiological factors in personality, *Occupations*, 1936, **14**, 733-744.

372. Hovland, C. I., and Sears, R. R., Experiments on motor conflict. I. Types of conflict and their modes of resolution, *J. Exp. Psychol.*, 1938, **23**, 477-493.

373. Hovland, C. I., and Sears, R. R., Minor studies of aggression. VI. Correlation of lynchings with economic indices, *J. Psychol.*, 1940, **9**, 301-310.

374. Howard, F. E., and Patry, F. L., *Mental Health*, Harper, New York, 1935.

375. Hudgins, C. V., Conditioning and voluntary control of the pupillary light reflex, *J. Gen. Psychol.*, 1933, **8**, 2-51.

376. Hull, C. L., *Hypnosis and Suggestibility*, Appleton-Century, New York, 1933.

377. Hull, C. L., and Huse, B., Comparative suggestibility in the trance and waking states, *Amer. J. Psychol.*, 1930, **42**, 279-286.

378. Hunt, J. McV., An instance of the social origin of conflict resulting in psychoses, *Amer. J. Orthopsychiat.*, 1938, **8**, 158-164.

379. Hunt, J. McV., and Willoughby, R. R., The effect of frustration on hoarding in rats, *Psychosom. Med.*, 1939, **1**, 309-319.

380. Husband, R. W., The comparative value of continual versus interrupted sleep, *J. Exp. Psychol.*, 1935, 18, 792-796.

381. Hutton, L.; Weber, H., and Wolfe, B., Individual psychology and the child (II), *Individual Psychology Pamphlet, No. 8*, Daniel, London, 1935.

382. Huxley, A., *Brave New World*, Doubleday, New York, 1932.

383. Hyman, H. T., Value of psychoanalysis as a therapeutic procedure, *J. Amer. Med. Assoc.*, 1936, 106, 326-329.

384. Itard, J., *The Wild Boy of Aveyron*, Appleton-Century, New York, 1932.

385. Jacobsen, C. F., A study of cerebral function in learning. The frontal lobes, *J. Comp. Neurol.*, 1931, 52, 271-340.

386. Jacobsen, C. F., Influence of motor and premotor area lesions upon the retention of acquired skilled movements in monkeys and chimpanzees, *Proc. Ass. Res. Nerv. Ment. Dis.*, 1934, 13, 225-247.

387. Jacobsen, C. F., Functions of frontal association areas in primates, *Arch. Neurol. Psychiat.*, 1935, 33, 558-569.

388. Jacobsen, C. F., and Elder, J. H., Studies of cerebral function in primates. II. The effect of temporal lobe lesions on delayed response in monkeys, *Comp. Psychol. Monog.*, 1936, 13, 61-65.

389. Jacobsen, C. F., and Nissen, H. W., Studies of cerebral function in primates. IV. The effects of frontal lobe lesions on the delayed alternation habit in monkeys, *J. Comp. Psychol.*, 1937, 23, 101-112.

390. Jacobsen, C. F.; Elder, J., and Haslerud, G., Studies in cerebral function in primates. I. The functions of the frontal association areas in monkeys, *Comp. Psychol. Monog.*, 1936, 13, 1-60.

391. Jacobsen, C. F.; Wolfe, J. B., and Jackson, T. A., An experimental analysis of the functions of the frontal association areas in primates, *J. Nerv. Ment. Dis.*, 1935, 82, 1-14.

392. Jacobson, E., *Progressive Relaxation*, Univ. of Chicago Press, Chicago, 1929.

393. Jameison, G. R., Suicide and mental disease, *Arch. Neurol. Psychiat.*, 1936, 36, 1-12.

394. Jameison, G. R., and Wall, J. H., Psychoses associated with hyperthyroidism, *Psychiat. Quart.*, 1936, **10**, 464-480.

395. Janet, P., *The Major Symptoms of Hysteria*, Macmillan, New York, 2nd ed., 1920.

396. Janet, P., *Principles of Psychotherapy*, Macmillan, New York, 1924.

397. Janet, P., *Psychological Healing*, Allen & Unwin, London, 1926.

398. Jekels, L., Der Wendepunkt im Leben Napoleons 1, *Imago*, 1914, **3**, 313-381.

399. Jekels, L., Zur Psychologie des Mitleids, *Imago*, 1930, **16**, 5-22.

400. Jelliffe, S. E., and White, W. A., *Diseases of the Nervous System*, Lea & Febiger, Philadelphia, 6th ed., 1935.

401. Jennings, H. S., *Biological Basis of Human Nature*, Norton, New York, 1930.

402. Johnson, W. B., and Terman, L. M., Personality characteristics of happily married, unhappily married and divorced persons, *Character and Pers.*, 1935, **3**, 290-311.

403. Jolliffe, N., Effects of vitamin deficiency on mental and emotional processes, in *The Inter-Relationship of Mind and Body*, Williams & Wilkins, Baltimore, 1939.

404. Jones, E., *Treatment of the Neuroses*, Baillere, London, 1920.

405. Jones, E., *Papers on Psycho-Analysis*, William Wood, Baltimore, 1938.

406. Joyce, J., *Portrait of the Artist as a Young Man*, Modern Library, New York, 1928.

407. Jung, C. G., *The Psychology of Dementia Praecox*, Nerv. & Ment. Dis. Pub., Washington, 1914.

408. Jung, C. G., *Psychology of the Unconscious*, Moffat, Yard, New York, 1916.

409. Jung, C. G., *Studies in Word Associations*, Heinemann, New York, 1919.

410. Jung, C. G., *Psychological Types or the Psychology of Individuation*, Harcourt, Brace, New York, 1923.

411. Kabat, H.; Anson, B. J.; Magoun, H. W., and Ranson, W. S., Electrical stimulation of points in forebrain; alterations in blood pressure, *Arch. Neurol. Psychiat.*, 1935, **34**, 931-955.

412. Kahn, E., *Psychopathic Personalities*, Yale Univ. Press, New Haven, 1931.

413. Kahn, E., Adjustment and its limits, *Amer. J. Psychiat.*, 1938, **94**, 1277-1290.

414. Kallmann, F. J., *The Genetics of Schizophrenia*, Augustin, New York, 1938.

415. Kamiat, A. H., Male masochism and culture, *Psychoanal. Rev.*, 1936, **23**, 34-91.

416. Kamiat, A. H., *Social Forces in Personality Stunting*, Sci-Art, Cambridge, Mass., 1939.

417. Kanner, L., *Child Psychiatry*, Thomas, Springfield, Illinois, 1935.

418. Kardiner, A., *The Bio-Analysis of the Epileptic Reaction*, Psychoanal. Quart. Press, Albany, 1932.

419. Kardiner, A., The role of economic security in the adaptation of the individual, *The Family*, 1936, 187-197.

420. Kardiner, A., Security, cultural restraints, intrasocial dependencies and hostilities, *The Family*, 1937, 183-196.

421. Kardiner, A., *The Individual and His Society*, Columbia Univ. Press, New York, 1939.

422. Kardiner, A., Freud's scientific legacy, *New Republic*, 1940, 368-370.

423. Karn, W., A case of experimentally induced neuroses in the cat, *J. Exp. Psychol.*, 1938, **22**, 589-592.

424. Karpf, F. B., Dynamic relationship therapy. The Freudian background, *Social Work Technique*, 1937, **2**, 56-64.

425. Katan, M., The understanding of schizophrenic speech, *Int. J. Psychoanal.*, 1939, **20**, 353-362.

426. Katzenelbogen, S., A critical appraisal of the "Shock Therapies" in the major psychoses, I. Insulin, *Psychiatry*, 1939, **2**, 493-505.

427. Kaufman, M. R., Religious delusions in schizophrenia, *Int. J. Psychoanal.*, 1939, **20**, 363-376.

428. Keller, H., *The World I Live in*, Methuen, London, 1933.

429. Kempf, E., *The Autonomic Functions and the Personality*, Nerv. & Ment. Dis. Pub., Washington, 1918.

430. Kerr, W. J.; Dalton, J. W., and Gliebe, P. A., Some physical phenomena associated with anxiety states and their relationship to hyperventilation, *Ann. Int. Med.*, 1937, **2**, 961-992.

431. Klein, M., *The Psychoanalysis of Children*, Norton, New York, 1932.

432. Klein, M., and Riviere, J., *Love, Hate and Reparation*, Hogarth, London, 1938.

433. Klopfer, B., The technic of Rorschach performance, *Rorschach Research Exchange*, 1937, 2, 1-14.

434. Klopfer, B., Theory and technic of Rorschach interpretation, *Rorschach Research Exchange*, 1939, 3, 152-194.

435. Klopfer, B.; Krugman, M.; Kelley, D. J.; Shakow, D., and Murphy, L., Shall the Rorschach method be standardized? *Amer. J. Orthopsychiat.*, 1939, 9, 514-528.

436. Knopf, O., Preliminary report on personality studies in thirty migraine patients, *J. Nerv. Ment. Dis.*, 1935, 82, 270-285, 400-414.

437. Knott, J. R.; Henry, C. E., and Hadley, J. M., Brain potentials during sleep: A comparative study of the dominant and non-dominant alpha groups, *J. Exp. Psychol.*, 1939, 24, 157-168.

438. Koffka, K., *Principles of Gestalt Psychology*, Harcourt, Brace, New York, 1935.

439. Köhler, W., *The Mentality of Apes*, Harcourt, Brace, New York, 1925.

440. Köhler, W., *Gestalt Psychology*, Liveright, New York, 1929.

441. Köhler, W., *The Place of Values in a World of Facts*, Liveright, New York, 1938.

442. Kovsharova, T. V., An attempt at an experimental investigation of psychoanalytic therapy, *Psychoanal. Quart.*, 1937, 6, 426-452.

443. Kraepelin, E., and Lange, J., *Psychiatrie*, Barth, Leipzig, 9th ed., 1927.

444. Krasnogorski, N. I., The conditioned reflexes and children's neuroses, *Amer. J. Dis. of Children*, 1925, 30, 753-768.

445. Kretschmer, E., *Physique and Character*, Harcourt, Brace, New York, 1925.

446. Kubie, L. S., *Practical Aspects of Psychoanalysis*, Norton, New York, 1936.

447. Kubie, L. S., The experimental induction of neurotic reactions in man, *Yale J. Biol. Med.*, 1939, 11, 541-545.

448. Kubie, L. S., A critical analysis of the concept of a repetition compulsion, *Int. J. Psychoanal.*, 1939, 20, 390-402.

449. Landau, E., Morphology and character, *Character and Pers.,* 1933, 1, 238-241.

450. Landes, R., The personality of the Ojibwa, *Character and Pers.,* 1937, 6, 51-60.

451. Landes, R., The abnormal among the Ojibwa Indians, *J. Abnorm. Soc. Psychol.,* 1938, 33, 14-33.

452. Landis, C., and Forbes, T. W., Studies of catatonia, *Psychiat. Quart.,* 1934, 8, 535-537.

453. Landis, C., and Hunt, W. A., *The Startle Pattern,* Farrar & Rinehart, New York, 1939.

454. Landis, C., and Page, J. D., *Modern Society and Mental Disease,* Farrar & Rinehart, New York, 1938.

455. Langdon-Brown, W.; Crookshank, F. G.; Young, J. C.; Gordon, G., and Bevan-Brown, C. M., Anorexia Nervosa, *Individual Psychology Pamphlets, No. 2,* Daniel, London, 1933.

456. Langdon-Brown, W.; Woodcock, O. H.; Young, J. C.; Pearson, S. V.; Ray, M. B.; Robb, M., and Crookshank, F. G., Individual psychology and psychosomatic disorders (I), *Individual Psychology Pamphlets, No. 4,* Daniel, London, 1933.

457. Lange, J., Facial lupus and personality, *Character and Pers.,* 1933, 2, 117-126.

458. Langford, W. S., Anxiety attacks in children, *Amer. J. Orthopsychiat.,* 1937, 7, 210-218.

459. Lasswell, H. D., *Psychopathology and Politics,* Univ. of Chicago Press, Chicago, 1930.

460. Lazarsfeld, P., An unemployed village, *Character and Pers.,* 1932, 1, 147-151.

461. Lederer, R. H., and Redfield, J., *Studies in Infant Behavior, V,* Univ. of Iowa, Iowa City, 1939.

462. Lee, P., and Kenworthy, M., *Mental Hygiene and Social Work,* Commonwealth Fund, New York, 1929.

463. Lehrman, P. R., Analysis of a conversion-hysteria superimposed on an old diffuse central nervous system lesion, *J. Nerv. Ment. Dis.,* 1921, 54, 31-39.

464. Lehrman, P. R., Some unconscious determinants in homicide, *Psychiat. Quart.,* 1939, 13, 605-621.

465. Lehrman, P. R., Psychopathological aspects of emotional divorce, *Psychoanal. Rev.,* 1939, 26, 1-10.

466. Leonard, W. E., *The Locomotive God*, Appleton-Century, New York, 1927.

467. Lerner, E., New techniques for tracing cultural factors in children's personality organization, *J. Educ. Sociol.*, 1937, **10**, 479-486.

468. Levy, D. M., Fingersucking and accessory movements in early infancy: An etiologic study, *Amer. J. Psychiat.*, 1928, **7**, 881-918.

469. Levy, D. M., On the problem of delinquency, *Amer. J. Orthopsychiat.*, 1932, **2**, 197-211.

470. Levy, D. M., Use of play technic as experimental procedure, *Amer. J. Orthopsychiat.*, 1933, **3**, 266-275.

471. Levy, D. M., Experiments on the sucking reflex and social behavior of dogs, *Amer. J. Orthopsychiat.*, 1934, **4**, 203-224.

472. Levy, D. M., Aggressive-submissive behavior and the Frohlich Syndrome, *Arch. Neurol. Psychiat.*, 1936, **36**, 991-1020.

473. Levy, D. M., Studies in sibling rivalry, *Res. Monograph No. 2*, Amer. Orthopsychiat. Assoc., 1937.

474. Levy, D. M., Primary affect hunger, *Amer. J. Psychiat.*, 1937, **94**, 643-652.

475. Levy, D. M., Attitude therapy, *Amer. J. Orthopsychiat.*, 1937, **7**, 103-113.

476. Levy, D. M., On instinct-satiation: an experiment on pecking behavior of chickens, *J. Gen. Psychol.*, 1938, **18**, 327-348.

477. Levy, D. M., Maternal overprotection, *Psychiatry*, 1938, **1**, 561-591, *Psychiatry*, 1939, **2**, 99-128, 563-597.

478. Levy, D. M., Release therapy, *Amer. J. Orthopsychiat.*, 1939, **9**, 713-736.

479. Levy, D. M., Sibling rivalry studies in children of primitive groups, *Amer. J. Orthopsychiat.*, 1939, **9**, 205-215.

480. Levy, D. M., and Tulchin, H. S., The resistant behavior of infants and children, *J. Exp. Psychol.*, 1925, **8**, 209-224.

481. Levy, J., Relationship therapy, *Amer. J. Orthopsychiat.*, 1938, **8**, 64-67.

482. Levy, J., and Munroe, R., *The Happy Family*, Knopf, New York, 1938.

483. Lewin, B. D., A study of the endocrine organs in the psychoses, *Amer. J. Psychiat.*, 1927, **7**, 391-458.

484. Lewin, B. D., Analysis and structure of a transient hypomania, *Psychoanal. Quart.*, 1932, 1, 43-58.

485. Lewin, K., Environmental forces, in *Handbook of Child Psychology*, Clark Univ. Press, Worcester, Mass., 1931.

486. Lewin, K., Some social psychological differences between the United States and Germany, *Character and Pers.*, 1934, 4, 265-293.

487. Lewin, K., Psycho-sociological problems of a minority group, *Character and Pers.*, 1934, 31, 175-187.

488. Lewin, K., *Dynamic Theory of Personality*, McGraw-Hill, New York, 1935.

489. Lewin, K., Psychology of success and failure, *Occupations*, 1936, 14, 921-930.

490. Lewin, K., Psychoanalysis and topographical psychology, *Bull. Menninger Clin.*, 1937, 1, 202-212.

491. Lewin, K.; Lippitt, R., and White, R. K., Patterns of aggressive behavior in experimentally created "social climates," *J. Soc. Psychol.*, 1939, 10, 271-299.

492. Lewis, N. D. C., *Constitutional Factors in Dementia Praecox*, Nerv. & Ment. Dis. Pub., Washington, 1923.

493. Lewis, N. D. C., and Hubbard, L. D., The mechanisms and prognostic aspects of the manic-depressive-schizophrenic combinations, *Assoc. Research Nerv. Ment. Dis.*, 1931, 11, 539-608.

494. Liddell, H. S., Nervous strain in domesticated animals and man, *Cornell Veterinarian*, 1936, 26, 107-112.

495. Liddell, H. S., The experimental neurosis and the problem of mental disorder, *Amer. J. Psychiat.*, 1938, 94, 1035-1041.

496. Lincoln, S. J., *The Dream in Primitive Cultures*, Williams & Wilkins, Baltimore, 1937.

497. Linton, R., *The Study of Man: An Introduction*, Appleton-Century, New York, 1936.

498. Linton, R., Culture, society and the individual, *J. Abnorm. Soc. Psychol.*, 1938, 33, 425-436.

499. Linton, R., The effects of culture on mental and emotional processes, in *The Inter-Relationship of Mind and Body*, Williams & Wilkins, Baltimore, 1939.

500. Lippmann, H., Neurotic delinquent, *Amer. J. Orthopsychiat.*, 1937, **7**, 114-121.

501. London, L. S., *Mental Therapy; Studies in Fifty Cases*, Covici Friede, New York, 2 vols., 1938.

502. Loomis, A. L.; Harvey, E. N., and Hobart, G., Electrical potentials of the human brain, *J. Exp. Psychol.*, 1936, **19**, 249-279.

503. Loomis, A. L.; Harvey, E. N., and Hobart, G., Cerebral states during sleep, as studied by human brain potentials, *J. Exp. Psychol.*, 1937, **21**, 127-144.

504. Lorand, S., *Psychoanalysis Today: Its Scope and Function*, Allen & Unwin, London, 1933.

505. Lorand, S., Anxiety as a medical problem, *N. Y. State J. Med.*, 1934, **34**, 2-4.

506. Lorand, S., Dynamics and therapy of depressive states, *Psychoanal. Rev.*, 1937, **24**, 337-349.

507. Lorand, S., and Moschcowitz, E., A psychoanalytic interpretation of the constitution in Graves' Syndrome, *J. Nerv. Ment. Dis.*, 1934, **72**, 136-152.

508. Louttit, C. M., *Clinical Psychology*, Harper, New York, 1936.

509. Lowenstein, P., and Svendson, M., Experimental modification of behavior of shy and withdrawn children, *Amer. J. Orthopsychiat.*, 1938, **8**, 639-653.

510. Löwy, I., Stupidity as exemption, *Int. J. Individ. Psychol.*, 1935, **1**, 102-110.

511. Lundholm, H., Laboratory neurosis, *Character and Pers.*, 1933, **2**, 127-133.

512. Luria, A. L., *Nature of Human Conflict*, Liveright, New York, 1932.

513. Luria, L. A., Endocrinology and the understanding and treatment of the exceptional child, *J. Amer. Med. Assoc.*, 1938, **110**, 1531-1536.

514. Lynn, J. G., and Lynn, D. R., Face-hand laterality in relation to personality, *J. Abnorm. Soc. Psychol.*, 1938, **32**, 291-322.

515. MacCurdy, J. T., *The War Neuroses and Shell Shock*, Univ. Press, Cambridge, 1918.

516. MacCurdy, J. T., *Problems in Dynamic Psychology*, Macmillan, New York, 1923.

517. MacDonald, M. W., Criminally aggressive behavior in passive, effeminate boys, *Amer. J. Orthopsychiat.*, 1938, **8**, 70-78.

518. McDougall, W., Four cases of regression in soldiers, *J. Abnorm. Psychol.*, 1920, **15**, 136-156.

519. McDougall, W., *Outline of Abnormal Psychology*, Scribner, New York, 1926.

520. McGranahan, D. V., A critical and experimental study of repression, *J. Abnorm. Soc. Psychol.*, 1940, **35**, 212-225.

521. Maier, N. R. F., *Studies of Abnormal Behavior in the Rat*, Harper, New York, 1939.

522. Mairet, P., *A. B. C. of Adler's Psychology*, Kegan Paul, London, 1928.

523. Malamud, W., Dreams and their relationship to recent impressions, *Arch. Neurol. Psychiat.*, 1931, **25**, 1081-1099.

524. Malamud, W., Dream analysis, *Arch. Neurol. Psychiat.*, 1934, **31**, 356-372.

525. Malinowski, B., *Sex and Repression in Savage Society*, Harcourt, Brace, New York, 1927.

526. Malinowski, B., *The Sexual Life of the Savage*, Liveright, New York, 1929.

527. Marcus, G., *Some Aspects of Relief in Family Casework*, based on a study made for the Charity Organization Society of New York, 1929.

528. Marsh, L. C., Group therapy and the psychiatric clinic, *J. Nerv. Ment. Dis.*, 1938, **82**, 393-398.

529. Martland, H. S., The pathology of acute and chronic alcoholism, in *Alcohol and Man*, Macmillan, New York, 1935.

530. Maslow, A. H., Individual psychology and the social behavior of animals, *Int. J. Individ. Psychol.*, 1935, **1**, 47-59.

531. Maslow, A. H., The role of dominance in the social and sexual behavior of infrahuman primates. III, A theory of sexual behavior, *J. Genet. Psychol.*, 1936, **48**, 310-338.

532. Maslow, A. H., Dominance-feeling, behavior and status, *Psychol. Rev.*, 1937, **44**, 404-429.

533. Maslow, A. H., Personality and culture patterns, in Stagner, R., *Psychology of Personality*, McGraw-Hill, New York, 1937.

534. Maslow, A. H., Dominance, personality and social behavior in women, *J. Soc. Psychol.*, 1939, **10**, 3-39.

535. Max, L. W., Experimental study of the motor theory of consciousness. Action-current responses in the deaf, dreaming, awakening, kinesthetic imagery and abstract thinking, *J. Comp. Psychol.*, 1937, **24**, 301-344.

536. Mead, M., *Coming of Age in Samoa*, Morrow, New York, 1928.

537. Mead, M., *Growing Up in New Guinea*, Morrow, New York, 1930.

538. Mead, M., The use of primitive material in the study of personality, *Character and Pers.*, 1934, **3**, 3-16.

539. Mead, M., *Sex and Temperament in Three Primitive Societies*, Morrow, New York, 1935.

540. Mead, M., *Competition and Cooperation Among Primitive Peoples*, McGraw-Hill, New York, 1937.

541. Mead, M., Researches in Bali, 1936-1939, *Transactions of the New York Academy of Science, Series II*, 1939.

542. Mead, M.; Cavan, R.; Dollard, J., and Wembridge, E., Culture and personality, *Amer. J. Sociol.*, 1936, **42**, 84-87.

543. Mekeel, H. S., Clinic and culture, *J. Abnorm. Soc. Psychol.*, 1935, **30**, 292-300.

544. Menninger, K. A., *The Human Mind*, Knopf, New York, 2nd ed., 1937.

545. Menninger, K. A., *Man Against Himself*, Harcourt, Brace, New York, 1938.

546. Menninger, K. A., The psychological factor in disease, *Bull. Menninger Clin.*, 1939, **3**, 14-19.

547. Menzies, R., Conditioned vasomotor responses in human subjects, *J. Psychol.*, 1937, **4**, 75-120.

548. Meyer, A., An attempt at analysis of neurotic constitution, *Amer. J. Psychol.*, 1903, **14**, 90-103.

549. Meyer, A., Problems of mental reaction types, mental cases, and disease, *Psychol. Bull.*, 1908, **5**, 245-261.

550. Meyer, A., Treatment of Paranoia and Paranoid States, in White and Jelliffe, *Modern Treatment of Nervous and Mental Disease*, 1913.

551. Meyer, A., Objective psychology and psychobiology, *J. Amer. Med. Assoc.*, 1915, **65**, 860-863.

552. Meyer, A., The aims and meaning of psychiatric diagnosis, *Amer. Med.-Psych. Assoc.*, 1917, **74**, 163-168.

553. Meyer, A., Inter-relations of the domain of neuropsychiatry, *Arch. Neurol. Psychiat.*, 1922, **9**, 111-121.

554. Meyer, A., *Therapy*, Third Salmon Lecture, New York, 1932.

555. Miles, W. R., Psychological effects of alcohol in man, in *Alcohol and Man*, Macmillan, New York, 1935.

556. Miller, C., and Slavson, S. R., Integration of individual and group therapy in the treatment of a problem boy, *Amer. J. Orthopsychiat.*, 1939, **9**, 792-798.

557. Miller, N. E.; Hubert, G., and Hamilton, J. B., Mental and behavioral changes following male hormone treatment of adult castration, hypogonadism and psychic impotence, *Proc. Soc. Exp. Biol.*, 1938, **38**, 538-540.

558. Mira, E., Myokinetic psychodiagnosis: A new technique of exploring the conative trends of personality, *Proc. Royal Soc. Med.*, 1940, **33**, 173-194.

559. Mischenchko, N. N., Conditions of the development of experimental sleep in man, *Med. Exp. Kharkov*, 1936, **8**, 57-66.

560. Mitrano, A. J., The clinical interpretation of psychometric data, *Proc. Amer. Assoc. Ment. Deficiency*, 1939, **43**, 156-160.

561. Mittelmann, B., Psychogenic factors and psychotherapy in hyperthyreosis and rapid heart imbalance, *J. Nerv. Ment. Dis.*, 1933, **77**, 465-488.

562. Mittelmann, B., Juvenile adiposogenital dystrophy. Neurological and psychopathological aspects. Results of organotherapy and psychotherapy, *Endocrinology*, 1938, **23**, 637-655.

563. Mittelmann, B., Euphoric reactions in the course of psychoanalytic treatment, *Psychoanal. Rev.*, 1940, **27**, 27-44.

564. Mittelmann, B., and Wolff, H. G., Affective states and gastric function: Experimental studies on patients with gastric ulcer. (To be published in *Psychosom. Med.*)

565. Mittelmann, B., and Wolff, H. G., Affective states and skin temperature: Experimental study of subjects with "cold hands" and Raynaud's Syndrome, *Psychosom. Med.*, 1939, **1**, 271-292.

566. Mittelmann, B., and Wolff, H. G., Psychoanalysis and experimental methods, *Psychol. Bull.*, 1939, **36**, 506.

567. Mohr, G. J., Psychoanalytic theory of personality, *Social Work*, 1939, **4**, 35-46.

568. Moreno, J. L., *Who Shall Survive?* Nerv. & Ment. Dis. Pub., Washington, 1934.

569. Moreno, J. L., Spontaneity training, a method of personality development, *J. Psychol.*, 1938, **6**, 81-88.

570. Moreno, J. L., Psychodramatic shock therapy: A sociometric approach to the problem of mental disorders, *Sociometry*, 1939, **2**, 1-30.

571. Morgan, C. D., and Murray, H. A., A method for investigating fantasies. The thematic apperception test, *Arch. Neurol. Psychiat.*, 1935, **34**, 289-306.

572. Morgan, C. T., and Morgan, J. C., Auditory induction of an abnormal pattern of behavior in rats, *J. Comp. Psychol.*, 1939, **27**, 505-508.

573. Morgan, J. J. B., *Keeping a Sound Mind*, Macmillan, New York, 1934.

574. Morgan, J. J. B., *The Psychology of Abnormal People*, Longmans, New York, 2nd ed., 1936.

575. Mosse, E. P., Painting-analysis in the treatment of neuroses, *Psychoanal. Rev.*, 1940, **27**, 65-82.

576. Mowrer, O. H., Authoritarianism versus "self-government" in the management of children's aggressive (anti-social) reactions as a preparation for citizenship in a democracy, *J. Soc. Psychol.*, 1939, **10**, 121-126.

577. Mowrer, O. H., An experimental analogue of "regression" with incidental observations on "reaction-formation," *J. Abnorm. Soc. Psychol.*, 1940, **35**, 56-87.

578. Mowrer, O. H., and Mowrer, W. M., Enuresis—A method for its study and treatment, *Amer. J. Orthopsychiat.*, 1938, **8**, 436-457.

579. Muncie, W., Postoperative states of excitement, *Arch. Neurol. Psychiat.*, 1934, **32**, 681-703.

580. Muncie, W., Depressions with tension—Their relation to the general problem of tension, *Arch. Neurol. Psychiat.*, 1934, **32**, 328-349.

581. Muncie, W., *Psychobiology and Psychiatry*, Mosby, St. Louis, 1939.

582. Murphy, G., *An Outline of Abnormal Psychology*, Boni & Liveright, New York, 1929.

583. Murphy, G., and Jensen, F., *Approaches to Personality*, Coward-McCann, New York, 1932.

584. Murphy, G.; Murphy, L., and Newcomb, T., *Experimental Social Psychology*, Harper, New York, rev. ed., 1937.

585. Murphy, L. B., *Social Behavior and Child Personality, An Exploratory Study of Some Roots of Sympathy*, Columbia Univ., New York, 1937.

586. Murray, H. A., and others, *Explorations in Personality*, Oxford Univ. Press, New York, 1938.

587. Myerson, A., *The Inheritance of Mental Diseases*, Williams & Wilkins, Baltimore, 1925.

588. Myerson, A., *The Psychology of Mental Disorders*, Macmillan, New York, 1928.

589. Meyerson, A., Effect of benzedrine sulfate on mood and fatigue in normal and neurotic persons, *Arch. Neurol. Psychiat.*, 1936, **36**, 816-22.

590. Myerson, A., The relationship of hereditary factors to mental processes, in *The Inter-Relationship of Mind and Body*, Williams & Wilkins, Baltimore, 1939.

591. Nadel, S. F., The typological approach to culture, *Character and Pers.*, 1936, **5**, 268-284.

592. Neustatter, L. W., *Modern Psychology in Practice*, Blakiston, Philadelphia, 1937.

593. Neymann, C. A., and Osborne, S. L., The treatment of dementia paralytica with hyperpyrexia by diathermy, *J. Amer. Med. Assoc.*, 1931, **96**, 7-11.

594. Nicole, J. E., and Fitzgerald, E. J., Ten years of malarial therapy, *Brit. J. Med.*, 1934, **1**, 426-427.

595. Nietzsche, F., *Works*, Modern Library, New York, 1937.

596. Nunberg, H., *Allgemeine Neurosenlehre auf Psychoanalytischer Grundlage*, Huber, Bern, 1932.

597. Oberndorf, P. C., On retaining the sense of reality in states of depersonalization, *Int. J. Psychoanal.*, 1939, **20**, 137-147.

598. O'Kelly, L. and Steckle, L., A note on long-enduring emotional responses in the rat, *J. Psychol.*, 1939, **8**, 125-131.

599. Orgler, H., *Alfred Adler: The Man and His Work*, Daniel, London, 1939.

600. Osborn, R., *Freud and Marx*, Equinox Co-Operative, New York, 1937.

601. Papanicolaou, G. N., and Shorr, E., The action of ovarian follicular hormone in the menopause, as indicated by vaginal smears, *Amer. J. Obstet. Gynec.*, 1936, **31**, 806-831.

602. Pavlov, I. P., *Conditioned Reflexes*, Oxford Univ. Press, New York, 1927.

603. Pavlov, I. P., *Lectures on Conditioned Reflex*, International Pub., New York, 1928.

604. Payne, S. M., A conception of femininity, *Brit. J. Med. Psychol.*, 1935, **15**, 18-33.

605. Peck, M., *The Meaning of Psychoanalysis*, Sun Dial Press, Inc., Garden City, 1938.

606. Penrose, L. S., *Mental Defect*, Farrar & Rinehart, New York, 1934.

607. Pfister, O. R., *The Psychoanalytic Method*, Moffat, Yard, New York, 1917.

608. Piaget, J., *Judgment and Reasoning in the Child*, Harcourt, Brace, New York, 1928.

609. Piaget, J., *The Child's Conception of the World*, Harcourt, Brace, New York, 1929.

610. Piotrowski, Z., The prognostic possibilities of the Rorschach method in insulin treatment, *Psychiat. Quart.*, 1938, **12** 679-689.

611. Piotrowski, Z., Rorschach manifestations of improvement in insulin treated schizophrenics, *Psychosom. Med.*, 1939, **1**, 508-526.

612. Plant, J., *Personality and the Cultural Pattern*, Commonwealth Fund, New York, 1937.

613. Pollock, H.; Malzberg, B., and Fuller, R., *Hereditary and Environmental Factors in the Causation of Manic Depressive Psychoses and Dementia Praecox*, State Hospital, Utica, 1939.

614. Postle, B., Folie à deux; report of a case of remission from a psychosis of more than 25 years' duration, *Arch. Neurol. Psychiat.*, 1940, **43**, 372-373.

615. Powdermaker, F.; Levis, H., and Touraine, G., Psychopathology and treatment of delinquent girls, *Amer. J. Orthopsychiat.*, 1937, 7, 58-71.

616. Prague, G., The psychiatrist's roles with his patients, *Amer. J. Psychiat.*, 1938, 95, 135-147.

617. Pratt, J., and Thomas, W., The endocrine treatment of menopausal phenomena, *J. Amer. Med. Assoc.*, 1937, 109, 1875-1877.

618. Prescott, D. A., *Emotions and the Educative Process*, American Council on Education, Washington, 1938.

619. Prince, M., *The Dissociation of a Personality*, Longmans, New York, 1905.

620. Prince, M., *Clinical and Experimental Studies in Personality* (A. A. Roback, ed.), Sci-Art, Cambridge, 2nd ed., 1938.

621. Prinzhorn, H., *Bilderei des Geistes Kranken*, Springer, Berlin, 2nd ed., 1923.

622. Prinzhorn, H., *Psychotherapy*, Smith, New York, 1932.

623. Rado, S., An oversolicitous mother: A contribution to the psychology of the ego, *Int. J. Psychoanal.*, 1928, 9, 219-226.

624. Rado, S., The problem of melancholia, *Int. J. Psychoanal.*, 1928, 9, 420-438.

625. Rado, S., Developments in the psychoanalytic conception and treatment of the neuroses, *Psychoanal. Quart.*, 1939, 8, 427-437.

626. Rahman, L.; Richardson, H. B., and Ripley, H. S. Anorexia nervosa, *Psychosom. Med.*, 1939, 1, 335-365.

627. Rank, O., *Psychoanalytische Beitrage zur Mythenforschung*, Psychoanal. Verlag, Vienna, 1919.

628. Rank, O., *Technik der Psychoanalyse*, Deuticke, Leipzig, 1926.

629. Rank, O., *The Trauma of Birth*, Harcourt, Brace, New York, 1929.

630. Ranson, S. W., The hypothalamus: Its significance for visceral innervation and emotional expression. The Weir Mitchell Oration. *Trans. of the Coll. of Phys. of Philadelphia, Series IV*, 1934, 2, 222-242.

631. Reese, H. H., Hypoglycemia and convulsive therapy in schizophrenia, *J. Amer. Med. Assoc.*, 1939, 112, 493-496.

632. Reese, H. H., and Sauthoff, A., Insulin and metrazol treatment in schizophrenia, *Wisconsin Med. J.*, 1938, **37**, 816-820.

633. Reich, W., *Die Funktion des Orgasmus*, Int. Psychoanal. Verlag, Leipzig, 1927.

634. Reich, W., *Characteranalyse*, published by the author, Berlin, 1933.

635. Ribble, M., Clinical studies of instinctive reactions in new babies, *Amer. J. Psychiat.*, 1938, **95**, 149-158.

636. Ribble, M., The significance of infantile sucking for the psychic development of the individual, *J. Nerv. Ment. Dis.*, 1939, **90**, 455-463.

637. Richmond, M., *What Is Social Casework?* Russell Sage Foundation, New York, 1922.

638. Rickman, J., *The Development of the Psycho-Analytical Theory of the Psychoses*, Balliere, London, 1928.

639. Rickman, J. (ed.), *On the Bringing Up of Children*, Kegan Paul, London, 1936.

640. Ripley, H. S.; Shorr, E., and Papanicolaou, G. N., The effect of treatment of depression in the menopause with estrogenic hormone, *Amer. J. Psychiat.*, 1940, **96**, 905-914.

641. Roback, A. A., Writing slips and personality, *Character and Pers.*, 1932, **1**, 137-146.

642. Roback, A. A., *Self-Consciousness, Self-Treated*, Sci-Art, Cambridge, 1936.

643. Robbins, S. B., Significance of infantile nutritional disturbances in alcoholism, *Psychoanal. Rev.*, 1935, **22**, 53-59.

644. Robbins, S. B., Escape into reality: A clinical note on spontaneous social recovery, *Psychoanal. Quart.*, 1937, **6**, 353-364.

645. Robbins, S. B., Neurotic disturbances in work, *Psychiatry*, 1939, **2**, 333-342.

646. Robinson, V., *A Changing Psychology in Social Case Work*, Univ. of North Carolina Press, Chapel Hill, 1930.

647. Robinson, V., *Supervision in Social Case Work*, Univ. of North Carolina Press, Chapel Hill, 1936.

648. Rogers, C. R., *The Clinical Treatment of the Problem Child*, Houghton Mifflin, Boston, 1939.

649. Rorschach, H., *Psychodiagnostik: Methodik und Ergebnisse eines Wahrnehmungs Diagnostischen Experiments*, Huber, Bern, 3rd ed., 1937.

650. Rorschach, H., and Oberholzer, E., The application of the interpretation of form to psychoanalysis, *J. Nerv. Ment. Dis.*, 1924, **60**, 225-248.

651. Rosanoff, A. J., *Manual of Psychiatry and Mental Hygiene*, Wiley, New York, 7th ed., 1938.

652. Rosanoff, A. J.; Handy, L. A., and Plesset, J. R., Mental disorders in triplets, *Amer. J. Psychol.*, 1939, **95**, 1139-1142.

653. Rosenthal, J. S., Typology in the light of the theory of conditioned reflexes, *Character and Pers.*, 1932, **1**, 56-59.

654. Rosenthal, J. S., *An Introduction to Analytical Psychotherapy*, Longmans, New York, 1932.

655. Rosenzweig, S., Preferences in the repetition of successful and unsuccessful activities as a function of age and personality, *J. Gen. Psychol.*, 1933, **42**, 423-441.

656. Rosenzweig, S., Types of reaction to frustration: A heuristic classification, *J. Abnorm. Soc. Psychol.*, 1934, **29**, 298-300.

657. Rosenzweig, S., A test for types of reaction to frustration, *Amer. J. Orthopsychiat.*, 1935, **5**, 395-403.

658. Rosenzweig, S., Some implicit common factors in diverse methods of psychotherapy, *Amer. J. Orthopsychiat.*, 1936, **6**, 412-415.

659. Rosenzweig, S., The experimental study of psychoanalytic concepts, *Character and Pers.*, 1937, **5**, 61-70.

660. Rosenzweig, S., The definition of ambivalence, *Brit. J. Med. Psychol.*, 1938, **17**, 223-226.

661. Rosenzweig, S., Frustration as an experimental problem, *Character and Pers.*, 1938, **7**, 126-128.

662. Rosenzweig, S., A dynamic interpretation of psychotherapy oriented toward research, *Psychiatry*, 1938, **1**, 521-26.

663. Rosenzweig, S., and Mason, G., An experimental study of memory in relation to the theory of repression, *Brit. J. Psychol.*, 1934, **24**, 247-265.

664. Ross, T. A., *The Common Neuroses: Their Treatment by Psychotherapy*, William Wood, Baltimore, and ed., 1937.

665. Rowe, A. W., and Lawrence, H. C., The male and female gonads, *Endocrinology*, 1928, **12**, 591-662.

666. Rowland, L. W., Will hypnotized persons try to harm themselves or others? *J. Abnorm. Soc. Psychol.*, 1939, **34**, 114-117.

667. Sadger, J., *Sleep Walking and Moon Walking*, Nerv. & Ment. Dis. Pub., Washington, 1920.

668. Sakel, M., The methodical use of hypoglycemia in the treatment of psychosis, *Amer. J. Psychiat.*, 1937, **94**, 111-129.

669. Sakel, M., Psychotherapeutic effect by chemical agents, in *The Inter-Relationship of Mind and Body*, Williams & Wilkins, Baltimore, 1939.

670. Sanders, J. J., An experimental demonstration of regression in the rat, *J. Exp. Psychol.*, 1937, **21**, 493-510.

671. Sapir, E., The emergence of the concept of personality in a study of cultures, *J. Soc. Psychol.*, 1934, **5**, 408-415.

672. Saudek, R., *The Psychology of Handwriting*, Doubleday Doran, New York, 1925.

673. Saul, L. J., Psychogenic factors in the etiology of the common cold and related symptoms, *Int. J. Psychoanal.*, 1938, **19**, 451-470.

674. Saul, L. J., Hostility in cases of essential hypertension, *Psychosom. Med.*, 1939, **1**, 153-216.

675. Saul, L. J., Psychoanalytic case records, *Psychoanal. Quart.*, 1939, **8**, 186-190.

676. Schilder, P. F., Über Halluzinationen (Vestibular), *Ztschr. f. d. ges. Neurol. und Psychiatr.*, 1919-20, **53**, 169-198.

677. Schilder, P. F., Vorstudien zu einer Psychologie der Manie, *Ztschr. f. d. ges. Neurol. und Psychiatr.*, 1921, **68**, 90-135.

678. Schilder, P., *Introduction to a Psychoanalytic Psychiatry*, Nerv. & Ment. Dis. Pub., Washington, 1928.

679. Schilder, P., *Studien zur Psychologie und Symptomatologie der Progressiven Paralyse*, Karger, Berlin, 1930.

680. Schilder, P., *The Image and Appearance of the Human Body*, Psyche Monographs, Kegan Paul, London, 1935.

681. Schilder, P. F., Psychoanalysis of space, *Int. J. Psychoanal.*, 1935, **16**, 274-295.

682. Schilder, P. F., Psychopathology of time, *J. Nerv. Ment. Dis.*, 1936, **83**, 530-546.

683. Schilder, P. F., The relation between social and personal disorganization, *Amer. J. Sociol.*, 1937, **42**, 832-839.

684. Schilder, P. F., *Psychotherapy*, Norton, New York, 1938.

685. Schilder, P. F., The social neurosis, *Psychoanal. Rev.*, 1938, **25**, 1-19.

686. Schilder, P. F., Notes on the psychology of metrazol treatment of schizophrenia, *J. Nerv. Ment. Dis.*, 1939, **89**, 133-144.

687. Schilder, P., and Kauders, O., *Hypnosis*, Nerv. & Ment. Dis. Pub., Washington, 1927.

688. Schilder, P. F., and Wechsler, D., What do children know about the interior of the body? *Int. J. Psychoanal.*, 1935, **16**, 355-360.

689. Schmalhausen, S. D., *The New Road to Progress*, Falcon, New York, 1934.

690. Schrotter, K., Experimentelle Traume, *Zentralblatt f. Psychoanalyse*, 1912, **2**, 638-646.

691. Seabrook, W., *Asylum*, Harcourt, Brace, New York, 1935.

692. Sears, R. R., Experimental studies of projection. I. Attribution of traits, *J. Soc. Psychol.*, 1936, **7**, 151-163.

693. Sears, R. R., Functional abnormalities of memory with special reference to amnesia, *Psychol. Bull.*, 1936, **33**, 229-274.

694. Sears, R. R., Experimental studies of projection. II. Ideas of reference, *J. Soc. Psychol.*, 1937, **8**, 389-400.

695. Sears, R. R., Initiation of the repression sequence by experienced failure, *J. Exp. Psychol.*, 1937, **20**, 570-580.

696. Sears, R. R., and Cohen, L. H., Hysterical anesthesia, analgesia and astereognosis, *Arch. Neurol. Psychiat.*, 1933, **29**, 206-271.

697. Sears, R., and Sears, P., Minor studies of aggression: V. Strength of frustration-reaction as a function of strength of drive, *J. Psychol.*, 1940, **9**, 297-300.

698. Sears, R.; Hovland, C., and Miller, N., Minor studies of aggression: I. Measurement of aggressive behavior, *J. Psychol.*, 1940, **9**, 275-296.

699. Seelman, K., A case of seeming feeblemindedness and its treatment in the elementary school, *Int. J. Individ. Psychol.*, 1935, **1**, 100-108.

700. Seif, L., Individual Psychology and Life-philosophy, *Individual Psychology Pamphlets*, No. 11A, Daniel, London, 1935.

701. Seif, L.; Rayner, D., and Zilahi, F., Individual Psychology and the Child (I), *Individual Psychology Pamphlets*, No. 7, Daniel, London, 1934.

702. Selling, L. S., Effect of conscious wish upon dream content, *J. Abnorm. Soc. Psychol.*, 1932, **27**, 122-128.

703. Selling, L. S., A suggestion relative to classifying nervous and mental disease, *Psychol. Rec.*, 1937, **17**, 217-226.

704. Sharpe, E. F., *Dream Analysis: A Practical Handbook in Psychoanalysis*, Norton, New York, 1938.

705. Shaw, C. R., *The Jack Roller*, Univ. of Chicago Press, Chicago, 1930.

706. Sheldon, W. H., and Stephens, S. S., A three-dimensional system for classifying human physiques. Paper read at Eastern Psychol. Assoc. Meetings, 1940.

707. Sherif, M., *Psychology of Social Norms*, Harper, New York, 1936.

708. Sherman, M., *Mental Hygiene and Education*, Longmans, New York, 1934.

709. Sherman, M., *Mental Conflicts and Personality*, Longmans, New York, 1938.

710. Sherman, M., and Henry, T., *Hollow Folk*, Crowell, New York, 1933.

711. Shipley, W. C., and Kant, F., The insulin-shock and metrazol treatments of schizophrenia, with emphasis on psychological aspects, *Psychol. Bull.*, 1940, **37**, 259-284.

712. Shipman, G., How to make your son a misfit, *Amer. Mercury*, 1938, **43**, 283-288.

713. Shirley, M., A behavior syndrome characterizing prematurely born children, *Child Development*, 1939, **10**, 115-128.

714. Shuttleworth, F. K., Rosanoff, Handy, and Plesset on the etiology of mental deficiency: A critical appraisal, *J. Educ. Psychol.*, 1938, **29**, 374-383.

715. Sidis, B., *Nervous Ills*, Badger, Boston, 1922.

716. Singer, G. H., The influence of sudden oppression on a racial minority, *J. Soc. Psychol.*, 1939, **10**, 127-145.

717. Slavson, S. R., Group therapy, *Ment. Hyg.*, 1940, **24**, 36-49.

718. Smith, G. M., A phobia originating before the age of three cured with aid of hypnotic recall, *Character and Pers.*, 1936, 5, 331-337.

719. Solomon, J., Active play therapy, *Amer. J. Orthopsychiat.*, 1938, 8, 479-498.

720. Sommerfield, W. A.; Kuenzel, W. M., and Todd, W. T., Studies in the alimentary canal of man. VIII. The time relationships of gastric peristalsis, *J. Laboratory and Clinical Med.*, 1931, 17, 151-165.

721. Stagner, R., *Psychology of Personality*, McGraw-Hill, New York, 1937.

722. Stagner, R., The role of parents in the development of emotional instability, *Amer. J. Orthopsychiat.*, 1938, 8, 122-129.

723. Stekel, W., *Conditions of Nervous Anxiety and Their Treatment*, Dodd, Mead, New York, 1923.

724. Stekel, W., *Peculiarities of Behavior*, Boni & Liveright, New York, 2 vols., 1924.

725. Stekel, W., *Technique of Analytical Psychotherapy*, Norton, New York, 1940.

726. Stephen, K., *Psychoanalysis and Medicine. A Study of the Wish to Fall Ill*, Macmillan, New York, 1933.

727. Stephen, K., Aggression in early childhood, *Brit. J. Med. Psychol.*, 1939, 18, 178-188.

728. Stern, A., Psychoanalytic investigation of and therapy in the border line group of neuroses, *Psychoanal. Quart.*, 1938, 7, 467-480.

729. Stogdill, R., Neurosis as learned behavior, *Psychol. Rev.*, 1934, 41, 497-507.

730. Stone, S., Psychiatry through the ages, *J. Abnorm. Soc. Psychol.*, 1937, 32, 131-160.

731. Strauss, H.; Rahm, W. E., Jr., and Barrera, S. E., Children with psychiatric disorders: I. Electroencephalographic studies, *Psychosom. Med.*, 1940, 2, 34-42.

732. Strecker, E. A., *Beyond the Clinical Frontiers*, Norton, New York, 1940.

733. Strickler, C. B., A quantitative study of post-hypnotic amnesia, *J. Abnorm. Psychol.*, 1929, 24, 108-119.

734. Sullivan, A., Ulcerative colitis and personality, *Amer. J. Psychiat.*, 1938, 95, 407-420.

735. Sulzberger, M. B., and Wolf, J., The treatment of warts by suggestion, *Med. Rev.*, 1934, **140**, 552-556.

736. Sumner, W. G., *Folkways*, Ginn, Boston, 1906.

737. Symonds, P. M., Some basic concepts in parent-child relationships, *Amer. J. Psychol.*, 1937, **50**, 195-206.

738. Symonds, P. M., A study of parental acceptance and rejection, *Amer. J. Orthopsychiat.*, 1938, **8**, 679-688.

739. Symonds, P. M., *The Psychology of Parent-Child Relationship*, Appleton-Century, New York, 1939.

740. Taylor, W. S., *Readings in Abnormal Psychology and Mental Hygiene*, Appleton-Century, New York, 1926.

741. Taylor, W. S., and Culler, E., The problem of the locomotive god, *J. Abnorm. Soc. Psychol.*, 1929, **24**, 342-399.

742. Tendler, A. D., A reorientation in psychotherapy, *Psychol. Clinic*, 1932, **21**, 253-259.

743. Terman, L. M., and Buttenweiser, P., Personality factors in marital compatibility, *J. Soc. Psychol.*, 1939, **6**, 143-171.

744. Terman, L.; Miles, C. C., and others, *Sex and Personality*, McGraw-Hill, New York, 1937.

745. Thomas, G., Psychic factors in rheumatoid arthritis, *Amer. J. Psychiat.*, 1936, **93**, 693-710.

746. Thompson, C., Development of awareness of transference in a markedly detached personality, *Int. J. Psychoanal.*, 1938, **19**, 299-309.

747. Thompson, C., Identification with the enemy and loss of the sense of self, *Psychoanal. Quart.*, 1940, **9**, 37-50.

748. Thorndike, E. L., *Educational Psychology, Vol. I, The Original Nature of Man*, Teachers College, New York, 1914.

749. Timasheff, N. S., The power phenomenon, *Amer. Sociol. Rev.*, 1938, **3**, 499-509.

750. Todd, T. W., The role of roentgenology in medical education. II. Observations on the alimentary tract of the medical student, *Amer. J. Roentgenology and Radium Therapy*, 1927, **17**, 305-315.

751. Todd, T. W., and Kuenzel, W., Studies in the alimentary tract of man. V. Disturbances of central origin in gastric responses, *J. Laboratory and Clinical Med.*, 1929, **15**, 142-154.

752. Todd, T. W., *Behavior Patterns of the Alimentary Tract*, Williams & Wilkins, Baltimore, 1930.

753. Todd, T. W., and Rowlands, M. C., Studies in the alimentary canal of man. VI. Emotional interference in gastric behavior patterns. *J. Comp. Psychol.*, 1930, **10**, 167-188.

754. Treadway, W. L., Drug addiction and measures for its prevention in the United States, *J. Amer. Med. Assoc.*, 1932, **99**, 372-375.

755. Tredgold, A. F., *Mental Deficiency*, William Wood, Baltimore, 1929.

756. Tulchin, S. H., *Intelligence and Crime. A Study of Penitentiary and Reformatory Offenders*, Univ. of Chicago Press, Chicago, 1939.

757. Uchimuta, Y., "Imu," a malady of the Ainu, *Lancet*, 1935, **228**, 1272-1275.

758. Veblen, T., *The Theory of the Leisure Class*, Macmillan, New York, 1899.

759. Von Meduna, L., and Friedman, E., The convulsive-irritative therapy of the psychoses, *J. Amer. Med. Assoc.*, 1939, **112**, 501-509.

760. Waller, J. V.; Kaufman, M. R., and Deutsch, F., Anorexia nervosa: A psychosomatic entity, *Psychosom. Med.*, 1940, **2**, 3-16.

761. Waller, W., *The Family: A Dynamic Interpretation*, Dryden Press, New York, 1938.

762. Wallin, J. E. W., *Minor Mental Maladjustments in Normal People*, Duke Univ. Press, Durham, 1939.

763. Warburg, B., Suicide, pregnancy and rebirth, *Psychoanal. Quart.*, 1938, **7**, 490-502.

764. Watson, J. B., *Behaviorism*, Norton, New York, rev. ed., 1930.

765. Watson, G., Mental hygiene and emotional adjustment, *Rev. Educ. Res.*, 1935, **5**, 245-258.

766. Wechsler, I. S., *A Text-book of Clinical Neurology*, Saunders, Philadelphia, 3rd ed., 1935.

767. Wechsler, I. S.; Jervis, G. A., and Potts, H. D., Experimental study of alcoholism and vitamin B deficiency in monkeys, *Bull. Neurol. Inst. N. Y.*, 1936, **5**, 453-465.

768. Wegrocki, H. J., A critique of cultural and statistical concepts of abnormality, *J. Abnorm. Soc. Psychol.*, 1939, **34**, 166-178.

769. Weisenburg, T.; Roe, A., and McBride, K. E., *Adult Intelligence*, Commonwealth Fund, New York, 1936.

770. Welch, L., The space and time of induced hypnotic dreams, *J. Psychol.*, 1936, 1, 171-178.

771. Wells, W. R., Experiments in waking hypnosis for instructional purposes, *J. Abnorm. Soc. Psychol.*, 1924, 18, 389-404.

772. Wells, W. R., Hypnotizability versus suggestibility, *J. Abnorm. Soc. Psychol.*, 1931, 25, 436-49.

773. Wells, W. R., Extent and duration of post-hypnotic amnesia, *J. Psychol.*, 1940, 9, 137-151.

774. Wells, W. R., Ability to resist artificially induced dissociation, *J. Abnorm. Soc. Psychol.*, 1940, 35, 261-272.

775. Wembridge, E. H., *Life Among the Lowbrows*, Houghton Mifflin, Boston, 1931.

776. Wender, L., The dynamics of group psychotherapy and its application, *J. Nerv. Ment. Dis.*, 1936, 84, 54-55.

777. Wertham, F., The active work therapy of Dr. Simon, *Arch. Neurol. Psychiat.*, 1930, 24, 150-160.

778. Wexberg, E., *Your Nervous Child*, Boni & Liveright, New York, 1927.

779. Wexberg, E., *Individual Psychology*, Cosmopolitan, New York, 1929.

780. Wexberg, E., *The Psychology of Sex*, Farrar & Rinehart, New York, 1931.

781. Wexberg, E.; Knopf, O., and Squires, H. C., Individual Psychology and Practice (I), *Individual Psychology Pamphlets*, No. 2, Daniel, London, 1934.

782. White, W. A., *Principles of Mental Hygiene*, Macmillan, New York, 1917.

783. White, W. A., *An Introduction to the Study of the Mind*, Nerv. & Ment. Dis. Pub., Washington, 1924.

784. White, W. A., *Forty Years in Psychiatry*, Nerv. & Ment. Dis. Pub., Washington, 1933.

785. White, W. A., *Outlines of Psychiatry*, Nerv. & Ment. Dis. Pub., Washington, 1935.

786. White, W. A., *Twentieth Century Psychiatry*, Norton, New York, 1936.

787. Wiersma, D., On pathological lying, *Character and Pers.*, 1933, **21**, 48-61.

788. Williams, F. E., *Russia, Youth, and the Present-day World*, Farrar & Rinehart, New York, 1934.

789. Williams, G. W., The effect of hypnosis on muscular fatigue, *J. Abnorm. Soc. Psychol.*, 1929, **24**, 318-329.

790. Witkin, H., Abnormal behavior in animals, *Psychol. League J.*, 1939, **3**, 75-83.

791. Witmer, H., Influence of parental attitudes on the social adjustment of the individual, *Amer. Sociol. Rev.*, 1937, **2**, 756-763.

792. Witmer, H., Some parallels between dynamic psychiatry and cultural anthropology, *Amer. J. Orthopsychiat.*, 1939, **9**, 95-102.

793. Wittels, F., *Freud and His Time*, Liveright, New York, 1931.

794. Wolfe, T., Dynamic aspects of cardiovascular symptomatology, *Amer. J. Psychol.*, 1934, **91**, 563-573.

795. Wolff, H. G., Personality features and reactions of subject with migraine, *Arch. Neurol. Psychiat.*, 1937, **37**, 895-921.

796. Wolff, H. G., and Curran, D., Nature of the delirium and allied states—The dysergastic reactions, *Arch. Neurol. Psychiat.*, 1935, **33**, 1175-1215.

797. Wolff, H. G., and Gantt, W. H., Caffeine sodiobenzoate, sodium isoamylethyl barbiturate, sodium bromide and chloral hydrate: Effect on the highest integrative functions, *Arch. Neurol. Psychiat.*, 1935, **33**, 1030-1057.

798. Wolff, W., The experimental study of forms of expression, *Character and Pers.*, 1933, **2**, 168-176.

799. Wolff, W., Involuntary self-expression in gait and other movements in an experimental study, *Character and Pers.*, 1935, **3**, 327-344.

800. Woodard, J. W., The relation of personality structure to the structure of culture, *Amer. Sociol. Rev.*, 1938, **3**, 637-651.

801. Woodworth, R. S., *Contemporary Schools of Psychology*, Ronald, New York, 1931.

802. Woodworth, R. S., *Experimental Psychology*, Holt, New York, 1938.

803. Yaskin, J. C., The psychoneuroses and neuroses, *Amer. J. Psychiat.*, 1936, **93**, 107-125.

804. Yates, D. H., An association-set method in psychotherapy, *Psychol. Bull.*, 1939, **36**, 506.

805. Young, K., Contribution of psychiatry to the study of group conflict, in *Social Conflict*, Univ. of Chicago Press, Chicago, 1931.

806. Young, P. C., Hypnotism, *Psychol. Bull.*, 1926, **23**, 504-523.

807. Young, P. C., Is rapport an essential characteristic of hypnosis? *J. Abnorm. Psychol.*, 1927, **22**, 130-139.

808. Young, W. C., and Rundlett, B., Hormonal induction of homosexual behavior in the spayed female guinea pig, *Psychosom. Med.*, 1939, **1**, 449-460.

809. Zachry, C. B., Contributions of psychoanalysis to the education of the adolescent, *Psychoanal. Quart.*, 1939, **8**, 98-107.

810. Zilboorg, G., The dynamics of the schizophrenic reactions related to pregnancy and childbirth, *Amer. J. Psychiat.*, 1929, **8**, 733-767.

811. Zilboorg, G., Affective reintegration in the schizophrenias, *Arch. Neurol. Psychiat.*, 1930, **24**, 335-347.

812. Zilboorg, G., The deeper layers of schizophrenic psychoses, *Amer. J. Psychiat.*, 1931, **11**, 493-518.

813. Zilboorg, G., Anxiety without affect, *Psychoanal. Quart.*, 1933, **2**, 48-67.

814. Zilboorg, G., *The Medical Man and the Witch During the Renaissance*, Johns Hopkins Press, Baltimore, 1935.

815. Zilboorg, G., Some sidelights on the psychology of murder, *J. Nerv. Ment. Dis.*, 1935, **81**, 442-444.

816. Zilboorg, G., Differential diagnostic types of suicide, *Arch. Neurol. Psychiat.*, 1936, **35**, 270-291.

817. Zilboorg, G., Considerations on suicide, with particular reference to that of the young, *Amer. J. Orthopsychiat.*, 1937, **7**, 15-31.

818. Zondek, H., *The Diseases of the Endocrine Glands*, Routledge, London, 1935.

819. Zweig, S., *Mental Healers: Mesmer, Eddy, Freud*, Viking, New York, 1932.

GLOSSARY

~~~~~~

Abulia: Diminution or loss of initiative and decisiveness; inability to make a decision.

Adaptation, adjustment: The sum total of the individual's reactions to the needs of his life situations; the preferred form for these reactions. (See *Life style.*)

Agitation: A restless, anxious, worried frame of mind, with motor manifestations, e.g., wringing the hands.

Agoraphobia: A morbid fear of open places.

Allergy: A reaction to eating, inhaling, or touching proteins which elicits certain symptoms (hay fever, asthma, hives, etc.).

Ambivalence: Contradictory attitudes (particularly love and hate) toward the same person or thing.

Ameliorative device: A psychological process which aims at relieving psychic distress.

Amentia: Feeble-mindedness. A mental state (psychotic reaction) characterized by apathy, disorientation, and impaired consciousness.

Amnesia: Inability consciously to recall events or personal identity.

Anesthesia: Loss of sensation, particularly touch, heat, pain, or cold.

Anorexia: Loss of appetite or ability to eat.

Anxiety, neurotic: Fear in the absence of actual danger.

Anxiety hysteria: A psychoneurotic reaction characterized by attacks of fear in response to situations of stress. Phobias are usually included.

Anxiety neurosis: A condition characterized by attacks or physiological signs of anxiety (e.g., palpitation). A colloquial term for any condition characterized by attacks of anxiety.

Apathy: Absence of emotional interest.

Aphasia: Impairment in the ability to use or understand language caused by a disturbance in certain parts of the brain.

Astasia-abasia: Inability to stand or walk, the patient having normal control of the legs while sitting or lying.

Asthma: A disease characterized by difficulty in breathing.

Ataxia: Disturbance of muscular coordination.

Atrophy: A wasting away of organ or tissue, particularly muscle.

Aura: Sensory experiences preceding epileptic seizures, such as seeing lights.

Automatic writing: Writing without full conscious control.

Autonomic nervous system: That part of the nervous system that regulates involuntary bodily functions.

Babinski reflex: Extension of the great toe (instead of normal flexion) when the sole of the foot is stroked.

Basic anxiety: The feeling of helplessness in a potentially hostile world.

Behaviorism: A system of psychology based exclusively on objectively observable phenomena.

Benign: Relatively mild, in contrast to malignant.

Blocking: Retardation of the flow of thought or associations to the point of stoppage.

Castration fear: A constellation of conscious and unconscious ideas centered about the fear of genital injury, including mutilation.

Catalepsy: A condition characterized by lack of response to stimuli, and by waxy rigidity of the limbs.

Catastrophic breakdown: A reaction to stress which entails incapacity in an indispensable psychological function and is accompanied by intense suffering.

Catastrophic fear: Anticipation of situations which imply destructive and unbearable distress and panic.

Catatonia: A condition in schizophrenic reactions, characterized by stupor, waxy flexibility, and periods of excitement.

Catharsis: The emotional discharge which occurs when a repressed traumatic experience is recalled and which is followed by relief; used sometimes also for sudden conscious realization of any repression.

Central nervous system: The brain and the spinal cord.

Character: The sum total of the individual's relatively permanent modes of behavior, attitudes, reaction patterns, and methods of coping with problems.

Character neurosis (neurotic character): Disturbances in character with or without symptoms.

Chorea: A disease of the nervous system characterized by involuntary muscular movements.

Chronic: Pertaining to a condition which progresses slowly and is long continued, or reaches this phase after an acute beginning.

Claustrophobia: A morbid fear of inclosed places.

Clinical methods: Methods of investigation, except laboratory and experimental procedures, which imply direct contact with and observation of the patient.

Coma: A state of profound unconsciousness characterized by absence of reflexes and the loss of nearly all bodily defense reactions (nonresponsiveness to pricks or to obstruction of breathing).

Compensation: The individual's attempt to make up for an undesirable trait and the consequent discomfort by emphasizing or exaggerating a desirable trait.

Complex: An affectively (emotionally) charged constellation of ideas.

Compromise formation: The process, conscious or unconscious or both, leading to the formation of symptoms and patterns of behavior which attempt to satisfy opposing needs.

Compulsion: The impulse to perform usually harmless and apparently senseless acts which the individual's judgment opposes and he wants to resist; also the performance of such acts.

Compulsion or obsessional neurosis: A psychoneurotic reaction characterized chiefly by compulsions and obsessional thoughts which seriously impair the individual's functioning.

Confabulation: The making up of stories and the readiness to give fluent but false answers to questions.

Conflict: A clash between conscious or unconscious impulses and needs.

Constellation: A pattern or syndrome of connected or correlated motives, impulses, ideas, and emotions.

Conversion hysteria: A psychoneurotic reaction in response to stress, characterized by a localized disturbance in bodily function but with no anatomical damage.

Coping: The individual's emotional and physical functioning in attempting to solve problems.

Coping reaction: Methods and devices used to avoid distress and to reach goals which are charged with fear and conflict.

Cretin: A feeble-minded individual whose condition is caused by a congenital deficiency of the thyroid gland.

Cultural conflicts: Conflicts engendered in the individual by opposing cultural demands and norms.

Cyclothymic: Temperamental make-up characterized by the alternation of optimism, cheerfulness, and planfulness, with sadness, pessimism, and worry.

Defense hostility: The tendency, conscious or unconscious or both, to hurt or attack someone who is feared; this serves as a defense against him.

Defense mechanisms: Psychological reaction patterns for avoiding psychic distress and danger.

Delirium: A mental state characterized by disorientation, difficulty in perception, and excitement, accompanied by illusions and hallucinations.

Delusion: An abnormal conscious belief which the individual defends in spite of reality or its logical absurdity.

Dementia: Mental deterioration; loss of intellectual capacities.

Dementia paralytica: See *Paresis.*

Dementia praecox: A term formerly used to denote a group of mental disorders which appear between the ages of fifteen and thirty and end in dementia. The term has been replaced by schizophrenia.

Depression: A prolonged mood of extreme sadness accompanied by decrease in initiative, difficulty in thinking, and self-debasing ideas.

Deprivation: The inability to satisfy a need or desire because of external obstacles. Some authors use the term synonymously with frustration; others restrict the latter to cases where psychological threat results from the deprivation. (See *Frustration.*)

Dipsomania: Periodic uncontrollable desire for and indulgence in alcohol.

Disorientation: Confusion or uncertainty concerning time, place, or people.

Displacement: The substitution of an object, circumstance, mode of expression, or body organ for the expression of an impulse, emotional reaction, or the function of another organ.

Dissociation: A condition in which the different mental processes lose their usual modifying influence upon one another.

Dominance feeling: A synonym for self-esteem.

Drive: A persistent or recurrent urge (motivation) to characteristic patterns of behavior. (See *Instinct.*)

Drive to power: An intense and persistent search for means which will enable the individual to control others. The drive is at least partly unconscious, is motivated by fear, and aims at safety and self-esteem.

Dynamic psychology: The approach to psychological phenomena which emphasizes the subjective experience of drivenness, the observable persistent striving, often unconscious, in certain directions and for certain goals in spite of obstacles. It emphasizes motivation, the integral interrelation between various psychological states, and the underlying (unconscious) meaning or purpose of any psychological state or bodily symptom.

Dystrophy: Faulty growth.

Echolalia: A symptom in schizophrenic reactions in which the patient echoes anything said to him.

Echopraxia: A condition in which the patient repeats mechanically the gestures and actions of another person.

Ego: The self. That part of the mental apparatus which controls conscious perception, thought, feeling, and behavior, and which attempts to guide the adjustment to external and internal reality.

Ego psychology: Aspects of psychoanalytic investigation and theory which emphasize the significance of anxiety, defense mechanisms, and character in psychopathology.

Elation: A strong feeling of cheerfulness, well-being, and satisfaction with oneself, often accompanied by an optimistic outlook and great energy.

Electrocardiography: A method of recording, by means of a special apparatus, the electrical changes caused by the contraction of the heart muscle.

Electroencephalography: A method of recording the electrical activity of the brain.

Encephalitis: Inflammation of the brain.

Encephalogram: An X-ray photograph of the brain made after the fluid in the ventricles has been withdrawn and replaced by air.

Enuresis: Involuntary discharge of urine; bed-wetting.

Epilepsy: A group of diseases characterized by generalized convulsions or loss of consciousness, or both.

Erogenous zones: Sensitive regions of the body whose stimulation gives rise to erotic excitement.

Etiology: The source or origin of a symptom or disease.

Euphoria: A feeling of marked well-being and of satisfaction with oneself and the world in general.

Exhibitionism: A sexual perversion, in which display of the genitals affords the maximal erotic pleasure. Also an excessive desire, conscious or unconscious, to display oneself in order to be looked at or admired.

Exophthalmic goiter: A condition characterized by bulging of the eyes, overfunctioning and enlargement of the thyroid gland, rapid pulse, restlessness, increased basal metabolism.

Expiation process: A psychological process and behavior by which the individual unconsciously seeks forgiveness for an impulse or an act.

Fantasy: A vivid and prolonged imaginary activity, usually fictitious in nature, which either is satisfying to the individual or is evoked by a strong emotion.

Fetichism: Predominant sexual interest in an inanimate object.

Free association: The spontaneous reporting of every thought as it becomes conscious, with a minimum of rational or ethical criticism.

Frigidity: Any impairment of the woman's ability to reach sexual gratification.

Frustration: A serious or threatening non-gratification of needs and desires because of environmental or intrapsychic obstacles. (See *Deprivation.*)

Frustration tolerance: The ability to experience deprivation or frustration without psychological disturbances.

Fugue: A period of "disassociation" (split consciousness) during which the individual is engaged in a complicated act away from his usual environment; he remembers nothing subsequently.

Functional psychoses: Mental disorders whose cause is primarily psychological rather than an anatomical or toxic damage to the nervous system.

Genetic: Pertaining to the origin, history, or development of anything.

Gestalt: Configuration. Any constantly observable pattern of functioning (action, sense perception, emotional reaction) whose parts are integrated into a whole.

Globus hystericus: A distressing and prolonged feeling of a "lump in the throat," often with choking sensations; correlated with partly unconscious emotional stress.

Goal object: That person or thing toward which, consciously or unconsciously, the drives or pleasure-seeking impulses are directed.

Gonad: A sexual gland; a testicle or ovary.

Grandiosity: Abnormal over-evaluation of the self.

Gratification: The act and experience of satisfying a bodily or psychological need.

Grave's disease: See *Exophthalmic goiter.*

Gyri: The convolutions of the brain.

Hallucination: An abnormal sensory experience that has no real and external stimulus.

Heredity: Traits, tendencies, and reaction patterns which are transmitted by the germ plasm.

Heterosexuality: Sexual interest in the opposite sex.

Homosexuality: Erotic relationship with an individual of one's own sex.

Hydrocephaly: An abnormal accumulation of fluid in the skull, often resulting in enlargement of the head and in mental defect.

Hyperaemia: A superabundance of blood in circulation in any part of the body.

Hyperkinetic: Pertaining to excessive general motor activity.

Hyperthyroidism: Over-abundant secretion from the thyroid gland.

Hypnoanalysis: A therapeutic technique which combines some psychoanalytical techniques with hypnosis.

Hypnosis: A mental state called a trance, which is characterized primarily by extreme responsiveness to suggestions.

Hypochondria: A neurotic reaction whose most conspicuous symptom is preoccupation with morbid sensations in various organs.

Hypomania: The mildest form of the manic phase of manic-depressive psychosis.

Hysteria: A term applied to diverse neurotic reactions by various writers. The syndromes are organic dysfunction with no anatomical pathology; attacks of anxiety and phobia, amnesia, and double personality. Most frequently it is used to characterize physical symptoms which have psychological rather than organic causes.

Identification: The process by which real or imagined characteristics of one person are reproduced in the personality of another by unconscious or partly unconscious mechanisms.

Idiomotor tendency: The tendency to react, without reasoning, to a stimulus, either overt or implied, when the attention is concentrated elsewhere.

Idiot: A feeble-minded person whose I.Q. is less than 25.

Imbecile: A person whose I.Q. is between 25 and 50.

Inadequacy: A conscious and unconscious disturbance of self-evaluation or self-esteem.

Incoherence: Disconnected and unrelated thoughts, utterances, or actions.

Inferiority complex: The constellation of ideas and feelings which centers around a conscious or unconscious self-evaluation in terms of inadequacy; the attitudes and reactions deriving from this, including (according to some writers) compensatory measures.

Inhibition, neurotic: The impairment or cessation of a function as the result of conflicts.

Insanity: Any psychological disorder, other than feeble-mindedness, which legally constitutes a person irresponsible and thereby warrants his commitment to an institution. The medical term is psychosis or mental disease.

Insecurity: The evaluation of the environment and of other people as rejecting, threatening, dangerous, or hostile, leading to feelings of rejection or isolation.

Instinct: A term given various meanings by different authors: an inborn bodily need which is gratified in a predetermined manner; any psychological reaction the tendency to which is inborn.

Integration: The process or result of establishing relations between parts and welding them into a functional whole.

Intelligence quotient: The mental age obtained by the Binet test, divided by the chronological age, multiplied by 100 to eliminate decimals.

Kleptomania: Compulsive stealing.

Lesion: A visible damage or abnormality in an organ.

Libido: The term used by Freud to denote either the life force, the drive for any activity, or the drive for pleasure.

Life style: The characteristic manner of perceiving, reacting to, and solving the problems of life.

Macrocephaly: A pathological condition characterized by an abnormal enlargement of the head.

Maladjusted individual: A person who is inadequately adjusted to, and therefore unable to cope adequately with, reality and his own needs; a person whose vital needs clash with reality. The term maladjusted is used variously to refer to any psychological disturbance, or to mild disturbances, particularly of behavior.

Manic-depressive psychosis: A psychotic reaction characterized by prolonged periods of excitement, etc. (mania), or by periods of depression, or both.

Masochism: A sexual perversion characterized by the need to experience pain in order to attain the maximal erotic satisfaction; conscious or unconscious desires to experience physical or psychological pain.

Megalomania: A psychotic condition characterized by delusions of grandeur.

Melancholia: Serious depression occurring during involution (40-60 years); the depressive phase of manic-depressive psychosis.

Menopause: Cessation of menstruation.

Mental conflict: The condition resulting when desires, needs, or impulses which are partly or completely incompatible are present simultaneously.

Mental hygiene: Therapeutic techniques for preventing or relieving mental and emotional disturbances before they become severe and incapacitating.

Microcephaly: A pathological condition characterized by an abnormally small cranium.

Migraine: Periodic attacks of severe headache, usually on only one side.

Mongolism: A form of feeble-mindedness characterized by many body disturbances, particularly by slanting eyes.

Moron: A person whose I.Q. is between 50 and 70.

Multiple personality: A character abnormality which causes an individual, in reacting to stress or conflict, to assume an entirely different personality and identity. This indicates that there are two or more fairly distinct, autonomous, and mutually exclusive mental integrations within the individual.

Mutism: Lack of speech, either because of reluctance to speak, as during a psychotic reaction, or failure of the speech function to develop.

Myxedema: A disease caused by adult hypothyroidism, resulting in increased weight, retardation of mental processes and action, and usually mental deficiency.

Narcissism: Love of self. In an abnormal reaction to stress, as in schizophrenia, this may reach the point of self-aggrandizement. The individual's selfish preoccupation with his pleasure-seeking impulses.

Negativism: Marked resistance; the tendency to do the opposite of what one is requested to do.

Neurasthenia: A psychoneurotic reaction characterized by sensations of fatigue; there is often also constipation and a feeling of pressure on the head.

Neurosis: Any psychological disturbance or symptom, or both. A psychological disturbance arising as a reaction to stress, but with no serious disturbance in the evaluation of reality (in contrast to psychosis); in this sense the term is synonymous with psychoneurosis.

Neurosyphilis: Syphilis of the nervous system.

Neurotic character: See *Character neurosis.*

Nihilistic delusion: The conviction or feeling that nothing exists.

Obsession: A persistently recurring and distressing thought upon which attention must be focused, even though it is adequately evaluated by the intellect and opposed by the will.

Obsessional neurosis: See *Compulsion or obsessional neurosis.*

Occipital: Pertaining to the back of the head.

Oedipus complex: Sexual attachment to the parent of the opposite sex and hostility toward the other parent.

Organic disease: A condition in which the abnormality of a tissue or organ can be inferred or demonstrated.

Orientation: Knowledge of time, place, and person; one's perspective of himself both as an individual and in relation to others.

Over-compensation: The development of excessively positive character traits and reaction patterns in an attempt to overcome feelings of inadequacy.

Over-protection: An attitude and course of action by which one person tries to guard another from extremely trivial risks; particularly characteristic of some mother-child relationships.

Overt: Objectively observable.

Paranoia: A psychotic reaction characterized by systematized and unshakable delusions.

Paresis: An organic psychotic reaction caused by syphilis of the brain; also called dementia paralytica.

Parkinsonian syndrome: A pathological condition caused by damage to certain groups of cells in the brain tissue, and manifested by muscular rigidity, coarse trembling, stooped posture, and mask-like expression.

Pathogenic: Causing disease or disturbance.

Pathological: Abnormal; indicating the presence of disease or structural damage.

Peptic ulcer: A "wound" of the inner lining of the stomach or the duodenum, caused by the action of a gastric juice upon a portion of this lining whose nutrition has been interfered with in some way.

Perseveration: The involuntary tendency to continue a response even if the stimulus has ceased or is altered; continued interest in an unsolved problem.

Personality: The integrated expression of the characteristic needs, goals, reaction patterns, and modes of handling situations.

Phobia: A neurotic reaction characterized by intense fear.

Play technique: A therapeutic method which uses toys and play to encourage and enable the child to express his conscious and unconscious emotional attitudes and conflicts in the presence of the therapist.

Prestige suggestion: Direct suggestion which depends for its effect upon the personality, reputation, and past success of the one who makes it.

Prognosis: Prediction of the probable outcome of an illness.

Projection: Ascribing to other persons modes of behavior, which in reality are unconscious wishes or character traits of the individual himself.

Projective methods: Investigation techniques in which, by reacting to an unstructured or loosely structured situation, the subject reveals (projects) his fantasies, needs, attitudes, and conflicts.

Psychasthenia: Literally, psychic or mental exhaustion. A psychoneurotic syndrome characterized by obsessions, compulsions, doubts, scruples (Janet). This classification is not used in this book.

Psyche: The human mind; the sum total of psychological processes.

Psychiatry: The branch of medicine which treats psychological illness and the mental aspects of organic disease.

Psychoanalysis: A psychological method of study and treatment which includes frequent interviews, free association, and dream analysis, and the interpretation to the patient of his reactions to daily events and to the analysis. The data, concepts, and theories resulting from the use of this method.

Psychogenic: Caused by psychological factors.

Psychoneurosis: A disturbance of psychological or physiological functions, or both, which arises as a reaction to external or internal stress, but does not seriously alter the evaluation of sensory or social reality. It is used in this book synonymously with neurosis, although some differentiate between them in various ways.

Psychopathology: More serious psychological disturbances; the study of these disturbances.

Psychosis: A disturbance in mental and emotional behavior, usually to an extent incompatible with social adjustment, and often accompanied by delusions and hallucinations. Disturbance of relation with, or perception of, reality.

Psychosomatic: Pertaining to the interrelations between bodily and psychological phenomena.

Psychotherapy: Treatment by psychological methods.

Pyromania: A morbid and usually compulsive tendency to start fires.

Rapport: An attitude of mutual trust, confidence, openness, and dependence between two individuals.

Rationalization: The process of "manufacturing" rational explanations for attitudes or acts to avoid the distress resulting from acknowledging their true motivations.

Reaction formation: The excessive development of the opposite of a repressed attitude which is disapproved of by the individual.

Regression: A method of reacting to difficulties in which adequate response patterns are relinquished in favor of the reaction patterns of childhood.

Rejection: Such attitudes and behavior, partly unconscious, toward another person as lead him to believe that he is not loved and valued as an individual.

Release: The freeing of blocked impulses; this is followed by relief of distress.

Repetition compulsion: The tendency to repeat reaction patterns regardless of whether they are pleasurable or painful.

Repression: The rejection and shutting out of the awareness of a reaction pattern (thought, feeling, impulse, memory) in order to avoid distress.

Resistance: Largely unconscious reluctance on the part of the patient to relinquish his existing mode of coping with situations.

Sadism: A sexual perversion characterized by the need to inflict physical pain in order to attain the maximal erotic gratification; a conscious or unconscious tendency to derive pleasure from hurting others.

Schizoid character: A personality type characterized by seclusiveness, lack of adequate emotional attachment, diminished initiative, and preoccupation with fantasies.

Schizophrenia: A psychotic reaction characterized by absence of emotional attachment and of the experience and expression of normal emotions, by extreme preoccupation, by unreal ideas, and by bizarre delusions, hallucinations, and behavior.

Security: The evaluation of the environment as essentially helpful and friendly, leading to a feeling of safety and acceptance.

Security system: The sum total of the attitudes and reaction patterns by which the individual maintains his safety and self-evaluation of worth and allays his expectation of potentially catastrophic distress.

Self-aggrandizement: A conscious or unconscious need or desire to over-estimate oneself. The reaction patterns which result from this.

Self-esteem: The self-evaluation of an individual; his estimate of worth, adequacy, strength, or power. Many near-synonyms are used by various writers—dominance-feeling, ascendance-submission, feeling of superiority or inferiority, self-regard, ego-strength, self-evaluation.

Self-evaluation: Synonym for self-esteem.

Somatic: Pertaining to the body.

Somatopsychic: Pertaining to both the body and the mind.

Somnambulism: A trance-like state in a period of sleep during which the individual carries out a complex activity which he does not remember later.

Stereotypy: Continued repetition of apparently senseless syllables, words, or movements.

Stomach ulcer: See *Peptic ulcer.*

Sublimation: The process of consciously gratifying unconscious sexual or aggressive impulses, in work, play, or art.

Submissive attitudes: Conscious or unconscious tendencies to obey or submit to another person which are motivated by fear of the other person and by desire for his protection.

Suggestibility: A permanent or temporary trait which makes a person receptive to the ideas, requests, and demands of others.

Suggestion: A request or command, overt or implied, with which the individual complies without logical reasoning, e.g., in hypnosis. A psychotherapeutic technique by which symptoms are cured by direct or implied authoritative assurance that they will disappear.

Symbol: The representation of an intended act, thought, or emotion by means of a substitute act or thought which has some parallel features.

Syndrome or symptom complex: A group of symptoms often found together and characteristic of a particular disorder or disease; by extension, any group of characteristics which can be integrated into a whole.

Tic: A periodic involuntary contraction of any muscle group, the resulting motion resembling an organized action, such as turning the head or licking the lips.

Trance: A sleep-like state in which the range of consciousness is narrowed and voluntary movements are suspended.

Transference: The sum total of the patient's attitudes toward the psychoanalyst which develop during the treatment, spring from the patient's fears, vital needs, and memory patterns, and are essentially non-logical in nature.

Traumatic: Pertaining to or resulting from injury; pertaining to any event which creates a significant psychological disturbance.

Traumatic neurosis: A psychoneurotic reaction to physical injury or threat of death. Shell shock is the best-known form.

Traumatic psychosis: A psychotic reaction resulting from brain injury.

Unconscious (referring to psychological processes): Inaccessible to consciousness by effort of voluntary attention.

Urticaria: Hives; itching red wheals or eruptions over the entire body. They may disappear in a few hours and new ones may appear.

Ventriculography: A diagnostic procedure involving the injection of air into the ventricles of the brain after the withdrawal of fluid. Following this, X-ray photographs are taken. The procedure is used chiefly for the diagnosis of brain tumors.

Verbigeration: A senseless or prolonged repetition of words or phrases.

Vicious circle: A series of psychological reactions which have the unconscious purpose of relieving stress, but which, because of their nature, lead to a renewal of the stress.

Waxy flexibility: A peculiar pliable rigidity of the muscle. Any part of the patient's body can be put into various positions which can be retained for a long time without any apparent fatigue.

APPENDIX I

PROJECTIVE METHODS OF EXAMINATION

The most important methods of examining the individual and arriving at a diagnosis are the interview and observation, supplemented by information obtained from the patient's relatives and friends and from laboratory tests. These methods have been described in earlier parts of the book. Other methods frequently used are personal inventory and association tests. In the former—the Bernreuter Personal Inventory Test, for example—the individual is asked to write answers to printed questions which are calculated to touch on his possible emotional problems. The chief value of such a procedure in colleges is that it quickly indicates the students who might most benefit from psychological treatment. In one form of the association test (Jung [409]) the subject is asked to name as quickly as he can the word he associates with stimulus words, some of which are relatively neutral, whereas others, such as "father," "sweetheart," are apt to be emotionally charged. From the nature of the replies, the relative length of time taken to respond, and the visible discomfort shown by the subject, the investigator can determine the points of stress in his emotional life. This test is primarily of experimental interest but can also yield valuable information regarding patients who are otherwise uncommunicative.

In the so-called projective methods of studying personality, the subject is confronted with an unstructured test situation and asked to organize it. The term "unstructured" implies that the nature of the objects or their interrelation in the situation is not strictly defined; on the contrary, the subject is free to handle and interpret them in any way he wishes. This process and its results are called "organization."

It is instructive to contrast projective methods with the method followed in intelligence tests. In the latter, the subject is confronted with a test situation which he is expected to handle in only one way, the "correct" way. The test situation is potentially structured. As Frank[1] (254) phrases it: "The standardized tests offer procedures for rating the individuals in terms of their socialization and how nearly they approximate to the acceptance and the use of culturally described patterns of belief, action, and speech." In projective methods of examination, we "induce the individual to reveal his way of organizing experience by giving him a field (objects, materials, experiences) with relatively little structure and cultural patterning so that the personality can project upon the plastic field his way of seeing life, his meanings, significances, patterns, and especially his feelings. Thus we elicit a projection of the individual personality's *private world*." Hence these methods are often called "projective" methods. We shall now describe several.

THE RORSCHACH TEST

The procedure.—The "unstructured" material in this test consists of a series of ten cards. On each one of these cards there appears a form which does not represent any definite object. These forms are commonly referred to as *ink blots*. Some are gray-black, others contain colors in addition. They were originally obtained by Rorschach by dropping ink on a sheet of paper which was then folded in the middle and pressed together, thus giving the ink drop an accidental symmetrical shape. The same ink blots are used in all the tests and are shown in the same sequence. Of the many originally used, the final ones were selected by Rorschach in many tests as the ones that best bring out variable responses. As the ink blots are shown, the subject is asked: "What might this be?" At the end of the test the examiner goes over his responses with him, attempting by apparently naïve questions to discover what qualities in the blots (colors, form, shading) he used in arriving at his concept.

Scoring.—The test is scored on the basis of the evaluation of each response and then on the relative percentage of various types of response in the total number of responses.

For instance, one subject describes Card 2 as two clowns with red hats playing pat-a-cake. Another subject sees an Indian arrowhead

---

[1] L. K. Frank, Projective methods for the study of personality, *Journal of Psychology*, 1939, **8**, 394-403.

where the first one saw the hands of the clowns. How are such responses evaluated? What is the significance of the relative frequency of one type of response and of another? This has been arrived at *empirically*. It has been found, for example, that active outgoing individuals have a different percentage of certain types of responses than rigidly repressed ones. Schizophrenics give different responses than manic-depressives. Therefore, we might say roughly that the various types of responses represent various tendencies in the subject.

1. The first aspect of the response to be considered is what "space" in the ink blot the subject chooses for interpretation; in other words, whether the response relates to the ink blot as a whole (W), to a frequently considered and obvious detail (D), or to a small and rarely seen detail (Dd). In the above examples, the first (two clowns) is a whole response; the second (arrowhead), an obvious detail.

W represents the generalizing tendencies, D represents the sense for the obvious, and Dd represents the interest partly for the minute and partly for the extravagant and queer.

2. Another aspect is the content—animals, human figures, objects, landscapes, plants, anatomical content, formless geological and geographical content, blood, cloud, etc. In the above examples the first response is a human, the second, an object response. Roughly, the more variegated the content, the wider are the subject's interests and education. The human responses indicate an interest in fellow humans; if, however, there are more parts than complete human figures in the test record, this usually indicates that the subject is an anxious person whose interest in human beings is rather an anxious preoccupation. Anatomical answers may be indicative of bodily preoccupation.

3. The third aspect is the way the subject integrates the chosen space and chosen content. This integration can be achieved in the following ways:

(a) The form of the chosen space determines the integration and thus the content of the interpretation (F). Such a form response may be "good" (+) or "bad" (—). It is good if the content seen by the subject is in harmony with the form on the card; thus the arrowhead response above is a (good) form response. It has been found that the higher the percentage of form responses the better the subject's control over his emotions; but that if the form percentage is too high, the presence of repression is indicated. The percentage of good responses in all the form responses (F+%) has been found to represent the subject's intelligence level; there is a fair interrelation between this measure and the I.Q. The intelligence level, however, is not determined solely on the basis of this percentage, for the number and quality of whole responses, of movement responses, of original responses (see below), the variety of content, etc., are all significant.

(b) A response is termed a movement response when in addition to the form a kinesthetic impression contributes to the integration, as, for example, two clowns *playing* pat-a-cake. The significance of movement responses can be roughly described as indicating reactiveness to inner stimuli, and hence rich inner emotional life, spontaneity, creativity, natural endowment. The movements may be human, as in the example just cited. Such responses indicate mature inner feelings. Movements of animals may indicate more elementary instinctual drives; movements of inanimate objects, unassimilated chaotic drives.

(c) The responses in which bright colors appear as the integrative agent are called color responses (C). Sometimes they appear with and in harmony with forms; sometimes they have the leading role and suggest the forms to the subject; and sometimes they appear independently, producing formless responses and becoming the sole determiners of the content attributed to the chosen space. These color responses represent the emotionality (affectivity) of the subject, particularly in response to external stimuli. In the first illustration the color red ("red hats") played a role, in good harmony with the form, in determining the subject's response. Where the colors only accompany the form (as in this example) they are indicative of an adaptive affectivity; where they determine the form ("flowers," "flames," etc.) they are usually indicative of unstable affectivity, of an uneven emotional discharge; where they appear independently (blood, lawn, sea) they are indicative of uncontrolled, impulsive, violent affectivity, of paroxysmal emotional discharges.

(d) When shadings of gray and black ("chiaroscuro") are the integrative agent, anxiety is indicated. Here again these light and dark effects appear—as did colors—in varied relations to forms, indicating more or less controlled or uncontrolled anxieties. In the best possible harmony with forms they are indicative of anxious, cautious, unfree adaptation.

(e) Other characteristics of the responses can be determined and evaluated. Thus responses which are frequently given by various subjects (P, popular) or responses which are rare and therefore original can be indicative of the subject's common sense or his originality respectively.

Interpretation.—After all the responses have been obtained, each one is evaluated. Thus, the response two clowns with red hats playing pat-a-cake is tabulated W M FC H meaning that the whole blot is used by the subject (W), that the figure is in motion (M), that color is used in conjunction with form for the hats (FC), and that the content is human (H). The second response (Indian arrowhead) is tabulated DF obj., that is, a detail (D), determined only by the form of the blot (F), in content an object (obj.). After each response is thus tabulated, the whole responses, movement responses, form responses, etc., are added up, and their percentages of the total determined and compared with previously established norms. It should be emphasized again, that no one single response or even the *absolute* sum of any one type of response determines the interpretation; it is their relationships to each other in the total number of responses.

Two persons give five movement responses. One has ten responses using color and very little pure F; the other has much F and almost no color. The first subject is probably an active, spontaneous, social individual (unless other evidence in the test contradicts this impression), whereas the second is likely to be a repressed introvert. An accurate view of the personality structure depends upon insight into the *interplay* of different forces, not upon an enumeration of traits. The skilled Rorschach expert not only must know all the subtle implications of the test (of which only the most obvious have been mentioned), but he must be an experienced clinician as well. The test is useless in the hands of an untrained examiner, but yields surprisingly detailed and accurate information about the personality structure when administered by an experienced tester. However, the test still awaits validation by the techniques most in favor with experimental psychologists.

THEMATIC APPERCEPTION TEST

Procedure.—The test material consists of three series of ten photographs each, each of which represents an independent scene. The pictures are presented to the subject with the following instructions:[1] "This is a test of your creative imagination. I shall show you a picture and I want you to make up a plot or story for which it might be used as an illustration. What is the relation of the individuals in the picture? What has happened to them? What are their present thoughts and feelings? What will be the outcome?" The following is an example of a response:

A student who was working for a Ph.D. in science had, as a child and adolescent, gone through poverty and pogroms, with his mother in Russia. "Recollections of those persecutions," he stated, "still prey on my mind: dead bodies with torn limbs dragged in heaps to the cemetery; my uncle forced to dig his own grave before my eyes; my aunt shot in cold blood at my hand; bombs thrown a few feet before me." His father had immigrated to America when the subject was six months old. There were frequent quarrels with the father after they came to America, in which he always took his mother's part. Recently his mother has been sick. He has been depressed lately.

Thematic Apperceptions.—Picture No. 13 shows on the floor against the couch, the huddled form of a boy with his head bowed on his right arm. Beside him on the floor is an object which resembles a revolver. The subject interpreted this as follows:

"Some great trouble has occurred. Someone he loved has shot herself. Probably it is his mother. She may have done it out of poverty. He, being fairly grown up, sees the misery of it all and would like to shoot himself. But he is young and braces up after a while. For some time he lives in misery—the first few months thinking of death.

[1] H. A. Murray, *Explorations in Personality*, Oxford University Press, New York, 1938, p. 532.

"Here, the possible death of the mother appears as one determinant of his present pessimism. The story is one variety of a large class of complex themas—the Tragic Love Thema."[1]

Scoring.—The hypothesis underlying Murray's scoring system is that the subject in making up his story projects into the strivings of the main figure (figure of identification) his own strivings which Murray designates as "needs"; the other figures, objects, and facts are also results of projection and represent the forces confronting the subject. Murray calls the latter "press" (e.g., "mother" in the above quotation).

Interpretation.—The predominance of needs and presses as obtained by scoring is considered to represent the predominant trends of the subject and of the presses he feels himself exposed to. The interpretation can be restricted to describing these tendencies and their relative order of dominance, or psychological knowledge can be used to draw out further conclusions from the co-existence of such factors, thus leading to personality description and even to formal psychiatric diagnosis.

PLAY TECHNIQUE

The play technique involves the use of toys to enable the child to reveal his needs and conflicts in the presence of the examiner (Klein [431], Freud [268], Homburger [360], Levy [470]). Some children start to play very easily; others are shy and need encouragement. Some toys are particularly well suited for the expression of the child's needs and conflicts. Wooden and iron-jointed dolls, doll houses and furniture, bathroom and bedroom sets, paper and crayons are particularly useful and give the child an opportunity to represent his own life as well as his fantasy world; but furniture and odds and ends can be used. A sink at which the children can play should be available if possible.

The following case is a good illustration of the play technique:[2]

The child was four and one-half years old, had feeding difficulties which were increasing in severity and imperiling the

---

[1] *Ibid.*, pp. 534-535.
[2] M. E. Fries, Play technique in the analysis of young children, *Psychoanal. Review*, 1937, 24, 233-245.

child's health; he was afraid to remain alone in a room by day and by night. The economic situation of the family was critical. He was an illegitimate child, both mother and grandmother had no work, and the aunt earned very little. The family's attitude towards cleanliness was pathological. Neither the grandmother nor the mother had ever dined at a restaurant or at a friend's, as they never could be certain that the food was clean. The child refused to drink from his cup if his mother first took a sip.

An example of the child's behavior during play is this: "William's behavior during the first hour was that of a pretty fearful child. He insisted upon his mother staying in the room and he refused to say a word while he played with the therapist. During the second hour he was willing to have his mother leave the room, and, once gone, began to talk. He was hesitant and frightened. He looked at me enquiringly to see if I would permit him to do this or that. His activity was so restricted that he reminded one of a cowed, beaten child. As he saw that I was friendly and uncritical, he slowly became more courageous in his play, so that by the end of the eleventh hour he was far more active and friendlier.

"William had asked for horses, which had been supplied. Right from the beginning he shoved one horse against the other. It was interesting to note the marked difference between his inhibited attitude towards people and his marked aggression in his play. He violently bumped one horse into the other and at the same time timidly looked up at me for my permission. One of the horses had a broken leg which I had repaired with adhesive plaster. This one he called 'The naughty, biting horse.' 'He is wild.' 'He knocks the other over.' 'He is dead.'

"He needed a hearse to continue his play, so I gave him an empty shoe box to which we attached a cord. He then placed the dead horse in the box and dragged the so-called hearse around my room. One rug he designated as the cemetery and here we buried the horse.

"The aggressiveness and the preoccupation with death in this play is quite evident in this shy and timid child. At later periods, he played a lot with the running water in the sink by his own initiative, expressing his fear in the conversation that mother would be angry, showing great anxiety at the end of one of the play hours.

"In still other interviews preoccupation with the sexual problem was evident in the child's play."

In the play technique the child's preoccupation with one problem or another as well as his manner of playing varies, depending on his immediate problems. The activity may be chiefly constructive or destructive, or, at still other times, reserved and inhibited, as when the child merely touches the toy.

The child's reactions in the daily sessions are correlated with the daily events of his life. In the course of prolonged observation, the child reveals in the examiner's presence all his significant conflicts about his daily existence. In the case just cited, the child showed his feeling of rejection, of frustration in the relationship with his family and in connection with his bodily functions, the hostility resulting from this, and the fear of abandonment and injury.

Many variations can be made in the play technique. Thus children can be confronted with the same play situation and the differences in their reactions studied (Levy [470]); or the investigator may interfere at definite points in the child's activity and thus study the child's reactions to frustrations.[1]

Interesting variations on the play techniques are the use of marionette shows (Bender [60, 62], Bender and Woltmann [66-67]). Moreno (569) has adults act out their difficulties dramatically on a stage.

EVALUATION OF PROJECTIVE METHODS

The significance and usefulness of projective methods can be summarized as follows:

"1. Apparently random reactions of the human individual are strictly determined by his personality make-up. The Rorschach Test, for example, illustrates how even an apparently indifferent type of activity, such as a seemingly unemotional perception, is deeply influenced by the individual's emotional life.

"2. Projective methods can be of great diagnostic significance. The

[1] See Lerner in *Studying Child-Personality*, edited by E. Lerner and L. B. Murphy, Monographs of the Society for Research in Child Development, 1941.

random reactions are elicited and recorded in well-controlled experimental situations and can therefore be classified and compared with such personality trends of the individual as can be established by talking with and observing him. The projective methods are the more useful for diagnostic purposes, the less familiar the stimulus is, the more it calls for a free organizing activity (reaction) of the subject, and the more it elicits responses which have classifiable characteristics that allow for immediate comparison with records obtained from other individuals."[1]

In this sense the best standardized test is the Rorschach Test. Its possible accuracy can be spectacularly demonstrated if it is given "blindly," that is, if someone administers the test and someone else interprets it. The latter can often give a very accurate diagnosis and a surprisingly good description of the subject's personality traits. The test can also be used as a sort of gauge of how far the treatment of a patient has progressed.

3. Projective methods can be of great therapeutic value. Procedures like the Rorschach or the Thematic Apperception Test have not been put to this use, but the play technique has. It is the established psychoanalytic procedure with children. The child acts out and reveals his needs and conflicts in the presence of the therapist who interprets his reactions to him. The factors in this type of cure are essentially the same as those in adult analysis. The sessions, of course, have to be held frequently and over a prolonged period of time, and psychological treatment of the individual on whom the child is dependent is indispensable.

SUGGESTED READINGS

A good description of personality inventory tests can be found in the respective sections of Murphy, Murphy, and Newcomb's *Experimental Social Psychology* (584) and in Allport's *Personality; a Psychological Interpretation* (27). Association tests are described by Jung, *Studies in Word Associations* (409) and in Rosanoff's *Manual of Psychiatry and Mental Hygiene* (651). A good introduction to the Rorschach Test are Klopfer's article, Theory and technique of Rorschach interpretation (434), and Rorschach and

[1] D. Rapaport, Projective testing, its problems and principles, to be published in the June, 1941, issue of the *Menninger Bulletin*.

Oberholzer's article (650). Rorschach's book, *Psychodiagnostik* (649), in German, is a classic.

The Thematic Apperception Test is presented with many other procedures in Murray's *Explorations in Personality* (586). An excellent article on play technique is one by Homburger (360). Also recommended are Melanie Klein, *The Psychoanalysis of Children* (431), Anna Freud's *Introduction to the Technic of Child Analysis* (268), and D. Levy's article, Use of play technique as experimental procedure (470). A comprehensive discussion of projective methods is given in Frank's article, Projective methods for the study of personality (254), and D. Rapaport's forthcoming article, Projective testing, its problems and principles, to be published in the June, 1941, issue of the *Menninger Bulletin*. For an extensive discussion of play technique in research, read *Studying Child-Personality*, edited by E. Lerner and L. B. Murphy; Monographs of the Society for Research in Child Development, 1941. See also Benjamin and Ebaugh's The diagnostic validity of the Rorschach test, *Amer. J. Psych.*, 1937-38, 94, 1163-1178; E. R. Balken and J. H. Masserman, The language of phantasy, *J. Psych.*, 1940, 10, 75-86; Beck (56).

APPENDIX II

THE MAGNITUDE OF THE PROBLEM OF MENTAL DISEASE: STATISTICAL DATA

~~~~~~

The magnitude of the problem of mental disease is best indicated by statistics on the size of the populations of state psychopathic hospitals. (See also Landis and Page, *Modern Society and Mental Disease* [454].) "It should be clearly recognized, however, that statistics of mental patients in hospitals do not directly measure the prevalence of mental disease either in the country as a whole or in the various states. Many persons having nervous and mental diseases never receive hospital treatment. The hospital cases probably cover most of the severe cases of mental disease, but fail to cover many cases of milder type."[1] Actually the loss in health and social economy is greater than is indicated by the figures. Furthermore, it should be recognized that only very severe cases of psychoneurotic reactions reach psychopathic hospitals; most of them are treated outside of institutions. Table I indicates the total state hospital population in various years. Table II indicates the number of first admissions in 1937 to various mental hospitals.

[1] *Patients in Hospitals for Mental Disease, 1937*, U. S. Department of Commerce, Washington, 1939.

TABLE I.—PATIENTS IN STATE HOSPITALS IN THE U. S. A. AT THE BEGINNING OF THE YEAR, 1926 TO 1938[1]

Year	Total Number on Books	In Hospital		In Family Care		On Parole or Otherwise Absent	
		Number	Number per 100,000 of Estimated Population	Number	Percentage	Number	Percentage
1938.......	424,118	374,043	288.1	893	0.2	49,182	11.6
1937.......	411,814	364,563	282.9	603	0.1	46,648	11.3
1936.......	398,006	353,604	276.2	...	...	44,402	11.2
1935.......	384,675	342,167	269.1	...	...	42,508	11.1
1934.......	373,607	332,094	263.1	...	...	41,513	11.1
1933.......	359,105	321,824	256.7	...	...	37,281	10.4
1932.......	340,037	305,031	244.8	...	...	35,006	10.3
1931.......	324,214	292,284	236.3	...	...	31,930	9.8
1930.......	312,088	280,252	228.8	...	...	31,836	10.2
1929.......	302,538	272,252	225.6	...	...	30,286	10.0
1928.......	294,062	264,511	222.2	...	...	29,551	10.0
1927.......	284,650	256,858	218.9	...	...	27,792	9.8
1926.......	272,716	246,486	217.2	...	...	26,230	9.6

[1] The figures are based on *Patients in Hospitals for Mental Disease*, 1937, U. S. Department of Commerce, Washington, 1939. The publication is obtainable on request from the Bureau of the Census, Washington, D. C.

TABLE II.—FIRST ADMISSIONS TO HOSPITALS FOR MENTAL DISEASE IN THE U. S. A., BY PSYCHOSIS, 1937[1]

Psychosis	Number	Percentage
Total..	110,082	100.0
With psychosis...............................	93,236	84.7
General paresis..................................	7,517	6.8
With other forms of syphilis of the C.N.S.............	1,629	1.5
With epidemic encephalitis..........................	373	0.3
With other infectious diseases.......................	639	0.6
Alcoholic..	5,639	5.1
Due to drugs and other exogenous poisons.............	653	0.6
Traumatic......................................	586	0.5
With cerebral arteriosclerosis.........................	11,543	10.5
With other disturbances of circulation.................	742	0.7
With convulsive disorders...........................	1,952	1.8
Senile..	8,530	7.7
Involutional psychoses..............................	3,677	3.3
Due to other metabolic, etc., diseases.................	1,393	1.3
Due to new growth.................................	174	0.2
With organic changes of the nervous system............	875	0.8
Psychoneuroses....................................	3,795	3.4
Manic-depressive..................................	12,626	11.5
Dementia praecox (schizophrenia).....................	20,658	18.8
Paranoia and paranoid conditions.....................	1,812	1.6
With psychopathic personality.......................	1,252	1.1
With mental deficiency..............................	3,099	2.8
Other, undiagnosed, and unknown.....................	4,072	3.7
Without psychosis.................................	16,846	15.3
Epilepsy...	583	0.5
Mental deficiency..................................	1,587	1.4
Alcoholism.......................................	8,453	7.7
Drug addiction....................................	934	0.8
Personality disorders due to epidemic encephalitis.........	123	0.1
Psychopathic personality............................	885	0.8
Primary behavior disorders..........................	349	0.3
Other, unclassified, and unknown.....................	3,932	3.6

[1] *Ibid.*

INDEX

Abeles, M., 398 ff.

Abnormal psychology, field of, 17

Abnormality, 9; analysis of, 27; anatomical and chemical disturbances causing, 32, 66-72; culture and, 22, 30, 33; difficulties in defining, 33 ff.; in typical case, 9-10; relation to character disturbances, 27-29; statistical approach to, 29-30

Abraham, K., 448, 463

Adjustment, and unity of personality, 19; analysis of, 17-18; in psychoanalytic therapy, 352-359; process of, to problems of life, 18-19; relation to hereditary and environmental factors, 204-205

Adler, Alfred, 20, 25, 27, 96, 140, 153, 155, 192, 204, 205, 226, 264, 270, 542

Advice in psychotherapy, 288

Affect hunger, meaning of, 250-253; relation to over-protection, 260

Aggression, anger, hostility, and, 60-62; as biological reaction, 23; as coping mechanism, 160-161; catharsis of, 118-119; definition of, 117-118; experimental study of, 215-217; in children, 235-236; relation to broken homes, 265-266; relation to frustration, 117-123

Aichhorn, A., 334

Alcohol, effects of, 512-513

Alcoholic psychotic reactions, see Psychosis, alcoholic.

Alcoholism, chronic, 515-516; psychodynamics of, 512-513; transmission of, 196; treatment of, 516-517

Alexander, F. G., 334, 359, 434, 435, 438, 444, 445, 446, 484

Allport, G. W., 45, 150, 620

Amnesia, as coping mechanism, 156; nature of, 305-307, 398-400; use of hypnosis in, 311-312

Anderson, O. D., 170, 175

Anesthesia in deep trance, 305, 313

Anger, in children, 236; relation to fear, 60-62

Animal neurosis, see Neurosis, animal.

Anthropology, contribution to understanding of abnormality, 22, 30, 207; suggested readings, 226

Anxiety, as distinguished from fear, 57, 62; basic, 53, 140; derivatives of, 55; in typical case, 3-4, 138-139; relation to alcoholism, 512-513; relation to cultural institutions, 208; significance of, 55; unconscious, 58

Anxiety hysteria, 376-381; as reaction to stress situations, 377-378; in typical case, 15; psychodynamics of, 378-380; treatment, 380-381

Arsenical treatment in paresis, 505

Arteriosclerotic-senile reactions, 498

Assault, 394-396

Asthma, 439

Attention, analysis of, 303

Aura, 523

Autobiography in psychotherapy, 298-299

Autocracy as experimental social condition, 214-217

Autonomic nervous system, role in psychopathology, 63-66